D1163359

VALUE
and
MAN

Property of Philosophy/
Religious Studies-UWEC

VALUE
and
MAN
READINGS IN PHILOSOPHY

LOUIS Z. HAMMER   Wellesley College

McGRAW-HILL BOOK COMPANY

New York
St. Louis
San Francisco
Toronto
London
Sydney

VALUE AND MAN: Readings in Philosophy

Copyright © 1966 by McGraw-Hill, Inc. All
Rights Reserved. Printed in the United States
of America. This book, or parts thereof, may
not be reproduced in any form without permission of the publishers.
Library of Congress Catalog Card Number 65-21584

25860

1234567890VB7210698765

Preface

This book originates in a conviction, developed through experience in teaching undergraduates, that the far-reaching reflections of philosophers can be successfully brought into focus for the beginning student by concentrating on problems related to our value-notions. Out of the wide variety of philosophic issues I have selected a number which are particularly important in specifying and clarifying our concepts of what constitutes human value. In choosing and organizing the readings I have tried to give the reader a way of approaching some of the most compelling problems of philosophy as they have been seen in the past and as they fit into today's philosophic frames. The readings have been chosen for their intrinsic merit as well, not the least part of which consists in the capacity to stimulate further thought.

Wherever possible, the selections have been arranged chronologically, to give a sense of historical development, and in many instances a thesis presented in one selection is attacked in another. Sometimes the views expressed are not in sharp opposition. Instead, the different selections consider different aspects of one issue or a number of related issues.

The arrangement has been made primarily by considering problem areas, but some attention has also been given to providing background for certain selections. For example, A. J. Ayer's presentation of the emotivist position in ethics is put in the part on language, thought, and meaning rather than among the readings on ethics, where it might have been placed, because this discussion can probably be better understood if the positivist approach to meaning is first considered. The reader will find that a number of other selections easily fit into more than one part. Plato's *Apology* of Socrates could be placed in the prologue or in the last part as appropriately as in the fourth part; Adolf Grünbaum's discussion of science and man could certainly be in the fifth part, and Merleau-Ponty's examination of freedom might be included with the existentialist writings of the last part. The teacher or the individual reader will very likely find it desirable to develop his own sequence, and nothing in the readings should prohibit that procedure.

It is my hope that through these selections I have enabled the reader to see and to participate in, with proper balance, both the constructive vision that has characterized traditional and recent philosophy and the critical rigor that strengthens and moves forward that vision. It is also my hope that the student who works through these selections will find himself impelled to look more deeply into one or more special branches of philosophy and that he will find himself bringing to bear on his studies in other fields the discipline of philosophic reflection.

The first expression of appreciation for making this book possible must be to the authors, living and dead, whose discipline, cultivation, and cogency of thought have made philosophy the exciting study that it is. A debt of gratitude is also owed to the publishers and holders of copyright who kindly consented to allow their material to be used.

I also wish to thank Drs. Paul Weiss, W. H. Werkmeister, and James W. Oliver, and Mr. David Cotton for advice and encouragement; Drs. William O'Neill and S. Morris Engel for suggesting readings to be included; Mr. Wallace K. Nethery for assistance in locating materials; and Mrs. Daphne M. Garey for generous and capable help in preparing portions of the manuscript. I am grateful also to the trustees of the Edmond de Rothschild Memorial Trust in the Humanities of the Hebrew University of Jerusalem for a fellowship granted me in 1964–1965, during which time work on the manuscript was completed.

Louis Z. Hammer

Contents

The Nature and Contemporary Situation of Philosophy

The teacher and the student of philosophy experience a difficulty from which their colleagues in other fields of study are relatively free. Because of the peculiar scope and generality of philosophic issues it is the philosophy teacher's misfortune—possibly it is his great advantage —to have to try repeatedly to establish for himself as well as for his students just what his field of study is. He must also reconcile the teaching of a certain body of works—traditional and contemporary— with what he knows is the real task of philosophy: the advancement of critical thought about fundamental human issues.

The reader will discover the precise character of many of these issues in the process of studying the selections in this book. Some of the most important are the nature and extent of knowledge, the issue as to whether or not man has free will, the question of what principles ought to guide human conduct, and the nature of science and its bearing on the determination of values.

Throughout this book philosophy will take hold of the reader bit by bit. The selections assembled here should reveal to him the excitement of philosophic thought and provoke him to decide for himself what philosophy has to offer, how it may offer it, and why he should bother to seek what is there. Also, the reader should be stimulated to compare his own increasingly definite notion of what philosophy is with the notions either suggested or explicitly put forward in the readings.

Without giving anything like a complete answer to the question, What is philosophy? I should like to suggest that the genuine focal point for the activity of philosophizing is at the intersection of two lines of inquiry. By a line of inquiry I mean a consideration or examination of a fundamental human issue—for example, the nature of knowledge —carried on by one person with at least a minimum of rigor.

But why should two intersecting lines of inquiry be imperative if philosophizing is to begin? The answer to this can perhaps be put best by saying that philosophizing begins as the inquiries of two different minds cross at a point where a common issue appears. At this point genuine philosophizing has its origin and center because a basis now exists for mutual critical thought, in which the strengths and deficiencies of the opinions and arguments of one side are drawn out and clarified by another. What I am describing is the movement of philosophical dialogue, an undertaking carefully preserved in the writings of Plato and some other thinkers and engaged in with varying degrees of tenacity and success on countless occasions throughout the history of thought.

Underlying all solitary reflection and treatise-making in philosophy must be the actual or potential interaction of at least two persons who respect the independence of one another's views. The impetus and sustaining context for philosophic activity lies in the mutual presence of man with man, in a search, if you will, for the conditions and first principles of human existence. This original context of philosophizing is never entirely superseded, no matter how solitary or technical philosophizing may become. The history of philosophy ranges from recondite and oracular pronouncement to mathematically precise and minute analysis, from writing that is mostly personal confession to treatises which follow the pattern of a formal deductive system. In spite of this range, the heart of the activity seems to lie in the approach most thoroughly practiced by Socrates, for it is here that the critical rigor which has characterized the best philosophizing has its foundation. No matter what rules are employed to ensure rigorous philosophic thought, the basic dialogical context of personal encounter, remaining at least in the background, probably more than any other factor preserves the vitality and cogency of the philosopher's enterprise.

It is often said that each of us has a world view, or peculiar outlook upon the universe and our own place in it. This world view may be implicit and uncritical or, more rarely, explicit and critically developed. In the latter case, one's world view has become a full-blown "philosophy"; this development has been accomplished by the activity of philosophizing.

However, I should like to caution the reader against supposing that philosophizing amounts merely to making explicit a presumed total philosophy which already exists implicitly. It is true, of course, that each of us, by the time he has become an adult, has developed definite attitudes toward matters which, when treated reflectively, become philosophic issues. But the act of philosophizing itself shapes and develops the elements of a world view to such an extent that there seems to be no good warrant for supposing that anything quite like a philosophy existed even implicitly before this act was undertaken. What is more, individual statements such as, "Man is free," or, "God is omnipotent," or, "The universe is infinite," no matter how philosophic their import, cannot be strung together to make a philosophy. The process of arriving at a philosophy, together with the result, constitute its content. The critical dialogue within which a set of philosophic statements is forged is as much that philosophy as are the basic statements themselves. Internal consistency, clarity of conception, and adequacy to encompass the complexity of all that is—these are the demands which a philosophy worthy of the name should satisfy.

This book has been put together on the assumption that one of the most helpful things a philosophy course can do for students is to aid them in sorting out, recognizing the interrelations among, and assessing the respective claims of, the many competing approaches both in and out of philosophy to issues affecting the determination of human value. What perspectives affecting our value-notions are taken in the sciences, in the arts, in traditional moral theory, or in religious thought? What are the claims of positivists, of "ordinary-language" philosophers, of existential thinkers? All these approaches contribute to the confusing array of ideas which form the world of contemporary thought and all make impressive claims to validity. A consideration of the nature of value-notions and of problems related to them has played an important role in the thought of a great many recent philosophers of quite different persuasions, and these issues are often immediately relevant to the daily lives of students. Moreover, contemporary approaches have antecedents in the philosophic tradition and cannot be understood without some acquaintance with the major elements of that tradition. Old ideas appear alongside new ones, and traditional problems must be rethought in modern forms of expression and in relation to recent developments outside of philosophy. The beginning student must enter philosophy as it is being practiced in his own day, but he must also hark back to earlier thought to get his bearings. Thus, a book of readings that will do justice to contemporary thought must provide a good deal of material from past philosophers.

The present philosophic scene shows a number of major concentrations of thought, some of an unusual and original character. Let us see how they may have come about.

The advent of modern science, probably more than any other circumstance, has thrown the activity of the philosopher into relief and has impelled many philosophers to conceive their tasks in new ways. Modern science has successfully advanced the claim that it employs a method which offers a reliable standard for explaining the connections among matters of fact. While the various sciences are certainly not uniform and while the patterns of scientific explanation differ, science, generally speaking, has preempted the task of investigating the causal relationships among events in the natural world.

This "take-over" by science has affected philosophers but it has not deprived them of something to do. Before modern science got fully under way, the speculations of philosophers about the natural world were given a great deal more credence than the same kinds of speculations would be given today. Some philosophers, in the face of modern science, have conceived the role of philosophy as mainly that of investigating the problems involved in the methods of the sciences or, in line with the modern interest in the nature of symbolism, of investigating the variety of issues resulting from the numerous ways in which language is employed. Within these confines philosophers have examined some fundamental problems in a cogent manner and have clarified many issues which earlier philosophers had not treated carefully.

Logical positivists have been interested in applying the concepts and symbolic notation of modern logic to the analysis of the theories and linguistic expressions of the positive sciences, sciences such as physics and chemistry. So-called *linguistic analysts* (or "ordinary-language" philosophers) have made close readings of linguistic usage in order to discover the sources of philosophical misconceptions—they have also been called "clinical" philosophers. Both have contributed some admirably precise and minute analyses.

Both philosophers of the positivist school and analytic philosophers tend to be critical of speculative philosophy, and both of these groups have been extremely influential on the contemporary scene, especially in the Anglo-American schools. Nevertheless, philosophers still exist who are interested in so-called "metaphysical" questions, that is, questions about the fundamental nature of the whole of reality, and they still write with vigor and imagination. Their speculative inquiries continue the great tradition of philosophic synthesis, attempting to provide fundamental categories, or types of concepts, under which all of reality might be conceived. Such metaphysical inquiry, it should be noted, does not interfere with scientific inquiry but rather complements it.

Another modern group of thinkers are called *existential philosophers*. These writers, insofar as we can treat them as a group, conceive philosophic thought to be inextricably bound up with the concreteness of human existing. They recognize that thought participates in timelessness and universality, but they believe that, if it is to be genuine, it must also insert itself into the crannies of temporal existence and remain bound to existential uncertainties and "ambiguities." These thinkers have frequently used highly figurative language and even imaginative literature and drama to express their views. Though their writing often has lacked the precision and clarity found in the work of most positivists and analysts, they have had much to say that is relevant to the problems and perplexities that any one of us encounters if we scrutinize our own being.

Generally, existential thinkers have rebelled against all-embracing philosophical systems as much as have, say, the positivists, but for a different reason. While positivist thinkers reject some forms of metaphysics because these metaphysical statements are not in any sense verifiable empirically, existential thinkers are most concerned to stress the uniqueness of man's existence, the conditions of which, according to these thinkers, can never be embraced in an all-inclusive set of categories.

Finally, it should be pointed out that the genius of philosophy for the dialogical form makes itself felt not only in the encounters between individual thinkers but also in the oppositions of philosophical schools or families. The more that interchange takes place among thinkers of opposing persuasions at the level of serious philosophic concern, the more likely it will be that some middle ground will show itself on which positivists and analysts, together with existential thinkers and traditional metaphysicians, can stand in productive exchange. In philosophizing, construction and critical dismemberment go hand in hand; neither is successful without some measure of the other. Apparently, also, philosophers find it easier to recognize the things that divide them from other thinkers than to be aware of the things which they hold in common.

Knowledge and Self-knowledge

In the selections from Plato's *Meno* and *Republic* with which we begin, one of the most basic issues of Western philosophy is raised: How is knowledge possible at all? This becomes in Plato's hands: How can we know our ignorance? Here we see the influence of Plato's teacher, Socrates, the chief character in many of the dialogues, who always protested that he knew nothing.

Plato asks, how can we know what is yet lacking to our knowledge? To raise this problem is to uncover something at the very center of knowledge: its dynamic character, its dependence on that which is not knowledge, its constant involvement with ignorance. To know something about knowledge we must first take note of our ignorance.

PROLOGUE

In the *Meno* Plato offers the thesis that knowledge is really the coming to light of what is already in the soul but lies hidden there. Plato's doctrine of *anamnesis* or "recollection," with its mythological overtones, focuses on an issue which has been one of the liveliest and most divisive in the philosophy of the Western world. The question might be put this way: Does knowledge derive primarily from the reports of our senses or primarily from some activity of the mind?

Those philosophers who have stood on the side of the senses have been called *empiricists*. Their stress has been on observation and the testing by experiment of what is proposed as knowledge. David Hume is a leading figure among them. Those who have held that knowledge derives from the mind's activity have been called *rationalists*. The emphasis of rationalist thinkers has been on the clarity and order of concepts. Descartes, often called the "father" of modern philosophy, was a chief exponent of rationalism. We shall consider the thought of Descartes and Hume in a moment.

First let us see where Plato's doctrine that knowledge is recollection takes him. In holding that knowledge is the mind's uncovering of what is already latent in it, Plato is siding with the rationalists. In his day, this issue of the foundation of our knowledge had already become an important one. A group called *Sophists,* for the most part instructors in the art of persuasive speech and pleaders of cases in the law courts, had taught that the shifting, inconstant, elusive content of our senses was all that was available for knowledge. On moral issues, the Sophists were relativists, who held that the individual man was the measure of all things.

Against this view Plato urged a doctrine of Ideas or Forms, unchanging, ideal models, of which the objects of our senses are only imperfect copies. The Forms, according to Plato, are the standard of what is real; they subsist in an independent realm and can be known only by the thinker who undergoes the proper course of reflection. To know the Forms is to achieve absolute knowledge, not subject to later revision as a result of experience and not varying from individual to individual. To know the Forms is, for Plato, to achieve true enlightenment.

The view that knowledge is recollection may be looked on as forming a transition between the popular view expressed by the Sophists, that what we call knowledge is a matter of sensory experience, and the view of Plato's maturity, that to know is to possess an intuition of the Forms. By locating our knowledge-producing activity in the mind's rediscovering what had come into it previously, he initiates a break with the Sophists' position. At the same time he lays a foundation for a view of knowledge that requires appeal to fixed eternal Ideas, a view that regards truth, beauty, and justice, or right action, as absolutes, independent of history, personal preference or opinion, and scientific experimentation.

The reader may now be in a position to see that to begin with a consideration of knowledge is to start from one of the pivotal points in reflecting on man and value. For in asking what knowledge is we may also ask whether knowledge is a value. To carry this investigation further, we might ask whether we can infer that knowledge is a value because it has some particular uses which we regard as valuable or whether we have some kind of direct apprehension of its value. Thus we can raise not only the question whether knowledge itself is a value, but also the question how we know that knowledge is a value or, for that matter, that anything else—truth, beauty, goodness, or the appeasing of hunger—is a value, if in fact it is. We have to ask whether there are different kinds of knowledge, whether to know a value, or to know what things are values, is different from knowing, say, an electron, a painting, the distance of a star, the roots of a quadratic equation, or the color of one's eyes. And in asking this, we are also asking about the limitations of knowledge, where it begins and where it ends.

It seems correct to say that one of the characteristic emphases of Western philosophy has been on the primacy of knowledge as a value. Plato did perhaps more than any other philosopher to advance this view, but one should keep in mind that later philosophers have regarded knowledge as a value without holding Plato's view of what knowledge is. While holding that knowledge is a value, Plato urged something more about knowledge. Plato seems to tell us that it is not a value only in and of itself, but that it establishes itself as a value as it orders other aspects of our being—sense awareness, feeling, willing.

To this view he gave a popular presentation in the most famous of his dialogues, the *Republic,* a work devoted to so many topics that scholars have had a difficult time stating just what the work's central theme is. It is undoubtedly concerned with ethical problems, that is, with problems about human conduct, but it is just as much concerned with the nature of knowledge and, more specifically, with a problem which Plato inherited from Socrates, the nature of self-knowledge. Socrates had taught that moral virtue *is* knowledge. In the *Republic* Plato emphasizes the interconnection of knowledge and the conduct of the good life, especially our knowledge of what goes to compose ourselves. In Plato's thought, knowledge, being, and value are inseparable. To achieve self-knowledge is to grasp oneself in one's passage from appearance to reality, from the Cave, as he says in his famous allegory, to the sun-illumined world outside. To know anything is to be able to speak of it in its right relationship to other things, and this holds in speaking of oneself as well as of chairs or beds or the sides of a triangle. Thus Plato was one of the first to see that the question of what is valuable is inevitably linked to the question of how we know what is valuable, and this in turn to the question of how we know anything at all, and this last to the question of what we ourselves are.

What we are and how we know ourselves are among the most difficult of all questions of knowledge. From an ethical standpoint, we might want to know what sort of entities we are in order that we might better know how we ought to act. But the problem of self-knowledge can be raised in a more fundamental way: Is it possible to know with certainty that we exist? Putting the question this way, we are asking not only about the existence of the Self, but also about the possibility of certain knowledge. Does it make sense to talk of something called the "Self" and, if so, what kind of sense? Is the Self a datum which we intuit, or is it something whose existence we infer from the observation of other things, or is its existence logically necessary and self-evident, so clear to the natural light of reason that anyone who can understand the meanings of words must see that it is so?

This last view of our knowledge of our existence we find expressed by Descartes, and it is characteristic of his general approach to knowledge. A creative mathematician, inventor of the science of analytic geometry, he attempted to order all our knowledge after the pattern of mathematical knowledge. The foundation for all our knowledge, according to Descartes, consists in what he calls "intuitions," an individual mind's direct acts of knowing truths. In order to see their truth, we need only grasp the meanings of the words used to express them. An example of such a truth would be the principle, "Things equal to the same things are equal to each other," or, he contends, his own famous statement, "Cogito, ergo sum," "I think, therefore I am." What is essential about these propositions is that their truth can be known independently of sense-experience.

Descartes utilized his method of "deliberate doubt" in order to arrive at what could be known with certainty, and it is the existence of oneself that he judged to be the most certain of all certainties, a truth confirmed in the very process of trying to doubt it. The reader must refer to Descartes's own account of this process in our selection from his *Meditations* in order to discover just how he employed it.

In attempting to discover what he himself is, Descartes makes a sharp distinction between body and mind, a distinction which has had a great influence on all modern philosophy. Body is that which is extended; mind is that which thinks. Descartes finds it easier to know that he is mind than to be certain that he is body. In considering mind and body as two distinct substances, Descartes set the problem for all subsequent philosophy of explaining in what way the two are related. Some philosophers have thought it a grave mistake ever to have separated them. We shall see that this is an issue of importance in the discussion of free will and determinism in Part I.

We find an empiricist's approach to the question of what we ourselves are in the analysis by David Hume of the idea of personal identity.

What is at stake in this examination is the ordinary man's belief that he is a Self, an entity enduring from moment to moment above the stream of experience. Like Descartes, Hume begins with an individual mind, but, unlike Descartes, he considers the data of the senses primary. Any concepts—Hume calls them "ideas"—must be derived from primary data of the senses: the reds, the blues, the rounds, the squares, the hards, the softs. Hume names the sense-data "impressions." In one's perception, for example, of a red rubber ball, the primary "given" is a "redness" of a certain spherical shape and a certain texture. The concept which I form of the ball is founded upon these basic impressions and is produced, according to Hume, after repeated experience, with the help of memory and habit. He holds that no expression is meaningful which is not based upon some sensuous element and contends that our senses do not provide any experience of a Self. In our next part we shall see him further arguing that there is no basis in our impressions for the belief in a necessary link between cause and effect. Our belief in a necessary causal relation, he maintains, is attributable to our habitually associating events which follow one another in time, and our belief in a Self is also produced by association and habit.

The selections from Descartes and Hume enable us to raise issues which are of the first importance in a consideration of human value. As individuals thinking about what we are, can we get any grasp upon ourselves? Can we say exactly what we mean when we use the term "person"? Is each one of us merely a bundle of perceptions? Should we look for personal identity among the data of the senses? Is the person to be identified with his mind, with his body, or with both? If with both, what is the relationship between mind and body? Do the reports of other persons affect an individual's establishing his self-identity? Can we make successful use of nonhuman models in talking of self-identity? Can experimental psychology provide us with any data affecting the problem of self-identity? The answers we give to these questions will help to determine our view of that entity—the person—which is the focal point for what we call value.

Knowledge as recollection

The divided line

Allegory of the cave

Plato (428/7-348/7 B.C.)

Plato reached manhood in the period of political strife and chaos that followed the death of Pericles (429 B.C.). He could see no prospect for reforming the politics of Athens, a city-state whose citizens had sentenced to death Socrates, his teacher, on trumped-up charges. Plato founded a school, the Academy, and turned to a life of philosophic reflection, to which he gave expression in a long series of dialogues. Through his depiction of Socrates's life and manner of inquiry, Plato hoped to restore in memory the character of this unusual man, who had described himself as a "gadfly" and "midwife" of ideas. (See the Apology *beginning on page 199.)*

Plato rejected the popular beliefs of his day, especially the view that knowledge derives from the senses, and developed instead his doctrine of the Forms, or intelligible essences, which belong to a realm independent of material things. In the dialogue Meno, *from which our first selection is taken, Socrates tries to show, in questioning the slave-boy, that what we call "learning" is simply recollecting what the soul, viewed as immortal, already knows. Knowledge, he maintains, comes neither from the senses nor from teaching; it is not information passed from one mind to another, but discovery of the content of the soul's reflection before it entered the body.*

Beginning with a discussion of "justice" or "right action" between Socrates and a group of younger men, the Republic *becomes an examination of the ideal state, taken as an enlarged model of the individual soul. But it is more than this; it is also a nontechnical account of a doctrine central to Plato's thought, that of the Forms, the intelligible objects of real knowledge said to have existence apart from the objects perceived by the senses.*

The famous discussion of the divided line and the allegory of the cave are memorable examples of Plato's poetic power. His capacity to unite abstract reflection with concrete imagery is probably unsurpassed in the literature of philosophy. But besides their literary merit, these passages focus on the important contribution, influential for many centuries, which Plato **5** *made to thought about value. He has etched in a remarkable manner the view of value as transcendent, belonging to an independent realm outside the world of material things and of the senses.*

From the *Meno*

... *Men.* O Socrates, I used to be told, before I knew you, that you were always doubting yourself and making others doubt; and now you are casting your spells over me, and I am simply getting bewitched and enchanted, and am at my wits' end. And if I may venture to make a jest upon you, you seem to me both in your appearance and in your power over others to be very like the flat torpedo fish, who torpifies those who come near him and touch him, as you have now torpified me, I think. For my soul and my tongue are really torpid. ... And I think that you are very wise in not voyaging and going away from home, for if you did in other places as you do in Athens, you would be cast into prison as a magician.

Soc. You are a rogue, Meno, and had all but caught me.

Men. What do you mean, Socrates?

Soc. I can tell why you made a simile about me.

Men. Why?

Soc. In order that I might make another simile about you. For I know that all beautiful youths like to have similes made about them—as well they may, since beautiful images, I take it, are naturally evoked by beauty—but I shall not return the compliment. As to my being a torpedo, if the torpedo is itself torpid as well as the cause of torpidity in others, then indeed I am a torpedo, but not otherwise; for I perplex others, not because I am clear, but because I am utterly perplexed myself. And now I know not what virtue is, and you seem to be in the same case, although you did once perhaps know before you touched me. However, I have no objection to join with you in the inquiry.

Reprinted from *The Dialogues of Plato,* trans. Benjamin Jowett, Oxford, The Clarendon Press, 4th ed., 1953. By permission of The Clarendon Press, Oxford.

Men. And how will you investigate, Socrates, that of which you know nothing at all? Where can you find a starting-point in the region of the unknown? And even if you happen to come full upon what you want, how will you ever know that this is the thing which you did not know?

Soc. I know, Meno, what you mean; but just see what a tiresome dispute you are introducing. You argue that a man cannot inquire either about that which he knows, or about that which he does not know; for if he knows, he has no need to inquire; and if not, he cannot; for he does not know the very subject about which he is to inquire.

Men. Well, Socrates, and is not the argument sound?

Soc. I think not.

Men. Why not?

Soc. I will tell you why: I have heard from certain men and women skilled in things divine that—

Men. What did they say?

Soc. They spoke of a glorious truth, as I conceive.

Men. What is it? and who are they?

Soc. Some of them are priests and priestesses, who have striven to learn how to give a reasonable account of the things with which they concern themselves: there are poets also, like Pindar, and the many others who are inspired. And they say—mark, now, and see whether their words are true—they say that the soul of man is immortal, and at one time has an end, which is termed dying, and at another time is born again, but is never destroyed. And the moral is, that a man ought to live always in perfect holiness. *"For in the ninth year Persephone sends the souls of those from whom she has received the penalty of ancient crime back again from beneath into the light of the sun above, and these are they who become noble kings and mighty men and great in wisdom and are for ever called saintly heroes."*

The soul, then, as being immortal and having been born again many times, and having seen all things that exist, whether in this world or in the world below, has knowledge of them all; and it is no wonder that she should be able to call to remembrance all that she ever knew about virtue, and about everything; for as all nature is akin, and the soul has learned all things, there is no difficulty in a man eliciting out of a single recollection all the rest—the process generally called "learning"—if he is strenuous and does not faint; for all inquiry and all learning is but recollection. And therefore we ought not to listen to this eristic argument about the impossibility of inquiry: for it will make us idle, and it is sweet to the sluggard; but the other doctrine will make us active and inquisitive. In that confiding, I will gladly inquire with you into the nature of virtue.

Men. Yes, Socrates; but what do you mean by saying that we do not learn, and that what we call learning is only a process of recollection? Can you teach me how this is?

Soc. I told you, Meno, just now that you were a rogue, and now you ask whether I can teach you, when I am saying that there is no teaching, but only recollection; and thus you imagine that you will expose me in a contradiction.

Men. Indeed, Socrates, I protest that I had no such intention. I only asked the question from habit; but if you can prove to me that what you say is true, I wish that you would.

Soc. It will be no easy matter, but I am willing to do my best for you. Suppose that you call one of your numerous attendants, whichever you like, that I may demonstrate on him.

Men. Certainly. Come hither, boy.

Soc. He is Greek, and speaks Greek, does he not?

Men. Yes, indeed; he was born in the house.

Soc. Attend now, and observe whether he learns of me or only remembers.

Men. I will.

Soc. Tell me, boy, do you know that a figure like this is a square?

Boy. I do.

Soc. And you know that a square figure has these four lines equal?

Boy. Certainly.

Soc. And these lines which I have drawn through the middle of the square are also equal?

Boy. Yes.

Soc. A square may be of any size?

Boy. Certainly.

Soc. And if one side of the figure be two feet long, and the other side two feet, how much will the whole be? Let me explain: if in one direction the space was two feet long, and in the other direction one foot, the whole space would be two feet taken once?

Boy. Yes.

Soc. But since this side is also two feet, there are twice two feet?

Boy. There are.

Soc. Then the square is twice two feet?

Boy. Yes.

Soc. And how many are twice two feet? count and tell me.

Boy. Four, Socrates.

Soc. And might there not be another figure twice as large as this, but of the same kind, and having like this all the lines equal?

Boy. Yes.

Soc. And how many feet will that be?

Boy. Eight feet.

Soc. And now try and tell me the length of the line which forms the side of that double square: this is two feet—what will that be?

Boy. Clearly, Socrates, it will be double.

Soc. Do you observe, Meno, that I am not teaching the boy anything, but only asking him questions; and now he fancies that he knows how long a line is necessary in order to produce a figure of eight square feet; does he not?

Men. Yes.

Soc. And does he really know?

Men. Certainly not.

Soc. He fancies that because the square is double, the line is double?

Men. True.

Soc. Now see him being brought step by step to recollect in regular order. (*To the boy.*) Tell me, boy, do you assert that a double space comes from a double line? Remember that I am not speaking of an oblong, but of a figure equal every way, and twice the size of this—that is to say of eight feet; and I want to know whether you still say that a double square comes from a double line?

Boy. Yes.

Soc. But does not this line become doubled if we add another such line here?

Boy. Certainly.

Soc. And four such lines, you say, will make a space containing eight feet?

Boy. Yes.

Soc. Let us describe such a figure: Would you not say that this is the figure of eight feet?

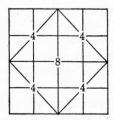

Boy. Yes.

Soc. And are there not these four divisions in the figure, each of which is equal to the figure of four feet?

Boy. True.

Soc. And is not that four times four?

Boy. Certainly.

Soc. And four times is not double?

Boy. No, indeed.

Soc. But how much?

Boy. Four times as much.

Soc. Therefore the double line, boy, has given a space, not twice, but four times as much.

Boy. True.

Soc. Four times four are sixteen—are they not?

Boy. Yes.

Soc. What line would give you a space of eight feet—for that gives a fourfold space, of sixteen feet, does it not?

Boy. Yes.

Soc. And the space of four feet is made from this half line?

Boy. Yes.

Soc. Good; and is not a space of eight feet twice the size of this, and half the size of the other?

Boy. Certainly.

Soc. Such a space, then, will be made out of a line greater than this one, and less than that one?

Boy. Yes; I think so.

Soc. Very good; I like to hear you say what you think. And now tell me, is not this a line of two feet and that of four?

Boy. Yes.

Soc. Then the line which forms the side of the eight foot space ought to be more than this line of two feet, and less than the other of four feet?

Boy. It ought.

Soc. Try and see if you can tell me how much it will be.

Boy. Three feet.

Soc. Then if we add a half to this line of two, that will be the line of three. Here are two and there is one; and on the other side, here are two also and there is one: and that makes the figure of which you speak?

Boy. Yes.

Soc. But if there are three feet this way and three feet that way, the whole space will be three times three feet?

Boy. That is evident.

Soc. And how much are three times three feet?

Boy. Nine.

Soc. And what was to be the number of feet in the doubled square?

Boy. Eight.

Soc. Then the eight foot space is not made out of a line of three feet?

Boy. No.

Soc. But from what line?—tell me exactly; and if you would rather not reckon, try and show me the line.

Boy. Indeed, Socrates, I do not know.

Soc. Do you see, Meno, what advances he has made in his power of recollection? He did not know at first, and he does not know now, what is the side of a figure of eight feet: but then he thought that he knew, and answered confidently as if he knew, and felt no difficulty;

now he feels a difficulty, and neither knows nor fancies that he knows.

Men. True.

Soc. Is he not better off in knowing his ignorance?

Men. I think that he is.

Soc. If we have made him doubt, and given him the "torpedo's shock," have we done him any harm?

Men. I think not.

Soc. We have certainly, as would seem, assisted him in some degree to the discovery of the truth; and now he will wish to remedy his ignorance, but then he would have been ready to tell all the world again and again that the double space should have a double side.

Men. True.

Soc. But do you suppose that he would ever have started to inquire into or to learn what he fancied that he knew, though he was really ignorant of it, until he had fallen into perplexity under the idea that he did not know, and had desired to know?

Men. I think not, Socrates.

Soc. Then he was the better for the torpedo's touch?

Men. I think so.

Soc. Mark now the further development. I shall only ask him, and not teach him, and he shall share the inquiry with me: and do you watch and see if you find me telling or explaining anything to him, instead of eliciting his opinion. Tell me, boy, is not this a square of four feet which I have drawn?

Boy. Yes.

Soc. And now I add another square equal to the former one?

Boy. Yes.

Soc. And a third, which is equal to either of them?

Boy. Yes.

Soc. Suppose that we fill up the vacant corner?

Boy. Very good.

Soc. Here, then, there are four equal spaces?

Boy. Yes.

Soc. And how many times larger is this space than this other?

Boy. Four times.

Soc. But we wanted one only twice as large, as you will remember.

Boy. True.

Soc. Now, does not this line, reaching from corner to corner, bisect each of these spaces?

Boy. Yes.

Soc. And are there not here four equal lines which contain this space?

Boy. There are.

Soc. Look and see how much this space is.

Boy. I do not understand.

Soc. Has not each interior cut off half of the four spaces?

Boy. Yes.

Soc. And how many such spaces are there in this section?

Boy. Four.

Soc. And how many in this?

Boy. Two.

Soc. And four is how many times two?

Boy. Twice.

Soc. So that this space is of how many feet?

Boy. Of eight feet.

Soc. And from what line do you get this figure?

Boy. From this.

Soc. That is, from the line which extends from corner to corner of the figure of four feet?

Boy. Yes.

Soc. And that is the line which the learned call the diagonal. And if this is the proper name, then you, Meno's slave, are prepared to affirm that the double space is the square of the diagonal?

Boy. Certainly, Socrates.

Soc. What do you say of him, Meno? Were not all these answers given out of his own head?

Men. Yes, they were all his own.

Soc. And yet, as we were just now saying, he did not know?

Men. True.

Soc. But still he had in him those notions of his—had he not?

Men. Yes.

Soc. Then he who does not know may still have true notions of that which he does not know?

Men. Apparently.

Soc. And at present these notions have just been stirred up in him, as in a dream; but if he were frequently asked the same questions, in different forms, he would know as accurately as anyone at last?

Men. I dare say.

Soc. Without anyone teaching him he will recover his knowledge for himself, if he is merely asked questions?

Men. Yes.

Soc. And this spontaneous recovery of knowledge in him is recollection?

Men. True.

Soc. And this knowledge which he now has must he not either have acquired at some time, or else possessed always?

Men. Yes.

Soc. But if he always possessed this knowledge he would always have known; or if he has acquired the knowledge he could not have acquired it in this life, unless he has been taught geometry. And he may be made to do the same with all geometry and every other branch of knowledge; has anyone ever taught him all this? You must know about him, if, as you say, he was born and bred in your house.

Men. And I am certain that no one ever did teach him.

Soc. And yet he has these notions?

Men. The fact, Socrates, is undeniable.

Soc. But if he did not acquire them in this life, then he must have had and learned them at some other time?

Men. Clearly he must.

Soc. Which must have been the time when he was not a man?

Men. Yes.

Soc. And if there are always to be true notions in him, both while he is and while he is not a man, which only need to be awakened into knowledge by putting questions to him, his soul must remain always possessed of this knowledge; for he must always either be or not be a man.

Men. Obviously.

Soc. And if the truth of all things always exists in the soul, then the soul is immortal. Wherefore be of good cheer, and try to dis-

cover by recollection what you do not now know, or rather what you do not remember.

Men. I feel, somehow, that I like what you are saying.

Soc. And I too like what I am saying. Some things I have said of which I am not altogether confident. But that we shall be better and braver and less helpless if we think that we ought to inquire, than we should have been if we thought that there was no knowing and no duty to seek to know what we do not know;— that is a belief for which I am ready to fight, in word and deed, to the utmost of my power.

Men. There again, Socrates, your words seem to me excellent.

Soc. Then, as we are agreed that a man should inquire about that which he does not know, shall you and I make an effort to inquire together into the nature of virtue?

Men. By all means, Socrates.

From the *Republic*

(*Socrates is conversing with Glaucon.*)

... But, Socrates, what is your own account of the Good? Is it knowledge, or pleasure, or something else? [1]

There you are! I exclaimed; I could see all along that you were not going to be content with what other people think.

Well, Socrates, it does not seem fair that you should be ready to repeat other people's opinions but not to state your own, when you have given so much thought to this subject.

And do you think it fair of anyone to speak as if he knew what he does not know?

No, not as if he knew, but he might give his opinion for what it is worth.

Why, have you never noticed that opinion without knowledge is always a shabby sort of thing? At the best it is blind. One who holds a true belief without intelligence is just like a

---

From *The Republic of Plato*, trans. F. M. Cornford, Oxford, The Clarendon Press, 1941. By permission of The Clarendon Press, Oxford.

[1] Here it begins to appear that the discussion is not confined to the "Human Good" but extends to the supreme Form, "Goodness itself."

blind man who happens to take the right road, isn't he? [2]

No doubt.

Well, then, do you want me to produce one of these poor blind cripples, when others could discourse to you with illuminating eloquence?

No, really, Socrates, said Glaucon, you must not give up within sight of the goal. We should be quite content with an account of the Good like the one you gave us of justice and temperance and the other virtues.

So shall I be, my dear Glaucon, much more than content! But I am afraid it is beyond my powers; with the best will in the world I should only disgrace myself and be laughed at. No, for the moment let us leave the question of the real meaning of good; to arrive at what I at any rate believe it to be would call for an effort too ambitious for an inquiry like ours. However, I will tell you, though only if you wish it, what I picture to myself as the offspring of the Good and the thing most nearly resembling it.

Well, tell us about the offspring, and you shall remain in our debt for an account of the parent.

I only wish it were within my power to offer, and within yours to receive, a settlement of the whole account. But you must be content now with the interest only; [3] and you must see to it that, in describing this offspring of the Good, I do not inadvertently cheat you with false coin.

We will keep a good eye on you. Go on.

First we must come to an understanding. Let me remind you of the distinction we drew earlier and have often drawn on other occasions,[4] between the multiplicity of things that

we call good or beautiful or whatever it may be and, on the other hand, Goodness itself or Beauty itself and so on. Corresponding to each of these sets of many things, we postulate a single Form or real essence, as we call it.

Yes, that is so.

Further, the many things, we say, can be seen, but are not objects of rational thought; whereas the Forms are objects of thought, but invisible.

Yes, certainly.

And we see things with our eyesight, just as we hear sounds with our ears and, to speak generally, perceive any sensible thing with our sense-faculties.

Of course.

Have you noticed, then, that the artificer who designed the senses has been exceptionally lavish of his materials in making the eyes able to see and their objects visible?

That never occurred to me.

Well, look at it in this way. Hearing and sound do not stand in need of any third thing, without which the ear will not hear nor sound be heard; [5] and I think the same is true of most, not to say all, of the other senses. Can you think of one that does require anything of the sort?

No, I cannot.

But there is this need in the case of sight and its objects. You may have the power of vision in your eyes and try to use it, and colour may be there in the objects; but sight will see nothing and the colours will remain invisible in the absence of a third thing peculiarly constituted to serve this very purpose.

By which you mean——?

Naturally I mean what you call light; and if light is a thing of value, the sense of sight and the power of being visible are linked together by a very precious bond, such as unites no other sense with its object.

No one could say that light is not a precious thing.

---

[2] At *Meno 97* the man who has a correct belief at second-hand about the way from Athens to Larisa is contrasted with one who has certain knowledge of the road from having travelled by it himself.

[3] The Greek has a play on two meanings of the word *tokos*—"offspring" and "interest" on a loan, "a breed for barren metal."

[4] Perhaps an allusion to the *Phaedo* (especially 78 E ff.), where the theory of Forms was first explicitly stated in similar terms. The earlier passage in the *Republic* is at 475 E ff.

[5] Plato held that the hearing of sound is caused by blows inflicted by the air (*Timaeus* 67 B, 80 A); but the air is hardly analogous to light.

And of all the divinities in the skies [6] is there one whose light, above all the rest, is responsible for making our eyes see perfectly and making objects perfectly visible?

There can be no two opinions: of course you mean the Sun.

And how is sight related to this deity? Neither sight nor the eye which contains it is the Sun, but of all the sense-organs it is the most sun-like; and further, the power it possesses is dispensed by the Sun, like a stream flooding the eye.[7] And again, the Sun is not vision, but it is the cause of vision and also is seen by the vision it causes.

Yes.

It was the Sun, then, that I meant when I spoke of that offspring which the Good has created in the visible world, to stand there in the same relation to vision and visible things as that which the Good itself bears in the intelligible world to intelligence and to intelligible objects.

How is that? You must explain further.

You know what happens when the colours of things are no longer irradiated by the daylight, but only by the fainter luminaries of the night: when you look at them, the eyes are dim and seem almost blind, as if there were no unclouded vision in them. But when you look at things on which the Sun is shining, the same eyes see distinctly and it becomes evident that they do contain the power of vision.

Certainly.

Apply this comparison, then, to the soul. When its gaze is fixed upon an object irradiated by truth and reality, the soul gains understanding and knowledge and is manifestly in possession of intelligence. But when it looks towards that twilight world of things that come into existence and pass away, its sight is dim and it has only opinions and beliefs which shift to and fro, and now it seems like a thing that has no intelligence.

That is true.

This, then, which gives to the objects of knowledge their truth and to him who knows them his power of knowing, is the Form or essential nature of Goodness. It is the cause of knowledge and truth; and so, while you may think of it as an object of knowledge, you will do well to regard it as something beyond truth and knowledge and, precious as these both are, of still higher worth. And, just as in our analogy light and vision were to be thought of as like the Sun, but not identical with it, so here both knowledge and truth are to be regarded as like the Good, but to identify either with the Good is wrong. The Good must hold a yet higher place of honour.

You are giving it a position of extraordinary splendour, if it is the source of knowledge and truth and itself surpasses them in worth. You surely cannot mean that it is pleasure.

Heaven forbid, I exclaimed. But I want to follow up our analogy still further. You will agree that the Sun not only makes the things we see visible, but also brings them into existence and gives them growth and nourishment; yet he is not the same thing as existence.[8] And so with the objects of knowledge: these derive from the Good not only their power of being known, but their very being and reality; and Goodness is not the same thing as being, but even beyond being, surpassing it in dignity and power.

Glaucon exclaimed with some amusement at my exalting Goodness in such extravagant terms.

It is your fault, I replied; you forced me to say what I think.

Yes, and you must not stop there. At any

---

[6] Plato held that the heavenly bodies are immortal living creatures, i.e., gods.

[7] Plato's theory of vision involves three kinds of fire or light: (1) daylight, a body of pure fire diffused in the air by the Sun; (2) the visual current or "vision," a pure fire similar to daylight, contained in the eye-ball and capable of issuing out in a stream directed towards the object seen; (3) the colour of the external object, "a flame streaming off from every body, having particles proportioned to those of the visual current, so as to yield sensation" when the two streams meet and coalesce (*Timaeus*, 45 B, 67 C).

[8] The ambiguity of *genesis* can hardly be reproduced. The Sun "gives things their *genesis*" (generation, birth), but "is not itself *genesis*" (becoming, the existence in time of things which begin and cease to exist, as opposed to the real being of eternal things in the intelligible world).

rate, complete your comparison with the Sun, if there is any more to be said.

There is a great deal more, I answered.

Let us hear it, then; don't leave anything out.

I am afraid much must be left unspoken. However, I will not, if I can help it, leave out anything that can be said on this occasion.

Please do not.

Conceive, then, that there are these two powers I speak of, the Good reigning over the domain of all that is intelligible, the Sun over the visible world—or the heaven as I might call it; only you would think I was showing off my skill in etymology.[9] At any rate you have these two orders of things clearly before your mind: the visible and the intelligible?

I have.

Now take a line divided into two unequal parts, one to represent the visible order, the other the intelligible; and divide each part again in the same proportion, symbolizing degrees of comparative clearness or obscurity. Then (A) one of the two sections in the visible world will stand for images. By images I mean first shadows, and then reflections in water or in close-grained, polished surfaces, and everything of that kind, if you understand.

Yes, I understand.

Let the second section (B) stand for the actual things of which the first are likenesses, the living creatures about us and all the works of nature or of human hands.

So be it.

Will you also take the proportion in which the visible world has been divided as corresponding to degrees of reality and truth, so that the likeness shall stand to the original in the same ratio as the sphere of appearances and belief to the sphere of knowledge?

Certainly.

Now consider how we are to divide the part which stands for the intelligible world. There are two sections. In the first (C) the mind uses as images those actual things which

themselves had images in the visible world; and it is compelled to pursue its inquiry by starting from assumptions and travelling, not up to a principle, but down to a conclusion. In the second (D) the mind moves in the other direction, from an assumption up towards a principle which is not hypothetical; and it makes no use of the images employed in the other section, but only of Forms, and conducts its inquiry solely by their means.

I don't quite understand what you mean.

Then we will try again; what I have just said will help you to understand. (C) You know, of course, how students of subjects like geometry and arithmetic begin by postulating odd and even numbers, or the various figures and the three kinds of angle, and other such data in each subject. These data they take as known; and, having adopted them as assumptions, they do not feel called upon to give any account of them to themselves or to anyone else, but treat them as self-evident. Then, starting from these assumptions, they go on until they arrive, by a series of consistent steps, at all the conclusions they set out to investigate.

Yes, I know that.

You also know how they make use of visible figures and discourse about them, though what they really have in mind is the originals of which these figures are images: they are not reasoning, for instance, about this particular square and diagonal which they have drawn, but about *the* Square and *the* Diagonal; and so in all cases. The diagrams they draw and the models they make are actual things, which may have their shadows or images in water; but now they serve in their turn as images, while the student is seeking to behold those realities which only thought can apprehend.[10]

True.

This, then, is the class of things that I spoke of as intelligible, but with two qualifications: first, that the mind, in studying them, is com-

---

[9] Some connected the word for heaven (οὐρανός) with ὁρᾶν "to see" (*Cratylus,* 396 B). It is sometimes used for the whole of the visible universe.

[10] Conversely, the fact that the mathematician can use visible objects as illustrations indicates that the realities and truths of mathematics are embodied, though imperfectly, in the world of visible and tangible things; whereas the counterparts of the moral Forms can only be beheld by thought.

pelled to employ assumptions, and, because it cannot rise above these, does not travel upwards to a first principle; and second, that it uses as images those actual things which have images of their own in the section below them and which, in comparison with those shadows and reflections, are reputed to be more palpable and valued accordingly.

I understand: you mean the subject-matter of geometry and of the kindred arts.

(D) Then by the second section of the intelligible world you may understand me to mean all that unaided reasoning apprehends by the power of dialectic, when it treats its assumptions, not as first principles, but as *hypotheses* in the literal sense, things "laid down" like a flight of steps up which it may mount all the way to something that is not hypothetical, the first principle of all; and having grasped this, may turn back and, holding on to the consequences which depend upon it, descend at last to a conclusion, never making use of any sensible object, but only of Forms, moving through Forms from one to another, and ending with Forms.

I understand, he said, though not perfectly; for the procedure you describe sounds like an enormous undertaking. But I see that you mean to distinguish the field of intelligible reality studied by dialectic as having a greater certainty and truth than the subject matter of the "arts," as they are called, which treat their assumptions as first principles. The students of these arts are, it is true, compelled to exercise thought in contemplating objects which the senses cannot perceive; but because they start from assumptions without going back to a first principle, you do not regard them as gaining true understanding about those objects, although the objects themselves, when connected with a first principle, are intelligible. And I think you would call the state of mind of the students of geometry and other such arts, not intelligence, but thinking, as being something between intelligence and mere acceptance of appearances.

You have understood me quite well enough, I replied. And now you may take, as corresponding to the four sections, these four states of mind: *intelligence* for the highest, *thinking*

for the second, *belief* for the third, and for the last *imagining*.[11] These you may arrange as the terms in a proportion, assigning to each a degree of clearness and certainty corresponding to the measure in which their objects possess truth and reality.

I understand and agree with you. I will arrange them as you say.

Next, said I, here is a parable to illustrate the degrees in which our nature may be enlightened or unenlightened. Imagine the condition of men living in a sort of cavernous chamber underground, with an entrance open to the light and a long passage all down the cave.[12] Here they have been from childhood, chained by the leg and also by the neck, so that they cannot move and can see only what is in front of them, because the chains will not let them turn their heads. At some distance higher up is the light of a fire burning behind them; and between the prisoners and the fire is a track [13] with a parapet built along it, like the screen at a puppet-show, which hides the performers while they show their puppets over the top.

I see, said he.

Now behind this parapet imagine persons carrying along various artificial objects, including figures of men and animals in wood or stone or other materials, which project above the parapet. Naturally, some of these persons will be talking, others silent.[14]

---

[11] Plato never uses hard and fast technical terms. The four here proposed are not defined or strictly employed in the sequel.

[12] The *length* of the "way in" (*eisodos*) to the chamber where the prisoners sit is an essential feature, explaining why no daylight reaches them.

[13] The track crosses the passage into the cave at right angles, and is *above* the parapet built along it.

[14] A modern Plato would compare his Cave to an underground cinema, where the audience watch the play of shadows thrown by the film passing before a light at their backs. The film itself is only an image of "real" things and events in the world outside the cinema. For the film Plato has to substitute the clumsier apparatus of a procession of artificial objects carried on their heads by persons who are merely part of the machinery, providing for the

It is a strange picture, he said, and a strange sort of prisoners.

Like ourselves, I replied; for in the first place prisoners so confined would have seen nothing of themselves or of one another, except the shadows thrown by the fire-light on the wall of the Cave facing them, would they?

Not if all their lives they had been prevented from moving their heads.

And they would have seen as little of the objects carried past.

Of course.

Now, if they could talk to one another, would they not suppose that their words referred only to those passing shadows which they saw? [15]

Necessarily.

And suppose their prison had an echo from the wall facing them? When one of the people crossing behind them spoke, they could only suppose that the sound came from the shadow passing before their eyes.

No doubt.

In every way, then, such prisoners would recognize as reality nothing but the shadows of those artificial objects.[16]

Inevitably.

Now consider what would happen if their release from the chains and the healing of their unwisdom should come about in this way. Suppose one of them set free and forced suddenly to stand up, turn his head, and walk with eyes lifted to the light; all these movements would be painful, and he would be too dazzled to make out the objects whose shadows he had been used to see. What do you think he would say, if someone told him that what he had formerly seen was meaningless illusion, but now, being somewhat nearer to reality and turned towards more real objects, he was getting a truer view? Suppose further that he were shown the various objects being carried by and were made to say, in reply to questions, what each of them was. Would he not be perplexed and believe the objects now shown him to be not so real as what he formerly saw? [17]

Yes, not nearly so real.

And if he were forced to look at the fire-light itself, would not his eyes ache, so that he would try to escape and turn back to the things which he could see distinctly, convinced that they really were clearer than these other objects now being shown to him?

Yes.

And suppose someone were to drag him away forcibly up the steep and rugged ascent and not let him go until he had hauled him out into the sunlight, would he not suffer pain and vexation at such treatment, and, when he had come out into the light, find his eyes so full of its radiance that he could not see a single one of the things that he was now told were real?

Certainly he would not see them all at once.

He would need, then, to grow accustomed before he could see things in that upper world.[18] At first it would be easiest to make out shadows, and then the images of men and things reflected in water, and later on the things themselves. After that, it would be easier to watch the heavenly bodies and the sky itself by night, looking at the light of the moon and stars rather than the Sun and the Sun's light in the day-time.

Yes, surely.

Last of all, he would be able to look at the Sun and contemplate its nature, not as it appears when reflected in water or any alien medium, but as it is in itself in its own domain.

No doubt.

And now he would begin to draw the conclusion that it is the Sun that produces

movement of the objects and the sounds whose echo the prisoners hear. The parapet prevents these persons' shadows from being cast on the wall of the Cave.

[15] Adam's text and interpretation. The prisoners, having seen nothing but shadows, cannot think their words refer to the objects carried past behind their backs. For them shadows (images) are the only realities.

[16] The state of mind called *eikasia* in the previous chapter.

[17] The first effect of Socratic questioning is perplexity.

[18] Here is the moral—the need of habituation by mathematical study before discussing moral ideas and ascending through them to the Form of the Good.

the seasons and the course of the year and controls everything in the visible world, and moreover is in a way the cause of all that he and his companions used to see.

Clearly he would come at last to that conclusion.

Then if he called to mind his fellow prisoners and what passed for wisdom in his former dwelling-place, he would surely think himself happy in the change and be sorry for them. They may have had a practice of honouring and commending one another, with prizes for the man who had the keenest eye for the passing shadows and the best memory for the order in which they followed or accompanied one another, so that he could make a good guess as to which was going to come next.[19] Would our released prisoner be likely to covet those prizes or to envy the men exalted to honour and power in the Cave? Would he not feel like Homer's Achilles, that he would far sooner "be on earth as a hired servant in the house of a landless man" [20] or endure anything rather than go back to his old beliefs and live in the old way?

Yes, he would prefer any fate to such a life.

Now imagine what would happen if he went down again to take his former seat in the Cave. Coming suddenly out of the sunlight, his eyes would be filled with darkness. He might be required once more to deliver his opinion on those shadows, in competition with the prisoners who had never been released, while his eyesight was still dim and unsteady; and it might take some time to become used to the darkness. They would laugh at him and say that he had gone up only to come back with his sight ruined; it was worth no one's while even to attempt the ascent. If they could lay hands on the man

who was trying to set them free and lead them up, they would kill him.[21]

Yes, they would.

Every feature in this parable, my dear Glaucon, is meant to fit our earlier analysis. The prison dwelling corresponds to the region revealed to us through the sense of sight, and the fire-light within it to the power of the Sun. The ascent to see the things in the upper world you may take as standing for the upward journey of the soul into the region of the intelligible; then you will be in possession of what I surmise, since that is what you wish to be told. Heaven knows whether it is true; but this, at any rate, is how it appears to me. In the world of knowledge, the last thing to be perceived and only with great difficulty is the essential Form of Goodness. Once it is perceived, the conclusion must follow that, for all things, this is the cause of whatever is right and good; in the visible world it gives birth to light and to the lord of light, while it is itself sovereign in the intelligible world and the parent of intelligence and truth. Without having had a vision of this Form no one can act with wisdom, either in his own life or in matters of state.

So far as I can understand, I share your belief.

Then you may also agree that it is no wonder if those who have reached this height are reluctant to manage the affairs of men. Their souls long to spend all their time in that upper world—naturally enough, if here once more our parable holds true. Nor, again, is it at all strange that one who comes from the contemplation of divine things to the miseries of human life should appear awkward and ridiculous when, with eyes still dazed and not yet accustomed to the darkness, he is compelled, in a law-court or elsewhere, to dispute about the shadows of justice or the images that cast those shadows, and to wrangle over the notions of what is right in the minds of men who have never beheld Justice itself.[22]

---

[19] The empirical politician, with no philosophic insight, but only a "knack of remembering what usually happens" (*Gorg.* 501 A). He has *eikasia* = conjecture as to what is likely (*eikos*).

[20] This verse, being spoken by the ghost of Achilles, suggests that the Cave is comparable with Hades.

[21] An allusion to the fate of Socrates.

[22] In the *Gorgias* 486 A, Callicles, forecasting the trial of Socrates, taunts him with the philosopher's inability to defend himself in a court.

It is not at all strange.

No; a sensible man will remember that the eyes may be confused in two ways—by a change from light to darkness or from darkness to light; and he will recognize that the same thing happens to the soul. When he sees it troubled and unable to discern anything clearly, instead of laughing thoughtlessly, he will ask whether, coming from a brighter existence, its unaccustomed vision is obscured by the darkness, in which case he will think its condition enviable and its life a happy one; or whether, emerging from the depths of ignorance, it is dazzled by excess of light. If so, he will rather feel sorry for it; or, if he were inclined to laugh, that would be less ridiculous than to laugh at the soul which has come down from the light.

That is a fair statement.

If this is true, then, we must conclude that education is not what it is said to be by some, who profess to put knowledge into a soul which does not possess it, as if they could put sight into blind eyes. On the contrary, our own account signifies that the soul of every man does possess the power of learning the truth and the organ to see it with; and that, just as one might have to turn the whole body round in order that the eye should see light instead of darkness, so the entire soul must be turned away from this changing world, until its eye can bear to contemplate reality and that supreme splendour which we have called the Good. Hence there may well be an art whose aim would be to effect this very thing, the conversion of the soul, in the readiest way; not to put the power of sight into the soul's eye, which already has it, but to ensure that, instead of looking in the wrong direction, it is turned the way it ought to be.

Yes, it may well be so.

It looks, then, as though wisdom were different from those ordinary virtues, as they are called, which are not far removed from bodily qualities, in that they can be produced by habituation and exercise in a soul which has not possessed them from the first. Wisdom, it seems, is certainly the virtue of some diviner faculty, which never loses its power, though its use for good or harm depends on the direction towards which it is turned. You must have noticed in dishonest men with a reputation for sagacity the shrewd glance of a narrow intelligence piercing the objects to which it is directed. There is nothing wrong with their power of vision, but it has been forced into the service of evil, so that the keener its sight, the more harm it works.

Quite true.

And yet if the growth of a nature like this had been pruned from earliest childhood, cleared of those clinging overgrowths which come of gluttony and all luxurious pleasure and, like leaden weights charged with affinity to this mortal world, hang upon the soul, bending its vision downwards; if, freed from these, the soul were turned round towards true reality, then this same power in these very men would see the truth as keenly as the objects it is turned to now.

Yes, very likely.

Is it not also likely, or indeed certain after what has been said, that a state can never be properly governed either by the uneducated who know nothing of truth or by men who are allowed to spend all their days in the pursuit of culture? The ignorant have no single mark before their eyes at which they must aim in all the conduct of their own lives and of affairs of state; and the others will not engage in action if they can help it, dreaming that, while still alive, they have been translated to the Islands of the Blest.

Quite true.

It is for us, then, as founders of a commonwealth, to bring compulsion to bear on the noblest natures. They must be made to climb the ascent to the vision of Goodness, which we called the highest object of knowledge; and, when they have looked upon it long enough, they must not be allowed, as they now are, to remain on the heights, refusing to come down again to the prisoners or to take any part in their labours and rewards, however much or little these may be worth.

Deliberate doubt and self-certainty

René Descartes (1596–1650)

Educated in his early years in a Jesuit college and all his life a devout Catholic, Descartes experienced at the age of twenty-three, with the force of a mystical vision, the revelation that the universe is to be interpreted as a mathematical structure, that nature is at bottom a mechanism to which logical form is the key. He developed the science of analytic geometry, applying algebraic symbols to describe geometrical figures. The clarity and exactness introduced into thought through mathematical symbolism represented to Descartes the model for all thinking, and he resolved to follow a deductive method founded on axioms that could be accepted as true without the trace of a doubt.

By his method of deliberate doubt, Descartes hoped to arrive at what could be known with certainty, not skeptically to doubt all things. He wanted to base his beliefs neither on the authority of previous thinkers nor on the shifting folkways of the world. He turned then to the evidence of his senses but reasoned that his senses offered no certainty, since what they presented might be "illusions and dreams." What was left, following this radical doubt, was the certainty that he, the doubter, existed in order to doubt. If the evidence of the senses is doubted, then there must be a person doubting who does not accept these sense impressions. Descartes concluded "I think, therefore I am."

One of his famous works, the Discourse on Method, *was originally the preface to a book on meteors and geometry. The title of this extremely influential work indicates the kind of influence it had. It turned attention to the possibility of unraveling the secrets of nature through lucid and precise description and through a method of individual reflection. Our selection is from an equally important work, the* Meditations.

Meditation I. Of the things which may be brought within the sphere of the doubtful.

It is now some years since I detected how many were the false beliefs that I had from my earliest youth admitted as true, and how doubtful was everything I had since constructed on this basis; and from that time I was convinced that I must once for all seriously undertake to rid myself of all the opinions which I

From *The Philosophical Works of Descartes,* tr. E. S. Haldane and G. R. T. Ross, Vol. I. Copyright, 1911, by Cambridge University Press. Used by permission.

18

had formerly accepted, and commence to build anew from the foundation, if I wanted to establish any firm and permanent structure in the sciences. But as this enterprise appeared to be a very great one, I waited until I had attained an age so mature that I could not hope that at any later date I should be better fitted to execute my design. This reason caused me to delay so long that I should feel that I was doing wrong were I to occupy in deliberation the time that yet remains to me for action. To-day, then, since very opportunely for the plan I have in view I have delivered my mind from every care [and am happily agitated by no passions] and since I have procured for myself an assured leisure in a peaceable retirement, I shall at last seriously and freely address myself to the general upheaval of all my former opinions.

Now for this object it is not necessary that I should show that all of these are false—I shall perhaps never arrive at this end. But inasmuch as reason already persuades me that I ought no less carefully to withhold my assent from matters which are not entirely certain and indubitable than from those which appear to me manifestly to be false, if I am able to find in each one some reason to doubt, this will suffice to justify my rejecting the whole. And for that end it will not be requisite that I should examine each in particular, which would be an endless undertaking; for owing to the fact that the destruction of the foundations of necessity brings with it the downfall of the rest of the edifice, I shall only in the first place attack those principles upon which all my former opinions rested.

All that up to the present time I have accepted as most true and certain I have learned either from the senses or through the senses; but it is sometimes proved to me that these senses are deceptive, and it is wiser not to trust entirely to any thing by which we have once been deceived.

But it may be that although the senses sometimes deceive us concerning things which are hardly perceptible, or very far away, there are yet many others to be met with as to which we cannot reasonably have any doubt, although

we recognise them by their means. For example, there is the fact that I am here, seated by the fire, attired in a dressing gown, having this paper in my hands and other similar matters. And how could I deny that these hands and this body are mine, were it not perhaps that I compare myself to certain persons, devoid of sense, whose cerebella are so troubled and clouded by the violent vapours of black bile, that they constantly assure us that they think they are kings when they are really quite poor, or that they are clothed in purple when they are really without covering, or who imagine that they have an earthenware head or are nothing but pumpkins or are made of glass. But they are mad, and I should not be any the less insane were I to follow examples so extravagant.

At the same time I must remember that I am a man, and that consequently I am in the habit of sleeping, and in my dreams representing to myself the same things or sometimes even less probable things, than do those who are insane in their waking moments. How often has it happened to me that in the night I dreamt that I found myself in this particular place, that I was dressed and seated near the fire, whilst in reality I was lying undressed in bed! At this moment it does indeed seem to me that it is with eyes awake that I am looking at this paper; that this head which I move is not asleep, that it is deliberately and of set purpose that I extend my hand and perceive it; what happens in sleep does not appear so clear nor so distinct as does all this. But in thinking over this I remind myself that on many occasions I have in sleep been deceived by similar illusions, and in dwelling carefully on this reflection I see so manifestly that there are no certain indications by which we may clearly distinguish wakefulness from sleep that I am lost in astonishment. And my astonishment is such that it is almost capable of persuading me that I now dream.

Now let us assume that we are asleep and that all these particulars, e.g. that we open our eyes, shake our head, extend our hands, and so on, are but false delusions; and let us reflect that possibly neither our hands nor our whole body are such as they appear to us to be. At the same time we must at least confess that the things which are represented to us in sleep are like painted representations which can only have been formed as the counterparts of something real and true, and that in this way those general things at least, i.e. eyes, a head, hands, and a whole body, are not imaginary things, but things really existent. For, as a matter of fact, painters, even when they study with the greatest skill to represent sirens and satyrs by forms the most strange and extraordinary, cannot give them natures which are entirely new, but merely make a certain medley of the members of different animals; or if their imagination is extravagant enough to invent something so novel that nothing similar has ever before been seen, and that then their work represents a thing purely fictitious and absolutely false, it is certain all the same that the colours of which this is composed are necessarily real. And for the same reason, although these general things, to wit, [a body], eyes, a head, hands, and such like, may be imaginary, we are bound at the same time to confess that there are at least some other objects yet more simple and more universal, which are real and true; and of these just in the same way as with certain real colours, all these images of things which dwell in our thoughts, whether true and real or false and fantastic, are formed.

To such a class of things pertains corporeal nature in general, and its extension, the figure of extended things, their quantity or magnitude and number, as also the place in which they are, the time which measures their duration, and so on.

That is possibly why our reasoning is not unjust when we conclude from this that Physics, Astronomy, Medicine and all other sciences which have as their end the consideration of composite things, are very dubious and uncertain; but that Arithmetic, Geometry and other sciences of that kind which only treat of things that are very simple and very general, without taking great trouble to ascertain whether they are actually existent or not, contain some measure of certainty and an element of the indubitable. For whether I am awake or asleep, two and three together always form five, and the square can never have more than four sides, and it does not seem possible that truths so clear and apparent can be suspected of any falsity [or uncertainty].

Nevertheless I have long had fixed in my mind the belief that an all-powerful God existed by whom I have been created such as I am. But how do I know that He has not brought it to pass that there is no earth, no heaven, no extended body, no magnitude, no place, and that nevertheless [I possess the perceptions of all these things and that] they seem to me to exist just exactly as I now see them? And, besides, as I sometimes imagine that others deceive themselves in the things which they think they know best, how do I know that I am not deceived every time that I add two and three, or count the sides of a square, or judge of things yet simpler, if anything simpler can be imagined? But possibly God has not desired that I should be thus deceived, for He is said to be supremely good. If, however, it is contrary to His goodness to have made me such that I constantly deceive myself, it would also appear to be contrary to His goodness to permit me to be sometimes deceived, and nevertheless I cannot doubt that He does permit this.

There may indeed be those who would prefer to deny the existence of a God so powerful, rather than believe that all other things are uncertain. But let us not oppose them for the present, and grant that all that is here said of a God is a fable; nevertheless in whatever way they suppose that I have arrived at the state of being that I have reached—whether they attribute it to fate or to accident, or make out that it is by a continual succession of antecedents, or by some other method—since to err and deceive oneself is a defect, it is clear that the greater will be the probability of my being so imperfect as to deceive myself ever, as is the Author to whom they assign my origin the less powerful. To these reasons I have certainly nothing to reply, but at the end I feel constrained to confess that there is nothing in all that I formerly believed to be true, of which I cannot in some measure doubt, and that not merely through want of thought or through levity, but for reasons which are very powerful and maturely considered; so that henceforth I ought not the less carefully to refrain from giving credence to these opinions than to that which is manifestly false, if I desire to arrive at any certainty [in the sciences].

But it is not sufficient to have made these remarks, we must also be careful to keep them in mind. For these ancient and commonly held opinions still revert frequently to my mind, long and familiar custom having given them the right to occupy my mind against my inclination and rendered them almost masters of my belief; nor will I ever lose the habit of deferring to them or of placing my confidence in them, so long as I consider them as they really are, i.e. opinions in some measure doubtful, as I have just shown, and at the same time highly probable, so that there is much more reason to believe in than to deny them. That is why I consider that I shall not be acting amiss, if, taking of set purpose a contrary belief, I allow myself to be deceived, and for a certain time pretend that all these opinions are entirely false and imaginary, until at last, having thus balanced my former prejudices with my latter [so that they cannot divert my opinions more to one side than to the other], my judgment will no longer be dominated by bad usage or turned away from the right knowledge of the truth. For I am assured that there can be neither peril nor error in this course, and that I cannot at present yield too much to distrust, since I am not considering the question of action, but only of knowledge.

I shall then suppose, not that God who is supremely good and the fountain of truth, but some evil genius not less powerful than deceitful, has employed his whole energies in deceiving me; I shall consider that the heavens, the earth, colours, figures, sound, and all other external things are nought but the illusions and dreams of which this genius has availed himself in order to lay traps for my credulity; I shall consider myself as having no hands, no eyes, no flesh, no blood, nor any senses, yet falsely believing myself to possess all these things; I shall remain obstinately attached to this idea, and if by this means it is not in my power to arrive at the knowledge of any truth, I may at least do what is in my power [i.e. suspend my judgment], and with firm purpose avoid giving credence to any false thing, or being imposed upon by this arch deceiver, however powerful and deceptive he may be. But this task is a laborious one, and insensibly a certain lassitude leads me into the course of my ordinary life. And just as a captive who in sleep enjoys an imaginary liberty, when he begins to suspect that his liberty is but a dream, fears to awaken, and conspires with these agreeable illusions that the deception may be prolonged, so insensibly of my own accord I fall back into my former opinions, and I dread awakening from this slumber, lest the laborious wakefulness which would follow the tranquillity of this repose should have to be spent not in daylight, but in the excessive darkness of the difficulties which have just been discussed.

Meditation II. Of the Nature of the Human Mind; and that it is more easily known than the Body.

The Meditation of yesterday filled my mind with so many doubts that it is no longer in my power to forget them. And yet I do not see in what manner I can resolve them; and, just as if I had all of a sudden fallen into very deep water, I am so disconcerted that I can neither make certain of setting my feet on the bottom, nor can I swim and so support myself on the surface. I shall nevertheless make an effort and follow anew the same path as that on which I yesterday entered, i.e. I shall proceed by setting aside all that in which the least doubt could be supposed to exist, just as if I had discovered that it was absolutely false; and I shall ever follow in this road until I have met with something which is certain, or at least, if I can do nothing else, until I have learned for certain that there is nothing in the world that is certain. Archimedes, in order that he might draw the terrestrial globe out of its place, and transport it elsewhere, demanded only that one point should be fixed and immoveable; in the same way I shall have the right to conceive high hopes if I am happy enough to discover one thing only which is certain and indubitable.

I suppose, then, that all the things that I see are false; I persuade myself that nothing has ever existed of all that my fallacious memory represents to me. I consider that I possess no senses; I imagine that body, figure, extension, movement and place are but the fictions of my mind. What, then, can be esteemed as true? Perhaps nothing at all, unless that there is nothing in the world that is certain.

But how can I know there is not something different from those things that I have just considered, of which one cannot have the slightest doubt? Is there not some God, or some other being by whatever name we call it, who puts these reflections into my mind? That is not necessary, for is it not possible that I am capable of producing them myself? I myself, am I not at least something? But I have already denied that I had senses and body. Yet I hesitate, for what follows from that? Am I so dependent on body and senses that I cannot exist without these? But I was persuaded that there was nothing in all the world, that there was no heaven, no earth, that there were no minds, nor any bodies: was I not then likewise persuaded that I did not exist? Not at all; of a surety I myself did exist since I persuaded myself of something [or merely because I thought of something]. But there is some deceiver or other, very powerful and very cunning, who ever employs his ingenuity in deceiving me. Then without doubt I exist also if he deceives me, and let him deceive me as much as he will, he can never cause me to be nothing so long as I think that I am something. So that after having reflected well and carefully examined all things, we must come to the definite conclusion that this proposition: I am, I exist, is necessarily true each time that I pronounce it, or that I mentally conceive it.

But I do not yet know clearly enough what I am, I who am certain that I am; and hence I must be careful to see that I do not imprudently take some other object in place of myself, and thus that I do not go astray in respect of this knowledge that I hold to be the most certain and most evident of all that I have formerly learned. That is why I shall now consider anew what I believed myself to be before I embarked upon these last reflections; and of my former opinions I shall withdraw all that might even in a small degree be invalidated by the reasons which I have just brought forward, in order that there may be nothing at all left beyond what is absolutely certain and indubitable.

What then did I formerly believe myself to be? Undoubtedly I believed myself to be a man. But what is a man? Shall I say a reasonable animal? Certainly not; for then I should have to inquire what an animal is, and what is reasonable; and thus from a single question I should insensibly fall into an infinitude of others more difficult; and I should not wish to waste the little time and leisure remaining to me in trying to unravel subtleties like these. But I shall rather stop here to consider the thoughts which of themselves spring up in my mind, and which were not inspired by anything beyond my own nature alone when I applied myself to the consideration of my being. In the first place, then, I considered myself as having a face, hands, arms, and all that system of members composed of bones and flesh as seen in a corpse which I designated by the name of body. In addition to this I considered that I was nourished, that I walked, that I felt, and that I thought, and I referred all these actions to the soul: but I did not stop to consider what the soul was, or if I did stop, I imagined that it was something extremely rare and subtle like a wind, a flame, or an ether, which was spread throughout my grosser parts. As to body I had no manner of doubt about its nature, but thought I had a very clear knowledge of it; and if I had desired to explain it according to the notions that I had then formed of it, I should have described it thus: By the body I understand all that which can be defined by a certain figure: something which can be confined in a certain place, and which can fill a given space in such a way that every other body will be excluded from it;

which can be perceived either by touch, or by sight, or by hearing, or by taste, or by smell: which can be moved in many ways not, in truth, by itself, but by something which is foreign to it, by which it is touched [and from which it receives impressions]: for to have the power of self-movement, as also of feeling or of thinking, I did not consider to appertain to the nature of body: on the contrary, I was rather astonished to find that faculties similar to them existed in some bodies.

But what am I, now that I suppose that there is a certain genius which is extremely powerful, and, if I may say so, malicious, who employs all his powers in deceiving me? Can I affirm that I possess the least of all those things which I have just said pertain to the nature of body? I pause to consider, I revolve all these things in my mind, and I find none of which I can say that it pertains to me. It would be tedious to stop to enumerate them. Let us pass to the attributes of soul and see if there is any one which is in me? What of nutrition or walking [the first mentioned]? But if it is so that I have no body it is also true that I can neither walk nor take nourishment. Another attribute is sensation. But one cannot feel without body, and besides I have thought I perceived many things during sleep that I recognised in my waking moments as not having been experienced at all. What of thinking? I find here that thought is an attribute that belongs to me; it alone cannot be separated from me. I am, I exist, that is certain. But how often? Just when I think; for it might possibly be the case if I ceased entirely to think, that I should likewise cease altogether to exist. I do not now admit anything which is not necessarily true: to speak accurately I am not more than a thing which thinks, that is to say a mind or a soul, or an understanding, or a reason, which are terms whose significance was formerly unknown to me. I am, however, a real thing and really exist; but what thing? I have answered: a thing which thinks.

And what more? I shall exercise my imagination [in order to see if I am not something more]. I am not a collection of members which we call the human body: I am not a subtle air distributed through these members, I am not a wind, a fire, a vapour, a breath, nor anything at all which I can imagine or conceive; because I have assumed that all these were nothing. Without changing that supposition I find that I only leave myself certain of the fact that I am somewhat. But perhaps it is true that these same things which I supposed were non-existent because they are unknown to me, are really not different from the self which I know. I am not sure about this, I shall not dispute about it now; I can only give judgment on things that are known to me. I know that I exist, and I inquire what I am, I whom I know to exist. But it is very certain that the knowledge of my existence taken in its precise significance does not depend on things whose existence is not yet known to me; consequently it does not depend on those which I can feign in imagination. And indeed the very term *feign* in imagination [1] proves to me my error, for I really do this if I image myself a something, since to imagine is nothing else than to contemplate the figure or image of a corporeal thing. But I already know for certain that I am, and that it may be that all these images, and, speaking generally, all things that relate to the nature of body are nothing but dreams [and chimeras]. For this reason I see clearly that I have as little reason to say, "I shall stimulate my imagination in order to know more distinctly what I am," than if I were to say, "I am now awake, and I perceive somewhat that is real and true: but because I do not yet perceive it distinctly enough, I shall go to sleep of express purpose, so that my dreams may represent the perception with greatest truth and evidence." And, thus, I know for certain that nothing of all that I can understand by means of my imagination belongs to this knowledge which I have of myself, and that it is necessary to recall the mind from this mode of thought with the utmost diligence in order that it may be able to know its own nature with perfect distinctness.

But what then am I? A thing which thinks.

[1] Or "form an image" (effingo).

What is a thing which thinks? It is a thing which doubts, understands, [conceives], affirms, denies, wills, refuses, which also imagines and feels.

Certainly it is no small matter if all these things pertain to my nature. But why should they not so pertain? Am I not that being who now doubts nearly everything, who nevertheless understands certain things, who affirms that one only is true, who denies all the others, who desires to know more, is averse from being deceived, who imagines many things, sometimes indeed despite his will, and who perceives many likewise, as by the intervention of the bodily organs? Is there nothing in all this which is as true as it is certain that I exist, even though I should always sleep and though he who has given me being employed all his ingenuity in deceiving me? Is there likewise any one of these attributes which can be distinguished from my thought, or which might be said to be separated from myself? For it is so evident of itself that it is I who doubts, who understands, and who desires, that there is no reason here to add anything to explain it. And I have certainly the power of imagining likewise; for although it may happen (as I formerly supposed) that none of the things which I imagine are true, nevertheless this power of imagining does not cease to be really in use, and it forms part of my thought. Finally, I am the same who feels, that is to say, who perceives certain things, as by the organs of sense, since in truth I see light, I hear noise, I feel heat. But it will be said that these phenomena are false and that I am dreaming. Let it be so; still it is at least quite certain that it seems to me that I see light, that I hear noise and that I feel heat. That cannot be false; properly speaking it is what is in me called feeling [2]; and used in this precise sense that is no other thing than thinking.

From this time I begin to know what I am with a little more clearness and distinction than before; but nevertheless it still seems to me, and I cannot prevent myself from think-

[2] Sentire.

ing, that corporeal things, whose images are framed by thought, which are tested by the senses, are much more distinctly known than that obscure part of me which does not come under the imagination. Although really it is very strange to say that I know and understand more distinctly these things whose existence seems to me dubious, which are unknown to me, and which do not belong to me, than others of the truth of which I am convinced, which are known to me and which pertain to my real nature, in a word, than myself. But I see clearly how the case stands: my mind loves to wander, and cannot yet suffer itself to be retained within the just limits of truth. Very good, let us once more give it the freest rein, so that, when afterwards we seize the proper occasion for pulling up, it may the more easily be regulated and controlled.

Let us begin by considering the commonest matters, those which we believe to be the most distinctly comprehended, to wit, the bodies which we touch and see; not indeed bodies in general, for these general ideas are usually a little more confused, but let us consider one body in particular. Let us take, for example, this piece of wax: it has been taken quite freshly from the hive, and it has not yet lost the sweetness of the honey which it contains; it still retains somewhat of the odour of the flowers from which it has been culled; its colour, its figure, its size are apparent; it is hard, cold, easily handled, and if you strike it with the finger, it will emit a sound. Finally all the things which are requisite to cause us distinctly to recognise a body, are met with in it. But notice that while I speak and approach the fire what remained of the taste is exhaled, the smell evaporates, the colour alters, the figure is destroyed, the size increases, it becomes liquid, it heats, scarcely can one handle it, and when one strikes it, no sound is emitted. Does the same wax remain after this change? We must confess that it remains; none would judge otherwise. What then did I know so distinctly in this piece of wax? It could certainly be nothing of all that the senses brought to my notice, since all these things which fall under taste, smell, sight, touch, and hearing, are found to be changed, and yet the same wax remains.

Perhaps it was what I now think, viz. that this wax was not that sweetness of honey, nor that agreeable scent of flowers, nor that particular whiteness, nor that figure, nor that sound, but simply a body which a little while before appeared to me as perceptible under these forms, and which is now perceptible under others. But what, precisely, is it that I imagine when I form such conceptions? Let us attentively consider this, and, abstracting from all that does not belong to the wax, let us see what remains. Certainly nothing remains excepting a certain extended thing which is flexible and movable. But what is the meaning of flexible and movable? Is it not that I imagine that this piece of wax being round is capable of becoming square and of passing from a square to a triangular figure? No, certainly it is not that, since I imagine it admits of an infinitude of similar changes, and I nevertheless do not know how to compass the infinitude by my imagination, and consequently this conception which I have of the wax is not brought about by the faculty of imagination. What now is this extension? Is it not also unknown? For it becomes greater when the wax is melted, greater when it is boiled, and greater still when the heat increases; and I should not conceive [clearly] according to truth what wax is, if I did not think that even this piece that we are considering is capable of receiving more variations in extension than I have ever imagined. We must then grant that I could not even understand through the imagination what this piece of wax is, and that it is my mind [3] alone which perceives it. I say this piece of wax in particular, for as to wax in general it is yet clearer. But what is this piece of wax which cannot be understood excepting by the [understanding or] mind? It is certainly the same that I see, touch, imagine, and finally it is the same which I have always believed it to be from the beginning. But what must partic-

ularly be observed is that its perception is neither an act of vision, nor of touch, nor of imagination, and has never been such although it may have appeared formerly to be so, but only an intuition [4] of the mind, which may be imperfect and confused as it was formerly, or clear and distinct as it is at present, according as my attention is more or less directed to the elements which are found in it, and of which it is composed.

Yet in the meantime I am greatly astonished when I consider [the great feebleness of mind] and its proneness to fall [insensibly] into error; for although without giving expression to my thoughts I consider all this in my own mind, words often impede me and I am almost deceived by the terms of ordinary language. For we say that we see the same wax, if it is present, and not that we simply judge that it is the same from its having the same colour and figure. From this I should conclude that I knew the wax by means of vision and not simply by the intuition of the mind; unless by chance I remember that, when looking from a window and saying I see men who pass in the street, I really do not see them, but infer that what I see is men, just as I say that I see wax. And yet what do I see from the window but hats and coats which may cover automatic machines? Yet I judge these to be men. And similarly solely by the faculty of judgment which rests in my mind, I comprehend that which I believed I saw with my eyes.

A man who makes it his aim to raise his knowledge above the common should be ashamed to derive the occasion for doubting from the forms of speech invented by the vulgar; I prefer to pass on and consider whether I had a more evident and perfect conception of what the wax was when I first perceived it, and when I believed I knew it by means of the external senses or at least by the common sense [5] as it is called, that is to say by the imaginative faculty, or whether my present conception is clearer now that I have most care-

[3] entendement F., mens L.

[4] inspectio.
[5] sensus communis.

fully examined what it is, and in what way it can be known. It would certainly be absurd to doubt as to this. For what was there in this first perception which was distinct? What was there which might not as well have been perceived by any of the animals? But when I distinguish the wax from its external forms, and when, just as if I had taken from it its vestments, I consider it quite naked, it is certain that although some error may still be found in my judgment, I can nevertheless not perceive it thus without a human mind.

But finally what shall I say of this mind, that is, of myself, for up to this point I do not admit in myself anything but mind? What then, I who seem to perceive this piece of wax so distinctly, do I not know myself, not only with much more truth and certainty, but also with much more distinctness and clearness? For if I judge that the wax is or exists from the fact that I see it, it certainly follows much more clearly that I am or that I exist myself from the fact that I see it. For it may be that what I see is not really wax, it may also be that I do not possess eyes with which to see anything; but it cannot be that when I see, or (for I no longer take account of the distinction) when I think I see, that I myself who think am nought. So if I judge that the wax exists from the fact that I touch it, the same thing will follow, to wit, that I am; and if I judge that my imagination, or some other cause, whatever it is, persuades me that the wax exists, I shall still conclude the same.

And what I have here remarked of wax may be applied to all other things which are external to me [and which are met with outside of me]. And further, if the [notion or] perception of wax has seemed to me clearer and more distinct, not only after the sight or the touch, but also after many other causes have rendered it quite manifest to me, with how much more [evidence] and distinctness must it be said that I now know myself, since all the reasons which contribute to the knowledge of wax, or any other body whatever, are yet better proofs of the nature of my mind! And there are so many other things in the mind itself which may contribute to the elucidation of its nature, that those which depend on body such as these just mentioned, hardly merit being taken into account.

But finally here I am, having insensibly reverted to the point I desired, for, since it is now manifest to me that even bodies are not properly speaking known by the senses or by the faculty of imagination, but by the understanding only, and since they are not known from the fact that they are seen or touched, but only because they are understood, I see clearly that there is nothing which is easier for me to know than my mind. But because it is difficult to rid oneself so promptly of an opinion to which one was accustomed for so long, it will be well that I should halt a little at this point, so that by the length of my meditation I may more deeply imprint on my memory this new knowledge.

Personal identity

David Hume (1711-1776)

Hume was born in Edinburgh, Scotland, and educated at the University in that city. He wrote a number of philosophical works which attracted little notice during his lifetime but achieved great influence after his death. His History of England *and his works on religion did bring him fame in his own day, but his enduring reputation as a philosopher rests on* A Treatise of Human Nature (*1739–1740*) *and* An Enquiry Concerning Human Understanding (*1748*).

Hume subscribed to the empiricist view that all knowledge of the world derives from, and is founded upon, experience. The data of the senses and of introspection he labels "impressions" and uses the word "ideas" for the thoughts and images produced in reflection upon impressions. There can be no idea in the mind, he holds, that is not based on some impression, and no verbal expression is meaningful which lacks a foundation in sense-data.

In the present selection from his Treatise *Hume tests the meaningfulness of the word "self" by seeking the impressions on which such an idea may be based. Our belief that each person possesses a self, he concludes, is not based on any impression of a self but is produced by the association of ideas. Human minds are no more than bundles of perceptions.*

There are some philosophers, who imagine we are every moment intimately conscious of what we call our Self; that we feel its existence and its continuance in existence; and are certain, beyond the evidence of a demonstration, both of its perfect identity and simplicity. The strongest sensation, the most violent passion, say they, instead of distracting us from this view, only fix it the more intensely, and make us consider their influence on *self* either by their pain or pleasure. To attempt a farther proof of this were to weaken its evidence; since no proof can be derived from any fact, of which we are so intimately conscious; nor is there any thing, of which we can be certain, if we doubt of this.

Unluckily all these positive assertions are contrary to that very experience, which is pleaded for them, nor have we any idea of *self*, after the manner it is here explained. For from what impression could this idea be derived? This question it is impossible to answer without a manifest contradiction and absurdity; and yet it is a question, which must necessarily be answered, if we would have the idea of self pass for clear and intelligible. It must be some one impression, that gives rise to every real idea. But self or person is not any one impression, but that to which our several impressions and ideas are supposed to have a reference. If any impression gives rise to the idea of self, that impression must continue invariably the same, through the whole course of our lives; since self is supposed to exist after that manner. But there is no impression constant and invariable. Pain and pleasure, grief and joy, passions and sensations succeed each other, and never all exist at the same time. It cannot, therefore, be from any of these impressions, or

From David Hume, "Of Personal Identity," from *A Treatise of Human Nature,* book I, part 4.

27

from any other, that the idea of self is derived; and consequently there is no such idea.

But farther, what must become of all our particular perceptions upon this hypothesis? All these are different, and distinguishable, and separable from each other, and may be separately considered, and may exist separately, and have no need of any thing to support their existence. After what manner, therefore, do they belong to self; and how are they connected with it? For my part, when I enter most intimately into what I call *myself*, I always stumble on some particular perception or other, of heat or cold, light or shade, love or hatred, pain or pleasure. I never can catch *myself* at any time without a perception, and never can observe any thing but the perception. When my perceptions are removed for any time, as by sound sleep; so long am I sensible of *myself*, and may truly be said not to exist. And were all my perceptions removed by death, and could I neither think, nor feel, nor see, nor love, nor hate after the dissolution of my body, I should be entirely annihilated, nor do I conceive what is farther requisite to make me a perfect non-entity. If any one upon serious and unprejudiced reflexion, thinks he has a different notion of *himself*, I must confess I can reason no longer with him. All I can allow him is, that he may be in the right as well as I, and that we are essentially different in this particular. He may, perhaps, perceive something simple and continued, which he calls *himself*; though I am certain there is no such principle in me.

But setting aside some metaphysicians of this kind, I may venture to affirm of the rest of mankind, that they are nothing but a bundle or collection of different perceptions, which succeed each other with an inconceivable rapidity, and are in a perpetual flux and movement. Our eyes cannot turn in their sockets without varying our perceptions. Our thought is still more variable than our sight; and all our other senses and faculties contribute to this change; nor is there any single power of the soul, which remains unalterably the same, perhaps for one moment. The mind is a kind of theatre, where several perceptions successively make their appearance; pass, re-pass, glide away, and mingle in an infinite variety of postures and situations.

There is properly no *simplicity* in it at one time, nor *identity* in different; whatever natural propension we may have to imagine that simplicity and identity. The comparison of the theatre must not mislead us. They are the successive perceptions only, that constitute the mind; nor have we the most distant notion of the place, where these scenes are represented, or of the materials, of which it is composed.

What then gives us so great a propension to ascribe an identity to these successive perceptions, and to suppose ourselves possest of an invariable and uninterrupted existence through the whole course of our lives? ...

We have a distinct idea of an object, that remains invariable and uninterrupted through a supposed variation of time; and this idea we call that of *identity* or *sameness*. We have also a distinct idea of several different objects existing in succession, and connected together by a close relation; and this to an accurate view affords as perfect a notion of *diversity*, as if there was no manner of relation among the objects. But though these two ideas of identity, and a succession of related objects be in themselves perfectly distinct, and even contrary, yet it is certain, that in our common way of thinking they are generally confounded with each other. That action of the imagination, by which we consider the uninterrupted and invariable object, and that by which we reflect on the succession of related objects, are almost the same to the feeling, nor is there much more effort of thought required in the latter case than in the former. The relation facilitates the transition of the mind from one object to another, and renders its passage as smooth as if it contemplated one continued object. This resemblance is the cause of the confusion and mistake, and makes us substitute the notion of identity, instead of that of related objects. However at one instant we may consider the related succession as variable or interrupted, we are sure the next to ascribe to it a perfect identity, and regard it as invariable and uninterrupted. Our propensity to this mistake is so great from the resemblance above-mentioned, that we fall into it before we are aware; and though we incessantly correct ourselves by reflexion, and return to a more accurate method of thinking, yet we cannot long sustain our philosophy, or take off this biass from the imagination. Our last resource is to yield to it, and boldly assert that these different related objects are in effect the same, however interrupted and variable. In order to justify to ourselves this absurdity, we often feign some new and unintelligible principle, that connects the objects together, and prevents their interruption or variation. Thus we feign the continued existence of the perceptions of our senses, to remove the interruption; and run into the notion of a *soul*, and *self*, and *substance*, to disguise the variation. But we may farther observe, that where we do not give rise to such a fiction, our propension to confound identity with relation is so great, that we are apt to imagine [1] something unknown and mysterious, connecting the parts, beside their relation; and this I take to be the case with regard to the identity we ascribe to plants and vegetables. And even when this does not take place, we still feel a propensity to confound these ideas, though we are not able fully to satisfy ourselves in that particular, nor find any thing invariable and uninterrupted to justify our notion of identity.

Thus the controversy concerning identity is not merely a dispute of words. For when we attribute identity, in an improper sense, to variable or interrupted objects, our mistake is not confined to the expression, but is commonly attended with a fiction, either of something invariable and uninterrupted, or of something mysterious and inexplicable, or at least with a propensity to such fictions. . . .

We now proceed to explain the nature of *personal identity*, which has become so great a question in philosophy, especially of late years in *England*, where all the abstruser sciences are studied with a peculiar ardour and application. . . .

It is evident, that the identity, which we

attribute to the human mind, however perfect we may imagine it to be, is not able to run the several different perceptions into one, and make them lose their characters of distinction and difference, which are essential to them. It is still true, that every distinct perception, which enters into the composition of the mind, is a distinct existence, and is different, and distinguishable, and separable from every other perception, either contemporary or successive. But, as, notwithstanding this distinction and separability, we suppose the whole train of perceptions to be united by identity, a question naturally arises concerning this relation of identity; whether it be something that really binds our several perceptions together, or only associates their ideas in the imagination. That is, in other words, whether in pronouncing concerning the identity of a person, we observe some real bond among his perceptions, or only feel one among the ideas we form of them. This question we might easily decide, if we would recollect what has been already proved at large, that the understanding never observes any real connexion among objects, and that even the union of cause and effect, when strictly examined, resolves itself into a customary association of ideas. For from thence it evidently follows, that identity is nothing really belonging to these different perceptions, and uniting them together; but is merely a quality, which we attribute to them, because of the union of their ideas in the imagination, when we reflect upon them. Now the only qualities, which can give ideas an union in the imagination, are these three relations abovementioned. These are the uniting principles in the ideal world, and without them every distinct object is separable by the mind, and may be separately considered, and appears not to have any more connexion with any other object, than if disjoined by the greatest difference and remoteness. It is, therefore, on some of these three relations of resemblance, contiguity and causation, that identity depends; and as the very essence of these relations consists in their producing an easy transition of ideas; it follows, that our notions of personal identity, proceed entirely from the smooth and uninterrupted progress of the thought along a

[1] If the reader is desirous to see how a great genius may be influenced by these seemingly trivial principles of the imagination, as well as the mere vulgar, let him read my Lord *Shaftsbury's* reasonings concerning the uniting principle of the universe, and the identity of plants and animals. See his *Moralists:* or, *Philosophical Rhapsody.*

train of connected ideas, according to the principles above-explained.

The only question, therefore, which remains, is, by what relations this uninterrupted progress of our thought is produced, when we consider the successive existence of a mind or thinking person. And here it is evident we must confine ourselves to resemblance and causation, and must drop contiguity, which has little or no influence in the present case.

To begin with *resemblance;* suppose we could see clearly into the breast of another, and observe that succession of perceptions, which constitutes his mind or thinking principle, and suppose that he always preserves the memory of a considerable part of past perceptions; it is evident that nothing could more contribute to the bestowing a relation on this succession amidst all its variations. For what is the memory but a faculty, by which we raise up the images of past perceptions? And as an image necessarily resembles its object, must not the frequent placing of these resembling perceptions in the chain of thought, convey the imagination more easily from one link to another, and make the whole seem like the continuance of one object? In this particular, then, the memory not only discovers the identity, but also contributes to its production, by producing the relation of resemblance among the perceptions. The case is the same whether we consider ourselves or others.

As to *causation;* we may observe, that the true idea of the human mind, is to consider it as a system of different perceptions or different existences, which are linked together by the relation of cause and effect, and mutually produce, destroy, influence, and modify each other. Our impressions give rise to their correspondent ideas; and these ideas in their turn produce other impressions. One thought chases another, and draws after it a third, by which it is expelled in its turn. In this respect, I cannot compare the soul more properly to anything than to a republic or commonwealth, in which the several members are united by the reciprocal ties of government and subordination, and give rise to other persons, who propagate the same republic in the incessant changes of its parts. And as the same individual republic may

not only change its members, but also its laws and constitutions; in like manner the same person may vary his character and disposition, as well as his impressions and ideas, without losing his identity. Whatever changes he endures, his several parts are still connected by the relation of causation. And in this view our identity with regard to the passions serves to corroborate that with regard to the imagination, by the making our distant perceptions influence each other, and by giving us a present concern for our past or future pains or pleasures.

As memory alone acquaints us with the continuance and extent of this succession of perceptions, it is to be considered, upon that account chiefly, as the source of personal identity. Had we no memory, we never should have any notion of causation, nor consequently of that chain of causes and effects, which constitute our self or person. But having once acquired this notion of causation from the memory, we can extend the same chain of causes, and consequently the identity of our persons beyond our memory, and can comprehend times, and circumstances, and actions, which we have entirely forgot, but suppose in general to have existed. For how few of our past actions are there, of which we have any memory? Who can tell me, for instance, what were his thoughts and actions on the first of *January* 1715, the 11th of *March* 1719, and the 3d of *August* 1733? Or will he affirm, because he has entirely forgot the incidents of these days, that the present self is not the same person with the self of that time; and by that means overturn all the most established notions of personal identity? In this view, therefore, memory does not so much *produce* as *discover* personal identity, by shewing us the relation of cause and effect among our different perceptions. It will be incumbent on those, who affirm that memory produces entirely our personal identity, to give a reason why we can thus extend our identity beyond our memory.

The whole of this doctrine leads us to a conclusion, which is of great importance in the present affair, *viz.* that all the nice and subtile questions concerning personal identity can never possibly be decided.

Causality, Free Will,
and Determinism

In the Prologue we encountered one of the most basic issues with which human thought has tried to deal, our knowledge of our own existence and nature. In this part the problem of self-knowledge is carried further, into the question of human freedom. By trying to answer this question we shall help to expand our view of the sort of beings we are. Is it proper to speak of our actions as "free"? What is our relationship to physical nature? Are human actions determined by antecedent conditions? Indeed, are there necessary causal connections in nature? Before we attempt to ponder the question whether man is free, let us consider causality in physical nature. Here we have to turn again to David Hume.

Hume's famous examination of the idea of necessary connection between cause and effect and his analysis of the notion of personal identity are examples of a freshness of thought that occasionally enters philosophy, waking other thinkers, in Immanuel Kant's words, from their "dogmatic slumbers." In pointing out that we do not find among our "impressions" any necessity in the relation between cause and effect, Hume stimulated a reexamination of our knowledge of causality that has had an important effect on the assumptions of the philosophers of science about the investigations of scientists. Hume's analysis, attributing the idea of necessary connection to our habit of associating events which follow one another in time, has led to a stress on the notion of "laws of nature," which express regularities rather than explain "causes." And since Hume presented the view that the principle of causality by which we interpret the world cannot be confirmed through the senses, philosophers have been led to ask themselves pointed questions about the foundations of our knowledge.

In a rejoinder to Hume and to many philosophers of science who have followed Hume on this point, Brand Blanshard argues against the view that causality in physical nature consists only of observed regularity. He maintains that the hypothesis of an intrinsic connection covers the observed facts of nature better than does the hypothesis of regularity merely by chance. He argues that Hume's view conflicts with both common sense and science and that the scientist is drawn toward the ideal of necessity found in mathematical relations. Blanshard maintains that causality means intrinsic connection, which in turn means necessary connection in the sense of logical necessity. The principle of the connection between cause and effect is, Blanshard holds, the principle of inference, and this involves conclusions following from premises by *necessity*. It is this element of logical necessity, without which there would be no inference, Blanshard maintains, that is present in the relation between cause and effect in physical nature. Is Blanshard right in identifying logical necessity with causal necessity?

He also argues that if causality were to mean only observed regularity, then we should have to regard every *unique* event, for example, a biological mutation which happens for the first time, as uncaused, and we should also be unable to say that a human action proceeded from a human self or from motives. Blanshard argues, then, that only on the hypothesis of a necessary intrinsic connection between cause and effect can we make proper sense of physical nature and of human action.

We have now reached one of the most fundamental issues in philosophy, an issue that is central to an inquiry into human value: the relation of human conduct to causal law. Is man subject in his actions to the principle of causality? We have already seen that Hume was able to raise some searching questions about our knowledge of the link between cause and effect among natural events, and we find Blanshard answering Hume, in part, with the argument that his view would not allow us to connect human action with a human agent. Thinkers who have inquired about the connections among events in the universe have tried to envision the type of relatedness among all events. Is the fabric of events so tightly woven that one event is fully determined by all other events? Or is there room for an element of chance, unpredictability, indeterminism? Is there an exact and universal relatedness amounting to necessity in nature, including human consciousness and will, or are we to allow for chance, spontaneity, and freedom of the will?

In the selection from William James we find the indeterminist position argued. Curiously enough, James maintains that it is the indeterminist position, rejecting necessity, that better accounts for the facts of human action. In reading James, one cannot help noticing his desire to show that human choice and decision do make a difference, that the human will is one of the factors contributing to chance in the universe, that feelings of regret or of joy in the outcome of events are justified, and that man is to be held accountable for what he does. James argues that if all human actions had to have happened as they did, which is what the determinist maintains, then we could not speak meaningfully of human choice and decision, and we should have no reason to feel regret or joy in any outcome. For James it is only on the hypothesis that a man could have made a different choice that he can lead a meaningful moral life.

Here, then, is an issue worth considering: May one regard human effort, creativity, and aspiration as leading values whether one is an indeterminist or a determinist? Or, more generally, will the very same things be values in a universe regarded as deterministic and in one regarded as indeterministic? Has James put forward important considerations for which the determinist cannot account? Or has James failed to answer the necessitarian's charge that the indeterminist has not provided a necessary link between human agents and their actions?

Adolf Grünbaum, in a discussion centered on the question whether science should treat man as it treats the rest of nature, defends determinism, arguing that we may regard human actions as voluntary and consider men responsible for their actions while maintaining that motives necessarily determine actions. In other words, given the motive that in fact prevailed, we could not have acted otherwise. Grünbaum contends that too often determinism is confused with fatalism, which says that no matter what men do, things will happen as they are going to happen. He argues that the determinist is not a fatalist; rather, the determinist believes that while human decisions do make a difference, these decisions are causally determined by a complex of antecedent conditions. Grünbaum also argues that only on the determinist view can one hold a theory of punishment that emphasizes education rather than retaliation, for only the determinist can argue that punishment may causally influence the criminal. Thus, for Grünbaum, the determinist position is entirely compatible with a meaningful moral life.

One of Grünbaum's chief points is that motives are causes of human actions, that certain sets of conditions causally influence what we do. In the concluding selection of this part, the French existentialist, Maurice Merleau-Ponty, presents a view of human freedom which directly challenges Grünbaum's position. Along with his compatriot Jean-Paul Sartre, Merleau-Ponty rejects the view that motives can be regarded simply as causes. He maintains that our decision, already taken at the level of existence, more basic than reflective deliberation, gives to a situation its significance as a motive. Rather than the motive causally determining our decision, it is only reflection on our choice which can disclose a motive.

While agreeing with Sartre in this argument, Merleau-Ponty disagrees with him on another important point. For Sartre, man is absolutely free; he is a pure consciousness that is sharply distinguished from a world which is meaningless without the acts by which he confers meaning on it. Merleau-Ponty, on the other hand, believes that the world is not altogether without meaning and that human freedom has its significance only in a constant involvement with the world. According to Sartre, man chooses himself at every moment and is always free to create himself anew. Sartre holds also that one must see man as either totally free or totally determined. Merleau-Ponty suggests, however, that it is impossible sharply to allocate to freedom that part of an action which comes from it, and to the world, or a man's "situation," that part which belongs to it as an obstacle to human freedom. Freedom is never so complete that a man can deal with the world entirely as he chooses. Any view that regards man as free must, Merleau-Ponty maintains, take into account the fact that human beings develop tendencies or inclinations to perform in certain ways, and that one can regard it as "probable" that a man, for example, will continue in a certain habit rather than throw it off. By our own choices we tend to "fix" ourselves in situations, and then these situations attain a weight that our freedom cannot disregard. A man is a combination of the general and the particular; he has a role to perform, and he alters that role. Freedom is always rooted in the objective world; our freedom is always set in a context of other persons and of general conditions. Man, however, being free, is never fully limited by any set of conditions. Merleau-Ponty, then, regards man as free, but he believes it necessary not to overlook those facts which suggest the opposite view. Such facts can be shown to be compatible with freedom, but only if we recognize that freedom is not absolute.

On Merleau-Ponty's view, freedom both characterizes man and constitutes a value for him. Man *is* free, and man also recognizes and values his freedom. Freedom must, to some extent, recognize itself as freedom, and, indeed, we should not be free if we were unable to see ourselves as free.

In answer to our earlier question as to whether the very same things will be values in a universe regarded as deterministic and in one regarded as indeterministic, we can say that in an indeterministic view of the universe, freedom itself, in the sense in which it has been discussed in this part, becomes a value. Generally speaking, it seems, the indeterminist makes of the chief tenet of his position—man's freedom—a value to be promoted, while the determinist argues that his position does not in the least diminish the importance of human choice.

The idea of necessary connection

David Hume (1711-1776)*

In the following selection from An Enquiry Concerning Human Understanding, *Hume analyzes critically the common notion of a necessary connection or power between cause and effect. He holds that we are unable to discover any impression which is the basis of such an idea and attributes our recognition of causal relations to habitual association of events regularly following one another. His probing and lucid analysis has had a lasting effect on subsequent philosophy.*

Part I

There are no ideas, which occur in metaphysics, more obscure and uncertain, than those of *power, force, energy* or *necessary connexion,* of which it is every moment necessary for us to treat in all our disquisitions. We shall, therefore, endeavour, in this section, to fix, if possible, the precise meaning of these terms, and thereby remove some part of that obscurity, which is so much complained of in this species of philosophy.

It seems a proposition, which will not admit of much dispute, that all our ideas are nothing but copies of our impressions, or, in other words, that it is impossible for us to *think* of any thing, which we have not antecedently *felt,* either by our external or internal senses. ... To be fully acquainted, therefore, with the idea of power or necessary connexion, let us examine its impression; and in order to find the impression with greater certainty, let us search for it in all the sources, from which it may possibly be derived.

When we look about us towards external objects, and consider the operation of causes,

From David Hume, *An Enquiry Concerning Human Understanding,* sec. 7.

* See the introductory note on Hume on page 27.

we are never able, in a single instance, to discover any power or necessary connexion; any quality, which binds the effect to the cause, and renders the one an infallible consequence of the other. We only find, that the one does actually, in fact, follow the other. The impulse of one billiard-ball is attended with motion in the second. This is the whole that appears to the *outward* senses. The mind feels no sentiment or *inward* impression from this succession of objects: Consequently, there is not, in any single, particular instance of cause and effect, any thing which can suggest the idea of power or necessary connexion.

From the first appearance of an object, we never can conjecture what effect will result from it. But were the power or energy of any cause discoverable by the mind, we could foresee the effect, even without experience; and might, at first, pronounce with certainty concerning it, by mere dint of thought and reasoning.

In reality, there is no part of matter, that does ever, by its sensible qualities, discover any power or energy, or give us ground to imagine, that it could produce any thing, or be followed by any other object, which we could denominate its effect. Solidity, extension, motion; these qualities are all complete in themselves, and never point out any other event which may **35** result from them. The scenes of the universe are continually shifting, and one object follows another in an uninterrupted succession; but the power or force, which actuates the whole machine, is entirely concealed from us, and never discovers itself in any of the sensible qualities of body. We know, that, in fact, heat is a constant attendant of flame; but what is the connexion between them, we have no room so much as to conjecture or imagine. It is impossible, therefore, that the idea of power can be derived from the contemplation of bodies, in single instances of their operation; because no bodies ever discover any power, which can be the original of this idea.

Since, therefore, external objects as they appear to the senses, give us no idea of power or necessary connexion, by their operation in particular instances, let us see, whether this idea be derived from reflection on the operations of our own minds, and be copied from any internal impression. It may be said, that we are every moment conscious of internal power; while we feel, that, by the simple command of our will, we can move the organs of our body, or direct the faculties of our mind. An act of volition produces motion in our limbs, or raises a new idea in our imagination. This influence of the will we know by consciousness. Hence we acquire the idea of power or energy; and are certain, that we ourselves and all other intelligent beings are possessed of power. . . .

We shall proceed to examine this pretension; and first with regard to the influence of volition over the organs of the body. This influence, we may observe, is a fact, which, like all other natural events, can be known only by experience, and can never be foreseen from any apparent energy or power in the cause, which connects it with the effect, and renders the one an infallible consequence of the other. The motion of our body follows upon the command of our will. Of this we are every moment conscious. But the means, by which this is effected; the energy, by which the will performs so extraordinary an operation; of this we are so far from being immediately conscious, that it must for ever escape our most diligent enquiry.

For *first*; is there any principle in all nature more mysterious than the union of soul with body; by which a supposed spiritual substance acquires such an influence over a material one, that the most refined thought is able to actuate the grossest matter? Were we empowered, by a secret wish, to remove mountains, or control the planets in their orbit; this extensive authority would not be more extraordinary, nor more beyond our comprehension. But if by consciousness we perceived any power or energy in the will, we must know this power; we must know its connexion with the effect; we must know the secret union of soul and body, and the nature of both these substances; by which the one is able to operate, in so many instances, upon the other.

Secondly, We are not able to move all the organs of the body with a like authority; though we cannot assign any reason besides experience, for so remarkable a difference between one and the other. Why has the will an influence over the tongue and fingers, not over the heart or liver? This question would never embarrass us, were we conscious of a power in the former case, not in the latter. . . .

Thirdly, We learn from anatomy, that the immediate object of power in voluntary motion, is not the member itself which is moved, but certain muscles, and nerves, and animal spirits, and, perhaps, something still more minute and more unknown, through which the motion is successively propagated, ere it reach the member itself whose motion is the immediate object of volition. Can there be a more certain proof, that the power, by which this whole operation is performed, so far from being directly and fully known by an inward sentiment or consciousness, is, to the last degree, mysterious and unintelligible? Here the mind wills a certain event: Immediately another event, unknown to ourselves, and totally different from the one intended, is produced: This event produces another, equally unknown: Till at last, through a long succession, the desired event is produced. But if the original power were felt, it must be known: Were it known, its effect also must be known; since all power is relative to its effect. And *vice versa*, if the effect be not known, the power cannot be known nor felt. How indeed can we be conscious of a power to move our limbs, when we have no such power; but only that to move certain animal spirits, which, though they produce at last the motion of our limbs, yet operate in such a manner as is wholly beyond our comprehension?

We may, therefore, conclude ... that our idea of power is not copied from any sentiment or consciousness of power within ourselves, when we give rise to animal motion, or apply our limbs to their proper use and office. That their motion follows the command of the will is a matter of common experience, like other natural events: But the power or energy by which this is effected, like that in other natural events, is unknown and inconceivable. . . .

The generality of mankind never find any difficulty in accounting for the more common and familiar operations of nature—such as the descent of heavy bodies, the growth of plants, the generation of animals, or the nourishment of bodies by food: But suppose that, in all these cases, they perceive the very force or energy of the cause, by which it is connected with its effect, and is for ever infallible in its operation. They acquire, by long habit, such a turn of mind, that, upon the appearance of the cause, they immediately expect with assurance its usual attendant, and hardly conceive it possible that any other event could result from it. It is only on the discovery of extraordinary phænomena, such as earthquakes, pestilence, and prodigies of any kind, that they find themselves at a loss to assign a proper cause, and to explain the manner in which the effect is produced by it. It is usual for men, in such difficulties to have recourse to some invisible intelligent principle as the immediate cause of that event which surprises them, and which, they think, cannot be accounted for from the common powers of nature. But philosophers, who carry their scrutiny a little farther, immediately perceive that, even in the most familiar events, the energy of the cause is as unintelligible as in the most unusual, and that we only learn by experience the frequent *Conjunction* of objects, without being ever able to comprehend anything like *Connexion* between them. . . .

Part II

But to hasten a conclusion of this argument, which is already drawn out to too great a length: We have sought in vain for an idea of power or necessary connexion in all the sources from which we could suppose it to be derived. It appears that, in single instances of the operation of bodies, we never can, by our utmost scrutiny, discover any thing but one event following another, without being able to comprehend any force or power by which the cause operates, or any connexion between it and its supposed effect. The same difficulty occurs in contemplating the operations of mind on body —where we observe the motion of the latter to follow upon the volition of the former, but are not able to observe or conceive the tie which binds together the motion and volition, or the energy by which the mind produces this effect. The authority of the will over its own faculties and ideas is not a whit more comprehensible: So that, upon the whole, there appears not, throughout all nature, any one instance of connexion which is conceivable by us. All events seem entirely loose and separate. One event follows another; but we never can observe any tie between them. They seem *conjoined*, but never *connected*. And as we can have no idea of any thing which never appeared to our outward sense or inward sentiment, the necessary conclusion *seems* to be that we have no idea of connexion or power at all, and that these words are absolutely without any meaning, when employed either in philosophical reasonings or common life.

But there still remains one method of avoiding this conclusion, and one source which we have not yet examined. When any natural object or event is presented, it is impossible for us, by any sagacity or penetration, to discover, or even conjecture, without experience, what event will result from it, or to carry our foresight beyond that object which is immediately present to the memory and senses. Even after one instance or experiment where we have observed a particular event to follow upon another, we are not entitled to form a general rule, or foretell what will happen in like cases; it being justly esteemed an unpardonable temerity to judge of the whole course of nature from one single experiment, however accurate or certain. But when one particular species of event has always, in all instances, been conjoined with another, we make no longer any scruple of foretelling one upon the appearance of the other, and of employing that reasoning, which can alone assure us of any matter of fact or existence. We then call the one object, *Cause*; the other, *Effect*. We suppose that there is some connexion between them; some power in the one, by which it infallibly produces the other, and operates with the greatest certainty and strongest necessity.

It appears, then, that this idea of a necessary connexion among events arises from a number of similar instances which occur of the constant conjunction of these events; nor can that idea ever be suggested by any one of these instances, surveyed in all possible lights and positions. But there is nothing in a number of instances, different from every single instance, which is supposed to be exactly similar; except only, that after a repetition of similar instances, the mind is carried by habit, upon the appearance of one event, to expect its usual attendant, and to believe that it will exist. This connexion, therefore, which we *feel* in the mind, this customary transition of the imagination from one object to its usual attendant, is the sentiment or impression from which we form the idea of power or necessary connexion. Nothing farther is in the case. Contemplate the subject on all sides; you will never find any other origin of that idea. This is the sole difference between one instance, from which we can never receive the idea of connexion, and a number of similar instances, by which it is suggested. The first time a man saw the communication of motion by impulse, as by the shock of two billiard balls, he could not pronounce that the one event was *connected*: but only that it was *conjoined* with the other. After he has observed several instances of this nature, he then pronounces them to be *connected*. What alteration has happened to give rise to this new idea of *connexion*? Nothing but that he now *feels*

these events to be *connected* in his imagination, and can readily foretell the existence of one from the appearance of the other. When we say, therefore, that one object is connected with another, we mean only that they have acquired a connexion in our thought, and give rise to this inference, by which they become proofs of each other's existence: A conclusion which is somewhat extraordinary, but which seems founded on sufficient evidence. Nor will its evidence be weakened by any general diffidence of the understanding, or sceptical suspicion concerning every conclusion which is new and extraordinary. No conclusions can be more agreeable to scepticism than such as make discoveries concerning the weakness and narrow limits of human reason and capacity.

And what stronger instance can be produced of the surprising ignorance and weakness of the understanding than the present? For surely, if there be any relation among objects which it imports to us to know perfectly, it is that of cause and effect. On this are founded all our reasonings concerning matter of fact or existence. By means of it alone we attain any assurance concerning objects which are removed from the present testimony of our memory and senses. The only immediate utility of all sciences, is to teach us, how to control and regulate future events by their causes. Our thoughts and enquiries are, therefore, every moment, employed about this relation: Yet so imperfect are the ideas which we form concerning it, that it is impossible to give any just definition of cause, except what is drawn from something extraneous and foreign to it. Similar objects are always conjoined with similar. Of this we have experience. Suitably to this experience, therefore, we may define a cause to be *an object, followed by another, and where all the objects similar to the first are followed by objects similar to the second*. Or in other words, *where, if the first object had not been, the second never had existed*. The appearance of a cause always conveys the mind, by a customary transition, to the idea of the effect. Of this also we have experience. We may, therefore, suitably to this experience, form another definition of cause, and call it, *an object fol-*

lowed by another, and whose appearance always conveys the thought to that other. But though both these definitions be drawn from circumstances foreign to the cause, we cannot remedy this inconvenience, or attain any more perfect definition, which may point out that circumstance in the cause, which gives it a connexion with its effect. We have no idea of this connexion, nor even any distinct notion what it is we desire to know, where we endeavour at a conception of it. We say, for instance, that the vibration of this string is the cause of this particular sound. But what do we mean by that affirmation? We either mean *that this vibration is followed by this sound, and that all similar vibrations have been followed by similar sounds: Or, that this vibration is followed by this sound, and that upon the appearance of one the mind anticipates the senses, and forms immediately an idea of the other.* We may consider the relation of cause and effect in either of these two lights; but beyond these, we have no idea of it.

To recapitulate, therefore, the reasonings of this section: Every idea is copied from some preceding impression or sentiment; and where we cannot find any impression, we may be certain that there is no idea. In all single instances of the operation of bodies or minds, there is nothing that produces any impression, nor consequently can suggest any idea of power or necessary connexion. But when many uniform instances appear, and the same object is always followed by the same event; we then begin to entertain the notion of cause and connexion. We then *feel* a new sentiment or impression, to wit, a customary connexion in the thought or imagination between one object and its usual attendant; and this sentiment is the original of that idea which we seek for. For as this idea arises from a number of similar instances, and not from any single instance, it must arise from that circumstance, in which the number of instances differ from every individual instance. But this customary connexion or transition of the imagination is the only circumstance in which they differ. In every other particular they are alike. The first instance which we saw of motion communicated by the shock of two billiard balls (to return to this obvious illustration) is exactly similar to any instance that may, at present, occur to us; except only, that we could not, at first, *infer* one event from the other; which we are enabled to do at present, after so long a course of uniform experience.

A defense of necessary connection

Brand Blanshard (b. 1892)

Brand Blanshard was born in Fredericksburg, Ohio, and was educated at the University of Michigan, Columbia University, Oxford, where he was a Rhodes Scholar, and Harvard, where he received the Ph.D. in 1921. Before joining the Yale faculty in 1945, he had taught at Michigan and Swarthmore. Blanshard has served as chairman of the Yale philosophy department and was Sterling Professor of Philosophy when he retired from regular teaching in 1961. Noted as a contemporary exponent of idealism and rationalism, he is the author of the two-volume The Nature of Thought *(1939), from which our selection is taken. He is completing a three-part work on reason, including the volumes* Reason and Goodness *(1960) and* Reason and Analysis *(1962).*

With the grace and clarity present in all his writings, Blanshard criticizes Hume's account of causality and the position taken by many philosophers of science who have followed Hume. He defends the hypothesis that there is an intrinsic and necessary causal connection between events and argues that the necessity that is present in causal relations is the necessity present in logical inference.

... There is ... good reason to think that not only in inference but also in many other mental processes the causal relation involves necessity. But what of causation in physical nature? This is the field in which most cases of causation are considered to fall, yet current philosophies of science are disposed to agree that no relation whatever is discoverable between physical cause and effect but one of regular conjunction. Certain it is that between the blow of a hammer and the sinking of a nail, or between the motion of one billiard-ball and that of a second, no one has shown the same transparent relation that appears in a course of inference and may be recognized under veils of varying depth in other processes of the mind. The challenge laid down by Hume to show *why* any particular physical event was followed by any other has not been met. Nor do we propose to add one more to the list of futile attempts to meet it. But we should be clear as to what is implied in the failure to meet it. Does such failure in particular cases show that causality generally is nothing but regular sequence? Very far from it. Indeed I think it can be shown that regular sequence is not enough, that there must be some intrinsic connection between cause and effect, and that this intrinsic connection probably is, or includes, one of logical necessity. We must dwell on this a little, since it is important for our position that it should be seen.

In order to overthrow the regular-sequence theory, nothing more, strictly speaking, need be shown than what has been contended for already. It will hardly be denied that

From Brand Blanshard, *The Nature of Thought*, Vol. II, 1939. Used by permission of the publishers, George Allen & Unwin, Ltd.

mental processes supply genuine cases of causality, and any case at all in which the relation involves necessity is enough to invalidate an account which asserts that it never does. But we are dealing now with causality in physical nature. It seems to me that even there the theory has been disposed of by certain criticisms that have recently been made of it.

One of the most persuasive of these has been offered by Professor Montague. It is substantially as follows. How do we proceed when in ordinary life we must calculate the probability of finding a sequence repeated, where the events that are conjoined are not known to be connected otherwise? Suppose we throw a die and get a six. The chances that six will be given in a single throw, we say, are one in six, or $\frac{1}{6}$. Assuming that there is nothing, to our knowledge, in the manner of throwing the die that will secure one side rather than another, what are the chances that a second throw will bring a like result? They will be $\frac{1}{6} \times \frac{1}{6}$ or $\frac{1}{36}$. What are the chances of getting three sixes in a row? They will be $(\frac{1}{6})^3$ or $\frac{1}{216}$. The likelihood of getting six sixes in a row would be one in a little less than 50,000, and if we carried the repetitions to ten or more, the figures would become astronomical. Now if we found that anyone, in throwing a die, kept getting sixes regularly, we should soon begin to harbour suspicions. We should accept his results tolerantly perhaps through two or three repetitions, or if we were extremely charitable, perhaps a few more; but there would soon come a time for the most naïve of us when the hypothesis of mere luck would impose such a strain on our belief as compared with the hypothesis of some sort of control, that we should think anyone a dupe who went on crediting it.

Now, says Mr. Montague, suppose that we throw water on fire. We cannot say what the chances are of getting any one result, say quenching the fire, because we can set no limit to the number of possible alternatives.[1] But we

can say something, he thinks, if one of these results goes on repeating itself to the exclusion of all others. If there is really nothing in event *a* that would compel or require event *b* to follow, then it is antecedently as likely, indeed enormously more likely, that *a* would be followed in a second case by something other than *b* than by *b* itself. And if, in spite of this, *b*, and *b* alone, continues to appear with *a*, is it not as naïve to suppose them unconnected by anything but chance as would be the like supposition about unfailing wins at dice? Yet that is essentially what the regularity theory, with its denial of intrinsic relation, commits us to. It says in effect that if water continues to quench fire, that is only "an outrageous run of luck."

Unfortunately, as Mr. Montague recognizes, the case is not quite so simple. For if you take seriously the hypothesis of merely chance conjunctions, then among the possibilities covered by that hypothesis is not only repetition of *a* with varying consequents but also its repetition with the same consequent. This will be less surprising if we reflect on the literal truth of the old adage that it is always the improbable that happens. Whatever side of a die comes up, the chances against it before it happened were five to one; yet it happened for all that. The simultaneous occurrence of the events composing the present universe is only one out of an infinite number of possibilities, and hence was all but infinitely improbable a moment ago; yet here it is. Similarly the repetition of *a* and *b* together a dozen times, or a hundred, or a thousand, is most unlikely beforehand, but still it is one of the possibilities conceivable under the reign of chance. And therefore it is absurd to offer it as evidence against the reign of chance.

Is there any effective rejoinder to this reply? On its own grounds I do not think there is.[2] Of an infinite number of chance combina-

---

[1] Strictly speaking, we cannot set such a limit in the other case either. We cannot a priori rule out the possibility that the die should stand

on one of its corners and spin there permanently.

[2] I say "not on its own grounds" because I think there are other ways in which the theory that all succession is chance succession can be attacked, e.g., through the direct exhibition of necessity in inference.

tions, the known history of the world may present one, and it might fairly be argued that any extension of that history, with any multiplication of its uniformities, could only produce another. Nevertheless, as a reply to the case just presented, the argument commits the fallacy of inexhaustive division. The question at issue is how the successions we actually find are to be interpreted or accounted for, and the original argument proceeded by offering the alternative of chance or some form of necessity, and then eliminating the first. The alternatives considered in the reply are not these at all; they are all of them combinations that would be possible under *one* of these, namely, the hypothesis of chance. The exponent of the view has been so eager to show that the hypothesis he prefers will cover the facts that he has forgotten that to the hypothesis under which all his combinations fall there is a further alternative which may cover the facts equally well. And when we turn from chance hypothesis to the hypothesis of an intrinsic connection, we find that it not only covers the facts equally well; it covers them vastly better. For on the chance hypothesis every successive repetition of a conjunction given in the past is the occurrence of the progressively more improbable,[3] while on the hypothesis of intrinsic connection, it is only a confirmation, more impressive at each recurrence, of what the hypothesis predicted. So far, neither theory can absolutely exclude its rival. But the chance hypothesis, while according with the known arrangement, would accord equally with any other. The hypothesis of connection accords selectively with the arrangement actually found.[4]

[3] Not, to be sure, if every length of run were to be counted as equally probable; but in that case, the hypothesis, as according equally with every conceivable arrangement, could neither be compared with any other, nor, therefore, urged in preference.

[4] This reply is stated a little differently from Professor Montague's, but I think it is in substance the same. For his discussions of the point, see *Proceedings of the Seventh International Congress of Philosophy,* 198ff., and the somewhat fuller account in *Ways of Knowing,* 199ff.

The view that cause and effect are connected by more than conjunctions, even in the physical realm, would thus appear more reasonable than its opposite. But further, even those who accept the regularity view are compelled, sometimes in the statement of this view itself, to assume that it is false. When they say that events have causes in the sense of regular and special antecedents, they intend this to apply to the future as well as to the past. But they have not experienced the future, and hence they must be using an *argument: Because b* has followed *a* in the past, it will continue to do so. Now unless *a* is connected with *b* by something more than mere conjunction, there is no ground for this argument whatever. What, apart from such connection, could be our reason for saying that uniform sequence in the past would carry with it uniform sequence in the future? We may say of course that when we have argued from such uniformities in the past to their continuance in the future, we have found our expectations verified, but plainly this will not do, for the uniform sequence of verification upon expectation is only another sequence, on a par with the original ones, and is entitled to no special privileges when the question is as to our right to argue from *any* past sequence to others. Again, if we make it a matter of probability, and say that a conjunction frequently recurrent is more likely to be maintained than broken, this either repeats the old assumption whose basis is in question, that the past is a guide to the future, or else is clearly false, since if *a* and *b* are really unconnected, there is no more reason to expect them to continue together than there is to expect an unloaded penny to go on giving heads because it has just done so ten times running. When this old puzzle about induction is raised, the answer usually given is that we "postulate" the uniformity of nature, viz., that the same cause is always followed by the same effect. But what is the status of this postulate? Is it merely an arbitrary assumption? Clearly not; in some sense it arises out of experience. Is it then a conclusion derived from experience? No, for, as has been pointed out times without number, the argument would be circular; unless we assumed "same cause, same effect," we could not argue that the same cause as in the past would be followed by the same effect. But then the question arises, what part *does* this assumption play in the argument? And the answer is that it is the *principle* of the inference, just as the principle of syllogism is the canon involved in any syllogistic reasoning. Now can the principle of an argument or inference be totally without necessity? We can only say that, if so, the "inference" to which it applies is no inference at all, and quite without cogency. We are not maintaining, of course, that the principle of uniformity has the clear and definite necessity of geometric demonstration, nor is that to be expected while the terms that pass muster as causes and effects remain so loose and vague. We do maintain, however, that the passage from past to future sequences is clearly an argument, that the principle of the argument, as of inferences generally, must be more than a chance conjunction of symbols or characters, and hence that the linkage between cause and effect in virtue of which we predict their future sequence is always implicitly taken as intrinsic.[5]

Indeed, whatever the difficulties of finding the true connection between cause and effect, the difficulties of holding that they are not connected at all except by *de facto* conjunction is far greater. We have no room here to develop these in full, but by way of rounding out our brief case against this theory, we may set down the following paradoxes. (1) If causality *means* regularity of sequence, every unique event must be regarded as uncaused. An unexampled biological sport could not even be set down as miracle since miracles are supposed to be caused; it would have to be an explosion of chance.[6] (2) No human action would ever

spring from a self or from a motive; there is no intrinsic connection between volition and behaviour, character and conduct, motive and performance. Strictly speaking, no one murders anyone, though in some cases homicide has unhappily and quite inexplicably associated itself with certain elements of a person's constitution. This association is the more unfortunate because, though wholly irrational, it is also permanent. Such a view conflicts at a thousand points with our everyday judgements about practical action and moral accountability; and though all these judgements may be mistaken, the fact that the sequence view would *require* that they be mistaken is enough to impose on it a heavy burden of proof.[7] (3) Note that we used the word "require." It was natural to use it, and those who hold the regularity view do frequently use it. Yet, as we have seen, if they hold any belief that is said to be required by their theory, its being required can have nothing to do with their holding it. (4) Nor is their explanation of how we came to suppose that causality involved more than association at all convincing. The usual explanation is Hume's, that the regular repetition of *a* and *b* together produced a habit of conjoining them in thought. But apart from the difficulty that a habit or even a thought of uniform conjunction is clearly different from the thought of necessity, what is meant here by "produced"? When one says that regular repetition produces a habit, does one mean only that there is a regular repetition of regular-repetition's-being-followed-by-a-habit? It does not seem likely. (5) Hume's confident denial that we could perceive anything more than sequence in the connection of particular events becomes more doubtful the more one thinks about it. Mr. Montague has pointed out that though the way the body acts upon the mind

---

[5] Cf. Mill's definition of cause as *unconditional* antecedent. On the argument involved in induction, see Ewing, *Idealism*, 151ff.; for the difficulties of the regular-sequence view, see Ewing, *ibid.*, and Ducasse, *Causation and Types of Necessity*, chaps. 1, 2, 5.

[6] The converse criticism is also sometimes urged, that there are regular sequences where

there is no causal or other intrinsic connection; day follows night, ruminants are cloven-footed, white tom-cats that have blue eyes are deaf. The argument is unconvincing. For there is usually, if not always, the suspicion that if the terms are not themselves connected intrinsically, they are both so connected with a third term.

[7] See Ewing, *op. cit.*, p. 162.

remains in darkness, still, when we resolve to attend to something more closely and "in consequence" succeed in doing so, we have a sense of "enforcement" that does not leave us wholly blank as to the mode of connection; and Mr. Whitehead has urged that in particular cases of perception we are immediately aware of being causally acted upon by some external agency. (6) The position would guarantee a scepticism that may be unavoidable, but is not to be accepted till necessary. It says that between the percept and its cause there is no intrinsic connection. Now since we have no access to nature except through impressons that are presumably produced in us causally, we must depend for knowledge of nature on an argument from the character of the impressions to the character of their source. Such argument would be rendered impossible by the sort of causation before us. (7) Stout and Ewing have held, rightly I think, that the memory of our own experiences would be rendered impossible by it. When I recall a particular event that happened yesterday, one of the factors that led to the recall was the occurrence of the past event itself. And when we say that this event "conditioned" this recall, we do not mean that all similar events are followed by such recalls, for we plainly have in mind one particular event happening at a point in past time. (8) Finally, to say that causality involves nothing but regular sequence brings one into sharp conflict with both common sense and science. The plain man has undoubtedly got it fixed in his head that when he drives a nail with a blow of his hammer, there is an inner connection between these events which is not to be found between either of them and, say, a storm in the Antilles. If it is objected that his views are worthless, it may be pointed out that science from its birth has suffered from the same obsession. To be sure, in some manuals like Mill's and Pearson's the uniformity view is insisted on, and Mr. Russell has even suggested that the name and notion of causality should be dropped by science.[8] But we do not believe that scientific thought,

even in physics, on which he too exclusively relies,[9] really has succeeded, or will succeed, in dispensing with it. The reason is that behind the scientist's desire to unbare the causes of things is his desire to understand, and his intuition that in mastering the cause of something he *has* to some extent understood it. We do not believe that the *only* reason why the scientific mind has rejected astrology is that the correlation between positions of the stars and the ups and downs of human fortune has been imperfectly made out. We do not believe that when the connection was revealed between tuberculosis and bacilli, physicians would have admitted that it gave no further understanding of the disease, but only a new fact, concomitant though wholly external. It is notorious that the physical scientist finds his ideal in mathematics; and if he continues to refine and purify his statements of abstract connection, it is surely because in doing so he feels himself approaching not only the precision but also the necessity of mathematical relations. Of course his conviction may have been a delusion from the beginning. But whoever says so assumes the burden of proof.[10]

For all these reasons we believe that the view which would deny to causality any intrinsic connection and reduce it to conjunction may be dismissed. *Some* intrinsic connection there must be. But of what sort? Does the insight that between cause and effect there is an intrinsic connection suffice to show that this

[8] Russell, *Mysticism and Logic*, p. 180.

[9] Cf. Stebbing, *Modern Introduction to Logic*, p. 289.

[10] We may repeat Bosanquet's question: "Is there any man of science who in his daily work, and apart from philosophic controversy, will accept a bare given conjunction as conceivably ultimate truth?" (*Distinction between Mind and its Objects*, pp. 59–60); and Ewing: "Thinkers and scientists looked for causes because they wished to *explain* events, and if they had seriously held from the beginning the views of causation which most realist philosophers hold to-day, half the inspiration of the scientific search for causes would have been missing and induction would never have been trusted at all," *op. cit.*, p. 176.

is also a *necessary* connection? We believe that it does.

Consider the meaning of "same cause, same effect," which we have seen to be the principle of all inductive causal argument. Why do we accept it? We have seen that if it is taken as expressive of conjunction only, no evidence for it and no argument under it are possible; and we have suggested that if it is accepted nevertheless, that is because we have an insight that is felt as justifying it. The nature of this insight will become clearer if we try for a moment to conceive the connection to be otherwise. Conceive a state of affairs in which there is causation but no uniformity; everything now has a cause, but the causes vary; everything produces effects, but the effects vary; the blow of the hammer sinks the nail today, but tomorrow under precisely the same conditions it fails to do so, and produces instead the *Melody in F* or a case of measles in Novgorod. We can talk thus, since we have just done it, but can we think thus? We cannot. For as Mr. Joseph says, "to say that anything may produce anything is to empty the word 'produce' of all its meaning." [11] Why? Because it implies that when *a* produces *x*, the *nature* of *a* had nothing to do with the result; that result could equally have appeared if nothing resembling *a* had been on the scene. But if *a*, in virtue of its nature, exercised no constraining influence at all, why say *it* produced something? *It* is a thing of special character; this character makes it what it is; and we should be talking idly if we said that *it* produced something when this character was in no way engaged.

To assert a causal connexion between *a* and *x* implies that *a* acts as it does because it is what it is. . . . For the causal relation which connects *a* with *x* connects a cause of the *nature a* with an effect of the *nature x*. The connexion is between them *as a* and *x*, and therefore must hold between any *a* and any *x*. . . . [12]

[11] Joseph, *Logic*, p. 407.
[12] *Ibid.*, pp. 408–409.

Now we suggest that when *a* is said to produce *x* in virtue of its nature as *a*, the connection referred to is not only an intrinsic relation but a necessary relation. There are two considerations that make us think so. (1) Reflection seems to show that necessity is part of our *meaning* when we call such relations intrinsic. If we lay down a yellow card, then to the right of it an orange card, and to the right of that a red one, they have spatial relations to each other, but those relations are not *prima facie* intrinsic, for so far as we can see there is nothing about a card of one colour *as such* to demand particular space relations to cards of other colours. Now consider the relations, not of the cards, but of the colours themselves. Regarded merely as colour, orange comes between red and yellow. And that relation is intrinsic in the present sense, since it is obviously determined by the natures of the three colours. But note that it is also necessary; we see that, yellow, orange and red being what they are, orange *must* come between the other two, and could not possibly fall elsewhere. Is this not the case with all relations that turn on the content or character of the terms? It seems to us that it is. Not that the necessity is seen with equal purity or clearness in all such cases, but that whenever we see that a relation depends on *a*'s being what it is, we see *that* the relation is necessary whether we can isolate the nexus or not. Whether the tendency to gratitude, for example, follows from the nature of modesty we may not be quite sure, but *if* we are, we are sure that modesty *must* carry with it this tendency. Indeed to say that something follows from the nature of *a*, but not necessarily, seems meaningless.

But is this necessity in the logical sense, or have we smuggled into the term some meaning that is allied, perhaps, but distinct? That the necessity is genuinely logical will be clearer from our second point. (2) To say that *a* produces *x* in virtue of being *a* and yet that, given *a*, *x* might not follow, is inconsistent with the laws of identity and contradiction. Of course if *a* were a cluster of qualities abstracted from their relations, and its modes of causal behaviour were another set conjoined with the former externally, then one could deny the latter and retain the former with perfect consistency. But we have seen that when we say *a* causes *x*, we do *not* mean that sort of conjunction; we mean an intrinsic relation, i.e. a relation in which *a*'s behaviour is the outgrowth or expression of *a*'s nature. And to assert that *a*'s behaviour, so conceived, could be different while *a* was the same would be to assert that something both did and did not issue from the nature of *a*. And that is self-contradiction. The statement would also, though perhaps not so apparently, conflict with the law of identity. It implies that a thing may remain itself when you have stripped from it everything which it is *such as* to be and do. To strip it of these things would be to strip it, so to speak, of the suchness that makes it what it is, i.e., to say that it is other than it is.

We are now in a position to see the upshot of our long argument about causality. There were two propositions, we said, which if established would carry with them the conclusion that everything that exists is related internally to everything else, i.e., is so related that without this relation it would not be what it is. These propositions were that everything is *causally* connected with everything else, directly or indirectly, and that being causally connected involved being connected by a relation of logical *necessity*. The first proposition, while perhaps undemonstrable, we found probable enough to commend itself to most philosophers and scientists, and the arguments against it were unconvincing. The second proposition has given us far more trouble. Does causality involve intelligible necessity? We have seen that in some cases it does unquestionably, for it does in every case of genuine inference. But can we say the same of causality generally? We saw that the principle could be extended to a great many other mental processes, though the presence of necessity was here less clearly discernible. But what about the enormous range of causal processes in physical nature? Was any hint or trace of really intelligible connection to be found among them? Many writers on scientific method have denied this, and have sought to commit science to the view that there is nothing in causality but regularity of sequence or functional dependence. This view we have found so full of paradoxical consequences as to be incredible. Its rejection left us with the result that between cause and effect there is some sort of intrinsic connection, a result confirmed by considering that ordinary inductive procedure involves an argument which without this would be invalid. But is this intrinsic connection necessary? Yes, for when anything is said to have a consequent or a consequence in virtue of its special nature, necessity is part of our meaning, and what follows can not be denied except on pain of self-contradiction. Note that in this we have made no such unredeemable claim as that we can see *why* a particular hammer-stroke should drive a particular nail. Despite all the changes in physics since the turn of the century, we are very far from the sort of insight into physical things that would enable us to isolate the nerve of a given physical interaction. But unless there is such a nerve, the principle is illusory on which all practice is conducted and all causal argument is based.

Now if all this is true, it is hard to see how the conclusion is to be resisted that the universe of existing things is a system in which all things are related internally. Let *a* and *x* be *any* two things in the universe. They are then related to each other causally. But if causally, then also intrinsically, and if intrinsically then also necessarily, in the sense that they causally act as they do in virtue of their nature or character, and that to deny such activity would entail denying them to be what they are. And to have this sort of relation to all other things is precisely what we mean by being related to them internally.

The dilemma of determinism

William James (1842-1910)

The son of an eminent father, and older brother of the novelist Henry James, William James was graduated from the Harvard Medical School and appointed to the Harvard faculty in 1872 as instructor of comparative anatomy and physiology. He soon became interested in psychology and in philosophical problems and in 1885 was appointed professor of psychology and philosophy. By 1876 he had founded the first experimental laboratory for psychology in America, and in 1890 he published his important text, The Principles of Psychology. *Later he turned his attention almost exclusively to philosophy, becoming the most celebrated exponent of the new American philosophy of pragmatism. His major philosophic works include* The Will to Believe *(1897)*, The Varieties of Religious Experience *(1902)*, Pragmatism *(1907)*, A Pluralistic Universe *(1909), and* Essays in Radical Empiricism, *published posthumously in 1912.*

Our selection was originally an address before the Harvard Divinity Students. In it James argues for indeterminism by attempting to show the conceptual difficulties to which the deterministic view leads. The essay exhibits James's characteristic force of language.

A common opinion prevails that the juice has ages ago been pressed out of the free-will controversy, and that no new champion can do more than warm up stale arguments which every one has heard. This is a radical mistake. I know of no subject less worn out, or in which inventive genius has a better chance of breaking open new ground,—not, perhaps, of forcing a conclusion or of coercing assent, but of deepening our sense of what the issue between the two parties really is, of what the ideas of fate and of free-will imply. . . .

The arguments I am about to urge all proceed on two suppositions: first, when we make

From William James, "The Dilemma of Determinism," an address to the Harvard Divinity 28 Students, first published in the *Unitarian Review*, 1884. Also available in William James, *Essays on Faith and Morals*, Longmans, Green & Co., Inc., New York, 1943.

theories about the world and discuss them with one another, we do so in order to attain a conception of things which shall give us subjective satisfaction; and, second, if there be two conceptions, and the one seems to us, on the whole, more rational than the other, we are entitled to suppose that the more rational one is the truer of the two. I hope that you are all willing to make these suppositions with me; for I am afraid that if there be any of you here who are not, they will find little edification in the rest of what I have to say. I cannot stop to argue the point; but I myself believe that all the magnificent achievements of mathematical and physical science—our doctrines of evolution, of uniformity of law, and the rest—proceed from our indomitable desire to cast the world into a more rational shape in our minds than the shape into which it is thrown there by the crude order of our experience. The **47** world has shown itself, to a great extent, plastic to this demand of ours for rationality. How much farther it will show itself plastic no one can say. Our only means of finding out is to try; and I, for one, feel as free to try conceptions of moral as of mechanical or of logical rationality. If a certain formula for expressing the nature of the world violates my moral demand, I shall feel as free to throw it overboard, or at least to doubt it, as if it disappointed my demand for uniformity of sequence, for example; the one demand being, so far as I can see, quite as subjective and emotional as the other is. The principle of causality, for example,—what is it but a postulate, an empty name covering simply a demand that the sequence of events shall some day manifest a deeper kind of belonging of one thing with another than the mere arbitrary juxtaposition which now phenomenally appears? It is as much an altar to an unknown god as the one that Saint Paul found at Athens. All our scientific and philosophic ideals are altars to unknown gods. Uniformity is as much so as is free-will. If this be admitted, we can debate on even terms. But if any one pretends that while freedom and variety are, in the first instance, subjective demands, necessity and uniformity are something altogether different, I do not see how we can debate at all.

To begin, then, I must suppose you acquainted with the usual arguments on the subject. I cannot stop to take up the old proofs from causation, from statistics, from the certainty with which we can foretell one another's conduct, from the fixity of character, and all the rest. But there are two *words* which usually encumber these classical arguments, and which we must immediately dispose of if we are to make any progress. One is the eulogistic word *freedom*, and the other is the opprobrious word *chance*. The word "chance" I wish to keep, but I wish to get rid of the word "freedom." Its eulogistic associations have so far overshadowed all the rest of its meaning that both parties claim the sole right to use it, and determinists to-day insist that they alone are

freedom's champions. Old-fashioned determinism was what we may call *hard* determinism. It did not shrink from such words as fatality, bondage of the will, necessitation, and the like. Nowadays, we have a *soft* determinism which abhors harsh words, and, repudiating fatality, necessity, and even predetermination, says that its real name is freedom; for freedom is only necessity understood, and bondage to the highest is identical with true freedom. . . .

Now, all this is a quagmire of evasion under which the real issue of fact has been entirely smothered. . . . But there *is* a problem, an issue of fact and not of words, an issue of the most momentous importance. . . .

Fortunately, no ambiguities hang about this word or about its opposite, indeterminism. Both designate an outward way in which things may happen, and their cold and mathematical sound has no sentimental associations that can bribe our partiality either way in advance. Now, evidence of an external kind to decide between determinism and indeterminism is . . . strictly impossible to find. Let us look at the difference between them and see for ourselves. What does determinism profess?

It professes that those parts of the universe already laid down absolutely appoint and decree what the other parts shall be. The future has no ambiguous possibilities hidden in its womb: the part we call the present is compatible with only one totality. Any other future complement than the one fixed from eternity is impossible. The whole is in each and every part, and welds it with the rest into an absolute unity, an iron block, in which there can be no equivocation or shadow of turning.

> "With earth's first clay they did the last man knead,
> And there of the last harvest sowed the seed.
> And the first morning of creation wrote
> What the last dawn of reckoning shall read."

Indeterminism, on the contrary, says that the parts have a certain amount of loose play on one another, so that the laying down of one of them does not necessarily determine what the others shall be. It admits that possibilities may be in excess of actualities, and that things not yet revealed to our knowledge may really in themselves be ambiguous. Of two alternative futures which we conceive, both may now be really possible; and the one become impossible only at the very moment when the other excludes it by becoming real itself. Indeterminism thus denies the world to be one unbending unit of fact. It says there is a certain ultimate pluralism in it; and, so saying, it corroborates our ordinary unsophisticated view of things. To that view, actualities seem to float in a wider sea of possibilities from out of which they are chosen; and, *somewhere*, indeterminism says, such possibilities exist, and form a part of truth.

Determinism, on the contrary, says they exist *nowhere*, and that necessity on the one hand and impossibility on the other are the sole categories of the real. Possibilities that fail to get realized are, for determinism, pure illusions: they never were possibilities at all. . . .

The issue, it will be seen, is a perfectly sharp one, which no eulogistic terminology can smear over or wipe out. The truth *must* lie with one side or the other, and its lying with one side makes the other false.

The question relates solely to the existence of possibilities, in the strict sense of the term, as things that may, but need not, be. Both sides admit that a volition, for instance, has occurred. The indeterminists say another volition might have occurred in its place: the determinists swear that nothing could possibly have occurred in its place. Now, can science be called in to tell us which of these two point-blank contradicters of each other is right? Science professes to draw no conclusions but such as are based on matters of fact, things that have actually happened; but how can any amount of assurance that something actually happened give us the least grain of information as to whether another thing might or might not have happened in its place? Only facts can be proved by other facts. With things that are possibilities and not facts, facts have

no concern. If we have no other evidence than the evidence of existing facts, the possibility-question must remain a mystery never to be cleared up.

And the truth is that facts practically have hardly anything to do with making us either determinists or indeterminists. Sure enough, we make a flourish of quoting facts this way or that; and if we are determinists, we talk about the infallibility with which we can predict one another's conduct; while if we are indeterminists, we lay great stress on the fact that it is just because we cannot foretell one another's conduct, either in war or statecraft or in any of the great and small intrigues and businesses of men, that life is so intensely anxious and hazardous a game. But who does not see the wretched insufficiency of this so-called objective testimony on both sides? What fills up the gaps in our minds is something not objective, not external. What divides us into possibility men and anti-possibility men is different faiths or postulates,—postulates of rationality. To this man the world seems more rational with possibilities in it,—to that man more rational with possibilities excluded; and talk as we will about having to yield to evidence, what makes us monists or pluralists, determinists or indeterminists, is at bottom always some sentiment like this.

The stronghold of the deterministic sentiment is the antipathy to the idea of chance. As soon as we begin to talk indeterminism to our friends, we find a number of them shaking their heads. This notion of alternative possibility, they say, this admission that any one of several things may come to pass, is, after all, only a roundabout name for chance; and chance is something the notion of which no sane mind can for an instant tolerate in the world. What is it, they ask, but barefaced crazy unreason, the negation of intelligibility and law? And if the slightest particle of it exist anywhere, what is to prevent the whole fabric from falling together, the stars from going out, and chaos from recommencing her topsy-turvy reign?

Remarks of this sort about chance will put an end to discussion as quickly as anything one can find. I have already told you that "chance" was a word I wished to keep and use. Let us then examine exactly what it means, and see whether it ought to be such a terrible bugbear to us. I fancy that squeezing the thistle boldly will rob it of its sting.

The sting of the word "chance" seems to lie in the assumption that it means something positive, and that if anything happens by chance, it must needs be something of an intrinsically irrational and preposterous sort. Now, chance means nothing of the kind. It is a purely negative and relative term, giving us no information about that of which it is predicated, except that it happens to be disconnected with something else,—not controlled, secured, or necessitated by other things in advance of its own actual presence. As this point is the most subtile one of the whole lecture, and at the same time the point on which all the rest hinges, I beg you to pay particular attention to it. What I say is that it tells us nothing about what a thing may be in itself to call it "chance." It may be a bad thing, it may be a good thing. It may be lucidity, transparency, fitness incarnate, matching the whole system of other things, when it has once befallen, in an unimaginably perfect way. All you mean by calling it "chance" is that this is not guaranteed, that it may also fall out otherwise. . . .

Nevertheless, many persons talk as if the minutest dose of disconnectedness of one part with another, the smallest modicum of independence, the faintest tremor of ambiguity about the future, for example, would ruin everything, and turn this goodly universe into a sort of insane sand-heap or nulliverse, no universe at all. Since future human volitions are as a matter of fact the only ambiguous things we are tempted to believe in, let us stop for a moment to make ourselves sure whether their independent and accidental character need be fraught with such direful consequences to the universe as these.

What is meant by saying that my choice of which way to walk home after the lecture is ambiguous and matter of chance as far as the present moment is concerned? It means that both Divinity Avenue and Oxford Street are called; but that only one, and that one *either* one, shall be chosen. Now, I ask you seriously to suppose that this ambiguity of my choice is real; and then to make the impossible hypothesis that the choice is made twice over, and each time falls on a different street. In other words, imagine that I first walk through Divinity Avenue, and then imagine that the powers governing the universe annihilate ten minutes of time with all that it contained, and set me back at the door of this hall just as I was before the choice was made. Imagine then that, everything else being the same, I now make a different choice and traverse Oxford Street. You, as passive spectators, look on and see the two alternative universes,—one of them with me walking through Divinity Avenue in it, the other with the same me walking through Oxford Street. Now, if you are determinists you believe one of these universes to have been from eternity impossible: you believe it to have been impossible because of the intrinsic irrationality or accidentality somewhere involved in it. But looking outwardly at these universes, can you say which is the impossible and accidental one, and which the rational and necessary one? I doubt if the most ironclad determinist among you could have the slightest glimmer of light on this point. In other words, either universe *after the fact* and once there would, to our means of observation and understanding, appear just as rational as the other. There would be absolutely no criterion by which we might judge one necessary and the other matter of chance. Suppose now we relieve the gods of their hypothetical task and assume my choice, once made, to be made forever. I go through Divinity Avenue for good and all. If, as good determinists, you now begin to affirm, what all good determinists punctually do affirm, that in the nature of things I *couldn't* have gone through Oxford Street,—had I done so it would have been chance, irrationality, insanity, a horrid gap in nature,—I simply call your attention to this, that your affirmation is what the Germans call a *Macht-*

spruch, a mere conception fulminated as a dogma and based on no insight into details. Before my choice, either street seemed as natural to you as to me. Had I happened to take Oxford Street, Divinity Avenue would have figured in your philosophy as the gap in nature; and you would have so proclaimed it with the best deterministic conscience in the world.

But what a hollow outcry, then, is this against a chance which, if it were present to us, we could by no character whatever distinguish from a rational necessity! ... The more one thinks of the matter, the more one wonders that so empty and gratuitous a hubbub as this outcry against chance should have found so great an echo in the hearts of men. It is a word which tells us absolutely nothing about what chances, or about the *modus operandi* of the chancing; and the use of it as a war-cry shows only a temper of intellectual absolutism, a demand that the world shall be a solid block, subject to one control,—which temper, which demand, the world may not be bound to gratify at all. In every outwardly verifiable and practical respect, a world in which the alternatives that now actually distract *your* choice were decided by pure chance would be by *me* absolutely undistinguished from the world in which I now live. I am, therefore, entirely willing to call it, so far as your choices go, a world of chance for me. To *yourselves,* it is true, those very acts of choice, which to me are so blind, opaque, and external, are the opposites of this, for you are within them and effect them. To you they appear as decisions; and decisions, for him who makes them, are altogether peculiar psychic facts. Self-luminous and self-justifying at the living moment at which they occur, they appeal to no outside moment to put its stamp upon them or make them continuous with the rest of nature. Themselves it is rather who seem to make nature continuous; and in their strange and intense function of granting consent to one possibility and withholding it from another, to transform an equivocal and double future into an inalterable and simple past.

But with the psychology of the matter we have no concern this evening. The quarrel which determinism has with chance fortunately has nothing to do with this or that psychological detail. It is a quarrel altogether metaphysical. Determinism denies the ambiguity of future volitions, because it affirms that nothing future can be ambiguous. But we have said enough to meet the issue. Indeterminate future volitions *do* mean chance. . . .

We have seen what determinism means: we have seen that indeterminism is rightly described as meaning chance; and we have seen that chance, the very name of which we are urged to shrink from as from a metaphysical pestilence, means only the negative fact that no part of the world, however big, can claim to control absolutely the destinies of the whole. But although, in discussing the word "chance," I may at moments have seemed to be arguing for its real existence, I have not meant to do so yet. We have not yet ascertained whether this be a world of chance or no; at most, we have agreed that it seems so. And I now repeat what I said at the outset, that, from any strict theoretical point of view, the question is insoluble. To deepen our theoretic sense of the *difference* between a world with chances in it and a deterministic world is the most I can hope to do; and this I may now at last begin upon, after all our tedious clearing of the way.

I wish first of all to show you just what the notion that this is a deterministic world implies. The implications I call your attention to are all bound up with the fact that it is a world in which we constantly have to make what I shall, with your permission, call judgments of regret. Hardly an hour passes in which we do not wish that something might be otherwise; and happy indeed are those of us whose hearts have never echoed the wish of Omar Khayam—

"That we might clasp, ere closed, the book of fate,
And make the writer on a fairer leaf
Inscribe our names, or quite obliterate.

"Ah! Love, could you and I with fate conspire

To mend this sorry scheme of things entire,
 Would we not shatter it to bits, and then
 Remould it nearer to the heart's desire?"

Now, it is undeniable that most of these regrets are foolish, and quite on a par in point of philosophic value with the criticisms on the universe of that friend of our infancy, the hero of the fable The Atheist and the Acorn,—

"Fool! had that bough a pumpkin bore,
 Thy whimsies would have worked no
  more," etc.

Even from the point of view of our own ends, we should probably make a botch of remodelling the universe. How much more then from the point of view of ends we cannot see! Wise men therefore regret as little as they can. But still some regrets are pretty obstinate and hard to stifle,—regrets for acts of wanton cruelty or treachery, for example, whether performed by others or by ourselves. Hardly any one can remain *entirely* optimistic after reading the confession of the murderer at Brockton the other day: how, to get rid of the wife whose continued existence bored him, he inveigled her into a desert spot, shot her four times, and then, as she lay on the ground and said to him, "You didn't do it on purpose, did you, dear?" replied, "No, I didn't do it on purpose," as he raised a rock and smashed her skull. Such an occurrence, with the mild sentence and self-satisfaction of the prisoner, is a field for a crop of regrets, which one need not take up in detail. We feel that, although a perfect mechanical fit to the rest of the universe, it is a bad moral fit, and that something else would really have been better in its place.

But for the deterministic philosophy the murder, the sentence, and the prisoner's optimism were all necessary from eternity; and nothing else for a moment had a ghost of a chance of being put into their place. To admit such a chance, the determinists tell us, would be to make a suicide of reason; so we must steel our hearts against the thought. And here our plot thickens, for we see the first of those difficult implications of determinism and monism which it is my purpose to make you feel. If this Brockton murder was called for by the rest of the universe, if it had to come at its preappointed hour, and if nothing else would have been consistent with the sense of the whole, what are we to think of the universe? Are we stubbornly to stick to our judgment of regret, and say, though it *couldn't* be, yet it *would* have been a better universe with something different from this Brockton murder in it? That, of course, seems the natural and spontaneous thing for us to do; and yet it is nothing short of deliberately espousing a kind of pessimism. The judgment of regret calls the murder bad. Calling a thing bad means, if it mean anything at all, that the thing ought not to be, that something else ought to be in its stead. Determinism, in denying that anything else can be in its stead, virtually defines the universe as a place in which what ought to be is impossible,—in other words, as an organism whose constitution is afflicted with an incurable taint, an irremediable flaw. The pessimism of a Schopenhauer says no more than this,—that the murder is a symptom; and that it is a vicious symptom because it belongs to a vicious whole, which can express its nature no otherwise than by bringing forth just such a symptom as that at this particular spot. Regret for the murder must transform itself, if we are determinists and wise, into a larger regret. It is absurd to regret the murder alone. Other things being what they are, *it* could not be different. What we should regret is that whole frame of things of which the murder is one member. I see no escape whatever from this pessimistic conclusion, if, being determinists, our judgment of regret is to be allowed to stand at all.

The only deterministic escape from pessimism is everywhere to abandon the judgment of regret. That this can be done, history shows to be not impossible. The devil, *quoad existentiam*, may be good. That is, although he be a *principle* of evil, yet the universe, with such a principle in it, may practically be a better universe than it could have been without. On every hand, in a small way, we find that a certain amount of evil is a condition by which a higher form of good is brought. There is nothing to prevent anybody from generalizing this view, and trusting that if we could but see things in the largest of all ways, even such matters as this Brockton murder would appear to be paid for by the uses that follow in their train. An optimism *quand même*, a systematic and infatuated optimism like that ridiculed by Voltaire in his Candide, is one of the possible ideal ways in which a man may train himself to look on life. Bereft of dogmatic hardness and lit up with the expression of a tender and pathetic hope, such an optimism has been the grace of some of the most religious characters that ever lived.

"Throb thine with Nature's throbbing breast,
And all is clear from east to west."

Even cruelty and treachery may be among the absolutely blessed fruits of time, and to quarrel with any of their details may be blasphemy. The only real blasphemy, in short, may be that pessimistic temper of the soul which lets it give way to such things as regrets, remorse, and grief.

Thus, our deterministic pessimism may become a deterministic optimism at the price of extinguishing our judgments of regret.

But does not this immediately bring us into a curious logical predicament? Our determinism leads us to call our judgments of regret wrong, because they are pessimistic in implying that what is impossible yet ought to be. But how then about the judgments of regret themselves? If they are wrong, other judgments, judgments of approval presumably, ought to be in their place. But as they are necessitated, nothing else *can* be in their place; and the universe is just what it was before,—namely, a place in which what ought to be appears impossible. We have got one foot out of the pessimistic bog, but the other one sinks all the deeper. We have rescued our actions from the bonds of evil, but our judgments are now held fast. When murders and treacheries cease to be sins, regrets are theoretic absurdities and errors. The theoretic and the active life thus play a kind of see-saw with each other on the ground of evil. The rise of either sends the other down. Murder and treachery cannot

be good without regret being bad: regret cannot be good without treachery and murder being bad. Both, however, are supposed to have been foredoomed; so something must be fatally unreasonable, absurd, and wrong in the world. It must be a place of which either sin or error forms a necessary part. From this dilemma there seems at first sight no escape. . . .

The only consistent way of representing a pluralism and a world whose parts may affect one another through their conduct being either good or bad is the indeterministic way. What interest, zest, or excitement can there be in achieving the right way, unless we are enabled to feel that the wrong way is also a possible and a natural way,—nay, more, a menacing and an imminent way? And what sense can there be in condemning ourselves for taking the wrong way, unless we need have done nothing of the sort, unless the right way was open to us as well? I cannot understand the willingness to act, no matter how we feel, without the belief that acts are really good and bad. I cannot understand the belief that an act is bad, without regret at its happening. I cannot understand regret without the admission of real, genuine possibilities in the world. Only *then* is it other than a mockery to feel, after we have failed to do our best, that an irreparable opportunity is gone from the universe, the loss of which it must forever after mourn.

If you insist that this is all superstition, that possibility is in the eye of science and reason impossibility, and that if I act badly 'tis that the universe was foredoomed to suffer this defect, you fall right back into the dilemma, the labyrinth, of pessimism, from out of whose toils we have just wound our way.

Now, we are of course free to fall back, if we please. For my own part, though, whatever difficulties may beset the philosophy of objective right and wrong, and the indeterminism it seems to imply, determinism, with its alternative of pessimism or romanticism, contains difficulties that are greater still. But you will remember that I expressly repudiated awhile ago the pretension to offer any arguments which could be coercive in a so-called scientific fashion in this matter. And I consequently find myself, at the end of this long talk, obliged to state my conclusions in an altogether personal way. This personal method of appeal seems to be among the very conditions of the problem; and the most any one can do is to confess as candidly as he can the grounds for the faith that is in him, and leave his example to work on others as it may.

Let me, then, without circumlocution say just this. The world is enigmatical enough in all conscience, whatever theory we may take up toward it. The indeterminism I defend, the free-will theory of popular sense based on the judgment of regret, represents that world as vulnerable, and liable to be injured by certain of its parts if they act wrong. And it represents their acting wrong as a matter of possibility or accident, neither inevitable nor yet to be infallibly warded off. In all this, it is a theory devoid either of transparency or of stability. It gives us a pluralistic, restless universe, in which no single point of view can ever take in the whole scene; and to a mind possessed of the love of unity at any cost, it will, no doubt, remain forever inacceptable. A friend with such a mind once told me that the thought of my universe made him sick, like the sight of the horrible motion of a mass of maggots in their carrion bed.

But while I freely admit that the pluralism and the restlessness are repugnant and irrational in a certain way, I find that every alternative to them is irrational in a deeper way. The indeterminism with its maggots, if you please to speak so about it, offends only the native absolutism of my intellect,—an absolutism which, after all, perhaps, deserves to be snubbed

and kept in check. But the determinism with its necessary carrion, to continue the figure of speech, and with no possible maggots to eat the latter up, violates my sense of moral reality through and through. When, for example, I imagine such carrion as the Brockton murder, I cannot conceive it as an act by which the universe, as a whole, logically and necessarily expresses its nature without shrinking from complicity with such a whole. And I deliberately refuse to keep on terms of loyalty with the universe by saying blankly that the murder, since it does flow from the nature of the whole, is not carrion. There are *some* instinctive reactions which I, for one, will not tamper with. . . .

Make as great an uproar about chance as you please, I know that chance means pluralism and nothing more. If some of the members of the pluralism are bad, the philosophy of pluralism, whatever broad views it may deny me, permits me, at least, to turn to the other members with a clean breast of affection and an unsophisticated moral sense. And if I still wish to think of the world as a totality, it lets me feel that a world with a *chance* in it of being altogether good, even if the chance never come to pass, is better than a world with no such chance at all. That "chance" whose very notion I am exhorted and conjured to banish from my view of the future as the suicide of reason concerning it, that "chance" is—what? Just this,—the chance that in moral respects the future may be other and better than the past has been. This is the only chance we have any motive for supposing to exist. Shame, rather, on its repudiation and its denial! For its presence is the vital air which lets the world live, the salt which keeps it sweet.

Science, causality, and man

Adolf Grünbaum (b. 1923)

Born in Cologne, Germany, Adolf Grünbaum came to the United States in 1938. He was educated at Wesleyan University and at Yale, where he received the Ph.D. He is at present Andrew Mellon Professor of Philosophy at the University of Pittsburgh, where his special field is the philosophy of science. Grünbaum has written widely on problems in this area, and he has done noted work in the mathematical theory of continuity. His book, Philosophical Problems of Space and Time, *appeared in 1964.*

In the following selection from one of his articles he discusses the issue of determinism or indeterminism in connection with the social sciences. Grünbaum points out that if scientific method is to be applicable to the problem of elucidating human nature, then the actions of human agents must display causal law. The remainder of his discussion is an attempt to prove that causality does characterize human behavior. He proceeds by attempting to refute the arguments commonly offered against determinism.

I. Introduction

In a paper entitled "Some Limitations of Science," Thomas Murray (1) of the United States Atomic Energy Commission wrote as follows: "However useful science is to investigate the privacy of tiny chambers called atoms, it is all but useless to investigate the inner and higher life of man. You can't examine free-will in a test tube. Yet, much of what man does for weal or woe springs from this inner life of free choice."

It is the aim of the present paper to show by reference to the issues raised by Murray that the scientific method is no less applicable to

From Adolf Grünbaum, "Science and Man," *Perspectives in Biology and Medicine,* Vol. V, No. 4, Summer 1962, published by The University of Chicago Press. Copyright 1962 by The University of Chicago. Used by permission of the author and publisher. (This paper was read at a meeting of the Pittsburgh Psychoanalytic Society on February 13, 1961.)

man's "inner life of free choice" than to atoms or to the processes occurring in test tubes.

I am not concerned with the emotional factors which may have inspired Murray's thesis that science "is all but useless to investigate the inner and higher life of man," but only with the intellectual considerations which have been adduced in support of it. These center on the claim that while causal and statistical laws characterize the physical world and thus make possible predictions and postdictions of the careers of physical processes, the consciousness characteristic of man in some sense intrinsically defies any such characterization by laws. And since scientific mastery of a domain requires successful predictions and/or postdictions which only the existence of laws makes possible, it is claimed that consciously directed human behavior is beyond the scope of scientific comprehensibility.

It is strange that this claim often finds adherents among executives like Murray, whose every step in the management of people is **55** based on the unwitting assumption of *causal* connections between *influences* on men and their *responses*. But it is precisely this *deterministic* conception of man which is repudiated by Murray. And in view of that conception's pivotal role in our inquiry, we shall need to make a careful assessment of its credentials. The deterministic conception of the *inorganic* sector of nature found its modern prototype in classical Newtonian mechanics, and in classical physics generally. These classical theories feature exceptionless functional dependencies relating the states of physical systems as follows: given the state of a physical system at one or more times, its state at other times is uniquely determined.

The deterministic conception of *human behavior* is inspired by the view that man is an integral part and product of nature and that his behavior can reasonably be held to exhibit scientifically ascertainable regularities just as any other *macroscopic* sector of nature.

The opponent of determinism, or "indeterminist," maintains that determinism is *logically incompatible* with the known fact that people respond meaningfully to moral imperatives. Specifically, the indeterminist says: If each one of us makes decisions which are determined by the sum total of all the relevant influences upon us (heredity, environmental background, the stimuli affecting us at the moment, etc.), then no man can help doing what he does. And then the consequences are allegedly as follows: (*a*) It is impossible to account for our feeling that we are able to act freely except by dismissing it as devoid of any factual foundation. (*b*) It is useless to try to choose between good and bad courses of action. (*c*) It is meaningless to hold people responsible for their acts. (*d*) It is unjust to punish people for wrong-doing, or reward and praise them for good deeds. (*e*) It is mere self-delusion to feel remorse or guilt for past misdeeds.

Furthermore, the indeterminist often makes the ominous declaration that if determinism became known to the masses of people and were accepted by them, moral chaos would result, because—so he claims—everyone would forthwith drop his inhibitions. The excuse would be that he cannot help acting uninhibitedly, and people would fatalistically sink into a state of futility, laziness, and indifference. Moreover, we are told that if determinism were believed, the great fighters against injustice in human history would give up raising their voices in protest, since the truth of determinism would allegedly make such efforts useless.

Thus, the indeterminist goes on to contend that there is a basic *inconsistency* in *any* deterministic *and* activistic socio-political theory, the alleged inconsistency being the following: to *advocate* a social activism with the aim of thereby bringing about a future state whose eventuation the given theory regards as assured by historical causation. This argument is applied to any kind of deterministic theory independently of whether the explanatory variables of the historical process are held by that theory to be economic, climatic, sexual, demographic, geopolitical, or the inscrutable will of God. Accordingly, the indeterminist objects to such diverse doctrines as (*a*) Justice Oliver Wendell Holmes' dictum that the inevitable comes to pass through effort, and (*b*) St. Augustine's (and Calvin's) belief in divine foreordination, when coupled with the advocacy of Christian virtue. And correlatively, the indeterminist claims that if determinism is true, it is futile for men to discuss how to optimize the achievement of their ends by a change in personal or group behavior.

A second group of arguments which I shall criticize centers on the view that human affection eludes scientific understanding because of the so-called "intangibility" or "unmeasurability" of love.

The third argument that we shall consider is based on one of the consequences of the postulates of quantum physics. Results formulated by the Heisenberg Uncertainty Principle, which I shall state, have been claimed to show that there is at last a physical basis for the ethical claims of the philosophical indeterminist.

I shall argue that the quantum mechanical indeterminacies characterizing individual microprocesses of physics are *irrelevant* to the free-will problem.

II. The argument from morality

To introduce the objections to the indeterminist's argument from morality, we must remind the addict to the narcotic of Norman Vincent Peale's "positive thinking" of the following stubborn fact. If determinism did actually make moral imperatives meaningless—which I shall argue it does not—then that would be simply tragic. But it could hardly be claimed that determinism is false on the mere grounds that its alleged consequences would be terrible. We would show concern for the sanity of anyone who would say that his house could not have burnt down because this fact would make him unhappy.

But is it actually the case that there are data from the field of human responses to moral rules which refute the deterministic hypothesis? I shall argue that the answer is decidedly negative.... Of course, determinism does exclude, as we shall see, *some* of the moral conceptions entertained by philosophical indeterminists like Murray. But I shall maintain that this involves no actual loss for ethics. And we have already seen that even if it did, this would not constitute evidence against determinism. I wish to emphasize, however, that I am *not* endeavoring to show that determinism is categorically true in the domain of human behavior but *only* that it is logically compatible with a meaningful system of moral rules. For the categorical truth of determinism can be established *not* by logical analysis alone but requires the working psychologist's empirical discovery of specific causal laws.

To establish the invalidity of the moral argument offered by the indeterminist, I shall now try to show that there is no incompatibility between the deterministic assumptions of scientific psychology, on the one hand, and the feelings of freedom which we actually do have, the meaningful assignment of responsibility, the infliction of punishment, and the existence of feelings of remorse or guilt on the other.

A. Confusion of determinism with fatalism

The first point to be made clear is that determinism should never be identified with the prescientific and appallingly primitive doctrine of fatalism. The fatalist says that, in every situation, regardless of what we do, the outcome will be unaffected by our efforts. By contrast, the determinist says that *if* we do such and such, *then* the effect will be thus and so, *and* that there are indeed causes for what we do. The fatalist thinks that every person is destined to die on a certain day *come what may*. If you go into combat, and if "some bullet has your name on it," you will be killed no matter what you do. Even if you fake an illness and are hospitalized, there will be a fire in your hospital bed or the nurse will be a psychopath and will poison you. The determinist maintains that a person will die on a certain day only if the conditions which lead to death materialize for that person on that day, as indeed they do at some time for each of us. Unlike fatalism, determinism allows causal efficacy to human actions under specifiable conditions.

The indeterminist illicitly identifies and confuses fatalism with determinism in several of his theses, as will now become apparent.

The predictions that might be made by contemporary historical determinists concerning the social organization of industrial society, for example, pertain to a society of which these forecasters are themselves members. Hence such predictions are self-referential. But these predictions are made by social prophets who, *qua* deterministic forecasters, consider their own society from *without* rather than as active contributors to its destiny. And the predictions made from that theoretically external perspective are *predicated* on the prior fulfilment of certain initial conditions which include the presence in that society of people—among whom they themselves may happen to be included—who are dissatisfied with the existing state of affairs and are therefore actively seeking the future realization of the externally predicted social state. To ignore that the determinist rests his social prediction in part on the existence of the latter initial conditions, just as much as a physicist makes a prediction of a thermal expansion conditional upon the presence of heat, is to commit the *fallacy of equating determinism with fatalism*. We see that the indeterminist has no valid grounds for maintaining that it is logically inconsistent for a historical determinist, *qua* participating citizen, to advocate that action be taken by his fellow-citizens to create the social system whose advent he is predicting on the basis of his theory. For it is plain now that the indeterminist's charge derives its semblance of plausibility from his confusion of determinism with fatalism in the context of self-referential predictions.

Equally fallacious is his claim that it is practically *futile* for a determinist to weigh alternative modes of social organization with a view to optimizing the organization of his own society. For the determinist does *not* maintain, in fatalist fashion, that the future state of society is independent of the decisions which men make in response to (*a*) facts (both physical and social), (*b*) their own *interpretation* of these facts (which, of course, is often false), and (*c*) their value-objectives. It is precisely because, on the deterministic theory, human decisions *are* causally dependent upon these factors that deliberation concerning optimal courses of action and social arrangements can be reasonably expected to issue in successful action rather than lose its significance by adventitiousness.

B. *Confusion of causal determination and compulsion*

The second, more fundamental point to bear in mind is that psychological laws do *not* force us to do or desire anything against our will. These laws merely state what, as a matter of fact, we do or desire under certain conditions. Thus, if there were a psychological law enabling us to predict that under certain conditions a man will desire to commit a certain act, this law would *not* be making him act in

a manner contrary to his own desires; for the desire would be his. It follows that neither the causes of our desires nor psychological laws, which state under what conditions our desires arise, *compel* us in any way to act in a manner contrary to our own will. There is in the indeterminist's thinking a confusion of physical and psychological law, on the one hand, with statutory law, on the other. Psychological laws do not coerce us against our will and cannot be broken. Only statutory laws can be and are often broken, when their directives contravene powerful desires. Anyone who steps off the top of the Empire State Building shouting defiance and insubordination to the law of gravitation will not break that law, but rather will give a pathetic illustration of its applicability.

We act under *compulsion*, in the sense relevant here, *when we are literally being physically restrained from without in implementing the desires which we have upon reacting to the total stimulus situation in our environment.* For example, if I am locked up and *therefore* cannot make an appointment, then I would be compelled to miss my appointment. Or, if a stronger man literally forces my hand to press a button which I do not wish to press, then I would be compelled to blow up a bridge. The meaning of "compulsion" intended here should *not*, of course, be identified with the meaning of that term familiar to students of neuroses. In the case of neurotic compulsion, *the compulsive person does what he wishes*, although his behavior is inspired by unwarranted anxiety and hence is insensitive to normally deterring factors.

To emphasize the meaning of "compulsion" relevant to the issue before us, I wish to point out that when a bank teller hands over cash during a stick-up upon feeling the revolver pressing against his ribs, he is *not* acting under *compulsion* in my sense, any more than you and I act under compulsion when deciding *not* to go out playing tennis during a heavy rain. When handing over the money in preference to being shot, the bank teller is doing what he genuinely wishes to do *under the given conditions*. The similarity of the bank-teller case to a case of genuine compulsion in my sense lies only in the fact that our legal system does *not* decree punishment either in a case of genuine compulsion, like having one's hand literally forced to blow up a bridge by pressing a button, or in a case of *voluntary* action, like that of the bank teller. For, although the bank teller is actually *physically free* to hold on to the money and sound the alarm, he is *not* punished for surrendering the money because the alternative to such surrender would be to sound the alarm *at the cost of his own life*. The armed bank robber can therefore be said to have "compelled" the teller to surrender the money *not* in our technical sense, but only in the sense that the robber's threat was the decisive determinant of the *particular kind of voluntary action* that was taken by the teller. Thus, what is common to genuine compulsion and voluntarily deciding to hand over money in preference to dying is that both of them are treated *as excusing conditions*. But *causal determination is not identical with what we have called compulsion*. For *voluntary* behavior does *not* cease to be voluntary and become "compelled" in our technical sense just because there are causes for that behavior. Hence the indeterminist is *not* entitled to assert that if determinism were true, the assignment of responsibility to people for their acts would be meaningless.

It should not be thought that the indeterminist is now prepared to surrender, for he has yet to use his strongest weapon. Says he: "We are all familiar with the fact that when we look back upon past conduct, we frequently feel very strongly that we could have done otherwise. For example, some one might have chosen to come here today via a route different from the one he actually did use. If the determinist is right in saying that our behavior was unavoidably determined by earlier causes, this retrospective feeling of freedom either should not exist or else it is fraudulent. In either case, the burden of proof rests upon the determinist." The determinist gladly accepts this challenge, and his reply is as follows: Let us carefully examine the content of the feeling that on a certain occasion we could have acted other than the way we did, in fact, act. What

do we find? Does the feeling we have inform us that we could have acted otherwise *under exactly the same kinds of relevant external and internal motivational conditions?* No, says the determinist, this feeling simply discloses that we were able to act in accord with our strongest desire at that time *instead of acting under compulsion* and that we could indeed have acted otherwise *if a different motive had prevailed at the time*. And this state of affairs is entirely in accord with determinism. Thus the determinist answer is that the content of this "consciousness of freedom" consists in our awareness that we were able to act in response to our strongest motive at the time, and that we were not "under compulsion" in that sense. We were able to do what we wanted. But the determinist reminds us that our feeling of "freedom" does *not* disclose that, given the motives which acted on us at the time and given their relative strength and temporal distribution, we could have acted differently from the way in which we did, in fact, act. *Neither do we feel that we could have responded to the weaker of two contending motives, or acted without a cause or motive, or chosen the motives which acted upon us.* I never wake up totally devoid of any content of consciousness and then ask my *blank* self: "With what motives shall I populate my consciousness this A.M.?" Nor do I even know what the indeterminist means by the supposition that we could have chosen our own character from scratch: every decision to shape or choose one's character must be one's own, i.e., must be made by an already existing personality, constituted by a set of dispositions. The notion of choosing one's character involves an infinite regress, because an initial "I" is presupposed in the making of the choice. Since the retrospective feeling of freedom that we have does *not* report any ability of making the kinds of choices envisioned by the indeterminist, its deliverances contain no facts incompatible with the claim of the determinist. When asked about her choice to marry Mr. Rosselini, Ingrid Bergman showed much insight by saying, that in retrospect, she could not have acted differently under the given (relevant) conditions.

The analysis we have offered is applicable at once to the case of remorse, regret, or guilt. We sometimes experience remorse over past conduct when we reconsider that conduct in the light of *different* motives. Once we bring a different set of motives to bear on a given situation, we may feel that a different decision is called for. If our motives do not change, we do not regret a past deed no matter how reprehensible it would otherwise appear. Many a killer has honestly declared that if he had to choose again, he would do again precisely what he had done. In that case, the relevant motives had not changed. *Regret is an expression of our emotion toward the disvalue and injustice which issued from our past conduct, as seen in the light of the new motives*. The regret we experience can then act as a *deterrent* against the repetition of past behavior which issued in disvalue. If the determinist expresses regret concerning past misconduct, he is applying motives of self-improvement to himself but not indulging in retroactive self-blame. Retroactive blame is futile, since the past will never return again. Thus, by responsibility the determinist does *not* mean retroactive blameworthiness, but rather *liability to reformative or educative punishment*. Punishment is educative in the sense that, when properly administered, it institutes counter-causes to the repetition of injurious conduct. For the determinist, punishment is never an end in itself. It is *not* intended as a revenge-catharsis. The determinist rejects as barbarous the primitive vengeful idea of retaliatory, retributive, or vindictive punishment. He condemns hurting a man simply because he has hurt others, for the same reason that he would condemn stealing from a thief or cheating a swindler. He fails to see how the damage done by the wrongdoer is remedied by the mere infliction of pain or sorrow on the culprit, *unless* such infliction of pain promises to act as a causal deterrent against the repetition of evil conduct. For the determinist, the decision whether pain is to be inflicted on the culprit and, if so, to what extent, is governed solely by the conduciveness of such punishment to reform and re-education of the culprit and repairing his damage, where

possible. The mathematics professor at the University of Pennsylvania whose three-year-old daughter was murdered by an adolescent in Philadelphia nobly disavowed all cave-man revenge. But he did ask for greater preventive efforts in diagnosing potentially homicidal but seemingly exemplary adolescents.

The implementation of this conception requires psychological and sociological research into *causal* connections and the institution of a *rational prison system*. If kindness rather than punishment were to deter the potential criminal, then it is clearly rational to be kind. The design and organization of the prison system must be set up accordingly, and the social cost would probably be less. Revenge seekers do not care whether prison hardens criminals further, nor whether the social cost of protecting society increases further. Their motto is that of the English schoolmaster: "Be pure in heart boys, or I'll flog you until you are."

On the determinist view of punishment as educative, "punishment" of the insane automatically takes the form of treatment, since their insanity lies in the fact that, among other things, (a) they act in a socially injurious way, and (b) they do not, because of a mental malfunction, provide a unified point, as it were, for applying a counter-motive by the usual kinds of punishment.

Insanity and punishment should *not* be judged by the McNaughton criterion: "Did the wrong-doer '*really know*' the difference between right and wrong at the time of the act?" For this criterion does *not* suffice to determine whether a man is sane in the sense of being deterred from repeating his crime by the same punishment that would deter the rest of us. Often a man who is judged sane by the *traditional* criterion does *not* respond to the standard punishment but is, in fact, attracted by the prospect of such punishment.

Our legal and penal system is to a certain extent an inconsistent and unresolved compromise between the revenge philosophy of medieval spiritism which prescribed tortures for the insane and a grudging recognition of some of the findings of modern science concerning the conditions breeding criminal behavior. For the determinist, there is no "tempering of justice with mercy": the punishment is never made more severe than is believed necessary to reform the criminal or prevent him from continuing his destructive behavior. "Tempering justice with mercy" is the philosophy of either a revenge-seeker who has qualms or a man who is torn between the revenge conception and the reformatory one.

The *New York Sun* editorially supported revenge in the Leopold parole case and said that reform is not enough, although it was not against throwing in a touch of mercy for good measure. On the other hand, the great attorney Clarence Darrow, who was as warmhearted as he was mistaken, used a revenge conception of punishment in conjunction with a belief in determinism to plead with his juries that criminals should be excused for their misdeeds, since they did not "choose their own character." But he and most of his juries failed to realize that the notion of choosing one's own character is self-contradictory, and hence this notion can hardly be used to characterize the conditions under which revengeful or vindictive punishment would be just.

Contrary to Darrow, we see that determinism does *not* entail the doctrine that *to understand all is to forgive all:* punishment that prevents or deters human beings from committing acts issuing in much greater pain than is inflicted by the punishment is the lesser evil.

It is apparent that the entire problem of responsibility can be solved within the domain of deterministic assumptions. Thus the issue is not *whether* conduct is determined but rather *by what factors* it is determined, when responsibility is to be assigned. Far from facing insuperable difficulties with the problem of responsibility, the determinist and the scientific psychologist now challenge the indeterminist to provide a logical foundation for the penal system. We recall that the indeterminist accused the determinist of cruelly punishing people who, if determinism is true, cannot help acting as they do. The determinist now turns the tables on his antagonist and accuses him of being gratuitously vengeful, on the grounds

that the indeterminist is committed by his own theory to a retaliatory theory of punishment. The indeterminist cannot consistently expect to achieve anything better than retaliation by inflicting punishment; for were he to admit that punishment will causally influence all or some of the criminals, then he would be abandoning the basis of his entire argument against the determinist.

C. Other arguments of the indeterminist

It is sometimes said that, when applied to man, the deterministic doctrine becomes untenable by virtue of becoming self-contradictory. This contention is often stated as follows: "The determinist, by his own doctrine, must admit that his very acceptance of determinism was causally conditioned or determined. Since he could not help accepting it, he cannot argue that he has chosen a true doctrine." To justify this claim, it is first pointed out rightly that determinism implies a causal determination of its own acceptance by its defenders. Then it is further maintained, however, that since the determinist could not, by his own theory, help accepting determinism, he can have no confidence in its truth. Thus it is asserted that the determinist's acceptance of his own doctrine was forced upon him. I submit that this inference involves a radical fallacy. The proponent of this argument is gratuitously invoking the view that if our beliefs have causes, these causes *force* the beliefs in question upon us, against our better judgment, as it were. Nothing could be further from the truth: this argument is another case of confusing *causation* with *compulsion*. My belief that I am now addressing you derives from the fact that your presence is causally inducing certain images on the retinas of my eyes, and that these images, in turn, cause me to infer that corresponding people are actually present before me. The reason why I do not suppose that I am now witnessing a performance of *Aïda* is that the images which Aïda, Radames, and Amneris would produce are not now in my visual field. The causal generation of a belief in no way detracts from its reliability. In fact, if a given belief were not produced in us by definite causes, we should have no reason to accept that belief as a correct description of the world, rather than some other belief arbitrarily selected. Far from making knowledge either adventitious or impossible, the deterministic theory about the origin of our beliefs alone provides the basis for thinking that our judgments of the world are or may be true. Knowing and judging are indeed causal processes in which the facts we judge are determining elements along with the cerebral mechanism employed in their interpretation. It follows that although the determinist's assent to his own doctrine is caused or determined, the truth of determinism is not jeopardized by this fact; if anything, it is made credible.

More generally, both true beliefs and false beliefs have psychological causes. The difference between a true or warranted belief and a false or unwarranted one must therefore be sought *not* in *whether* the belief in question is caused; instead, the difference must be sought in the particular *character* of the psychological causal factors which issued in the entertaining of the belief: *a warrantedly held belief, which has the presumption of being true, is one to which a person gave assent in response to awareness of supporting evidence.* Assent in the face of awareness of a *lack* of supporting evidence is irrational, although there are indeed psychological causes in such cases for giving assent.

The irrationality of unsupported beliefs is not at all mitigated, of course, by their prevalence or even by the fact that they may be prompted by deep-seated instinctual needs of man. This requires mention because writers such as Jules Masserman and some of the other existentialist writers have drawn the appalling inference that beliefs growing out of deep, emotionally-inspired commitments can legitimately be regarded as true (2). And the reason they give for this atavistic conclusion is that every system of ideas must begin with certain principles of reasoning which cannot themselves be validated within the framework

of that system and which are allegedly espoused as a matter of sheer commitment. According to this view, believing on the basis of evidence constitutes merely one possible kind of commitment. I submit that if this were so, the only thing that could justify the ordinary beliefs of Dr. Masserman and the rest of us against the beliefs of one of his psychotic patients who claims to be Napoleon is that those with our kind of commitment to evidence happen to *outnumber* the psychotics sufficiently to be able to confine them to mental institutions. For, by his own premises, Dr. Masserman cannot claim that the criterion of evidence—which tells him that his patient is *not* Napoleon—is a uniquely distinguished avenue for gaining true knowledge of the world. But it clearly and demonstrably is that. For what makes a factual belief true is that it asserts what is the case, i.e., that it corresponds to reality. And the very existence of the state of affairs truly affirmed by the belief will then manifest itself to us under appropriate conditions *in the form of evidence for it.* That those of us who make claims to knowledge contingent on the availability of supporting evidence are not simply making *one* of several alternative and equally legitimate commitments seems to me to be clear from the following fact: the beliefs which we have formed about our physical environment on the basis of evidence are sufficiently in tune with reality to enable us to confine psychotics to mental institutions, whereas the well-laid schemes of intelligent psychotics usually fail because of insufficient sensitivity on their part to the evidence.

Contrary to Jules Masserman, therefore, the truth of a belief can thus never be determined by the role of that belief in satisfying emotional needs, however deep-seated. Rebellion against a religious father may drive a son to examine the question of the existence of a theistic God, and the son may find that there is no evidence for this belief. Emotional rebellion against an irreligious father may have the same outcome or not. But in either case, the truth of the belief is *not* dependent on its psychogenesis or on the needs it satisfies, however imperative these needs may be. And one is distressed, therefore, to find such writers as Gregory Zilboorg becoming exponents of irrationality on the strength of finding so much of it among their patients.

I hope that these considerations have shown, therefore, that it is entirely possible to give a *causal* account of both rational *and* irrational beliefs and behavior. And since a causal account is based on principles and regularities which are based on evidence, it follows that we can indeed give a rational explanation of why it is that people do behave irrationally under certain conditions, no less than we can provide a causal account of their rational behavior.

Lastly, a remark on the belief that determinism would lead to moral cynicism: why should my belief that my motives for wishing to help someone are caused lessen my readiness to implement my desire to help that person? Lincoln's view that his own beliefs (ethical and other) were causally determined did not weaken in the least his desire to abolish Negro slavery, as demanded by his ethical theory; and similarly for Augustine, Calvin, Spinoza, and a host of lesser men.

III. Is love measurable?

Let us now turn to the contention that love is scientifically intractable in the sense of *not* lending itself to description by laws, because it is "intangible" or *not amenable to measurement*. Its proponents do not, of course, mean mere intangibility in the purely etymological sense that would accord to the sense of touch a preferred status as an avenue of scientific knowledge. But awareness of our reasons for *not* regarding that sense as having unique reliability will throw light on the issue of the alleged intangibility or non-measurability of love. These reasons emerge from the following twofold considerations.

a) As far as vision alone is concerned, we can interpret the visually bent appearance of a stick partially immersed in water as follows: the stick bends when partially immersed and then unbends when taken out. By means of pure vision, we are quite ignorant of any optical theories of refraction. But the sense of touch is invoked by some to declare that sight deceived us as to the condition of the stick: touch tells us that the partially immersed stick is straight. Hence, here touch presumably corrects sight.

b) But the inverse order of trustworthiness prevails among the senses of sight and touch in regard to ascertaining the dimensions of a distressing cavity in one's tooth: tactile exploration with the tongue suggests a huge crater but the dentist's mirror is held to tell the true story visually.

How can we oscillate like that in accepting the verdicts of a given sense organ in one case and not in the other? The answer was given by Immanuel Kant when he said that percepts without concepts are blind. *Theories* are used to assess the significance of observational findings, and the same holds true for *measures*, whether in physics or psychology. For some measures are totally devoid of theoretical significance, while others function in a powerfully fruitful way by virtue of being lawfully linked to other quantities, as we shall now see.

Suppose that I were to define the "Mathew-measure" of a person at a given time as follows: blood count, multiplied by the number of hairs, divided by the square root of the height, the measure being plus or minus depending on whether the person is Rh $+$ or $-$. I venture to say that although this is a perfectly well-defined measure, no physiologist would be interested in it. Again, suppose that I were to define "the George-index of a piece of metal" as follows: $3/2$ π, times its mass, times the square root of its electrical conductivity, divided by 45 times its volume. The George-index plays no role in metallurgy. Neither is the Mathew-measure of interest to the physiologist. And why not? Because these respective measures or indices are not lawfully (predictively) related to *other* properties whose occurrence is of concern to the physiologist or metallurgist. Similarly, there are a host of perfectly trivial measures of love that one could introduce and which are unavailing, *not* because they fail to be measures, but because they are explanatorily sterile. Thus, consider the following measures of love: disregarding ethical or legal complications, how much electric shock or how much imprisonment up to ten years would a man be willing to stand to marry the woman he loves? Apart from its impracticality, the sterility of this measure lies in the fact that it is not predictively related to whether a man will exhibit *other* types of behavior which his wife may expect from him by virtue of his love. Thus, there is no "intangibility" of love in the sense of lack of measures per se. On the other hand, if the "intangibility" of love is held to lie in the purely inferential, indirect knowledge we have of *other* people's feelings of affection toward us, then indeed neutrinos, nuclear forces, and the interiors of stars would also have to be deemed "intangible" and scientifically intractable, which they are surely not.

But, you might say, do we not have reason to think that in the human domain there simply aren't *any* theoretically fruitful measures at all, and correlatively no regularities, whereas in physical science there are some celebratedly successful measures and laws? This seems to me a misleading oversimplification. First of all, there are a host of reliable indices of the presence of love which we generally regard as obvious because of their familiarity. It is banal to say that the willful and knowing throwing of sulphuric acid by a man into the face of another for pay is a reliable index of deficient affection and even callous indifference to human suffering. And it is equally trite to predict that under the usual assumed initial conditions, the vast majority of undergraduates will stay away from their college campuses during vacations. Similarly, people are unimpressed when a businessman makes dependable forecasts of the economic fortunes of neighborhood grocery stores in small communities. But they ask economists to predict the state of the U.S. national economy for the next ten years. Why? Because the exigencies of life confer great urgency on the immediate solution of highly complex problems by the social scientist. . . . To be sure, there are social demands made on the physical scientist also. But almost any discovery by him issuing in a change in the externals of life will be hailed as an indication of the power of the scientific method to deal

with inanimate nature and will be contrasted with the failure of the psychiatrist to find the cause and cure of schizophrenia and of the political scientist to devise an immediately workable disarmament agreement. And we recall that Lawrence Kubie has deplored the fact that psychoanalysis was no sooner born when it was confronted with the demand to administer therapy. When people say that the physical sciences are more successful than the social sciences, what *measure* of success do they use? *I believe that the implicit measure is very often the relative social urgency of the problems which these disciplines leave unsolved.* It is clear that in any such comparison, the social sciences are bound to end up on the bottom. *But, this purely pragmatic measure has none of the derogatory implications for the scientific intractability of man which Murray and his supporters claim.*

IV. Does quantum physics have any bearing on the freedom of the will?

Although we saw that there is no incompatibility between determinism and the *feeling* of freedom, it might be supposed that the discovery of micro-indeterminism in quantum theory has shown that the causal conception of human decision processes has to be abandoned and that grave doubt has been cast on the amenability of human behavior to scientific mastery. I wish to devote the remainder of my remarks to showing why I do *not* think that this is so.

There is an important class of experimental results in physics which seems to compel the conclusion that micro-entities like electrons cannot be held to be particles in the classical sense. That is, they cannot be assumed to be entities characterized by the simultaneous possession of such sharply defined pairs of attributes as exact positions and velocities, attributes which specified the state of a particle in classical mechanics and which we shall call "conjugates." . . . Instead, the experimental findings would seem to support the conclusion that (*a*) of any pair of the classical conjugate properties of state, like exact position and velocity, *at most one* characterizes the electron in any given experimental context, and that (*b*) sharp position and velocity of microparticles cannot be measured simultaneously because they do not jointly exist to be measured. Thus, the evidence in question shows that the repudiation of the particle conception of the electron does *not* rest on the *mere* fact that sharply defined values of position and velocity are not simultaneously measurable or are *operationally incompatible* (4).

In classical physics, pairs of conjugates were held to characterize a particle simultaneously. We can therefore call this classical *joint*-ascribability the "theoretical *con*junctiveness" of these properties, and contrast it with the opposing claim of the new quantum theory that these properties are theoretically *dis*junctive in the sense that *at most one* of them can characterize the micro-entity at any given time. Bohr has formulated the philosophical upshot of the discoveries of quantum theory by saying that conjugate properties are "complementary." By this he means two things. First, the complementarity of conjugates asserts that they are theoretically disjunctive, because the experimental arrangements under which a sharp value of one of two conjugates can be said to characterize the micro-entity in question are physically *incompatible* with the conditions under which a sharp value of the corresponding other conjugate parameter belongs to the micro-entity; contrary to the classical conception, these conjugate properties do *not* belong to microphysical objects *independently* of the experimental arrangement into which they enter but are *context-dependent*: that is to say, they are relevant only to particular interactions in which the micro-object is coupled indivisibly to a particular kind of observational macro-setup. Second, Bohr speaks of complementarity to convey the fact that in any account of the totality of all interactions of micro-entities with observational macro-apparatus, there is a need for *each* of the conjugate properties taken separately. The so-called Heisenberg Uncertainty Principle gives mathematical expression to this complementarity of conjugates in the form of certain inequalities. . . .

In the classical physics of closed systems,

there was a one-to-one or unique functional relation between the values of the *complete* set of state variables at one or more times and the corresponding values at other times. In particle mechanics, the theoretical conjunctiveness of exact position and velocity is a *necessary condition* for a deterministic prediction or retrodiction: no classical physicist would claim a deterministic linkage between the mere position of a particle at a given time and its state at other times, but requires both position *and* velocity at a given time to predict or postdict the state of the particle at other times. But the quantum mechanical thesis is that the necessary condition for a classical deterministic prediction *cannot* be fulfilled: for the classical state attributes are *not* theoretically *con*junctive but merely *disjunctive*, so that the necessary condition for a deterministic relation between the attributes of individual events in space and time is *not* fulfilled. No wonder then that the new theory regards a *statistical* description of atomic phenomena not as merely an expression of our ignorance but as a reflection of an irreducible feature of the physical facts themselves.

I now wish to examine the import of this quantum mechanical indeterminism for the possibility of the scientific study of man by stating what conclusions, if any, seem to me to be warranted by the logic of the situation.

Earlier, I have argued that our retrospective feeling of freedom that we could have acted otherwise does *not* tell us that our decisions are uncaused in the sense that they could have been different under the same kinds of relevant circumstances; so far as I can see, our feeling of freedom merely discloses that often we can do what we wish, but *not* that we can will what desires we shall have. As we saw, the very concept of "I" or of self already involves a set of dispositions which come into play when this self finds itself with desires that it has not chosen.

I therefore regard as wholly ill-conceived the quest for indeterministic neurological correlates of the non-existent kind of feeling of freedom postulated by the philosophical free willist. For the non-existence of the latter kind of feeling seems to me to make it idle to try to find quantum processes in the nervous system which are its supposed physical correlates. But what of the neurological correlate of the feeling of freedom which I do experience; that is, the feeling that I can often do what I wish under given circumstances and that under *other* circumstances I might well have different desires and act differently? Here I cannot see that the evidence warrants any more than the following cautious statement made by Niels Bohr in stating the conclusions of his essay "Light and Life" (3):

> I should like to emphasize that considerations of the kind here mentioned are entirely opposed to any attempt of seeking new possibilities for a spiritual influence on the behavior of matter in the statistical description of atomic phenomena. For instance, it is impossible from our standpoint, to attach an unambiguous meaning to the view sometimes expressed that the probability of the occurrence of certain atomic processes in the body might be under the direct influence of the will. In fact, according to the generalized interpretation of the psycho-physical parallelism, the freedom of the will is to be considered as a feature of conscious life which corresponds to functions of the organism that not only evade a causal mechanical description but resist even a physical analysis carried to the extent required for an unambiguous application of the statistical laws of atomic mechanics.

What then is the bearing of quantum physics on the freedom of the will? It seems to me to be the following: even if the retrospective feeling of freedom *did* disclose anything incompatible with the causal generation of our decisions—which it does not—the discoveries of quantum physics could *not* be adduced to show that this feeling has a foundation in fact.

So much for arguments which rest on the supposition that *the feeling of freedom* poses a problem to whose solution either quantum theory or its alleged philosophical lessons are relevant. But what of the import of quantum theory for the existence of regularities in human conduct and its predictability *apart from any invocation of the feeling of freedom?* Does that theory provide grounds for impugning the possibility of a science of man?

Perhaps there are cases in which the human eye responds to as little energy as a single photon or in which a neuron is triggered by a physical process sufficiently microscopic to be subject to quantum uncertainties. If these processes of vision or neural excitation then issue in decisions and actions on the part of humans in whose bodies they transpire, then one can say that quantum uncertainties enter into human macro-conduct and one can speak of a corresponding reduction in predictability *in principle*. But unless it is shown that a significant number of human decisions fall into this category, it would seem that the vast bulk if not all human decisions and acts involve physical agencies of such magnitude that quantum uncertainties become irrelevant to them and classical deterministic characterization holds to all intents and purposes.

It is hoped that this discussion of the alleged intangibility of man's inner life and of the bearing of quantum indeterminacy on human freedom has served to support the view that there are very important respects in which science can *and* ought to deal with man as with the rest of nature.

References

1. T. E. Murray: *Chemical Engineering Progress*, 48:22, 1952.
2. J. Masserman: *Amer. J. Psychiat.*, 110:324, 1953.
3. N. Bohr: *Atomic Physics and Human Knowledge*, John Wiley & Sons, Inc., New York, 1958, p. 11.
4. A. Grünbaum: *J. Philosophy*, 54:713, 1957.

What is freedom?

Maurice Merleau-Ponty (1907-1961)

Merleau-Ponty, a leading French existentialist, was born in the province of Normandy. He received the main part of his philosophical education at the Ecole Normale Supérieur in Paris, where he became a friend of Jean-Paul Sartre. He developed an early interest in the relations between the sciences of biology and psychology, and much of his philosophic work was influenced by Gestalt psychology. Merleau-Ponty joined the faculty of the Sorbonne in 1950 and was elected to the Collège de France in 1952.

His analysis of freedom owes a great deal to the use of a method which has achieved importance in its own right and as a pathway to existentialist thought. The method is called "phenomenological" and was developed primarily by the German-Jewish philosopher, Edmund Husserl (1859-1938). Basically it is a way of giving exact accounts of the meaning structures of phenomena (any of the items of which the mind is aware) and of describing the acts and correlated objects of consciousness. Merleau-Ponty attempts to ground his view of freedom in a precise account of what an examination of our mental acts reveals about freedom.

Among his important works translated into English are The Structure of Behavior *(1942),* Phenomenology of Perception *(1945), from which our selection is taken, and* In Praise of Philosophy *(1953).*

... Again, it is clear that no causal relationship is conceivable between the subject and his body, his world or his society. Only at the cost of losing the basis of all my certainties can I question what is conveyed to me by my presence to myself. Now the moment I turn to myself in order to describe myself, I have a glimpse of an anonymous flux,[1] a comprehensive project in which there are so far no "states of consciousness," nor, *a fortiori*, qualifications of any sort. For myself I am neither "jealous," nor "inquisitive," nor "hunchbacked," nor "a civil servant." It is often a matter of surprise that the cripple or the invalid can put up with himself. The reason is that such people are not for themselves deformed or at death's door. Until the final coma, the dying man is inhabited by a consciousness, he is all that he sees, and enjoys this much of an outlet. Consciousness can never objectify itself into invalid-consciousness or cripple-consciousness, and even if the old man complains of his age or the cripple of his deformity, they can do so only by comparing themselves with others, or seeing themselves through the eyes of others, that is, by taking a statistical and objective view of themselves, so that such complaints are never absolutely genuine: when he is back in the heart of his own consciousness, each one of us

From Maurice Merleau-Ponty, *Phenomenology of Perception,* tr. Colin Smith. Copyright, 1962, by Routledge & Kegan Paul, Ltd. Used by permission of Routledge & Kegan Paul, Ltd. and The Humanities Press, Inc.

[1] In the sense in which, with Husserl, we have taken this word.

feels beyond his limitations and thereupon resigns himself to them. They are the price which we automatically pay for being in the world, a formality which we take for granted. Hence we may speak disparagingly of our looks and still not want to change our face for another. No idiosyncrasy can, seemingly, be attached to the insuperable generality of consciousness, nor can any limit be set to this immeasurable power of escape. In order to be determined (in the two senses of that word) by an external factor, it is necessary that I should be a thing. Neither my freedom nor my universality can admit of any eclipse. It is inconceivable that I should be free in certain of my actions and determined in others: how should we understand a dormant freedom that gave full scope to determinism? And if it is assumed that it is snuffed out when it is not in action, how could it be rekindled? If *per impossibile* I had once succeeded in *making myself into* a thing, how should I subsequently reconvert myself to consciousness? Once I am free, I am not to be counted among things, and I must then be uninterruptedly free. Once my actions cease to be mine, I shall never recover them, and if I lose my hold on the world, it will never be restored to me. It is equally inconceivable that my liberty should be attenuated; one cannot be to some extent free, and if, as is often said, motives incline me in a certain direction, one of two things happens: either they are strong enough to force me to act, in which case there is no freedom, or else they are not strong enough, and then freedom is complete, and as great in the worst torments as in the peace of one's home. We ought, therefore, to reject not only the idea of causality, but also that of motivation.[2] The alleged motive does not burden my decision; on the contrary my decision lends the motive its force. Everything that I "am" in virtue of nature or history—hunchbacked, handsome or Jewish—I never am completely for myself, as we have just explained: and I may well be these things for other people, nevertheless I remain free to posit another person as a consciousness whose views strike

through to my very being, or on the other hand merely as an object. It is also true that this option is itself a form of constraint: if I am ugly, I have the choice between being an object of disapproval or disapproving of others. I am left free to be a masochist or a sadist, but not free to ignore others. But this dilemma, which is given as part of the human lot, is not one for me as pure consciousness: it is still I who cause the other to be for me, and who cause us both to be as members of mankind. Moreover, even if existence as a human being were imposed upon me, the manner alone being left to my choice, and considering this choice itself and ignoring the small number of forms it might take, it would still be a free choice. If it is said that my temperament inclines me particularly to either sadism or masochism, it is still merely a manner of speaking, for my temperament exists only for the second order knowledge that I gain about myself when I see myself as others see me, and in so far as I recognize it, confer value upon it, and in that sense, choose it. What misleads us on this, is that we often look for freedom in the voluntary deliberation which examines one motive after another and seems to opt for the weightiest or most convincing. In reality the deliberation follows the decision, and it is my secret decision which brings the motives to light, for it would be difficult to conceive what the force of a motive might be in the absence of a decision which it confirms or to which it runs counter. When I have abandoned a project, the motives which I thought held me to it suddenly lose their force and collapse. In order to resuscitate them, an effort is required on my part to reopen time and set me back to the moment preceding the making of the decision. Even while I am deliberating, already I find it an effort to suspend time's flow, and to keep open a situation which I feel is closed by a decision which is already there and which I am holding off. That is why it so often happens that after giving up a plan I experience a feeling of relief: "After all, I wasn't so very particular"; the debate was purely a matter of form, and the deliberation a mere parody, for I had decided against from the start.

[2] See J. P. Sartre, *L'Être et le Néant*, pp. 508ff.

We often see the weakness of the will brought forward as an argument against freedom. And indeed, although I can will myself to adopt a course of conduct and act the part of a warrior or a seducer, it is not within my power to be a warrior or seducer with ease and in a way that "comes naturally"; really to *be* one, that is. But neither should we seek freedom in the act of will, which is, in its very meaning, something short of an act. We have recourse to an act of will only in order to go against our true decision, and, as it were, for the purpose of proving our powerlessness. If we had really and truly made the conduct of the warrior or the seducer our own, then we should *be* one or the other. Even what are called obstacles to freedom are in reality deployed by it. An unclimbable rock face, a large or small, vertical or slanting rock, are things which have no meaning for anyone who is not intending to surmount them, for a subject whose projects do not carve out such determinate forms from the uniform mass of the *in itself* and cause an orientated world to arise—a significance in things. There is, then, ultimately nothing that can set limits to freedom, except those limits that freedom itself has set in the form of its various initiatives, so that the subject has simply the external world that he gives himself. . . .

The result, however, of this first reflection on freedom would appear to be to rule it out altogether. If indeed it is the case that our freedom is the same in all our actions, and even in our passions, if it is not to be measured in terms of our conduct, and if the slave displays freedom as much by living in fear as by breaking his chains, then it cannot be held that there is such a thing as *free action*, freedom being anterior to all actions. In any case it will not be possible to declare: "Here freedom makes its appearance," since free action, in order to be discernible, has to stand out against a background of life from which it is entirely, or almost entirely, absent. We may say in this case that it is everywhere, but equally nowhere. In the name of freedom we reject the idea of acquisition, since freedom has become a primordial acquisition and, as it

were, our state of nature. Since we do not have to provide it, it is the gift granted to us of having no gift, it is the nature of consciousness which consists in having no nature, and in no case can it find external expression or a place in our life. The idea of action, therefore, disappears: nothing can pass from us to the world, since we are nothing that can be specified, and since the non-being which constitutes us could not possibly find its way into the world's plenum. There are merely intentions immediately followed by their effects, and we are very near to the Kantian idea of an intention which is tantamount to the act, which Scheler countered with the argument that the cripple who would like to be able to save a drowning man and the good swimmer who actually saves him do not have the same experience of autonomy. The very idea of choice vanishes, for to choose is to choose *something* in which freedom sees, at least for a moment, a symbol of itself. There is free choice only if freedom comes into play in its decision, and posits the situation chosen as a situation of freedom. A freedom which has no need to be exercised because it is already acquired could not commit itself in this way: it knows that the following instant will find it, come what may, just as free and just as indeterminate. The very notion of freedom demands that our decision should plunge into the future, that something should have been *done* by it, that the subsequent instant should benefit from its predecessor and, though not necessitated, should be at least required by it. If freedom is doing, it is necessary that what it does should not be immediately undone by a new freedom. Each instant, therefore, must not be a closed world; one instant must be able to commit its successors and, a decision once taken and action once begun, I must have something acquired at my disposal, I must benefit from my impetus, I must be inclined to carry on, and there must be a bent or propensity of the mind. It was Descartes who held that conservation demands a power as great as does creation; a view which implies a realistic notion of the instant. It is true that the instant is not a philosopher's fiction. It is the point at which one project is brought to fruition and another begun [3]—the point at which my gaze is transferred from one end to another, it is the *Augen-Blick*. But this break in time cannot occur unless each of the two spans is of a piece. Consciousness, it is said, is, though not atomized into instants, at least haunted by the spectre of the instant which it is obliged continually to exorcise by a free act. We shall soon see that we have indeed always the power to interrupt, but it implies in any case a power to *begin*, for there would be no severance unless freedom had taken up its abode somewhere and were preparing to move it. Unless there are cycles of behaviour, open situations requiring a certain completion and capable of constituting a background to either a confirmatory or transformatory decision, we never experience freedom. The choice of an intelligible character is excluded, not only because there is no time anterior to time, but because choice presupposes a prior commitment and because the idea of an initial choice involves a contradiction. If freedom is to have *room* [4] in which to move, if it is to be describable as freedom, there must be something to hold it away from its objectives, it must have a *field*, which means that there must be for it special possibilities, or realities which tend to cling to being. As J. P. Sartre himself observes, dreaming is incompatible with freedom because, in the realm of imagination, we have no sooner taken a certain significance as our goal than we already believe that we have intuitively brought it into being, in short, because there is no obstacle and nothing *to do*.[5] It is established that freedom is not to be confused with those abstract decisions of will at grips with motives or passions, for the classical conception of deliberation is relevant only to a freedom "in bad faith" which secretly harbours antagonistic motives without being prepared to act on them, and so itself manufactures the alleged proofs of its impotence. We can see,

beneath these noisy debates and these fruitless efforts to "construct" us, the tacit decisions whereby we have marked out round ourselves the field of possibility, and it is true that nothing is done as long as we cling to these fixed points, and everything is easy as soon as we have weighed anchor. This is why our freedom is not to be sought in spurious discussion on the conflict between a style of life which we have no wish to reappraise and circumstances suggestive of another: the real choice is that between our whole character and our manner of being in the world. But either this total choice is never mentioned, since it is the silent upsurge of our being in the world, in which case it is not clear in what sense it could be said to be ours, since this freedom glides over itself and is the equivalent of a fate—or else our choice of ourselves is a genuine choice, a conversion involving our whole existence. In this case, however, there is presupposed a previous acquisition which the choice sets out to modify and it founds a new tradition: this leads us to ask whether the perpetual severance in terms of which we initially defined freedom is not simply the negative aspect of our universal commitment to a world, and whether our indifference to each determinate thing does not express merely our involvement in all; whether the ready-made freedom from which we started is not reducible to a power of initiative which cannot be transformed into *doing* without taking up the world as posited in some shape or form, and whether, in short, concrete and actual freedom is not to be found in this exchange. . . .

When I say that this rock is unclimbable, it is certain that this attribute, like that of being big or little, straight and oblique, and indeed like all attributes in general, can be conferred upon it only by the project of climbing it, and by a human presence. It is, therefore, freedom which brings into being the obstacles to freedom, so that the latter can be set over against it as its bounds. However, it is clear that, one and the same project being given, one rock will appear as an obstacle, and another, being more negotiable, as a means. My freedom, then, does

[3] *Ibid.*, p. 544.
[4] "avoir du champ"; in this sentence there is a play on the word "champ"—field [Translator's note].
[5] Sartre, *op. cit.*, p. 562.

not so contrive it that this way there is an obstacle, and that way a way through, it arranges for there to be obstacles and ways through in general; it does not draw the particular outline of this world, but merely lays down its general structures. It may be objected that there is no difference; if my freedom conditions the structure of the "there is," that of the "here" and the "there," it is present wherever these structures arise. We cannot distinguish the quality of "obstacle" from the obstacle itself, and relate one to freedom and the other to the world in itself which, without freedom, would be merely an amorphous and unnameable mass. It is not, therefore, outside myself that I am able to find a limit to my freedom. But should I not find it in myself? We must indeed distinguish between my express intentions, for example the plan I now make to climb those mountains, and general intentions which evaluate the potentialities of my environment. Whether or not I have decided to climb them, these mountains appear high to me, because they exceed my body's power to take them in its stride, and, even if I have just read *Micromégas*, I cannot so contrive it that they are small for me. Underlying myself as a thinking subject, who am able to take my place at will on Sirius or on the earth's surface, there is, therefore, as it were a natural self which does not budge from its terrestrial situation and which constantly adumbrates absolute valuations. What is more, my projects as a thinking being are clearly modelled on the latter; if I elect to see things from the point of view of Sirius, it is still to my terrestrial experience that I must have recourse in order to do so; I may say, for example, that the Alps are *molehills*. In so far as I have hands, feet, a body, I sustain around me intentions which are not dependent upon my decisions and which affect my surroundings in a way which I do not choose. These intentions are general in a double sense: firstly in the sense that they constitute a system in which all possible objects are simultaneously included; if the mountain appears high and upright, the tree appears small and sloping; and

furthermore in the sense that they are not of my own making, they originate from outside me, and I am not surprised to find them in all psycho-physical subjects organized as I am. Hence, as Gestalt psychology has shown, there are for me certain shapes which are particularly favoured, as they are for other men, and which are capable of giving rise to a psychological science and rigorous laws. The grouping of dots

  ..   ..

is always perceived as six pairs of dots with two millimetres between each pair, while one figure is always perceived as a cube, and another as a plane mosaic. It is as if, on the hither side of our judgement and our freedom, someone were assigning such and such a significance to such and such a given grouping. It is indeed true that perceptual structures do not always force themselves upon the observer; there are some which are ambiguous. But these reveal even more effectively the presence within us of spontaneous evaluation: for they are elusive shapes which suggest constantly changing meanings to us. Now a pure consciousness is capable of anything except being ignorant of its intentions, and an absolute freedom cannot choose itself as hesitant, since that amounts to allowing itself to be drawn in several directions, and since, the possibilities being *ex hypothesi* indebted to freedom for all the strength they have, the weight that freedom gives to one is thereby withdrawn from the rest. We *can* break up a shape by looking at it awry, but this too is because freedom uses the gaze along with its spontaneous evaluations. Without the latter, we would not have a world, that is, a collection of things which emerge from a background of formlessness by presenting themselves to our body as "to be touched," "to be taken," "to be climbed over." We should never be aware of adjusting ourselves to things and reaching them where they are, beyond us, but would be conscious only of restricting our thoughts to the immanent objects of our intentions, and we should not be in the world, ourselves implicated in the spectacle and, so to speak, intermingled with things, we should simply enjoy the spectacle of a universe. It is, therefore, true that there are no obstacles in themselves, but the self which qualifies them as such is not some acosmic subject; it runs ahead of itself in relation to things in order to confer upon them the form of things. . . .

This is true not only of an impersonal and, generally speaking, abstract function such as "external perception." There is something comparable present in all evaluations. It has been perceptively remarked that pain and fatigue can never be regarded as causes which "act" upon my liberty, and that, in so far as I may experience either at any given moment, they do not have their origin outside me, but always have a significance and express my attitude towards the world. Pain makes me give way and say what I ought to have kept to myself, fatigue makes me break my journey. We all know the moment at which we decide no longer to endure pain or fatigue, and when, simultaneously, they become intolerable in fact. Tiredness does not halt my companion because he likes the clamminess of his body, the heat of the road and the sun, in short, because he likes to feel himself in the midst of things, to feel their rays converging upon him, to be the cynosure of all this light, and an object of touch for the earth's crust. My own fatigue brings me to a halt because I dislike it, because I have chosen differently my manner of being in the world, because, for instance, I endeavour, not to be in nature, but rather to win the recognition of others. I am free in relation to fatigue to precisely the extent that I am free in relation to my being in the world, free to make my way by transforming it.[6] But here once more we must recognize a sort of sedimentation of our life: an attitude towards the world, when it has received frequent confirmation, acquires a favoured status for us. Yet since freedom does not tolerate any motive in its path, my habitual being in the world is at each moment equally precarious, and the complexes which I have allowed to develop over the years always remain equally soothing, and the free act can with no difficulty blow them sky-high. However, having built our life upon an

[6] Sartre, *op. cit.*, pp. 531ff.

inferiority complex which has been operative for twenty years, it is not *probable* that we shall change. It is clear what a summary rationalism might say in reply to such a hybrid notion: there are no degrees of possibility; either the free act is no longer possible, or it is still possible, in which case freedom is complete. In short, "probable" is meaningless. It is a notion belonging to statistical thought, which is not thought at all, since it does not concern any particular thing actually existing, any moment of time, any concrete event. "It is improbable that Paul will give up writing bad books" means nothing, since Paul may well decide to write no more such books. The probable is everywhere and nowhere, a reified fiction, with only a psychological existence; it is not an ingredient of the world. And yet we have already met it a little while ago in the perceived *world*. The mountain is great or small to the extent that, as a perceived thing, it is to be found in the field of my possible actions, and in relation to a level which is not only that of my individual life, but that of "any man." Generality and probability are not fictions, but phenomena; we must therefore find a phenomenological basis for statistical thought. It belongs necessarily to a being which is fixed, situated and surrounded by things in the world. "It is improbable" that I should at this moment destroy an inferiority complex in which I have been content to live for twenty years. That means that I have committed myself to inferiority, that I have made it my abode, that this past, though not a fate, has at least a specific weight and is not a set of events over there, at a distance from me, but the atmosphere of my present. The rationalist's dilemma: either the free act is possible, or it is not—either the event originates in me or is imposed on me from outside, does not apply to our relations with the world and with our past. Our freedom does not destroy our situation, but gears itself to it: as long as we are alive, our situation is open, which implies both that it calls up specially favoured modes of resolution, and also that it is powerless to bring one into being by itself. . . .

We therefore recognize, around our initiatives and around that strictly individual project which is oneself, a zone of generalized existence and of projects already formed, significances which trail between ourselves and things and which confer upon us the quality of man, bourgeois or worker. Already generality intervenes, already our presence to ourselves is mediated by it and we cease to be pure consciousness, as soon as the natural or social constellation ceases to be an unformulated *this* and crystallizes into a situation, as soon as it has a meaning—in short, as soon as we exist. Every thing appears to us through a medium to which it lends its own fundamental quality; this piece of wood is neither a collection of colours and tactile data, not even their total *Gestalt*, but something from which there emanates a woody essence; these "sense-data" modulate a certain theme or illustrate a certain style which is the wood itself, and which creates, round this piece of wood and the perception I have of it, a horizon of significance. The natural world, as we have seen, is nothing other than the place of all possible themes and styles. It is indissolubly an unmatched individual and a significance. Correspondingly, the generality and the individuality of the subject, subjectivity qualified and pure, the anonymity of the One and the anonymity of consciousness are not two conceptions of the subject between which philosophy has to choose, but two stages of a unique structure which is the concrete subject. Let us consider, for example, sense experience. I lose myself in this red which is before me, without in any way qualifying it, and it seems that this experience brings me into contact with a pre-human subject. Who perceives this red? It is nobody who can be named and placed among other perceiving subjects. For, between this experience of red which I have, and that about which other people speak to me, no direct comparison will ever be possible. I am here in my own point of view, and since all experience, in so far as it derives from impression, is in the same way strictly my own, it seems that a unique and unduplicated subject enfolds them all. Suppose I formulate a thought, the God of Spinoza, for example; this thought as it is in my living experience is

a certain landscape to which no one will ever have access, even if, moreover, I manage to enter into a discussion with a friend on the subject of Spinoza's God. However, the very individuality of these experiences is not quite unadulterated. For the thickness of this red, its thisness, the power it has of reaching me and saturating me, are attributable to the fact that it requires and obtains from my gaze a certain vibration, and imply that I am familiar with a world of colours of which this one is a particular variation. The concrete colour red, therefore, stands out against a background of generality, and this is why, even without transferring myself to another's point of view, I grasp myself in perception as *a* perceiving subject, and not as unclassifiable consciousness. I feel, all round my perception of red, all the regions of my being unaffected by it, and that region set aside for colours, "vision," through which the perception finds its way into me. Similarly my thought about the God of Spinoza is only apparently a strictly unique experience, for it is the concretion of a certain cultural world, the Spinozist philosophy, or of a certain philosophic style in which I immediately recognize a "Spinozist" idea. There is therefore no occasion to ask ourselves why the thinking subject or consciousness perceives itself as a man, or an incarnate or historical subject, nor must we treat this apperception as a second order operation which it somehow performs starting from its absolute existence: the absolute flow takes shape beneath its own gaze as "*a* consciousness," or a man, or an incarnate subject, because it is a field of presence —to itself, to others and to the world—and because this presence throws it into the natural and cultural world from which it arrives at an understanding of itself. We must not envisage this flux as absolute contact with oneself, as an absolute density with no internal fault, but on the contrary as a being which is in pursuit of itself outside. If the subject made a constant and at all times peculiar choice of himself, one might wonder why his experience always ties up with itself and presents him with objects and definite historical phases, why we have a general notion of time valid through all times, and why finally the experience of each one of us links up with that of others. But it is the question itself which must be questioned: for what is given, is not one fragment of time followed by another, one individual flux, then another; it is the taking up of each subjectivity by itself, and of subjectivities by each other in the generality of a single nature, the cohesion of an intersubjective life and a world. The present mediates between the For Oneself and the For Others, between individuality and generality. True reflection presents me to myself not as idle and inaccessible subjectivity, but as identical with my presence in the world and to others, as I am now realizing it: I am all that I see, I am an intersubjective field, not despite my body and historical situation, but, on the contrary, by being this body and this situation, and through them, all the rest.

What, then, becomes of the freedom we spoke about at the outset, if this point of view is taken? I can no longer pretend to be a cipher, and to choose myself continually from the starting point of nothing at all. If it is through subjectivity that nothingness appears in the world, it can equally be said that it is through the world that nothingness comes into being. I am a general refusal to be anything, accompanied surreptitiously by a continual acceptance of such and such a qualified form of being. *For even this general refusal is still one manner of being, and has its place in the world.* It is true that I can at any moment interrupt my projects. But what *is* this power? It is the power to begin something else, for we never remain suspended in nothingness. We are always in a plenum, in being, just as a face, even in repose, even in death, is always doomed to express something (there are people whose faces, in death, bear expressions of surprise, or peace, or discretion), and just as silence is still a modality of the world of sound. I may defy all accepted form, and spurn everything, for there is no case in which I am utterly committed: but in this case I do not withdraw into my freedom, I commit myself elsewhere. Instead of thinking about my bereavement, I look at my nails, or have lunch, or engage in politics. Far from its being the case that my freedom is

always unattended, it is never without an accomplice, and its power of perpetually tearing itself away finds its fulcrum in my universal commitment in the world. My actual freedom is not on the hither side of my being, but before me, in things. We must not say that I continually choose myself, on the excuse that I *might* continually refuse what I am. Not to refuse is not the same thing as to choose. We could identify drift and action only by depriving the implicit of all phenomenal value, and at every instant arraying the world before us in perfect transparency, that is, by destroying the world's "worldliness." Consciousness holds itself responsible for everything, and takes everything upon itself, but it has nothing of its own and makes its life in the world. We are led to conceive freedom as a choice continually remade as long as we do not bring in the notion of a generalized or natural time. We have seen that there is no natural time, if we understand thereby a time of things without subjectivity. There is, however, at least a generalized time, and this is what the common notion of time envisages. It is the perpetual reiteration of the sequence of past, present and future. It is, as it were, a constant disappointment and failure. This is what is expressed by saying that it is continuous: the present which it brings to us is never a present for good, since it is already over when it appears, and the future has, in it, only the appearance of a goal towards which we make our way, since it quickly comes into the present, whereupon we turn towards a fresh future. This time is the time of our bodily functions, which like it, are cyclic, and it is also that of nature with which we co-exist. It offers us only the adumbration and the abstract form of a commitment, since it continually erodes itself and undoes that which it has just done. As long as we place in opposition, with no mediator, the For Itself and the In Itself, and fail to perceive, between ourselves and the world, this natural foreshadowing of a subjectivity, this prepersonal time which rests upon itself, acts are needed to sustain the upsurge of time, and everything becomes equally a matter of choice, the respiratory reflex no less than the moral decision, conservation no less than creation. As far as we are concerned, consciousness attributes this power of universal constitution to itself only if it ignores the event which upholds it and is the occasion of its birth. A consciousness for which the world "can be taken for granted," which finds it "already constituted" and present even in consciousness itself, does not *absolutely* choose either its being or its manner of being.

What then is freedom? To be born is both to be born of the world and to be born into the world. The world is already constituted, but also never completely constituted; in the first case we are acted upon, in the second we are open to an infinite number of possibilities. But this analysis is still abstract, for we exist in both ways *at once*. There is, therefore, never determinism and never absolute choice, I am never a thing and never bare consciousness. In fact, even our own pieces of initiative, even the situations which we have chosen, bear us on, once they have been entered upon by virtue of a state rather than an act. The generality of the "rôle" and of the situation comes to the aid of decision, and in this exchange between the situation and the person who takes it up, it is impossible to determine precisely the "share contributed by the situation" and the "share contributed by freedom." Let us suppose that a man is tortured to make him talk. If he refuses to give the names and addresses which it is desired to extract from him, this does not arise from a solitary and unsupported decision: the man still feels himself to be with his comrades, and, being still involved in the common struggle, he is as it were incapable of talking. Or else, for months or years, he has, in his mind, faced this test and staked his whole life upon it. Or finally, he wants to prove, by coming through it, what he has always thought and said about freedom. These motives do not cancel out freedom, but at least ensure that it does not go unbuttressed in being. What withstands pain is not, in short, a bare consciousness, but the prisoner with his comrades or with those he loves and under whose gaze he lives; or else the awareness of his proudly willed solitude, which again is a certain mode of the *Mit-Sein*. And probably

the individual in his prison daily reawakens these phantoms, which give back to him the strength he gave to them. But conversely, in so far as he has committed himself to this action, formed a bond with his comrades or adopted this morality, it is because the historical situation, the comrades, the world around him seemed to him to expect that conduct from him. The analysis could be pursued endlessly in this way. We choose our world and the world chooses us. What is certain, in any case, is that we can at no time set aside within ourselves a redoubt to which being does not find its way through, without seeing this freedom, immediately and by the very fact of being a living experience, take on the appearance of being and become a motive and a buttress. Taken concretely, freedom is always a meeting of the inner and the outer—even the prehuman and prehistoric freedom with which we began—and it shrinks without ever disappearing altogether in direct proportion to the lessening of the *tolerance* allowed by the bodily and institutional data of our lives. There is, as Husserl says, on the one hand a "field of freedom" and on the other a "conditioned freedom"; [7] not that freedom is absolute within the limits of this field and non-existent outside it (like the perceptual field, this one has no traceable boundaries), but because I enjoy immediate and remote possibilities. Our commitments sustain our power and there is no freedom without some power. Our freedom, it is said, is either total or non-existent. This dilemma belongs to objective thought and its stable-companion, analytical reflection. If indeed we place ourselves within being, it must necessarily be the case that our actions must have their origin outside us, and if we revert to constituting consciousness, they must originate within. But we have learnt precisely to recognize the order of phenomena. We are involved in the world and with others in an inextricable tangle. The idea of situation rules out absolute freedom at the source of our commitments, and equally, indeed, at their terminus. No commitment, not even commitment

[7] Fink, *Vergegenwärtigung und Bild*, p. 285.

in the Hegelian State, can make me leave behind all differences and free me for anything. This universality itself, from the mere fact of its being experienced, would stand out as a particularity against the world's background, for existence both generalizes and particularizes everything at which it aims, and cannot ever be finally complete.

The synthesis of *in itself* and *for itself* which brings Hegelian freedom into being has, however, its truth. In a sense, it is the very definition of existence, since it is effected at every moment before our eyes in the phenomenon of presence, only to be quickly re-enacted, since it does not conjure away our finitude. By taking up a present, I draw together and transform my past, altering its significance, freeing and detaching myself from it. But I do so only by committing myself somewhere else. Psychoanalytical treatment does not bring about its cure by producing direct awareness of the past, but in the first place by binding the subject to his doctor through new existential relationships. It is not a matter of giving scientific assent to the psychoanalytical interpretation, and discovering a notional significance for the past; it is a matter of reliving this or that as significant, and this the patient succeeds in doing only by seeing his past in the perspective of his co-existence with the doctor. The complex is not dissolved by a non-instrumental freedom, but rather displaced by a new pulsation of time with its own supports and motives. The same applies in all cases of coming to awareness: they are real only if they are sustained by a new commitment. Now this commitment too is entered into in the sphere of the implicit, and is therefore valid only for a certain temporal cycle. The choice which we make of our life is always based on a certain givenness. My freedom can draw life away from its spontaneous course, but only by a series of unobtrusive deflections which necessitate first of all following its course—not by any absolute creation. All explanations of my conduct in terms of my past, my temperament and my environment are therefore true, provided that they be regarded not as separable contributions, but as moments of my total being, the significance

of which I am entitled to make explicit in various ways, without its ever being possible to say whether I confer their meaning upon them or receive it from them. I am a psychological and historical structure, and have received, with existence, a manner of existing, a style. All my actions and thoughts stand in a relationship to this structure, and even a philosopher's thought is merely a way of making explicit his hold on the world, and what he is. The fact remains that I am free, not in spite of, or on the hither side of, these motivations, but by means of them. For this significant life, this certain significance of nature and history which I am, does not limit my access to the world, but on the contrary is my means of entering into communication with it. It is by being unrestrictedly and unreservedly what I am at present that I have a chance of moving forward; it is by living my time that I am able to understand other times, by plunging into the present and the world, by taking on deliberately what I am fortuitously, by willing what I will and doing what I do, that I can go further. I can pass freedom by, only if I try to get over my natural and social situation by refusing, in the first place, to take it up, instead of using it as a way into the natural and human world. Nothing determines me from outside, not because nothing acts upon me, but, on the contrary, because I am from the start outside myself and open to the world. We are *true* through and through, and have with us, by the mere fact of belonging to the world, and not merely being in the world in the way that things are, all that we need to transcend ourselves. We need have no fear that our choices or actions restrict our liberty, since choice and action alone cut us loose from our anchorage. Just as reflection borrows its wish for absolute sufficiency from the perception which causes a thing to appear, and as in this way idealism tacitly uses that "primary opinion" which it would like to destroy as opinion, so freedom flounders in the contradictions of commitment, and fails to realize that, without the roots which it thrusts into the world, it would not be freedom at all. Shall I make this promise? Shall I risk my life for so little? Shall I give up my liberty in order to save liberty? There is no theoretical reply to these questions. But there are these *things* which stand, irrefutable, there is before you this person whom you love, there are these men whose existence around you is that of slaves, and *your* freedom cannot be willed without leaving behind its singular relevance, and without willing freedom *for all*. Whether it is a question of things or of historical situations, philosophy has no function other than to teach us once more to see them clearly, and it is true to say that it comes into being by destroying itself as separate philosophy. But what is here required is silence, for only the hero lives out his relation to men and the world. "Your son is caught in the fire; you are the one who will save him. . . . If there is an obstacle, you would be ready to give your shoulder provided only that you can charge down that obstacle. Your abode is your act itself. Your act is you. . . . You give yourself in exchange. . . . Your significance shows itself, effulgent. It is your duty, your hatred, your love, your steadfastness, your ingenuity. . . . Man is but a network of relationships, and these alone matter to him." [8]

[8] A. de Saint-Exupéry, *Pilote de Guerre,* pp. 171 and 174.

God, Faith,

and Religious Thought

PART II

If God exists, what difference does his existence make to man? Is man in a position to know whether or not God exists? Why should God's existence pose a problem for man's thought? What would it mean to "know" God? What sorts of argument might be offered for his existence? Is belief in God, together with the practices associated with such belief, equivalent to being "religious"? What does it mean to live in a religious culture, and how would human values appear within such a culture? What relation ought one's religious belief bear to his personal conduct? Is God a value among other values, is he the highest value, or does he have some special relation to value?

In this part we are concerned with problems of belief in the God of theistic religions and with the bearing which such belief might have on one's attitude toward issues of value. The God of theistic religions is a personal God, who is a being apart from the universe and who yet has some kind of intercommunication with man. Not all religions are theistic. A pantheistic religion, for example, would not accept a God who is a being apart from the universe. Such a religion would recognize the universe itself as divine.

We saw in the previous parts something of the variety of questions which could be raised in connection with our knowledge, whether it be of the sensible world, of ourselves, or of value. The questions which arise in the readings of this part seem to be of a special kind because they are centered about the idea of a being utterly unlike any of the actual things or even the persons of our experience. With the exception of Hume and Dewey, the writers in this part are men who hold a belief in the God of theism and have wanted to clarify and defend that belief.

One of the oldest problems in the sphere of religious thought has to do with the effect of God's omniscience on man's capacity to originate his actions. If God knows everything, then he must know in advance how human beings will act, down to the least detail. Doesn't this foreknowledge impose constraint on man's action? If the answer to this question is yes, what becomes of human freedom and of man's accountability for his actions? Theistic thinkers, such as Augustine, have usually wanted to defend both theses: that God is all-knowing and knows in advance what man will do; and that man, nevertheless, has free will. How to show that the two theses are logically compatible is one of the problems which Augustine sets himself.

Augustine's solution of this problem is to view the human will as a power which God has given us. When we act voluntarily, we exercise our power to will, and God foreknows just how we shall exercise that power. But his foreknowledge in no way deprives us of the power to will. Since we always possess the power of willing, our will is free rather than necessitated. When we sin, even though God has prior knowl-ledge that we shall sin, he does not compel us to do so and may justly punish us.

Augustine is concerned also with another theological question. If God is the creator of all things, including men who sin, are not the sins of men imputable to him? But if they are, then how can God be said to be all good? Here Augustine argues that in creating men free, free even to sin, God is expressing his goodness. Men are creatures essentially of soul, and soul is superior to material things and always constitutes an intrinsic dignity in man. (The view of soul as superior to body or matter Augustine takes from Plato.) That men are souls which are free to sin does not mean that God is responsible for sin; it is only because God is thoroughly good that men have been created with free will. God's goodness also expresses itself in giving the sinner grace by which he is enabled to turn back to God.

The reader ought to compare the approach to the problem of free will taken in the context of religious belief by Augustine with the approaches taken by the secular writers of the first part. Does the issue of free will versus determinism raised in the previous part shift its meaning when introduced within a religious context? Do the facts of human experience referred to by the nonreligious thinkers in the course of their arguments bear upon Augustine's problem? Or, to put the question in a more general way, does the fact that one of the terms in our argument is God affect the relevant considerations and the conclusions that our thinking can reach?

This question leads to our next selection, the "ontological" argument of Anselm. This is one of the most celebrated and oft-discussed bits of reasoning in the whole history of religious thought and one of the most interesting for students of philosophy, even though it was offered by Anselm to support a belief in God already held rather than to convince the nonbeliever. Ontology is commonly defined as the science of being. The argument is called ontological because it turns on the recognition of the kind of being which God is said to be. If we say of God that he is a perfect being, and if we recognize that nonexistence would be an imperfection, then we must conclude that God exists. God, who is the highest of all possible beings, that is, a perfect being, cannot lack existence, for then he would fall short of perfection.

One noticeable feature of this argument is that it makes no appeal to experience. It consists solely of drawing conclusions said to be implicit in the meanings of the word "God." It is not surprising that Descartes, with his rationalist theory of knowledge, developed his version of the ontological argument, which derives from the Platonist, Augustine. One of the chief attacks on the validity of the argument was made by Immanuel Kant, a thinker concerned with the limits of reason. Kant urged that all Anselm proves is that in thinking of God I cannot help *thinking* of him as existent and that this in no way establishes his real existence.

A feature of Anselm's argument of particular interest for an inquiry into value is simply the idea of a perfect being. One might ask in what way such a perfect being might play a part in the value experiences of his imperfect creatures. Does God in some way bestow value on man's existence? Does he require man to attain certain values which he also reveals to man? If so, do all of man's values depend on God? If just some of them depend upon him, then which ones? Can man fully fathom his relationship to God in respect to knowledge of value, or must this relationship remain obscure?

Our selection from Thomas Aquinas concentrates on distinguishing the range of things our reason can know unaided by divine revelation from the things that are revealed by God and grasped through faith. As Thomas sees it, man can arrive at truths about God by his own powers of reflection. Thomas bases his entire system on the thought of the ancient Greek philosopher, Aristotle, and endeavors to show that the truths of reason are compatible with, but need to be supplemented by, the truths of faith. Thomas offers a series of proofs of God's existence which are based on our knowledge of the universe and are thus quite distinct from Anselm's proof. Thomas, in fact, rejects Anselm's ontological argument.

It is interesting to consider whether it is by faith or by reason that we discover the relationship between reason and faith. Can reason demonstrate that revealed religion is needed to supplement reason, or is this an item of faith which Thomas considers "reasonable"?

To speak of the relationship between faith and reason is also to speak of the relationship between God and man and of the manner in which man obtains the idea of God. Thought about God has had a historical connection with philosophic thought generally, and it is with the philosophic background of two main currents of Christian thought that our selection from Etienne Gilson is concerned. One is that followed by Augustine, deriving from Plato, the other followed by Thomas Aquinas, deriving from Aristotle. Gilson shows how the idea of man's knowledge of God is intimately connected with the idea of man. He points out that Augustine accepted Plato's view of man as essentially soul, a timeless essence which can obtain knowledge of what is real, or truth. Plato believes that soul possesses truth because it is itself of the same nature as truth, which is a Form or essence, and that nature is divine. But, as a Christian thinker, Augustine cannot regard man as divine. He says that man possesses divine truth only because God causes him to possess it; it does not belong to him essentially. What man knows of God is revealed to him by God, who influences man's reason to perceive the truth.

Thomas Aquinas, on the other hand, following Aristotle, views man as an individual substance which is a unity of soul and body. To know, or to possess truth, is to understand what substances are and what it is "to be." Thomas stresses man's concrete existence and focuses on the act of existing common to all creatures. Perceiving this act of existing in all substances, he is led, by human reason alone, to grasp God as a pure act of existing. Unlike Augustine, he is able to say that man can reach truth about God by his unaided philosophical reflection, because he does not start out regarding truth as something divine or above man.

This selection helps to point up the importance of the question of God's existence, a question which has held an exceedingly significant position in religious thought. If the very essence of God is to exist, then religious thought must be ocupied with the manner in which man can know God's existence, can deal with it conceptually, and is affected by it in his own existence.

This concern with God's existence is reflected in the proofs of his existence. David Hume examines one of the arguments for his existence, based upon our knowledge of nature—an argument which, from the presence of an orderly design in the universe, argues to the existence of God as the author of that design. Hume tries to expose the logical difficulties which stand in the way of employing such an argument. Is the presence of a being called God the only explanation which will account for what appear to be orderly relationships among events and objects in the universe? This question also involves asking in what sense the universe as a whole can be said to be a "design." Can the universe be properly called a design, and, if so, does this design imply a designer somewhat as a house or a watch implies an architect or watchmaker?

Hume's examination of this argument is significant not only for its treatment of the particular issue but also because it is an example of an unusually keen philosophical discussion and, furthermore, because it has a bearing on the question of the relation between faith and reason. The force of the discussion may depend not only on its convincingness as a piece of argumentation but also on one's attitude toward the employment of reason and human experience in connection with objects of faith. One who already accepts God founds his acceptance usually on a whole complex of factors, of which reason is only one. It is legitimate to ask what role logical reason and experience should be given in the religious outlook.

Is there a sense in which one can be "religious" and yet make no claim that a supreme being beyond the world of experience exists? In our selection John Dewey examines the "religious" as an attitude which may be present in all our experience, not just in those experiences associated with organized religion. He contrasts this attitude with the institutions and doctrines which constitute the "religions." While Dewey takes a standpoint outside of any one of the traditional religions and attacks the "supernatural," he tries to preserve and clarify a feature of experience, the recognition and intelligent pursuit of ideal goals. The "religious," in Dewey's conception, becomes a value that can be realized in a great variety of situations. What is at issue here is the reference of sentences employing the adjective "religious." Should this word be used to refer to a quality present in a wide range of seemingly unrelated experiences involving no appeal to a being beyond the world, or should its reference be limited to a special set of actions and experiences centering about the alleged reality of a divine being? One should consider whether Dewey is primarily describing how a great many people actually use the adjective "religious," or whether he is primarily proposing a new way of using it. If the former, then we should ask what evidence he might have that people do use the word this way; if the latter, then we should want to know what the advantages are of using the word in the way he proposes.

The discussion by Dewey raises the question of how religion is related to other aspects of culture. While religions have shown a genius for preserving traditional practice and doctrine, they have also tried to meet the demands of a changing climate of thought. The contemporary Protestant theologian Paul Tillich faces the secular culture of the contemporary world with the interests of a theistic world view. Tillich tries to specify the conditions for a culture in which religious life, directed toward a theistic God, emerges from the same source as, and is firmly joined with, so-called secular life. The growing lack of rapport between those who are God-centered and those who are man-centered has been widely noticed and poses one of the chief difficulties for thinkers who want to achieve a rapprochement between theistic and humanistic values. Tillich tries to provide a base for common thought by speaking of religion as man's "ultimate concern." Even the atheist has "ultimate concern," since he bothers to deny the existence of God. Some questions to consider in connection with Tillich's essay are these: What conditions must a religious symbol meet? Are these conditions such that the significance of the symbol can be grasped only by one who already believes? Can the interests of secular culture always be made compatible with those of religious life? If not, how do we determine priorities?

Reinhold Niebuhr's discussion of the ethic of Jesus is especially relevant at this point, since it makes extremely vivid the discrepancy that can be discovered between the religious life and the requirements of a stable, mutually responsible community. Theologians such as Niebuhr, who regard Christian religion as relevant to social problems, have had to struggle to hold in active relationship the "hard sayings" of Jesus, which seem "antisocial," and the requirements of prudence in practical social life. More broadly, some religious thinkers make the claim that reason is essentially opposed to faith, that revealed religion in its highest reaches involves commands which reason must reject. Some thinkers find at times an unbridgeable gap between the principles and policies which the best efforts of man's reason can produce and the absolute demands of the God of faith. Should the thinker who regards man's thought and God's word as sometimes irreconcilable be prepared to put reason aside when he judges this step to be necessary? Should he recognize a legitimate sphere of interest called the "social order"? Should he see its values as ultimate, or should he be prepared for faith to dictate a total renunciation of these values? If he renounces the social order, then God is for him not only the revealer of the highest values, "the Giver of every good and perfect gift," but himself a value so high as to invalidate all mundane values and all products of man's reason. Does Niebuhr adequately meet the difficulty of employing the ethic of Jesus as a standard for judging life in the social order?

The selection by Niebuhr also raises the question of how to interpret the writings and other symbols of religious expression. In addition, it suggests the presence of an approach to human values altogether different from the religious—that of independent philosophic reflection. It thus points us toward our next part, on ethical thought.

God's foreknowledge

and man's free will

St. Augustine (354-430)

Aurelius Augustinus, who became Bishop of Hippo in North Africa, was first trained in Roman thought. Led by his reading of Cicero to pursue philosophical and theological studies, he came to accept the teachings of the Persian religion of Manichaeism, which he later rejected under the influence of the Neoplatonists. After a period of skepticism, and counseled by St. Ambrose, Bishop of Milan, Augustine underwent a dramatic conversion to Christianity. Afterward he wrote extensively on Christian doctrine and exerted an influence greater than that of any early medieval thinker. He wrote numerous polemical works against the enemies of the Church, and his Confessions, *in which he gives an account of his early life and conversion, is one of the most famous of all autobiographies. Among his other most important works are* On the Trinity, The City of God, *and* On Free Will, *from which our selection is taken.*

Here Augustine presents and solves the problem arising from the apparent conflict between God's foreknowledge and man's free will. The discussion is carried on in the form of a dialogue between two persons, Evodius and Augustine. It is an example of a theological problem examined through careful development of an argument.

Ev.—... I have a deep desire to know how it can be that God knows all things beforehand and that, nevertheless, we do not sin by necessity. Whoever says that anything can happen otherwise than as God has foreknown it, is attempting to destroy the divine foreknowledge with the most insensate impiety. If God foreknew that the first man would sin—and that anyone must concede who acknowledges with me that God has foreknowledge of all

Reprinted from *Augustine, Earlier Writings,* tr. J. H. S. Burleigh, published 1953, The Westminster Press and Student Christian Movement Press, Ltd. Used by permission.

future events—I do not say that God did not make him, for he made him good, nor that the sin of the creature whom he made good could be prejudicial to God. On the contrary, God showed his goodness in making man, his justice in punishing his sin, and his mercy in delivering him. I do not say, therefore, that God did not make man. But this I say. Since God foreknew that man would sin, that which God foreknew must necessarily come to pass. How then is the will free when there is apparently this unavoidable necessity?

Aug.—You have knocked vigorously. May God in his mercy grant us his presence and open the door to those who knock. But I verily believe that the vast majority of men are troubled by that question for no other reason than that they do not ask it in a pious fashion. They are swifter to make excuses for their sins than to make confession of them. Some are glad to hold the opinion that there is no divine providence presiding over human affairs. They commit themselves, body and soul, to fortuitous circumstances, and deliver themselves to be carried about and tormented by lusts. They deny that there is any divine judgment, and deceive human judges when they are accused. They imagine that they are driven on by the favour of fortune. In sculpture or painting they are wont to represent Fortune as blind, either because they are better than the goddess by whom they think they are ruled, or because they confess that in their sentiments they are afflicted with that same blindness. In the case of such people it is not absurd to admit that they do everything by chance, seeing that they stumble in all that they do. But against this opinion, so full of foolish and senseless error, we have, I think, sufficiently spoken in our second disputation. Others do not venture to deny that the providence of God presides over human affairs, but they would rather indulge in the wicked error of believing that providence is weak or unjust or evil than confess their sins with suppliant piety. If all these would suffer themselves to be persuaded to believe that the goodness, justice and power of God are greater far, and far superior to any thought they can have of goodness, justice or might, if they would but take thought to themselves, they would know that they owe thanks to God, even if he had willed them to be somewhat lower in the scale of being than they actually are, and with all that is within them they would exclaim with the Psalmist: "I have spoken: Lord have mercy upon me; heal my soul for I have sinned against thee" (Ps. 41:5). So by stages the divine mercy would bring them to wisdom. They would be neither inflated by what they discover, nor rebellious when they fail to find the truth; by learning they would become better prepared to see the truth, and by recognizing their ignorance they would become more patient in seeking it. I am quite sure that these are your views too. Now first answer a few questions I am going to put to you, and you will see how easily I can find a solution to your tremendous problem.

Your trouble is this. You wonder how it can be that these two propositions are not contradictory and incompatible, namely that God has foreknowledge of all future events, and that we sin voluntarily and not by necessity. For if, you say, God foreknows that a man will sin, he must necessarily sin. But if there is necessity there is no voluntary choice in sinning, but rather fixed and unavoidable necessity. You are afraid that by that reasoning the conclusion may be reached either that God's foreknowledge of all future events must be impiously denied, or, if that cannot be denied, that sin is committed not voluntarily but by necessity. Isn't that your difficulty? *Ev.*—Exactly that. *Aug.*—You think, therefore, that all things of which God has foreknowledge happen by necessity and not voluntarily. *Ev.*—Yes. Absolutely. *Aug.*—Try an experiment, and examine yourself a little, and tell me what kind of will you are going to have tomorrow. Will you want to sin or to do right? *Ev.*—I do not know. *Aug.*—Do you think God also does not know? *Ev.*—I could in no wise think that. *Aug.*—If God knows what you are going to will tomorrow, and foresees what all men are going to will in the future, not only those who are at present alive but all who will ever be, much more will he foresee what he is going to do with the just and the impious? *Ev.*—Certainly if I say that God has foreknowledge of my deeds, I should say with even greater confidence that he has foreknowledge of his own acts, and foresees with complete certainty what he is going to do. *Aug.*—Don't you see that you will have to be careful lest someone say to you that, if all things of which God has foreknowledge are done by necessity and not voluntarily, his own future acts will be done not voluntarily but by necessity? *Ev.*—When I said that all future events of which God has foreknowledge happen by necessity, I was having regard only to things which happen within his creation, and not to things which happen in God himself. Indeed, in God nothing happens. Everything is eternal. *Aug.*—God, then, is not active within his creation? *Ev.*—He determined once for all how the order of the universe he created was to go on, and he never changes his mind. *Aug.*—Does he never make anyone happy? *Ev.*—Indeed he does. *Aug.*—He does it precisely at the time when the man in question actually becomes happy. *Ev.*—That is so. *Aug.*—If, then, for example, you yourself are happy one year from now, you will be made happy at that time. *Ev.*—Exactly. *Aug.*—God knows today what he is going to do a year hence? *Ev.*—He eternally had that foreknowledge, but I agree that he has it now, if indeed it is to happen so.

Aug.—Now tell me, are you not God's creature? And will not your becoming happy take place within your experience? *Ev.*—Certainly I am God's creature, and if I become happy it will be within my experience. *Aug.*—If God, then, makes you happy, your happiness will come by necessity and not by the exercise of your will? *Ev.*—God's will is my necessity. *Aug.*—Will you then be happy against your will? *Ev.*—If I had the power to be happy, I should be so at once. For I wish to be happy but am not, because not I but God makes me happy. *Aug.*—The truth simply cries out against you. You could not imagine that "having in our power" means anything else than "being able to do what we will." Therefore there is nothing so much in our power as is the will itself. For as soon as we will [*volumus*] immediately will [*voluntas*] is there. We can say rightly that we do not grow old voluntarily but necessarily, or that we do not die voluntarily but from necessity, and so with other similar things. But who but a raving fool would say that it is not voluntarily that we will? Therefore though God knows how we are going to will in the future, it is not proved that we do not voluntarily will anything. When you said that you did not make yourself happy, you said it as if I had denied it. What I say is that when you become happy in the future it will take place not against your will but in accordance with your willing. Therefore, though God has foreknowledge of your happiness in the future, and though nothing can happen other-

wise than as he has foreknown it (for that would mean that there is no foreknowledge) we are not thereby compelled to think that you will not be happy voluntarily. That would be absurd and far from true. God's foreknowledge, which is even to-day quite certain that you are to be happy at a future date, does not rob you of your will to happiness when you actually attain happiness. Similarly if ever in the future you have a culpable will, it will be none the less your will because God had foreknowledge of it.

Observe, pray, how blind are those who say that if God has foreknowledge of what I am going to will, since nothing can happen otherwise than as he has foreknown it, therefore I must necessarily will what he has foreknown. If so, it must be admitted that I will, not voluntarily but from necessity. Strange folly! Is there, then, no difference between things that happen according to God's foreknowledge where there is no intervention of man's will at all, and things that happen because of a will of which he has foreknowledge? I omit the equally monstrous assertion of the man I mentioned a moment ago, who says I must necessarily so will. By assuming necessity he strives to do away with will altogether. If I must necessarily will, why need I speak of willing at all? But if he puts it in another way, and says that, because he must necessarily so will, his will is not in his own power, he can be countered by the answer you gave me when I asked whether you could become happy against your will. You replied that you would be happy now if the matter were in your power, for you willed to be happy but could not achieve it. And I added that the truth cries out against you; for we cannot say we do not have the power unless we do not have what we will. If we do not have the will, we may think we will but in fact we do not. If we cannot will without willing, those who will have will, and all that is in our power we have by willing. Our will would not be will unless it were in our power. Because it is in our power, it is free. We have nothing that is free which is not in our power, and if we have something it cannot be nothing. Hence it is not necessary to deny that God has foreknowledge of all things, while at the same time our wills are our own. God has foreknowledge of our will, so that of which he has foreknowledge must come to pass. In other words, we shall exercise our wills in the future because he has foreknowledge that we shall do so; and there can be no will or voluntary action unless it be in our power. Hence God has also foreknowledge of our power to will. My power is not taken from me by God's foreknowledge. Indeed I shall be more certainly in possession of my power because he whose foreknowledge is never mistaken, foreknows that I shall have the power. Ev.—Now I no longer deny that whatever God has foreknown must necessarily come to pass, nor that he has foreknowledge of our sins, but in such a way that our wills remain free and within our power.

Aug.—What further difficulty do you have? Perhaps you have forgotten what we established in our first disputation, and now wish to deny that we sin voluntarily and under no compulsion from anything superior, inferior or equal to us. Ev.—I do not venture to deny that at all. But I must confess I do not yet see how God's foreknowledge of our sins and our freedom of will in sinning can be other than mutually contradictory. We must confess that God is just and knows all things beforehand. But I should like to know with what justice he punishes sins which must necessarily be committed; or how they are not necessarily committed when he knows that they will be committed; or how the Creator is to escape having imputed to him anything that happens necessarily in his creature.

Aug.—Why do you think our free will is opposed to God's foreknowledge? Is it because it is foreknowledge simply, or because it is God's foreknowledge? Ev.—In the main because it is God's foreknowledge. Aug.—If you knew in advance that such and such a man would sin, there would be no necessity for him to sin. Ev.—Indeed there would, for I should have no real foreknowledge unless I knew for certain what was going to happen. Aug.—So it is foreknowledge generally and not God's foreknowledge specially that causes the events

foreknown to happen by necessity? There would be no such thing as foreknowledge unless there was certain foreknowledge. Ev.—I agree. But why these questions? Aug.—Unless I am mistaken, you would not directly compel the man to sin, though you knew beforehand that he was going to sin. Nor does your prescience in itself compel him to sin even though he was certainly going to sin, as we must assume if you have real prescience. So there is no contradiction here. Simply you know beforehand what another is going to do with his own will. Similarly God compels no man to sin, though he sees beforehand those who are going to sin by their own will.

Why then should he not justly punish sins which, though he had foreknowledge of them, he did not compel the sinner to commit? Just as you apply no compulsion to past events by having them in your memory, so God by his foreknowledge does not use compulsion in the case of future events. Just as you remember your past actions, though all that you remember were not actions of your own, so God has foreknowledge of all his own actions, but is not the agent of all that he foreknows. Of evil actions he is not the agent but the just punisher. From this you may understand with what justice God punishes sins, for he has no responsibility for the future actions of men though he knows them beforehand. If he ought not to award punishment to sinners because he knew beforehand that they would sin, he ought not to reward the righteous, because he knew equally that they would be righteous. Let us confess that it belongs to his foreknowledge to allow no future event to escape his knowledge, and that it belongs to his justice to see that no sin goes unpunished by his judgment. For sin is committed voluntarily and not by any compulsion from his foreknowledge.

As to your third question how the Creator is to escape having imputed to him anything that happens necessarily in his creature, it is fitting for us to remember the rule of piety which says that we owe thanks to our Creator. That will provide us with the answer. His lavish goodness should be most justly praised even if he had made us with some lower rank in his creation. Though our soul be soiled with sins it is nevertheless loftier and better than if it were changed into visible light. And yet light is an eminent part of creation, as you can see by considering how much God is praised for it, even by souls wholly given over to bodily sense. Wherefore, though sinful souls are censured, do not let that provoke you to say in your heart that it would have been better if they did not exist. They are censured because they are compared with what they might have been if they had not willed to sin. God, their Maker, is to be gloriously praised for the human faculties with which he has endowed them, not only because he justly subjects them to his order when they sin, but also because he made them such that, even when soiled with sin, they are not surpassed in dignity by corporeal light, for which also God is rightly praised.

Possibly you would not go so far as to say that it would have been better if sinful souls did not exist, but take care also not to say that they should have been other than they are. Whatever better argument true reason may suggest to you, know at least that God made them, and that he is author of all good things. For it is not true reason but envious weakness that bids you think that anything ought to have been made better than it is, and that nothing inferior should have been made at all. That is as if you looked at the heavens and concluded that the earth ought not to have been made. That is all wrong. You would be quite right to find fault if you saw that the earth had been made, and no heavens, for then you might say the earth ought to have been made according to your ideal conception of the heavens. But now you see that your ideal earth has been made, only it is called not earth but heaven. I believe that since you have not been defrauded of the better creation you ought not to grudge that there is an inferior creation which we call the earth. In the earth again there is such a variety among its parts that you can think of nothing of an earthly nature which God has not made somewhere in the totality of his work. For the earth contains land of all kinds, passing by gradual stages from the most

fruitful and pleasant to the most deceitful and infertile tracts, so that you can only find fault with one kind of land by comparing it with a better kind. So you ascend through all the grades of land with their varying praiseworthy qualities, and when you find the very best land you are glad that there are the other kinds as well. And yet what a difference there is between earth, in all its variety, and heaven! Water and air are interposed. Of these four elements various other forms and species of things are made, innumerable to us but all numbered by God. There may be things in the natural realm which you would never have thought of yourself, but the wholly and purely rational cannot but be. You can think of nothing better in the creation which the Creator did not think of. When the human soul says: "This is better than that," and if it says so truly, it will say so because of its relation to the divine reasons on which it depends. If it understands what it says, it does so likewise because of its relation to these reasons. Let it therefore believe that God has made what true reason knows he must have made, even if it is not evident in created things. If the heavens were invisible, but true reason led to the conclusion that such a thing must have been created, we ought to believe that it has been created though it do not appear to the eye. For thought would have no idea that it ought to have been created if it did not have some relation to the reasons through which all things were created. What does not exist can no more be thought than have true existence.

Many err because, beholding the better things with their minds, they look for them also with their eyes in the wrong places. That would be as if someone, who by reason understood perfect rotundity, should be annoyed that he did not observe it in a nut, assuming that he never saw any other round object besides that fruit. So when some people see with true reason that there are better creatures who, though they have free will, have ever adhered to God and have never sinned, they look at the sins of men and lament not that they may cease from sin but simply that men have been created at all. They say: "He did not create us such that we should will ever to enjoy his unchangeable truth and never to sin." Do not let them cry out or be annoyed. He did not compel them to sin by the mere fact that he created them and gave them power to choose good or evil as they would. He made them so far like those angels who never sinned and never will sin. If you delight in a creature which by voluntary perseverance never sins, there is no doubt you rightly prefer it to a sinful creature. Just as you give it the preference in your thought, so God gives it the preference in his universal order. You may believe that there are such creatures in the loftier regions of the heavens. For if God showed his goodness in creating creatures whom he knew beforehand would sin, he would show his goodness no less in creating creatures whom he knew beforehand would never sin.

Those sublime creatures have their happiness perpetually in the eternal enjoyment of their Creator; and their happiness they merit by their perpetual will to hold fast to righteousness. Below them sinful creatures have their proper order. By their sins they have lost happiness, but they have not lost the capacity to recover it. Herein they are superior to those creatures whose will is to remain perpetually in sin. Between these two extremes—those who continue in the will to righteousness and those who continue in the will to sin—there is this middle class who by the humility of repentance recover their exalted rank. But God did not withhold the lavishness of his bounty even from his creatures who he knew beforehand would not only sin but would continue in the will to sin; for he showed it in creating them. An errant horse is better than a stone that cannot err because it has neither motion nor feeling of its own. So a creature which sins by its own free will is more excellent than one which cannot sin because it has no free will. I would praise wine that was good of its kind, and would censure the man who drank it to excess. And yet I would hold the man whom I had censured, even while he was drunk, to be superior to the wine which made him drunk, even though I had praised it. So the corporeal creature is rightly to be praised in its own

order, though those are to be censured who use it to excess and are thereby turned away from perception of the truth. And those perverse people, drunkards or the like, are to be preferred to the thing, laudable in its own order, greediness for which made them vain; not indeed because of their vices but because of the dignity of their nature which still remains.

Soul is universally superior to body. No soul can fall so far in sinfulness as to be changed into body. Its quality as soul cannot be taken from it, and it cannot in any way lose that which makes it superior to body. Now among corporeal objects light holds the first place. Consequently the worst soul is superior to the first of corporeal things. It is of course possible that some body may be preferable to the body in which a soul resides, but it cannot be preferred to the soul itself. Why, then, should not God be praised with all possible praise, who made souls that were to abide in the laws of righteousness, even if he also made other souls which he knew beforehand would sin or even persevere in sin? For even these are better than things that cannot sin because they have not reason or free choice of will. They are even better than the most splendid brilliance of bodies of any kind, though some people [the Manichees], greatly erring, venerate light as if it were the substance of God most high. In the order of corporeal creatures, from the sidereal choir down to the number of our hairs, the beauty of good things is so perfectly graded that it is a sign of lack of understanding to ask: "What is this?" or "To what purpose is that?" All things are created each in its own order. How much more does it show lack of understanding to ask such questions about any soul whatever? No matter how great a diminution of its glory it may suffer or what defects it may exhibit, nevertheless it will always and without any doubt surpass in dignity every kind of body.

Reason has a different standard of judgment from that of utility. Reason judges by the light of truth, and correctly subordinates lesser things to those that are greater. Utility, guided by experience of convenience, often attributes a higher value to things which reason convinces us are of lesser rank. Reason sets a vast difference in value between celestial and terrestrial bodies, but what carnal man would not prefer that several stars should be wanting in the heavens, than that one shrub should be lacking in his field or one cow from his herd? Older men pay no attention to, or at least are prepared patiently to correct, the judgments of children, who prefer the death of a man (except one of those bound to them by the ties of happy affection), to the death of a favourite sparrow, especially if the man was an object of terror to them, and the sparrow was tuneful and beautiful. So, if there are people, unskilled in judging the values of things, who praise God for his lesser creatures, finding them more easily appreciated by their carnal senses, and do not praise him for his better and superior creatures, or praise him less than they ought, or try to find fault with his creatures and to point out how they might have been better, or even do not believe that he created them, those who have advanced some way towards wisdom either entirely scorn such judgments or hear them with good-natured patience if they cannot correct them or until they are corrected.

Such being the case, it is far from the truth that the sins of the creature must be attributed to the Creator, even though those things must necessarily happen which he has foreknown. So much so that when you say you can find no reason why whatever necessarily happens in the creature should not be attributed to him, I on the contrary find no way, and I assert that none exists or can be found, of attributing to him what is done, necessarily no doubt, but also by the will of the sinner. If anyone says, I should prefer not to exist than to exist in unhappiness, I shall reply: That is a lie; for you are miserable now, and yet you do not wish to die, simply because you wish to exist. You don't want to be miserable but you want to continue in life all the same. Give thanks, therefore, because you exist, as you wish to do, so that the misery you do not wish may be taken from you. You exist as you wish to do, but you are unhappy against your will. If you are ungrateful for your existence you are rightly compelled to be unhappy, which you do not wish. I praise the goodness of the Creator because, even when you are ungrateful, you have what you wish. And I praise the justice of the Orderer of things because for your ingratitude you suffer what you do not wish.

The ontological argument

St. Anselm (1033-1109)

St. Anselm, who spent the last six years of his life in England as Archbishop of Canterbury, was a member of the Benedictine Order and became Abbot of the Monastery of Bec in Normandy, a major center of learning in the Europe of his time. His thinking, in which theological and philosophical problems are interwoven, belongs to the tradition of St. Augustine, to whom he is indebted for the form of his well-known ontological argument for the existence of God. The following selection from his Proslogium *contains the statement of that proof.*

The proof is called "ontological" because it is based upon the nature or being of God. ("Ontology" is commonly defined as the science of being.) The argument turns on our saying that God is a perfect being and on our recognizing that not to exist is an imperfection. Hence the being who is the highest of all possible beings, that is, perfect, must exist.

Anselm's ontological argument has been often contested and is the subject of much controversy even in our own day. St. Thomas Aquinas and Immanuel Kant, among other philosophers, rejected it. The reader should recognize that the argument is offered by one who already holds a theistic belief.

. . . I do not endeavor, O Lord, to penetrate thy sublimity, for in no wise do I compare my understanding with that; but I long to understand in some degree thy truth, which my heart believes and loves. For I do not seek to understand that I may believe, but I believe in order to understand. For this also I believe,—that unless I believed, I should not understand.

And so, Lord, do thou, who dost give understanding to faith, give me, so far as thou knowest it to be profitable, to understand that thou art as we believe; and that thou art that which we believe. And, indeed, we believe that thou art a being than which nothing greater can be conceived. Or is there no such nature, since the fool hath said in his heart, there is no God?

From St. Anselm, *Proslogium* in *St. Anselm: Basic Writings,* tr. S. N. Deane. Second edition, copyright 1961 by The Open Court Publishing Company, La Salle, Illinois. Used by permission.

(Psalms xiv. 1). But, at any rate, this very fool, when he hears of this being of which I speak—a being than which nothing greater can be conceived—understands what he hears, and what he understands is in his understanding; although he does not understand it to exist.

For, it is one thing for an object to be in the understanding, and another to understand that the object exists. When a painter first conceives of what he will afterwards perform, he has it in his understanding, but he does not yet understand it to be, because he has not yet performed it. But after he has made the painting, he both has it in his understanding, and he understands that it exists, because he has made it.

Hence, even the fool is convinced that something exists in the understanding, at least, than which nothing greater can be conceived. For, when he hears of this, he understands it. And whatever is understood, exists in the understanding. And assuredly that, than which nothing greater can be conceived, cannot exist in the understanding alone. For, suppose it exists in the understanding alone: then it can be conceived to exist in reality; which is greater.

Therefore, if that, than which nothing greater can be conceived, exists in the understanding alone, the very being, than which nothing greater can be conceived, is one, than which a greater can be conceived. But obviously this is impossible. Hence, there is no doubt that there exists a being, than which nothing greater can be conceived, and it exists both in the understanding and in reality.

And it assuredly exists so truly, that it cannot be conceived not to exist. For, it is possible to conceive of a being which cannot be conceived not to exist; and this is greater than one which can be conceived not to exist. Hence, if that, than which nothing greater can be conceived, can be conceived not to exist, it is not that, than which nothing greater can be conceived. But this is an irreconcilable contradiction. There is, then, so truly a being than which nothing greater can be conceived to exist, that it cannot even be conceived not to exist; and this being thou art, O Lord, our God.

So truly, therefore, dost thou exist, O Lord, my God, that thou canst not be conceived not to exist; and rightly. For, if a mind could conceive of a being better than thee, the creature would rise above the Creator; and this is most absurd. And, indeed, whatever else there is, except thee alone, can be conceived not to exist. To thee alone, therefore, it belongs to exist more truly than all other beings, and hence in a higher degree than all others. For, whatever else exists does not exist so truly, and hence in a less degree it belongs to it to exist. Why, then, has the fool said in his heart, there is no God (Psalms xiv. 1), since it is so evident, to a rational mind, that thou dost exist in the highest degree of all? Why, except that he is dull and a fool?

But how has the fool said in his heart what he could not conceive; or how is it that he could not conceive what he said in his heart? since it is the same to say in the heart, and to conceive.

But, if really, nay, since really, he both conceived, because he said in his heart; and did not say in his heart, because he could not conceive; there is more than one way in which a thing is said in the heart or conceived. For, in one sense, an object is conceived, when the word signifying it is conceived; and in another, when the very entity, which the object is, is understood.

In the former sense, then, God can be conceived not to exist; but in the latter, not at all. For no one who understands what fire and water are can conceive fire to be water, in accordance with the nature of the facts themselves, although this is possible according to the words. So, then, no one who understands what God is can conceive that God does not exist; although he says these words in his heart, either without any, or with some foreign, signification. For, God is that than which a greater cannot be conceived. And he who thoroughly understands this, assuredly understands that this being so truly exists, that not even in concept can it be non-existent. Therefore, he who understands that God so exists, cannot conceive that he does not exist.

I thank thee, gracious Lord, I thank thee; because what I formerly believed by thy bounty, I now so understand by thine illumination, that if I were unwilling to believe that thou dost exist, I should not be able not to understand this to be true.

What art thou, then, Lord God, than whom nothing greater can be conceived? But what art thou, except that which, as the highest of all beings, alone exists through itself, and creates all other things from nothing? For, whatever is not this is less than a thing which can be conceived of. But this cannot be conceived of thee. What good, therefore, does the supreme Good lack, through which every good is? Therefore, thou art just, truthful, blessed, and whatever it is better to be than not to be. For it is better to be just than not just; better to be blessed than not blessed.

Faith and reason

St. Thomas Aquinas (1224-1274)

St. Thomas is regarded as one of the most notable minds among the Scholastics or "Schoolmen" of the Middle Ages. A member of the Dominican Order, which was founded to preach Christian doctrine, he turned to the writings of Aristotle in order to summarize all philosophy and theology. In the years from 1259 to 1264 he produced his great Summa Contra Gentiles, *an extensive survey of Christian doctrine intended to convince non-Christians of the reasonableness of Christian beliefs. His other great compendium, the* Summa Theologica, *was written for believers. Begun in 1265, it was unfinished at the time of his death.*

St. Thomas sought to order and justify Christian doctrine through the use of reason and to harmonize Christian belief with Greek philosophy, notably that of Aristotle.

In the following selection from the Summa Contra Gentiles *he maintains that truths about God are of two kinds: those which can be reached by human reason and those which lie beyond human reason, depending upon God's revelation to be known. These two kinds of truths, he holds, are mutually consistent; reason and faith are mutually confirming.*

In what way it is possible to make known the divine truth

Since, however, not every truth is to be made known in the same way, *and it is the part of an educated man to seek for conviction in each subject, only so far as the nature of the subject allows,* as the Philosopher [1] most rightly observes as quoted by Boethius, it is necessary to show first of all in what way it is possible to make known the aforesaid truth.

Now in those things which we hold about God there is truth in two ways. For certain things that are true about God wholly surpass the capability of human reason, for instance that God is three and one: while there are certain things to which even natural reason can attain, for instance that God is, that God is one, and others like these, which even the philosophers proved demonstratively of God, being guided by the light of natural reason.

That certain divine truths wholly surpass the capability of human reason, is most clearly evident. For since the principle of all the knowledge which the reason acquires about a thing, is the understanding of that thing's essence, because according to the Philosopher's teaching the principle of a demonstration is *what a thing is,* it follows that our knowledge about a thing will be in proportion to our understanding of its essence. Wherefore, if the human intellect comprehends the essence of a particular thing, for instance a stone or a triangle, no truth about that thing will surpass the capability of

From St. Thomas Aquinas, *Summa Contra Gentiles,* Bk. 1, Ch. 3-8, tr. English Dominican Fathers. Copyright 1924 by Burns & Oates. Ltd. Used by permission of Burns & Oates, Ltd., London, and Benziger Bros., Inc., New York.

94   [1] [Aristotle. Ed.]

human reason. But this does not happen to us in relation to God, because the human intellect is incapable by its natural power of attaining to the comprehension of His essence: since our intellect's knowledge, according to the mode of the present life, originates from the senses: so that things which are not objects of sense cannot be comprehended by the human intellect, except in so far as knowledge of them is gathered from sensibles. Now sensibles cannot lead our intellect to see in them what God is, because they are effects unequal to the power of their cause. And yet our intellect is led by sensibles to the divine knowledge so as to know about God that He is, and other such truths, which need to be ascribed to the first principle. Accordingly some divine truths are attainable by human reason, while others altogether surpass the power of human reason.

Again. The same is easy to see from the degrees of intellects. For if one of two men perceives a thing with his intellect with greater subtlety, the one whose intellect is of a higher degree understands many things which the other is altogether unable to grasp; as instanced in a yokel who is utterly incapable of grasping the subtleties of philosophy. Now the angelic intellect surpasses the human intellect more than the intellect of the cleverest philosopher surpasses that of the most uncultured. For an angel knows God through a more excellent effect than does man, for as much as the angel's essence, through which he is led to know God by natural knowledge, is more excellent than sensible things, even than the soul itself, by which the human intellect mounts to the knowledge of God. And the divine intellect surpasses the angelic intellect much more than the angelic surpasses the human. For the divine intellect by its capacity equals the divine essence, wherefore God perfectly understands of Himself what He is, and He knows all things that can be understood about Him: whereas the angel knows not what God is by his natural knowledge, because the angel's essence, by which he is led to the knowledge of God, is an effect unequal to the power of its cause. Consequently an angel is unable by his natural knowledge to grasp all that God understands

about Himself: nor again is human reason capable of grasping all that an angel understands by his natural power. Accordingly just as a man would show himself to be a most insane fool if he declared the assertions of a philosopher to be false because he was unable to understand them, so, and much more, a man would be exceedingly foolish, were he to suspect of falsehood the things revealed by God through the ministry of His angels, because they cannot be the object of reason's investigations.

Furthermore. The same is made abundantly clear by the deficiency which every day we experience in our knowledge of things. For we are ignorant of many of the properties of sensible things, and in many cases we are unable to discover the nature of those properties which we perceive by our senses. Much less therefore is human reason capable of investigating all the truths about that most sublime essence.

With this the saying of the Philosopher is in accord (2 *Metaph.*) where he says that *our intellect in relation to those primary things which are most evident in nature is like the eye of a bat in relation to the sun.*

To this truth Holy Writ also bears witness. For it is written (Job xi. 7): *Peradventure thou wilt comprehend the steps of God and wilt find out the Almighty perfectly?* and (xxxvi. 26): *Behold God is great, exceeding our knowledge,* and (1 Cor. xiii. 9): *We know in part.*

Therefore all that is said about God, though it cannot be investigated by reason, must not be forthwith rejected as false, as the Manicheans and many unbelievers have thought.

That the truth about divine things which is attainable by reason is fittingly proposed to man as an object of belief

While then the truth of the intelligible things of God is twofold, one to which the inquiry of reason can attain, the other which surpasses the whole range of human reason, both are fittingly proposed by God to man as an object of belief. We must first show this with regard to that truth which is attainable by the inquiry of reason, lest it appears to some, that since it can be attained by reason, it was useless to make it an object of faith by supernatural inspiration. Now three disadvantages would result if this truth were left solely to the inquiry of reason. One is that few men would have knowledge of God: because very many are hindered from gathering the fruit of diligent inquiry, which is the discovery of truth, for three reasons. Some indeed on account of an indisposition of temperament, by reason of which many are naturally indisposed to knowledge: so that no efforts of theirs would enable them to reach to the attainment of the highest degree of human knowledge, which consists in knowing God. Some are hindered by the needs of household affairs. For there must needs be among men some that devote themselves to the conduct of temporal affairs, who would be unable to devote so much time to the leisure of contemplative research as to reach the summit of human inquiry, namely the knowledge of God. And some are hindered by laziness. For in order to acquire the knowledge of God in those things which reason is able to investigate, it is necessary to have a previous knowledge of many things: since almost the entire consideration of philosophy is directed to the knowledge of God: for which reason metaphysics, which is about divine things, is the last of the parts of philosophy to be studied. Wherefore it is not possible to arrive at the inquiry about the aforesaid truth except after a most laborious study: and few are willing to take upon themselves this labour for the love of a knowledge, the natural desire for which has nevertheless been instilled into the mind of man by God.

The second disadvantage is that those who would arrive at the discovery of the aforesaid truth would scarcely succeed in doing so after a long time. First, because this truth is so profound, that it is only after long practice that the human intellect is enabled to grasp it by means of reason. Secondly, because many things are required beforehand, as stated above. Thirdly, because at the time of youth, the mind, when tossed about by the various movements of the passions, is not fit for the knowl-edge of so sublime a truth, whereas *calm gives prudence and knowledge,* as stated in 7 *Phys.* Hence mankind would remain in the deepest darkness of ignorance, if the path of reason were the only available way to the knowledge of God: because the knowledge of God which especially makes men perfect and good, would be acquired only by the few, and by these only after a long time.

The third disadvantage is that much falsehood is mingled with the investigations of human reason, on account of the weakness of our intellect in forming its judgments, and by reason of the admixture of phantasms. Consequently many would remain in doubt about those things even which are most truly demonstrated, through ignoring the force of the demonstration: especially when they perceive that different things are taught by the various men who are called wise. Moreover among the many demonstrated truths, there is sometimes a mixture of falsehood that is not demonstrated, but assumed for some probable or sophistical reason which at times is mistaken for a demonstration. Therefore it was necessary that definite certainty and pure truth about divine things should be offered to man by the way of faith.

Accordingly the divine clemency has made this salutary commandment, that even some things which reason is able to investigate must be held by faith: so that all may share in the knowledge of God easily, and without doubt or error.

Hence it is written (Eph. iv. 17, 18): That *henceforward you walk not as also the Gentiles walk in the vanity of their mind, having their understanding darkened:* and (Isa. liv. 13): *All thy children shall be taught of the Lord.*

That those things which cannot be investigated by reason are fittingly proposed to man as an object of faith

It may appear to some that those things which cannot be investigated by reason ought not to be proposed to man as an object of faith: because divine wisdom provides for each thing according to the mode of its nature. We must therefore prove that it is necessary also for those things which surpass reason to be proposed by God to man as an object of faith.

For no man tends to do a thing by his desire and endeavour unless it be previously known to him. Wherefore since man is directed by divine providence to a higher good than human frailty can attain in the present life, as we shall show in the sequel, it was necessary for his mind to be bidden to something higher than those things to which our reason can reach in the present life, so that he might learn to aspire, and by his endeavours to tend to something surpassing the whole state of the present life. And this is especially competent to the Christian religion, which alone promises goods spiritual and eternal: for which reason it proposes many things surpassing the thought of man: whereas the old law which contained promises of temporal things, proposed few things that are above human inquiry. It was with this motive that the philosophers, in order to wean men from sensible pleasures to virtue, took care to show that there are other goods of greater account than those which appeal to the senses, the taste of which things affords much greater delight to those who devote themselves to active or contemplative virtues.

Again it is necessary for this truth to be proposed to man as an object of faith in order that he may have truer knowledge of God. For then alone do we know God truly, when we believe that He is far above all that man can possibly think of God, because the divine essence surpasses man's natural knowledge, as stated above. Hence by the fact that certain things about God are proposed to man, which surpass his reason, he is strengthened in his opinion that God is far above what he is able to think.

There results also another advantage from this, namely, the checking of presumption which is the mother of error. For some there are who presume so far on their wits that they think themselves capable of measuring the whole nature of things by their intellect, in that they esteem all things true which they see, and false which they see not. Accordingly, in order that man's mind might be freed from this presumption, and seek the truth humbly, it was necessary that certain things far surpassing his intellect should be proposed to man by God.

Yet another advantage is made apparent by the words of the Philosopher (10 *Ethic.*). For when a certain Simonides maintained that man should neglect the knowledge of God, and apply his mind to human affairs, and declared that *a man ought to relish human things, and a mortal, mortal things:* the Philosopher contradicted him, saying that *a man ought to devote himself to immortal and divine things as much as he can.* Hence he says (11 *De Animal.*) that though it is but little that we perceive of higher substances, yet that little is more loved and desired than all the knowledge we have of lower substances. He says also (2 *De Cœlo et Mundo*) that when questions about the heavenly bodies can be answered by a short and probable solution, it happens that the hearer is very much rejoiced. All this shows that however imperfect the knowledge of the highest things may be, it bestows very great perfection on the soul: and consequently, although human reason is unable to grasp fully things that are above reason, it nevertheless acquires much perfection, if at least it hold things, in any way whatever, by faith.

Wherefore it is written (Ecclus. iii. 25): *Many things are shown to thee above the understanding of men,* and (1 Cor. ii. 10, 11): *The things . . . that are of God no man knoweth, but the Spirit of God: but to us God hath revealed them by His Spirit.*

That it is not a mark of levity to assent to the things that are of faith, although they are above reason

Now those who believe this truth, of *which reason affords a proof,* believe not lightly, as though *following foolish fables* (2 Pet. i. 16). For divine Wisdom Himself, Who knows all things most fully, deigned to reveal to man *the secrets of God's wisdom:* and by suitable arguments proves His presence, and the truth of His doctrine and inspiration, by performing works surpassing the capability of the whole of nature, namely, the wondrous healing of the sick, the raising of the dead to life, a marvellous control over the heavenly bodies, and what excites yet more wonder, the inspiration of human minds, so that unlettered and simple persons are filled with the Holy Ghost, and in one instant are endowed with the most sublime wisdom and eloquence. And after considering these arguments, convinced by the strength of the proof, and not by the force of arms, nor by the promise of delights, but—and this is the greatest marvel of all—amidst the tyranny of persecutions, a countless crowd of not only simple but also of the wisest men, embraced the Christian faith, which inculcates things surpassing all human understanding, curbs the pleasures of the flesh, and teaches contempt of all worldly things. That the minds of mortal beings should assent to such things, is both the greatest of miracles, and the evident work of divine inspiration, seeing that they despise visible things and desire only those that are invisible. And that this happened not suddenly nor by chance, but by the disposition of God, is shown by the fact that God foretold that He would do so by the manifold oracles of the prophets, whose books we hold in veneration as bearing witness to our faith. This particular kind of proof is alluded to in the words of Heb. ii. 3, 4: *Which*, namely the salvation of mankind, *having begun to be declared by the Lord, was confirmed with us by them that heard Him, God also bearing witness by signs and wonders, and divers . . . distributions of the Holy Ghost.*

Now such a wondrous conversion of the world to the Christian faith is a most indubitable proof that such signs did take place, so that there is no need to repeat them, seeing that there is evidence of them in their result. For it would be the most wondrous sign of all if without any wondrous signs the world were persuaded by simple and lowly men to believe things so arduous, to accomplish things so difficult, and to hope for things so sublime. Although God ceases not even in our time to work miracles through His saints in confirmation of the faith.

On the other hand those who introduced the errors of the sects proceeded in contrary fashion, as instanced by Mohammed, who enticed peoples with the promise of carnal pleasures, to the desire of which the concupiscence of the flesh instigates. He also delivered commandments in keeping with his promises, by giving the reins to carnal pleasure, wherein it is easy for carnal men to obey: and the lessons of truth which he inculcated were only such as can be easily known to any man of average wisdom by his natural powers: yea rather the truths which he taught were mingled by him with many fables and most false doctrines. Nor did he add any signs of supernatural agency, which alone are a fitting witness to divine inspiration, since a visible work that can be from God alone, proves the teacher of truth to be invisibly inspired: but he asserted that he was sent in the power of arms, a sign that is not lacking even to robbers and tyrants. Again, those who believed in him from the outset were not wise men practised in things divine and human, but beastlike men who dwelt in the wilds, utterly ignorant of all divine teaching; and it was by a multitude of such men and the force of arms that he compelled others to submit to his law.

Lastly, no divine oracles of prophets in a previous age bore witness to him; rather did he corrupt almost all the teaching of the Old and New Testaments by a narrative replete with fables, as one may see by a perusal of his law. Hence by a cunning device, he did not commit the reading of the Old and New Testament Books to his followers, lest he should thereby be convicted of falsehood. Thus it is evident that those who believe his words believe lightly.

That the truth of reason is not in opposition to the truth of the Christian faith

Now though the aforesaid truth of the Christian faith surpasses the ability of human reason, nevertheless those things which are naturally instilled in human reason cannot be opposed to this truth. For it is clear that those things which are implanted in reason by nature, are most true, so much so that it is impossible to think them to be false. Nor is it lawful to deem false that which is held by faith, since it is so evidently confirmed by God. Seeing then that the false alone is opposed to the true, as evidently appears if we examine their definitions, it is impossible for the aforesaid truth of faith to be contrary to those principles which reason knows naturally.

Again. The same thing which the disciple's mind receives from its teacher is contained in the knowledge of the teacher, unless he teach insincerely, which it were wicked to say of God. Now the knowledge of naturally known principles is instilled into us by God, since God Himself is the author of our nature. Therefore the divine Wisdom also contains these principles. Consequently whatever is contrary to these principles, is contrary to the divine Wisdom; wherefore it cannot be from God. Therefore those things which are received by faith from divine revelation cannot be contrary to our natural knowledge.

Moreover. Our intellect is stayed by contrary arguments, so that it cannot advance to the knowledge of truth. Wherefore if conflicting knowledges were instilled into us by God, our intellect would thereby be hindered from knowing the truth. And this cannot be ascribed to God.

Furthermore. Things that are natural are unchangeable so long as nature remains. Now contrary opinions cannot be together in the same subject. Therefore God does not instil into man any opinion or belief contrary to natural knowledge.

Hence the Apostle says (Rom. x. 8): *The word is nigh thee even in thy heart and in thy mouth. This is the word of faith which we preach.* Yet because it surpasses reason some look upon it as though it were contrary thereto; which is impossible.

This is confirmed also by the authority of Augustine who says (*Gen. ad lit.* ii): *That which truth shall make known can nowise be in opposition to the holy books whether of the Old or of the New Testament.*

From this we may evidently conclude that whatever arguments are alleged against the teachings of faith, they do not rightly proceed from the first self-evident principles instilled by nature. Wherefore they lack the force of demonstration, and are either probable or sophistical arguments, and consequently it is possible to solve them.

In what relation human reason stands to the truth of faith

It would also seem well to observe that sensible things from which human reason derives the source of its knowledge, retain a certain trace of likeness to God, but so imperfect that it proves altogether inadequate to manifest the substance itself of God. For effects resemble their causes according to their own mode, since like action proceeds from like agent; and yet the effect does not always reach to a perfect likeness to the agent. Accordingly human reason is adapted to the knowledge of the truth of faith, which can be known in the highest degree only by those who see the divine substance, in so far as it is able to put together certain probable arguments in support thereof, which nevertheless are insufficient to enable us to understand the aforesaid truth as though it were demonstrated to us or understood by us in itself. And yet however weak these arguments may be, it is useful for the human mind to be practised therein, so long as it does not pride itself on having comprehended or demonstrated: since although our view of the sublimest things is limited and weak, it is most pleasant to be able to catch but a glimpse of them, as appears from what has been said.

The authority of Hilary is in agreement with this statement: for he says (*De Trin.*) while speaking of this same truth: *Begin by believing these things, advance and persevere; and though I know thou wilt not arrive, I shall rejoice at thy advance. For he who devoutly follows in pursuit of the infinite, though he never come up with it, will always advance by setting forth. Yet pry not into that secret, and meddle not in the mystery of the birth of the infinite, nor presume to grasp that which is the summit of understanding: but understand that there are things thou canst not grasp.*

Of the order and mode of procedure in this work

Accordingly, from what we have been saying it is evident that the intention of the wise man must be directed to the twofold truth of divine things and to the refutation of contrary errors: and that the research of reason is able to reach to one of these, while the other surpasses every effort of reason. And I speak of a twofold truth of divine things, not on the part of God Himself Who is Truth one and simple, but on the part of our knowledge, the relation of which to the knowledge of divine things varies.

Wherefore in order to deduce the first kind of truth we must proceed by demonstrative arguments whereby we can convince our adversaries. But since such arguments are not available in support of the second kind of truth, our intention must be not to convince our opponent by our arguments, but to solve the arguments which he brings against the truth, because, as shown above, natural reason cannot be opposed to the truth of faith. In a special way may the opponent of this kind of truth be convinced by the authority of Scripture confirmed by God with miracles: since we believe not what is above human reason save because God has revealed it. In support, however, of this kind of truth, certain probable arguments must be adduced for the practice and help of the faithful, but not for the conviction of our opponents, because the very insufficiency of these arguments would rather confirm them in their error, if they thought that we assented to the truth of faith on account of such weak reasonings.

With the intention then of proceeding in the manner laid down, we shall first of all endeavour to declare that truth which is the object of faith's confession and of reason's researches, by adducing arguments both demonstrative and probable, some of which we have gathered from the writings of the philosophers and of holy men, so as thereby to confirm the truth and convince our opponents. After this, so as to proceed from the more to the less manifest, we shall with God's help proceed to declare that truth which surpasses reason, by refuting the arguments of our opponents, and by setting forth the truth of faith by means of probable arguments and authority.

Seeing then that we intend by the way of reason to pursue those things about God which human reason is able to investigate, the first object that offers itself to our consideration consists in those things which pertain to God in Himself; the second will be the procession of creatures from Him; and the third the relation of creatures to Him as their end. Of those things which we need to consider about God in Himself, we must give the first place (this being the necessary foundation of the whole of this work), to the question of demonstrating that there is a God: for unless this be established, all questions about divine things are out of court.

God and existence

Etienne Gilson (b. 1884)

Born in Paris and educated at the Sorbonne, Gilson has achieved interna-
tional eminence as a historian and interpreter of medieval thought. He
taught medieval philosophy at the Sorbonne from 1921 to 1932, when he
was elected to the Collège de France. Since 1929, except for the war years,
he has divided his time between Paris and the Institute of Medieval Studies
in Toronto. He has served in the French Senate and as delegate to UNESCO.
His books include The Spirit of Medieval Philosophy (*1932*), The Unity
of Philosophical Experience (*1937*), Being and Some Philosophers (*1949*),
as well as noted studies of Descartes, St. Augustine, St. Thomas Aquinas,
St. Bernard, and St. Bonaventure. He is the author also of a monumental
history of medieval philosophy and of numerous articles.

In God and Philosophy (*1941*), *his Terry Lectures at Yale University,*
Gilson considers the manner in which philosophical thought has dealt with
the nature of God. In the present selection he is particularly concerned with
the Thomistic development of the idea of God as "a pure Act of existence."
He contrasts the Thomistic conception of man and God with that of St.
Augustine and shows how the Augustinian view derives from Platonic and
Neoplatonic sources.

. . . A pure Act of existing, taken as such and without any limitation, necessarily is all that which it is possible to be. We cannot even say that such a God has knowledge, or love, or anything else; he is it in his own right, for the very reason that, were he not everything and anything that it is possible to be, he could be called "He who is" but with some added qualification. If, as is part of Christian faith, such a God begets in virtue of his infinite fecundity, he must beget somebody else, that is another person, but not something else, that is another God. Otherwise, there would be two absolute acts of existing, each of which would include the totality of being, which is absurd. If, on the other hand, such a God

actually is, or exists, his self-sufficiency is so perfect that there can be no necessity for anything else to exist. Nothing can be added to him; nothing can be subtracted from him; and since nothing can share in his being without at once being himself; "He who is" can eternally enjoy the fullness of his own perfection, of his own beatitude, without needing to grant existence to anybody else, or to anything whatsoever.

Yet it is a fact that there is something which is not God. Men, for instance, are not such an eternal act of absolute existence. There are therefore some beings that are radically different from God at least in this that, unlike him, they might not have existed, and still may, at a certain time, cease to exist. Thus to be, or exist, is not at all to be, or exist, as God himself is, or exists. It is therefore not to be an inferior sort of god; rather, it is not

From Etienne Gilson, *God and Philosophy*, Ch. II. Copyright, 1941, Yale University Press. Used by permission.

to be a god at all. The only possible explanation for the presence of such finite and contingent beings is that they have been freely given existence by "Him who is," and not as parcels of his own existence, which, because it is absolute and total, is also unique, but as finite and partial imitations of what He himself eternally is in his own right. This act whereby "He who is" causes to exist something that, of itself, is not, is what is called, in Christian philosophy, "creation." Whence there follows, that whereas all that which the Christian God begets must of necessity share in the oneness of God, all that which does not share in his oneness must of necessity be not begotten but created.

Such is, in fact, the Christian world of Saint Augustine. On the one side, God, one in the Trinity of a single, self-existing substance; on the other side, all that which, because it has but a received existence, is not God. Unlike the Plotinian dividing line which we have seen running between the One and all that is begotten by the One, the Christian dividing line runs between God, including his own begotten Word, and all that is created by God. As one among God's creatures, man finds himself therein excluded from the order of the divine. Between "Him who is" and ourselves, there is the infinite metaphysical chasm which separates the complete self-sufficiency of His own existence from the intrinsic lack of necessity of our own existence. Nothing can bridge such a chasm, save a free act of the divine will only. This is why, from the time of Saint Augustine up to our own days, human reason has been up against the tremendously difficult task of reaching a transcendent God whose pure act of existing is radically distinct from our own borrowed existence. How can man, who out of himself is not, living in a world of things which out of themselves are not, reach, by means of reason alone, "Him who is"? Such is, to a Christian, the fundamental problem of natural theology.

In his effort to solve this problem, Augustine had nothing to help him but the philosophical technique of Plato in the revised edition of Plotinos. Here again, the philosophical eagerness of the Christian convert took him beyond the data of the problem straight to its solution. Interpreting Plato's doctrine of reminiscence, Plotinos had described dialectics as an effort of the human soul to rid itself of all material images so as to contemplate the intelligible Ideas in the light of the first Intellect, who is the supreme god. Was not this exactly what Saint John himself had, if not philosophically established, at least clearly suggested in the first chapter of his gospel? When Plotinos and Saint John thus met in the mind of Augustine, their combination was instantaneous. Reading the gospel into Plotinos' *Enneads*, he found there that the soul of man, though it "bears witness of the light," yet itself "is not that light; but the Word of God, being God, is that true light that lighteth every man that cometh into the world." Why should not men use this constant presence of the divine light in their souls as an always open way to the Christian God?

This is precisely what Augustine did, or, at least, what he tried to do, for the task proved to be a much more difficult one than he himself had imagined. In inheriting the philosophical world of Plato, Augustine had fallen heir to Plato's man. Now, man, as Plato conceived him, was not the substantial unity of body and soul; he was essentially a soul. Instead of saying that man *has* a soul, we should therefore say that man *is* a particular soul, that is to say, an intelligent, intelligible, and eternally living substance, which, though it now happens to be conjoined to a body, has always existed before it and is ultimately destined to outlive it. In Plato's own words, man is "a soul using a body," but he is no more his body than a worker is the tools he uses or than any one of us is his own garments.

By accepting this definition of man, Augustine was putting himself in an exceedingly awkward philosophical position. In Plato's doctrine, and still more clearly in that of Plotinos, to be a purely intelligible, living, and immortal substance was exactly to be a god. Human souls then are just so many gods. When a man philosophizes and, discarding his body, focuses his mind upon intelligible truth, he simply behaves like a god who remembers to be a god. Rightly to philosophize then is nothing else, for each and every one of us, than to behave as becomes the god which each and every one of us actually is. True, we all are but individual Intelligences radiated by the supreme Intellect, and therefore by the One. For this very reason, just as we are by and in the One, we also know, and contemplate, by and in the light of the supreme Intellect who eternally emanates from the One. Yet, when all is said and done, we nevertheless are so many gods, lesser gods as we may be, patiently working our way back into the company of our fellow gods. Dialectics, as Plato and Plotinos understood it, was but the method which enables man to achieve a sort of philosophical salvation, by progressively raising him to the full awareness of his own divinity. A god may eventually forget himself but he cannot possibly stand in need of being saved.

This is the fundamental reason why Saint Augustine has found it so hard to reach the Christian God by means of methods borrowed from Plato and Plotinos. To him, as to them, all that was immaterial, intelligible, and true was divine in its own right; but, whereas, in Plato's philosophy, man was naturally entitled to the possession of truth as a divinity is entitled to the possession of things divine, he could no longer appear as entitled to it in a Christian philosophy where, metaphysically speaking, man in no way belongs in the divine order. Hence this important consequence, that man was bound to appear to Augustine as a creature endowed with something that was divine in its own right. If truth is divine, and if man is not a god, man should not be possessed of truth. In fact, however, man is; consequently, the only conceivable way for Augustine to account for the paradoxical presence of intelligible truth, which is divine, in man, who is not a god, was to consider man as knowing in the permanent light of a supremely intelligible and self-subsisting truth, that is, in the light of God.

Time and again, under a variety of different forms, Augustine has attempted the same demonstration of the existence of God as the only conceivable cause of the presence of truth in the human mind. His God is the intelligible sun whose light shines upon human reason and enables it to know truth; he is the inner master who teaches man from within; his eternal and unchangeable ideas are the supreme rules whose influence submits our reason to the necessity of divine truth. As demonstrations, the arguments of Saint Augustine are very effective. Granting that truth is superhuman and divine in its own right, the bare fact that man knows truth conclusively proves the existence of God. But why should we grant Augustine that truth is a more than human object of knowledge? The only reason why he himself thought so was a merely accidental one. Augustine's implicit reasoning seems to have run as follows: Plato and Plotinos consider man as a god because man is possessed of truth; now man is emphatically not a god; hence man cannot possibly be possessed of truth. Taken in itself, such an argument is perfectly correct; it would even be a perfectly conclusive one if it were true to say that truth is too good a thing to be considered as naturally attainable by man.

What happened to Saint Augustine is only too clear. An unsurpassed exponent of Christian wisdom, he never had the philosophy of his theology. The God of Augustine is the true Christian God, of whose pure Act of existing nothing better can be said than: He is; but when Augustine undertakes to describe existence in philosophical terms, he at once falls back upon the Greek identification of being with the notions of immateriality, intelligibility, immutability, and unity. Every such thing is divine; since truth is such, truth is divine. Immaterial, intelligible, and immutable, truth belongs in the order of that which truly is, or exists. Consequently, it belongs to God. Similarly the God of Augustine is the true creator of all things; but when it comes to defining creation, Augustine naturally understands it in accordance with his own notion of being. To create is to give being, and since to be is to be both intelligible and one, Augustine understands creation as the divine gift of that sort of existence which consists in rhythm, numbers, forms, beauty, order, and unity. Like all Christians, but unlike the Greeks, Augustine has a quite clear notion of what it is to create something "out of nothing." It is to make it to be. What still remains Greek in Augustine's thought is his very notion of what it is to be. His ontology, or science of being, is an "essential" rather than an "existential" one. In other words, it exhibits a marked tendency to reduce the existence of a thing to its essence, and to answer the question: What is it for a thing to be? by saying: It is to be that which it is.

A most sensible answer indeed, but perhaps not the deepest conceivable one in philosophy, and certainly not a perfectly suitable one for a Christian philosopher speculating on a world created by the Christian God. For reasons which I will later try to make clear, it was not easy to go beyond Saint Augustine, because the limit he had reached was the limit of Greek ontology itself, and therefore just about the very limit which the human mind can reach in matters of metaphysics. When, nine centuries after the death of Saint Augustine, a new and decisive progress in natural theology was made, its occasional cause was the discovery of another Greek metaphysical universe by another Christian theologian. This time the metaphysical universe was that of Aristotle, and the name of the theologian was Thomas Aquinas.

"The religious side of Plato's thought," Gilbert Murray rightly says, "was not revealed in its full power till the time of Plotinos in the third century A.D.: that of Aristotle, one might say without undue paradox, not till its exposition by Aquinas in the thirteenth." Let us add only this, that the "explanation" of Aristotle by Thomas Aquinas might perhaps be more justly called its metamorphosis in the light of Christian revelation. The self-thinking Thought of Aristotle has certainly become an essential element of the natural theology of Saint Thomas Aquinas, but not without first undergoing the metaphysical transformation that turned him into the *Qui est,* or "He who is" of the Old Testament.

Why, Saint Thomas asks, do we say that *Qui est* is the most proper name among all those that can be given to God? And his answer is because it signifies "to be": *ipsum esse.* But what is it to be? In answering this most difficult of all metaphysical questions, we must carefully distinguish between the meaning of two words which are both different and yet intimately related: *ens,* or "being," and *esse,* or "to be." To the question: What is being? the correct answer is: Being is that which is, or exists. If, for instance, we ask this same question with regard to God, the correct answer would be: The being of God is an infinite and boundless ocean of substance. But *esse,* or "to be," is something else and much harder to grasp because it lies more deeply hidden in the metaphysical structure of reality. The word "being," as a noun, designates some substance; the word "to be"—or *esse*—is a verb, because it designates an act. To understand this is also to reach, beyond the level of essence, the deeper level of existence. For it is quite true to say that all that which is a substance must of necessity have also both an essence and an existence. In point of fact, such is the natural order followed by our rational knowledge: we first conceive certain beings, then we define their essences, and last we affirm their existences by means of a judgment. But the metaphysical order of reality is just the reverse of the order of human knowledge: what first comes into it is a certain act of existing which, because it is *this* particular act of existing, circumscribes at once a certain essence and causes a certain substance to come into being. In this deeper sense, "to be" is the primitive and fundamental act by virtue of which a certain being actually is, or exists. In Saint Thomas' own words: *dicitur esse ipse actus essentiae—* "to be" is the very act whereby an essence is.

A world where "to be" is the act par excellence, the act of all acts, is also a world wherein, for each and every thing, existence is the original energy whence flows all that which deserves the name of being. Such an existential world can be accounted for by no other cause than a supremely existential God. The strange thing is that, historically speaking, things seem to have worked the other way around. Philosophers have not inferred the supreme existentiality of God from any previous knowledge of the existential nature of things; on the contrary, the self-revelation of the existentiality of God has helped philosophers toward the realization of the existential nature of things. In other words, philosophers were not able to reach, beyond essences, the existential energies which are their very causes, until the Jewish-Christian Revelation had taught them that "to be" was the proper name of the Supreme Being. The decisive progress achieved by metaphysics in the light of Christian faith has not been to realize that there must be a first being, cause of being in all things. The greatest among the Greeks already knew it. When, for instance, Aristotle was positing his first self-thinking Thought as the supreme being, he certainly conceived it as a pure Act and as an infinitely powerful energy; still, his god was but the pure Act of a Thought. This infinitely powerful actuality of a self-thinking principle most certainly deserves to be called a pure Act, but it was a pure Act in the order of knowing, not in that of existence. Now nothing can give what it has not. Because the supreme Thought of Aristotle was not "He who is," it could not give existence: hence the world of Aristotle was not a created world. Because the supreme Thought of Aristotle was not the pure Act of existing, its self-knowledge did not entail the knowledge of all being, both actual and possible: the god of Aristotle was not a providence; he did not even know a world which he did not make and which he could not possibly have made because he was the thought of a Thought, nor did he know the self-awareness of "Him who is."

I would not like to minimize the philosophical indebtedness of Thomas Aquinas to Aristotle. He himself would not forgive me for making him guilty of such an ingratitude. As a philosopher, Thomas Aquinas was not a pupil of Moses, but of Aristotle, to whom he owed his method, his principles, up to even his all-important notion of the fundamental actuality of being. My only point is that a

decisive metaphysical progress or, rather, a true metaphysical revolution was achieved when somebody began to translate all the problems concerning being from the language of essences into that of existences. From its earliest origins, metaphysics had always obscurely aimed at becoming existential; from the time of Saint Thomas Aquinas it has always been so, and to such an extent that metaphysics has regularly lost its very existence every time it has lost its existentiality.

The metaphysics of Thomas Aquinas was, and it still remains, a climax in the history of natural theology. No wonder then that it was so soon followed by an anticlimax. Human reason feels at home in a world of things, whose essences and laws it can grasp and define in terms of concepts; but shy and ill at ease in a world of existences, because to exist is an act, not a thing. And we know it but too well. Every time a lecturer begins a sentence by saying: "As a matter of fact," you know at once that the man is at his wit's end. Granting that something is, he can tell you a great deal concerning that which it is; what he cannot do is to account for the very existence of the thing. How could he, if existence is a principle, and the innermost first principle of what the thing is? When dealing with facts as facts, or with things that happen as mere happenings, our *ultima ratio* always is and that's that. Obviously, to ask us to view the universe as a world of particular existential acts all related to a supreme and absolute Self-Existence is to stretch the power of our essentially conceptual reason almost to the breaking point. We know that we must do it, but we wonder if we can, because we are not sure that the thing can be done at all.

This, at least, is a point about which several among the successors of Thomas Aquinas have entertained grave doubts. Themselves Christian theologians, and sometimes very great ones, they had no hesitations concerning the true name of the true God. Their real difficulty was, granting that God is "He who is," can such a God be attained by means of philosophical reason alone, unaided by Revelation? A perfectly relevant question indeed. After all, these theologians knew full well that philosophers had never thought of giving God such a name until they had learned it from Moses, who himself had learned it from God. Hence the marked tendency, even in such a great metaphysician as Duns Scotus, to question the possibility of human reason's reaching, by means of philosophy alone, the absolutely existing and absolutely all-powerful Christian God.

The reason for this hesitancy is simple. The human mind feels shy before a reality of which it can form no proper concept. Such, precisely, is existence. It is hard for us to realize that "I am" is an active verb. It is perhaps still more difficult for us to see that "it is" ultimately points out, not that which the thing is, but the primitive existential act which causes it both to be and to be precisely that which it is. He who begins to see this, however, also begins to grasp the very stuff our universe is made of. He even begins obscurely to perceive the supreme cause of such a world.

Why had the Greek mind spontaneously stopped at the notion of nature, or of essence, as at an ultimate explanation? Because, in our human experience, existence is always that of a particular essence. We directly know only individual and sensible existing things whose existence merely consists in being this and that individual thing. The existence of an oak tree obviously limits itself to being an oak tree or, rather, to being this one particular oak tree, and the same could be said of everything else. What does this mean, if not that the essence of any and every thing is not existence itself, but only one of the many possible sharings in existence? This fact is best expressed by the fundamental distinction of "being" and "what is" so clearly laid down by Thomas Aquinas. It does not mean that existence is distinct from essence as a thing from another thing. Once more, existence is not a thing, but the act that causes a thing both to be and to be what it is. This distinction merely expresses the fact that, in our human experience, there is no thing whose essence it is "to be," and not "to-be-a-certain-thing." The definition of no empirically given thing is existence; hence its essence is not existence, but existence must be conceived as distinct from it.

How then are we to account for the existence of a world made up of such things? You can take them all one after the other and ask yourself why each of them is, or exists; the essence of no one of them will ever yield the answer to your question. Since the nature of no one of them is "to be," the most exhaustive scientific knowledge of what they are will not so much as suggest the beginning of an answer to the question: Why are they? This world of ours is a world of change; physics, chemistry, biology can teach us the laws according to which change actually happens in it; what these sciences cannot teach us is why this world, taken together with its laws, its order, and its intelligibility, is, or exists. If the nature of no known thing is "to be," the nature of no known thing contains in itself the sufficient reason for its own existence. But it points to its sole conceivable cause. Beyond a world wherein "to be" is everywhere at hand, and where every nature can account for what other natures are but not for their common existence, there must be some cause whose very essence it is "to be." To posit such a being whose essence is a pure Act of existing, that is, whose essence is not to be this and that, but "to be," is also to posit the Christian God as the supreme cause of the universe. A most deeply hidden God, "He who is" is also a most obvious God. By revealing to the metaphysician that they cannot account for their own existence, all things point to the fact that there is such a supreme cause wherein essence and existence coincide. Here at last, Thomas Aquinas and Augustine ultimately meet. Because his own existential metaphysics has succeeded in forcing its way through that crust of essences which is but the outer coating of reality, Thomas Aquinas can see the pure Act of existing as one sees the presence of the cause in any one of its effects.

To reach this point was probably to reach the *ultima Thule* of the metaphysical world. Saint Augustine had reached it on the strength of Christian faith, on the very day he had heard all things proclaim, in the language of the Bible: "We created not ourselves, but were created by Him who abideth for ever." To Augustine, however, "He who abideth for ever" essentially remained the self-existing "eternal Truth, true Love and loved Eternity." Saint Thomas Aquinas has reached it on the strength of straight metaphysical knowledge, where he says that "all knowing beings implicitly know God in any and every thing that they know." It was impossible to go further, because human reason cannot go further than the highest of all metaphysical principles. One might have expected at least this, that once in possession of so fundamental a truth, men would carefully preserve it. But they did not. Its loss almost immediately followed its discovery. How and why it has been lost is therefore the problem to which we now have to turn our attention.

The argument from design

David Hume (1711-1776) *

In the famous Dialogues Concerning Natural Religion (*1779*) *Hume examines the possibility of proving anything about God's existence or his nature from a consideration of the nature of the world. The three speakers are Cleanthes, a theist who believes that God's existence is susceptible of proof, Demea, a theist who denies that human reason can prove God's existence, and Philo, a skeptic. Our selection is Part 2 of the* Dialogues. *Here the argument from design is stated and then refuted. The universe is regarded as a great machine, and the argument seeks to prove the existence of a maker from the fact that there is orderliness in the working of this machinelike universe.*

I must own, Cleanthes, said Demea, that nothing can more surprise me, than the light, in which you have, all along, put this argument. By the whole tenor of your discourse, one would imagine that you were maintaining the Being of a God, against the cavils of Atheists and Infidels; and were necessitated to become a champion for that fundamental principle of all religion. But this, I hope, is not by any means a question among us. No man; no man, at least, of common sense, I am persuaded, ever entertained a serious doubt with regard to a truth, so certain and self-evident. The question is not concerning the being, but the nature of God. This, I affirm, from the infirmities of human understanding, to be altogether incomprehensible and unknown to us. The essence of that supreme mind, his attributes, the manner of his existence, the very nature of his duration; these and every particular, which regards so divine a Being, are mysterious to men. Finite, weak, and blind creatures, we ought to humble ourselves in his august presence, and, conscious of our frailties,

adore in silence his infinite perfections, which eye hath not seen, ear hath not heard, neither hath it entered into the heart of man to conceive them. They are covered in a deep cloud from human curiosity: It is profaneness to attempt penetrating through these sacred obscurities: And next to the impiety of denying his existence, is the temerity of prying into his nature and essence, decrees and attributes.

But lest you should think, that my *piety* has here got the better of my *philosophy*, I shall support my opinion, if it needs any support, by a very great authority. I might cite all the divines almost, from the foundation of Christianity, who have ever treated of this or any other theological subject: But I shall confine myself, at present, to one equally celebrated for piety and philosophy. It is Father Malebranche, who, I remember, thus expresses himself.[1] "One ought not so much (says he) to call God a spirit, in order to express positively what he is, as in order to signify that he is not matter. He is a Being infinitely perfect: Of this we cannot doubt. But in the same manner as we ought not to imagine, even supposing him corporeal, that he is clothed with a human

From David Hume, *Dialogues Concerning Natural Religion*, 1779, part 2.

* See the introductory note on Hume on page 27.

[1] *Recherche de la Vérité*, liv. 3, chap. 9.

body, as the Anthropomorphites asserted, under colour that that figure was the most perfect of any; so neither ought we to imagine, that the Spirit of God has human ideas, or bears *any* resemblance to our spirit; under colour that we know nothing more perfect than a human mind. We ought rather to believe, that as he comprehends the perfections of matter without being material ... he comprehends also the perfections of created spirits, without being spirit, in the manner we conceive spirit: That his true name is, *He that is*, or, in other words, Being without restriction, All Being, the Being infinite and universal."

After so great an authority, Demea, replied Philo, as that which you have produced, and a thousand more, which you might produce, it would appear ridiculous in me to add my sentiment, or express my approbation of your doctrine. But surely, where reasonable men treat these subjects, the question can never be concerning the *Being*, but only the Nature of the Deity. The former truth, as you well observe, is unquestionable and self-evident. Nothing exists without a cause; and the original cause of this universe (whatever it be) we call God; and piously ascribe to him every species of perfection. Whoever scruples this fundamental truth, deserves every punishment, which can be inflicted among philosophers, to wit, the greatest ridicule, contempt and disapprobation. But as all perfection is entirely relative, we ought never to imagine, that we comprehend the attributes of this divine Being, or to suppose, that his perfections have any analogy or likeness to the perfections of a human creature. Wisdom, Thought, Design, Knowledge; these we justly ascribe to him; because these words are honourable among men, and we have no other language or other conceptions, by which we can express our adoration of him. But let us beware, lest we think, that our ideas any wise correspond to his perfections, or that his attributes have any resemblance to these qualities among men. He is infinitely superior to our limited view and comprehension; and is more the object of worship in the temple, than of disputation in the schools.

In reality, Cleanthes, continued he, there is no need of having recourse to that affected scepticism, so displeasing to you, in order to come at this determination. Our ideas reach no farther than our experience: We have no experience of divine attributes and operations: I need not conclude my syllogism: You can draw the inference yourself. And it is a pleasure to me (and I hope to you too) that just reasoning and sound piety here concur in the same conclusion, and both of them establish the adorably mysterious and incomprehensible nature of the Supreme Being.

Not to lose any time in circumlocutions, said Cleanthes, addressing himself to Demea, much less in replying to the pious declamations of Philo; I shall briefly explain how I conceive this matter. Look round the world: contemplate the whole and every part of it: You will find it to be nothing but one great machine, subdivided into an infinite number of lesser machines, which again admit of subdivisions, to a degree beyond what human senses and faculties can trace and explain. All these various machines, and even their most minute parts, are adjusted to each other with an accuracy, which ravishes into admiration all men, who have ever contemplated them. The curious adapting of means to ends, throughout all nature, resembles exactly, though it much exceeds, the productions of human contrivance; of human design, thought, wisdom, and intelligence. Since therefore the effects resemble each other, we are led to infer, by all the rules of analogy, that the causes also resemble; and that the Author of Nature is somewhat similar to the mind of man; though possessed of much larger faculties, proportioned to the grandeur of the work, which he has executed. By this argument *a posteriori*, and by this argument alone, do we prove at once the existence of a Deity, and his similarity to human mind and intelligence.

I shall be so free, Cleanthes, said Demea, as to tell you, that from the beginning, I could not approve of your conclusion concerning the similarity of the Deity to men; still less can I approve of the mediums, by which you endeavour to establish it. What! No demonstration of the Being of a God! No abstract arguments! No proofs *a priori!* Are these, which have hitherto been so much insisted on by philosophers, all fallacy, all sophism? Can we reach no farther in this subject than experience and probability? I will not say, that this is betraying the cause of a deity: But surely, by this affected candour, you give advantage to Atheists, which they never could obtain, by the mere dint of argument and reasoning.

What I chiefly scruple in this subject, said Philo, is not so much, that all religious arguments are by Cleanthes reduced to experience, as that they appear not to be even the most certain and irrefragable of that inferior kind. That a stone will fall, that fire will burn, that the earth has solidity, we have observed a thousand and a thousand times; and when any new instance of this nature is presented, we draw without hesitation the accustomed inference. The exact similarity of the cases gives us a perfect assurance of a similar event; and a stronger evidence is never desired nor sought after. But wherever you depart, in the least, from the similarity of the cases, you diminish proportionably the evidence; and may at last bring it to a very weak *analogy*, which is confessedly liable to error and uncertainty. After having experienced the circulation of the blood in human creatures, we make no doubt that it takes place in Titius and Mævius: but from its circulation in frogs and fishes, it is only a presumption, though a strong one, from analogy, that it takes place in men and other animals. The analogical reasoning is much weaker, when we infer the circulation of the sap in vegetables from our experience, that the blood circulates in animals; and those, who hastily followed that imperfect analogy, are found, by more accurate experiments, to have been mistaken.

If we see a house, Cleanthes, we conclude, with the greatest certainty, that it had an architect or builder; because this is precisely that species of effect, which we have experienced to proceed from that species of cause. But surely you will not affirm, that the universe bears such a resemblance to a house, that we can with the same certainty infer a similar cause, or that the analogy is here entire and perfect. The dissimilitude is so striking, that the utmost you can here pretend to is a guess, a conjecture, a presumption concerning a similar cause; and how that pretension will be received in the world, I leave you to consider.

It would surely be very ill received, replied Cleanthes; and I shall be deservedly blamed and detested, did I allow, that the proofs of a Deity amounted to no more than a guess or conjecture. But is the whole adjustment of means to ends in a house and in the universe so slight a resemblance? The œconomy of final causes? The order, proportion, and arrangement of every part? Steps of a stair are plainly contrived, that human legs may use them in mounting; and this inference is certain and infallible. Human legs are also contrived for walking and mounting; and this inference, I allow, is not altogether so certain, because of the dissimilarity which you remark; but does it, therefore, deserve the name only of presumption or conjecture?

Good God! cried Demea, interrupting him, where are we? Zealous defenders of religion allow, that the proofs of a Deity fall short of perfect evidence! And you, Philo, on whose assistance I depended, in proving the adorable mysteriousness of the Divine Nature, do you assent to all these extravagant opinions of Cleanthes? For what other name can I give them? Or why spare my censure, when such principles are advanced, supported by such an authority, before so young a man as Pamphilus?

You seem not to apprehend, replied Philo, that I argue with Cleanthes in his own way; and by showing him the dangerous consequences of his tenets, hope at last to reduce him to our opinion. But what sticks most with you, I observe, is the representation which Cleanthes has made of the argument *a posteriori*; and finding, that that argument is likely to escape your hold and vanish into air, you think it so disguised, that you can scarcely believe it to be set in its true light. Now, however much I may dissent, in other respects, from the dangerous principles of Cleanthes, I must allow, that he has fairly represented that argument; and I shall endeavour so to state the matter to you, that you will entertain no farther scruples with regard to it.

Were a man to abstract from every thing which he knows or has seen, he would be altogether incapable, merely from his own ideas, to determine what kind of scene the universe must be, or to give the preference to one state or situation of things above another. For as nothing which he clearly conceives, could be esteemed impossible or implying a contradiction, every chimera of his fancy would be upon an equal footing; nor could he assign any just reason, why he adheres to one idea or system, and rejects the others, which are equally possible.

Again; after he opens his eyes, and contemplates the world, as it really is, it would be impossible for him, at first, to assign the cause of any one event; much less, of the whole of things or of the universe. He might set his Fancy a rambling; and she might bring him in an infinite variety of reports and representations. These would all be possible; but being all equally possible, he would never, of himself, give a satisfactory account for his preferring one of them to the rest. Experience alone can point out to him the true cause of any phenomenon.

Now, according to this method of reasoning, Demea, it follows (and is, indeed, tacitly allowed by Cleanthes himself) that order, arrangement, or the adjustment of final causes is not, of itself, any proof of design; but only so far as it has been experienced to proceed from that principle. For aught we can know *a priori*, matter may contain the source or spring of order originally, within itself, as well as mind does; and there is no more difficulty in conceiving, that the several elements, from an internal unknown cause, may fall into the most exquisite arrangement, than to conceive that their ideas, in the great, universal mind, from a like internal, unknown cause, fall into that arrangement. The equal possibility of both these suppositions is allowed. But by experience we find (according to Cleanthes), that there is a difference between them. Throw several pieces of steel together, without shape or form; they will never arrange themselves so as to compose a watch: Stone, and mortar, and wood, without an architect, never erect a

house. But the ideas in a human mind, we see, by an unknown, inexplicable œconomy, arrange themselves so as to form the plan of a watch or house. Experience, therefore, proves, that there is an original principle of order in mind, not in matter. From similar effects we infer similar causes. The adjustment of means to ends is alike in the universe, as in a machine of human contrivance. The causes, therefore, must be resembling.

I was from the beginning scandalised, I must own, with this resemblance, which is asserted, between the Deity and human creatures; and must conceive it to imply such a degradation of the Supreme Being as no sound Theist could endure. With your assistance, therefore, Demea, I shall endeavour to defend what you justly called the adorable mysteriousness of the Divine Nature, and shall refute this reasoning of Cleanthes, provided he allows, that I have made a fair representation of it.

When Cleanthes had assented, Philo, after a short pause, proceeded in the following manner.

That all inferences, Cleanthes, concerning fact, are founded on experience, and that all experimental reasonings are founded on the supposition, that similar causes prove similar effects, and similar effects similar causes; I shall not, at present, much dispute with you. But observe, I entreat you, with what extreme caution all just reasoners proceed in the transferring of experiments to similar cases. Unless the cases be exactly similar, they repose no perfect confidence in applying their past observation to any particular phenomenon. Every alteration of circumstances occasions a doubt concerning the event; and it requires new experiments to prove certainly, that the new circumstances are of no moment or importance. A change in bulk, situation, arrangement, age, disposition of the air, or surrounding bodies; any of these particulars may be attended with the most unexpected consequences: And unless the objects be quite familiar to us, it is the highest temerity to expect with assurance, after any of these changes, an event similar to that which before fell under our observation. The slow and deliberate steps of philosophers, here, if any where, are distinguished from the precipitate march of the vulgar, who, hurried on by the smallest similitudes, are incapable of all discernment or consideration.

But can you think, Cleanthes, that your usual phlegm and philosophy have been preserved in so wide a step as you have taken, when you compared to the universe, houses, ships, furniture, machines; and from their similarity in some circumstances inferred a similarity in their causes? Thought, design, intelligence, such as we discover in men and other animals, is no more than one of the springs and principles of the universe, as well as heat or cold, attraction or repulsion, and a hundred others, which fall under daily observation. It is an active cause, by which some particular parts of nature, we find, produce alterations on other parts. But can a conclusion, with any propriety, be transferred from parts to the whole? Does not the great disproportion bar all comparison and inference? From observing the growth of a hair, can we learn any thing concerning the generation of a man? Would the manner of a leaf's blowing, even though perfectly known, afford us any instruction concerning the vegetation of a tree?

But allowing that we were to take the *operations* of one part of nature upon another for the foundation of our judgment concerning the *origin* of the whole (which never can be admitted), yet why select so minute, so weak, so bounded a principle as the reason and design of animals is found to be upon this planet? What peculiar privilege has this little agitation of the brain which we call *thought*, that we must thus make it the model of the whole universe? Our partiality in our own favour does indeed present it on all occasions; but sound philosophy ought carefully to guard against so natural an illusion.

So far from admitting, continued Philo, that the operations of a part can afford us any just conclusion concerning the origin of the whole, I will not allow any one part to form a rule for another part, if the latter be very remote from the former. Is there any reasonable ground to conclude, that the inhabitants of other planets possess thought, intelligence, reason, or any thing similar to these faculties in men? When Nature has so extremely diversified her manner of operation in this small globe; can we imagine, that she incessantly copies herself throughout so immense a universe? And if thought, as we may well suppose, be confined merely to this narrow corner, and has even there so limited a sphere of action; with what propriety can we assign it for the original cause of all things? The narrow views of a peasant, who makes his domestic œconomy the rule for the government of kingdoms, is in comparison a pardonable sophism.

But were we ever so much assured, that a thought and reason, resembling the human, were to be found throughout the whole universe, and were its activity elsewhere vastly greater and more commanding than it appears in this globe; yet I cannot see, why the operations of a world, constituted, arranged, adjusted, can with any propriety be extended to a world, which is in its embryo-state, and is advancing towards that constitution and arrangement. By observation, we know somewhat of the œconomy, action, and nourishment of a finished animal; but we must transfer with great caution that observation to the growth of a fœtus in the womb, and still more, to the formation of an animalcule in the loins of its male parent. Nature, we find, even from our limited experience, possesses an infinite number of springs and principles, which incessantly discover themselves on every change of her position and situation. And what new and unknown principles would actuate her in so new and unknown a situation as that of the formation of a universe, we cannot, without the utmost temerity, pretend to determine.

A very small part of this great system, during a very short time, is very imperfectly discovered to us: and do we thence pronounce decisively concerning the origin of the whole?

Admirable conclusion! Stone, wood, brick, iron, brass, have not, at this time, in this minute globe of earth, an order or arrangement without human art and contrivance: therefore the universe could not originally attain its order and arrangement, without something similar to human art. But is a part of nature a rule for another part very wide of the former? Is it a rule for the whole? Is a very small part a rule for the universe? Is nature in one situation, a certain rule for nature in another situation, vastly different from the former?

And can you blame me, Cleanthes, if I here imitate the prudent reserve of Simonides, who, according to the noted story, being asked by Hiero, *What God was?* desired a day to think of it, and then two days more; and after that manner continually prolonged the term, without ever bringing in his definition or description? Could you even blame me, if I had answered at first *that I did not know*, and was sensible that this subject lay vastly beyond the reach of my faculties? You might cry out sceptic and rallier as much as you pleased: but having found, in so many other subjects, much more familiar, the imperfections and even contradictions of human reason, I never should expect any success from its feeble conjectures, in a subject, so sublime, and so remote from the sphere of our observation. When two *species* of objects have always been observed to be conjoined together, I can *infer*, by custom, the existence of one wherever I *see* the existence of the other: and this I call an argument from experience. But how this argument can have place, where the objects, as in the present case, are single, individual, without parallel, or specific resemblance, may be difficult to explain. And will any man tell me with a serious countenance, that an orderly universe must arise from some thought and art, like the human; because we have experience of it? To ascertain this reasoning, it were requisite, that we had experience of the origin of worlds; and it is not sufficient surely, that we have seen ships and cities arise from human art and contrivance...

Philo was proceeding in this vehement manner, somewhat between jest and earnest, as it appeared to me; when he observed some signs of impatience in Cleanthes, and then immediately stopped short. What I had to suggest, said Cleanthes, is only that you would not abuse terms, or make use of popular expressions to subvert philosophical reasonings. You know, that the vulgar often distinguish reason from experience, even where the question relates only to matter of fact and existence; though it is found, where that *reason* is properly analysed, that it is nothing but a species of experience. To prove by experience the origin of the universe from mind is not more contrary to common speech than to prove the motion of the earth from the same principle. And a caviller might raise all the same objections to the Copernican system, which you have urged against my reasonings. Have you other earths, might he say, which you have seen to move? Have ...

Yes! cried Philo, interrupting him, we have other earths. Is not the moon another earth, which we see to turn round its centre? Is not Venus another earth, where we observe the same phenomenon? Are not the revolutions of the sun also a confirmation, from analogy, of the same theory? All the planets, are they not earths, which revolve about the sun? Are not the satellites moons, which move round Jupiter and Saturn, and along with these primary planets, round the sun? These analogies and resemblances, with others, which I have not mentioned, are the sole proofs of the Copernican system: and to you it belongs to consider, whether you have any analogies of the same kind to support your theory.

In reality, Cleanthes, continued he, the modern system of astronomy is now so much received by all inquirers, and has become so essential a part even of our earliest education, that we are not commonly very scrupulous in examining the reasons upon which it is founded. It is now become a matter of mere curiosity to study the first writers on that subject, who had the full force of prejudice to encounter, and were obliged to turn their arguments on every side, in order to render them popular and convincing. But if we peruse Galilæo's famous Dialogues concerning the system of the world, we shall find, that that great genius, one of the sublimest that ever existed, first bent all his endeavours to prove, that there was no foundation for the distinction commonly made between elementary and celestial substances. The schools, proceeding from the illusions of sense, had carried this distinction very far; and had established the latter substances to be ingenerable, incorruptible, unalterable, impassable; and had assigned all the opposite qualities to the former. But Galilæo, beginning with the moon, proved its similarity in every particular to the earth; its convex figure, its natural darkness when not illuminated, its density, its distinction into solid and liquid, the variations of its phases, the mutual illuminations of the earth and moon, their mutual eclipses, the inequalities of the lunar surface, etc. After many instances of this kind, with regard to all the planets, men plainly saw, that these bodies became proper objects of ex-

perience; and that the similarity of their nature enabled us to extend the same arguments and phenomena from one to the other.

In this cautious proceeding of the astronomers, you may read your own condemnation, Cleanthes; or rather may see, that the subject in which you are engaged exceeds all human reason and inquiry. Can you pretend to show any such similarity between the fabric of a house, and the generation of a universe? Have you ever seen nature in any such situation as resembles the first arrangement of the elements? Have worlds ever been formed under your eye? and have you had leisure to observe the whole progress of the phenomenon, from the first appearance of order to its final consummation? If you have, then cite your experience, and deliver your theory.

Religion versus the "religious"

John Dewey (1859-1952)

Educated at the University of Vermont and at Johns Hopkins University, Dewey taught at the University of Michigan and the University of Chicago before going to Columbia University, where he remained from 1904 to 1929. A prolific writer, whose interests extended into many fields, Dewey has had a great impact on contemporary philosophy as well as on educational, psychological, and social theory. While at the University of Chicago he organized and directed the Laboratory School, in which his educational theories were put to the test of practice.

A developer of the philosophy known as "pragmatism," Dewey was profoundly concerned with the nature and use of human intelligence. His numerous writings probe the condition of man within nature and society.

Dewey was deeply devoted to the practice of democratic liberalism and called for a reconstruction of philosophic conceptions in logic, morals, and social thought in line with the spirit of investigation in the sciences. In the present selection from his Terry Lectures at Yale University, he tries to extend his conception of "experience" to the religious sphere, distinguishing between "religion, a religion, and the religious." He urges the emancipation of the religious from the supernatural and the recognition of the possibilities for a common faith inherent in the religious phase of experience.

Never before in history has mankind been so much of two minds, so divided into two camps, as it is today. Religions have traditionally been allied with ideas of the supernatural, and often have been based upon explicit beliefs about it. Today there are many who hold that nothing worthy of being called religious is possible apart from the supernatural. Those who hold this belief differ in many respects. They range from those who accept the dogmas and sacraments of the Greek and Roman Catholic church as the only sure means of access to the supernatural to the theist or mild deist. Between them are the many Protestant denominations who think the Scriptures, aided by a pure conscience, are adequate avenues to supernatural truth and power. But they agree in one point: the necessity for a Supernatural Being and for an immortality that is beyond the power of nature.

The opposed group consists of those who think the advance of culture and science has completely discredited the supernatural and with it all religions that were allied with belief in it. But they go beyond this point. The extremists in this group believe that with elimination of the supernatural not only must historic religions be dismissed but with them everything of a religious nature. When historical knowledge has discredited the claims made for the supernatural character of the persons said to have founded historic religions; **115**

From John Dewey, *A Common Faith*, Lect. I. Copyright, 1934, by Yale University Press. Used by permission.

when the supernatural inspiration attributed to literatures held sacred has been riddled, and when anthropological and psychological knowledge has disclosed the all-too-human source from which religious beliefs and practices have sprung, everything religious must, they say, also go.

There is one idea held in common by these two opposite groups: identification of the religious with the supernatural. The question I shall raise in these chapters concerns the ground for and the consequences of this identification: its reasons and its value. In the discussion I shall develop another conception of the nature of the religious phase of experience, one that separates it from the supernatural and the things that have grown up about it. I shall try to show that these derivations are encumbrances and that what is genuinely religious will undergo an emancipation when it is relieved from them; that then, for the first time, the religious aspect of experience will be free to develop freely on its own account.

This view is exposed to attack from both the other camps. It goes contrary to traditional religions, including those that have the greatest hold upon the religiously minded today. The view announced will seem to them to cut the vital nerve of the religious element itself in taking away the basis upon which traditional religions and institutions have been founded. From the other side, the position I am taking seems like a timid halfway position, a concession and compromise unworthy of thought that is thoroughgoing. It is regarded as a view entertained from mere tendermindedness, as an emotional hangover from childhood indoctrination, or even as a manifestation of a desire to avoid disapproval and curry favor.

The heart of my point, as far as I shall develop it in this first section, is that there is a difference between religion, *a* religion, and the religious; between anything that may be denoted by a noun substantive and the quality of experience that is designated by an adjective. It is not easy to find a definition of religion in the substantive sense that wins general acceptance. However, in the *Oxford Dictionary* I find the following: "Recognition on the part

of man of some unseen higher power as having control of his destiny and as being entitled to obedience, reverence and worship."

This particular definition is less explicit in assertion of the supernatural character of the higher unseen power than are others that might be cited. It is, however, surcharged with implications having their source in ideas connected with the belief in the supernatural, characteristic of historic religions. Let us suppose that one familiar with the history of religions, including those called primitive, compares the definition with the variety of known facts and by means of the comparison sets out to determine just what the definition means. I think he will be struck by three facts that reduce the terms of the definition to such a low common denominator that little meaning is left.

He will note that the "unseen powers" referred to have been conceived in a multitude of incompatible ways. Eliminating the differences, nothing is left beyond the bare reference to something unseen and powerful. This has been conceived as the vague and undefined Mana of the Melanesians; the Kami of primitive Shintoism; the fetish of the Africans; spirits, having some human properties, that pervade natural places and animate natural forces; the ultimate and impersonal principle of Buddhism; the unmoved mover of Greek thought; the gods and semi-divine heroes of the Greek and Roman Pantheons; the personal and loving Providence of Christianity, omnipotent, and limited by a corresponding evil power; the arbitrary Will of Moslemism; the supreme legislator and judge of deism. And these are but a few of the outstanding varieties of ways in which the invisible power has been conceived.

There is no greater similarity in the ways in which obedience and reverence have been expressed. There has been worship of animals, of ghosts, of ancestors, phallic worship, as well as of a Being of dread power and of love and wisdom. Reverence has been expressed in the human sacrifices of the Peruvians and Aztecs; the sexual orgies of some Oriental religions; exorcisms and ablutions; the offering of the humble and contrite mind of the Hebrew prophet, the elaborate rituals of the Greek and Roman Churches. Not even sacrifice has been uniform; it is highly sublimated in Protestant denominations and in Moslemism. Where it has existed it has taken all kinds of forms and been directed to a great variety of powers and spirits. It has been used for expiation, for propitiation and for buying special favors. There is no conceivable purpose for which rites have not been employed.

Finally, there is no discernible unity in the moral motivations appealed to and utilized. They have been as far apart as fear of lasting torture, hope of enduring bliss in which sexual enjoyment has sometimes been a conspicuous element; mortification of the flesh and extreme asceticism; prostitution and chastity; wars to extirpate the unbeliever; persecution to convert or punish the unbeliever, and philanthropic zeal; servile acceptance of imposed dogma, along with brotherly love and aspiration for a reign of justice among men.

I have, of course, mentioned only a sparse number of the facts which fill volumes in any well-stocked library. It may be asked by those who do not like to look upon the darker side of the history of religions why the darker facts should be brought up. We all know that civilized man has a background of bestiality and superstition and that these elements are still with us. Indeed, have not some religions, including the most influential forms of Christianity, taught that the heart of man is totally corrupt? How could the course of religion in its entire sweep not be marked by practices that are shameful in their cruelty and lustfulness, and by beliefs that are degraded and intellectually incredible? What else than what we find could be expected, in the case of people having little knowledge and no secure method of knowing; with primitive institutions, and with so little control of natural forces that they lived in a constant state of fear?

I gladly admit that historic religions have been relative to the conditions of social culture in which peoples lived. Indeed, what I am concerned with is to press home the logic of this method of disposal of outgrown traits of past religions. Beliefs and practices in a religion that now prevails are by this logic relative to the present state of culture. If so much flexibility has obtained in the past regarding an unseen power, the way it affects human destiny, and the attitudes we are to take toward it, why should it be assumed that change in conception and action has now come to an end? The logic involved in getting rid of inconvenient aspects of past religions compels us to inquire how much in religions now accepted are survivals from outgrown cultures. It compels us to ask what conception of unseen powers and our relations to them would be consonant with the best achievements and aspirations of the present. It demands that in imagination we wipe the slate clean and start afresh by asking what would be the idea of the unseen, of the manner of its control over us and the ways in which reverence and obedience would be manifested, if whatever is basically religious in experience had the opportunity to express itself free from all historic encumbrances.

So we return to the elements of the definition that has been given. What boots it to accept, in defense of the universality of religion, a definition that applies equally to the most savage and degraded beliefs and practices that have related to unseen powers and to noble ideals of a religion having the greatest share of moral content? There are two points involved. One of them is that there is nothing left worth preserving in the notions of unseen powers, controlling human destiny to which obedience, reverence and worship are due, if we glide silently over the nature that has been attributed to the powers, the radically diverse ways in which they have been supposed to control human destiny, and in which submission and awe have been manifested. The other point is that when we begin to select, to choose, and say that some present ways of thinking about the unseen powers are better than others; that the reverence shown by a free and self-respecting human being is better than the servile obedience rendered to an arbitrary power by frightened men; that we should believe that control of human destiny is exercised by a wise and loving spirit rather than by madcap ghosts or sheer force—when I say, we begin to choose, we have entered upon a road that has not yet come to an end. We have reached a point that invites us to proceed farther.

For we are forced to acknowledge that concretely there is no such thing as religion in the singular. There is only a multitude of religions. "Religion" is a strictly collective term and the collection it stands for is not even of the kind illustrated in textbooks of logic. It has not the unity of a regiment or assembly but that of any miscellaneous aggregate. Attempts to prove the universality prove too much or too little. It is probable that religions have been universal in the sense that all the peoples we know anything about have had *a* religion. But the differences among them are so great and so shocking that any common element that can be extracted is meaningless. The idea that religion is universal proves too little in that the older apologists for Christianity seem to have been better advised than some modern ones in condemning every religion but one as an impostor, as at bottom some kind of demon worship or at any rate a superstitious figment. Choice among religions is imperative, and the necessity for choice leaves nothing of any force in the argument from universality. Moreover, when once we enter upon the road of choice, there is at once presented a possibility not yet generally realized.

For the historic increase of the ethical and ideal content of religions suggests that the process of purification may be carried further. It indicates that further choice is imminent in which certain values and functions in experience may be selected. This possibility is what I had in mind in speaking of the difference between the religious and a religion. I am not proposing a religion, but rather the emancipation of elements and outlooks that may be called religious. For the moment we have a religion, whether that of the Sioux Indian or of Judaism or of Christianity, that moment the ideal factors in experience that may be called religious take on a load that is not inherent in them, a load of current beliefs and of institutional practices that are irrelevant to them.

I can illustrate what I mean by a common phenomenon in contemporary life. It is widely supposed that a person who does not accept any religion is thereby shown to be a non-religious person. Yet it is conceivable that the present depression in religion is closely connected with the fact that religions now prevent, because of their weight of historic encumbrances, the religious quality of experience from coming to consciousness and finding the expression that is appropriate to present conditions, intellectual and moral. I believe that such is the case. I believe that many persons are so repelled from what exists as a religion by its intellectual and moral implications, that they are not even aware of attitudes in themselves that if they came to fruition would be genuinely religious. I hope that this remark may help make clear what I mean by the distinction between "religion" as a noun substantive and "religious" as adjectival.

To be somewhat more explicit, a religion (and as I have just said there is no such thing as religion in general) always signifies a special body of beliefs and practices having some kind of institutional organization, loose or tight. In contrast, the adjective "religious" denotes nothing in the way of a specifiable entity, either institutional or as a system of beliefs. It does not denote anything to which one can specifically point as one can point to this and that historic religion or existing church. For it does not denote anything that can exist by itself or that can be organized into a particular and distinctive form of existence. It denotes attitudes that may be taken toward every object and every proposed end or ideal. . . .

With increase of mechanisms of control, the element of fear has, relatively speaking, subsided. Some optimistic souls have even concluded that the forces about us are on the whole essentially benign. But every crisis, whether of the individual or of the community, reminds man of the precarious and partial nature of the control he exercises. When man, individually and collectively, has done his uttermost, conditions that at different times and places have given rise to the ideas of Fate and Fortune, of Chance and Providence, remain. It is the part of manliness to insist upon the capacity of mankind to strive to direct natural and social forces to humane ends. But unqualified absolutistic statements about the omnipotence of such endeavors reflect egoism rather than intelligent courage.

The fact that human destiny is so interwoven with forces beyond human control renders it unnecessary to suppose that dependence and the humility that accompanies it have to find the particular channel that is prescribed by traditional doctrines. What is especially significant is rather the form which the sense of dependence takes. Fear never gave stable perspective in the life of anyone. It is dispersive and withdrawing. Most religions have in fact added rites of communion to those of expiation and propitiation. For our dependence is manifested in those relations to the environment that support our undertakings and aspirations as much as it is in the defeats inflicted upon us. The essentially unreligious attitude is that which attributes human achievement and purpose to man in isolation from the world of physical nature and his fellows. Our successes are dependent upon the coöperation of nature. The sense of the dignity of human nature is as religious as is the sense of awe and reverence when it rests upon a sense of human nature as a coöperating part of a larger whole. Natural piety is not of necessity either a fatalistic acquiescence in natural happenings or a romantic idealization of the world. It may rest upon a just sense of nature as the whole of which we are parts, while it also recognizes that we are parts that are marked by intelligence and purpose, having the capacity to strive by their aid to bring conditions into greater consonance with what is humanly desirable. Such piety is an inherent constituent of a just perspective in life.

Understanding and knowledge also enter into a perspective that is religious in quality. Faith in the continued disclosing of truth through directed coöperative human endeavor is more religious in quality than is any faith in a completed revelation. It is of course now usual to hold that revelation is not completed in the sense of being ended. But religions hold that the essential framework is settled in its significant moral features at least, and that new elements that are offered must be judged by conformity to this framework. Some fixed doctrinal apparatus is necessary for *a* religion. But faith in the possibilities of continued and rigorous inquiry does not limit access to truth to any channel or scheme of things. It does not first say that truth is universal and then add there is but one road to it. It does not depend for assurance upon subjection to any dogma or item of doctrine. It trusts that the natural interactions between man and his environment will breed more intelligence and generate more knowledge provided the scientific methods that define intelligence in operation are pushed further into the mysteries of the world, being themselves promoted and improved in the operation. There is such a thing as faith in intelligence becoming religious in quality—a fact that perhaps explains the efforts of some religionists to disparage the possibilities of intelligence as a force. They properly feel such faith to be a dangerous rival.

Lives that are consciously inspired by loyalty to such ideals as have been mentioned are still comparatively infrequent to the extent of that comprehensiveness and intensity which arouse an ardor religious in function. But before we infer the incompetency of such ideals and of the actions they inspire, we should at least ask ourselves how much of the existing situation is due to the fact that the religious factors of experience have been drafted into supernatural channels and thereby loaded with irrelevant encumbrances. A body of beliefs and practices that are apart from the common and natural relations of mankind must, in the degree in which it is influential, weaken and sap the force of the possibilities inherent in such relations. Here lies one aspect of the emancipation of the religious from religion.

Any activity pursued in behalf of an ideal end against obstacles and in spite of threats of personal loss because of conviction of its general and enduring value is religious in quality. Many a person, inquirer, artist, philanthropist, citizen, men and women in the humblest walks of life, have achieved, without presumption and without display, such unification of themselves and of their relations to the conditions of existence. It remains to extend their spirit and inspiration to ever wider numbers. If I have said anything about religions and religion that seems harsh, I have said those things because of a firm belief that the claim on the part of religions to possess a monopoly of ideals and of the supernatural means by which alone, it is alleged, they can be furthered, stands in the way of the realization of distinctively religious values inherent in natural experience.

For that reason, if for no other, I should be sorry if any were misled by the frequency with which I have employed the adjective "religious" to conceive of what I have said as a disguised apology for what have passed as religions. The opposition between religious values as I conceive them and religions is not to be bridged. Just because the release of these values is so important, their identification with the creeds and cults of religions must be dissolved.

Religion and secular culture

Paul Tillich (1886-1965)

Tillich was already well known in Germany as a social thinker when he was forced to flee the Nazis. He is now generally recognized as the leading Protestant theologian in the United States and one of the foremost spokesmen in the world for "liberal" Protestantism. He had taught at Union Theological Seminary and at Harvard, where he had been University Professor.

Influenced by existentialism and by modern studies of symbolism, Tillich is especially noted for his three-volume Systematic Theology *(1951–1963). In his books, lectures, and sermons he has developed his conception of what he calls "ultimate concern." His Terry Lectures, entitled* The Courage To Be *(1952), deal with the problem of existential dread and meaninglessness.*

In the following selection, originally a lecture given in 1946 at the University of Chicago, Tillich discusses his conception of a "theonomous" culture, in which man's religious life and cutural life spring from one ground and are indissolubly united. Tillich also discusses his view of religion as man's ultimate concern and examines the nature of religious symbols.

Introduction

The technical problem of a lecture on religion and secular culture is the implicit demand to give in one paper the content of at least two volumes, namely, that of a philosophy of religion and that of a philosophy of culture. Since this cannot be done except in terms of an abstract and unconvincing summary, I intend to limit myself to one central concept, namely, that of a "theonomous" culture, and to develop this concept in a kind of autobiographical retrospect from the end of the first World War to the end of the second, adding some systematic analyses of the theonomous character of symbols.

Reprinted from *The Protestant Era,* by Paul Tillich, by permission of The University of Chicago Press. Copyright 1948 by The University of Chicago Press.

I

When we returned from the first World War, we found a deep gap between the cultural revolution and the religious tradition in central and eastern Europe. The Lutheran and the Roman and Greek Catholic churches rejected the cultural and—with some exceptions on the part of Roman Catholicism—the political revolutions. They rejected them as the rebellious expression of a secular autonomy. The revolutionary movements, on the other hand, repudiated the churches as the expression of a transcendent heteronomy. It was very obvious to those of us who had spiritual ties with both sides that this situation was intolerable and, in the long run, disastrous for religion as well as for culture. We believed that it was possible to close the gap, partly by creating movements such as religious socialism, partly by a fresh **121** interpretation of the mutual immanence of religion and culture within each other. History, however, has shown that it was too late for such an attempt to be successful at that time. It proved impossible to break down the secular ideology and the mechanistic (non-Marxist) materialism of the labor parties. The Old Guard prevailed against us and against the youth of their own movement. In the religious realm not only the conservative representatives of "ruling-class Christianity" (the European counterpart to American "suburban Christianity") ostracized us; we were also attacked by that dynamic theology which in this country is called "neo-orthodoxy" and which united prophetic powers with a non-prophetic detachment from culture, thus confirming and deepening the gap. Our attempt was frustrated; but we did not and do not accept defeat in so far as the truth of our conception is concerned; for we do not accept the idea, which a consistent pragmatism can hardly avoid, that victory is a method of pragmatic verification.

The first of my attempts to analyze the mutual immanence of religion and culture was made in a lecture which I read in Berlin immediately after the end of the war, entitled "The Idea of a Theology of Culture." It was written with the enthusiasm of those years in which we believed that a new beginning, a period of radical transformation, a fulfilment of time, or, as we call it with a New Testament term, a kairos had come upon us, in spite of breakdown and misery. We did *not*, however, share the feeling of many American religious and secular humanists of the twenties; we did *not* believe that the Kingdom of God, consisting in peace, justice, and democracy, had been established. Very early we saw those demonic structures of reality which during the past months have been recognized by all thoughtful people in this country. But we also saw a new chance, a moment pregnant with creative possibilities. The breakdown of bourgeois civilization in central and eastern Europe could pave the way for a reunion of religion and secular culture. That was what we hoped for and what religious socialism fought for, and to it we tried to give a philosophical and

theological basis. The idea of a "theonomous culture" seemed to be adequate for this aim; it became the principle of philosophies of religion and of culture which proposed to fill the gap from both sides.

The churches had rejected the secularized autonomy of modern culture; the revolutionary movements had rejected the transcendent heteronomy of the churches. Both had rejected something from which, in the last analysis, they themselves lived; and this something is theonomy. The words "autonomy," "heteronomy," and "theonomy" answer the question of the *nomos* or the law of life in three different ways: Autonomy asserts that man as the bearer of universal reason is the source and measure of culture and religion—that he is his own law. Heteronomy asserts that man, being unable to act according to universal reason, must be subjected to a law, strange and superior to him. Theonomy asserts that the superior law is, at the same time, the innermost law of man himself, rooted in the divine ground which is man's own ground: the law of life transcends man, although it is, at the same time, his own. Applying these concepts to the relation between religion and culture, we called an autonomous culture the attempt to create the forms of personal and social life without any reference to something ultimate and unconditional, following only the demands of theoretical and practical rationality. A heteronomous culture, on the other hand, subjects the forms and laws of thinking and acting to authoritative criteria of an ecclesiastical religion or a political quasi-religion, even at the price of destroying the structures of rationality. A theonomous culture expresses in its creations an ultimate concern and a transcending meaning not as something strange but as its own spiritual ground. "Religion is the substance of culture and culture the form of religion." This was the most precise statement of theonomy.

With these distinctions it was possible to create a theonomous analysis of culture, a "theology of culture," so to speak, which shows its theonomous ground not only where it is clearly indicated, as in the archaic periods of the great cultures and the early and high Middle Ages of our Western civilization, but also in those periods in which heteronomy was victorious, as in the later Middle Ages and in Arabic and Protestant orthodoxy, and even in autonomous or secular epochs, such as classical Greece, the Renaissance, the Enlightenment, and the nineteenth century. No cultural creation can hide its religious ground or its rational formation. Against ecclesiastical heteronomy it is always possible to show that all the rites, doctrines, institutions, and symbols of a religious system constitute a religious culture which is derived from the surrounding general culture—from its social and economic structure, its character traits, its opinions and philosophy, its linguistic and artistic expressions, its complexes, its traumas, and its longings. It is possible to show that, if such a special religious culture be imposed on dissenters or foreign cultures, it is not the ultimate, with its justified claim to grasp the hearts of men, but something provisional and conditioned which uses the religious ultimacy for *its* claims. The Thomistic philosophy, as well as the Protestant ideal of personality, is a transitory form of religious culture, but neither has any claim to ultimacy and finality; and the same holds true of the Greek concepts in the dogma of the church, of the feudal pattern of the Roman hierarchy, of the patriarchalistic ethics of Lutheranism, of the democratic ideals of sectarian Protestantism, and even of the cultural traditions which, for instance, are embodied in the biblical language and world view. Theonomous thinking sides with autonomous criticism, if such forms of religious culture present themselves as absolutes.

But more important in our situation was and is the other task of a theonomous analysis of culture: to show that in the depth of every autonomous culture an ultimate concern, something unconditional and holy, is implied. It is the task of deciphering the style of an autonomous culture in all its characteristic expressions and of finding their hidden religious significance. This we did with all possible tools of historical research and comparative interpretation and empathic understanding and with a special effort in regard to such stages

of civilization as were utterly secular, as, for instance, the later nineteenth century. Autonomous culture is secularized in the degree to which it has lost its ultimate reference, its center of meaning, its spiritual substance. The Renaissance was a step toward autonomy, but still in the spiritual power of an unwasted medieval heritage. The Enlightenment quickly lost its Protestant and sectarian substance and became in some—though not in many—of its expressions completely secular. The later nineteenth century, with its subjection to the technical pattern of thought and action, shows the character of an extremely emptied and secularized autonomy in an advanced stage of disintegration. But even here the religious substance, a remnant of something ultimate, was noticeable and made the transitory existence of such a culture possible. However, more than in the disintegrating bourgeois autonomy, the religious reference was effective in the movements which protested—often with a prophetic passion—against this situation. Theonomous analysis was able to decipher puzzling experiences, such as the visionary destruction of bourgeois idealism and naturalism in art and literature by expressionism and surrealism; it was able to show the religious background of the rebellion of the vital and unconscious side of man's personality against the moral and intellectual tyranny of consciousness; it was able to interpret the quasi-religious, fanatical, and absolutistic character of the reactions of the twentieth century as against the nineteenth. It was able to do all this without special reference to organized religion, the churches being only a part of the whole picture, but with a decisive reference to the religious element which was and is hidden in all these antireligious and anti-Christian movements. In all of them there is an ultimate, unconditional, and all-determining concern, something absolutely serious and therefore holy, even if expressed in secular terms.

So the gap between religion and culture is filled: religion is more than a system of special symbols, rites, and emotions, directed toward a highest being; religion is ultimate concern; it is the state of being grasped by something unconditional, holy, absolute. As such it gives meaning, seriousness, and depth to all culture and creates out of the cultural material a religious culture of its own. The contrast between religion and culture is reduced to the duality of religious and secular culture with innumerable transitions between them. The revolutionary movements, for instance, represent an ultimate concern, a religious principle, hidden but effective within them. The Lutheran churches, for example, represent a special cultural period in which an ultimate concern, a religious principle, has embodied itself manifestly and directly. Both are religious and both are cultural at the same time. Why, then, the difference? The answer can only be that the Kingdom of God has not yet come, that God is not yet all in all, whatever this "not yet" may mean. Asked what the proof is for the fall of the world, I like to answer: religion itself, namely, a religious culture beside a secular culture, a temple beside a town hall, a Lord's Supper beside a daily supper, prayer beside work, meditation beside research, *caritas* beside *eros*. But although this duality can never be overcome in time, space, and history, it makes a difference whether the duality is deepened into a bridgeless gap, as in periods in which autonomy and heteronomy fight with each other, or whether the duality is recognized as something which should not be and which is overcome fragmentarily by anticipation, so to speak, in a theonomous period. The kairos which we believed to be at hand was the coming of a new theonomous age, conquering the destructive gap between religion and secular culture.

But history took another path, and the question of religion and culture cannot be answered simply in those terms. A new element has come into the picture, the experience of the "end." Something of it appeared after the first World War; but we did not feel it in its horrible depth and its incredible thoroughness. We looked at the beginning of the new more than at the end of the old. We did not realize the price that mankind has to pay for the coming of a new theonomy; we still believed in transitions without catastrophes. We did not see the

possibility of final catastrophes as the true prophets, the prophets of doom, announced them. Therefore, our theonomous interpretation of history had a slight tinge of romanticism, though it tried to avoid any kind of utopianism. This has come to an end because the end itself has appeared like a flash of lightning before our eyes; and not only among the ruins of central and eastern Europe but also within the abundance of this country has it been seen. While after the first World War the mood of a new beginning prevailed, after the second World War a mood of the end prevails. A present theology of culture is, above all, a theology of the end of culture, not in general terms but in a concrete analysis of the inner void of most of our cultural expressions. Little is left in our present civilization which does not indicate to a sensitive mind the presence of this vacuum, this lack of ultimacy and substantial power in language and education, in politics and philosophy, in the development of personalities, and in the life of communities. Who of us has never been shocked by this void when he has used traditional or untraditional secular or religious language to make himself understandable and has not succeeded and has then made a vow of silence to himself, only to break it a few hours later? This is symbolic of our whole civilization. Often one gets the impression that only those cultural creations have greatness in which the experience of the void is expressed; for it can be expressed powerfully only on the basis of a foundation which is deeper than culture, which is ultimate concern, even if it accepts the void, even in respect to religious culture. Where this happens, the vacuum of disintegration can become a vacuum out of which creation is possible, a "sacred void," so to speak, which brings a quality of waiting, of "not yet," of a being broken from above, into all our cultural creativity. It is not an empty criticism, however radical and justified such criticism may be. It is not an indulgence in paradoxes that prevents the coming-down to concreteness. It is not cynical detachment, with its ultimate spiritual dishonesty. It is simple cultural work out of, and qualified by, the experience of the sacred void.

This is the way—perhaps the only way—in which our time can reach a theonomous union between religion and culture.

One thing is clear: the experience of the end by no means undermines the idea of theonomy. On the contrary, it is its strongest confirmation. Two events may illustrate this. The first is the turn of Karl Barth from a theology of radical detachment from culture, religious as well as secular, to an equally radical attachment to the fight against a demonically distorted cultural system. Barth suddenly realized that culture can never be indifferent toward the ultimate. If it ceases to be theonomous, it first becomes empty, and then it falls, at least for a time, under demonic control. The demand for a merely matter-of-fact culture is dishonesty or illusion, and a catastrophic illusion at that. This leads to the second event to which I want to refer: the change of attitude toward culture in this country. It was truly symbolic for the collapse of our secular autonomy when the atom scientists raised their voices and preached the end, not unconditionally but with conditions of salvation which present-day humanity is hardly willing to fulfil. It was and is a symptom of a changed mood when some of these men and others with them, statesmen, educators, psychologists, physicians, sociologists, not to speak of artists and poets, whose visions anticipated our cultural predicament long ago—when these people cry for religion as the saving power of our culture. They do it often in the ugly and false phraseology which demands the undergirding of culture by religion, as if religion were a tool for a higher purpose. But even in this inadequate form the ideal of a theonomous culture is transparent.

II

After this historical and dialectical interpretation of the relation between religion and secular culture, I want to show the truth of the underlying assertion by analyzing some religious symbols and their significance for the cultural situation out of which they are taken. Religious symbols use a finite reality in order to express our relation to the infinite. But the finite reality they use is not an arbitrary means for an end, something strange to it; it participates in the power of the ultimate for which it stands. A religious symbol is double edged. It expresses not only what is symbolized but also that through which it is symbolized.

The terms for "salvation" in many languages are derived from roots like *salvus, saos*, whole, *heil*, which all designate health, the opposite of disintegration and disruption. Salvation is healing in the ultimate sense; it is final cosmic and individual healing. In such theonomous terminology the work of the physician stands symbolically for the ultimate restitution. But the decisive question is whether it stands so by chance or by inner necessity. If it is a symbol by chance, it can be replaced by any other symbol and is in reality not even a symbol but only a metaphor. This is the situation in a secularized culture, in which religious salvation and medical healing are separated. In a theonomous culture, healing is an expression of salvation and, consequently, can become a genuine symbol of the saving power of the ultimate. It is perhaps a symptom of the longing for a new theonomy that everywhere attempts at co-operation among ministers, physicians, and psychiatrists are being made.

Medieval historians know that the official welcome offered to princes, kings, and emperors by city authorities often was given in messianic terminology. Not this or that king was greeted but *the* king of peace, the messianic king. Now, it is obvious that the term "king," applied, for instance, to Yahweh or to his Messiah, is a symbol of something which infinitely transcends every human king. Nevertheless, the symbol is not arbitrary. The king is called by God. The grace that is upon him is divine grace. The symbol works in both directions. It gives the king—and that means the political realm—theonomous dignity; and it makes the kingship of God a genuine symbol. When the king became a functionary of an autonomous state, he became either a tyrant (and was removed) or a puppet without the power of religious symbolism. We use kingship still as a traditional, but no longer as a genuine, symbol.

The Christian church as the mystical body of Christ is a strictly theonomous symbol. It has meaning only so long as the organic unity, including a spiritual center, is seriously applied to human communities. In this case human relations have the character of a mutual edification on the basis of a common ultimate concern. "Body" is a genuine symbol and not an exchangeable metaphor. It lost its symbolic power when the church became a voluntary covenant of individuals and society became the realm of social contracts for preliminary purposes. The nineteenth-century philosophical and political organologists made a mistake when they tried to save the idea of the organic "body politic" without its theonomous foundation. And this is, generally speaking, the reason for the unavoidable frustration of all politics and ethics and philosophies of restoration. They try to re-establish theonomy on an autonomous foundation.

Personality is the most emphasized ideal of modern religious and secular humanism. Personality is considered as the most necessary symbol for God. God is even described as the person in whom all human perfections are perfectly embodied. In this case the disintegration of a symbol has occurred, and the result has been its large-scale removal. In classical theology, "person" was used only for the three principles in the divine life, not for God himself; and "personality" was not used at all in this connection. The idea of God in classical theology united personal with supra-personal traits. God was less and more than personal, as well as personal; he was the unity of all potentialities. In this sense personal symbolism could be applied to him on the basis of man's real existence, which unites prepersonal and postpersonal elements with personality. In the degree to which first Protestantism, then humanism, neglected the nonpersonal elements in man—his vital and mystical side—for the sake of consciousness, God became one person alongside others. He ceased to be the supporting and transcending center of every personal life. But as such he was superfluous, one more autonomous personality beside the others, although exceeding them in power and value.

The persons were left alone, centered in themselves and very soon unable to stand this situation of monadic loneliness. The symbol and, along with it, the reality from which it was taken disintegrated in mutual interdependence. When God became *a* person, man's personality was driven into neurotic disintegration.

In classical theology God is, first of all, Being as such. *Deus est esse.* Being in this sense is not the most abstract category, as a mistaken nominalism asserts; it is the power of Being in everything that is, in everything that participates in Being. So long as this is the basic statement about God, we are in a theonomous situation because it implies that every finite reality is rooted in the creative ground, in Being itself. Therefore, it is possible to find the traces of the ultimate in everything, and the scientific approach to Being is an approach to that which concerns us unconditionally. When Being lost its symbolic power under the influence of nominalism and when, more definitely in the second half of the Renaissance, Being became the object for a subject, to be calculated and controlled, God ceased to be Being itself and Being ceased to be divine. If today you say that God is Being, it sounds almost blasphemous. The consequence of this whole development was that science observed the relation of all beings to one another and the calculable rules of their behavior, but that it lost Being itself, its unity, its power, its meaning. Science had destroyed the unity of reality *before* it learned to split up any given structure of reality. Science openly confesses that it no longer has anything to do with Being, but only with equations. When Being as a symbol was lost, Being itself was lost. If it is denied that *Deus est esse, Deus* as well as *esse* is given up.

If God is called *ipsum esse*, Being itself, he can also, and must, be called *ipsum verum*, the true itself. But if God is a being beside others which may or may not exist, or a person beside others whom we may or may not discover, a statement like *Deus est veritas*, "God is truth," has no meaning. There is perhaps no point in the history of human thought at which the transition from theonomy to a cleavage between autonomous culture and heteronomous religion is more obvious and more clearly discussed than in this question. In a recent paper about the two types of philosophy of religion, I have tried to show how the first slight break in theonomous thinking occurred when Thomas Aquinas interpreted the Augustinian-Franciscan principle that God is truth (and, therefore, immediately certain more than anything else, including myself) in Aristotelian terms and said that God is immediately certain for himself but not for us. We need mediating discourse and ecclesiastical authority to reach him. This gap was deepened by Duns Scotus and made insuperable by the nominalists who in this, as in many other respects, opened the way toward a secular culture. If the statement that God is the true has itself lost its symbolic power, two consequences follow. The first one is that there is no truth about God in terms of the prius of all other truth, that the truth about God is secondary, and this necessarily leads to a secular world without God. The second consequence is that within this secular world the idea of truth is reduced to the realm of observable and, if possible, calcuable relations, while the truth about existence itself and its meaning for us is left to emotions and opinions, a situation most useful for the rise and victory of uncontrolled authorities. Being and truth are lost if they cannot be applied to God any more, and God is lost if Being is mere objectivity and truth mere subjectivity. The two-edged character of any symbol used for God is manifest even in concepts like "being" and "truth" which, if applied to God, unite a symbolic and a nonsymbolic element.

I want to close with a few words concerning that realm of culture which is not an independent realm but is the way of communicating all other realms to those who are to be shaped by them, namely, education. In doing so, I give, at the same time, homage to the genius of this place. The theonomous word for education is "initiation." While the word "education" points to the *terminus a quo*, the "where from," the word "initiation" points to the

terminus ad quem, the "where to." Secular culture has lost an ultimate and commanding *terminus ad quem*, because it has lost an ultimate and unconditional concern. In the Diotima speech in Plato's *Symposium* we see, still retained, the steps of initiation into the ultimate wisdom. And in his myth of the cave in the *Republic* we learn that the way to wisdom implies a radical transformation, a liberation from bondage and darkness. Such ideas presuppose that there is a level in life, the most and ultimately the *only* important one, which cannot be approached directly. It is the level of gnosis or *sapientia* or "wisdom," in distinction from the level of *episteme* or *scientia* or "science." It is the level of Being and truth as such before they split into subject and object; and, therefore, it has the character of a mystery. Everything which is merely object can be approached directly with scientific reasoning and technical tools. That which precedes mere objectivity needs initiation. Innumerable rites of initiation in all nations up to Christian baptism and confirmation show that mankind was conscious of the sacred depth in things which cannot be approached in ordinary ways. When the element of initiation was lost, education lost the *terminus ad quem* and is now desperately looking for it. But no abundance of highest possibility shown to the coming generations can replace something ultimate that is necessary. Are we able to show it to them by initiation as well as by education? We *cannot* do it today in terms of special contents, whether they be religious or secular. But we *can* do it by accepting the void which is the destiny of our period, by accepting it as a "sacred void" which may qualify and transform thinking and acting. I have not tried to present a well-balanced synthesis between religion and secular culture. I have tried to show their *one* theonomous root and the void which neccessarily has followed their separation, and perhaps something of the longing of our time for a new theonomy, for an ultimate concern in all our concerns.

The ethic of Jesus

Reinhold Niebuhr (b. 1892)

Born in Missouri, the son of a German Evangelical pastor, Niebuhr was educated at the Lutheran Theological Seminary in St. Louis and at Yale University. In 1915 he was assigned to a small church in Detroit, where he remained for thirteen years. During this pastorate he developed his own interpretation of Christianity, which he calls "prophetic Christianity." He became a strong advocate of the view that the church must be concerned with social and economic conditions and gained the respect both of members of organized labor groups and of intellectuals. His influence was strongly felt during the thirty years in which he was professor of Christian ethics at Union Theological Seminary in New York City. Among his most important works are Moral Man and Immoral Society *(1932)*, An Interpretation of Christian Ethics *(1935)*, The Nature and Destiny of Man *(1941–1943)*, and* Christianity and Power Politics *(1940)*.

In the following selection Niebuhr conducts a searching examination of the strict ethical requirements in the Gospels and seeks to understand their significance in relation to an ethic of prudence and the requirements of social order. His analysis stresses the different demands of a stable society of man and what he calls the "peace of the City of God."

The ethic of Jesus is the perfect fruit of prophetic religion. Its ideal of love has the same relation to the facts and necessities of human experience as the God of prophetic faith has to the world. It is drawn from, and relevant to, every moral experience. It is immanent in life as God is immanent in the world. It transcends the possibilities of human life in its final pinnacle as God transcends the world. It must, therefore, be confused neither with the ascetic ethic of world-denying religions nor with the prudential morality of naturalism, designed to guide good people to success and happiness in this world. It is easily confused with the former because of its un-

From *An Interpretation of Christian Ethics* by Reinhold Niebuhr. Copyright Harper & Brothers. Reprinted by permission of Harper & Row, Publishers, Incorporated.

compromising attitude toward all the impulses of nature; but it never condemns natural impulse as inherently bad. It may be confused with the latter because the transcendent character of its love ideal is implicit rather than explicit in the teachings of Jesus. The ethic proceeds logically from the presuppositions of prophetic religion. In prophetic religion God, as creator and judge of the world, is both the unity which is the ground of existence and the ultimate unity, the good which is, to use Plato's phrase, on the other side of existence. In as far as the world exists at all it is good; for existence is possible only when chaos is overcome by unity and order. But the unity of the world is threatened by chaos, and its meaningfulness is always under the peril of meaninglessness. The ultimate confidence in the meaningfulness of life, therefore, rests upon a faith in the final unity, which transcends the world's chaos as certainly as it is basic to the world's order....

The rigorism of the gospel ethic and its failure to make concessions to even the most inevitable and "natural" self-regarding impulses may best be judged by analyzing the attitude of Jesus toward various natural expressions of human life. Every form of self-assertion is scrutinized and condemned in words which allow of no misinterpretation.

The very basis of self-love is the natural will to survive. In man the animal impulse to maintain life becomes an immediate temptation to assert the self against the neighbor. Therefore, in the ethic of Jesus, concern for physical existence is prohibited: "Take no thought for your life, what ye shall eat, or what ye shall drink; nor yet for your body, what ye shall put on. Is not the life more than meat and the body more than raiment? Behold the fowls of the air: for they sow not, neither do they reap, nor gather into barns; yet your heavenly Father feedeth them. Are ye not much better than they? ... Therefore take no thought, saying, What shall we eat? or, What shall we drink? or, Wherewithall shall we be clothed? For after all these things do the Gentiles seek; for your heavenly Father knoweth that ye have need of all these things." The prudent conscience will have an immediately unfavorable reaction to these words. No life can be lived in such unconcern for the physical basis of life. Those who try to make the ethic of Jesus a guide to prudent conduct have, therefore, been anxious to point out that the naïve faith in God's providential care which underlies these injunctions had more relevance in the simple agrarian life of Palestine than in the economic complexities of modern urban existence. But it must be noted that they cannot be followed absolutely even in simple agrarian life. The fact is that this word contains a completely unprudential rigorism in the ethic of Jesus which appears again and again.

The most natural expansion of the self is the expansion through possessions. Therefore the love of possessions as a form of self-assertion meets the same uncompromising rigor. "Lay not up for yourselves treasures upon earth ... for where your treasure is, there will your heart be also.... No man can serve two masters.... Ye cannot serve God and mammon." Here the religious orientation of the ethic is perfectly clear. Love of possession is a distraction which makes love and obedience to God impossible. God demands absolute obedience. Thus the rich young ruler who has kept all the commandments is advised, "Go and sell that thou hast, and give to the poor." This word has been used to establish a basis for an ascetic ethic, but it probably was not meant as a rule in the thought of Jesus. It was meant rather as a test of complete devotion to the sovereignty of God. In the same manner the poor widow is praised above those who gave of their superfluity because she "gave all she had." Somewhat in the same category is the parable of the great supper from which some of the guests excluded themselves because of their preoccupation with the land or the oxen they had bought and the wife one had married. In all these instances the attitude toward wealth is not determined by any socio-moral considerations, but rather by the conviction that wealth is a source of distraction. The key to Jesus' attitude on wealth is most succinctly stated in the words, "Where your treasure is there will your heart be also."

The most penetrating analyses of the character of self-love are to be found in Jesus' excoriation of pride, particularly the pride of good people. Pride is a subtle form of self-love. It feeds not on the material advantages which more greedy people seek, but upon social approval. His strictures against the Pharisees were partly directed against their social pride. "All their works they do for to be seen of men ... and love the uppermost rooms at feasts and the chief seats in the synagogues and greetings in the markets and to be called of men, Rabbi, Rabbi." In the same spirit is the advice to dinner guests, at the house of one of the chief Pharisees "when he marked how they chose out the chief rooms." ... "But when thou art bidden, go and sit down in the lowest room.... For whosoever exalteth himself shall be abased: and he that humbleth himself shall be exalted." Incidentally in this case the subjection of egoistic pride is justified not only in religious terms, but in terms of prudential morality. It is pointed out that the effort of the proud to reach exalted positions in society actually results in a loss of respect, while humility leads to social approval: "When he that bade thee cometh, he may say unto thee, Friend, go up higher: then shalt thou have worship in the presence of them that sit at meat with thee." This note of prudence is somewhat at variance with the general more purely religious orientation of Jesus' ethic. The same emphasis is found in the words "Whosoever will be great among you, shall be your minister: and whosoever of you will be the chiefest, shall be the servant of all." Pride is the form of egoism which corrupts the spirits of all those who possess some excellency of knowledge or achievement which distinguishes them from the crowd, so that they forget their common humanity and their equal unworthiness in the sight of God. But the spiritual pride and self-righteousness which fails to detect the alloy of sin in the relative virtues achieved according to moral codes belongs in yet another category and must be dealt with separately.

Jesus' attitude toward vindictiveness and his injunction to forgive the enemy reveals more clearly than any other element in his ethic his intransigence against forms of self-assertion which have social and moral approval in any natural morality. Resentment against injustice is both the basis, and the egoistic corruption of, all forms of corrective justice. Every communal punishment of murder is a refinement of early customs of blood vengeance. The early community permitted and even encouraged blood vengeance because it felt that the destruction of life within the community was wrong; but it left punishment in the hands of a blood relative because the vindictive passion of the injured family was more potent than the community's more dispassionate disapproval of murder. From the first restraints upon blood vengeance to the last refinements of corrective justice, the egoistic element of vindictiveness remains both an

inevitable and a dangerous alloy in the passion for justice. It is inevitable because men never judge injustice so severely as it ought to be judged until their life, or life in their intimate circle, is destroyed by it. It is dangerous because, informed not by a passion for all life, but by attachment to a particular life, it may, and frequently does, do as much injury to life as it seeks to correct. But it remains inevitable however dangerous it may be. Self-assertion when the self is in peril or the victim of injustice expresses itself as a natural impulse even in persons who know its dangers and disapprove the logic which underlies it.

Neither its inevitability nor its moral or social justification in immediate situations qualifies the rigor of Jesus' position. Men are enjoined to "love their enemies," to "forgive, not seven times, but seventy times seven," to resist evil, to turn the other cheek, to go the second mile, to bless them that curse you and do good to them that hate you. In all these injunctions both resistance and resentment are forbidden. The self is not to assert its interests against those who encroach upon it, and not to resent the injustice done to it. The modern pulpit would be saved from much sentimentality if the thousands of sermons which are annually preached upon these texts would contain some suggestions of the impossibility of these ethical demands for natural man in his immediate situations. Nowhere is the ethic of Jesus in more obvious conflict with both the impulses and the necessities of ordinary men in typical social situations.

The justification for these demands is put in purely religious and not in socio-moral terms. We are to forgive because God forgives; we are to love our enemies because God is impartial in his love. The points of reference are vertical and not horizontal. Neither natural impulses nor social consequences are taken into consideration. It is always possible, of course, that absolute ethical attitudes have desirable social consequences. To do good to an enemy may prompt him to overcome his enmity; and forgiveness of evil may be a method of redemption which commends itself to the most prudent. It must be observed, however, that no appeal to social consequences could ever fully justify these demands of Jesus. Non-resistance may shame an aggressor into goodness, but it may also prompt him to further aggression. Furthermore, if the action is motivated by regard for social consequences it will hardly be pure enough to secure the consequences which are supposed to justify it. Upon that paradox all purely prudential morality is shattered. Therefore Jesus admonishes the disciples who rejoice that "the devils are subject unto us in thy name" not to rejoice in success—"rejoice not that the devils are subject unto you, but rather rejoice because your names are written in heaven." One might paraphrase that injunction as follows: Find your satisfaction not in the triumph over evil in existence, but rather in the conformity of your life to its ultimate essence. Jesus' attitude toward the woman taken in adultery and his confounding word to the self-righteous judges, "Let him who is without sin cast the first stone," shows the relation of his idea of contrition to that of forgiveness. We are to forgive those who wrong society not only because God forgives, but because we know that in the sight of God we also are sinners. This insight into, and emphasis upon, the sins of the righteous is derived from the religious perspective; but it has a very practical relevance to the problems of society. The society which punishes criminals is never so conscious as it might be of the degree to which it is tainted with, and responsible for, the very sins which it abhors and punishes. Yet an unqualified insistence upon guiltlessness as a prerequisite of the right to punish would invalidate every measure required for the maintenance of social order. It is, therefore, impossible to construct a socio-moral policy from this religio-moral insight of Jesus', as, for instance, Tolstoi attempted in his objection to jails and other forms of social punishment. Society must punish criminals, or at least quarantine them, even if the executors of judgment are self-righteous sinners who do not realize to what degree they are involved in the sins they seek to suppress. But this fact does not invalidate the insight which sees the relative good and the relative evil in both judges and criminals from a high perspective.

The effort to elaborate the religio-moral thought of Jesus into a practical socio-moral or even politico-moral system usually has the effect of blunting the very penetration of his moral insights. When, for instance, liberal Christianity defines the doctrine of non-resistance, so that it becomes merely an injunction against violence in conflict, it ceases to provide a perspective from which the sinful element in all resistance, conflict, and coercion may be discovered. Its application prompts moral complacency rather than contrition, and precisely in those groups in which the evils which flow from self-assertion are most covert. This is the pathos of the espousal of Christian pacifism by the liberal Church, ministering largely to those social groups who have the economic power to be able to dispense with the more violent forms of coercion and therefore condemn them as un-Christian.

The love absolutism in the ethic of Jesus expresses itself in terms of a universalism, set against all narrower forms of human sympathy, as well as in terms of a perfectionism which maintains a critical vigor against the most inevitable and subtle forms of self-assertion. The universalistic element appears in the injunctions which require that the life of the neighbor be affirmed beyond the bounds set by natural human sympathy. Love within the bounds of consanguinity and intimate community is regarded as devoid of special merit: "For if ye love them which love you, what thanks have ye? Do not even the publicans the same?" An all-embracing love is enjoined because God's love is like that. In Professor Torrey's recent translation of the four gospels, Matt. 5:48 is rendered in words which fit in perfectly with the general logic of Jesus' thought: "Be therefore all-including in your good-will, as your Heavenly Father includes all."

The universalism in Jesus' ethic has affinities with Stoic universalism, but there are also important differences between them. In Stoicism life beyond the narrow bonds of class, community, and race is to be affirmed because all life reveals a unifying divine principle. Since the divine principle is reason, the logic of Stoicism tends to include only the intelligent in the divine community. An aristocratic condescension, therefore, corrupts Stoic universalism. In the thought of Jesus men are to be loved not because they are equally divine, but because God loves them equally; and they are to be forgiven (the highest form of love) because all (the self included) are equally far from God and in need of his grace. This difference between Stoicism and the gospel ethic is important because it marks a real distinction between pantheism and prophetic religion. The ultimate moral demands upon man can never be affirmed in terms of the actual facts of human existence. They can be affirmed only in terms of a unity and a possibility, a divine reality which transcends human existence. The order of human existence is too imperiled by chaos, the goodness of man too corrupted by sin, and the possibilities of man too obscured by natural handicaps to make human order and human virtue and human possibilities solid bases of the moral imperative.

The universalistic note in the thought of Jesus is reinforced by his critical attitude toward the family. This attitude is particularly significant because he was not an ascetic in his family ethic. On the contrary, he had a sacramental conception of the family relation. Yet family loyalty is seen as a possible hindrance to a higher loyalty. When apprised of the presence of the members of his family he answers ruthlessly: "Who is my mother, or my brethren? . . . For whosoever shall do the will of God, the same is my brother, and my sister, and mother." In the same spirit is his advice to the young man who desired to withhold his discipleship until he could perform the last act of filial piety, "Let the dead bury the dead"; and also the uncompromising words "He that loveth father or mother more than me is not worthy of me" (given an even more ruthless form in Luke 14: 26, "If any man come to me, and hate not his father, and mother, and wife, and children, and brethren, and sisters, yea, and his own life also, he cannot be my disciple"). Surely this is not an ethic which can give us specific guidance in the detailed prob-

lems of social morality where the relative claims of family, community, class, and nation must be constantly weighed. One is almost inclined to agree with Karl Barth that this ethic "is not applicable to the problems of contemporary society nor yet to any conceivable society." It is oriented by only one vertical religious reference, to the will of God; and the will of God is defined in terms of all-inclusive love. Under the perspective of that will the realities of the world of human egoism, and the injustices and tyrannies arising from it, are fully revealed. We see the actual facts more clearly and realize that the world of nature is also a world of sin. But there is no advice on how we may hold the world of sin in check until the coming of the Kingdom of God. The ethic of Jesus may offer valuable insights to and sources of criticism for a prudential social ethic which deals with present realities; but no such social ethic can be directly derived from a pure religious ethic. . . .

The ethical demands made by Jesus are incapable of fulfillment in the present existence of man. They proceed from a transcendent and divine unity of essential reality, and their final fulfillment is possible only when God transmutes the present chaos of this world into its final unity. The logic of this thought is obviously under the influence of the later apocalypses of Jewish prophecy in which the hope for a "good time" and a "fulfilled time" becomes transmuted into the expectation of the end of time. These later apocalypses were the consequence of a logic inherent in the moral life, a logic which recognizes that the ultimate moral demands upon the human spirit proceed from a unity which transcends all conceivable possibilities in the order of nature and history in which human life moves. Placing the final fulfillment at the end of time and not in a realm above temporality is to remain true to the genius of prophetic religion and to state mythically what cannot be stated rationally. If stated rationally the world is divided between the temporal and the eternal and only the eternal forms above the flux of temporality have significance. To state the matter mythically is to do justice to the fact that the eternal can only be fulfilled in the temporal. But since myth is forced to state a paradoxical aspect of reality in terms of concepts connoting historical sequence, it always leads to historical illusions. Jesus, no less than Paul, was not free of these historical illusions. He expected the coming of the Messianic kingdom in his lifetime; at least that seems to have been his expectation before the crisis in his ministry. Even when he faced the cross rather than triumph he merely postponed the ultimate triumph to a later future, though to a rather proximate one.

Apocalypticism in terms of a specific interpretation of history may thus be regarded as the consequence and not the cause of Jesus' religion and ethic. The apocalypse is a mythical expression of the impossible possibility under which all human life stands. The Kingdom of God is always at hand in the sense that impossibilities are really possible, and lead to new actualities in given moments of history. Nevertheless every actuality of history reveals itself, after the event, as only an approximation of the ideal; and the Kingdom of God is therefore not here. It is in fact always coming but never here.

The historical illusions which resulted inevitably from this mythical statement of the situation in which the human spirit finds itself do not destroy the truth in the myth; no more than the discovery that the fall of man was not actual history destroys the mythical truth in the story of the fall. Nevertheless it must be admitted that the ethical rigor of the early church was maintained through the hope of the second coming of Christ and the establishment of his Kingdom. When the hope of the *parousia* waned the rigor of the Christian ethic was gradually dissipated and the Church, forced to come to terms with the relativities of politics and economics and the immediate necessities of life, made unnecessary compromises with these relativities which frequently imperiled the very genius of prophetic religion. But the mistakes which resulted, both from illusions about the course of history and from the adjustments which had to be made when the illusions vanished, do not invalidate the basic insights of prophetic religion. They merely present Christian ethics afresh with the problem of compromise, the problem of creating and maintaining tentative harmonies of life in the world in terms of the possibilities of the human situation, while yet at the same time preserving the indictment upon all human life of the impossible possibility, the law of love. . . .

The full dimension of human life includes not only an impossible ideal, but realities of sin and evil which are more than simple imperfections and which prove that the ideal is something more than the product of a morbidly sensitive religious fantasy. Anything less than perfect love in human life is destructive of life. All human life stands under an impending doom because it does not live by the law of love. Egoism is always destructive. The wages of sin is death. The destruction of our contemporary civilization through its injustice and through the clash of conflicting national wills is merely one aspect and one expression of the destruction of sin in the world.

Confronted with this situation humanity always faces a double task. The one is to reduce the anarchy of the world to some kind of immediately sufferable order and unity; and the other is to set these tentative and insecure unities and achievements under the criticism of the ultimate ideal. When they are not thus challenged, what is good in them becomes evil and each tentative harmony becomes the cause of a new anarchy. With Augustine we must realize that the peace of the world is gained by strife. That does not justify us either in rejecting such a tentative peace or in accepting it as final. The peace of the city of God can use and transmute the lesser and insecure peace of the city of the world; but that can be done only if the peace of the world is not confused with the ultimate peace of God.

Norms, Value, and Ethical Thought

PART III

We saw in the preceding part that religious thinkers have been occupied with aspects of human conduct. In this part our interest is in thinkers who do not assume the active presence of God in human affairs but attempt, by independent philosophic reflection, to arrive at conclusions about how human beings ought to act. Such thought is called philosophic ethics and is related to the moral judgments we make in everyday life. Many important philosophers have written works on the problems of ethics. In these works they have examined such concepts as good and evil, right and wrong, duty and obligation, reason and emotion, freedom and responsibility.

The field of ethics is said to be *normative* rather than *descriptive* because it is primarily concerned with what *ought* to be the case rather than with what *is* the case. Moral philosophers have formulated moral principles and sometimes specific rules for human conduct. It is the concern with standards or "norms" of conduct that distinguishes ethics from a descriptive study. Not all ethical writings, however, are purely normative. Purported description of human behavior or of the conditions for such behavior, has often been a part of ethical writings. Nevertheless, the key concepts of ethics, such as good, right, and duty, involve sentences using the normative terms "ought" and "should."

In our opening selection the Finnish philosopher, G. H. von Wright, helps us to see what sorts of things norms are, and what it means to speak of normative statements. He analyzes the use of these terms in "ordinary language" (see Part VII for descriptions of "ordinary-language" philosophy), and maintains that our understanding of the nature of moral principles depends on our seeing how they are related "to the other main types of norm and to the value-notions of good and evil."

He begins by distinguishing "description" from "prescription." The laws of nature are descriptive, but the laws of a state are prescriptive. Any statement that issues a command or prohibition or grants a permission is a prescription, and prescriptions form one of the main types of norm. Rules, such as the rules of a game or of English grammar, are another type of norm, and a third type consists of what von Wright calls "technical norms" or directives. These express necessary relationships between means and ends. He maintains that moral norms, with which ethical thought is concerned, fall somewhere between these main types and are related to them but are not exactly equivalent to any of them.

Von Wright's analysis should make it easier, in general, for us to keep in mind what is being talked about when normative discourse is mentioned. In particular, it provides a framework within which to view the variety of moral principles offered in the readings that follow. It also provides a background for an issue discussed in this part at the end of our selection from Hume.

One of the most important problems running through all the readings in this part and many in later parts concerns the relationship between the "is" and the "ought," between descriptive and normative statements. It was Hume who insisted that an "ought" cannot be derived from an "is." In other words, beginning with what we know to be the case, we cannot infer, that is, argue validly to, statements about what we should do or about what ought to be the case. Putting the matter as a logician would, unless we have as one of our premises a sentence which contains "ought" we cannot have an "ought" in our conclusion.

Now, why should this be such an important matter for moral thought? One of the chief reasons is that the attempt has frequently been made to found ethics, or moral reasoning, on some body of knowledge, usually, in our time, on the natural or social sciences. With the advent of scientific attitudes of thought and the marked development of scientific research into almost every conceivable area, it has seemed reasonable to many people to try to use this rapidly accumulating body of information to solve the most perplexing problem that faces human beings—the development of principles to govern their own actions. Instead of relying on custom, habit, convention, why not once and for all place moral reasoning on a secure foundation, that of experimentally confirmed knowledge? In the last paragraph of our selection Hume tells us pointedly that this cannot be done. Is Hume right? Many philosophers have thought so, but others have questioned whether the distinction between descriptive and normative is as sharp as Hume makes it. Is there not perhaps an element of valuation in the descriptions that we make? Are not the ethical proposals offered by philosophers subject to confirmation by social scientists? (See the selection from Gordon Allport in Part V.)

To think further about this matter we must see what ethical theories have been like. Not all ethical theories have chosen the same kind of standard for judging the morality of actions. Some theories have said that we must appeal to the consequences of an action in order to determine whether the action should be performed. In other words, they deny that an act should be performed because of some intrinsic qualities which it possesses. Only the result to which it will lead, the future state of affairs which it will generate, justifies an action, and this consideration of the result may require taking into account the special circumstances of every case. Such theories are usually called "teleological" (from Greek *telos*: goal or end) because they emphasize the moral end or good to be promoted rather than the character of the action itself.

Some teleological theories have been "egoistic," claiming that the goal of action should be only one's own good. Others have been "universalistic," requiring that the goal of action be the greatest good of the greatest number. What this goal should be has also been a matter of dispute. Hedonists identify the good with pleasure, and they have argued the questions whether pleasure is equivalent to happiness and whether it is a positive bodily state or freedom from pain. Other theorists have rejected pleasure as the good and have adopted some form of "self-realization" as the goal of action. But these theorists have differed in their conception of what the self is and of how it is to be realized.

Our first example of ethical theories, that of Aristotle, falls into the classification of teleological theories which take self-realization as the goal of action. Men seek happiness as the end of life, but, says Aristotle, happiness is "an activity of the soul in accordance with perfect virtue." Thus moral action is action through which the soul seeks to perfect itself. But what are the characteristics of such action? Can they be described with any precision? In our selection from the *Nicomachean Ethics*, Aristotle presents a view of the moral virtues as a mean between two extremes, one an excess, the other a defect. Courage, for example, is viewed as a mean between rashness and cowardice, temperance as a mean between the excess of self-indulgence and the defect of sensuous indifference or insensibility. Aristotle adds to his doctrine of the "golden mean" the claim that men become courageous or just or temperate only by doing courageous, just, or temperate acts.

One should consider how the doctrine of the mean takes into account individual differences among men—Aristotle says that it is "the mean relative to us"—and in what way habit plays a role in the moral life. One should also bear in mind that Aristotle regards ethics as a kind of practical science which can achieve only a limited exactness suited to its subject matter. This will be an issue of importance in Part V: Can the modern sciences of human behavior achieve the precision of the mathematical and physical sciences? Is the notion of causal law utilized in the natural sciences applicable to the behavioral sciences? Do the patterns of scientific explanation and the confirmed body of scientific knowledge constitute the sources from which we can draw conclusions about what is desirable in human conduct?

In the reading from Epicurus we have a classic statement of egoistic hedonism, in which the stress is placed on freedom from pain rather than on positive pleasure. It should be noted that while the moral doctrines of Epicurus are founded on the materialistic atomism of the philosopher Democritus, allowance is made for spontaneity in human action. Should moral theories be derived from a philosophic view of the basic nature of all reality? Are any of them actually derived exclusively from that kind of source, or do independent observation and preference influence their formulation?

We have already mentioned some respects in which the views expressed in our selection from Hume are significant for thought about human value. Hume's moral theory is important also for its assessment of the relation between reason and emotion. For Hume, reason is limited to judgments about matters of fact and their relations. All matters of value are matters of preference and are emotional; they have their independent source in the feelings and are not derived from reason. In matters of morals, says Hume, "Reason is, and ought always to be, the slave of the passions, and can have no other office but to serve and obey them." That is to say, reason is able to answer factual questions relevant to moral decisions but cannot dictate a moral decision.

Morality for Hume, it appears, is a matter of habitual disposition, custom, and convention and moral controversies can only be decided by a sampling of opinion to determine preferences. Thus Hume sharpens for us one of the major questions in ethics: Can moral action be guided by universal principles founded on a knowledge of human nature—whether a priori or empirical—or is it to be guided ultimately only by preference and custom?

Let us look at an attempt to answer Hume from a new approach. One of the major divisions of ethical thought includes theories which hold that the notions of right and duty are fundamental in morality rather than the notion of good. These theories, called "deontological" (from Greek *dei*: it is right), hold that rightness or wrongness are intrinsic properties of actions and are determined without appeal to consequences. They stress performance of duty, which they recognize as unconditionally binding. Deontological theorists differ among themselves. Some hold that we discern the rightness or wrongness of specific acts; others limit our judgment to certain types of acts; and still others, notably Immanuel Kant, hold that we recognize one supreme moral law from which we justify specific rules of conduct.

In his moral theory Kant tried to present a rationale for what he believed to be the manner in which people think about morals. Moral worth resides in the proper intention, in the "good will" which acts from duty. Duty is respect for law, not for some particular rule but for law itself, the very essence of law, which is perfect universality and reason. Thus the morality suited to a rational being is to follow only those rules of conduct which he can consistently will that all men shall follow. Kant meant to exclude preference and the consequences of actions and to promote as the supreme moral guide the "categorical imperative" which commands the a priori test of universality. Did Kant succeed in his attempt to found ethics on an appeal to duty rather than to consequences? Can morality be reduced to one supreme principle extracted from the idea of reason?

In his exposition and defense of utilitarianism John Stuart Mill argues for a view directly opposed to the Kantian position. Mill is apparently a hedonist in that he takes pleasure to be the good or, what he regards as its equivalent, happiness, but he is a universal hedonist in that he asserts that it is not merely the individual's good which counts but the good of the greatest number. His position is that of a utilitarian. There may be occasions, he holds, on which one must sacrifice his own individual good for the good of a larger number.

Mill's utilitarian position is interesting for the distinction it makes among pleasures of different qualities. Mill's utilitarian predecessor, Jeremy Bentham, had recognized only quantitative differences among pleasures and had outlined a "calculus" of pleasure. Mill, however, says that pleasures also differ qualitatively, so that a lesser amount of a higher (usually more intellectual) pleasure is more desirable than a greater amount of a qualitatively inferior pleasure. Does one remain a hedonist if he regards some pleasures as "higher" than others? By what standard are the higher pleasures distinguished from the lower? Must not this standard be something other than pleasure?

The tendency of many thinkers in the ethical tradition to speak of absolute ends or goals of conduct comes under attack in our final selection, chosen from the writings of the American philosopher John Dewey. One of the chief proponents of the philosophic position known as "Pragmatism," Dewey lays the stress in his moral theory, as in other phases of his thought, on intelligent discovery, creative advance in ideas, and "reconstruction" of outmoded concepts. In our selection Dewey argues that instead of viewing some states of affairs as intrinsically ends, and others as mere means, we recognize that what is now viewed as an end may later become a means to a further end, and so on indefinitely. Thus, in place of fixed ends and definite means, he substitutes his notion of a continuum of means and ends.

In later writings Dewey advocated applying the methods of the natural sciences to the facts of moral choice and developing a systematic classification of valuations with a view toward conforming moral decision to the facts of actual situations. Dewey takes what has been called a "naturalistic" position in ethics. He identifies the value term "good" with a definite set of "natural" qualities characterizing some distinct experience. In place of the notion of fixed ends or "good" as a single set of natural qualities, Dewey asks us to recognize a multiplicity of "goods," each a set of experiences embedded in a concrete environmental situation and inseparable from objective conditions. The question has been raised by the British philosopher G. E. Moore as to whether the term "good" is to be defined naturalistically. Moore argues that it should not be, that it is an indefinable term standing for a simple, nonnatural quality, and that we can know intuitively what things are good, without being able to say what "good" is.

Here we have another phase of the argument over the relation of our knowledge to our moral judgments. Is Dewey right in believing that better moral choices will result from better knowledge of the dynamic processes of interaction between the human organism and its environment? Or is moral choice a matter of habit and preference only? Is it perhaps based on an unanalyzable intuition to which our highly organized knowledge is irrelevant?

On norms in general

Georg Henrik von Wright (b. 1916)

A native of Helsinki, Finland, G. H. von Wright studied there before World War II with Eino Kaila and then with C. D. Broad and Ludwig Wittgenstein at Cambridge University in England. He has been professor of philosophy at the University of Helsinki and at Cambridge, and visiting professor at Cornell University and the University of California in the United States, as well as Gifford Lecturer (1959, 1960) at St. Andrew's University in Scotland. Since 1961 he has been research professor at the Academy of Finland.

His chief publications are The Logical Problem of Induction *(1941, 1957),* A Treatise on Induction and Probability *(1951),* An Essay in Modal Logic *(1951),* Logical Studies *(1957),* The Varieties of Goodness *(1963),* Norm and Action *(1963), the work from which our selection is taken, and* The Logic of Preference *(1963).*

In our selection von Wright untangles what he considers the main kinds of norms and tries to clarify what is meant by normative statements. In the process he helps us to order our thinking about moral principles, which constitute a distinct type of norm. This examination has direct bearing on the discussions of ethical problems in the selections which follow.

1. The word "norm" in English, and the corresponding word in other languages, is used in many senses and often with an unclear meaning. It can hardly be said to be a well-established term in the English philosophic vocabulary. This can be said, however, of the adjective "normative."

"Norm" has several partial synonyms which are good English. "Pattern," "standard," "type" are such words. So are "regulation," "rule," and "law." Directions of use and prescriptions are perhaps not often called "norms," but we should not hesitate to call them "normative."

From Georg Henrik von Wright, *Norm and Action: A Logical Enquiry.* Copyright, 1963, by Georg Henrik von Wright. Used by permission of the author and the publishers, Routledge & Kegan Paul, Ltd., and The Humanities Press, Inc.

Since the field of meaning of "norm" is not only heterogeneous but also has vague boundaries, it would probably be futile to try to create a General Theory of Norms covering the whole field. The theory of norms must be somehow restricted in its scope.

When constructing a restricted theory of norms, however, it is as well to remember that the various meanings of "norm" are not logically unrelated. The word is not "ambiguous" in the ordinary sense. A restricted theory of norms runs the risk of being defective if it does not pay due attention to conceptual affinities and logical relationships between the various parts of the whole field of meaning.

In this chapter I shall try to single out and briefly characterize some of the chief meanings of the word "norm" or, as we could also say, species or types of norms.

2. We have said that *one* of the meanings of "norm" is *law*. The word "law," however, is used in at least three typically different senses. First, we speak of the *laws of the state*. Secondly, we speak of the *laws of nature*. Thirdly, we speak of *laws of logic* (and mathematics).

Obviously, the laws of nature and the laws of the state are very different. Yet the identity of name is no pure coincidence.

Thus, with the Greeks the conception of the world as a *kosmos* or harmonious order seems to have been connected historically with their conception of the city-state as a just and lawful order for a human community. The natural philosophy of the pre-Socratics has been called a projection of ideals of a social order on to the entire universe. In the philosophy of Plato we could say, this idea of the world as a *kosmos* is projected back on to human conditions and made a pattern or standard of the good life.

With the Greek conception of law as the conditions of equilibrium and harmony may be contrasted the Hebrew (Old Testament) conception of it as the expression of a commanding sovereign will. The idea of God as lawgiver may be regarded as an analogy or a projection on to a supernatural plane of the idea of a sovereign chief or king in a human community. As the king gives laws to those over whom he is set to rule, so in a similar manner God rules the whole universe by His law or "word." The Christian idea of a king "by the grace of God" is a projection back on to human affairs of this idea of a supreme lord of the universe. The idea of the worldly kingdom is given a foundation in the same supernatural idea, for which it originally set the pattern.

As *we* tend to see it, the laws of nature and the laws of the state are *toto coelo* logically different in spite of affinities in the origins of the ideas of the two "laws." The difference can be briefly characterized as follows:

The laws of nature are *descriptive*. They describe the regularities which man thinks he has discovered in the course of nature. They are true or false. Nature does not, except metaphorically, "obey" its laws. If a discrepancy is found to exist between the description and the

actual course of nature it is the description, and not the course of nature, that must be corrected.—This is a superficial characterization of what the laws of nature are. But I think it is *basically* correct.

The laws of the state are *prescriptive*. They lay down regulations for the conduct and intercourse of men. They have no truth-value. Their aim is to influence behaviour. When men disobey the laws the authority behind the laws tries, in the first place, to correct the behaviour of men. Sometimes, however, the authority alters the laws—perhaps in order to make them conform more to the capacities and demands of "human nature."

The contrast "prescriptive/descriptive" can be used for distinguishing norms from things which are not norms. The laws of nature are descriptive, not prescriptive—and *therefore* they are not norms. That is: we thus delineate the use of the word "norm"; we draw the boundaries of the concept. Under another use of the term the laws of nature can perfectly well be called "norms."

Someone may think that the attribute "prescriptive" gives the clue to a general characterization of norms. Normative discourse is prescriptive discourse, it is often said. With prescriptive discourse is then contrasted descriptive, and sometimes also evaluative, discourse.

To identify the meaning of "normative" with that of "prescriptive" and "norm" with "prescription" would, however, be too narrowing. Besides, "prescriptive" and "prescription" are words with a vague meaning and must be made more precise in order to be useful. As we shall soon see, there are things which we may without hesitation wish to call norms, but to which the attributes "prescriptive" and "descriptive" both appear equally inappropriate.

3. Let us briefly consider the meaning of "law" in the phrase "laws of logic (mathematics)." The laws of logic were often in the past also called the Laws of Thought.

On closer inspection we find that there are, in logic and mathematics, several *types* of proposition which are or may be called "laws." We need not here inquire into these distinctions. As examples of laws of logic, we shall instance the Law of Excluded Middle in the formulation "Every proposition is either true or false" and the Law of Contradiction in the formulation "No proposition is both true and false."

Are such laws "descriptive" or "prescriptive"? If the first, *what* do they describe? The way people think? This suggestion is not very satisfactory. For, first of all, it is not clear in itself what it *means* to think according to the law, for example, that no proposition is both true and false. Secondly, the idea that the laws of logic describe how people think seems difficult to reconcile with the notion that these laws are *a priori* and thus true independently of experience—including experience of how people think.

The *a priori* nature of the laws of logic seems easier to reconcile with a view of them as prescriptive laws. Shall we then say that the laws of logic prescribe how we *ought to* think and how we *may* and *must not* think? Perhaps we can say this, but it is also obvious on reflection that the *sense* in which the laws of logic "prescribe" (order, permit, prohibit) is a different sense from that in which the laws of the state prescribe.

Here the idea suggests itself that the laws of logic and mathematics prescribe how one ought to think and calculate in order to think and calculate correctly. The laws of logic do not aim at making people think correctly, as the laws of the state can be said to aim at making people behave in a certain way. The laws of logic provide a standard whereby to judge *whether* people think correctly or not. This seems to be a good way of characterizing the difference between the two types of law and the different senses in which they "prescribe."

Yet to say that the laws of logic prescribe how people have to think in order to think correctly is a challenging and dangerous way of talking. It suggests that the "prescriptive" function of the laws of logic is secondary to a "descriptive" function of them as stating principles of correct thinking. Primarily, the laws of logic and mathematics state *truths* about the logical and mathematical entities—propositions,

relations, inferences, numbers, etc. This they also do overtly when formulated in the usual way, as, *e.g.*, when we say, "Every proposition *is* either true or false."

Thus the view of the laws of logic as prescriptive of the way people ought to think leads to a view of these laws as being, primarily, descriptive. What, on this new view, the laws of logic describe is not, however, how people think, but how the logical entities are constituted.

This view of logic (and mathematics) is connected with great difficulties. It seems to presuppose a peculiar "ontology" of the logical (mathematical) entities. This ontology is sometimes called *Platonism* or *Realism* in the philosophy of logic (mathematics). On this view, the laws of logic (mathematics) are at the same time very much like and yet significantly different from the laws of nature. Both types of law have a truth-value. But laws of the first type are necessarily true; laws of the second type contingently so. Both types of law describe the properties and relations of some entities. But the entities with which laws of the first type deal are eternal and imperishable, whereas the entities with which the laws of the second type deal are mutable and contingently existing. This is a superficial characterization. But I think it catches hold of something typical.

The main alternative to a realistic (Platonistic) position in the philosophy of logic (mathematics) is sometimes called a *nominalist* or *conventionalist* position. It has many variants. Some of them seem just as implausible and difficult to defend as some radically Platonistic view. I shall here refrain from giving even a superficial characterization of the conventionalist position as such. I shall only hint at the status which the *laws* of logic (mathematics) will acquire if we reject a Platonistic philosophy.

We could then compare these laws to the *rules of a game*. Playing a game is an activity, and so is thinking and calculating. The rules of, say, chess determine which moves are permitted and which not, and sometimes require a certain move to be made. *In a similar sense* it may be suggested, the rules of logic determine which inferences and affirmations are "possible" (correct, legitimate, permitted) in thinking. Of a person who does not play in accordance with the rules of chess, we would say either that he plays *incorrectly* or that he does not play *chess*. We would say the first, *e.g.*, if he wanted to follow the rules but did not know or understand what they demanded of him. Or we would say it if he is trying to cheat his opponent. We would say the second, *e.g.*, if he did not care about following the rules, or consciously and consistently played according to different rules. *In a similar sense*, the suggestion runs, we say of a person who does not infer according to the rules of logic either that he infers incorrectly or that he does not "infer" at all. And we say the one or the other on roughly the same grounds as those which determine our reactions to the player.

The "Platonist" would argue that the above analogy breaks down at this point: Whereas the man who plays against the rules of a game sins only against the *rules*, the man who thinks against the rules of logic is in conflict with *truth*. The rules of a game are man-made and can be altered by convention or at will. The standards of truth are not conventional. That there is some truth in this argument is obvious. What this truth is and what implications it has for the analogy between the laws of logic and the rules of a game is, however, *not* obvious.

We raised the question whether the laws of logic and mathematics are descriptive or prescriptive. We have found that neither characterization appears quite to the point. These laws may be called descriptive, but not in the same clear sense in which the laws of nature are descriptive. They may also be called prescriptive, but in a rather different sense from that in which the laws of the state are prescriptive. The comparison of the laws of logic (mathematics) to the rules of a game suggested a new characterization of these laws. According to this new characterization, the laws of logic (mathematics) neither describe nor prescribe, but *determine* something. Irrespective of what we think of the comparison in other respects,

we can agree to the usefulness of this characterization. It suits the laws of logic (mathematics) *better* than either the attribute "descriptive" or the attribute "prescriptive."

4. The rules of a game are the prototype and standard example of a main type of norm. We shall here reserve the name *rule* as a technical term for this type.

Playing a game is a human activity. It is performed according to standardized patterns, which can be called *moves* in the game. The rules of the game *determine*, as I shall say, these moves or patterns—and thereby also the game "itself" and the activity of playing it. We could say that, when viewed from the point of view of the game itself, the rules determine which are the *correct* moves, and when viewed from the point of view of the activity of playing, the rules determine which are the *permitted* moves. It is understood that moves which are not correct are *prohibited* to players of the game, and that a move which is the only correct move in a certain situation in the game is *obligatory* when one is playing the game.

The *rules of grammar* (morphology and syntax) of a natural language are another example of the same main type of norm as the rules of a game. To the moves of a game as patterns correspond the set forms of correct speech. To play or the activity of playing a game corresponds speech or the activity of speaking (and writing) a language. Of a person who does not speak according to the rules of grammar, we say either that he speaks incorrectly or that he does not speak *that language*. The grounds for saying the one or the other are very much the same as the grounds for saying of a person either that he plays a game incorrectly or does not play *it* at all. But the rules of grammar have a much greater flexibility and mutability than the rules of a game. They are in a constant process of growth. What the rules *are* at any given moment in the history of a language may not be possible to tell with absolute completeness and precision.

The rules of a logical and mathematical *calculus* are in some respects even more like the rules of a game (such as, *e.g.*, chess) than are the rules of grammar of a natural language. (Games and calculi have a much poorer "history" than natural languages.) In at least one important respect, however, the rules of a calculus are more like rules of grammar than like rules of a game. Calculating, like speaking a language, is a play with *symbols*. Calculi and languages have a *semantic* dimension, which games, on the whole, lack.

5. A second main type of norms, beside rules, I shall call *prescriptions* or *regulations*. We have already met with one sub-type of such norms, *viz.* the laws of the state.

I shall regard the following features as characteristic of norms which are prescriptions:

Prescriptions are *given* or *issued* by someone. They "flow" from or have their "source" in the will of a norm-giver or, as we shall also say, a norm-*authority*. They are, moreover, addressed or directed to some agent or agents, whom we shall call norm-*subject(s)*. The authority of a norm can normally be said to want the subject(s) to adopt a certain conduct. The giving of the norm can then be said to manifest the authority's will to make the subject(s) behave in a certain way. In order to make its will *known* to the subject(s), the authority *promulgates* the norm. In order to make its will *effective*, the authority attaches a *sanction* or threat of punishment to the norm. In all these respects the norms which we call prescriptions differ characteristically from the norms which we call rules.

Generally speaking, prescriptions are commands or permissions, given by someone in a position of authority to someone in a position of subject. Military commands are an example of prescriptions. So are the orders and permissions given by parents to children. Traffic-rules and other regulations issued by a magistrate largely have this character too. The decisions of a law-court may be said to have a prescriptive aspect or component.

6. A group of norms which are in some respects like rules and in other respects like prescriptions are *customs*.

Customs may be regarded as a species of habits. A habit is primarily a regularity in an individual's behaviour, a disposition or tendency to do similar things on similar occasions or in recurrent circumstances. Habits are acquired and not innate. Customs may be regarded as *social* habits. They are patterns of behaviour for the members of a community. They are acquired by the community in the course of its history, and imposed on its members rather than acquired by them individually.

Customs have to do with the way people greet each other, eat, dress, get married, bury their dead, etc. Ceremony, fashion, and manner are sister-categories of custom. It is a custom of my country, but not of the Anglo-Saxon countries, to thank the hosts or the heads of a family when the meal is finished. This is regularly done. A member of the community who— either exceptionally or habitually—does not do this is regarded with disapproval. A "foreigner" to the community may be excused for not knowing or not adopting the custom.

Habits and customs, *qua* regularities of behaviour, show a certain resemblance to the regularities of nature, which natural scientists study. Social anthropology is largely a *science des mœurs*. It is "descriptive" in much the same sense in which natural science is descriptive.

Yet there is a difference "in principle" between regularities of behaviour, such as customs, and laws of nature. This difference is *not* that the former regularities are "statistical" and admit of exceptions, the latter regularities "nomic" and exceptionless. There seems to be no objection to calling *some* statistical regularities "laws of nature." It is not the bare existence of exceptions to a rule that constitutes the difference "in principle" between customs and regularities in nature. The difference lies in the *way* in which exceptions may occur. There is a sense in which the human individual can "break" the rule of custom and in which the course of nature cannot "break" its (causal or statistical) laws.

We can characterize this difference between customs and laws of nature by saying that the former present a genuinely normative or prescriptive aspect which the latter lack. Customs are "normlike" in the sense that they *influence* conduct; they exert a "normative pressure" on the individual members of the community whose customs they are. The existence of this pressure is reflected in the various punitive measures whereby the community reacts to those of its members who do not conform to its customs. In this respect customs are entirely unlike laws of nature, and resemble, not so much norms which are rules, as norms which are prescriptions.

Yet there are important differences too between customs and prescriptions. Customs, first of all, are not *given* by any authority to subjects. If we can speak of an authority behind the customs at all this authority would be the community itself, including both its past and present members. Customs could aptly be characterized as *anonymous* norms or prescriptions. But this characterization must not encourage any mysticism about the nature of the community as norm-giver.

Another difference between customs and prescriptions is that the former do not require promulgation by means of symbolic marks. They need not be "written down" anywhere in so many words. On this ground they could also be called *implicit* prescriptions. It is an interesting problem whether, within an animal or other community without a language, customs which exert a normative pressure on the members are (logically) possible.

There are some respects in which customs are more like rules than like prescriptions. Customs determine, or as it were "define," ways of living which are characteristic of a certain community. A member who does not live in accordance with custom is seldom sought out for punishment in the same way as he who breaks the laws. The awkwardness of his position is more like that of a child who stands aside and does not want to join in the games of his playmates. He becomes a "stranger" to his community rather than an "outlaw."

7. A third main type of norms, beside rules and prescriptions, are those which I shall call *directives* or *technical norms*. They are, approximately speaking, concerned with the *means* to be used for the sake of attaining a certain *end*.

"Directions for use" are examples of technical norms. In them is presupposed that the person who follows the directions, aims at the thing (end, result), with a view to the attainment of which those directions are laid down.

I shall regard as the standard formulation of technical norms, conditional sentences, in whose antecedent there is mention of some wanted thing, and in whose consequent there is mention of something that must (has to, ought to) or must not be done. An example would be "If you want to make the hut habitable, you ought to heat it."

Shall we say that the sentence quoted is "descriptive" or "prescriptive"? The proper answer, it seems to me, is that it is neither.

Compare the sentence under discussion with the sentence "If the house is to be made habitable, it ought to be heated." This last sentence I would not hesitate to call (purely) descriptive. It says that heating the house is a *necessary condition* of making the house habitable. This is (or is not) true, independently of whether anyone wants to make the house habitable and aims at this as an end. An equivalent formulation of the sentence would be "Unless the house is heated, it will not be habitable." We could say that the normal use of either is to make a statement about men's living conditions. The truth which the statement affirms is a kind of primitive "law of nature."

A statement to the effect that something is (or is not) a necessary condition of something else I shall call an *anankastic statement*. A (type of) sentence the normal use of which is for making an anankastic statement, I shall call an *anankastic sentence*. A sentence which is used for making an anankastic statement can also be said to express an *anankastic proposition*.

It would be a mistake, I think, to identify technical norms with anankastic propositions. There is, however, an essential (logical) connexion between the two. In giving the directive "If you want to make the hut habitable, you ought to heat it," it is (logically) *presupposed* that if the hut is not being heated it will not become habitable.

Another confusion to be avoided is that between technical norms and what I propose to call *hypothetical norms*. By the latter I understand, approximately speaking, norms concerning that which ought to or may or must not be done should a certain contingency arise. Hypothetical norms, too, are usually formulated by means of conditional sentences. For example: "If the dog barks, don't run." This sentence would normally be used for prescribing a certain mode of conduct, in case a certain thing should happen. The norm which the sentence enunciates is a prescription.

In the "background" of a hypothetical norm (prescription) too there is often an anankastic proposition. Why must I not run, if the dog starts to bark? If I run, the dog may attack me. Therefore, if I want to escape being attacked by the barking dog I must not run. Here the technical norm—or the underlying anankastic proposition—explains why the hypothetical prescription was given to me. But this connexion is accidental, not essential. Neither the technical norm nor the anankastic relationship is (logically) presupposed in the giving of the hypothetical norm (prescription). Even if there existed no technical norm or anankastic relationship in the background, the hypothetical order not to run, if—could be given to a person.

A man argues with himself: "I want to make the hut habitable. Unless it is heated, it will not become habitable. Therefore I ought to heat it." I shall call this type of argument a *practical inference*. In it the person who conducts the argument extracts, as it were, a prescription for his own conduct from a technical norm. Such "autonomous" prescriptions given by a man to himself are, however, very unlike the "heteronomous" prescriptions, categorical or hypothetical, given by a norm-authority to some norm-subject(s). It is doubtful whether one should call the former "prescriptions" at all.

8. What is the position of so-called moral norms (principles, rules) in the division of norms into main groups?

An answer to the question might be easier if we could give obvious examples of moral norms. This, however, is not altogether easy. One example which appears relatively uncontroversial (as an example) is the principle that promises ought to be kept. It is, however, an example of a moral norm of a rather special character. Other examples would be that children ought to honour their parents, that one must not punish the innocent, or that one should love one's neighbour as oneself.

Are moral norms to be classified along with rules of a game, *i.e.*, do they determine (define) a practice? It seems to me that, *on the whole*, moral norms are *not* like rules (in the sense which we here give to the term). But some moral norms present this aspect too. It is an aspect of the obligation to keep promises that this obligation is inherent in or is a logical feature of the institution of giving and taking promises. "By definition," one could say, promises ought to be kept. But this is only one aspect, beside others, of the obligation in question.

Are moral norms to be classified with the *customs* of a society (community)? It is noteworthy that the word "moral" derives from the Latin *mos*, which means custom. Some moral philosophers have sought to reduce ethics to a branch of a general *science des mœurs*. It seems to me that *some* moral ideas can be profitably viewed by the philosopher too against a background of the customs (traditions) of a community. This might be true, for example, of moral ideas in matters relating to sexual life. Other moral norms, however, seem to have no significant place in this perspective. To try to explain the obligation to keep promises, for example, in terms of the "normative pressure" of customs seems utterly out of place.

Are moral norms prescriptions? If we think they are, we must also be able to tell *whose* prescriptions *to whom* they are. Who *gave* the moral law?

A contract is a kind of promise. The legal

obligations which people have under contract are therefore obligations to keep a kind of promise. The legal norms which institute these obligations are prescriptions. They can truly be called somebody's prescriptions to somebody— in spite of the fact that their authority is not a human individual or "physical" person. But the *moral* norm to the effect that promises ought to be kept cannot become identified with the sum total of such legal prescriptions "supporting" it. The laws of the state frequently have a "moral content" or are concerned with "moral matters." The same is true of the prescriptions which parents issue for the conduct of children. In the moral life of man prescriptions thus play a prominent role. This is no mere accident; it is a logical feature of morality. But this logical tie between moral norms and prescriptions does not, so far as I can see, reduce the former to a species of the latter.

Some think that moral norms are the commands of God to men. The moral law is the law of God. To take this view of morality is to regard moral norms as prescriptions. These prescriptions, however, are not only of a very special *kind*. They must, perhaps, be thought of as prescriptions in a special *sense* of the term. This is so because of the peculiar nature of the (supernatural) authority who is their source.

The chief alternative in the history of ethics to the view of morality as the laws of God is a teleological view of it. On the first view, moral norms are a kind of prescription—or prescriptions in some special sense of the term. On the second view, moral norms are a kind of technical norm or directives for the attainment of certain ends. But what end or ends? The happiness of the individual or the welfare of a community? Eudaimonism and utilitarianism are variants of a teleological ethics. It would seem that the ends, relative to which certain modes of conduct are morally obligatory or permissible, cannot be specified independently of considerations of good and evil. This holds true also of happiness and welfare as proposed ultimate ends of moral action.

In view of the difficulties encountered by both a law-conception of moral norms and a teleological conception of them, it might be suggested that moral norms are *sui generis*. They are "conceptually autonomous," a group of norms standing by themselves, and not prescriptions for conduct in conformity with the will of a moral authority or directives for the attainment of moral ends. The view of moral norms as *sui generis* is sometimes called the *deontologist* position in ethics.

This is not the place for detailed criticism of deontologism in ethics. As a proposed way out of difficulties, this position seems to me to be definitely unsatisfactory. The peculiarity of moral norms, as I see them, is not that they form an autonomous group of their own; it is rather that they have complicated logical affinities to the other main types of norm and to the value-notions of good and evil. To understand the nature of moral norms is therefore not to discover some unique feature in them; it is to survey their complex relationships to a number of *other* things.

9. The norms of various categories, of which we have so far been talking, are mainly norms concerned with that which ought to or may or must not be *done*. Laws of nature and other anankastic propositions are, on the whole, not concerned with action; but these we have decided not to call "norms."

There is, however, a group of norms which are immediately concerned, not with action, but with things that ought to or may or must not *be*. German writers sometimes make a distinction between *Tunsollen* and *Seinsollen*.[1] In Anglo-Saxon writings the distinction is not very often referred to.[2]

Following G. E. Moore,[3] I shall call norms which are concerned with being rather than

[1] See, for example, Nicolai Hartmann, *Ethik*, 1925, Teil I, Abschnitt VI, Kap. 18–19. Max Scheler, in *Der Formalismus in der Ethik und die materiale Wertethik*, 1916, uses the terms "ideales Sollen" and "normatives Sollen."

[2] An exception is G. E. Moore, who draws the distinction very neatly in his paper "The Nature of Moral Philosophy," in *Philosophical Studies*, 1922.

[3] *Op. cit.*, pp. 320f.

with doing, *ideal rules*. Ideal rules are referred to, for example, when we say that a man ought to be generous, truthful, just, temperate, etc., and also when we say that a soldier in the army should be brave, hardy, and disciplined; a schoolmaster patient with children, firm, and understanding; a watchman alert, observant, and resolute; and so forth.

We also say of cars, watches, hammers, and other implements, which are used to serve various purposes, that they ought to have certain properties and should not have others. The question may be raised whether such statements should be counted as stating ideal rules or as anankastic propositions about the relations of means to ends. That question will not be discussed here.

Ideal rules are closely connected with the concept of *goodness*. The properties which we say a craftsman, administrator, or judge ought to possess are characteristic, not of *every* craftsman, administrator, or judge, but of a *good* craftsman, administrator, or judge. The person who has the properties of a good so-and-so in a supreme degree, we often call an *ideal* so-and-so. The same holds true of watches, cars, and other things which serve various human purposes.

The features which ideal rules require to be present in good members of a class or kind of human beings can be termed the *virtues* characteristic of men of that class or kind. In an extended sense of "virtue," roughly corresponding to the Greek *arete*, the characteristic properties of good instruments are often called virtues also.

It is natural to call ideal rules concerning men in general, as distinct from men of a particular class or profession, *moral* rules or ideals. It is useful to distinguish between moral *principles*, which are norms of moral action, and moral *ideals*, which set the pattern of a good man.

It may be thought that ideal rules are reducible to norms of action. The concepts of a brave, generous, just, etc., *act*, it may be argued, are primary to the concepts of a brave, generous, just, etc., *man*. The man who does

brave acts is "by definition" a brave man, and so forth. This, however, would be to take a much too simple-minded view of the relationship in question. Yet it is also clear that "education" (in the broadest sense) towards ideals will have to make use of prescriptions and other norms of conduct.

There is a certain similarity between ideal rules and technical norms. Striving for the ideal resembles the pursuit of an end. It would, however, be a mistake to think of the ideal rules as norms concerning means to ends. In order to be a good teacher, a man ought to have such and such qualities. In order to fetch a book from the top shelf of his bookcase, he ought to use a ladder. But those qualities of a man which determine his goodness as a teacher are not *causally* related to the ideal—as the use of a ladder may be a causal prerequisite of fetching a book from a shelf. The former relation is conceptual (logical). The ideal rules determine a concept, *e.g.* the concept of a (good) teacher or soldier. In this they are similar to rules of a game. It is because of this similarity that we have given them here the name "rules."

10. Our discussion, in the preceding sections, of the field of meaning of the word "norm" has led us to distinguish between three major groups or types of norms. We have called them *rules*, *prescriptions*, and *directives*.

As a prototype of rules we instance the rules of a game. Rules of grammar also belong to this type of norm. Perhaps the so-called laws or rules of logic and mathematics should also be counted as belonging to it.

As prescriptions we count commands, permissions, and prohibitions, which are given or issued to agents concerning their conduct. The laws of the state are prescriptions.

Directives we also call technical norms. They presuppose ends of human action and necessary relationships of acts to these ends.

In addition to these three main groups of norms we mentioned three minor groups of particular importance. They are *customs*, *moral principles*, and *ideal rules*. It is characteristic of the minor groups that they show affinities to more than one of the major groups—they fall, so to speak, "between" the major groups.

Thus, customs resemble rules in that they determine, *quasi* define, certain patterns of conduct—and prescriptions in that they exert a "normative pressure" on the members of a community to conform to those patterns.

On the nature of moral principles there has been much controversy and disagreement. Some philosophers regard them as a kind of prescription—say, as the commands or laws of God to men. Others regard them as some sort of technical norm or directive of how to secure ends of a peculiar nature. Irrespective of which view one accepts as basically true, one cannot deny that moral principles have important relationships both to prescriptions *and* to technical norms. The prescriptive aspect of morality, moreover, is related to custom. The "technical" aspect of morality is related to ideals of the good life and man.

Ideal rules, finally, can be said to hold a position between technical norms about means to an end and rules which determine a pattern or standard.

Moral virtue

Aristotle (384-323 B.C.)

Aristotle was the son of a physician at the Macedonian court. He was sent to Athens in his eighteenth year to study at Plato's Academy and he remained there until the death of Plato in 348 B.C. For about thirteen years thereafter he traveled widely and for about three years during that period was tutor to the young Alexander of Macedon. Returning to Athens, he founded his own school, called the Lyceum, where he remained until driven out shortly before his death by the Athenians in their revolt against Macedon.

Throughout his life Aristotle carried on scientific observation, especially in biology. He had an unusual capacity for careful analysis, which he applied to an enormous range of subjects. His investigations covered logic, metaphysics, physics, biology, astronomy, psychology, politics, ethics, and aesthetics. His thought exerted a profound influence on Western culture for many centuries. Though strongly influenced by Plato, Aristotle's thinking reveals the mark of his work as an experimental scientist and shows little of the approach of the mathematician.

In his Nicomachean Ethics, *from which our selection is taken, he directs his analytical mind to the issues of human conduct. In Book II, which is reproduced here, he presents his account of moral virtue as a mean between two extremes.*

. . . 13. Since happiness is an activity of soul in accordance with perfect virtue, we must consider the nature of virtue; for perhaps we shall thus see better the nature of happiness. The true student of politics, too, is thought to have studied virtue above all things; for he wishes to make his fellow citizens good and obedient to the laws. As an example of this we have the lawgivers of the Cretans and the Spartans, and any others of the kind that there may have been. And if this inquiry belongs to political science, clearly the pursuit of it will

From Aristotle, *Nichomachean Ethics,* tr. W. D. Ross, Bks. I–II. Copyright, 1915, by the Clarendon Press. Used by permission of the Clarendon Press, Oxford.

be in accordance with our original plan. But clearly the virtue we must study is human virtue; for the good we were seeking was human good and the happiness human happiness. By human virtue we mean not that of the body but that of the soul; and happiness also we call an activity of soul. But if this is so, clearly the student of politics must know somehow the facts about soul, as the man who is to heal the eyes or the body as a whole must know about the eyes or the body; and all the more since politics is more prized and better than medicine; but even among doctors the best educated spend much labour on acquiring knowledge of the body. The student of politics, then, must study the soul, and must study it **151** with these objects in view, and do so just to the extent which is sufficient for the questions we are discussing; for further precision is perhaps something more laborious than our purposes require.

Some things are said about it, adequately enough, even in the discussions outside our school, and we must use these; e.g. that one element in the soul is irrational and one has a rational principle. Whether these are separated as the parts of the body or of anything divisible are, or are distinct by definition but by nature inseparable, like convex and concave in the circumference of a circle, does not affect the present question.

Of the irrational element one division seems to be widely distributed, and vegetative in its nature, I mean that which causes nutrition and growth; for it is this kind of power of the soul that one must assign to all nurslings and to embryos, and this same power to full-grown creatures; this is more reasonable than to assign some different power to them. Now the excellence of this seems to be common to all species and not specifically human; for this part or faculty seems to function most in sleep, while goodness and badness are least manifest in sleep (whence comes the saying that the happy are no better off than the wretched for half their lives; and this happens naturally enough, since sleep is an inactivity of the soul in that respect in which it is called good or bad), unless perhaps to a small extent some of the movements actually penetrate to the soul, and in this respect the dreams of good men are better than those of ordinary people. Enough of this subject, however; let us leave the nutritive faculty alone, since it has by its nature no share in human excellence.

There seems to be also another irrational element in the soul—one which in a sense, however, shares in a rational principle. For we praise the rational principle of the continent man and of the incontinent, and the part of their soul that has such a principle, since it urges them aright and towards the best objects; but there is found in them also another element naturally opposed to the rational principle, which fights against and resists that principle.

For exactly as paralysed limbs when we intend to move them to the right turn on the contrary to the left, so is it with the soul; the impulses of incontinent people move in contrary directions. But while in the body we see that which moves astray, in the soul we do not. No doubt, however, we must none the less suppose that in the soul too there is something contrary to the rational principle, resisting and opposing it. In what sense it is distinct from the other elements does not concern us. Now even this seems to have a share in a rational principle, as we said; at any rate in the continent man it obeys the rational principle—and presumably in the temperate and brave man it is still more obedient; for in him it speaks, on all matters, with the same voice as the rational principle.

Therefore the irrational element also appears to be twofold. For the vegetative element in no way shares in a rational principle, but the appetitive, and in general the desiring element in a sense shares in it, in so far as it listens to and obeys it; this is the sense in which we speak of "taking account" of one's father or one's friends, not that in which we speak of "accounting" for a mathematical property. That the irrational element is in some sense persuaded by a rational principle is indicated also by the giving of advice and by all reproof and exhortation. And if this element also must be said to have a rational principle, that which has a rational principle (as well as that which has not) will be twofold, one subdivision having it in the strict sense and in itself, and the other having a tendency to obey as one does one's father.

Virtue too is distinguished into kinds in accordance with this difference; for we say that some of the virtues are intellectual and others moral, philosophic wisdom and understanding and practical wisdom being intellectual, liberality and temperance moral. For in speaking about a man's character we do not say that he is wise or has understanding but that he is good-tempered or temperate; yet we praise the wise man also with respect to his state of mind; and of states of mind we call those which merit praise virtues.

Book II

1. Virtue, then, being of two kinds, intellectual and moral, intellectual virtue in the main owes both its birth and its growth to teaching (for which reason it requires experience and time), while moral virtue comes about as a result of habit, whence also its name *ethike* is one that is formed by a slight variation from the word *ethos* (habit). From this it is also plain that none of the moral virtues arises in us by nature; for nothing that exists by nature can form a habit contrary to it nature. For instance the stone which by nature moves downwards cannot be habituated to move upwards, not even if one tries to train it by throwing it up ten thousand times; nor can fire be habituated to move downwards, nor can anything else that by nature behaves in one way be trained to behave in another. Neither by nature, then, nor contrary to nature do the virtues arise in us; rather we are adapted by nature to receive them, and are made perfect by habit.

Again, of all the things that come to us by nature we first acquire the potentiality and later exhibit the activity (this is plain in the case of the senses; for it was not by often seeing or often hearing that we got these senses, but on the contrary we had them before we used them, and did not come to have them by using them); but the virtues we get by first exercising them, as also happens in the case of the arts as well. For the things we have to learn before we can do them, we learn by doing them, e.g. men become builders by building and lyre-players by playing the lyre; so too we become just by doing just acts, temperate by doing temperate acts, brave by doing brave acts.

This is confirmed by what happens in states; for legislators make the citizens good by forming habits in them, and this is the wish of every legislator, and those who do not effect it miss their mark, and it is in this that a good constitution differs from a bad one.

Again, it is from the same causes and by the same means that every virtue is both produced and destroyed, and similarly every art; for it is from playing the lyre that both good and bad lyre-players are produced. And the corresponding statement is true of builders and of all the rest; men will be good or bad builders as a result of building well or badly. For if this were not so, there would have been no need of a teacher, but all men would have been born good or bad at their craft. This, then, is the case with the virtues also; by doing the acts that we do in our transactions with other men we become just or unjust, and by doing the acts that we do in the presence of danger, and being habituated to feel fear or confidence, we become brave or cowardly. The same is true of appetites and feelings of anger; some men become temperate and good-tempered, others self-indulgent and irascible, by behaving in one way or the other in the appropriate circumstances. Thus, in one word, states of character arise out of like activities. This is why the activities we exhibit must be of a certain kind; it is because the states of character correspond to the differences between these. It makes no small difference, then, whether we form habits of one kind or of another from our very youth; it makes a very great difference, or rather *all* the difference.

2. Since, then, the present inquiry does not aim at theoretical knowledge like the others (for we are inquiring not in order to know what virtue is, but in order to become good, since otherwise our inquiry would have been of no use), we must examine the nature of actions, namely how we ought to do them; for these determine also the nature of the states of character that are produced, as we have said. Now, that we must act according to the right rule is a common principle and must be assumed—it will be discussed later, i.e. both what the right rule is, and how it is related to the other virtues. But this must be agreed upon beforehand, that the whole account of matters of conduct must be given in outline and not precisely, as we said at the very beginning that the accounts we demand must be in accordance with the subject-matter; matters concerned with conduct and questions of what is good for us have no fixity, any more than matters

of health. The general account being of this nature, the account of particular cases is yet more lacking in exactness; for they do not fall under any art or precept but the agents themselves must in each case consider what is appropriate to the occasion, as happens also in the art of medicine or of navigation.

But though our present account is of this nature we must give what help we can. First, then, let us consider this, that it is the nature of such things to be destroyed by defect and excess, as we see in the case of strength and of health (for to gain light on things imperceptible we must use the evidence of sensible things); both excessive and defective exercise destroys the strength, and similarly drink or food which is above or below a certain amount destroys the health, while that which is proportionate both produces and increases and preserves it. So too is it, then, in the case of temperance and courage and the other virtues. For the man who flies from and fears everything and does not stand his ground against anything becomes a coward, and the man who fears nothing at all but goes to meet every danger becomes rash; and similarly the man who indulges in every pleasure and abstains from none becomes self-indulgent, while the man who shuns every pleasure, as boors do, becomes in a way insensible; temperance and courage, then, are destroyed by excess and defect, and preserved by the mean.

But not only are the sources and causes of their origination and growth the same as those of their destruction, but also the sphere of their actualization will be the same; for this is also true of the things which are more evident to sense, e.g. of strength; it is produced by taking much food and undergoing much exertion, and it is the strong man that will be most able to do these things. So too is it with the virtues; by abstaining from pleasures we become temperate, and it is when we have become so that we are most able to abstain from them; and similarly too in the case of courage; for by being habituated to despise things that are terrible and to stand our ground against them we become brave, and it is when we have become so that we shall be most able to stand our ground against them.

3. We must take as a sign of states of character the pleasure or pain that ensues on acts; for the man who abstains from bodily pleasures and delights in this very fact is temperate, while the man who is annoyed at it is self-indulgent, and he who stands his ground against things that are terrible and delights in this or at least is not pained is brave, while the man who is pained is a coward. For moral excellence is concerned with pleasures and pains; it is on account of the pleasure that we do bad things, and on account of the pain that we abstain from noble ones. Hence we ought to have been brought up in a particular way from our very youth, as Plato says, so as both to delight in and to be pained by the things that we ought; for this is the right education.

Again, if the virtues are concerned with actions and passions, and every passion and every action is accompanied by pleasure and pain, for this reason also virtue will be concerned with pleasures and pains. This is indicated also by the fact that punishment is inflicted by these means; for it is a kind of cure, and it is the nature of cures to be effected by contraries.

Again, as we said but lately, every state of soul has a nature relative to and concerned with the kind of things by which it tends to be made worse or better; but it is by reason of pleasures and pains that men become bad, by pursuing and avoiding these—either the pleasures and pains they ought not or when they ought not or as they ought not, or by going wrong in one of the other similar ways that may be distinguished. Hence men even define the virtues as certain states of impassivity and rest; not well, however, because they speak absolutely, and do not say "as one ought" and "as one ought not" and "when one ought or ought not," and the other things that may be added. We assume, then, that this kind of excellence tends to do what is best with regard to pleasures and pains, and vice does the contrary.

The following facts also may show us that virtue and vice are concerned with these same things. There being three objects of choice and three of avoidance, the noble, the advantageous, the pleasant, and their contraries, the base, the injurious, the painful, about all of these the good man tends to go right and the bad man to go wrong, and especially about pleasure; for this is common to the animals, and also it accompanies all objects of choice; for even the noble and the advantageous appear pleasant.

Again, it has grown up with us all from our infancy; this is why it is difficult to rub off this passion, engrained as it is in our life. And we measure even our actions, some of us more and others less, by the rule of pleasure and pain. For this reason, then, our whole inquiry must be about these; for to feel delight and pain rightly or wrongly has no small effect on our actions.

Again, it is harder to fight with pleasure than with anger, to use Heraclitus' phrase, but both art and virtue are always concerned with what is harder; for even the good is better when it is harder. Therefore for this reason also the whole concern both of virtue and of political science is with pleasures and pains; for the man who uses these well will be good, he who uses them badly bad.

That virtue, then, is concerned with pleasures and pains, and that by the acts from which it arises it is both increased and, if they are done differently, destroyed, and that the acts from which it arose are those in which it actualizes itself—let this be taken as said.

4. The question might be asked, what we mean by saying that we must become just by doing just acts, and temperate by doing temperate acts; for if men do just and temperate acts, they are already just and temperate, exactly as, if they do what is in accordance with the laws of grammar and of music, they are grammarians and musicians.

Or is this not true even of the arts? It is possible to do something that is in accordance with the laws of grammar, either by chance or at the suggestion of another. A man will be a grammarian, then, only when he has both done something grammatical and done it grammatically; and this means doing it in accordance with the grammatical knowledge in himself.

Again, the case of the arts and that of the virtues are not similar; for the products of the arts have their goodness in themselves, so that it is enough that they should have a certain character, but if the acts that are in accordance with the virtues have themselves a certain character it does not follow that they are done justly or temperately. The agent also must be in a certain condition when he does them; in the first place he must have knowledge, secondly he must choose the acts, and choose them for their own sakes, and thirdly his action must proceed from a firm and unchangeable character. These are not reckoned in as conditions of the possession of the arts, except the bare knowledge; but as a condition of the possession of the virtues knowledge has little or no weight, while the other conditions count not for a little but for everything, i.e. the very conditions which result from often doing just and temperate acts.

Actions, then, are called just and temperate when they are such as the just or the temperate man would do; but it is not the man who does these that is just and temperate, but the man who also does them *as* just and temperate men do them. It is well said, then, that it is by doing just acts that the just man is produced, and by doing temperate acts the temperate man; without doing these no one would have even a prospect of becoming good.

But most people do not do these, but take refuge in theory and think they are being philosophers and will become good in this way, behaving somewhat like patients who listen attentively to their doctors, but do none of the things they are ordered to do. As the latter will not be made well in body by such a course of treatment, the former will not be made well in soul by such a course of philosophy.

5. Next we must consider what virtue is. Since things that are found in the soul are of three kinds—passions, faculties, states of character, virtue must be one of these. By passions I mean appetite, anger, fear, confidence, envy, joy, friendly feeling, hatred, longing, emulation, pity, and in general the feelings that are accompanied by pleasure or pain; by faculties the things in virtue of which we are said to be capable of feeling these, e.g. of becoming angry

or being pained or feeling pity; by states of character the things in virtue of which we stand well or badly with reference to the passions, e.g. with reference to anger we stand badly if we feel it violently or too weakly, and well if we feel it moderately; and similarly with reference to the other passions.

Now neither the virtues nor the vices are *passions*, because we are not called good or bad on the ground of our passions, but are so called on the ground of our virtues and our vices, and because we are neither praised nor blamed for our passions (for the man who feels fear or anger is not praised, nor is the man who simply feels anger blamed, but the man who feels it in a certain way), but for our virtues and our vices we *are* praised or blamed.

Again, we feel anger and fear without choice, but the virtues are modes of choice or involve choice. Further, in respect of the passions we are said to be moved, but in respect of the virtues and the vices we are said not to be moved but to be disposed in a particular way.

For these reasons also they are not *faculties*; for we are neither called good nor bad, nor praised nor blamed, for the simple capacity of feeling the passions; again, we have the faculties by nature, but we are not made good or bad by nature; we have spoken of this before.

If, then, the virtues are neither passions nor faculties, all that remains is that they should be *states of character*.

Thus we have stated what virtue is in respect of its genus.

6. We must, however, not only describe virtue as a state of character, but also say what sort of state it is. We may remark, then, that every virtue or excellence both brings into good condition the thing of which it is the excellence and makes the work of that thing be done well; e.g. the excellence of the eye makes both the eye and its work good; for it is by the excellence of the eye that we see well. Similarly the excellence of the horse makes a horse both good in itself and good at running and at carrying its rider and at awaiting the attack of the enemy. Therefore, if this is true in every case, the virtue of man also will be the state of character which makes a man good and which makes him do his own work well.

How this is to happen we have stated already, but it will be made plain also by the following consideration of the specific nature of virtue. In everything that is continuous and divisible it is possible to take more, less, or an equal amount, and that either in terms of the thing itself or relatively to us; and the equal is an intermediate between excess and defect. By the intermediate in the object I mean that which is equidistant from each of the extremes, which is one and the same for all men; by the intermediate relatively to us that which is neither too much nor too little—and this is not one, nor the same for all. For instance, if ten is many and two is few, six is the intermediate, taken in terms of the object; for it exceeds and is exceeded by an equal amount; this is intermediate according to arithmetical proportion. But the intermediate relatively to us is not to be taken so; if ten pounds are too much for a particular person to eat and two too little, it does not follow that the trainer will order six pounds; for this also is perhaps too much for the person who is to take it, or too little—too little for Milo [a famous wrestler], too much for the beginner in athletic exercises. The same is true of running and wrestling. Thus a master of any art avoids excess and defect, but seeks the intermediate and chooses this—the intermediate not in the object but relatively to us.

If it is thus, then, that every art does its work well—by looking to the intermediate and judging its works by this standard (so that we often say of good works of art that it is not possible either to take away or to add anything, implying that excess and defect destroy the goodness of works of art, while the mean preserves it; and good artists, as we say, look to this in their work), and if, further, virtue is more exact and better than any art, as nature also is, then virtue must have the quality of aiming at the intermediate. I mean moral virtue; for it is this that is concerned with passions and actions, and in these there is excess, defect, and the intermediate. For instance, both fear and confidence and appetite and anger and pity and in general pleasure and pain may be felt both too much and too little, and in both cases not well; but to feel them at the right times, with reference to the right objects, towards the right people, with the right motive, and in the right way, is what is both intermediate and best, and this is characteristic of virtue. Similarly with regard to actions also there is excess, defect, and the intermediate. Now virtue is concerned with passions and actions, in which excess is a form of failure, and so is defect, while the intermediate is praised and is a form of success; and being praised and being successful are both characteristics of virtue. Therefore virtue is a kind of mean, since, as we have seen, it aims at what is intermediate.

Again, it is possible to fail in many ways (for evil belongs to the class of the unlimited, as the Pythagoreans conjectured, and good to that of the limited), while to succeed is possible only in one way (for which reason also one is easy and the other difficult—to miss the mark easy, to hit it difficult); for these reasons also, then, excess and defect are characteristic of vice, and the mean of virtue;

For men are good in but one way, but bad in many.

Virtue, then, is a state of character concerned with choice, lying in a mean, i.e. the mean relative to us, this being determined by a rational principle, and by that principle by which the man of practical wisdom would determine it. Now it is a mean between two vices, that which depends on excess and that which depends on defect; and again it is a mean because the vices respectively fall short of or exceed what is right in both passions and actions, while virtue both finds and chooses that which is intermediate. Hence in respect of its substance and the definition which states its essence virtue is a mean, with regard to what is best and right an extreme.

But not every action nor every passion admits of a mean; for some have names that already imply badness, e.g. spite, shamelessness, envy, and in the case of actions adultery, theft, murder; for all of these and suchlike things

imply by their names that they are themselves bad, and not the excesses or deficiencies of them. It is not possible, then, ever to be right with regard to them; one must always be wrong. Nor does goodness or badness with regard to such things depend on committing adultery with the right woman, at the right time, and in the right way, but simply to do any of them is to go wrong. It would be equally absurd, then, to expect that in unjust, cowardly, and voluptuous action there should be a mean, an excess, and a deficiency; for at that rate there would be a mean of excess and of deficiency, an excess of excess, and a deficiency of deficiency. But as there is no excess and deficiency of temperance and courage because what is intermediate is in a sense an extreme, so too of the actions we have mentioned there is no mean nor any excess and deficiency, but however they are done they are wrong; for in general there is neither a mean of excess and deficiency, nor excess and deficiency of a mean.

7. We must, however, not only make this general statement, but also apply it to the individual facts. For among statements about conduct those which are general apply more widely, but those which are particular are more genuine, since conduct has to do with individual cases, and our statements must harmonize with the facts in these cases. We may take these cases from our table. With regard to feelings of fear and confidence courage is the mean; of the people who exceed, he who exceeds in fearlessness has no name (many of the states have no name), while the man who exceeds in confidence is rash, and he who exceeds in fear and falls short in confidence is a coward. With regard to pleasures and pains—not all of them, and not so much with regard to the pains—the mean is temperance, the excess self-indulgence. Persons deficient with regard to the pleasures are not often found; hence such persons also have received no name. But let us call them "insensible."

With regard to giving and taking of money the mean is liberality, the excess and the defect prodigality and meanness. In these actions people exceed and fall short in contrary ways;

the prodigal exceeds in spending and falls short in taking, while the mean man exceeds in taking and falls short in spending. (At present we are giving a mere outline or summary, and are satisfied with this; later these states will be more exactly determined.) With regard to money there are also other dispositions—a mean, magnificence (for the magnificent man differs from the liberal man; the former deals with large sums, the latter with small ones), an excess, tastelessness and vulgarity, and a deficiency, niggardliness; these differ from the states opposed to liberality, and the mode of their difference will be stated later.

With regard to honour and dishonour the mean is proper pride, the excess is known as a sort of "empty vanity," and the deficiency is undue humility; and as we said liberality was related to magnificence, differing from it by dealing with small sums, so there is a state similarly related to proper pride, being concerned with small honours while that is concerned with great. For it is possible to desire honour as one ought, and more than one ought, and less, and the man who exceeds in his desires is called ambitious, the man who falls short unambitious, while the intermediate person has no name. The dispositions also are nameless, except that that of the ambitious man is called ambition. Hence the people who are at the extremes lay claim to the middle place; and we ourselves sometimes call the intermediate person ambitious and sometimes unambitious, and sometimes praise the ambitious man and sometimes the unambitious. The reason of our doing this will be stated in what follows; but now let us speak of the remaining states according to the method which has been indicated.

With regard to anger also there is an excess, a deficiency, and a mean. Although they can scarcely be said to have names, yet since we call the intermediate person good-tempered let us call the mean good temper; of the persons at the extremes let the one who exceeds be called irascible, and his vice irascibility, and the man who falls short an inirascible sort of person, and the deficiency inirascibility.

There are also three other means, which have a certain likeness to one another, but differ from one another: for they are all concerned with intercourse in words and actions, but differ in that one is concerned with truth in this sphere, the other two with pleasantness; and of this one kind is exhibited in giving amusement, the other in all the circumstances of life. We must therefore speak of these too, that we may the better see that in all things the mean is praiseworthy, and the extremes neither praiseworthy nor right, but worthy of blame. Now most of these states also have no names, but we must try, as in the other cases, to invent names ourselves so that we may be clear and easy to follow. With regard to truth, then, the intermediate is a truthful sort of person and the mean may be called truthfulness, while the pretence which exaggerates is boastfulness and the person characterized by it a boaster, and that which understates is mock modesty and the person characterized by it mock-modest. With regard to pleasantness in the giving of amusement the intermediate person is ready-witted and the disposition ready wit, the excess is buffoonery and the person characterized by it a buffoon, while the man who falls short is a sort of boor and his state is boorishness. With regard to the remaining kind of pleasantness, that which is exhibited in life in general, the man who is pleasant in the right way is friendly and the mean is friendliness, while the man who exceeds is an obsequious person if he has no end in view, a flatterer if he is aiming at his own advantage, and the man who falls short and is unpleasant in all circumstances is a quarrelsome and surly sort of person.

There are also means in the passions and concerned with the passions; since shame is not a virtue, and yet praise is extended to the modest man. For even in these matters one man is said to be intermediate, and another to exceed, as for instance the bashful man who is ashamed of everything; while he who falls short or is not ashamed of anything at all is shameless, and the intermediate person is modest. Righteous indignation is a mean between envy and spite, and these states are concerned with the pain and pleasures that are felt at the fortunes of our neighbours; the man who is characterized by righteous indignation is pained at undeserved good fortune, the envious man, going beyond him, is pained at all good fortune, and the spiteful man falls so far short of being pained that he even rejoices. But these states there will be an opportunity of describing elsewhere; with regard to justice, since it has not one simple meaning, we shall, after describing the other states, distinguish its two kinds and say how each of them is a mean; and similarly we shall treat also of the rational virtues.

8. There are three kinds of disposition, then, two of them vices, involving excess and deficiency respectively, and one a virtue, viz. the mean, and all are in a sense opposed to all; for the extreme states are contrary both to the intermediate state and to each other, and the intermediate to the extremes; as the equal is greater relatively to the less, less relatively to the greater, so the middle states are excessive relatively to the deficiencies, deficient relatively to the excesses, both in passions and in actions. For the brave man appears rash relatively to the coward, and cowardly relatively to the rash man; and similarly the temperate man appears self-indulgent relatively to the insensible man, insensible relatively to the self-indulgent, and the liberal man prodigal relatively to the mean man, mean relatively to the prodigal. Hence also the people at the extremes push the intermediate man each over to the other, and the brave man is called rash by the coward, cowardly by the rash man, and correspondingly in the other cases.

These states being thus opposed to one another, the greatest contrariety is that of the extremes to each other, rather than to the intermediate; for these are further from each other than from the intermediate, as the great is further from the small and the small from the great than both are from the equal. Again, to the intermediate some extremes show a certain likeness, as that of rashness to courage and that of prodigality to liberality; but the extremes show the greatest unlikeness to each other; now contraries are defined as the things that are furthest from each other, so that things that are further apart are more contrary.

To the mean in some cases the deficiency, in some the excess is more opposed; e.g. it is not rashness, which is an excess, but cowardice, which is a deficiency, that is more opposed to courage, and not insensibility, which is a deficiency, but self-indulgence, which is an excess, that is more opposed to temperance. This happens from two reasons, one being drawn from the thing itself; for because one extreme is nearer and liker to the intermediate, we oppose not this but rather its contrary to the intermediate. E.g., since rashness is thought liker and nearer to courage, and cowardice more unlike, we oppose rather the latter to courage; for things that are further from the intermediate are thought more contrary to it. This, then, is one cause, drawn from the thing itself; another is drawn from ourselves; for the things to which we ourselves more naturally tend seem more contrary to the intermediate. For instance, we ourselves tend more naturally to pleasures, and hence are more easily carried away towards self-indulgence than towards propriety. We describe as contrary to the mean, then, rather the directions in which we more often go to great lengths; and therefore self-indulgence, which is an excess, is the more contrary to temperance.

9. That moral virtue is a mean, then, and in what sense it is so, and that it is a mean between two vices, the one involving excess, the other deficiency, and that it is such because its character is to aim at what is intermediate in passions and in actions, has been sufficiently stated. Hence also it is no easy task to be good. For in everything it is no easy task to find the middle, e.g. to find the middle of a circle is not for every one but for him who knows; so, too, any one can get angry—that is easy—or give or spend money; but to do this to the right person, to the right extent, at the right time, with the right motive, and in the right way, *that* is not for every one, nor is it easy; wherefore goodness is both rare and laudable and noble.

Hence he who aims at the intermediate must first depart from what is the more contrary to it, as Calypso advises—

Hold the ship out beyond that surf and
spray.

For of the extremes one is more erroneous, one
less so; therefore, since to hit the mean is hard
in the extreme, we must as a second best, as
people say, take the least of the evils; and this
will be done best in the way we describe.

But we must consider the things towards
which we ourselves also are easily carried away;
for some of us tend to one thing, some to another; and this will be recognizable from the
pleasure and the pain we feel. We must drag
ourselves away to the contrary extreme; for we
shall get into the intermediate state by drawing
well away from error, as people do in straight-
ening sticks that are bent.

Now in everything the pleasant or pleasure
is most to be guarded against; for we do not
judge it impartially. We ought, then, to feel
towards pleasure as the elders of the people
felt towards Helen, and in all circumstances
repeat their saying; for if we dismiss pleasure
thus we are less likely to go astray. It is by

doing this, then, (to sum the matter up) that
we shall best be able to hit the mean.

But this is no doubt difficult, and especially
in individual cases; for it is not easy to determine both how and with whom and on what
provocation and how long one should be angry;
for we too sometimes praise those who fall
short and call them good-tempered, but sometimes we praise those who get angry and call
them manly. The man, however, who deviates
little from goodness is not blamed, whether he
do so in the direction of the more or of the
less, but only the man who deviates more
widely; for *he* does not fail to be noticed. But
up to what point and to what extent a man
must deviate before he becomes blameworthy it
is not easy to determine by reasoning, any more
than anything else that is perceived by the
senses; such things depend on particular facts,
and the decision rests with perception. So
much, then, is plain, that the intermediate
state is in all things to be praised, but that we
must incline sometimes towards the excess,
sometimes towards the deficiency; for so shall
we most easily hit the mean and what is right.

Doctrines of hedonism

Epicurus (342/1-270 B.C.)

Most of what is commonly believed about the life of Epicurus comes from the biography written by Diogenes Laertius, about four centuries after the death of Epicurus. Though there is little to go on, and most of it uncertain, it is believed that Epicurus grew up on the island of Samos, an Athenian colony. In his eighteenth year he is supposed to have gone to Athens, where he probably studied the philosophies of Plato and of Democritus, a materialist. When he was about forty-eight, Epicurus is said to have founded a school in the outskirts of Athens and to have taught and practiced his philosophy thereafter.

Epicurus taught that pleasure was the good, basing his theory on the atomistic materialism of Democritus. He especially emphasized the avoidance of pain and held that prudence and honor were essential to a life of pleasure. Our selection is the whole of his Principal Doctrines.

I. The blessed and immortal nature knows no trouble itself nor causes trouble to any other, so that it is never constrained by anger or favour. For all such things exist only in the weak.

II. Death is nothing to us: for that which is dissolved is without sensation; and that which lacks sensation is nothing to us.

III. The limit of quantity in pleasures is the removal of all that is painful. Wherever pleasure is present, as long as it is there, there is neither pain of body nor of mind, nor of both at once.

IV. Pain does not last continuously in the flesh, but the acutest pain is there for a very short time, and even that which just exceeds the pleasure in the flesh does not continue for many days at once. But chronic illnesses permit a predominance of pleasure over pain in the flesh.

V. It is not possible to live pleasantly without living prudently and honourably and justly, [nor again to live a life of prudence, honour, and justice] without living pleasantly. And the man who does not possess the pleasant life, is not living prudently and honourably and justly, [and the man who does not possess the virtuous life], cannot possibly live pleasantly.

VI. To secure protection from men anything is a natural good, by which you may be able to attain this end.

VII. Some men wished to become famous and conspicuous, thinking that they would thus win for themselves safety from other men. Wherefore if the life of such men is safe, they have obtained the good which nature craves; but if it is not safe, they do not possess that for which they strove at first by the instinct of nature.

VIII. No pleasure is a bad thing in itself: but the means which produce some pleasures bring with them disturbances many times greater than the pleasures.

IX. If every pleasure could be intensified so that it lasted and influenced the whole organ-

From Cyril Bailey, *Epicurus: The Extant Remains.* Copyright, 1926, by the Clarendon Press. Used by permission of the Clarendon Press, Oxford.

ism or the most essential parts of our nature, pleasures would never differ from one another.

X. If the things that produce the pleasures of profligates could dispel the fears of the mind about the phenomena of the sky and death and its pains, and also teach the limits of desires (and of pains), we should never have cause to blame them: for they would be filling themselves full with pleasures from every source and never have pain of body or mind, which is the evil of life.

XI. If we were not troubled by our suspicions of the phenomena of the sky and about death, fearing that it concerns us, and also by our failure to grasp the limits of pains and desires, we should have no need of natural science.

XII. A man cannot dispel his fear about the most important matters if he does not know what is the nature of the universe but suspects the truth of some mythical story. So that without natural science it is not possible to attain our pleasures unalloyed.

XIII. There is no profit in securing protection in relation to men, if things above and things beneath the earth and indeed all in the boundless universe remain matters of suspicion.

XIV. The most unalloyed source of protection from men, which is secured to some extent by a certain force of expulsion, is in fact the immunity which results from a quiet life and the retirement from the world.

XV. The wealth demanded by nature is both limited and easily procured; that demanded by idle imaginings stretches on to infinity.

XVI. In but few things chance hinders a wise man, but the greatest and most important matters reason has ordained and throughout the whole period of life does and will ordain.

XVII. The just man is most free from trouble, the unjust most full of trouble.

XVIII. The pleasure in the flesh is not increased, when once the pain due to want is removed, but is only varied: and the limit as regards pleasure in the mind is begotten by the reasoned understanding of these very pleasures and of the emotions akin to them, which used to cause the greatest fear to the mind.

XIX. Infinite time contains no greater pleas-

ure than limited time, if one measures by reason the limits of pleasure.

XX. The flesh perceives the limits of pleasure as unlimited and unlimited time is required to supply it. But the mind, having attained a reasoned understanding of the ultimate good of the flesh and its limits and having dissipated the fears concerning the time to come, supplies us with the complete life, and we have no further need of infinite time: but neither does the mind shun pleasure, nor, when circumstances begin to bring about the departure from life, does it approach its end as though it fell short in any way of the best life.

XXI. He who has learned the limits of life knows that that which removes the pain due to want and makes the whole of life complete is easy to obtain; so that there is no need of actions which involve competition.

XXII. We must consider both the real purpose and all the evidence of direct perception, to which we always refer the conclusions of opinion; otherwise, all will be full of doubt and confusion.

XXIII. If you fight against all sensations, you will have no standard by which to judge even those of them which you say are false.

XXIV. If you reject any single sensation and fail to distinguish between the conclusion of opinion as to the appearance awaiting confirmation and that which is actually given by the sensation or feeling, or each intuitive apprehension of the mind, you will confound all other sensations as well with the same groundless opinion, so that you will reject every standard of judgement. And if among the mental images created by your opinion you affirm both that which awaits confirmation and that which does not, you will not escape error, since you will have preserved the whole cause of doubt in every judgement between what is right and what is wrong.

XXV. If on each occasion instead of referring your actions to the end of nature, you turn to some other nearer standard when you are making a choice or an avoidance, your actions will not be consistent with your principles.

XXVI. Of desires, all that do not lead to a sense of pain, if they are not satisfied, are not necessary, but involve a craving which is easily dispelled, when the object is hard to procure or they seem likely to produce harm.

XXVII. Of all the things which wisdom acquires to produce the blessedness of the complete life, far the greatest is the possession of friendship.

XXVIII. The same conviction which has given us confidence that there is nothing terrible that lasts for ever or even for long, has also seen the protection of friendship most fully completed in the limited evils of this life.

XXIX. Among desires some are natural ‹and necessary, some natural› but not necessary, and others neither natural nor necessary, but due to idle imagination.

XXX. Wherever in the case of desires which are physical, but do not lead to a sense of pain, if they are not fulfilled, the effort is intense, such pleasures are due to idle imagination, and it is not owing to their own nature that they fail to be dispelled, but owing to the empty imaginings of the man.

XXXI. The justice which arises from nature is a pledge of mutual advantage to restrain men from harming one another and save them from being harmed.

XXXII. For all living things which have not been able to make compacts not to harm one another or be harmed, nothing ever is either just or unjust; and likewise too for all tribes of men which have been unable or unwilling to make compacts not to harm or be harmed.

XXXIII. Justice never is anything in itself, but in the dealings of men with one another in any place whatever and at any time it is a kind of compact not to harm or be harmed.

XXXIV. Injustice is not an evil in itself, but only in consequence of the fear which attaches to the apprehension of being unable to escape those appointed to punish such actions.

XXXV. It is not possible for one who acts in secret contravention of the terms of the compact not to harm or be harmed, to be confident that he will escape detection, even if at present he escapes a thousand times. For up to the time of death it cannot be certain that he will indeed escape.

XXXVI. In its general aspect justice is the same for all, for it is a kind of mutual advantage in the dealings of men with one another: but with reference to the individual peculiarities of a country or any other circumstances the same thing does not turn out to be just for all.

XXXVII. Among actions which are sanctioned as just by law, that which is proved on examination to be of advantage in the requirements of men's dealings with one another, has the guarantee of justice, whether it is the same for all or not. But if a man makes a law and it does not turn out to lead to advantage in men's dealings with each other, then it no longer has the essential nature of justice. And even if the advantage in the matter of justice shifts from one side to the other, but for a while accords with the general concept, it is none the less just for that period in the eyes of those who do not confound themselves with empty sounds but look to the actual facts.

XXXVIII. Where, provided the circumstances have not been altered, actions which were considered just, have been shown not to accord with the general concept in actual practice, then they are not just. But where, when circumstances have changed, the same actions which were sanctioned as just no longer lead to advantage, there they were just at the time when they were of advantage for the dealings of fellow-citizens with one another; but subsequently they are no longer just, when no longer of advantage.

XXXIX. The man who has best ordered the element of disquiet arising from external circumstances has made those things that he could akin to himself and the rest at least not alien: but with all to which he could not do even this, he has refrained from mixing, and has expelled from his life all which it was of advantage to treat thus.

XL. As many as possess the power to procure complete immunity from their neighbours, these also live most pleasantly with one another, since they have the most certain pledge of security, and after they have enjoyed the fullest intimacy, they do not lament the previous departure of a dead friend, as though he were to be pitied.

Descriptive and normative

David Hume (1711-1776)*

In the following selection from A Treatise of Human Nature *Hume argues that the emotions, rather than reason, are the basis of our moral lives. Reason, he contends, is concerned only with matters of fact and their relations. Moral questions, however, are questions of liking and disliking, praising or blaming, approving and disapproving; they are passional and not rational. In the last paragraph Hume makes an extremely important observation: Statements telling us what* ought *to be the case cannot be inferred from statements which tell us what* is *the case.*

...It has been observed, that nothing is ever present to the mind but its perceptions; and that all the actions of seeing, hearing, judging, loving, hating, and thinking, fall under this denomination. The mind can never exert itself in any action which we may not comprehend under the term of *perception*; and consequently that term is no less applicable to those judgments by which we distinguish moral good and evil, than to every other operation of the mind. To approve of one character, to condemn another, are only so many different perceptions.

Now, as perceptions resolve themselves into two kinds, viz. *impressions* and *ideas*, this distinction gives rise to a question, with which we shall open up our present inquiry concerning morals, *whether it is by means of our* ideas *or* impressions *we distinguish betwixt vice and virtue, and pronounce an action blamable or praiseworthy?* This will immediately cut off all loose discourses and declamations, and reduce us to something precise and exact on the present subject.

From David Hume, *A Treatise of Human Nature,* book III, part 1.

* See the introductory note on Hume on page 27.

164

Those who affirm that virtue is nothing but a conformity to reason; that there are eternal fitnesses and unfitnesses of things, which are the same to every rational being that considers them; that the immutable measure of right and wrong impose an obligation, not only on human creatures, but also on the Deity himself: all these systems concur in the opinion, that morality, like truth, is discerned merely by ideas, and by their juxtaposition and comparison. In order, therefore, to judge of these systems, we need only consider whether it be possible from reason alone, to distinguish betwixt moral good and evil, or whether there must concur some other principles to enable us to make that distinction.

If morality had naturally no influence on human passions and actions, it were in vain to take such pains to inculcate it; and nothing would be more fruitless than that multitude of rules and precepts with which all moralists abound. Philosophy is commonly divided into *speculative* and *practical*; and as morality is always comprehended under the latter division, it is supposed to influence our passions and actions, and to go beyond the calm and indolent judgments of the understanding. And this is confirmed by common experience, which informs us, that men are often governed by their duties, and are deterred from some actions by the opinion of injustice, and impelled to others by that of obligation.

Since morals, therefore, have an influence on the actions and affections, it follows, that they cannot be derived from reason; and that because reason alone, as we have already proved, can never have any such influence. Morals excite passions, and produce or prevent actions. Reason of itself is utterly impotent in this particular. The rules of morality, therefore, are not conclusions of our reason.

No one, I believe, will deny the justness of this inference; nor is there any other means of evading it, than by denying that principle, on which it is founded. As long as it is allowed, that reason has no influence on our passions and actions, it is in vain to pretend that morality is discovered only by a deduction of reason. An active principle can never be founded on an inactive; and if reason be inactive in itself, it must remain so in all its shapes and appearances, whether it exerts itself in natural or moral subjects, whether it considers the powers of external bodies, or the actions of rational beings. . . .

Reason is the discovery of truth or falsehood. Truth or falsehood consists in an agreement or disagreement either to the *real* relations of ideas, or to *real* existence and matter of fact. Whatever therefore is not susceptible of this agreement or disagreement, is incapable of being true or false, and can never be an object of our reason. Now, it is evident our passions, volitions, and actions, are not susceptible of any such agreement or disagreement; being original facts and realities, complete in themselves, and implying no reference to other passions, volitions, and actions. It is impossible, therefore, they can be pronounced either true or false, and be either contrary or conformable to reason.

This argument is of double advantage to our present purpose. For it proves *directly*, that actions do not derive their merit from a conformity to reason, nor their blame from a contrariety to it; and it proves the same truth more *indirectly*, by showing us, that as reason can never immediately prevent or produce any action by contradicting or approving of it, it cannot be the source of moral good and evil, which are found to have that influence. Actions may be laudable or blamable; but they cannot be reasonable or unreasonable: laudable or blamable, therefore, are not the same with reasonable or unreasonable. The merit and demerit of actions frequently contradict, and sometimes control our natural propensities. But reason has no such influence. Moral distinctions, therefore, are not the offspring of reason. Reason is wholly inactive, and can never be the source of so active a principle as conscience, or a sense of morals.

But perhaps it may be said, that though no will or action can be immediately contradictory to reason, yet we may find such a contradiction in some of the attendants of the actions, that is, in its causes or effects. The action may cause a judgment, or may be *obliquely* caused by one, when the judgment concurs with a passion; and by an abusive way of speaking, which philosophy will scarce allow of, the same contrariety may, upon that account, be ascribed to the action. How far this truth or falsehood may be the source of morals, it will now be proper to consider.

It has been observed, that reason, in a strict and philosophical sense, can have an influence on our conduct only after two ways: either when it excites a passion, by informing us of the existence of something which is a proper object of it; or when it discovers the connection of causes and effects, so as to afford us means of exerting any passion. These are the only kinds of judgment which can accompany our actions, or can be said to produce them in any manner; and it must be allowed, that these judgments may often be false and erroneous. A person may be affected with passion, by supposing a pain or pleasure to lie in an object which has no tendency to produce either of these sensations, or which produces the contrary to what is imagined. A person may also take false measures for the attaining of his end, and may retard, by his foolish conduct, instead of forwarding the execution of any object. These false judgments may be thought to affect the passions and actions, which are connected with them, and may be said to render them un-reasonable, in a figurative and improper way of speaking. But though this be acknowledged, it is easy to observe, that these errors are so far from being the source of all immorality, that they are commonly very innocent, and draw no manner of guilt upon the person who is so unfortunate as to fall into them. They extend not beyond a mistake of *fact*, which moralists have not generally supposed criminal, as being perfectly involuntary. I am more to be lamented than blamed, if I am mistaken with regard to the influence of objects in producing pain or pleasure, or if I know not the proper means of satisfying my desires. No one can ever regard such errors as a defect in my moral character. A fruit, for instance, that is really disagreeable, appears to me at a distance, and, through mistake, I fancy it to be pleasant and delicious. Here is one error. I choose certain means of reaching this fruit, which are not proper for my end. Here is a second error; nor is there any third one, which can ever possibly enter into our reasonings concerning actions. I ask, therefore, if a man in this situation, and guilty of these two errors, is to be regarded as vicious and criminal, however unavoidable they might have been? Or if it be possible to imagine, that such errors are the sources of all immorality?

And here it may be proper to observe, that if moral distinctions be derived from the truth or falsehood of those judgments, they must take place wherever we form the judgments; nor will there be any difference, whether the question be concerning an apple or a kingdom, or whether the error be avoidable or unavoidable.

For as the very essence of morality is supposed to consist in an agreement or disagreement to reason, the other circumstances are entirely arbitrary, and can never either bestow on any action the character of virtuous or vicious, or deprive it of that character. To which we may add, that this agreement or disagreement, not admitting of degrees, all virtues and vices would of course be equal.

Should it be pretended, that though a mistake of *fact* be not criminal, yet a mistake of *right* often is; and that this may be the source of immorality: I would answer, that it is impossible such a mistake can ever be the original source of immorality, since it supposes a real right and wrong; that is, a real distinction in morals, independent of these judgments. A mistake, therefore, of right, may become a species of immorality; but it is only a secondary one, and is founded on some other antecedent to it.

As to those judgments which are the *effects* of our actions, and which, when false, give occasion to pronounce the actions contrary to truth and reason; we may observe, that our actions never cause any judgment, either true or false, in ourselves, and that it is only on others they have such an influence. It is certain that an action, on many occasions, may give rise to false conclusions in others; and that a person, who, through a window, sees any lewd behavior of mine with my neighbor's wife, may be so simple as to imagine she is certainly my own. In this respect my action resembles somewhat a lie or falsehood; only with this difference, which is material, that I perform not the action with any intention of giving rise to a false judgment in another, but merely to satisfy my lust and passion. It causes, however, a mistake and false judgment by accident; and the falsehood of its effects may be ascribed, by some odd figurative way of speaking, to the action itself. But still I can see no pretext of reason for asserting, that the tendency to cause such an error is the first spring or original source of all immorality.[1]

---

[1] One might think it were entirely superfluous to prove this, if a late author, who has had the good fortune to obtain some reputation, had not seriously affirmed, that such a falsehood is the foundation of all guilt and moral deformity. That we may discover the fallacy of his hypothesis, we need only consider, that a false conclusion is drawn from an action, only by means of an obscurity of natural principles, which makes a cause be secretly interrupted in its operation, by contrary causes, and renders the connection betwixt two objects uncertain and variable. Now, as a like uncertainty and variety of causes take place, even in natural objects, and produce a like error in our judg-

Thus, upon the whole, it is impossible that the distinction betwixt moral good and evil can be made by reason; since that distinction has an influence upon our actions, of which reason alone is incapable. Reason and judgment may, indeed, be the mediate cause of an action, by prompting or by directing a passion; but it is not pretended that a judgment of this kind, either in its truth or falsehood, is attended with virtue or vice. And as to the judgments, which are caused by our judgments, they can still less bestow those moral qualities on the actions which are their causes.

But, to be more particular, and to show that those eternal immutable fitnesses and unfit-

nesses of things cannot be defended by sound philosophy, we may weigh the following considerations.

If the thought and understanding were alone capable of fixing the boundaries of right and wrong, the character of virtuous and vicious either must lie in some relations of objects, or must be a matter of fact which is discovered by our reasoning. This consequence is evident. As the operations of human understanding divide themselves into two kinds, the comparing of ideas, and the inferring of matter of fact, were virtue discovered by the understanding, it must be an object of one of these operations; nor is there any third operation

---

ment, if that tendency to produce error were the very essence of vice and immorality, it should follow, that even inanimate objects might be vicious and immoral.

It is in vain to urge, that inanimate objects act without liberty and choice. For as liberty and choice are not necessary to make an action produce in us an erroneous conclusion, they can be, in no respect, essential to morality; and I do not readily perceive, upon this system, how they can ever come to be regarded by it. If the tendency to cause error be the origin of immorality, that tendency and immorality would in every case be inseparable.

Add to this, that if I had used the precaution of shutting the window, while I indulged myself in those liberties with my neighbor's wife, I should have been guilty of no immorality; and that because my action, being perfectly concealed, would have had no tendency to produce any false conclusion.

For the same reason, a thief, who steals in by a ladder at a window, and takes all imaginable care to cause no disturbance, is in no respect criminal. For either he will not be perceived, or if he be it is impossible he can produce any error, nor will any one, from these circumstances, take him to be other than what he really is.

It is well known, that those who are squint-sighted do very readily cause mistakes in others, and that we imagine they salute or are talking to one person, while they address themselves to another. Are they, therefore, upon that account, immoral?

Besides, we may easily observe, that in all those arguments there is an evident reasoning in a circle. A person who takes possession of *another's* goods, and uses them as his *own,* in a

manner declares them to be his own; and this falsehood is the source of the immorality of injustice. But is property, or right, or obligation, intelligible without an antecedent morality?

A man that is ungrateful to his benefactor, in a manner affirms that he never received any favors from him. But in what manner? Is it because it is his duty to be grateful? But this supposes that there is some antecedent rule of duty and morals. Is it because human nature is generally grateful, and makes us conclude that a man who does any harm, never receives any favor from the person he harmed? But human nature is not so generally grateful as to justify such a conclusion; or, if it were, is an exception to a general rule in every case criminal, for no other reason than because it is an exception?

But what may suffice entirely to destroy this whimsical system is, that it leaves us under the same difficulty to give a reason why truth is virtuous and falsehood vicious, as to account for the merit or turpitude of any other action. I shall allow, if you please, that all immorality is derived from this supposed falsehood in action, provided you can give me any plausible reason why such a falsehood is immoral. If you consider rightly of the matter, you will find yourself in the same difficulty as at the beginning.

This last argument is very conclusive; because, if there be not an evident merit or turpitude annexed to this species of truth or falsehood, it can never have any influence upon our actions. For who ever thought of forbearing any action, because others might possibly draw false conclusions from it? Or who ever performed any, that he might give rise to true conclusions?

of the understanding which can discover it. There has been an opinion very industriously propagated by certain philosophers, that morality is susceptible of demonstration; and though no one has ever been able to advance a single step in those demonstrations, yet it is taken for granted that this science may be brought to an equal certainty with geometry or algebra. Upon this supposition, vice and virtue must consist in some relations; since it is allowed on all hands, that no matter of fact is capable of being demonstrated. Let us therefore begin with examining this hypothesis, and endeavor, if possible, to fix those moral qualities which have been so long the objects of our fruitless researches; point out distinctly the relations which constitute morality or obligation, that we may know wherein they consist, and after what manner we must judge of them.

If you assert that vice and virtue consist in relations susceptible of certainty and demonstration, you must confine yourself to those *four* relations which alone admit of that degree of evidence; and in that case you run into absurdities from which you will never be able to extricate yourself. For as you make the very essence of morality to lie in the relations, and as there is no one of these relations but what is applicable, not only to an irrational but also to an inanimate object, it follows, that even such objects must be susceptible of merit or demerit. *Resemblance, contrariety, degrees in quality*, and *proportions in quantity and number;* all these relations belong as properly to matter, as to our actions, passions, and volitions. It is unquestionable, therefore, that morality lies not in any of these relations, nor the sense of it in their discovery.

Should it be asserted, that the sense of morality consists in the discovery of some relation distinct from these, and that our enumeration was not complete when we comprehended all demonstrable relations under four general heads; to this I know not what to reply, till some one be so good as to point out to me this new relation. It is impossible to refute a system which has never yet been explained. In such a manner of fighting in the dark, a man loses his blows in the air, and often places them where the enemy is not present.

I must therefore, on this occasion, rest contented with requiring the two following conditions of any one that would undertake to clear up this system. *First*, as moral good and evil belong only to the actions of the mind, and are derived from our situation with regard to external objects, the relations from which these moral distinctions arise must lie only betwixt internal actions and external objects, and must not be applicable either to internal actions, compared among themselves, or to external objects, when placed in opposition to other external objects. For as morality is supposed to attend certain relations, if these relations could belong to internal actions considered singly, it would follow, that we might be guilty of crimes in ourselves, and independent of our situation with respect to the universe; and in like manner, if these moral relations could be applied to external objects, it would follow, that even inanimate beings would be susceptible of moral beauty and deformity. Now, it seems difficult to imagine that any relation can be discovered betwixt our passions, volitions, and actions, compared to external objects, which relation might not belong either to these passions and volitions, or to these external objects, compared among *themselves.*

But it will be still more difficult to fulfil the *second* condition, requisite to justify this system. According to the principles of those who maintain an abstract rational difference betwixt moral good and evil, and a natural fitness and unfitness of things, it is not only supposed, that these relations, being eternal and immutable, are the same, when considered by every rational creature, but their *effects* are also supposed to be necessarily the same; and it is concluded they have no less, or rather a greater, influence in directing the will of the Deity, than in governing the rational and virtuous of our own species. These two particulars are evidently distinct. It is one thing to know virtue, and another to conform the will to it. In order, therefore, to prove that the measures of right and wrong are eternal laws, *obligatory* on every rational mind, it is not sufficient to show the relations upon which they are founded: we must also point out the connection betwixt the relation and the will; and must prove that this connection is so necessary, that in every well-disposed mind, it must take place and have its influence; though the difference betwixt these minds be in other respects immense and infinite. Now, besides what I have already proved, that even in human nature no relation can ever alone produce any action; besides this, I say, it has been shown, in treating of the understanding, that there is no connection of cause and effect, such as this is supposed to be, which is discoverable otherwise than by experience, and of which we can pretend to have any security by the simple consideration of the objects. All beings in the universe, considered in themselves, appear entirely loose and independent of each other. It is only by experience we learn their influence and connection; and this influence we ought never to extend beyond experience.

Thus it will be impossible to fulfil the *first* condition required to the system of eternal rational measures of right and wrong; because it is impossible to show those relations, upon which such a distinction may be founded: and it is as impossible to fulfil the *second* condition; because we cannot prove *a priori*, that these relations, if they really existed and were perceived, would be universally forcible and obligatory.

But to make these general reflections more clear and convincing, we may illustrate them by some particular instances, wherein this character of moral good or evil is the most universally acknowledged. Of all crimes that human creatures are capable of committing, the most horrid and unnatural is ingratitude, especially when it is committed against parents, and appears in the more flagrant instances of wounds and death. This is acknowledged by all mankind, philosophers as well as the people: the question only arises among philosophers, whether the guilt or moral deformity of this action be discovered by demonstrative reasoning, or be felt by an internal sense, and by means of some sentiment, which the reflecting on such an action naturally occasions. This question will soon be decided against the former opinion, if we can show the same relations in other objects, without the notion of any guilt or iniquity attending them. Reason or science is nothing but the comparing of ideas, and the discovery of their relations; and if the same relations have different characters, it must evidently follow, that those characters are not discovered merely by reason. To put the affair, therefore, to this trial, let us choose any inanimate object, such as an oak or elm; and let us suppose, that, by the dropping of its seed, it produces a sapling below it, which, springing up by degrees, at last overtops and destroys the parent tree: I ask, if, in this instance, there be wanting any relation which is discoverable in parricide or ingratitude? Is not the one tree the cause of the other's existence; and the latter the cause of the destruction of the former, in the same manner as when a child murders his parent? It is not sufficient to reply, that a choice or will is wanting. For in the case of parricide, a will does not give rise to any *different* relations, but is only the cause from which the action is derived; and consequently produces the *same* relations, that in the oak or elm arise from some other principles. It is a will or choice that determines a man to kill his parent: and they are the laws of matter and motion, that determine a sapling to destroy the oak from which it sprung. Here then the same relations have different causes; but still the relations are the same: and as their discovery is not in both cases attended with a notion of immorality, it follows, that that notion does not arise from such a discovery.

But to choose an instance still more resembling; I would fain ask any one, why incest in the human species is criminal, and why the very same action, and the same relations in animals, have not the smallest moral turpitude and deformity? If it be answered, that this action is innocent in animals, because they have not reason sufficient to discover its turpitude; but that man, being endowed with that faculty, which *ought* to restrain him to his duty, the same action instantly becomes criminal to him. Should this be said, I would reply, that this is evidently arguing in a circle. For, before reason can perceive this turpitude, the turpitude must exist; and consequently is independent of the decisions of our reason, and is their object more properly than their effect. According to this system, then, every animal that has sense and appetite and will, that is, every animal must be susceptible of all the same virtues and vices, for which we ascribe praise and blame to human creatures. All the difference is, that our superior reason may serve to discover the vice or virtue, and by that means may augment the blame or praise: but still this discovery supposes a separate being in these moral distinctions, and a being which depends only on the will and appetite, and which, both in thought and reality, may be distinguished from reason. Animals are susceptible of the same relations with respect to each other as the human species, and therefore would also be susceptible of the same morality, if the essence of morality consisted in these relations. Their want of a sufficient degree of reason may hinder them from perceiving the duties and obligations of morality, but can never hinder these duties from existing; since they must antecedently exist, in order to their being perceived. Reason must find them, and can never produce them. This argument deserves to be weighed, as being, in my opinion, entirely decisive.

Nor does this reasoning only prove, that morality consists not in any relations that are the objects of science; but if examined, will prove with equal certainty, that it consists not in any *matter of fact*, which can be discovered by the understanding. This is the *second* part of our argument; and if it can be made evident, we may conclude, that morality is not an object of reason. But can there be any difficulty in proving, that vice and virtue are not matters of fact, whose existence we can infer by reason? Take any action allowed to be vicious; wilful murder, for instance. Examine it in all lights, and see if you can find that matter of fact, or real existence, which you call *vice*. In whichever way you take it, you find only certain passions, motives, volitions, and thoughts. There is no other matter of fact in the case. The vice entirely escapes you, as long as you consider the object. You never can find it, till you turn your reflection into your own breast, and find a sentiment of disapprobation, which arises in you, towards this action. Here is a matter of fact; but it is the object of feeling, not of reason. It lies in yourself, not in the object. So that when you pronounce any action or character to be vicious, you mean nothing, but that from the constitution of your nature you have a feeling or sentiment of blame from the contemplation of it. Vice and virtue, therefore, may be compared to sounds, colors, heat, and cold, which, according to modern philosophy, are not qualities in objects, but perceptions in the mind: and this discovery in morals, like that other in physics, is to be regarded as a considerable advancement of the speculative sciences; though, like that too, it has little or no influence on practice. Nothing can be more real, or concern us more, than our own sentiments of pleasure and uneasiness; and if these be favorable to virtue, and unfavorable to vice, no more can be requisite to the regulation of our conduct and behavior.

I cannot forbear adding to these reasonings an observation, which may, perhaps, be found of some importance. In every system of morality which I have hitherto met with, I have always remarked, that the author proceeds for some time in the ordinary way of reasoning, and establishes the being of a God, or makes observations concerning human affairs; when of a sudden I am surprised to find, that instead of the usual copulations of propositions, *is*, and *is not*, I meet with no proposition that is not connected with an *ought*, or an *ought not*. This change is imperceptible; but is, however, of the last consequence. For as this *ought*, or *ought not*, expresses some new relation or affirmation, it is necessary that it should be observed and explained; and at the same time that a reason should be given, for what seems altogether inconceivable, how this new relation can be a deduction from others, which are entirely different from it. But as authors do not commonly use this precaution, I shall presume to recommend it to the readers; and am persuaded, that this small attention would subvert all the vulgar systems of morality, and let us see, that the distinction of vice and virtue is not founded merely on the relations of objects, nor is perceived by reason.

THIS COMPLIMENTARY COPY IS SENT TO YOU AT THIS TIME
IN ORDER TO GIVE YOU AN OPPORTUNITY TO EXAMINE
IT IN ADVANCE OF ITS OFFICIAL PUBLICATION DATE --
JANUARY 2 OF NEXT YEAR.   BOOKSTORES MAY PLACE
THIS BOOK ON SALE ON OR AFTER JANUARY 2.

McGRAW-HILL BOOK COMPANY

Duty, will, and the moral law

Immanuel Kant (1724-1804)

Kant was born and educated in Königsberg, East Prussia. There he spent all of his outwardly uneventful life and eventually held a professorship at the University. One hears much of the regularity of his personal life, especially in his later years. Yet Kant was a thinker of wide interests and of deep imagination. His philosophical views were highly original and exerted a profound influence on the subsequent course of philosophy. His best-known book, the Critique of Pure Reason *(1781), is a searching and complex work which inaugurated a philosophical revolution. Its impact on discussion in the theory of knowledge and metaphysics is felt today.*

Kant produced important works in ethical theory, the Fundamental Principles of the Metaphysic of Morals *(1785) and the* Critique of Practical Reason *(1788), as well as works in aesthetics, philosophy of religion, politics, and history.*

Our selection consists of the first section of his earlier statement of his ethical views, the Fundamental Principles. *In it he offers a study of "the common idea of duty and of moral laws." He is trying to exhibit the rational structure underlying the way in which we ordinarily approach moral issues. Kant contends that our knowledge in moral matters is grounded entirely on pure reason, that is, it is a priori and has nothing to do with the actual outcome of our actions. Moral worth consists in a good will, and we have a good will when we are motivated not by desire or "inclinations," but by the recognition of our duty.*

Nothing can possibly be conceived in the world, or even out of it, which can be called good, without qualification, except a Good Will. Intelligence, wit, judgment, and the other *talents* of the mind, however they may be named, or courage, resolution, perseverance, as qualities of temperament, are undoubtedly good and desirable in many respects; but these gifts of nature may also become extremely bad and mischievous if the will which is to make use of them, and which, therefore, constitutes what is called *character*, is not good. It is the

From Immanuel Kant, *Fundamental Principles of the Metaphysic of Morals*, tr. by T. K. Abbott, 1898, sec. I.

same with the *gifts of fortune*. Power, riches, honour, even health, and the general well-being and contentment with one's condition which is called *happiness*, inspire pride, and often presumption, if there is not a good will to correct the influence of these on the mind, and with this also to rectify the whole principle of acting, and adapt it to its end. The sight of a being who is not adorned with a single feature of a pure and good will, enjoying unbroken prosperity, can never give pleasure to an impartial rational spectator. Thus a good will appears to constitute the indispensable condition even of being worthy of happiness.

There are even some qualities which are of **171**

service to this good will itself, and may facilitate its action, yet which have no intrinsic unconditional value, but always presuppose a good will, and this qualifies the esteem that we justly have for them, and does not permit us to regard them as absolutely good. Moderation in the affections and passions, self-control, and calm deliberation are not only good in many respects, but even seem to constitute part of the intrinsic worth of the person; but they are far from deserving to be called good without qualification, although they have been so unconditionally praised by the ancients. For without the principles of a good will, they may become extremely bad; and the coolness of a villain not only makes him far more dangerous, but also directly makes him more abominable in our eyes than he would have been without it.

A good will is good not because of what it performs or effects, not by its aptness for the attainment of some proposed end, but simply by virtue of the volition, that is, it is good in itself, and considered by itself is to be esteemed much higher than all that can be brought about by it in favour of any inclination, nay, even of the sum-total of all inclinations. Even if it should happen that, owing to special disfavour of fortune, or the niggardly provision of a step-motherly nature, this will should wholly lack power to accomplish its purpose, if with its greatest efforts it should yet achieve nothing, and there should remain only the good will (not, to be sure, a mere wish, but the summoning of all means in our power), then, like a jewel, it would still shine by its own light, as a thing which has its whole value in itself. Its usefulness or fruitlessness can neither add to nor take away anything from this value. It would be, as it were, only the setting to enable us to handle it the more conveniently in common commerce, or to attract to it the attention of those who are not yet connoisseurs, but not to recommend it to true connoisseurs, or to determine its value.

There is, however, something so strange in this idea of the absolute value of the mere will, in which no account is taken of its utility, that notwithstanding the thorough assent of even common reason to the idea, yet a suspicion must arise that it may perhaps really be the product of mere high-flown fancy, and that we may have misunderstood the purpose of nature in assigning reason as the governor of our will. Therefore we will examine this idea from this point of view.

In the physical constitution of an organized being, that is, a being adapted suitably to the purposes of life, we assume it as a fundamental principle that no organ for any purpose will be found but what is also the fittest and best adapted for that purpose. Now in a being which has reason and a will, if the proper object of nature were its *conservation*, its *welfare*, in a word, its *happiness*, then nature would have hit upon a very bad arrangement in selecting the reason of the creature to carry out this purpose. For all the actions which the creature has to perform with a view to this purpose, and the whole rule of its conduct, would be far more surely prescribed to it by instinct, and that end would have been attained thereby much more certainly than it ever can be by reason. Should reason have been communicated to this favoured creature over and above, it must only have served it to contemplate the happy constitution of its nature, to admire it, to congratulate itself thereon, and to feel thankful for it to the beneficent cause, but not that it should subject its desires to that weak and delusive guidance, and meddle bunglingly with the purpose of nature. In a word, nature would have taken care that reason should not break forth into *practical exercise*, nor have the presumption, with its weak insight, to think out for itself the plan of happiness, and of the means of attaining it. Nature would not only have taken on herself the choice of the ends, but also of the means, and with wise foresight would have entrusted both to instinct.

And, in fact, we find that the more a cultivated reason applies itself with deliberate purpose to the enjoyment of life and happiness, so much the more does the man fail of true satisfaction. And from this circumstance there arises in many, if they are candid enough to confess it, a certain degree of *misology*, that is, hatred of reason, especially in the case of those who are most experienced in the use of it, because after calculating all the advantages they derive, I do not say from the invention of all the arts of common luxury, but even from the sciences (which seem to them to be after all only a luxury of the understanding), they find that they have, in fact, only brought more trouble on their shoulders, rather than gained in happiness; and they end by envying, rather than despising, the more common stamp of men who keep closer to the guidance of mere instinct, and do not allow their reason much influence on their conduct. And this we must admit, that the judgment of those who would very much lower the lofty eulogies of the advantages which reason gives us in regard to the happiness and satisfaction of life, or who would even reduce them below zero, is by no means morose or ungrateful to the goodness with which the world is governed, but that there lies at the root of these judgments the idea that our existence has a different and far nobler end, for which, and not for happiness, reason is properly intended, and which must, therefore, be regarded as the supreme condition to which the private ends of man must, for the most part, be postponed.

For as reason is not competent to guide the will with certainty in regard to its objects and the satisfaction of all our wants (which it to some extent even multiplies), this being an end to which an implanted instinct would have led with much greater certainty; and since, nevertheless, reason is imparted to us as a practical faculty, *i.e.* as one which is to have influence on the *will*, therefore, admitting that nature generally in the distribution of her capacities has adapted the means to the end, its true destination must be to produce a *will*, not merely good as a *means* to something else, but *good in itself*, for which reason was absolutely necessary. This will then, though not indeed the sole and complete good, must be the supreme good and the condition of every other, even of the desire of happiness. Under these circumstances, there is nothing inconsistent with the wisdom of nature in the fact that the cultivation of the reason, which is

requisite for the first and unconditional purpose, does in many ways interfere, at least in this life, with the attainment of the second, which is always conditional, namely, happiness. Nay, it may even reduce it to nothing, without nature thereby failing of her purpose. For reason recognizes the establishment of a good will as its highest practical destination, and in attaining this purpose is capable only of a satisfaction of its own proper kind, namely, that from the attainment of an end, which end again is determined by reason only, notwithstanding that this may involve many a disappointment to the ends of inclination.

We have then to develop the notion of a will which deserves to be highly esteemed for itself, and is good without a view to anything further, a notion which exists already in the sound natural understanding, requiring rather to be cleared up than to be taught, and which in estimating the value of our actions always takes the first place, and constitutes the condition of all the rest. In order to do this, we will take the notion of duty, which includes that of a good will, although implying certain subjective restrictions and hindrances. These, however, far from concealing it, or rendering it unrecognizable, rather bring it out by contrast, and make it shine forth so much the brighter.

I omit here all actions which are already recognized as inconsistent with duty, although they may be useful for this or that purpose, for with these the question whether they are done *from duty* cannot arise at all, since they even conflict with it. I also set aside those actions which really conform to duty, but to which men have *no* direct *inclination*, performing them because they are impelled thereto by some other inclination. For in this case we can readily distinguish whether the action which agrees with duty is done *from duty*, or from a selfish view. It is much harder to make this distinction when the action accords with duty, and the subject has besides a *direct* inclination to it. For example, it is always a matter of duty that a dealer should not overcharge an inexperienced purchaser; and wherever there is much commerce the prudent tradesman does not overcharge, but keeps a fixed price for everyone, so that a child buys of him as well as any other. Men are thus *honestly* served; but this is not enough to make us believe that the tradesman has so acted from duty and from principles of honesty: his own advantage required it; it is out of the question in this case to suppose that he might besides have a direct inclination in favour of the buyers, so that, as it were, from love he should give no advantage to one over another. Accordingly the action was done neither from duty nor from direct inclination, but merely with a selfish view.

On the other hand, it is a duty to maintain one's life; and, in addition, everyone has also a direct inclination to do so. But on this account the often anxious care which most men take for it has no intrinsic worth, and their maxim has no moral import. They preserve their life *as duty requires*, no doubt, but not *because duty requires*. On the other hand, if adversity and hopeless sorrow have completely taken away the relish for life; if the unfortunate one, strong in mind, indignant at his fate rather than desponding or dejected, wishes for death, and yet preserves his life without loving it—not from inclination or fear, but from duty—then his maxim has a moral worth.

To be beneficent when we can is a duty; and besides this, there are many minds so sympathetically constituted that, without any other motive of vanity or self-interest, they find a pleasure in spreading joy around them, and can take delight in the satisfaction of others so far as it is their own work. But I maintain that in such a case an action of this kind, however proper, however amiable it may be, has nevertheless no true moral worth, but is on a level with other inclinations, *e.g.* the inclination to honour, which, if it is happily directed to that which is in fact of public utility and accordant with duty, and consequently honourable, deserves praise and encouragement, but not esteem. For the maxim lacks the moral import, namely, that such actions be done *from duty*, not from inclination. Put the case that the mind of that philanthropist was clouded by sorrow of his own,

extinguishing all sympathy with the lot of others, and that while he still has the power to benefit others in distress, he is not touched by their trouble because he is absorbed with his own; and now suppose that he tears himself out of this dead insensibility, and performs the action without any inclination to it, but simply from duty, then first has his action its genuine moral worth. Further still; if nature has put little sympathy in the heart of this or that man; if he, supposed to be an upright man, is by temperament cold and indifferent to the sufferings of others, perhaps because in respect of his own he is provided with the special gift of patience and fortitude, and supposes, or even requires, that others should have the same—and such a man would certainly not be the meanest product of nature—but if nature had not specially framed him for a philanthropist, would he not still find in himself a source from whence to give himself a far higher worth than that of a good-natured temperament could be? Unquestionably. It is just in this that the moral worth of the character is brought out which is incomparably the highest of all, namely, that he is beneficent, not from inclination, but from duty.

To secure one's own happiness is a duty, at least indirectly; for discontent with one's condition, under a pressure of many anxieties and amidst unsatisfied wants, might easily become a great *temptation to transgression of duty*. But here again, without looking to duty, all men have already the strongest and most intimate inclination to happiness, because it is just in this idea that all inclinations are combined in one total. But the precept of happiness is often of such a sort that it greatly interferes with some inclinations, and yet a man cannot form any definite and certain conception of the sum of satisfaction of all of them which is called happiness. It is not then to be wondered at that a single inclination, definite both as to what it promises and as to the time within which it can be gratified, is often able to overcome such a fluctuating idea, and that a gouty patient, for instance, can choose to enjoy what he likes, and to suffer what he may, since, according to his calculation, on this occasion at least, he has [only] not sacrificed the enjoyment of the present moment to a possibly mistaken expectation of a happiness which is supposed to be found in health. But even in this case, if the general desire for happiness did not influence his will, and supposing that in his particular case health was not a necessary element in this calculation, there yet remains in this, as in all other cases, this law, namely, that he should promote his happiness not from inclination but from duty, and by this would his conduct first acquire true moral worth.

It is in this manner, undoubtedly, that we are to understand those passages of Scripture also in which we are commanded to love our neighbour, even our enemy. For love, as an affection, cannot be commanded, but beneficence for duty's sake may; even though we are not impelled to it by any inclination—nay, are even repelled by a natural and unconquerable aversion. This is *practical* love, and not *pathological*—a love which is seated in the will, and not in the propensions of sense—in principles of action and not of tender sympathy; and it is this love alone which can be commanded.

The second [1] proposition is: That an action done from duty derives its moral worth, *not from the purpose* which is to be attained by it, but from the maxim by which it is determined, and therefore does not depend on the realization of the object of the action, but merely on the *principle of volition* by which the action has taken place, without regard to any object of desire. It is clear from what precedes that the purposes which we may have in view in our actions, or their effects regarded as ends and springs of the will, cannot give to actions any unconditional or moral worth. In what, then, can their worth lie, if it is not to consist in the will and in reference to its expected effect? It cannot lie anywhere but in the *principle of the will* without regard to the ends which can be attained by the action. For the will stands between its *a priori* principle, which is formal, and its *a posteriori* spring,

which is material, as between two roads, and as it must be determined by something, it follows that it must be determined by the formal principle of volition when an action is done from duty, in which case every material principle has been withdrawn from it.

The third proposition, which is a consequence of the two preceding, I would express thus: *Duty is the necessity of acting from respect for the law.* I may have *inclination* for an object as the effect of my proposed action, but I cannot have *respect* for it, just for this reason, that it is an effect and not an energy of will. Similarly, I cannot have respect for inclination, whether my own or another's; I can at most, if my own, approve it; if another's, sometimes even love it; *i.e.* look on it as favourable to my own interest. It is only what is connected with my will as a principle, by no means as an effect—what does not subserve my inclination, but overpowers it, or at least in case of choice excludes it from its calculation—in other words, simply the law of itself, which can be an object of respect, and hence a command. Now an action done from duty must wholly exclude the influence of inclination, and with it every object of the will, so that nothing remains which can determine the will except objectively the *law*, and subjectively *pure respect* for this practical law, and consequently the maxim [2] that I should follow this law even to the thwarting of all my inclinations.

Thus the moral worth of an action does not lie in the effect expected from it, nor in any principle of action which requires to borrow its motive from this expected effect. For all these effects—agreeableness of one's condition, and even the promotion of the happiness of others—could have been also brought about by other causes, so that for this there would have been no need of the will of a rational being; whereas it is in this alone that the supreme

[1] [The first proposition was that to have moral worth an action must be done from duty.]

[2] A *maxim* is the subjective principle of volition. The objective principle (*i.e.* that which would also serve subjectively as a practical principle to all rational beings if reason had full power over the faculty of desire) is the practical *law*.

and unconditional good can be found. The pre-eminent good which we call moral can therefore consist in nothing else than *the conception of law* in itself, *which certainly is only possible in a rational being*, in so far as this conception, and not the expected effect, determines the will. This is a good which is already present in the person who acts accordingly, and we have not to wait for it to appear first in the result.[3]

But what sort of law can that be, the conception of which must determine the will, even without paying any regard to the effect expected from it, in order that this will may be called good absolutely and without qualification? As I have deprived the will of every impulse which could arise to it from obedience to any law, there remains nothing but the universal conformity of its actions to law in general, which alone is to serve the will as a principle, *i.e.* I am never to act otherwise than so *that I could also will that my maxim should become a universal law*. Here, now, it is the simple conformity to law in general, without assuming any particular law applicable to certain actions, that serves the will as its principle, and must so serve it, if duty is not to be a vain delusion and a chimerical notion. The common reason of men in its practical judgments perfectly coincides with this, and always has in view the principle here suggested. Let the question be, for example: May I when in dis-

tress make a promise with the intention not to keep it? I readily distinguish here between the two significations which the question may have: Whether it is prudent, or whether it is right, to make a false promise? The former may undoubtedly often be the case. I see clearly indeed that it is not enough to extricate myself from a present difficulty by means of this subterfuge, but it must be well considered whether there may not hereafter spring from this lie much greater inconvenience than that from which I now free myself, and as, with all my supposed *cunning*, the consequences cannot be so easily foreseen but that credit once lost may be much more injurious to me than any mischief which I seek to avoid at present, it should be considered whether it would not be more *prudent* to act herein according to a universal maxim, and to make it a habit to promise nothing except with the intention of keeping it. But it is soon clear to me that such a maxim will still only be based on the fear of consequences. Now it is a wholly different thing to be truthful from duty, and to be so from apprehension of injurious consequences. In the first case, the very notion of the action already implies a law for me; in the second case, I must first look about elsewhere to see what results may be combined with it which would affect myself. For to deviate from the principle of duty is beyond all doubt wicked; but to be unfaithful to my maxim of prudence may often

[3] It might be here objected to me that I take refuge behind the word *respect* in an obscure feeling, instead of giving a distinct solution of the question by a concept of the reason. But although respect is a feeling, it is not a feeling *received* through influence, but is *self-wrought* by a rational concept, and, therefore, is specifically distinct from all feelings of the former kind, which may be referred either to inclination or fear. What I recognize immediately as a law for me, I recognize with respect. This merely signifies the consciousness that my will is *subordinate* to a law, without the intervention of other influences on my sense. The immediate determination of the will by the law, and the consciousness of this, is called *respect,* so that this is regarded as an *effect* of the law on the subject, and not as the *cause* of it. Respect is properly the conception of a worth which thwarts

my self-love. Accordingly it is something which is considered neither as an object of inclination nor of fear, although it has something analogous to both. The *object* of respect is the *law* only, and that, the law which we impose on *ourselves,* and yet recognize as necessary in itself. As a law, we are subjected to it without consulting self-love; as imposed by us on ourselves, it is a result of our will. In the former aspect it has an analogy to fear, in the latter to inclination. Respect for a person is properly only respect for the law (of honesty, &c.) of which he gives us an example. Since we also look on the improvement of our talents as a duty, we consider that we see in a person of talents, as it were, the *example of a law* (viz. to become like him in this by exercise), and this constitutes our respect. All so-called moral *interest* consists simply in *respect* for the law.

be very advantageous to me, although to abide by it is certainly safer. The shortest way, however, and an unerring one, to discover the answer to this question whether a lying promise is consistent with duty, is to ask myself, Should I be content that my maxim (to extricate myself from difficulty by a false promise) should hold good as a universal law, for myself as well as for others? and should I be able to say to myself, "Every one may make a deceitful promise when he finds himself in a difficulty from which he cannot otherwise extricate himself"? Then I presently become aware that while I can will the lie, I can by no means will that lying should be a universal law. For with such a law there would be no promises at all, since it would be in vain to allege my intention in regard to my future actions to those who would not believe this allegation, or if they over-hastily did so, would pay me back in my own coin. Hence my maxim, as soon as it should be made a universal law, would necessarily destroy itself.

I do not, therefore, need any far-reaching penetration to discern what I have to do in order that my will may be morally good. Inexperienced in the course of the world, incapable of being prepared for all its contingencies, I only ask myself: Canst thou also will that thy maxim should be a universal law? If not, then it must be rejected, and that not because of a disadvantage accruing from it to myself or even to others, but because it cannot enter as a principle into a possible universal legislation, and reason extorts from me immediate respect for such legislation. I do not indeed as yet *discern* on what this respect is based (this the philosopher may inquire), but at least I understand this, that it is an estimation of the worth which far outweighs all worth of what is recommended by inclination, and that the necessity of acting from *pure* respect for the practical law is what constitutes duty, to which every other motive must give place, because it is the condition of a will being good *in itself*, and the worth of such a will is above everything.

Thus, then, without quitting the moral knowledge of common human reason, we have arrived at its principle. And although, no doubt, common men do not conceive it in such an abstract and universal form, yet they always have it really before their eyes, and use it as the standard of their decision. Here it would be easy to show how, with this compass in hand, men are well able to distinguish, in every case that occurs, what is good, what bad, conformably to duty or inconsistent with it, if, without in the least teaching them anything new, we only, like Socrates, direct their attention to the principle they themselves employ; and that, therefore, we do not need science and philosophy to know what we should do to be honest and good, yea, even wise and virtuous. Indeed we might well have conjectured beforehand that the knowledge of what every man is bound to do, and therefore also to know, would be within the reach of every man, even the commonest. Here we cannot forbear admiration when we see how great an advantage the practical judgment has over the theoretical in the common understanding of men. In the latter, if common reason ventures to depart from the laws of experience and from the perceptions of the senses, it falls into mere inconceivabilities and self-contradictions, at least into a chaos of uncertainty, obscurity, and instability. But in the practical sphere it is just when the common understanding excludes all sensible springs from practical laws that its power of judgment begins to show itself to advantage. It then becomes even subtle, whether it be that it chicanes with its own conscience or with other claims respecting what is to be called right, or whether it desires for its own instruction to determine honestly the worth of actions; and, in the latter case, it may even have as good a hope of hitting the mark as any philosopher whatever can promise himself. Nay, it is almost more sure of doing so, because the philosopher cannot have any other principle, while he may easily perplex his judgment by a multitude of considerations foreign to the matter, and so turn aside from the right way. Would it not therefore be wiser in moral concerns to acquiesce in the judgment of common reason, or at most only to call in philosophy for the purpose of rendering the system of morals more complete and intelligible, and its rules more convenient for use (especially for disputation), but not so as to draw off the common understanding from its happy simplicity, or to bring it by means of philosophy into a new path of inquiry and instruction?

Innocence is indeed a glorious thing, only, on the other hand, it is very sad that it cannot well maintain itself, and is easily seduced. On this account even wisdom—which otherwise consists more in conduct than in knowledge—yet has need of science, not in order to learn from it, but to secure for its precepts admission and permanence. Against all the commands of duty which reason represents to man as so deserving of respect, he feels in himself a powerful counterpoise in his wants and inclinations, the entire satisfaction of which he sums up under the name of happiness. Now reason issues its commands unyieldingly, without promising anything to the inclinations, and, as it were, with disregard and contempt for these claims, which are so impetuous, and at the same time so plausible, and which will not allow themselves to be suppressed by any command. Hence there arises a natural *dialectic*, i.e. a disposition, to argue against these strict laws of duty and to question their validity, or at least

their purity and strictness; and, if possible, to make them more accordant with our wishes and inclinations, that is to say, to corrupt them at their very source, and entirely to destroy their worth—a thing which even common practical reason cannot ultimately call good.

Thus is the *common reason of man* compelled to go out of its sphere, and to take a step into the field of a *practical philosophy*, not to satisfy any speculative want (which never occurs to it as long as it is content to be mere sound reason), but even on practical grounds, in order to attain in it information and clear instruction respecting the source of its principle, and the correct determination of it in opposition to the maxims which are based on wants and inclinations, so that it may escape from the perplexity of opposite claims, and not run the risk of losing all genuine moral principles through the equivocation into which it easily falls. Thus, when practical reason cultivates itself, there insensibly arises in it a dialectic which forces it to seek aid in philosophy, just as happens to it in its theoretic use; and in this case, therefore, as well as in the other, it will find rest nowhere but in a thorough critical examination of our reason.

Utilitarianism

John Stuart Mill (1806-1873)

A child prodigy, son of the economist and social thinker James Mill, John Stuart Mill achieved a reputation as a philosopher, an exponent of utilitarianism, and a leader of liberal reform, which eventually outshone the brilliant name of his father. Following a period of depression at the age of twenty-one, described in his famous Autobiography (1873), *Mill enjoyed a successful career in the London office of the East India Company, maintained a lifelong interest in public affairs, and in his writings made notable contributions to logic and to moral and political philosophy.*

Mill's Utilitarianism (1863) *shows the influence of his mentor, Jeremy Bentham, but departs fundamentally from the Benthamite position. Whereas Bentham's version of the principle of "utility" admits no differences in quality among pleasures, Mill recognizes that some pleasures are intrinsically superior to others and suggests also that moral virtue may be valuable in itself apart from the desirable consequences produced by virtuous action.*

The reader might ask himself whether Mill's account of utilitarianism, admitting qualitative as well as quantitative differences among pleasures, doesn't destroy the "greatest happiness principle" on which this moral theory is said to rest.

A passing remark is all that needs be given to the ignorant blunder of supposing that those who stand up for utility as the test of right and wrong use the term in that restricted and merely colloquial sense in which utility is opposed to pleasure. An apology is due to the philosophical opponents of utilitarianism, for even the momentary appearance of confounding them with anyone capable of so absurd a misconception; which is the more extraordinary, inasmuch as the contrary accusation, of referring everything to pleasure, and that, too, in its grossest form, is another of the common charges against utilitarianism: and, as has been pointedly remarked by an able writer, the same sort of persons, and often the very same persons, denounce the theory "as impracticably dry when the word 'utility' precedes the word 'pleasure,' and as too practicably voluptuous when the word 'pleasure' precedes the word 'utility.'" Those who know anything about the matter are aware that every writer, from Epicurus to Bentham, who maintained the theory of utility, meant by it, not something to be contradistinguished from pleasure, but pleasure itself, together with exemption from pain; and instead of opposing the useful to the agreeable or the ornamental, have always declared that the useful means these, among other things. Yet the common herd, including the herd of writers, not only in newspapers and periodicals, but in books of weight and pretension, are perpetually falling into this shallow mistake. Having caught up the word "utilitarian," while knowing nothing whatever about it but

From John Stuart Mill, *Utilitarianism*, 1863, chap. 2.

179

its sound, they habitually express by it the rejection or the neglect of pleasure in some of its forms: of beauty, of ornament, or of amusement. Nor is the term thus ignorantly misapplied solely in disparagement, but occasionally in compliment, as though it implied superiority to frivolity and the mere pleasures of the moment. And this perverted use is the only one in which the word is popularly known, and the one from which the new generation are acquiring their sole notion of its meaning. Those who introduced the word, but who had for many years discontinued it as a distinctive appellation, may well feel themselves called upon to resume it if by doing so they can hope to contribute anything towards rescuing it from this utter degradation.[1]

The creed which accepts as the foundation of morals "utility" or the "greatest happiness principle" holds that actions are right in proportion as they tend to promote happiness, wrong as they tend to produce the reverse of happiness. By happiness is intended pleasure, and the absence of pain; by unhappiness, pain, and the privation of pleasure. To give a clear view of the moral standard set up by the theory, much more requires to be said; in particular, what things it includes in the ideas of pain and pleasure; and to what extent this is left an open question. But these supplementary explanations do not affect the theory of life on which this theory of morality is grounded—namely, that pleasure and freedom from pain are the only things desirable as ends; and that all desirable things (which are as numerous in

---

[1] The author of this essay has reason for believing himself to be the first person who brought the word "utilitarian" into use. He did not invent it, but adopted it from a passing expression in Mr. Galt's *Annals of the Parish*. After using it as a designation for several years, he and others abandoned it from a growing dislike to anything resembling a badge or watchword of sectarian distinction. But as a name for one single opinion, not a set of opinions—to denote the recognition of utility as a standard, not any particular way of applying it—the term supplies a want in the language, and offers, in many cases, a convenient mode of avoiding tiresome circumlocution.

the utilitarian as in any other scheme) are desirable either for the pleasure inherent in themselves, or as means to the promotion of pleasure and the prevention of pain.

Now such a theory of life excites in many minds, and among them in some of the most estimable in feeling and purpose, inveterate dislike. To suppose that life has (as they express it) no higher end than pleasure—no better and nobler object of desire and pursuit—they designate as utterly mean and groveling; as a doctrine worthy only of swine, to whom the followers of Epicurus were, at a very early period, contemptuously likened; and modern holders of the doctrine are occasionally made the subject of equally polite comparisons by its German, French, and English assailants.

When thus attacked, the Epicureans have always answered that it is not they, but their accusers, who represent human nature in a degrading light, since the accusation supposes human beings to be capable of no pleasures except those of which swine are capable. If this supposition were true, the charge could not be gainsaid, but would then be no longer an imputation; for if the sources of pleasure were precisely the same to human beings and to swine, the rule of life which is good enough for the one would be good enough for the other. The comparison of the Epicurean life to that of beasts is felt as degrading, precisely because a beast's pleasures do not satisfy a human being's conceptions of happiness. Human beings have faculties more elevated than the animal appetites and, when once made conscious of them, do not regard anything as happiness which does not include their gratification. I do not, indeed, consider the Epicureans to have been by any means faultless in drawing out their scheme of consequences from the utilitarian principle. To do this in any sufficient manner, many Stoic, as well as Christian, elements require to be included. But there is no known Epicurean theory of life which does not assign to the pleasures of the intellect, of the feelings and imagination, and of the moral sentiments, a much higher value as pleasures than to those of mere sensation. It must be admitted, however, that utilitarian writers in general have placed the superiority of mental over bodily pleasures chiefly in the greater permanency, safety, uncostliness, etc., of the former—that is, in their circumstantial advantages rather than in their intrinsic nature. And on all these points utilitarians have fully proved their case; but they might have taken the other and, as it may be called, higher ground with entire consistency. It is quite compatible with the principle of utility to recognize the fact that some kinds of pleasure are more desirable and more valuable than others. It would be absurd that, while, in estimating all other things, quality is considered as well as quantity, the estimation of pleasures should be supposed to depend on quantity alone.

If I am asked what I mean by difference of quality in pleasures, or what makes one pleasure more valuable than another, merely as a pleasure, except its being greater in amount, there is but one possible answer. Of two pleasures, if there be one to which all or almost all who have experience of both give a decided preference, irrespective of any feeling of moral obligation to prefer it, that is the more desirable pleasure. If one of the two is, by those who are competently acquainted with both, placed so far above the other that they prefer it, even though knowing it to be attended with a greater amount of discontent, and would not resign it for any quantity of the other pleasure which their nature is capable of, we are justified in ascribing to the preferred enjoyment a superiority in quality so far outweighing quantity as to render it, in comparison, of small account.

Now it is an unquestionable fact that those who are equally acquainted with and equally capable of appreciating and enjoying both, do give a most marked preference to the manner of existence which employs their higher faculties. Few human creatures would consent to be changed into any of the lower animals for a promise of the fullest allowance of a beast's pleasures; no intelligent human being would consent to be a fool, no instructed person would be an ignoramus, no person of feeling and conscience would be selfish and base, even though

they should be persuaded that the fool, the dunce, or the rascal is better satisfied with his lot than they are with theirs. They would not resign what they possess more than he for the most complete satisfaction of all the desires which they have in common with him. If they ever fancy they would, it is only in cases of unhappiness so extreme that to escape from it they would exchange their lot for almost any other, however undesirable in their own eyes. A being of higher faculties requires more to make him happy, is capable probably of more acute suffering, and certainly accessible to it at more points, than one of an inferior type; but in spite of these liabilities, he can never really wish to sink into what he feels to be a lower grade of existence. We may give what explanation we please of this unwillingness; we may attribute it to pride, a name which is given indiscriminately to some of the most and to some of the least estimable feelings of which mankind are capable: we may refer it to the love of liberty and personal independence, an appeal to which was with the Stoics one of the most effective means for the inculcation of it; to the love of power or to the love of excitement, both of which do really enter into and contribute to it; but its most appropriate appellation is a sense of dignity, which all human beings possess in one form or other, and in some, though by no means in exact, proportion to their higher faculties, and which is so essential a part of the happiness of those in whom it is strong that nothing which conflicts with it could be otherwise than momentarily an object of desire to them. Whoever supposes that this preference takes place at a sacrifice of happiness—that the superior being, in anything like equal circumstances, is not happier than the inferior—confounds the two very different ideas of happiness and content. It is indisputable that the being whose capacities of enjoyment are low has the greatest chance of having them fully satisfied; and a highly endowed being will always feel that any happiness which he can look for, as the world is constituted, is imperfect. But he can learn to bear its imperfections, if they are at all bearable; and they will not make him envy the being who is indeed unconscious of the imperfections, but only because he feels not at all the good which those imperfections qualify. It is better to be a human being dissatisfied than a pig satisfied; better to be Socrates dissatisfied than a fool satisfied. And if the fool, or the pig, are of a different opinion, it is because they only know their own side of the question. The other party to the comparison knows both sides. . . .

According to the greatest happiness principle, as above explained, the ultimate end, with reference to and for the sake of which all other things are desirable—whether we are considering our own good or that of other people—is an existence exempt as far as possible from pain, and as rich as possible in enjoyments, both in point of quantity and quality; the test of quality and the rule for measuring it against quantity being the preference felt by those who, in their opportunities of experience, to which must be added their habits of self-consciousness and self-observation, are best furnished with the means of comparison. This, being, according to the utilitarian opinion, the end of human action, is necessarily also the standard of morality, which may accordingly be defined "the rules and precepts for human conduct," by the observance of which an existence such as has been described might be, to the greatest extent possible, secured to all mankind; and not to them only, but, so far as the nature of things admits, to the whole sentient creation.

Against this doctrine, however, arises another class of objectors who say that happiness, in any form, cannot be the rational purpose of human life and action; because, in the first place, it is unattainable; and they contemptuously ask, What right hast thou to be happy? — a question which Mr. Carlyle clenches by the addition, What right, a short time ago, hadst thou even *to be?* Next they say that men can do *without* happiness; that all noble human beings have felt this, and could not have become noble but by learning the lesson of *Entsagen*, or renunciation; which lesson, thoroughly learnt and submitted to, they affirm to be the beginning and necessary condition of all virtue.

The first of these objections would go to the root of the matter were it well founded; for if no happiness is to be had at all by human beings, the attainment of it cannot be the end of morality or of any rational conduct. Though, even in that case, something might still be said for the utilitarian theory, since utility includes not solely the pursuit of happiness, but the prevention or mitigation of unhappiness; and if the former aim be chimerical, there will be all the greater scope and more imperative need for the latter, so long at least as mankind think fit to live, and do not take refuge in the simultaneous act of suicide recommended under certain conditions by Novalis. When, however, it is thus positively asserted to be impossible that human life should be happy, the assertion, if not something like a verbal quibble, is at least an exaggeration. If by happiness be meant a continuity of highly pleasurable excitement, it is evident enough that this is impossible. A state of exalted pleasure lasts only moments or in some cases, and with some intermissions, hours or days, and is the occasional brilliant flash of enjoyment, not its permanent and steady flame. Of this the philosophers who have taught that happiness is the end of life were as fully aware as those who taunt them. The happiness which they meant was not a life of rapture; but moments of such, in an existence made up of few and transitory pains, many and various pleasures, with a decided predominance of the active over the passive, and having as the foundation of the whole not to expect more from life than it is capable of bestowing. A life thus composed, to those who have been fortunate enough to obtain it, has always appeared worthy of the name of happiness. And such an existence is even now the lot of many, during some considerable portion of their lives. The present wretched education and wretched social arrangements are the only real hindrance to its being attainable by almost all.

The objectors perhaps may doubt whether human beings, if taught to consider happiness as the end of life, would be satisfied with such a moderate share of it. But great numbers of mankind have been satisfied with much less,

The main constituents of a satisfied life appear to be two, either of which by itself is often found sufficient for the purpose: tranquility and excitement. With much tranquility, many find that they can be content with very little pleasure; with much excitement, many can reconcile themselves to a considerable quantity of pain. There is assuredly no inherent impossibility of enabling even the mass of mankind to unite both, since the two are so far from being incompatible that they are in natural alliance, the prolongation of either being a preparation for, and exciting a wish for, the other. It is only those in whom indolence amounts to a vice that do not desire excitement after an interval of repose; it is only those in whom the need of excitement is a disease that feel the tranquility which follows excitement dull and insipid, instead of pleasurable in direct proportion to the excitement which preceded it. When people who are tolerably fortunate in their outward lot do not find in life sufficient enjoyment to make it valuable to them, the cause generally is caring for nobody but themselves. To those who have neither public nor private affections, the excitements of life are much curtailed, and in any case dwindle in value as the time approaches when all selfish interests must be terminated by death; while those who leave after them objects of personal affection, and especially those who have also cultivated a fellow-feeling with the collective interests of mankind, retain as lively an interest in life on the eve of death as in the vigor of youth and health. Next to selfishness, the principal cause which makes life unsatisfactory is want of mental cultivation. A cultivated mind —I do not mean that of a philosopher, but any mind to which the fountains of knowledge have been opened, and which has been taught, in any tolerable degree, to exercise its faculties— finds sources of inexhaustible interest in all that surrounds it: in the objects of nature, the achievements of art, the imaginations of poetry, the incidents of history, the ways of mankind, past and present, and their prospects in the future. It is possible, indeed, to become indifferent to all this, and that too without having exhausted a thousandth part of it, but only when one has had from the beginning no moral or human interest in these things, and has sought in them only the gratification of curiosity.

Now there is absolutely no reason in the nature of things why an amount of mental culture sufficient to give an intelligent interest in these objects of contemplation should not be the inheritance of every one born in a civilized country. As little is there an inherent necessity that any human being should be a selfish egotist, devoid of every feeling or care but those which center in his own miserable individuality. Something far superior to this is sufficiently common even now, to give ample earnest of what the human species may be made. Genuine private affections and a sincere interest in the public good are possible, though in unequal degrees, to every rightly brought up human being. In a world in which there is so much to interest, so much to enjoy, and so much also to correct and improve, every one who has this moderate amount of moral and intellectual requisites is capable of an existence which may be called enviable; and unless such a person, through bad laws or subjection to the will of others, is denied the liberty to use the sources of happiness within his reach, he will not fail to find this enviable existence, if he escape the positive evils of life, the great sources of physical and mental suffering—such as indigence, disease, and the unkindness, worthlessness, or premature loss of objects of affection. The main stress of the problem lies, therefore, in the contest with these calamities from which it is a rare good fortune entirely to escape; which, as things now are, cannot be obviated, and often cannot be in any material degree mitigated. Yet no one whose opinion deserves a moment's consideration can doubt that most of the great positive evils of the world are in themselves removable, and will, if human affairs continue to improve, be in the end reduced within narrow limits. Poverty, in any sense implying suffering, may be completely extinguished by the wisdom of society combined with the good sense and providence of individuals. Even that most intractable of enemies, disease, may be indefinitely reduced in dimensions by good physical and moral education and proper control of noxious influences, while the progress of science holds out a promise for the future of still more direct conquests over this detestable foe. And every advance in that direction relieves us from some, not only of the chances which cut short our own lives, but, what concerns us still more, which deprive us of those in whom our happiness is wrapt up. As for vicissitudes of fortune and other disappointments connected with worldly circumstances, these are principally the effect either of gross imprudence, of ill-regulated desires, or of bad or imperfect social institutions. All the grand sources, in short, of human suffering are in a great degree, many of them almost entirely, conquerable by human care and effort; and though their removal is grievously slow—though a long succession of generations will perish in the breach before the conquest is completed, and this world becomes all that, if will and knowledge were not wanting, it might easily be made—yet every mind sufficiently intelligent and generous to bear a part, however small and inconspicuous, in the endeavor will draw a noble enjoyment from the contest itself, which he would not for any bribe in the form of selfish indulgence consent to be without.

And this leads to the true estimation of what is said by the objectors concerning the possibility and the obligation of learning to do without happiness. Unquestionably it is possible to do without happiness; it is done involuntarily by nineteen-twentieths of mankind, even in those parts of our present world which are least deep in barbarism; and it often has to be done voluntarily by the hero or the martyr, for the sake of something which he prizes more than his individual happiness. But this something, what is it, unless the happiness of others or some of the requisites of happiness? It is noble to be capable of resigning entirely one's own portion of happiness, or chances of it; but, after all, this self-sacrifice must be for some end; it is not its own end; and if we are told that its end is not happiness but virtue, which is better than happiness, I ask, would the sacrifice be made if the hero or martyr did not believe that it would earn for others immunity from similar sacrifices? Would it be made if he

thought that his renunciation of happiness for himself would produce no fruit for any of his fellow creatures, but to make their lot like his, and place them also in the condition of persons who have renounced happiness? All honor to those who can abnegate for themselves the personal enjoyment of life when by such renunciation they contribute worthily to increase the amount of happiness in the world; but he who does it or professes to do it for any other purpose is no more deserving of admiration than the ascetic mounted on his pillar. He may be an inspiriting proof of what men *can* do, but assuredly not an example of what they *should*.

Though it is only in a very imperfect state of the world's arrangements that any one can best serve the happiness of others by the absolute sacrifice of his own, yet, so long as the world is in that imperfect state, I fully acknowledge that the readiness to make such a sacrifice is the highest virtue which can be found in man. I will add that in this condition of the world, paradoxical as the assertion may be, the conscious ability to do without happiness gives the best prospect of realizing such happiness as is attainable. For nothing except that consciousness can raise a person above the chances of life, by making him feel that, let fate and fortune do their worst, they have not power to subdue him; which, once felt, frees him from excess of anxiety concerning the evils of life, and enables him, like many a Stoic in the worst times of the Roman Empire, to cultivate in tranquility the sources of satisfaction accessible to him, without concerning himself about the uncertainty of their duration any more than about their inevitable end.

Meanwhile, let utilitarians never cease to claim the morality of self-devotion as a possession which belongs by as good a right to them as either to the Stoic or to the Transcendentalist. The utilitarian morality does recognize in human beings the power of sacrificing their own greatest good for the good of others. It only refuses to admit that the sacrifice is itself a good. A sacrifice which does not increase or tend to increase the sum total of happiness, it considers as wasted. The only self-renunciation which it applauds is devotion to the happiness, or to some of the means of happiness, of others, either of mankind collectively or of individuals within the limits imposed by the collective interests of mankind.

I must again repeat what the assailants of utilitarianism seldom have the justice to acknowledge, that the happiness which forms the utilitarian standard of what is right in conduct is not the agent's own happiness but that of all concerned. As between his own happiness and that of others, utilitarianism requires him to be as strictly impartial as a disinterested and benevolent spectator. In the golden rule of Jesus of Nazareth, we read the complete spirit of the ethics of utility. "To do as you would be done by," and "to love your neighbor as yourself," constitute the ideal perfection of utilitarian morality. As the means of making the nearest approach to this ideal, utility would enjoin, first, that laws and social arrangements should place the happiness or (as, speaking practically, it may be called) the interest of every individual as nearly as possible in harmony with the interest of the whole; and, secondly, that education and opinion, which have so vast a power over human character, should so use that power as to establish in the mind of every individual an indissoluble association between his own happiness and the good of the whole, especially between his own happiness and the practice of such modes of conduct, negative and positive, as regard for the universal happiness prescribes; so that not only he may be unable to conceive the possibility of happiness to himself, consistently with conduct opposed to the general good, but also that a direct impulse to promote the general good may be in every individual one of the habitual motives of action, and the sentiments connected therewith may fill a large and prominent place in every human being's sentient existence. If the impugners of the utilitarian morality represented it to their own minds in this its true character, I know not what recommendation possessed by any other morality they could possibly affirm to be wanting to it; what more beautiful or more exalted developments of human nature any other ethical system can be supposed to foster, or what springs of action,

not accessible to the utilitarian, such systems rely on for giving effect to their mandates.

The objectors to utilitarianism cannot always be charged with representing it in a discreditable light. On the contrary, those among them who entertain anything like a just idea of its disinterested character sometimes find fault with its standard as being too high for humanity. They say it is exacting too much to require that people shall always act from the inducement of promoting the general interests of society. But this is to mistake the very meaning of a standard of morals, and confound the rule of action with the motive of it. It is the business of ethics to tell us what are our duties, or by what test we may know them; but no system of ethics requires that the sole motive of all we do shall be a feeling of duty; on the contrary, ninety-nine hundredths of all our actions are done from other motives, and rightly so done if the rule of duty does not condemn them. It is the more unjust to utilitarianism that this particular misapprehension should be made a ground of objection to it, inasmuch as utilitarian moralists have gone beyond almost all others in affirming that the motive has nothing to do with the morality of the action, though much with the worth of the agent. He who saves a fellow creature from drowning does what is morally right, whether his motive be duty or the hope of being paid for his trouble; he who betrays the friend that trusts him is guilty of a crime, even if his object be to serve another friend to whom he is under greater obligations. But to speak only of actions done from the motive of duty, and in direct obedience to principle: it is a misapprehension of the utilitarian mode of thought to conceive it as implying that people should fix their minds upon so wide a generality as the world, or society at large. The great majority of good actions are intended not for the benefit of the world, but for that of individuals, of which the good of the world is made up; and the thoughts of the most virtuous man need not on these occasions travel beyond the particular persons concerned, except so far as is necessary to assure himself that in benefiting them he is not violating the rights, that is, the legitimate and authorized expectations, of any one else. The multiplication of happiness is, according to the utilitarian ethics, the object of virtue: the occasions on which any person (except one in a thousand) has it in his power to do this on an extended scale, in other words, to be a public benefactor, are but exceptional; and on these occasions alone is he called on to consider public utility; in every other case, private utility, the interest or happiness of some few persons, is all he has to attend to. Those alone the influence of whose actions extends to society in general need concern themselves habitually about so large an object. In the case of abstinences indeed—of things which people forbear to do from moral considerations, though the consequences in the particular case might be beneficial—it would be unworthy of an intelligent agent not to be consciously aware that the action is of a class which, if practiced generally, would be generally injurious, and that this is the ground of the obligation to abstain from it. The amount of regard for the public interest implied in this recognition is no greater than is demanded by every system of morals, for they all enjoin to abstain from whatever is manifestly pernicious to society.

The same considerations dispose of another reproach against the doctrine of utility, founded on a still grosser misconception of the purpose of a standard of morality, and of the very meaning of the words "right" and "wrong." It is often affirmed that utilitarianism renders men cold and unsympathizing; that it chills their moral feelings towards individuals; that it makes them regard only the dry and hard consideration of the consequences of actions, not taking into their moral estimate the qualities from which those actions emanate. If the assertion means that they do not allow their judgment respecting the rightness or wrongness of an action to be influenced by their opinion of the qualities of the person who does it, this is a complaint not against utilitarianism, but against any standard of morality at all; for certainly no known ethical standard decides an action to be good or bad because it is done by a good or a bad man, still less because done by an amiable, a brave, or a benevolent man,

or the contrary. These considerations are relevant, not to the estimation of actions, but of persons; and there is nothing in the utilitarian theory inconsistent with the fact that there are other things which interest us in persons besides the rightness and wrongness of their actions. The Stoics, indeed, with the paradoxical misuse of language which was part of their system, and by which they strove to raise themselves above all concern about anything but virtue, were fond of saying that he who has that has everything; that he, and only he, is rich, is beautiful, is a king. But no claim of this description is made for the virtuous man by the utilitarian doctrine. Utilitarians are quite aware that there are other desirable possessions and qualities besides virtue, and are perfectly willing to allow to all of them their full worth. They are also aware that a right action does not necessarily indicate a virtuous character, and that actions which are blamable often proceed from qualities entitled to praise. When this is apparent in any particular case, it modifies their estimation, not certainly of the act, but of the agent. I grant that they are, notwithstanding, of opinion that in the long run the best proof of a good character is good actions; and resolutely refuse to consider any mental disposition as good of which the predominant tendency is to produce bad conduct. This makes them unpopular with many people; but it is an unpopularity which they must share with every one who regards the distinction between right and wrong in a serious light; and the reproach is not one which a conscientious utilitarian need be anxious to repel.

If no more be meant by the objection than that many utilitarians look on the morality of actions, as measured by the utilitarian standards, with too exclusive a regard, and do not lay sufficient stress upon the other beauties of character which go towards making a human being lovable or admirable, this may be admitted. Utilitarians who have cultivated their moral feelings, but not their sympathies, nor their artistic perceptions, do fall into this mistake; and so do all other moralists under the same conditions. What can be said in excuse for other moralists is equally available for them, namely, that, if there is to be any error, it is better that it should be on that side. As a matter of fact, we may affirm that among utilitarians, as among adherents of other systems, there is every imaginable degree of rigidity and of laxity in the application of their standard; some are even puritanically rigorous, while others are as indulgent as can possibly be desired by sinner or by sentimentalist. But on the whole, a doctrine which brings prominently forward the interest that mankind have in the repression and prevention of conduct which violates the moral law, is likely to be inferior to no other in turning the sanctions of opinion against such violations. It is true, the question, "What does violate the moral law?" is one on which those who recognize different standards of morality are likely now and then to differ. But difference of opinion on moral questions was not first introduced into the world by utilitarianism, while that doctrine does supply, if not always an easy, at all events a tangible and intelligible, mode of deciding such differences.

The nature of aims

John Dewey (1859-1952)*

Dewey's concern with "reconstruction" of philosophical conceptions extended especially to moral theory. He rejected the search of traditional moral theorists for fixed standards and ends of conduct. Dewey rethought the traditional distinction between means and ends in moral situations and regarded the distinction between instrumental and intrinsic value as misleading. In our selection from his Human Nature and Conduct *(1922) he brings this thinking to bear on the problem of aims in conduct. Among Dewey's writings on moral issues are* Ethics *(with James H. Tufts, 1908; rev. ed., 1932),* Reconstruction in Philosophy *(1920; 2d ed., 1948), and* The Theory of Valuation *(1939).*

Our problem now concerns the nature of ends, that is ends-in-view or aims. The essential elements in the problem have already been stated. It has been pointed out that the ends, objectives, of conduct are those foreseen consequences which influence present deliberation and which finally bring it to rest by furnishing an adequate stimulus to overt action. Consequently ends arise and function within action. They are not, as current theories too often imply, things lying beyond activity at which the latter is directed. They are not strictly speaking ends or termini of action at all. They are terminals of deliberation, and so turning points *in* activity. Many opposed moral theories agree however in placing ends beyond action, although they differ in their notions of what the ends are. The utilitarian sets up pleasure as such an outside-and-beyond, as something necessary to induce action and in which it terminates. Many harsh critics of utilitarian-

ism have however agreed that there is some end in which action terminates, a final goal. They have denied that pleasure is such an outside aim, and put perfection or self-realization in its place. The entire popular notion of "ideals" is infected with the conception of some fixed end beyond activity at which we should aim. According to this view ends-in-themselves come before aims. We have a moral aim only as our purpose coincides with some end-in-itself. We *ought* to aim at the latter whether we actually do or not.

When men believed that fixed ends existed for all normal changes in nature, the conception of similar ends for men was but a special case of a general belief. If the changes in a tree from acorn to full-grown oak were regulated by an end which was somehow immanent or potential in all the less perfect forms, and if change was simply the effort to realize a perfect or complete form, then the acceptance of a like view for human conduct was consonant with the rest of what passed for science. Such a view, consistent and systematic, was foisted by Aristotle upon western culture and endured for two thousand years. When the notion was expelled from natural science by

From *Human Nature and Conduct*, by John Dewey, copyright 1922; renewed 1950. Used by permission of Holt, Rinehart and Winston, Inc., publishers.

* See the introductory note on Dewey on page 115.

the intellectual revolution of the seventeenth century, logically, it should also have disappeared from the theory of human action. But man is not logical and his intellectual history is a record of mental reserves and compromises. He hangs on to what he can in his old beliefs even when he is compelled to surrender their logical basis. So the doctrine of fixed ends-in-themselves at which human acts are—or should be—directed and by which they are regulated if they are regulated at all persisted in morals, and was made the cornerstone of orthodox moral theory. The immediate effect was to dislocate moral from natural science, to divide man's world as it never had been divided in prior culture. One point of view, one method and spirit animated inquiry into natural occurrences; a radically opposite set of ideas prevailed about man's affairs. Completion of the scientific change begun in the seventeenth century thus depends upon a revision of the current notion of ends of action as fixed limits and conclusions.

In fact, ends are ends-in-view or aims. They arise out of natural effects or consequences which in the beginning are hit upon, stumbled upon so far as any purpose is concerned. Men *like* some of the consequences and *dislike* others. Henceforth (or till attraction and repulsion alter) attaining or averting similar consequences are aims or ends. These consequences constitute the meaning and value of an activity as it comes under deliberation. Meantime of course imagination is busy. Old consequences are enhanced, recombined, modified in imagination. Invention operates. Actual consequences, that is effects which have happened in the past, become possible future consequences of acts still to be performed. This operation of imaginative thought complicates the relation of ends to activity, but it does not alter the substantial fact: Ends are foreseen consequences which arise in the course of activity and which are employed to give activity added meaning and to direct its further course. They are in no sense ends *of* action. In being ends of *deliberation* they are redirecting pivots *in* action.

Men shoot and throw. At first this is done as an "instinctive" or natural reaction to some situation. The result when it is observed gives a new meaning to the activity. Henceforth men in throwing and shooting think of it in terms of its outcome; they act intelligently or have an end. Liking the activity in its acquired meaning, they not only "take aim" when they throw instead of throwing at random, but they find or make targets at which to aim. This is the origin and nature of "goals" of action. They are ways of defining and deepening the meaning of activity. Having an end or aim is thus a characteristic of *present* activity. It is the means by which an activity becomes adapted when otherwise it would be blind and disorderly, or by which it gets meaning when otherwise it would be mechanical. In a strict sense an end-in-view is a *means* in present action; present action is not a means to a remote end. Men do not shoot because targets exist, but they set up targets in order that throwing and shooting may be more effective and significant.

A mariner does not sail towards the stars, but by noting the stars he is aided in conducting his present activity of sailing. A port or harbor is his objective, but only in the sense of *reaching* it not of taking possession of it. The harbor stands in his thought as a significant point at which his activity will need re-direction. Activity will not cease when the port is attained, but merely the *present direction* of activity. The port is as truly the beginning of another mode of activity as it is the termination of the present one. The only reason we ignore this fact is because it is empirically taken for granted. We know without thinking that our "ends" are perforce beginnings. But theories of ends and ideals have converted a theoretical ignoring which is equivalent to practical acknowledgment into an intellectual denial, and have thereby confused and perverted the nature of ends.

Even the most important among all the consequences of an act is not necessarily its aim. Results which are objectively most important may not even be thought of at all; ordinarily a man does not think in connection with exercise of his profession that it will sustain him and his family in existence. The end-thought-of is uniquely important, but it is indispensable to state the respect in which it is important. It gives the decisive clew to the act to be performed under the existing circumstances. It is that particular foreseen object that will stimulate the act which relieves existing troubles, straightens out existing entanglements. In a temporary annoyance, even if only that caused by the singing of a mosquito, the thought of that which gives relief may engross the mind in spite of consequences much more important, objectively speaking. Moralists have deplored such facts as evidence of levity. But the remedy, if a remedy be needed, is not found in insisting upon the importance of ends in general. It is found in a change of the dispositions which make things either immediately troublesome or tolerable or agreeable.

When ends are regarded as literally ends to action rather than as directive stimuli to present choice they are frozen and isolated. It makes no difference whether the "end" is "natural" good like health or a "moral" good like honesty. Set up as complete and exclusive, as demanding and justifying action as a means to itself, it leads to narrowness; in extreme cases fanaticism, inconsiderateness, arrogance and hypocrisy. Joshua's reputed success in getting the sun to stand still to serve his desire is recognized to have involved a miracle. But moral theorists constantly assume that the continuous course of events can be arrested at the point of a particular object; that men can plunge with their own desires into the unceasing flow of changes, and seize upon some object as their end irrespective of everything else. The use of intelligence to discover the object that will best operate as a releasing and unifying stimulus in the existing situation is discounted. One reminds one's self that one's end is justice or charity or professional achievement or putting over a deal for a needed public improvement, and further questionings and qualms are stilled.

It is customary to suppose that such methods merely ignore the question of the morality of the means which are used to secure the end desired. Common sense revolts against the maxim, conveniently laid off upon Jesuits or other far-away people, that the end justifies the means. There is no incorrectness in saying that the question of means employed is overlooked in such cases. But analysis would go further it it were also pointed out that overlooking means is only a device for failing to note those ends, or consequences, which, if they were noted would be seen to be so evil that action would be estopped. Certainly nothing can justify or condemn means except ends, results. But we have to include consequences impartially. Even admitting that lying will save a man's soul, whatever that may mean, it would still be true that lying will have other consequences, namely, the usual consequences that follow from tampering with good faith and that lead lying to be condemned. It is wilful folly to fasten upon some single end or consequence which is liked, and permit the view of that to blot from perception all other undesired and undesirable consequences. It is like supposing that when a finger held close to the eye covers up a distant mountain the finger is really larger than the mountain. Not *the* end—in the singular—justifies the means; for there is no such thing as the single all-important end. To suppose that there is such an end is like working over again, in behalf of our private wishes, the miracle of Joshua in arresting the course of nature. It is not possible adequately to characterize the presumption, the falsity and the deliberate perversion of intelligence involved in refusal to note the plural effects that flow from any act, a refusal adopted in order that we may justify an act by picking out that one consequence which will enable us to do what we wish to do and for which we feel the need of justification.

Yet this assumption is continually made. It is made by implication in the current view of purposes or ends-in-view as objects in themselves, instead of means to unification and liberation of present conflicting, confused habits and impulses. There is something almost sinister in the desire to label the doctrine that the end justifies the means with the name of some one obnoxious school. Politicians, especially if they have to do with the foreign affairs of a nation and are called statesmen, almost uniformly act upon the doctrine that the welfare of their own country justifies any measure irrespective of all the demoralization it works. Captains of industry, great executives in all lines, usually work upon this plan. But they are not the original offenders by any means. Every man works upon it so far as he permits himself to become so absorbed in one aspect of what he is doing that he loses a view of its varied consequences, hypnotizing his attention by consideration of just those consequences which in the abstract are desirable and slurring over other consequences equally real. Every man works upon this principle who becomes overinterested in any cause or project, and who uses its desirability in the abstract to justify himself in employing any means that will assist him in arriving, ignoring all the collateral "ends" of his behavior. It is frequently pointed out that there is a type of executive-man whose conduct seems to be as non-moral as the action of the forces of nature. We all tend to relapse into this non-moral condition whenever we want any one thing intensely. In general, the identification of the end prominent in conscious desire and effort with *the* end is part of the technique of avoiding a reasonable survey of consequences. The survey is avoided because of a subconscious recognition that it would reveal desire in its true worth and thus preclude action to satisfy it—or at all events give us an uneasy conscience in striving to realize it. Thus the doctrine of the isolated, complete or fixed end limits intelligent examination, encourages insincerity, and puts a pseudo-stamp of moral justification upon success at any price.

Moralistic persons are given to escaping this evil by falling into another pit. They deny that consequences have anything at all to do with the morality of acts. Not ends but motives they say justify or condemn acts. The thing to do, accordingly, is to cultivate certain motives or dispositions, benevolence, purity, love of perfection, loyalty. The denial of consequences thus turns out formal, verbal. In reality a consequence is set up at which to aim, only it is a subjective consequence. "Meaning well" is selected as *the* consequence or end to be cul-

tivated at all hazards, an end which is all-justifying and to which everything else is offered up in sacrifice. The result is a sentimental futile complacency rather than the brutal efficiency of the executive. But the root of both evils is the same. One man selects some external consequence, the other man a state of internal feeling, to serve as the end. The doctrine of meaning well as *the* end is if anything the more contemptible of the two, for it shrinks from accepting any responsibility for actual results. It is negative, self-protective and sloppy. It lends itself to complete self-deception.

Why have men become so attached to fixed, external ends? Why is it not universally recognized that an end is a device of intelligence in guiding action, instrumental to freeing and harmonizing troubled and divided tendencies? The answer is virtually contained in what was earlier said about rigid habits and their effect upon intelligence. Ends are, in fact, literally endless, forever coming into existence as new activities occasion new consequences. "Endless ends" is a way of saying that there are no ends—that is no fixed self-enclosed finalities. While however we cannot actually prevent change from occurring we can and do regard it as evil. We strive to retain action in ditches already dug. We regard novelties as dangerous, experiments as illicit and deviations as forbidden. Fixed and separate ends reflect a projection of our own fixed and non-interacting compartmental habits. We see only consequences which correspond to our habitual courses. As we have said, men did not begin to shoot because there were ready-made targets to aim at. They made things into targets by shooting at them, and then made special targets to make shooting more significantly interesting. But if generation after generation were shown targets they had had no part in constructing, if bows and arrows were thrust into their hands, and pressure were brought to bear upon them to keep them shooting in season and out, some wearied soul would soon propound to willing listeners the theory that shooting was unnatural, that man was naturally wholly at rest, and that targets existed in order that men might be forced to be active; that the duty of shooting and the virtue of hitting are externally imposed and fostered, and that otherwise there would be no such thing as a shooting-activity—that is, morality.

The doctrine of fixed ends not only diverts attention from examination of consequences and the intelligent creation of purpose, but, since means and ends are two ways of regarding the same actuality, it also renders men careless in their inspection of existing conditions. An aim not framed on the basis of a survey of those present conditions which are to be employed as means of its realization simply throws us back upon past habits. We then do not do what we intended to do but what we have got used to doing, or else we thrash about in a blind ineffectual way. The result is failure. Discouragement follows, assuaged perhaps by the thought that in any case the end is too ideal, too noble and remote, to be capable of realization. We fall back on the consoling thought that our moral ideals are too good for this world and that we must accustom ourselves to a gap between aim and execution. Actual life is then thought of as a compromise with the best, an enforced second or third best, a dreary exile from our true home in the ideal, or a temporary period of troubled probation to be followed by a period of unending attainment and peace. At the same time, as has been repeatedly pointed out, persons of a more practical turn of mind accept the world "as it is," that is as past customs have made it to be, and consider what advantages for themselves may be extracted from it. They form aims on the basis of existing habits of life which may be turned to their own private account. They employ intelligence in framing ends and selecting and arranging means. But intelligence is confined to manipulation; it does not extend to construction. It is the intelligence of the politician, administrator and professional executive—the kind of intelligence which has given a bad meaning to a word that ought to have a fine meaning, opportunism. For the highest task of intelligence is to grasp and realize genuine opportunity, possibility.

Roughly speaking, the course of forming aims is as follows. The beginning is with a wish, an emotional reaction against the present state of things and a hope for something different. Action fails to connect satisfactorily with surrounding conditions. Thrown back upon itself, it projects itself in an imagination of a scene which if it were present would afford satisfaction. This picture is often called an aim, more often an ideal. But in itself it is a fancy which may be only a phantasy, a dream, a castle in the air. In itself it is a romantic embellishment of the present; at its best it is material for poetry or the novel. Its natural home is not in the future but in the dim past or in some distant and supposedly better part of the present world. Every such idealized object is suggested by something actually experienced, as the flight of birds suggests the liberation of human beings from the restrictions of slow locomotion on dull earth. It becomes an aim or end only when it is worked out in terms of concrete conditions available for its realization, that is in terms of "means."

This transformation depends upon study of the conditions which generate or make possible the fact observed to exist already. The fancy of the delight of moving at will through the air became an actuality only after men carefully studied the way in which a bird although heavier than air actually sustains itself in air. A fancy becomes an aim, in short, when some past sequence of known cause-and-effect is projected into the future, and when by assembling its causal conditions we strive to generate a like result. We have to fall back upon what has already happened naturally without design, and study it to see *how* it happened, which is what is meant by causation. This knowledge joined to wish creates a purpose. Many men have doubtless dreamed of ability to have light in darkness without the trouble of oil, lamps and friction. Glow-worms, lightning, the sparks of cut electric conductors suggest such a possibility. But the picture remained a dream until an Edison studied all that could be found out about such casual phenomena of light, and then set to work to search out and gather together the means for reproducing their operation. The great trouble with what passes for moral ends and ideals is that they do not get beyond the stage of fancy of something agreeable and desirable based upon an emotional wish; very often, at that, not even an original wish, but the wish of some leader which has been conventionalized and transmitted through channels of authority. Every gain in natural science makes possible new aims. That is, the discovery of how things *do* occur makes it possible to conceive of their happening at will, and gives us a start on selecting and combining the conditions, the means, to command their happening. In technical matters, this lesson has been fairly well learned. But in moral matters, men still largely neglect the need of studying the way in which results similar to those which we desire actually happen. Mechanism is despised as of importance only in low material things. The consequent divorce of moral ends from scientific study of natural events renders the former impotent wishes, compensatory dreams in consciousness. In *fact* ends or consequences are still determined by fixed habit and the force of circumstance. The evils of idle dreaming and of routine are experienced in conjunction. "Idealism" must indeed come first—the imagination of some better state generated by desire. But unless ideals are to be dreams and idealism a synonym for romanticism and phantasy-building, there must be a most realistic study of actual conditions and of the mode or law of natural events, in order to give the imagined or ideal object definite form and solid substance—to give it, in short, practicality and constitute it a working end.

The acceptance of fixed ends in themselves is an aspect of man's devotion to an ideal of certainty. This affection was inevitably cherished as long as men believed that the highest things in physical nature are at rest, and that science is possible only by grasping immutable forms and species: in other words, for much the greater part of the intellectual history of mankind. Only reckless sceptics would have dared entertain any idea of ends except as fixed in themselves as long as the whole structure of science was erected upon the immobile. Behind however the conception of fixity whether in science or morals lay adherence to certainty of "truth," a clinging to something fixed, born of fear of the new and of attachment to possessions. When the classicist condemns concession to impulse and holds up to admiration the patterns tested in tradition, he little suspects how much he is himself affected by unavowed impulses—timidity which makes him cling to authority, conceit which moves him to be himself the authority who speaks in the name of authority, possessive impulse which fears to risk acquisition in new adventures. Love of certainty is a demand for guarantees in advance of action. Ignoring the fact that truth can be bought only by the adventure of experiment, dogmatism turns truth into an insurance company. Fixed ends upon one side and fixed "principles"—that is authoritative rules—on the other, are props for a feeling of safety, the refuge of the timid and the means by which the bold prey upon the timid.

The Individual,
Liberty, and the State

Thought about the principles of human conduct embraces a wider acreage than the traditional problems of ethics, which concentrate on the acts of individuals. Man's social and political life must also be taken into account if human conduct is to be seen in all its ramifications. That man is, as Aristotle says, a social and political animal, seems to be as fundamental a fact about him as the fact that he is born and dies. Indeed, in civilized society human beings are unable to be born and to die without acknowledging their inescapable presence in a social and political context. Society and the body politic support the individual man in countless ways, and he cannot even express his identity adequately without mentioning the social and political groups in which he is included.

To surrender some authority to a political body has seemed a necessary means to ensure the order requisite to a productive life. But on what principles this surrender of authority is to be based, and just how far it can go before the power of political bodies becomes oppressive and intolerable, is a matter of continued controversy.

To arrive at intelligent conclusions on the questions of the principles and limits of government requires some consideration of the ends which government ought to serve. Often speculative thought on the ends of government has been tied to premises consisting of certain propositions about the nature of man, God, and human destiny, though some thinkers would contend that such premises are not needed, that political thought may be carried on without recourse to metaphysics. Here, as in ethical thought, many different approaches can be made, and here, too, problems of method and knowledge arise.

Recent decades have seen the accelerated development of political science, economics, and sociology, disciplines which are usually included among the sciences of man. What bearing do inquiries conducted in these fields have on the determination of the aims and ends of social organization and government? Is it possible to make these adolescent sciences value-free, that is, independent of the biases and preferences of the investigators who must choose the problems and collect and organize the data? Is it desirable to attempt to do so? In general, what effect must an investigator's own immersion in a milieu of social and political attitudes and ideas have on the information which he obtains and the hypotheses which he constructs?

We should keep these questions in mind while considering the philosophic political thought presented in this part of the book and also in preparing for the part which follows. Most of the writers in Part IV propose a definite conception of the state and of the relation of individuals to it. What are the connections between fact, hypothesis, and value in these writings? Are their studies of society, economics, and government primarily a kind of practical science for the guidance of policy makers? Are they a true theoretic science (see the next part)? Or are they primarily arguments for the acceptance of certain cherished views of the writers?

Political thought must constantly keep in view the fundamental difference between the abstract entity called the "State" and the concrete individuals who are members of the State. How to make the authority of the State consonant with the interests of its members is one of the most difficult problems of statecraft. One of the great ironies that history reveals is the fate of the man who challenges the idol of conventional authority, not in order to destroy but to vivify and strengthen the life of the community. Socrates was such a man, the "gadfly" of Athens, committed to a daily round of poverty and free inquiry. In the *Apology* of Socrates, written by Plato, Socrates is represented at his trial defending himself against the trumped-up charges brought by his accusers. His account of the way he has spent his life puts in sharp relief the question of how to effect a harmony between the values of an individual, the proper interests of the social order, and the need of government for self-criticism.

The *Apology* gives us a portrait of an unusual man, for whom the daily life of a citizen committed to the highest communal values was a constant inquiry into matters of many kinds—ethical, aesthetic, judicial, religious. Is it true in every state and at all times that, as Socrates maintains, the man who would serve the State with his wisdom, as a critic of it, must not hold public office? Is there a duty, in Thoreau's phrase, of "civil disobedience"? If so, what are the limits of such disobedience and how are they to be discerned? Was Socrates practicing civil disobedience, and does he defend himself on that ground? Or, does he claim that he, more than most men, but in his own peculiar way, was obedient to the State? Do the demands of loyalty and obedience to the State vary with the nature of political systems?

These same issues concern John Stuart Mill in his famous essay *On Liberty*. Mill is especially occupied with the problem of freedom of thought and expression, the foundation of a free society. The principle which he asserts and defends is that restrictions on the freedom of the individual are justified only when harm to others will result if he is allowed to do as he pleases. How the harm resulting to others is to be defined and recognized is an important issue that we must raise in considering Mill's principle.

Another point made by Mill bears on the large question of the nature of knowledge. Liberty of thought and expression, Mill maintains, is not an isolated value but directly affects the level of understanding in a society and its prospects for improving its knowledge. This is an exceedingly important matter in our own time and for the foreseeable future. Some observers hold that today the chief problem of the world's leading societies is not the production and distribution of goods, the dissemination of material wealth and resources, but the acquisition of new knowledge. Research and development of concepts and techniques now play a major role—some would say *the* major role—in the activities of governments and private individuals. What are the conditions which societies must meet in order to promote such inquiry? Is Mill's principle a desirable one as it stands? Does it need modification?

Before considering Mill's arguments for liberty of expression, the reader will want to inquire into the idea of a civilized society. Thomas Hobbes's account of the "state of nature" and of the reasons which impel men to form a civil society is a classic of political thought, though a much disputed one. The idea of a social contract which Hobbes presents has been criticized by those who point out that as a matter of fact states have come into existence through violence and conquest. One needs then to ask whether Hobbes means this as a factual, literal account of what happened historically or as a kind of mythical presentation of the differences between two conditions—of nature and of civilized society. Are such speculative accounts illuminating? In what sense, if any, can we claim that they provide knowledge?

It is interesting also to note what Hobbes says about rights: In the state of nature all men can equally claim a right to all things; in a civil society a man voluntarily relinquishes a part of his claim in order to gain protection from other men. In the state of nature no man may claim that *his* rights have been infringed since the things he claims could have been claimed equally by others. Is this a legitimate doctrine of individual rights? Where do the so-called "rights" of individuals come from? From God, nature, the tolerance of other men, political constitutions, or perhaps some combination of any of these?

John Locke argues that man has a natural right to private property prior to the establishment of a civil society. It is the work an individual has done on some portion of nature, Locke holds, which gives him his right in that property, and it is labor that establishes value. In Locke's view, men form societies for "the enjoyment of their properties in peace and safety," and governments have the right to tax only to ensure property rights. The reader should ask himself whether the abundance of unsettled land in Locke's day might not have helped to shape his theory.

Ought private property to enjoy the privileged status which Locke accords it? Is it feasible in complex urban societies to regard labor as the factor which establishes property value? Underlying Locke's view is the (for him) self-evident principle that an individual has a right to dispose as he sees fit both of his person and of his labor and consequently of anything to which his labor is attached. The reader should examine with care this supposedly self-evident principle. Is its truth apparent? What role should such principles play in the making of moral or political theories? Are there superior bases on which to found a theory of government? If so, what may they be?

Mill's essay On Liberty has already been introduced. In connection with it, one might ask at this point whether any so-called self-evident principles play a part in Mill's thinking. What might be the fate of such principles in a society which affords the kind of liberty of expression which Mill champions?

The selection from Engels is a classic statement of "Marxist" revolutionary doctrine, touching on economic and political theory and on the philosophy of history. Many questions might be raised with respect to it.

Among the most important are questions of the same sort as those we have been asking concerning other positions. What are the chief grounds for the view presented? Does Engels appeal to evidence, to self-evident principles, or to a wider philosophic system to undergird the view he advances? Do the facts of history, which seemingly play a significant part in his argument, admit of other interpretations? Does he make predictions about the future or proposals for future action or both? Is there a "necessity" in historical events? Does the word "necessity," when it is used to describe the conflict of interests in societies, have the same sense that it has when used to describe individual action? In what sense is Engels a materialist, and is his materialist view justified? Is this a view also of human nature, or is it limited to historical economic forces? What bearing might doctrines of free will or of determinism have on political theory?

Albert Camus shows how a world view involving a religious and philosophic outlook can have bearing on the actions of government, the specific issue being capital punishment. Are the reasons offered by Camus for rejecting capital punishment the kind that ought to be considered by the makers of social and political policy? Should the wider range of beliefs, including religious beliefs, be invoked in deciding practical issues? Is the issue of capital punishment a practical issue only, or is it a matter of principle as well? Can the two kinds of issues be easily separated? Is Camus right in characterizing the present age as one which rejects a God who judges mankind? Is he right in believing that the rejection of such a God entails abolishing capital punishment? What is the precise chain of argument?

The defense of Socrates

Plato (428/7-348/7 B.C.)*

The Apology is generally thought to be one of Plato's earliest works. In it Plato portrays the man whom he most revered—Socrates—as he appeared when he was tried by the citizens of Athens in 399 B.C. The Apology raises a number of interesting questions about the different demands of the private and public spheres. It is especially concerned with the role of the critic in the free society and with the difference between speaking the truth and saying what is merely persuasive and pleasing. What is central in it is the life and character of Socrates himself and the attitudes which he judged to be appropriate to a man who is "free" in the deepest sense. Our selection is the entire dialogue.

CHARACTERS

Socrates

Meletus

Scene—The Court of Justice

Soc. I cannot tell what impression my accusers have made upon you, Athenians. For my own part, I know that they nearly made me forget who I was, so believable were they; and yet they have scarcely uttered one single word of truth. But of all their many falsehoods, the one which astonished me most was when they said that I was a clever speaker, and that you must be careful not to let me mislead you. I thought that it was most impudent of them not to be ashamed to talk in that way; for as soon as I open my mouth they will be refuted, and I shall prove that I am not a clever speaker in any way at all—unless, indeed, by a clever speaker they mean a man who speaks the truth. If that is their meaning, I agree with them that I am a much greater

orator than they. My accusers, then I repeat, have said little or nothing that is true; but from me you shall hear the whole truth. Certainly you will not hear an elaborate speech, Athenians, dressed up, like theirs, with words and phrases. I will say to you what I have to say, without preparation, and in the words which come first, for I believe that my cause is just; so let none of you expect anything else. Indeed, my friends, it would hardly be seemly for me, at my age, to come before you like a young man with his specious phrases. But there is one thing, Athenians, which I do most earnestly beg and entreat of you. Do not be surprised and do not interrupt with shouts if in my defense I speak in the same way that I am accustomed to speak in the market-place, at the tables of the money-changers, where many of you have heard me, and elsewhere. The truth is this. I am more than seventy years old, and this is the first time that I have ever come before a law court; so your manner of speech here is quite strange to me. If I had been really a stranger, you would have forgiven me for speaking in the language and the fashion of my native country; and so now I ask you to grant me what I think I have a right to claim. Never mind the style of my

Plato, *The Apology*, translated by F. J. Church.

* See the introductory note on Plato on page 5.

speech—it may be better or it may be worse—give your whole attention to the question, Is what I say just, or is it not? That is what makes a good judge, as speaking the truth makes a good advocate.

I have to defend myself, Athenians, first against the old false accusations of my old accusers, and then against the later ones of my present accusers. For many men have been accusing me to you, and for very many years, who have not uttered a word of truth; and I fear them more than I fear Anytus and his associates, formidable as they are. But, my friends, those others are still more formidable; for they got hold of most of you when you were children, and they have been more persistent in accusing me untruthfully and have persuaded you that there is a certain Socrates, a wise man, who speculates about the heavens, and who investigates things that are beneath the earth, and who can make the weaker reason appear the stronger. These men, Athenians, who spread abroad this report are the accusers whom I fear; for their hearers think that persons who pursue such inquiries never believe in the gods. Then they are many, and their attacks have been going on for a long time, and they spoke to you when you were at the age most readily to believe them, for you were all young, and many of you were children, and there was no one to answer them when they attacked me. And the most unreasonable thing of all is that I do not even know their names: I cannot tell you who they are except when one happens to be a comic poet. But all the rest who have persuaded you, from motives of resentment and prejudice, and sometimes, it may be, from conviction, are hardest to cope with. For I cannot call any one of them forward in court to cross-examine him. I have, as it were, simply to spar with shadows in my defense, and to put questions which there is no one to answer. I ask you, therefore, to believe that, as I say, I have been attacked by two kinds of accusers—first, by Meletus and his associates, and, then, by those older ones of whom I have spoken. And, with your leave, I will defend myself first against my old accusers; for you heard their accusa-

tions first, and they were much more forceful than my present accusers are.

Well, I must make my defense, Athenians, and try in the short time allowed me to remove the prejudice which you have been so long a time acquiring. I hope that I may manage to do this, if it be good for you and for me, and that my defense may be successful; but I am quite aware of the nature of my task, and I know that it is a difficult one. Be the outcome, however, as is pleasing to God, I must obey the law and make my defense.

Let us begin from the beginning, then, and ask what is the accusation which has given rise to the prejudice against me, which was what Meletus relied on when he brought his indictment. What is the prejudice which my enemies have been spreading about me? I must assume that they are formally accusing me, and read their indictment. It would run somewhat in this fashion: Socrates is a wrongdoer, who meddles with inquiries into things beneath the earth and in the heavens, and who makes the weaker reason appear the stronger, and who teaches others these same things. That is what they say; and in the comedy of Aristophanes [*Clouds*] you yourselves saw a man called Socrates swinging round in a basket and saying that he walked the air, and prattling a great deal of nonsense about matters of which I understand nothing, either more or less. I do not mean to disparage that kind of knowledge if there is any one who is wise about these matters. I trust Meletus may never be able to prosecute me for that. But the truth is, Athenians, I have nothing to do with these matters, and almost all of you are yourselves my witnesses of this. I beg all of you who have heard me discussing, and they are many, to inform your neighbors and tell them if any of you have ever heard me discussing such matters, either more or less. That will show you that the other common stories about me are as false as this one.

But the fact is that not one of these is true. And if you have heard that I undertake to educate men, and make money by so doing, that is not true either, though I think that it would be a fine thing to be able to educate men, as Gorgias of Leontini, and Prodicus of Ceos, and Hippias of Elis do. For each of them, my friends, can go into any city, and persuade the young men to leave the society of their fellow citizens, with any of whom they might associate for nothing, and to be only too glad to be allowed to pay money for the privilege of associating with themselves. And I believe that there is another wise man from Paros residing in Athens at this moment. I happened to meet Callias, the son of Hipponicus, a man who has spent more money on sophists than everyone else put together. So I said to him (he has two sons), Callias, if your two sons had been foals or calves, we could have hired a trainer for them who would have made them perfect in the virtue which belongs to their nature. He would have been either a groom or a farmer. But whom do you intend to take to train them, seeing that they are men? Who understands the virtue which belongs to men and to citizens? I suppose that you must have thought of this, because of your sons. Is there such a person, said I, or not? Certainly there is, he replied. Who is he, said I, and where does he come from, and what is his fee? Evenus, Socrates, he replied, from Paros, five minae. Then I thought that Evenus was a fortunate person if he really understood this art and could teach so cleverly. If I had possessed knowledge of that kind, I should have been conceited and disdainful. But, Athenians, the truth is that I do not possess it.

Perhaps some of you may reply: But, Socrates, what is the trouble with you? What has given rise to these prejudices against you? You must have been doing something out of the ordinary. All these stories and reports of you would never have arisen if you had not been doing something different from other men. So tell us what it is, that we may not give our verdict in the dark. I think that that is a fair question, and I will try to explain to you what it is that has raised these prejudices against me and given me this reputation. Listen, then: some of you, perhaps, will think that I am joking, but I assure you that I will tell you the whole truth. I have gained this reputation, Athenians, simply by reason of a certain wisdom. But by what kind of wisdom? It is by just that wisdom which is perhaps human wisdom. In that, it may be, I am really wise. But the men of whom I was speaking just now must be wise in a wisdom which is greater than human wisdom, or else I cannot describe it, for certainly I know nothing of it myself, and if any man says that I do, he lies and speaks to arouse prejudice against me. Do not interrupt me with shouts, Athenians, even if you think that I am boasting. What I am going to say is not my own: I will tell you who says it, and he is worthy of your respect. I will bring the god of Delphi to be the witness of my wisdom, if it is wisdom at all, and of its nature. You remember Chaerephon. From youth upwards he was my comrade; and also a partisan of your democracy, sharing your recent exile and returning with you. You remember, too, Chaerephon's character—how vehement he was in carrying through whatever he took in hand. Once he went to Delphi and ventured to put this question to the oracle—I entreat you again, my friends, not to interrupt me with your shouts—he asked if there was any man who was wiser than I. The priestess answered that there was no one. Chaerephon himself is dead, but his brother here will confirm what I say.

Now see why I tell you this. I am going to explain to you how the prejudice against me has arisen. When I heard of the oracle I began to reflect: What can the god mean by this riddle? I know very well that I am not wise, even in the smallest degree. Then what can he mean by saying that I am the wisest of men? It cannot be that he is speaking falsely, for he is a god and cannot lie. For a long time I was at a loss to understand his meaning. Then, very reluctantly, I turned to seek for it in this manner: I went to a man who was reputed to be wise, thinking that there, if anywhere, I should prove the answer wrong, and meaning to point out to the oracle its mistake, and to say, You said that I was the wisest of men, but this man is wiser than I am. So I examined the man—I need not tell you his name, he was a politician—but this was the result, Athenians. When I conversed with him I came to see that, though a great many persons, and most of all he himself, thought that he was wise, yet he was not wise. Then I tried to prove to him that he was not wise, though he fancied that he was; and by so doing I made him indignant, and many of the bystanders. So when I went away, I thought to myself, I am wiser than this man: neither of us knows anything that is really worthwhile, but he thinks that he has knowledge when he has not, while I, having no knowledge, do not think that I have. I seem, at any rate, to be a little wiser than he is on this point: I do not think that I know what I do not know. Next I went to another man who was reputed to be still wiser than the last, with exactly the same result. And there again I made him, and many other men, indignant.

Then I went on to one man after another, seeing that I was arousing indignation every day, which caused me much pain and anxiety. Still I thought that I must set the god's command above everything. So I had to go to every man who seemed to possess any knowledge, and investigate the meaning of the oracle. Athenians, I must tell you the truth; by the dog, this was the result of the investigation which I made at the god's bidding: I found that the men whose reputation for wisdom stood highest were nearly the most lacking in it, while others who were looked down on as common people were much more intelligent. Now I must describe to you the wanderings which I undertook, like Heraclean labors, to prove the oracle irrefutable. After the politicians, I went to the poets, tragic, dithyrambic, and others, thinking that there I should find myself manifestly more ignorant than they. So I took up the poems on which I thought that they had spent most pains, and asked them what they meant, hoping at the same time to learn something from them. I am ashamed to tell you the truth, my friends, but I must say it. Almost any one of the bystanders could have talked about the works of these poets better than the poets themselves. So I soon found that it is not by wisdom that the poets create their works, but by a certain innate power and by inspiration, like soothsayers and prophets, who say

many fine things, but who understand nothing of what they say. The poets seemed to me to be in a similar situation. And at the same time I perceived that, because of their poetry, they thought that they were the wisest of men in other matters, too, which they were not. So I went away again, thinking that I had the same advantage over the poets that I had over the politicians.

Finally, I went to the artisans, for I knew very well that I possessed no knowledge at all worth speaking of, and I was sure that I should find that they knew many fine things. And in that I was not mistaken. They knew what I did not know, and so far they were wiser than I. But, Athenians, it seemed to me that the skilled artisans made the same mistake as the poets. Each of them believed himself to be extremely wise in matters of the greatest importance because he was skilful in his own art: and this presumption of theirs obscured their real wisdom. So I asked myself, on behalf of the oracle, whether I would choose to remain as I was, without either their wisdom or their ignorance, or to possess both, as they did. And I answered to myself and to the oracle that it was better for me to remain as I was.

From this examination, Athenians, has arisen much fierce and bitter indignation, and from this a great many prejudices about me, and people say that I am "a wise man." For the bystanders always think that I am wise myself in any matter wherein I refute another. But, my friends, I believe that the god is really wise, and that by this oracle he meant that human wisdom is worth little or nothing. I do not think that he meant that Socrates was wise. He only made use of my name, and took me as an example, as though he would say to men: He among you is the wisest who, like Socrates, knows that in truth his wisdom is worth nothing at all. Therefore I still go about testing and examining every man whom I think wise, whether he be a citizen or a stranger, as the god has commanded me; and whenever I find that he is not wise, I point out to him, on the god's behalf, that he is not wise. I am so busy in this pursuit that I have never had leisure to take any part worth mentioning in public matters or to look after my private affairs. I am in great poverty as the result of my service to the god.

Besides this, the young men who follow me about, who are the sons of wealthy persons and have the most leisure, take pleasure in hearing men cross-examined. They often imitate me among themselves; then they try their hands at cross-examining other people. And, I imagine, they find plenty of men who think that they know a great deal when in fact they know little or nothing. Then the persons who are cross-examined get angry with me instead of with themselves, and say that Socrates is an abomination and corrupts the young. When they are asked, Why, what does he do? what does he teach? they do not know what to say; but, not to seem at a loss, they repeat the stock charges against all philosophers, and allege that he investigates things in the air and under the earth, and that he teaches people to disbelieve in the gods, and to make the weaker reason appear the stronger. For, I suppose, they would not like to confess the truth, which is that they are shown up as ignorant pretenders to knowledge that they do not possess. So they have been filling your ears with their bitter prejudices for a long time, for they are ambitious, energetic, and numerous; and they speak vigorously and persuasively against me. Relying on this, Meletus, Anytus, and Lycon have attacked me. Meletus is indignant with me on the part of the poets, Anytus on the part of the artisans and politicians, and Lycon on the part of the orators. And so, as I said at the beginning, I shall be surprised if I am able, in the short time allowed me for my defense, to remove from your minds this prejudice which has grown so strong. What I have told you, Athenians, is the truth: I neither conceal nor do I suppress anything, small or great. Yet I know that it is just this plainness of speech which rouses indignation. But that is only a proof that my words are true, and that the prejudice against me, and the causes of it, are what I have said. And whether you look for them now or hereafter, you will find that they are so.

What I have said must suffice as my defense against the charges of my first accusers. I will try next to defend myself against Meletus, that "good patriot," as he calls himself, and my later accusers. Let us assume that they are a new set of accusers, and read their indictment, as we did in the case of the others. It runs thus. He says that Socrates is a wrongdoer who corrupts the youth, and who does not believe in the gods whom the state believes in, but in other new divinities. Such is the accusation. Let us examine each point in it separately. Meletus says that I do wrong by corrupting the youth. But I say, Athenians, that he is doing wrong, for he is playing a solemn joke by lightly bringing men to trial, and pretending to have a zealous interest in matters to which he has never given a moment's thought. Now I will try to prove to you that it is so.

Come here, Meletus. Is it not a fact that you think it very important that the young should be as excellent as possible?

Mel. It is.

Soc. Come then, tell the judges who is it who improves them? You care so much, you must know. You are accusing me, and bringing me to trial, because, as you say, you have discovered that I am the corrupter of the youth. Come now, reveal to the gentlemen who improves them. You see, Meletus, you have nothing to say; you are silent. But don't you think that this is shameful? Is not your silence a conclusive proof of what I say—that you have never cared? Come, tell us, my good sir, who makes the young better citizens?

Mel. The laws.

Soc. That, my friend, is not my question. What man improves the young, who starts with the knowledge of the laws?

Mel. The judges here, Socrates.

Soc. What do you mean, Meletus? Can they educate the young and improve them?

Mel. Certainly.

Soc. All of them? or only some of them?

Mel. All of them.

Soc. By Hera, that is good news! Such a large supply of benefactors! And do the listeners here improve them, or not?

Mel. They do.

Soc. And do the senators?

Mel. Yes.

Soc. Well then, Meletus, do the members of the assembly corrupt the young or do they again all improve them?

Mel. They, too, improve them.

Soc. Then all the Athenians, apparently, make the young into good men except me, and I alone corrupt them. Is that your meaning?

Mel. Most certainly; that is my meaning.

Soc. You have discovered me to be most unfortunate. Now tell me: do you think that the same holds good in the case of horses? Does one man do them harm and everyone else improve them? On the contrary, is it not one man only, or a very few—namely, those who are skilled with horses—who can improve them, while the majority of men harm them if they use them and have anything to do with them? Is it not so, Meletus, both with horses and with every other animal? Of course it is, whether you and Anytus say yes or no. The young would certainly be very fortunate if only one man corrupted them, and everyone else did them good. The truth is, Meletus, you prove conclusively that you have never thought about the youth in your life. You exhibit your carelessness in not caring for the very matters about which you are prosecuting me.

Now be so good as to tell us, Meletus, is it better to live among good citizens or bad ones? Answer, my friend. I am not asking you at all a difficult question. Do not the bad harm their associates and the good do them good?

Mel. Yes.

Soc. Is there any man who would rather be injured than benefited by his companions? Answer, my good sir; you are obliged by the law to answer. Does any one like to be injured?

Mel. Certainly not.

Soc. Well then, are you prosecuting me for corrupting the young and making them worse, intentionally or unintentionally?

Mel. For doing it intentionally.

Soc. What, Meletus? Do you mean to say that you, who are so much younger than I, are yet so much wiser than I that you know that bad citizens always do evil, and that good

citizens do good, to those with whom they come in contact, while I am so extraordinarily stupid as not to know that, if I make any of my companions evil, he will probably injure me in some way, and as to commit this great evil, as you allege, intentionally? You will not make me believe that, nor anyone else either, I should think. Either I do not corrupt the young at all or, if I do, I do so unintentionally: so that you are lying in either case. And if I corrupt them unintentionally, the law does not call upon you to prosecute me for an error which is unintentional, but to take me aside privately and reprove and instruct me. For, of course, I shall cease from doing wrong involuntarily, as soon as I know that I have been doing wrong. But you avoided associating with me and educating me; instead you bring me up before the court, where the law sends persons, not for instruction, but for punishment.

The truth is, Athenians, as I said, it is quite clear that Meletus has never cared at all about these matters. However, now tell us, Meletus, how do you say that I corrupt the young? Clearly, according to your indictment, by teaching them not to believe in the gods the state believes in, but other new divinities instead. You mean that I corrupt the young by that teaching, do you not?

Mel. Yes, most certainly I mean that.

Soc. Then in the name of these gods of whom we are speaking, explain yourself a little more clearly to me and to these gentlemen here. I cannot understand what you mean. Do you mean that I teach the young to believe in some gods, but not in the gods of the state? Do you accuse me of teaching them to believe in strange gods? If that is your meaning, I myself believe in some gods, and my crime is not that of absolute atheism. Or do you mean that I do not believe in the gods at all myself, and that I teach other people not to believe in them either?

Mel. I mean that you do not believe in the gods in any way whatever.

Soc. You amaze me, Meletus! Why do you say that? Do you mean that I believe neither the sun nor the moon to be gods, like other men?

Mel. I swear he does not, judges; he says that the sun is a stone, and the moon earth.

Soc. My dear Meletus, do you think that you are prosecuting Anaxagoras? You must have a very poor opinion of these men, and think them illiterate, if you imagine that they do not know that the works of Anaxagoras of Clazomenae are full of these doctrines. And so young men learn these things from me, when they can often buy places in the theatre for a drachma at most, and laugh at Socrates were he to pretend that these doctrines, which are very peculiar doctrines, too, were his own. But please tell me, do you really think that I do not believe in the gods at all?

Mel. Most certainly I do. You are a complete atheist.

Soc. No one believes that, Meletus, not even you yourself. It seems to me, Athenians, that Meletus is very insolent and reckless, and that he is prosecuting me simply out of insolence, recklessness and youthful bravado. For he seems to be testing me, by asking me a riddle that has no answer. Will this wise Socrates, he says to himself, see that I am joking and contradicting myself? or shall I outwit him and everyone else who hears me? Meletus seems to me to contradict himself in his indictment: it is as if he were to say, Socrates is a wrongdoer who does not believe in the gods, but who believes in the gods. But that is mere joking.

Now, my friends, let us see why I think that this is his meaning. Do you answer me, Meletus; and do you, Athenians, remember the request which I made to you at the start, and do not interrupt me with shouts if I talk in my usual way.

Is there any man, Meletus, who believes in the existence of things pertaining to men and not in the existence of men? Make him answer the question, my friends, without these interruptions. Is there any man who believes in the existence of horsemanship and not in the existence of horses? or in flute-playing and not in flute-players? There is not, my friend. If you will not answer, I will tell both you and the judges. But you must answer my next question. Is there any man who believes in the existence of divine things and not in the existence of divinities?

Mel. There is not.

Soc. I am very glad that these gentlemen have managed to extract an answer from you. Well then, you say that I believe in divine beings, whether they be old or new ones, and that I teach others to believe in them; at any rate, according to your statement, I believe in divine beings. That you have sworn in your indictment. But if I believe in divine beings, I suppose it follows necessarily that I believe in divinities. Is it not so? It is. I assume that you grant that, as you do not answer. But do we not believe that divinities are either gods themselves or the children of the gods? Do you admit that?

Mel. I do.

Soc. Then you admit that I believe in divinities. Now, if these divinities are gods, then, as I say, you are joking and asking a riddle, and asserting that I do not believe in the gods, and at the same time that I do, since I believe in divinities. But if these divinities are the illegitimate children of the gods, either by the nymphs or by other mothers, as they are said to be, then, I ask, what man could believe in the existence of the children of the gods, and not in the existence of the gods? That would be as strange as believing in the existence of the offspring of horses and asses, and not in the existence of horses and asses. You must have indicted me in this manner, Meletus, either to test me or because you could not find any crime that you could accuse me of with truth. But you will never contrive to persuade any man with any sense at all that a belief in divine things and things of the gods does not necessarily involve a belief in divinities, and in the gods, and in heroes.

But in truth, Athenians, I do not think that I need say very much to prove that I have not committed the crime for which Meletus is prosecuting me. What I have said is enough to prove that. But I repeat it is certainly true, as I have already told you, that I have aroused much indignation. That is what will cause my condemnation if I am condemned; not Meletus nor Anytus either, but that prejudice and suspicion of the multitude which have been the destruction of many good men before me, and I think will be so again. There is no fear that I shall be the last victim.

Perhaps some one will say: Are you not ashamed, Socrates, of leading a life which is very likely now to cause your death? I should answer him with justice, and say: My friend, if you think that a man of any worth at all ought to reckon the chances of life and death when he acts, or that he ought to think of anything but whether he is acting rightly or wrongly, and as a good or a bad man would act, you are mistaken. According to you, the demigods who died at Troy would be foolish, and among them the son of Thetis, who thought nothing of danger when the alternative was disgrace. For when his mother—and she was a goddess—addressed him, when he was burning to slay Hector, in this fashion, "My son, if you avenge the death of your comrade Patroclus and slay Hector, you will die yourself, for 'fate awaits you straightway after Hector's death' "; when he heard this, he scorned danger and death; he feared much more to live a coward and not to avenge his friend. "Let me punish the evildoer and straightway die," he said, "that I may not remain here by the beaked ships jeered at, encumbering the earth." Do you suppose that he thought of danger or of death? For this, Athenians, I believe to be the truth. Wherever a man's station is, whether he has chosen it of his own will, or whether he has been placed at it by his commander, there it is his duty to remain and face the danger without thinking of death or of any other thing except dishonor.

When the generals whom you chose to command me, Athenians, assigned me my station at Potidaea and at Amphipolis and at Delium, I remained where they placed me and ran the risk of death, like other men. It would be very strange conduct on my part if I were to desert my station now from fear of death or of any other thing when God has commanded me—as I am persuaded that he has done—to spend my life in searching for wisdom, and in examining myself and others. That would indeed be a very strange thing:

then certainly I might with justice be brought to trial for not believing in the gods, for I should be disobeying the oracle, and fearing death and thinking myself wise when I was not wise. For to fear death, my friends, is only to think ourselves wise without really being wise, for it is to think that we know what we do not know. For no one knows whether death may not be the greatest good that can happen to man. But men fear it as if they knew quite well that it was the greatest of evils. And what is this but that shameful ignorance of thinking that we know what we do not know? In this matter, too, my friends, perhaps I am different from the multitude; and if I were to claim to be at all wiser than others, it would be because, not knowing very much about the other world, I do not think I know. But I do know very well that it is evil and disgraceful to do wrong, and to disobey my superior, whoever he is, whether man or god. I will never do what I know to be evil, and shrink in fear from what I do not know to be good or evil. Even if you acquit me now, and do not listen to Anytus' argument that, if I am to be acquitted, I ought never to have been brought to trial at all, and that, as it is, you are bound to put me to death because, as he said, if I escape, all your sons will be utterly corrupted by practising what Socrates teaches. If you were therefore to say to me: Socrates, this time we will not listen to Anytus; we will let you go, but on this condition, that you give up this investigation of yours, and philosophy; if you are found following those pursuits again, you shall die. I say, if you offered to let me go on these terms, I should reply: Athenians, I hold you in the highest regard and affection, but I will be persuaded by the god rather than by you; and as long as I have breath and strength I will not give up philosophy and exhorting you and declaring the truth to every one of you whom I meet, saying, as I am accustomed, "My good friend, you are a citizen of Athens, a city which is very great and very famous for its wisdom and strength—are you not ashamed of caring so much for the making of money and for fame and prestige, when you neither think nor care about wisdom and truth and the improvement of your soul?" And if he disputes my words and says that he does care about these things, I shall not at once release him and go away: I shall question him and cross-examine him and test him. If I think that he does not possess virtue, though he says that he does, I shall reproach him for undervaluing the most valuable things, and overvaluing those that are less valuable. This I shall do to everyone whom I meet, young or old, citizen or stranger, but especially to citizens, for they are more nearly akin to me. For know that the god has commanded me to do so. And I think that no greater good has ever befallen you in Athens than my service to the god. For I spend my whole life in going about and persuading you all to give your first and greatest care to the improvement of your souls, and not till you have done that to think of your bodies or your wealth; and telling you that virtue does not come from wealth, but that wealth, and every other good thing which men have, whether in public or in private, comes from virtue. If then I corrupt the youth by this teaching, these things must be harmful; but if any man says that I teach anything else, there is nothing in what he says. And therefore, Athenians, I say, whether you are persuaded by Anytus or not, whether you acquit me or not, be sure I shall not change my way of life; no, not if I have to die for it many times.

Do not interrupt me, Athenians, with your shouts. Remember the request which I made to you, and do not interrupt my words. I think that it will profit you to hear them. I am going to say something more to you, at which you may be inclined to protest, but do not do that. Be sure that if you put me to death, who am what I have told you that I am, you will do yourselves more harm than me. Meletus and Anytus can do me no harm: that is impossible, for I am sure it is not allowed that a good man be injured by a worse. They may indeed kill me, or drive me into exile, or deprive me of my civil rights; and perhaps Meletus and others think those things great evils. But I do not think so. I think it is a much greater evil to do what he is doing now, and to try to put a man to death unjustly. And

now, Athenians, I am not arguing in my own defense at all, as you might expect me to do, but rather in yours in order you may not make a mistake about the gift of the god to you by condemning me. For if you put me to death, you will not easily find another who, if I may use a ludicrous comparison, clings to the state as a sort of gadfly to a horse that is large and well-bred but rather sluggish from its size, and needing to be aroused. It seems to me that the god has attached me like that to the state, for I am constantly alighting upon you at every point to rouse, persuade, and reproach each of you all day long. You will not easily find anyone else, my friends, to fill my place; and if you are persuaded by me, you will spare my life. You are indignant, as drowsy persons are, when they are awakened, and, of course, if you are persuaded by Anytus, you could easily kill me with a single blow, and then sleep on undisturbed for the rest of your lives, unless the god in his care for you sends another to rouse you. And you may easily see that it is the god who has given me to your city; for it is not human the way in which I have neglected all my own interests and permitted my private affairs to be neglected now for so many years, while occupying myself unceasingly in your interests, going to each of you privately, like a father or an elder brother, trying to persuade him to care for virtue. There would have been a reason for it, if I had gained any advantage by this, or if I had been paid for my exhortations; but you see yourselves that my accusers, though they accuse me of everything else without shame, have not had the impudence to say that I ever either exacted or demanded payment. Of that they have no evidence. And I think that I have sufficient evidence of the truth of what I say—my poverty.

Perhaps it may seem strange to you that, though I go about giving this advice privately and meddling in others' affairs, yet I do not venture to come forward in the assembly and advise the state. You have often heard me speak of my reason for this, and in many places: it is that I have a certain divine sign, which is what Meletus has caricatured in his indictment. I have had it from childhood. It is a kind of voice which, whenever I hear it, always turns me back from something which I was going to do, but never urges me to act. It is this which forbids me to take part in politics. And I think it does well to forbid me. For, Athenians, it is quite certain that, if I had attempted to take part in politics, I should have perished at once and long ago without doing any good either to you or to myself. And do not be indignant with me for telling the truth. There is no man who will preserve his life for long, either in Athens or elsewhere, if he firmly opposes the multitude, and tries to prevent the commission of much injustice and illegality in the state. He who would really fight for justice must do so as a private citizen, not as an office-holder, if he is to preserve his life, even for a short time.

I will prove to you that this is so by very strong evidence, not by mere words, but by what you value highly, actions. Listen then to what has happened to me, that you may know that there is no man who could make me consent to do wrong from the fear of death, but that I would perish at once rather than give way. What I am going to tell you may be a commonplace in the law court; nevertheless it is true. The only office that I ever held in the state, Athenians, was that of Senator. When you wished to try the ten generals who did not rescue their men after the battle of Arginusae, as a group, which was illegal, as you all came to think afterwards, the tribe Antiochis, to which I belong, held the presidency. On that occasion I alone of all the presidents opposed your illegal action and gave my vote against you. The speakers were ready to suspend me and arrest me; and you were clamoring against me, and crying out to me to submit. But I thought that I ought to face the danger, with law and justice on my side, rather than join with you in your unjust proposal, from fear of imprisonment or death. That was when the state was democratic. When the oligarchy came in, the Thirty sent for me, with four others, to the council-chamber, and ordered us to bring Leon the Salaminian from Salamis, that they might put him to death.

They were in the habit of frequently giving similar orders to many others, wishing to implicate as many as possible in their crimes. But, then, I again proved, not by mere words, but by my actions, that, if I may speak bluntly, I do not care a straw for death; but that I do care very much indeed about not doing anything unjust or impious. That government with all its powers did not terrify me into doing anything unjust; but when we left the council-chamber, the other four went over to Salamis and brought Leon across to Athens; and I went home. And if the rule of the Thirty had not been destroyed soon afterwards, I should very likely have been put to death for what I did then. Many of you will be my witnesses in this matter.

Now do you think that I could have remained alive all these years if I had taken part in public affairs, and had always maintained the cause of justice like an honest man, and had held it a paramount duty, as it is, to do so? Certainly not, Athenians, nor could any other man. But throughout my whole life, both in private and in public, whenever I have had to take part in public affairs, you will find I have always been the same and have never yielded unjustly to anyone; no, not to those whom my enemies falsely assert to have been my pupils. But I was never anyone's teacher. I have never withheld myself from anyone, young or old, who was anxious to hear me discuss while I was making my investigation; neither do I discuss for payment, and refuse to discuss without payment. I am ready to ask questions of rich and poor alike, and if any man wishes to answer me, and then listen to what I have to say, he may. And I cannot justly be charged with causing these men to turn out good or bad, for I never either taught or professed to teach any of them any knowledge whatever. And if any man asserts that he ever learned or heard anything from me in private which everyone else did not hear as well as he, be sure that he does not speak the truth.

Why is it, then, that people delight in spending so much time in my company? You have heard why, Athenians. I told you the whole truth when I said that they delight in hearing me examine persons who think that they are wise when they are not wise. It is certainly very amusing to listen to that. And, I say, the god has commanded me to examine men, in oracles and in dreams and in every way in which the divine will was ever declared to man. This is the truth, Athenians, and if it were not the truth, it would be easily refuted. For if it were really the case that I have already corrupted some of the young men, and am now corrupting others, surely some of them, finding as they grew older that I had given them bad advice in their youth, would have come forward today to accuse me and take their revenge. Or if they were unwilling to do so themselves, surely their relatives, their fathers or brothers, or others, would, if I had done them any harm, have remembered it and taken their revenge. Certainly I see many of them in Court. Here is Crito, of my own deme and of my own age, the father of Critobulus; here is Lysanias of Sphettus, the father of Aeschines; here is also Antiphon of Cephisus, the father of Epigenes. Then here are others whose brothers have spent their time in my company—Nicostratus, the son of Theozotides and brother of Theodotus—and Theodotus is dead, so he at least cannot entreat his brother to be silent; here is Paralus, the son of Demodocus and the brother of Theages; here is Adeimantus, the son of Ariston, whose brother is Plato here; and Aeantodorus, whose brother is Aristodorus. And I can name many others to you, some of whom Meletus ought to have called as witnesses in the course of his own speech; but if he forgot to call them then, let him call them now—I will yield the floor to him—and tell us if he has any such evidence. No, on the contrary, my friends, you will find all these men ready to support me, the corrupter, the injurer, of their relatives, as Meletus and Anytus call me. Those of them who have been already corrupted might perhaps have some reason for supporting me, but what reason can their relatives have who are grown up, and who are uncorrupted, except the reason of truth and justice—that they know very well that Meletus is a liar, and that I am speaking the truth?

Well, my friends, this, and perhaps more like this, is pretty much what I have to say in my defense. There may be some one among you who will be indignant when he remembers how, even in a less important trial than this, he begged and entreated the judges, with many tears, to acquit him, and brought forward his children and many of his friends and relatives in Court in order to appeal to your feelings; and then finds that I shall do none of these things, though I am in what he would think the supreme danger. Perhaps he will harden himself against me when he notices this: it may make him angry, and he may cast his vote in anger. If it is so with any of you—I do not suppose that it is, but in case it should be so—I think that I should answer him reasonably if I said: My friend, I have relatives, too, for, in the words of Homer, "I am not born of an oak or a rock" but of flesh and blood; and so, Athenians, I have relatives, and I have three sons, one of them a lad, and the other two still children. Yet I will not bring any of them forward before you and implore you to acquit me. And why will I do none of these things? It is not from arrogance, Athenians, nor because I lack respect for you—whether or not I can face death bravely is another question—but for my own good name, and for your good name, and for the good name of the whole state. I do not think it right, at my age and with my reputation, to do anything of that kind. Rightly or wrongly, men have made up their minds that in some way Socrates is different from the mass of mankind. And it will be shameful if those of you who are thought to excel in wisdom, or in bravery, or in any other virtue, are going to act in this fashion. I have often seen men of reputation behaving in an extraordinary way at their trial, as if they thought it a terrible fate to be killed, and as though they expected to live for ever if you did not put them to death. Such men seem to me to bring shame upon the state, for any stranger would suppose that the best and most eminent Athenians, who are selected by their fellow citizens to hold office, and for other honors, are no better than women. Those of you, Athenians, who have any reputation at all ought not to do these things, and you ought not to allow us to do them; you should show that you will be much more ready to condemn men who make the state ridiculous by these pitiful pieces of acting, than men who remain quiet.

But apart from the question of reputation, my friends, I do not think that it is right to entreat the judge to acquit us, or to escape condemnation in that way. It is our duty to convince him by reason. He does not sit to give away justice as a favor, but to pronounce judgment; and he has sworn, not to favor any man whom he would like to favor, but to judge according to law. And, therefore, we ought not to encourage you in the habit of breaking your oaths; and you ought not to allow yourselves to fall into this habit, for then neither you nor we would be acting piously. Therefore, Athenians, do not require me to do these things, for I believe them to be neither good nor just nor pious; and, more especially, do not ask me to do them today when Meletus is prosecuting me for impiety. For were I to be successful and persuade you by my entreaties to break your oaths, I should be clearly teaching you to believe that there are no gods, and I should be simply accusing myself by my defense of not believing in them. But, Athenians, that is very far from the truth. I do believe in the gods as no one of my accusers believes in them: and to you and to God I commit my cause to be decided as is best for you and for me.

(He is found guilty by 281 votes to 220.)

I am not indignant at the verdict which you have given, Athenians, for many reasons. I expected that you would find me guilty; and I am not so much surprised at that as at the numbers of the votes. I certainly never thought that the majority against me would have been so narrow. But now it seems that if only thirty votes had changed sides, I should have escaped. So I think that I have escaped Meletus, as it is; and not only have I escaped him, for it is perfectly clear that if Anytus and Lycon had not come forward to accuse me, too, he would not have obtained the fifth part of the votes,

and would have had to pay a fine of a thousand drachmae.

So he proposes death as the penalty. Be it so. And what alternative penalty shall I propose to you, Athenians? What I deserve, of course, must I not? What then do I deserve to pay or to suffer for having determined not to spend my life in ease? I neglected the things which most men value, such as wealth, and family interests, and military commands, and popular oratory, and all the political appointments, and clubs, and factions, that there are in Athens; for I thought that I was really too honest a man to preserve my life if I engaged in these matters. So I did not go where I should have done no good either to you or to myself. I went, instead, to each one of you privately to do him, as I say, the greatest of services, and tried to persuade him not to think of his affairs until he had thought of himself and tried to make himself as good and wise as possible, nor to think of the affairs of Athens until he had thought of Athens herself; and to care for other things in the same manner. Then what do I deserve for such a life? Something good, Athenians, if I am really to propose what I deserve; and something good which it would be suitable to me to receive. Then what is a suitable reward to be given to a poor benefactor who requires leisure to exhort you? There is no reward, Athenians, so suitable for him as a public maintenance in the Prytaneum. It is a much more suitable reward for him than for any of you who has won a victory at the Olympic games with his horse or his chariots. Such a man only makes you seem happy, but I make you really happy; and he is not in want, and I am. So if I am to propose the penalty which I really deserve, I propose this—a public maintenance in the Prytaneum.

Perhaps you think me stubborn and arrogant in what I am saying now, as in what I said about the entreaties and tears. It is not so, Athenians; it is rather that I am convinced that I never wronged any man intentionally, though I cannot persuade you of that, for we have discussed together only a little time. If there were a law at Athens, as there is elsewhere, not to finish a trial of life and death in a single day, I think that I could have persuaded you; but now it is not easy in so short a time to clear myself of great prejudices. But when I am persuaded that I have never wronged any man, I shall certainly not wrong myself, or admit that I deserve to suffer any evil, or propose any evil for myself as a penalty. Why should I? Lest I should suffer the penalty which Meletus proposes when I say that I do not know whether it is a good or an evil? Shall I choose instead of it something which I know to be an evil, and propose that as a penalty? Shall I propose imprisonment? And why should I pass the rest of my days in prison, the slave of successive officials? Or shall I propose a fine, with imprisonment until it is paid? I have told you why I will not do that. I should have to remain in prison, for I have no money to pay a fine with. Shall I then propose exile? Perhaps you would agree to that. Life would indeed be very dear to me if I were unreasonable enough to expect that strangers would cheerfully tolerate my discussions and reasonings when you who are my fellow citizens cannot endure them, and have found them so irksome and odious to you that you are seeking now to be relieved of them. No, indeed, Athenians, that is not likely. A fine life I should lead for an old man if I were to withdraw from Athens and pass the rest of my days in wandering from city to city, and continually being expelled. For I know very well that the young men will listen to me wherever I go, as they do here; and if I drive them away, they will persuade their elders to expel me; and if I do not drive them away, their fathers and kinsmen will expel me for their sakes.

Perhaps some one will say, "Why cannot you withdraw from Athens, Socrates, and hold your peace?" It is the most difficult thing in the world to make you understand why I cannot do that. If I say that I cannot hold my peace because that would be to disobey the god, you will think that I am not in earnest and will not believe me. And if I tell you that no better thing can happen to a man than to discuss virtue every day and the other matters about which you have heard me arguing and examining myself and others, and that an unexamined life is not worth living, then you will believe me still less. But that is so, my friends, though it is not easy to persuade you. And, what is more, I am not accustomed to think that I deserve any punishment. If I had been rich, I would have proposed as large a fine as I could pay: that would have done me no harm. But I am not rich enough to pay a fine unless you are willing to fix it at a sum within my means. Perhaps I could pay you a mina, so I propose that. Plato here, Athenians, and Crito, and Critobulus, and Apollodorus bid me propose thirty minae, and they will be sureties for me. So I propose thirty minae. They will be sufficient sureties to you for the money.

(He is condemned to death.)

You have not gained very much time, Athenians, and, as the price of it, you will have an evil name for all who wish to revile the state, and they will say that you put Socrates, a wise man, to death. For they will certainly call me wise, whether I am wise or not, when they want to reproach you. If you would have waited for a little while, your wishes would have been fulfilled in the course of nature; for you see that I am an old man, far advanced in years, and near to death. I am saying this not to all of you, only to those who have voted for my death. And to them I have something else to say. Perhaps, my friends, you think that I have been convicted because I was wanting in the arguments by which I could have persuaded you to acquit me, if, that is, I had thought it right to do or to say anything to escape punishment. It is not so. I have been convicted because I was wanting, not in arguments, but in impudence and shamelessness— because I would not plead before you as you would have liked to hear me plead, or appeal to you with weeping and wailing, or say and do many other things which I maintain are unworthy of me, but which you have been accustomed to from other men. But when I was defending myself, I thought that I ought not to do anything unworthy of a free man because of the danger which I ran, and I have not

Property of Philosophy/
Religious Studies-UWEC

changed my mind now. I would very much rather defend myself as I did, and die, than as you would have had me do, and live. Both in a lawsuit and in war, there are some things which neither I nor any other man may do in order to escape from death. In battle, a man often sees that he may at least escape from death by throwing down his arms and falling on his knees before the pursuer to beg for his life. And there are many other ways of avoiding death in every danger if a man is willing to say and to do anything. But, my friends, I think that it is a much harder thing to escape from wickedness than from death, for wickedness is swifter than death. And now I, who am old and slow, have been overtaken by the slower pursuer: and my accusers, who are clever and swift, have been overtaken by the swifter pursuer—wickedness. And now I shall go away, sentenced by you to death; and they will go away, sentenced by truth to wickedness and injustice. And I abide by this award as well as they. Perhaps it was right for these things to be so; and I think that they are fairly measured.

And now I wish to prophesy to you, Athenians, who have condemned me. For I am going to die, and that is the time when men have most prophetic power. And I prophesy to you who have sentenced me to death that a far more severe punishment than you have inflicted on me will surely overtake you as soon as I am dead. You have done this thing, thinking that you will be relieved from having to give an account of your lives. But I say that the result will be very different. There will be more men who will call you to account, whom I have held back, though you did not recognize it. And they will be harsher toward you than I have been, for they will be younger, and you will be more indignant with them. For if you think that you will restrain men from reproaching you for not living as you should, by putting them to death, you are very much mistaken. That way of escape is neither possible nor honorable. It is much more honorable and much easier not to suppress others, but to make yourselves as good as you can. This is my parting prophecy to you who have condemned me.

With you who have acquitted me I should like to discuss this thing that has happened, while the authorities are busy, and before I go to the place where I have to die. So, remain with me until I go: there is no reason why we should not talk with each other while it is possible. I wish to explain to you, as my friends, the meaning of what has happened to me. A wonderful thing has happened to me, judges—for you I am right in calling judges. The prophetic sign has been constantly with me all through my life till now, opposing me in quite small matters if I were not going to act rightly. And now you yourselves see what has happened to me—a thing which might be thought, and which is sometimes actually reckoned, the supreme evil. But the divine sign did not oppose me when I was leaving my house in the morning, nor when I was coming up here to the court, nor at any point in my speech when I was going to say anything; though at other times it has often stopped me in the very act of speaking. But now, in this matter, it has never once opposed me, either in my words or my actions. I will tell you what I believe to be the reason. This thing that has come upon me must be a good; and those of us who think that death is an evil must needs be mistaken. I have a clear proof that that is so; for my accustomed sign would certainly have opposed me if I had not been going to meet with something good.

And if we reflect in another way, we shall see that we may well hope that death is a good. For the state of death is one of two things: either the dead man wholly ceases to be and loses all consciousness or, as we are told, it is a change and a migration of the soul to another place. And if death is the absence of all consciousness, and like the sleep of one whose slumbers are unbroken by any dreams, it will be a wonderful gain. For if a man had to select that night in which he slept so soundly that he did not even dream, and had to compare with it all the other nights and days of his life, and then had to say how many days and nights in his life he had spent better and more pleasantly than this night, I think that a private person, nay, even the great King himself, would find them easy to count, compared with the others. If that is the nature of death, I for one count it a gain. For then it appears that all time is nothing more than a single night. But if death is a journey to another place, and what we are told is true—that there are all who have died—what good could be greater than this, my judges? Would a journey not be worth taking, at the end of which, in the other world, we should be released from the self-styled judges here and should find the true judges who are said to sit in judgment below, such as Minos and Rhadamanthus and Aeacus and Triptolemus, and the other demigods who were just in their own lives? Or what would you not give to discuss with Orpheus and Musaeus and Hesiod and Homer? I am willing to die many times if this be true. And for my own part I should find it wonderful to meet there Palamedes, and Ajax, the son of Telamon, and the other men of old who have died through an unjust judgment, and in comparing my experiences with theirs. That I think would be no small pleasure. And, above all, I could spend my time in examining those who are there, as I examine men here, and in finding out which of them is wise, and which of them thinks himself wise when he is not wise. What would we not give, my judges, to be able to examine the leader of the great expedition against Troy, or Odysseus, or Sisyphus, or countless other men and women whom we could name? It would be an infinite happiness to discuss with them and to live with them and to examine them. Assuredly there they do not put men to death for doing that. For besides the other ways in which they are happier than we are, they are immortal, at least if what we are told is true.

And you, too, judges, must face death hopefully, and believe this as a truth that no evil can happen to a good man, either in life or after death. His fortunes are not neglected by the gods; and what has happened to me today has not happened by chance. I am persuaded that it was better for me to die now, and to be released from trouble; and that was the reason why the sign never turned me back. And so I am not at all angry with my accusers or with those who have condemned me to die. Yet it was not with this in mind that they accused me and condemned me, but meaning to do me an injury. So far I may blame them.

Yet I have one request to make of them. When my sons grow up, punish them, my friends, and harass them in the same way that I have harassed you, if they seem to you to care for riches or for any other thing more than virtue; and if they think that they are something when they are really nothing, reproach them, as I have reproached you, for not caring for what they should, and for thinking that they are great men when really they are worthless. And if you will do this, I myself and my sons will have received justice from you.

But now the time has come, and we must go away—I to die, and you to live. Whether life or death is better is known to God, and to God only.

The state of nature

Thomas Hobbes (1588-1679)

Thomas Hobbes, who was born in the year of the defeat of the Spanish Armada, was the son of a vicar. He was graduated from Magdalen College, Oxford, in 1608, and the same year was appointed tutor to the son of William Cavendish, first Earl of Devonshire. Most of Hobbes's long life was spent in the household of the Devonshire family as tutor and secretary. This employment afforded him an opportunity for trips abroad, during which he was able to meet many of the intellectuals of Europe. At home, the prominence of the Devonshire family allowed him to become familiar with many of the leading personalities of English life.

Hobbes wrote many works on nature, man, society, and government. He believed that all ultimate explanations of physical and psychological events must be in terms of material bodies and motion. In this sense he was a materialist. By far his best-known work is Leviathan *(1651), a book which considers many fundamental questions about man, society, and government and which brought its author great esteem as a political writer, especially outside his homeland. Our selection is from a work written some years before* Leviathan *but published in English in the same year. It contains Hobbes's famous view of the state of nature, in which man's life is "solitary, poor, nasty, brutish, and short."*

The faculties of human nature may be reduced unto four kinds; bodily strength, experience, reason, passion. Taking the beginning of this following doctrine from these, we will declare, in the first place, what manner of inclinations men who are endued with these faculties bear towards each other, and whether, and by what faculty they are born apt for society, and to preserve themselves against mutual violence; then proceeding, we will show what advice was necessary to be taken for this business, and what are the conditions of society, or of human peace; that is to say, (changing the words only), what are the fundamental *laws of nature.*

From Thomas Hobbes, *Philosophical Rudiments Concerning Government and Society,* London, 1651, chap. 1. Based on the Molesworth edition of 1841.

2. The greatest part of those men who have written aught concerning commonwealths, either suppose, or require us or beg of us to believe, that man is a creature born fit [1] for society. The Greeks call him ζῷον πολιτικόν; and on this foundation they so build up the doctrine of civil society, as if for the preservation of peace, and the government of mankind, there were nothing else necessary than that men should agree to make certain covenants

[1] *Born fit.* Since we now see actually a constituted society among men, and none living out of it, since we discern all desirous of congress and mutual correspondence, it may seem a wonderful kind of stupidity, to lay in the very threshold of this doctrine such a stumbling block before the reader, as to deny *man to be born fit for society.* Therefore I must more plainly say, that it is true indeed, that to man by nature, or as man, that is, as soon as he is

and conditions together, which themselves should then call laws. Which axiom, though received by most, is yet certainly false; and an error proceeding from our too slight contemplation of human nature. For they who shall more narrowly look into the causes for which men come together, and delight in each other's company, shall easily find that this happens not because naturally it could happen no otherwise, but by accident. For if by nature one man should love another, that is, as man, there could no reason be returned why every man should not equally love every man, as being equally man; or why he should rather frequent those, whose society affords him honour or profit. We do not therefore by nature seek society for its own sake, but that we may receive some honour or profit from it; these we desire primarily, that secondarily. How, by what advice, men do meet, will be best known by observing those things which they do when they are met. For if they meet for traffic, it is plain every man regards not his fellow, but his business; if to discharge some office, a certain market-friendship is begotten, which hath more of jealousy in it than true love, and whence factions sometimes may arise, but good will never; if for pleasure and recreation of mind, every man is wont to please himself most with those things which stir up laughter, whence he may, according to the nature of that which is ridiculous, by comparison of another man's defects and infirmities, pass the more current in his own opinion. And although this be sometimes innocent and without offence, yet it is mani-

fest they are not so much delighted with the society, as their own vain glory. But for the most part, in these kinds of meeting we wound the absent; their whole life, sayings, actions are examined, judged, condemned. Nay, it is very rare but some present receive a fling as soon as they part; so as his reason was not ill, who was wont always at parting to go out last. And these are indeed the true delights of society, unto which we are carried by nature, that is, by those passions which are incident to all creatures, until either by sad experience or good precepts it so fall out, which in many it never happens, that the appetite of present matters be dulled with the memory of things past: without which the discourse of most quick and nimble men on this subject, is but cold and hungry.

But if it so happen, that being met they pass their time in relating some stories, and one of them begins to tell one which concerns himself; instantly every one of the rest most greedily desires to speak of himself too; if one relates some wonder, the rest will tell you miracles, if they have them; if not, they will feign them. Lastly, that I may say somewhat of them who pretend to be wiser than others: if they meet to talk of philosophy, look, how many men, so many would be esteemed masters, or else they not only love not their fellows, but even persecute them with hatred. So clear is it by experience to all men who a little more narrowly consider human affairs, that all free congress ariseth either from mutual poverty, or from vain glory, whence the parties met en-

---

born, solitude is an enemy; for infants have need of others to help them to live, and those of riper years to help them to live well. Wherefore I deny not that men (even nature compelling) desire to come together. But civil societies are not mere meetings, but bonds, to the making whereof faith and compacts are necessary; the virtue whereof to children and fools, and the profit whereof to those who have not yet tasted the miseries which accompany its defect, is altogether unknown; whence it happens, that those, because they know not what society is, cannot enter into it; these, because ignorant of the benefit it brings, care not for it. Manifest therefore it is, that all men, because they are

born in infancy, are born unapt for society. Many also, perhaps most men, either through defect of mind or want of education, remain unfit during the whole course of their lives; yet have they, infants as well as those of riper years, a human nature. Wherefore man is made fit for society not by nature, but by education. Furthermore, although man were born in such a condition as to desire it, it follows not, that he therefore were born fit to enter into it. For it is one thing to desire, another to be in capacity fit for what we desire; for even they, who through their pride, will not stoop to equal conditions, without which there can be no society, do yet desire it.

deavour to carry with them either some benefit, or to leave behind them that same εὐδοχιμεῖν, some esteem an honour with those, with whom they have been conversant. The same is also collected by reason out of the definitions themselves of *will, good, honour, profitable*. For when we voluntarily contract society, in all manner of society we look after the object of the will, that is, that which everyone of those who gather together, propounds to himself for good. Now, whatsoever seems good, is pleasant, and relates either to the senses, or the mind. But all the mind's pleasure is either glory, (or to have a good opinion of one's self), or refers to glory in the end; the rest are sensual, or conducing to sensuality, which may be all comprehended under the word *conveniences*. All society therefore is either for gain, or for glory; that is, not so much for love of our fellows, as for the love of ourselves. But no society can be great or lasting, which begins from vain glory. Because that glory is like honour; if all men have it no man hath it, for they consist in comparison and precellence. Neither doth the society of others advance any whit the cause of my glorying in myself; for every man must account himself, such as he can make himself without the help of others. But though the benefits of this life may be much furthered by mutual help; since yet those may be better attained to by dominion than by the society of others, I hope no body will doubt, but that men would much more greedily be carried by nature, if all fear were removed, to obtain dominion, than to gain society. We must therefore resolve, that the original of all great and lasting societies consisted not in the mutual good will men had towards each other, but in the mutual fear[2] they had of each other.

[2] *The mutual fear*. It is objected: it is so improbable that men should grow into civil societies out of fear, that if they had been afraid, they would not have endured each other's looks. They presume, I believe, that to fear is nothing else than to be affrighted. I comprehend in this word *fear*, a certain foresight of future evil; neither do I conceive flight the sole property of fear, but to distrust, suspect, take heed, provide so that they may not fear, is also incident to the fearful. They who go to sleep, shut their

3. The cause of mutual fear consists **partly** in the natural equality of men, partly in their mutual will of hurting: whence it comes to pass, that we can neither expect from others, nor promise to ourselves the least security. For if we look on men full-grown, and consider how brittle the frame of our human body is, which perishing, all its strength, vigour, and wisdom itself perisheth with it; and how easy a matter it is, even for the weakest man to kill the strongest: there is no reason why any man trusting to his own strength, should conceive himself made by nature above others. They are equals, who can do equal things one against the other; but they who can do the greatest things, namely, kill, can do equal things. All men therefore among themselves are by nature equal; the inequality we now discern, hath its spring from the civil law.

4. All men in the state of nature have a desire and will to hurt, but not proceeding from the same cause, neither equally to be condemned. For one man, according to that natural equality which is among us, permits as much to others as he assumes to himself; which is an argument of a temperate man, and one that rightly values his power. Another, supposing himself above others, will have a license to do what he lists, and challenges respect and honour, as due to him before others; which is an argument of a fiery spirit. This man's will to hurt ariseth from vain glory, and the false esteem he hath of his own strength; the other's from the necessity of defending

doors; they who travel, carry their swords with them, because they fear thieves. Kingdoms guard their coasts and frontiers with forts and castles; cities are compact with walls; and all for fear of neighbouring kingdoms and towns. Even the strongest armies, and most accomplished for fight, yet sometimes parley for peace, as fearing each other's power, and lest they might be overcome. It is through fear that men secure themselves by flight indeed, and in corners, if they think they cannot escape otherwise; but for the most part, by arms and defensive weapons; whence it happens, that daring to come forth they know each other's spirits. But then if they fight, civil society ariseth from the victory; if they agree, from their agreement.

himself, his liberty, and his goods, against this man's violence.

5. Furthermore, since the combat of wits is the fiercest, the greatest discords which are, must necessarily arise from this contention. For in this case it is not only odious to contend against, but also not to consent. For not to approve of what a man saith, is no less than tacitly to accuse him of an error in that thing which he speaketh: as in very many things to dissent, is as much as if you accounted him a fool whom you dissent from. Which may appear hence, that there are no wars so sharply waged as between sects of the same religion, and factions of the same commonweal, where the contestation is either concerning doctrines or politic prudence. And since all the pleasure and jollity of the mind consists in this, even to get some, with whom comparing, it may find somewhat wherein to triumph and vaunt itself; it is impossible but men must declare sometimes some mutual scorn and contempt, either by laughter, or by words, or by gesture, or some sign or other; than which there is no greater vexation of mind, and than from which there cannot possibly arise a greater desire to do hurt.

6. But the most frequent reason why men desire to hurt each other, ariseth hence, that many men at the same time have an appetite to the same thing; which yet very often they can neither enjoy in common, nor yet divide it; whence it follows that the strongest must have it, and who is strongest must be decided by the sword.

7. Among so many dangers therefore, as the natural lusts of men do daily threaten each other withal, to have a care of one's self is so far from being a matter scornfully to be looked upon, that one has neither the power nor wish to have done otherwise. For every man is desirous of what is good for him, and shuns what is evil, but chiefly the chiefest of natural evils, which is death; and this he doth by a certain impulsion of nature, no less than that whereby a stone moves downward. It is therefore neither absurd nor reprehensible, neither against the dictates of true reason, for a man to use all his endeavours to preserve and de-

fend his body and the members thereof from death and sorrows. But that which is not contrary to right reason, that all men account to be done justly, and with right. Neither by the word *right* is anything else signified, than that liberty which every man hath to make use of his natural faculties according to right reason. Therefore the first foundation of natural right is this, that *every man as much as in him lies endeavour to protect his life and members.*

8. But because it is in vain for a man to have a right to the end, if the right to the necessary means be denied him, it follows, that since every man hath a right to preserve himself, he must also be allowed a right *to use all the means, and do all the actions, without which he cannot preserve himself.*

9. Now whether the means which he is about to use, and the action he is performing, be necessary to the preservation of his life and members or not, he himself, by the right of nature, must be judge. For if it be contrary to right reason that I should judge of mine own peril, say, that another man is judge. Why now, because he judgeth of what concerns me, by the same reason, because we are equal by nature, will I judge also of things which do belong to him. Therefore it agrees with right reason, that is, it is the right of nature that I judge of his opinion, that is, whether it conduce to my preservation or not.

10. Nature hath given to *every one a right to all;* that is, it was lawful for every man, in the bare state of nature,[3] or before such time as men had engaged themselves by any covenants or bonds, to do what he would, and

[3] *In the bare state of nature.* This is thus to be understood: what any man does in the bare state of nature, is injurious to no man; not that in such a state he cannot offend God, or break the laws of nature; for injustice against men presupposeth human laws, such as in the state of nature there are none. Now the truth of this proposition thus conceived, is sufficiently demonstrated to the mindful reader in the articles immediately foregoing; but because in certain cases the difficulty of the conclusion makes us forget the premises, I will contract this argument, and make it most evident to a single view. Every man hath right to protect himself, as

against whom he thought fit, and to possess, use, and enjoy all what he would, or could get. Now because whatsoever a man would, it therefore seems good to him because he wills it, and either it really doth, or at least seems to him to contribute towards his preservation, (but we have already allowed him to be judge, in the foregoing article, whether it doth or not, insomuch as we are to hold all for necessary whatsoever he shall esteem so), and by the 7th article it appears that by the right of nature those things may be done, and must be had, which necessarily conduce to the protection of life and members, it follows, that in the state of nature, to have all, and do all, is lawful for all. And this is that which is meant by that common saying, *nature hath given all to all*. From whence we understand likewise, that in the state of nature profit is the measure of right.

11. But it was the least benefit for men thus to have a common right to all things. For the effects of this right are the same, almost, as if there had been no right at all. For although any man might say of every thing, *this is mine*, yet could he not enjoy it, by reason of his neighbour, who having equal right and equal power, would pretend the same thing to be his.

12. If now to this natural proclivity of men, to hurt each other, which they derive from their passions, but chiefly from a vain esteem of themselves, you add, the right of all to all, wherewith one by right invades, the other by right resists, and whence arise perpetual jealousies and suspicions on all hands, and how hard a thing it is to provide against an enemy invading us with an intention to oppress and ruin, though he come with a small number, and no great provision; it cannot be denied but that the natural state of men, before they entered into society, was a mere war, and that not simply, but a war of all men against all men. For what is WAR, but that same time in which the will of contesting by force is fully declared, either by words or deeds? The time remaining is termed PEACE.

13. But it is easily judged how disagreeable a thing to the preservation either of mankind, or of each single man, a perpetual war is. But it is perpetual in its own nature; because in regard of the equality of those that strive, it cannot be ended by victory. For in this state the conqueror is subject to so much danger, as it were to be accounted a miracle, if any, even the most strong, should close up his life with many years and old age. They of America are examples hereof, even in this present age: other nations have been in former ages; which now indeed are become civil and flourishing, but were then few, fierce, short-lived, poor, nasty, and deprived of all that pleasure and beauty of life, which peace and society are wont to bring with them. Whosoever therefore holds, that it had been best to have continued in that state in which all things were lawful for all men, he contradicts himself. For every man by natural necessity desires that which is good for him: nor is there any that esteems a war of all against all, which necessarily adheres to such a state, to be good for him. And so it happens, that through fear of each other we think it fit to rid ourselves of this condition, and to get some fellows; that if

---

appears by the seventh article. The same man therefore hath a right to use all the means which necessarily conduce to this end, by the eighth article. But those are the necessary means which he shall judge to be such, by the ninth article. He therefore hath a right to make use of, and to do all whatsoever he shall judge requisite for his preservation; wherefore by the judgment of him that doth it, the thing done is either right or wrong, and therefore right. True it is therefore in the bare state of nature, &c. But if any man pretend somewhat to tend necessarily to his preservation, which yet he himself doth not

confidently believe so, he may offend against the laws of nature, as in the third chapter of this book is more at large declared. It hath been objected by some: if a son kill his father, doth he him no injury? I have answered, that a son cannot be understood to be at any time in the state of nature, as being under the power and command of them to whom he owes his protection as soon as ever he is born, namely, either his father's or his mother's, or him that nourished him; as is demonstrated in the ninth chapter.

there needs must be war, it may not yet be against all men, nor without some helps.

14. Fellows are gotten either by constraint, or by consent; by constraint, when after fight the conqueror makes the conquered serve him, either through fear of death, or by laying fetters on him: by consent, when men enter into society to help each other, both parties consenting without any constraint. But the conqueror may by right compel the conquered, or the strongest the weaker, (as a man in health may one that is sick, or he that is of riper years a child), unless he will choose to die, to give caution of his future obedience. For since the right of protecting ourselves according to our own wills, proceeded from our danger, and our danger from our equality, it is more consonant to reason, and more certain for our conservation, using the present advantage to secure ourselves by taking caution, than when they shall be full grown and strong, and got out of our power, to endeavour to recover that power again by doubtful fight. And on the other side, nothing can be thought more absurd, than by discharging whom you already have weak in your power, to make him at once both an enemy and a strong one. From whence we may understand likewise as a corollary in the natural state of men, that *a sure and irresistible power confers the right of dominion and ruling over those who cannot resist*; insomuch, as the right of all things that can be done, adheres essentially and immediately unto this omnipotence hence arising.

15. Yet cannot men expect any lasting preservation, continuing thus in the state of nature, that is, of war, by reason of that equality of power, and other human faculties they are endued withal. Wherefore to seek peace, where there is any hopes of obtaining it, and where there is none, to enquire out for auxiliaries of war, is the dictate of right reason, that is, the law of nature. . . .

Private property

John Locke (1632-1704)

Locke was educated at Oxford. He was a friend of the chemist Robert Boyle and expressed his interest in the new science of his time through the study and practice of medicine. He helped to put the medicine of England on an empirical footing, that is, on a basis of observation and demonstration. In An Essay Concerning Human Understanding *(1690) he developed an empiricist theory of knowledge. Deeply interested in the political conflicts of his day, he championed in his writings the cause of civil liberty and religious toleration. His political views had a strong influence on Thomas Jefferson and other Founding Fathers of our own republic. His principal political writings are* Two Treatises of Civil Government *(1690) and* Letters on Toleration *(1689, 1690).*

Our selection is from Locke's Second Treatise on Civil Government, *one of the most influential of all works of political thought. In his discussion of property Locke holds that man has a natural right to private property, a right which he secures through labor. Locke bases this view on what is for him the self-evident principle than an individual has a right to dispose as he sees fit of his person and labor and consequently of anything to which his labor is attached. The reader should examine this supposedly self-evident principle with great care.*

Whether we consider natural reason, which tells us that men, being once born, have a right to their preservation, and consequently to meat and drink and such other things as Nature affords for their subsistence, or Revelation, which gives us an account of those grants God made of the world to Adam, and to Noah and his sons, it is very clear that God, as King David says (Psalm cxv. 16), "has given the earth to the children of men," given it to mankind in common. But, this being supposed, it seems to some a very great difficulty how any one should ever come to have a property in anything, I will not content myself to answer,

that, if it be difficult to make out property upon a supposition that God gave the world to Adam and his posterity in common, it is impossible that any man but one universal monarch should have any property upon a supposition that God gave the world to Adam and his heirs in succession, exclusive of all the rest of his posterity; but I shall endeavour to show how men might come to have a property in several parts of that which God gave to mankind in common, and that without any express compact of all the commoners.

God, who hath given the world to men in common, hath also given them reason to make use of it to the best advantage of life and convenience. The earth and all that is therein is given to men for the support and comfort of their being. And though all the fruits it nat-

From John Locke, *The Second Treatise on Civil Government,* chap. 5, in *Two Treatises of Civil Government.* First published in 1690. Many editions.

urally produces, and beasts it feeds, belong to mankind in common, as they are produced by the spontaneous hand of Nature, and nobody has originally a private dominion exclusive of the rest of mankind in any of them, as they are thus in their natural state, yet being given for the use of men, there must of necessity be a means to appropriate them some way or other before they can be of any use, or at all beneficial, to any particular men. The fruit or venison which nourishes the wild Indian, who knows no enclosure, and is still a tenant in common, must be his, and so his, *i.e.*, a part of him, that another can no longer have any right to it, before it can do him any good for the support of his life.

Though the earth and all inferior creatures be common to all men, yet every man has a property in his own person. This nobody has any right to but himself. The labour of his body and the work of his hands, we may say, are properly his. Whatsoever, then, he removes out of the state that Nature hath provided and left it in, he hath mixed his labour with, and joined to it something that is his own, and thereby makes it his property. It being by him removed from the common state Nature placed it in, it hath by this labour something annexed to it that excludes the common right of other men. For this labour being the unquestionable property of the labourer, no man but he can have a right to what that is once joined to, at least where there is enough, and as good left in common for others.

He that is nourished by the acorns he picked up under an oak, or the apples he gathered from the trees in the wood, has certainly appropriated them to himself. Nobody can deny but the nourishment is his. I ask, then, when did they begin to be his? when he digested? or when he ate? or when he boiled? or when he brought them home? or when he picked them up? And it is plain, if the first gathering made them not his, nothing else could. That labour put a distinction between them and common. That added something to them more than Nature, the common mother of all, had done, and so they became his private right. And will any one say he had no right to those

acorns or apples he thus appropriated, because he had not the consent of all mankind to make them his? Was it a robbery thus to assume to himself what belonged to all in common? If such a consent as that was necessary, man had starved, notwithstanding the plenty God had given him. We see in commons, which remain so by compact, that it is the taking any part of what is common, and removing it out of the state Nature leaves it in, which begins the property, without which the common is of no use. And the taking of this or that part does not depend on the express consent of all the commoners. Thus, the grass my horse has bit, the turfs my servant has cut, and the ore I have dug in any place, where I have a right to them in common with others, become my property without the assignation or consent of anybody. The labour that was mine, removing them out of that common state they were in, hath fixed my property in them.

By making an explicit consent of every commoner necessary to any one's appropriating to himself any part of what is given in common, children or servants could not cut the meat which their father or master had provided for them in common without assigning to every one his peculiar part. Though the water running in the fountain be every one's, yet who can doubt but that in the pitcher is his only who drew it out? His labour hath taken it out of the hands of Nature where it was common, and belonged equally to all her children, and hath thereby appropriated it to himself.

Thus this law of reason makes the deer that Indian's who hath killed it; it is allowed to be his goods who hath bestowed his labour upon it, though, before, it was the common right of every one. And amongst those who are counted the civilised part of mankind, who have made and multiplied positive laws to determine property, this original law of Nature for the beginning of property, in what was before common, still takes place, and by virtue thereof, what fish any one catches in the ocean, that great and still remaining common of mankind; or what ambergris any one takes up here is by the labour that removes it out of that common state Nature left it in, made his property who takes that pains about it. And even amongst us, the hare that any one is hunting is thought his who pursues her during the chase. For being a beast that is still looked upon as common, and no man's private possession, whoever has employed so much labour about any of that kind as to find and pursue her has thereby removed her from the state of Nature wherein she was common, and hath begun a property.

It will, perhaps, be objected to this, that if gathering the acorns or other fruits of the earth, etc., makes a right to them, then any one may engross as much as he will. To which I answer, Not so. The same law of Nature that does by this means give us property, does also bound that property too. "God has given us all things richly," (1 Tim. VI. 17) is the voice of reason confirmed by inspiration. But how far has He given it us—"to enjoy"? As much as any one can make use of to any advantage of life before it spoils, so much he may by his labour fix a property in. Whatever is beyond this is more than his share, and belongs to others. Nothing was made by God for man to spoil or destroy. And thus considering the plenty of natural provisions there was a long time in the world, and the few spenders, and to how small a part of that provision the industry of one man could extend itself and engross it to the prejudice of others, especially keeping within the bounds set by reason of what might serve for his use, there could be then little room for quarrels or contentions about property so established.

But the chief matter of property being now not the fruits of the earth and the beasts that subsist on it, but the earth itself, as that which takes in and carries with it all the rest, I think it is plain that property in that too is acquired as the former. As much land as a man tills, plants, improves, cultivates, and can use the product of, so much is his property. He by his labour does, as it were, enclose it from the common. Nor will it invalidate his right to say everybody else has an equal title to it, and therefore he cannot appropriate, he cannot enclose, without the consent of all his fellow-commoners, all mankind. God, when He gave the world in common to all mankind, commanded man also to labour, and the penury of his condition required it of him. God and his reason commanded him to subdue the earth, *i.e.*, improve it for the benefit of life, and therein lay out something upon it that was his own, his labour. He that, in obedience to this command of God, subdued, tilled, and sowed any part of it, thereby annexed to it something that was his property, which another had no title to, nor could without injury take from him.

Nor was this appropriation of any parcel of land, by improving it, any prejudice to any other man, since there was still enough and as good left, and more than the yet unprovided could use. So that, in effect, there was never the less left for others because of his enclosure for himself. For he that leaves as much as another can make use of, does as good as take nothing at all. Nobody could think himself injured by the drinking of another man, though he took a good draught, who had a whole river of the same water left him to quench his thirst. And the case of land and water, where there is enough of both, is perfectly the same.

God gave the world to men in common, but since He gave it them for their benefit and the greatest conveniences of life they were capable to draw from it, it cannot be supposed He meant it should always remain common and uncultivated. He gave it to the use of the industrious and rational (and labour was to be his title to it); not to the fancy or covetousness of the quarrelsome and contentious. He that had as good left for his improvement as was already taken up, needed not complain, ought not to meddle with what was already improved by another's labour; if he did, it is plain he desired the benefit of another's pains, which he had no right to, and not the ground which God had given him, in common with others, to labour on, and whereof there was as good left as that already possessed, and more than he knew what to do with, or his industry could reach to. . . .

The measure of property Nature has well set, by the extent of men's labour and the conveniency of life. No man's labour could subdue or appropriate all, nor could his enjoyment consume more than a small part; so that it was impossible for any man, this way, to entrench upon the right of another, or acquire to himself a property to the prejudice of his neighbour, who would still have room for as good and as large a possession (after the other had taken out his) as before it was appropriated. This measure did confine every man's possession to a very moderate proportion, and such as he might appropriate to himself without injury to anybody, in the first ages of the world, when men were more in danger to be lost, by wandering from their company, in the then vast wilderness of the earth than to be straitened for want of room to plant in.

The same measure may be allowed still, without prejudice to anybody, as full as the world seems. For, supposing a man or family, in the state they were at first, peopling of the world by the children of Adam or Noah, let him plant in some inland vacant places of America. We shall find that the possessions he could make himself, upon the measures we have given, would not be very large, nor, even to this day, prejudice the rest of mankind, or give them reason to complain or think themselves injured by this man's encroachment, though the race of men have now spread themselves to all the corners of the world, and do infinitely exceed the small number that was at the beginning. . . . I dare boldly affirm, that the same rule of propriety, viz., that every man should have as much as he could make use of, would hold still in the world, without straitening anybody, since there is land enough in the world to suffice double the inhabitants, had not the invention of money, and the tacit agreement of men to put a value on it, introduced (by consent) larger possessions and a right to them; which, how it has done, I shall by and by show more at large.

This is certain, that in the beginning, before the desire of having more than men needed had altered the intrinsic value of things, which depends only on their usefulness to the life of man, or had agreed that a little piece of yellow metal, which would keep without wasting or decay, should be worth a great piece of flesh or a whole heap of corn, though men had a right to appropriate by their labour, each one

to himself, as much of the things of Nature as he could use, yet this could not be much, nor to the prejudice of others, where the same plenty was still left, to those who would use the same industry.

Before the appropriation of land, he who gathered as much of the wild fruit, killed, caught, or tamed as many of the beasts as he could—he that so employed his pains about any of the spontaneous products of Nature as any way to alter them from the state Nature put them in, by placing any of his labour on them, did thereby acquire a propriety in them; but if they perished in his possession without their due use—if the fruits rotted or the venison putrefied before he could spend it, he offended against the common law of Nature, and was liable to be punished: he invaded his neighbour's share, for he had no right farther than his use called for any of them, and they might serve to afford him conveniencies of life.

The same measures governed the possession of land, too. Whatsoever he tilled and reaped, laid up and made use of before it spoiled, that was his peculiar right; whatsoever he enclosed, and could feed and made use of, the cattle and product was also his. But if either the grass of his enclosure rotted on the ground, or the fruit of his planting perished without gathering and laying up, this part of the earth, notwithstanding his enclosure, was still to be looked on as waste, and might be the possession of any other. Thus, at the beginning, Cain might take as much ground as he could till and make it his own land, and yet leave enough to Abel's sheep to feed on: a few acres would serve for both their possessions. But as families increased, and industry enlarged their stocks, their possessions enlarged with the need of them; but yet it was commonly without any fixed property in the ground they made use of, till they incorporated, settled themselves together, and built cities, and then, by consent, they came in time to set out the bounds of their distinct territories and agree on limits between them and their neighbours, and, by laws within themselves, settled the properties of those of the same society. For we see that in that part of the world which was first inhabited, and therefore like to be best peopled, even as low down as Abraham's time, they wandered with their flocks and their herds, which was their substance, freely up and down—and this Abraham did in a country where he was a stranger; whence it is plain that, at least, a great part of the land lay in common, that the inhabitants valued it not, nor claimed property in any more than they made use of; but when there was not room enough in the same place for their herds to feed together, they, by consent, as Abraham and Lot did (Gen. xiii. 5), separated and enlarged their pasture where it best liked them. And for the same reason, Esau went from his father and his brother, and planted in Mount Seir (Gen. xxxvi. 6).

And thus, without supposing any private dominion and property in Adam over all the world, exclusive of all other men, which can no way be proved, nor any one's property be made out from it, but supposing the world, given as it was to the children of men in common, we see how labour could make men distinct titles to several parcels of it for their private uses, wherein there could be no doubt of right, no room for quarrel.

Nor is it so strange as, perhaps, before consideration, it may appear, that the property of labour should be able to overbalance the community of land, for it is labour indeed that puts the difference of value on everything; and let any one consider what the difference is between an acre of land planted with tobacco or sugar, sown with wheat or barley, and an acre of the same land lying in common without any husbandry upon it, and he will find that the improvement of labour makes the far greater part of the value. I think it will be but a very modest computation to say, that of the products of the earth useful to the life of man, nine-tenths are the effects of labour. Nay, if we will rightly estimate things as they come to our use, and cast up the several expenses about them—what in them is purely owing to Nature and what to labour—we shall find that in most of them ninety-nine hundredths are wholly to be put on the account of labour.

There cannot be a clearer demonstration of

anything than several nations of the Americans are of this, who are rich in land and poor in all the comforts of life; whom Nature, having furnished as liberally as any other people with the materials of plenty, *i.e.*, a fruitful soil, apt to produce in abundance what might serve for food, raiment, and delight; yet, for want of improving it by labour, have not one hundredth part of the conveniencies we enjoy, and a king of a large and fruitful territory there feeds, lodges, and is clad worse than a day labourer in England.

To make this a little clearer, let us but trace some of the ordinary provisions of life, through their several progresses, before they come to our use, and see how much they receive of their value from human industry. Bread, wine, and cloth are things of daily use and great plenty; yet, notwithstanding acorns, water, and leaves, or skins must be our bread, drink and clothing, did not labour furnish us with these more useful commodities. For whatever bread is more worth than acorns, wine than water, and cloth or silk than leaves, skins or moss, that is wholly owing to labour and industry. The one of these being the food and raiment which unassisted Nature furnishes us with; the other, provisions which our industry and pains prepare for us, which how much they exceed the other in value, when any one hath computed, he will then see how much labour makes the far greatest part of the value of things we enjoy in this world; and the ground which produces the materials is scarce to be reckoned in as any, or at most, but a very small part of it; so little, that even amongst us, land that is left wholly to nature, that hath no improvement of pasturage, tillage, or planting, is called, as indeed it is, waste; and we shall find the benefit of it amount to little more than nothing.

An acre of land that bears here twenty bushels of wheat, and another in America, which, with the same husbandry, would do the like, are, without doubt, of the same natural, intrinsic value. But yet the benefit mankind receives from one in a year is worth five pounds, and the other possibly not worth a penny; if all the profit an Indian received from it were to be valued and sold here, at least I may truly say, not one thousandth. It is labour, then, which puts the greatest part of value upon land, without which it would scarcely be worth anything; it is to that we owe the greatest part of all its useful products; for all that the straw, bran, bread, of that acre of wheat, is more worth than the product of an acre of as good land which lies waste is all the effect of labour. For it is not barely the ploughman's pains, the reaper's and thresher's toil, and the baker's sweat, is to be counted into the bread we eat; the labour of those who broke the oxen, who dug and wrought the iron and stones, who felled and framed the timber employed about the plough, mill, oven, or any other utensils, which are a vast number, requisite to this corn, from its sowing to its being made bread, must all be charged on the account of labour, and received as an effect of that; Nature and the earth furnished only the almost worthless materials as in themselves. It would be a strange catalogue of things that industry provided and made use of, about every loaf of bread before it came to our use, if we could trace them; iron, wood, leather, bark, timber, stone, bricks, coals, lime, cloth, dyeing-drugs, pitch, tar, masts, ropes, and all the materials made use of in the ship that brought any of the commodities made use of by any of the workmen, to any part of the work, all which it would be almost impossible, at least too long, to reckon up.

From all which is evident, that though the things of Nature are given in common, man (by being master of himself, and proprietor of his own person, and the actions or labour of it) had still in himself the great foundation of property; and that which made up the great part of what he applied to the support or comfort of his being, when invention and arts had improved the conveniencies of life, was perfectly his own, and did not belong in common to others.

Thus labour, in the beginning, gave a right of property, wherever any one was pleased to employ it, upon what was common, which remained a long while, the far greater part, and is yet more than mankind makes use of. Men at first, for the most part, contented themselves with what unassisted Nature offered to their necessities; and though afterwards, in some parts of the world, where the increase of people

and stock, with the use of money, had made land scarce, and so of some value, the several communities settled the bounds of their distinct territories, and, by laws, within themselves, regulated the properties of the private men of their society, and so, by compact and agreement, settled the property which labour and industry began. And the leagues that have been made between several states and kingdoms, either expressly or tacitly disowning all claim and right to the land in the other's possession, have, by common consent, given up their pretences to their natural common right, which originally they had to those countries; and so have, by positive agreement, settled a property amongst themselves, in distinct parts of the world; yet there are still great tracts of ground to be found, which, the inhabitants thereof not having joined with the rest of mankind in the consent of the use of their common money, lie waste, and are more than the people who dwell on it, do, or can make use of, and so still lie in common; though this can scarce happen amongst that part of mankind that have consented to the use of money.

The greatest part of things really useful to the life of man, and such as the necessity of subsisting made the first commoners of the world look after—as it doth the Americans now—are generally things of short duration, such as—if they are not consumed by use—will decay and perish of themselves. Gold, silver, and diamonds are things that fancy or agreement hath put the value on, more than real use and the necessary support of life. Now of those good things which Nature hath provided in common, every one had a right (as hath been said) to as much as he could use, and property in all he could effect with his labour; all that his industry could extend to, to alter from the state Nature had put it in, was his. He that gathered a hundred bushels of acorns or apples had thereby a property in them; they were his goods as soon as gathered. He was only to look that he used them before they spoiled, else he took more than his share, and robbed others. And, indeed, it was a foolish thing, as well as dishonest, to hoard up more than he could make use of. If he gave away a part to anybody else, so that it perished not uselessly in his possession, these he also made use of. And if he also bartered away plums that would have rotted in a week, for nuts that would last good for his eating a whole year, he did no injury; he wasted not the common stock, destroyed no part of the portion of goods that belonged to others, so long as nothing perished uselessly in his hands. Again, if he would give his nuts for a piece of metal, pleased with its colour, or exchange his sheep for shells, or wool for a sparkling pebble or a diamond, and keep those by him all his life, he invaded not the right of others; he might heap up as much of these durable things as he pleased, the exeeding of the bounds of his just property not lying in the largeness of his possession, but the perishing of anything uselessly in it.

And thus came in the use of money; some lasting thing that men keep without spoiling, and that, by mutual consent, men would take in exchange for the truly useful but perishable supports of life.

And as different degrees of industry were apt to give men possessions in different proportions, so this invention of money gave them the opportunity to continue and enlarge them. For supposing an island, separate from all possible commerce with the rest of the world, wherein there were but a hundred families, but there were sheep, horses, and cows, with other useful animals, wholesome fruits, and land enough for corn for a hundred thousand times as many, but nothing in the island, either because of its commonness or perishableness, fit to supply the place of money. What reason could any one have there to enlarge his possessions beyond the use of his family, and a plentiful supply to its consumption, either in what their own industry produced, or they could barter for like perishable, useful commodities with others? Where there is not something both lasting and scarce, and so valuable to be hoarded up, there men will not be apt to enlarge their possessions of land, were it never so rich, never so free for them to take. For I ask, what would a man value ten thousand or an hundred thousand acres of excellent land, ready cultivated and well stocked, too, with cattle, in the middle of the inland parts

of America, where he had no hopes of commerce with other parts of the world, to draw money to him by the sale of the product? It would not be worth the enclosing, and we should see him give up again to the wild common of Nature whatever was more than would supply the conveniencies of life, to be had there for him and his family.

Thus, in the beginning, all the world was America, and more so than that is now; for no such thing as money was anywhere known. Find out something that hath the use and value of money amongst his neighbours, you shall see the same man will begin presently to enlarge his possessions.

But since gold and silver, being little useful to the life of man, in proportion to food, raiment, and carriage, has its value only from the consent of men—whereof labour yet makes in great part the measure—it is plain that the consent of men have agreed to a disproportionate and unequal possession of the earth—I mean out of the bounds of society and compact; for in governments the laws regulate it; they having, by consent, found out and agreed in a way how a man may, rightfully and without injury, possess more than he himself can make use of by receiving gold and silver, which may continue long in a man's possession without decaying for the overplus, and agreeing those metals should have a value.

And thus, I think, it is very easy to conceive, without any difficulty, how labour could at first begin a title of property in the common things of Nature, and how the spending it upon our uses bounded it; so that there could then be no reason of quarrelling about title, nor any doubt about the largeness of possession it gave. Right and conveniency went together. For as a man had a right to all he could employ his labour upon, so he had no temptation to labour for more than he could make use of. This left no room for controversy about the title, nor for encroachment on the right of others. What portion a man carved to himself was easily seen; and it was useless, as well as dishonest, to carve himself too much, or take more than he needed.

On liberty

John Stuart Mill (1806-1873)*

Mill's famous essay, On Liberty, *a portion of which is given below, contains both a statement of the limits of society's legitimate power over the individual and an argument for the social utility of liberty. It was Mill's firm belief that "the greatest happiness of the greatest number" could be achieved only in a society which was unwavering in its respect for personal liberty. The essay in which he vigorously defends this thesis is one of the strongest statements of a chief value of democratic society.*

... The object of this Essay is to assert one very simple principle, as entitled to govern absolutely the dealings of society with the individual in the way of compulsion and control, whether the means used be physical force in the form of legal penalties, or the moral coercion of public opinion. That principle is, that the sole end for which mankind are warranted, individually or collectively, in interfering with the liberty of action of any of their number, is self-protection. That the only purpose for which power can be rightfully exercised over any member of a civilized community, against his will, is to prevent harm to others. His own good, either physical or moral, is not a sufficient warrant. He cannot rightfully be compelled to do or forbear because it will be better for him to do so, because it will make him happier, because, in the opinions of others, to do so would be wise, or even right. These are good reasons for remonstrating with him, or reasoning with him, or persuading him, or entreating him, but not for compelling him, or visiting him with any evil in case he do otherwise. To justify that, the conduct from which it is desired to deter him, must be calculated to produce evil to some one else.

The only part of the conduct of any one, for which he is amenable to society, is that which concerns others. In the part which merely concerns himself, his independence is, of right, absolute. Over himself, over his own body and mind, the individual is sovereign. ...

The time, it is to be hoped, is gone by, when any defense would be necessary of the "liberty of the press" as one of the securities against corrupt or tyrannical government. No argument, we may suppose, can now be needed, against permitting a legislature or an executive, not identified in interest with the people, to prescribe opinions to them, and determine what doctrines or what arguments they shall be allowed to hear. This aspect of the question, besides, has been so often and so triumphantly enforced by preceding writers, that it needs not be specially insisted on in this place. Though the law of England, on the subject of the press, is as servile to this day as it was in the time of the Tudors, there is little danger of its being actually put in force against political discussion, except during some temporary panic, when fear of insurrection drives ministers and judges from their propriety;[1] and, speaking

From John Stuart Mill, *On Liberty,* London, 1859.

* See the introductory note on Mill on page 179.

[1] These words had scarcely been written, when, as if to give them an emphatic contradiction, occurred the Government Press Prosecutions of 1858. That ill-judged interference with the lib-

generally, it is not, in constitutional countries, to be apprehended, that the government, whether completely responsible to the people or not, will often attempt to control the expression of opinion, except when in doing so it makes itself the organ of the general intolerance of the public. Let us suppose, therefore, that the government is entirely at one with the people, and never thinks of exerting any power of coercion unless in agreement with what it conceives to be their voice. But I deny the right of the people to exercise such coercion, either by themselves or by their government. The power itself is illegitimate. The best government has no more title to it than the worst. It is as noxious, or more noxious, when exerted in accordance with public opinion, than when in opposition to it. If all mankind minus one, were of one opinion, and only one person were of the contrary opinion, mankind would be no more justified in silencing that one person, than he, if he had the power, would be justified in silencing mankind. Were an opinion a personal possession of no value except to the owner; if to be obstructed in the enjoyment of it were simply a private injury, it would make some difference whether the injury was inflicted only on a few persons or on many. But the peculiar evil of silencing the expression of an opinion is, that it is robbing the human race; posterity as well as the existing

generation; those who dissent from the opinion, still more than those who hold it. If the opinion is right, they are deprived of the opportunity of exchanging error for truth: if wrong, they lose, what is almost as great a benefit, the clearer perception and livelier impression of truth, produced by its collision with error.

It is necessary to consider separately these two hypotheses, each of which has a distinct branch of the argument corresponding to it. We can never be sure that the opinion we are endeavoring to stifle is a false opinion; and if we were sure, stifling it would be an evil still.

First: the opinion which it is attempted to suppress by authority may possibly be true. Those who desire to suppress it, of course deny its truth; but they are not infallible. They have no authority to decide the question for all mankind, and exclude every other person from the means of judging. To refuse a hearing to an opinion, because they are sure that it is false, is to assume that *their* certainty is the same thing as *absolute* certainty. All silencing of discussion is an assumption of infallibility. Its condemnation may be allowed to rest on this common argument, not the worse for being common.

Unfortunately for the good sense of mankind, the fact of their fallibility is far from carrying the weight in their practical judg-

---

erty of public discussion has not, however, induced me to alter a single word in the text, nor has it at all weakened my conviction that, moments of panic excepted, the era of pains and penalties for political discussion has, in our own country, passed away. For, in the first place, the prosecutions were not persisted in; and, in the second, they were never, properly speaking, political prosecutions. The offense charged was not that of criticizing institutions, or the acts or persons of rulers, but of circulating what was deemed an immoral doctrine, the lawfulness of Tyrannicide.

If the arguments of the present chapter are of any validity, there ought to exist the fullest liberty of professing and discussing, as a matter of ethical conviction, any doctrine, however immoral it may be considered. It would, therefore, be irrelevant and out of place to examine here, whether the doctrine of Tyrannicide de-

serves that title. I shall content myself with saying that the subject has been at all times one of the open questions of morals; that the act of a private citizen in striking down a criminal, who, by raising himself above the law, has placed himself beyond the reach of legal punishment or control, has been accounted by whole nations, and by some of the best and wisest of men, not a crime, but an act of exalted virtue; and that, right or wrong, it is not of the nature of assassination, but of civil war. As such, I hold that the instigation to it, in a specific case, may be a proper subject of punishment, but only if an overt act has followed, and at least a probable connection can be established between the act and the instigation. Even then, it is not a foreign government, but the very government assailed, which alone, in the exercise of self-defense, can legitimately punish attacks directed against its own existence.

ment, which is always allowed to it in theory; for while every one well knows himself to be fallible, few think it necessary to take any precautions against their own fallibility, or admit the supposition that any opinion, of which they feel very certain, may be one of the examples of the error to which they acknowledge themselves to be liable. Absolute princes, or others who are accustomed to unlimited deference, usually feel this complete confidence in their own opinions on nearly all subjects. People more happily situated, who sometimes hear their opinions disputed, and are not wholly unused to be set right when they are wrong, place the same unbounded reliance only on such of their opinions as are shared by all who surround them, or to whom they habitually defer: for in proportion to a man's want of confidence in his own solitary judgment, does he usually repose, with implicit trust, on the infallibility of "the world" in general. And the world, to each individual, means the part of it with which he comes in contact; his party, his sect, his church, his class of society: the man may be called, by comparison, almost liberal and large-minded to whom it means anything so comprehensive as his own country or his own age. Nor is his faith in this collective authority at all shaken by his being aware that other ages, countries, sects, churches, classes, and parties have thought, and even now think, the exact reverse. He devolves upon his own world the responsibility of being in the right against the dissentient worlds of other people; and it never troubles him that mere accident has decided which of these numerous worlds is the object of his reliance, and that the same causes which make him a Churchman in London, would have made him a Buddhist or a Confucian in Pekin. Yet it is as evident in itself, as any amount of argument can make it, that ages are no more infallible than individuals; every age having held many opinions which subsequent ages have deemed not only false but absurd; and it is as certain that many opinions, now general, will be rejected by future ages, as it is that many, once general, are rejected by the present.

The objection likely to be made to this argument would probably take some such form as the following. There is no greater assumption of infallibility in forbidding the propagation of error, than in any other thing which is done by public authority on its own judgment and responsibility. Judgment is given to men that they may use it. Because it may be used erroneously, are men to be told that they ought not to use it at all? To prohibit what they think pernicious, is not claiming exemption from error, but fulfilling the duty incumbent on them, although fallible, of acting on their conscientious conviction. If we were never to act on our opinions, because those opinions may be wrong, we should leave all our interests uncared for, and all our duties unperformed. An objection which applies to all conduct, can be no valid objection to any conduct in particular. It is the duty of governments, and of individuals, to form the truest opinions they can; to form them carefully, and never impose them upon others unless they are quite sure of being right. But when they are sure (such reasoners may say), it is not conscientiousness but cowardice to shrink from acting on their opinions, and allow doctrines which they honestly think dangerous to the welfare of mankind, either in this life or in another, to be scattered abroad without restraint, because other people, in less enlightened times, have persecuted opinions now believed to be true. Let us take care, it may be said, not to make the same mistake: but governments and nations have made mistakes in other things, which are not denied to be fit subjects for the exercise of authority: they have laid on bad taxes, made unjust wars. Ought we therefore to lay on no taxes, and, under whatever provocation, make no wars? Men, and governments, must act to the best of their ability. There is no such thing as absolute certainty, but there is assurance sufficient for the purposes of human life. We may, and must, assume our opinion to be true for the guidance of our own conduct: and it is assuming no more when we forbid bad men to pervert society by the propagation of opinions which we regard as false and pernicious.

I answer, that it is assuming very much more. There is the greatest difference between presuming an opinion to be true, because, with every opportunity for contesting it, it has not been refuted, and assuming its truth for the purpose of not permitting its refutation. Complete liberty of contradicting and disproving our opinion, is the very condition which justifies us in assuming its truth for purposes of action; and on no other terms can a being with human faculties have any rational assurance of being right.

When we consider either the history of opinion, or the ordinary conduct of human life, to what is it to be ascribed that the one and the other are no worse than they are? Not certainly to the inherent force of the human understanding; for, on any matter not self-evident, there are ninety-nine persons totally incapable of judging of it, for one who is capable; and the capacity of the hundredth person is only comparative; for the majority of the eminent men of every past generation held many opinions now known to be erroneous, and did or approved numerous things which no one will now justify. Why is it, then, that there is on the whole a preponderance among mankind of rational opinions and rational conduct? If there really is this preponderance—which there must be unless human affairs are, and have always been, in an almost desperate state—it is owing to a quality of the human mind, the source of everything respectable in man either as an intellectual or as a moral being, namely, that his errors are corrigible. He is capable of rectifying his mistakes, by discussion and experience. Not by experience alone. There must be discussion, to show how experience is to be interpreted. Wrong opinions and practices gradually yield to fact and argument: but facts and arguments, to produce any effect on the mind, must be brought before it. Very few facts are able to tell their own story, without comments to bring out their meaning. The whole strength and value, then, of human judgment, depending on the one property, that it can be set right when it is wrong, reliance can be placed on it only when the means of setting it right are kept constantly at hand. In the case of any person whose judgment is really deserving of

confidence, how has it become so? Because he has kept his mind open to criticism of his opinions and conduct. Because it has been his practice to listen to all that could be said against him; to profit by as much of it as was just, and expound to himself, and upon occasion to others, the fallacy of what was fallacious. Because he has felt, that the only way in which a human being can make some approach to knowing the whole of a subject, is by hearing what can be said about it by persons of every variety of opinion, and studying all modes in which it can be looked at by every character of mind. No wise man ever acquired his wisdom in any mode but this; nor is it in the nature of human intellect to become wise in any other manner. The steady habit of correcting and completing his own opinion by collating it with those of others, so far from causing doubt and hesitation in carrying it into practice, is the only stable foundation for a just reliance on it: for, being cognizant of all that can, at least obviously, be said against him, and having taken up his position against all gainsayers—knowing that he has sought for objections and difficulties, instead of avoiding them, and has shut out no light which can be thrown upon the subject from any quarter—he has a right to think his judgment better than that of any person, or any multitude, who have not gone through a similar process.

It is not too much to require that what the wisest of mankind, those who are best entitled to trust their own judgment, find necessary to warrant their relying on it, should be submitted to by that miscellaneous collection of a few wise and many foolish individuals, called the public. The most intolerant of churches, the Roman Catholic Church, even at the canonization of a saint, admits, and listens patiently to, a "devil's advocate." The holiest of men, it appears, cannot be admitted to posthumous honors, until all that the devil could say against him is known and weighed. If even the Newtonian philosophy were not permitted to be questioned, mankind could not feel as complete assurance of its truth as they now do. The beliefs which we have most warrant for, have no safeguard to rest on, but a standing invitation to the whole world to prove them unfounded. If the challenge is not accepted, or is accepted and the attempt fails, we are far enough from certainty still; but we have done the best that the existing state of human reason admits of; we have neglected nothing that could give the truth a chance of reaching us: if the lists are kept open, we may hope that if there be a better truth, it will be found when the human mind is capable of receiving it; and in the meantime we may rely on having attained such approach to truth, as is possible in our own day. This is the amount of certainty attainable by a fallible being, and this the sole way of attaining it.

Strange it is, that men should admit the validity of the arguments for free discussion, but object to their being "pushed to an extreme"; not seeing that unless the reasons are good for an extreme case, they are not good for any case. Strange that they should imagine that they are not assuming infallibility, when they acknowledge that there should be free discussion on all subjects which can possibly be *doubtful*, but think that some particular principle or doctrine should be forbidden to be questioned because it is so *certain*, that is, because *they are certain* that it is certain. To call any proposition certain, while there is any one who would deny its certainty if permitted, but who is not permitted, is to assume that we ourselves, and those who agree with us, are the judges of certainty, and judges without hearing the other side.

In the present age—which has been described as "destitute of faith, but terrified at scepticism"—in which people feel sure, not so much that their opinions are true, as that they should not know what to do without them—the claims of an opinion to be protected from public attack are rested not so much on its truth, as on its importance to society. There are, it is alleged, certain beliefs, so useful, not to say indispensable to well-being, that it is as much the duty of governments to uphold those beliefs, as to protect any other of the interests of society. In a case of such necessity, and so directly in the line of their duty, something less than infallibility may, it is maintained,

warrant, and even bind, governments, to act on their own opinion, confirmed by the general opinion of mankind. It is also often argued, and still oftener thought, that none but bad men would desire to weaken these salutary beliefs; and there can be nothing wrong, it is thought, in restraining bad men, and prohibiting what only such men would wish to practice. This mode of thinking makes the justification of restraints on discussion not a question of the truth of doctrines, but of their usefulness; and flatters itself by that means to escape the responsibility of claiming to be an infallible judge of opinions. But those who thus satisfy themselves, do not perceive that the assumption of infallibility is merely shifted from one point to another. The usefulness of an opinion is itself matter of opinion: as disputable, as open to discussion, and requiring discussion as much, as the opinion itself. There is the same need of an infallible judge of opinions to decide an opinion to be noxious, as to decide it to be false, unless the opinion condemned has full opportunity of defending itself. And it will not do to say that the heretic may be allowed to maintain the utility or harmlessness of his opinion, though forbidden to maintain its truth. The truth of an opinion is part of its utility. If we would know whether or not it is desirable that a proposition should be believed, is it possible to exclude the consideration of whether or not it is true? In the opinion, not of bad men, but of the best men, no belief which is contrary to truth can be really useful; and can you prevent such men from urging that plea, when they are charged with culpability for denying some doctrine which they are told is useful, but which they believe to be false? Those who are on the side of received opinions, never fail to take all possible advantage of this plea; you do not find *them* handling the question of utility as if it could be completely abstracted from that of truth: on the contrary, it is, above all, because their doctrine is the "truth," that the knowledge or the belief of it is held to be so indispensable. There can be no fair discussion of the question of usefulness, when an argument so vital may be employed on one side, but not on the other. And in point of fact, when law or public feeling do not permit the truth of an opinion to be disputed, they are just as little tolerant of a denial of its usefulness. The utmost they allow is an extenuation of its absolute necessity, or of the positive guilt of rejecting it.

In order more fully to illustrate the mischief of denying a hearing to opinions because we, in our own judgment, have condemned them, it will be desirable to fix down the discussion to a concrete case; and I choose, by preference, the cases which are least favorable to me—in which the argument against freedom of opinion, both on the score of truth and on that of utility, is considered the strongest. Let the opinions impugned be the belief in a God and in a future state, or any of the commonly received doctrines of morality. To fight the battle on such ground, gives a great advantage to an unfair antagonist; since he will be sure to say (and many who have no desire to be unfair will say it internally), Are these the doctrines which you do not deem sufficiently certain to be taken under the protection of law? Is the belief in a God one of the opinions, to feel sure of which, you hold to be assuming infallibility? But I must be permitted to observe, that it is not the feeling sure of a doctrine (be it what it may) which I call an assumption of infallibility. It is the undertaking to decide that question *for others*, without allowing them to hear what can be said on the contrary side. And I denounce and reprobate this pretension not the less, if put forth on the side of my most solemn convictions. However positive any one's persuasion may be, not only of the falsity but of the pernicious consequences—not only of the pernicious consequences, but (to adopt expressions which I altogether condemn) the immorality and impiety of an opinion; yet if, in pursuance of that private judgment, though backed by the public judgment of his country or his contemporaries, he prevents the opinion from being heard in its defense, he assumes infallibility. And so far from the assumption being less objectionable or less dangerous because the opinion is called immoral or impious, this is the case of all others in which it is most fatal. These are exactly the occasions on which the

men of one generation commit those dreadful mistakes, which excite the astonishment and horror of posterity. It is among such that we find the instances memorable in history, when the arm of the law has been employed to root out the best men and the noblest doctrines; with deplorable success as to the men, though some of the doctrines have survived to be (as if in mockery) invoked, in defense of similar conduct toward those who dissent from *them*, or from their received interpretation.

Mankind can hardly be too often reminded, that there was once a man named Socrates, between whom and the legal authorities and public opinion of his time, there took place a memorable collision. Born in an age and country abounding in individual greatness, this man has been handed down to us by those who best knew both him and the age, as the most virtuous man in it; while *we* know him as the head and prototype of all subsequent teachers of virtue, the source equally of the lofty inspiration of Plato and the judicious utilitarianism of Aristotle, *"i maëstri di color che sanno,"* the two headsprings of ethical as of all other philosophy. This acknowledged master of all the eminent thinkers who have since lived—whose fame, still growing after more than two thousand years, all but outweighs the whole remainder of the names which make his native city illustrious—was put to death by his countrymen, after a judicial conviction, for impiety and immorality. Impiety, in denying the gods recognized by the State; indeed his accuser asserted (see the *Apologia*) that he believed in no gods at all. Immorality, in being, by his doctrines and instructions, a "corruptor of youth." Of these charges the tribunal, there is every ground for believing, honestly found him guilty, and condemned the man who probably of all then born had deserved best of mankind, to be put to death as a criminal. . . .

It will be said, that we do not now put to death the introducers of new opinions: we are not like our fathers who slew the prophets, we even build sepulchres to them. It is true we no longer put heretics to death; and the amount of penal infliction which modern feeling would probably tolerate, even against the most obnoxious opinions, is not sufficient to extirpate them. But let us not flatter ourselves that we are yet free from the stain even of legal persecution. Penalties for opinion, or at least for its expression, still exist by law; and their enforcement is not, even in these times, so unexampled as to make it at all incredible that they may some day be revived in full force. In the year 1857, at the summer assizes of the county of Cornwall, an unfortunate man,[2] said to be of unexceptionable conduct in all relations of life, was sentenced to twenty-one months' imprisonment, for uttering, and writing on a gate, some offensive words concerning Christianity. Within a month of the same time, at the Old Bailey, two persons, on two separate occasions,[3] were rejected as jurymen, and one of them grossly insulted by the judge and by one of the counsel, because they honestly declared that they had no theological belief; and a third, a foreigner,[4] for the same reason, was denied justice against a thief. This refusal of redress took place in virtue of the legal doctrine, that no person can be allowed to give evidence in a court of justice, who does not profess belief in a God (any god is sufficient) and in a future state; which is equivalent to declaring such persons to be outlaws, excluded from the protection of the tribunals; who may not only be robbed or assaulted with impunity, if no one but themselves, or persons of similar opinions, be present, but any one else may be robbed or assaulted with impunity, if the proof of the fact depends on their evidence. The assumption on which this is grounded is that the oath is worthless, of a person who does not believe in a future state; a proposition which betokens much ignorance of history in those who assent to it (since it is historically true that a large proportion of infidels in all ages have been persons of distinguished integrity and honor);

and would be maintained by no one who had the smallest conception how many of the persons in greatest repute with the world, both for virtues and for attainments, are well known, at least to their intimates, to be unbelievers. The rule, besides, is suicidal, and cuts away its own foundation. Under pretense that atheists must be liars, it admits the testimony of all atheists who are willing to lie, and rejects only those who brave the obloquy of publicly confessing a detested creed rather than affirm a falsehood. A rule thus self-convicted of absurdity so far as regards its professed purpose, can be kept in force only as a badge of hatred, a relic of persecution; a persecution, too, having the peculiarity, that the qualification for undergoing it, is the being clearly proved not to deserve it. The rule, and the theory it implies, are hardly less insulting to believers than to infidels. For if he who does not believe in a future state, necessarily lies, it follows that they who do believe are only prevented from lying, if prevented they are, by the fear of hell. We will not do the authors and abettors of the rule the injury of supposing, that the conception which they have formed of Christian virtue is drawn from their own consciousness.

These, indeed, are but rags and remnants of persecution, and may be thought to be not so much an indication of the wish to persecute, as an example of that very frequent infirmity of English minds, which makes them take a preposterous pleasure in the assertion of a bad principle, when they are no longer bad enough to desire to carry it really into practice. But unhappily there is no security in the state of the public mind, that the suspension of worse forms of legal persecution, which has lasted for about the space of a generation, will continue. In this age the quiet surface of routine is as often ruffled by attempts to resuscitate past evils, as to introduce new benefits. What is boasted of at the present time as the revival of religion, is always, in narrow and uncultivated minds, at least as much the revival of bigotry; and where there is the strong permanent leaven of intolerance in the feelings of a people, which at all times abides in the middle classes of this country, it needs but little to

---

[2] Thomas Pooley, Bodmin Assizes, July 31, 1857. In December following, he received a free pardon from the Crown.

[3] George Jacob Holyoake, August 17, 1857; Edward Truelove, July, 1857.

[4] Baron de Gleichen, Marlborough-street Police Court, August 4, 1857.

provoke them into actively persecuting those whom they have never ceased to think proper objects of persecution.[5] For it is this—it is the opinions men entertain, and the feelings they cherish, respecting those who disown the beliefs they deem important, which makes this country not a place of mental freedom. For a long time past, the chief mischief of the legal penalties is that they strengthen the social stigma. It is that stigma which is really effective, and so effective is it, that the profession of opinions which are under the ban of society is much less common in England, than is, in many other countries, the avowal of those which incur risk of judicial punishment. In respect to all persons but those whose pecuniary circumstances make them independent of the goodwill of other people, opinion, on this subject, is as efficacious as law; men might as well be imprisoned, as excluded from the means of earning their bread. Those whose bread is already secured, and who desire no favors from men in power, or from bodies of men, or from the public, have nothing to fear from the open avowal of any opinions, but to be ill-thought of and ill-spoken of, and this it ought not to require a very heroic mold to enable them to bear. There is no room for any appeal *ad misericordiam* in behalf of such persons. But though we do not now inflict so much evil on those who think differently from us, as it was formerly our custom to do, it may be that we do ourselves as much evil as ever by our treatment of them. Socrates was put to death, but the Socratic philosophy rose like the sun in heaven, and spread its illumination over the whole intellectual firmament. Christians were cast to the lions, but the Christian church grew up a stately and spreading tree, overtopping the older and less vigorous growths, and stifling them by its shade. Our merely social intolerance kills no one, roots out no opinions, but induces men to disguise them, or to abstain from any active effort for their diffusion. With us, heretical opinions do not perceptibly gain, or even lose, ground in each decade or generation; they never blaze out far and wide, but continue to smolder in the narrow circles of thinking and studious persons among whom they originate, without ever lighting up the general affairs of mankind with either a true or a deceptive light. And thus is kept up a state of things very satisfactory to some minds, because, without the unpleasant process of fining or imprisoning anybody, it maintains all prevailing opinions outwardly undisturbed, while it does not absolutely interdict the exercise of reason by dissentients afflicted with the malady of thought. A convenient plan for having peace in the intellectual world, and keeping all things going on therein very much as they do already. But the price paid for this sort of intellectual

---

[5] Ample warning may be drawn from the large infusion of the passions of a persecutor, which mingled with the general display of the worst parts of our national character on the occasion of the Sepoy insurrection. The ravings of fanatics or charlatans from the pulpit may be unworthy of notice; but the heads of the Evangelical party have announced as their principle for the government of Hindoos and Mohammedans, that no schools be supported by public money in which the Bible is not taught, and by necessary consequence that no public employment be given to any but real or pretended Christians. An under-Secretary of State, in a speech delivered to his constituents on November 12, 1857, is reported to have said: "Toleration of their faith" (the faith of a hundred millions of British subjects), "the superstition which they called religion, by the British Government, had had the effect of retarding the ascendancy of the British name, and preventing the salutary growth of Christianity.... Toleration was the great corner-stone of the religious liberties of this country; but do not let them abuse that precious word toleration. As he understood it, it meant the complete liberty to all, freedom of worship, *among Christians, who worshipped upon the same foundation.* It meant toleration of all sects and denominations of *Christians who believed in the one mediation."* I desire to call attention to the fact, that a man who has been deemed fit to fill a high office in the government of this country, under a liberal Ministry, maintains the doctrine that all who do not believe in the divinity of Christ are beyond the pale of toleration. Who, after this imbecile display, can indulge the illusion that religious persecution has passed away, never to return?

pacification, is the sacrifice of the entire moral courage of the human mind. A state of things in which a large portion of the most active and inquiring intellects find it advisable to keep the general principles and grounds of their convictions within their own breasts, and attempt, in what they address to the public, to fit as much as they can of their own conclusions to premises which they have internally renounced, cannot send forth the open, fearless characters, and logical, consistent intellects who once adorned the thinking world. The sort of men who can be looked for under it, are either mere conformers to commonplace, or time-servers for truth, whose arguments on all great subjects are meant for their hearers, and are not those which have convinced themselves. Those who avoid this alternative, do so by narrowing their thoughts and interest to things which can be spoken of without venturing within the region of principles, that is, to small practical matters, which would come right of themselves, if but the minds of mankind were strengthened and enlarged, and which will never be made effectually right until then: while that which would strengthen and enlarge men's minds, free and daring speculation on the highest subjects, is abandoned.

Those in whose eyes this reticence on the part of heretics is no evil, should consider in the first place, that in consequence of it there is never any fair and thorough discussion of heretical opinions; and that such of them as could not stand such a discussion, though they may be prevented from spreading, do not disappear. But it is not the minds of heretics that are deteriorated most by the ban placed on all inquiry which does not end in the orthodox conclusions. The greatest harm done is to those who are not heretics, and whose whole mental development is cramped, and their reason cowed, by the fear of heresy. Who can compute what the world loses in the multitude of promising intellects combined with timid characters, who dare not follow out any bold, vigorous, independent train of thought, lest it should land them in something which would admit of being considered irreligious or immoral? Among them we may occasionally see some man of deep conscientiousness, and subtle and refined understanding, who spends a life in sophisticating with an intellect which he cannot silence, and exhausts the resources of ingenuity in attempting to reconcile the promptings of his conscience and reason with orthodoxy, which yet he does not, perhaps, to the end succeed in doing. No one can be a great thinker who does not recognize, that as a thinker it is his first duty to follow his intellect to whatever conclusions it may lead. Truth gains more even by the errors of one who, with due study and preparation, thinks for himself, than by the true opinions of those who only hold them because they do not suffer themselves to think. Not that it is solely, or chiefly, to form great thinkers, that freedom of thinking is required. On the the contrary, it is as much and even more indispensable, to enable average human beings to attain the mental stature which they are capable of. There have been, and may again be, great individual thinkers, in a general atmosphere of mental slavery. But there never has been, nor ever will be, in that atmosphere, an intellectually active people. When any people has made a temporary approach to such a character, it has been because the dread of heterodox speculation was for a time suspended. Where there is a tacit convention that principles are not to be disputed; where the discussion of the greatest questions which can occupy humanity is considered to be closed, we cannot hope to find that generally high scale of mental activity which has made some periods of history so remarkable. Never when controversy avoided the subjects which are large and important enough to kindle enthusiasm, was the mind of a people stirred up from its foundations, and the impulse given which raised even persons of the most ordinary intellect to something of the dignity of thinking beings. Of such we have had an example in the condition of Europe during the times immediately following the Reformation; another, though limited to the Continent and to a more cultivated class, in the speculative movement of the latter half of the eighteenth century; and a third, of still briefer duration, in the intellectual fermentation of Germany during the Goethian and

Fichtean period. These periods differed widely in the particular opinions which they developed; but were alike in this, that during all three the yoke of authority was broken. In each, an old mental despotism had been thrown off, and no new one had yet taken its place. The impulse given at these three periods has made Europe what it now is. Every single improvement which has taken place either in the human mind or in institutions, may be traced distinctly to one or other of them. Appearances have for some time indicated that all three impulses are wellnigh spent; and we can expect no fresh start, until we again assert our mental freedom.

Let us now pass to the second division of the argument, and dismissing the supposition that any of the received opinions may be false, let us assume them to be true, and examine into the worth of the manner in which they are likely to be held, when their truth is not freely and openly canvassed. However unwillingly a person who has a strong opinion may admit the possibility that his opinion may be false, he ought to be moved by the consideration that however true it may be, if it is not fully, frequently, and fearlessly discussed, it will be held as a dead dogma, not a living truth.

There is a class of persons (happily not quite so numerous as formerly) who think it enough if a person assents undoubtingly to what they think true, though he has no knowledge whatever of the grounds of the opinion, and could not make a tenable defense of it against the most superficial objections. Such persons, if they can once get their creed taught from authority, naturally think that no good, and some harm, comes of its being allowed to be questioned. Where their influence prevails, they make it nearly impossible for the received opinion to be rejected wisely and considerately, though it may still be rejected rashly and ignorantly; for to shut out discussion entirely is seldom possible, and when it once gets in, beliefs not grounded on conviction are apt to give way before the slightest semblance of an argument. Waiving, however, this possibility —assuming that the true opinion abides in the mind, but abides as a prejudice, a belief in-

dependent of, and proof against, argument— this is not the way in which truth ought to be held by a rational being. This is not knowing the truth. Truth, thus held, is but one superstition the more accidentally clinging to the words which enunciate a truth.

If the intellect and judgment of mankind ought to be cultivated, a thing which Protestants at least do not deny, on what can these faculties be more appropriately exercised by any one, than on the things which concern him so much that it is considered necessary for him to hold opinions on them? If the cultivation of the understanding consists in one thing more than in another, it is surely in learning the grounds of one's own opinions. Whatever people believe, on subjects on which it is of the first importance to believe rightly, they ought to be able to defend against at least the common objections. But, some one may say, "Let them be *taught* the grounds of their opinions. It does not follow that opinions must be merely parroted because they are never heard controverted. Persons who learn geometry do not simply commit the theorems to memory, but understand and learn likewise the demonstrations; and it would be absurd to say that they remain ignorant of the grounds of geometrical truths, because they never hear any one deny, and attempt to disprove them." Undoubtedly: and such teaching suffices on a subject like mathematics, where there is nothing at all to be said on the wrong side of the question. The peculiarity of the evidence of mathematical truths is, that all the argument is on one side. There are no objections, and no answers to objections. But on every subject on which difference of opinion is possible, the truth depends on a balance to be struck between two sets of conflicting reasons. Even in natural philosophy, there is always some other explanation possible of the same facts; some geocentric theory instead of heliocentric, some phlogiston instead of oxygen; and it has to be shown why that other theory cannot be the true one: and until this is shown, and until we know how it is shown, we do not understand the grounds of our opinion. But when we turn to subjects infinitely more complicated, to morals, religion, politics, social relations, and the business of life, three-fourths of the arguments for every disputed opinion consist in dispelling the appearances which favor some opinion different from it. The greatest orator, save one, of antiquity, has left it on record that he always studied his adversary's case with as great, if not with still greater, intensity than even his own. What Cicero practiced as the means of forensic success, requires to be imitated by all who study any subject in order to arrive at the truth. He who knows only his own side of the case, knows little of that. His reasons may be good, and no one may have been able to refute them. But if he is equally unable to refute the reasons on the opposite side; if he does not so much as know what they are, he has no ground for preferring either opinion. The rational position for him would be suspension of judgment, and unless he contents himself with that, he is either led by authority, or adopts, like the generality of the world, the side to which he feels most inclination. Nor is it enough that he should hear the arguments of adversaries from his own teachers, presented as they state them, and accompanied by what they offer as refutations. That is not the way to do justice to the arguments, or bring them into real contact with his own mind. He must be able to hear them from persons who actually believe them; who defend them in earnest, and do their very utmost for them. He must know them in their most plausible and persuasive form; he must feel the whole force of the difficulty which the true view of the subject has to encounter and dispose of; else he will never really possess himself of the portion of truth which meets and removes that difficulty. Ninety-nine in a hundred of what are called educated men are in this condition; even of those who can argue fluently for their opinions. Their conclusion may be true, but it might be false for anything they know: they have never thrown themselves into the mental position of those who think differently from them, and considered what such persons may have to say; and consequently they do not, in any proper sense of the word, know the doctrine which they themselves profess. They do not know

those parts of it which explain and justify the remainder; the considerations which show that a fact which seemingly conflicts with another is reconcilable with it, or that, of two apparently strong reasons, one and not the other ought to be preferred. All that part of the truth which turns the scale, and decides the judgment of a completely informed mind, they are strangers to; nor is it ever really known, but to those who have attended equally and impartially to both sides, and endeavored to see the reasons of both in the strongest light. So essential is this discipline to a real understanding of moral and human subjects, that if opponents of all important truths do not exist, it is indispensable to imagine them, and supply them with the strongest arguments which the most skilful devil's advocate can conjure up. . . .

But what! (it may be asked) Is the absence of unanimity an indispensable condition of true knowledge? Is it necessary that some part of mankind should persist in error, to enable any to realize the truth? Does a belief cease to be real and vital as soon as it is generally received —and is a proposition never thoroughly understood and felt unless some doubt of it remains? As soon as mankind have unanimously accepted a truth, does the truth perish within them? The highest aim and best result of improved intelligence, it has hitherto been thought, is to unite mankind more and more in the acknowledgment of all important truths: and does the intelligence only last as long as it has not achieved its object? Do the fruits of conquest perish by the very completeness of the victory?

I affirm no such thing. As mankind improve, the number of doctrines which are no longer disputed or doubted will be constantly on the increase: and the well-being of mankind may almost be measured by the number and gravity of the truths which have reached the point of being uncontested. The cessation, on one question after another, of serious controversy, is one of the necessary incidents of the consolidation of opinion; a consolidation as salutary in the case of true opinions, as it is dangerous and noxious when the opinions are erroneous. But though this gradual narrowing of the bounds of diversity of opinion is necessary in both senses of the term, being at once inevitable and indispensable, we are not therefore obliged to conclude that all its consequences must be beneficial. The loss of so important an aid to the intelligent and living apprehension of a truth, as is afforded by the necessity of explaining it to, or defending it against, opponents, though not sufficient to outweigh, is no trifling drawback from, the benefit of its universal recognition. Where this advantage can no longer be had, I confess I should like to see the teachers of mankind endeavoring to provide a substitute for it; some contrivance for making the difficulties of the question as present to the learner's consciousness, as if they were pressed upon him by a dissentient champion, eager for his conversion.

But instead of seeking contrivances for this purpose, they have lost those they formerly had. The Socratic dialectics, so magnificently exemplified in the dialogues of Plato, were a contrivance of this description. They were essentially a negative discussion of the great questions of philosophy and life, directed with consummate skill to the purpose of convincing any one who had merely adopted the commonplaces of received opinion, that he did not understand the subject—that he as yet attached no definite meaning to the doctrines he professed; in order that, becoming aware of his ignorance, he might be put in the way to attain a stable belief, resting on a clear apprehension both of the meaning of doctrines and of their evidence. The school disputations of the middle ages had a somewhat similar object. They were intended to make sure that the pupil understood his own opinion, and (by necessary correlation) the opinion opposed to it, and could enforce the grounds of the one and confute those of the other. These last-mentioned contests had indeed the incurable defect, that the premises appealed to were taken from authority, not from reason; and, as a discipline to the mind, they were in every respect inferior to the powerful dialectics which formed the intellects of the "Socratici viri": but the modern mind owes far more to both than it is generally willing to admit, and the present modes of education contain nothing which in

the smallest degree supplies the place either of the one or of the other. A person who derives all his instruction from teachers or books, even if he escape the besetting temptation of contenting himself with cram, is under no compulsion to hear both sides; accordingly it is far from a frequent accomplishment, even among thinkers, to know both sides; and the weakest part of what everybody says in defense of his opinion, is what he intends as a reply to antagonists. It is the fashion of the present time to disparage negative logic—that which points out weaknesses in theory or errors in practice, without establishing positive truths. Such negative criticism would indeed be poor enough as an ultimate result; but as a means to attaining any positive knowledge or conviction worthy the name, it cannot be valued too highly; and until people are again systematically trained to it, there will be few great thinkers, and a low general average of intellect, in any but the mathematical and physical departments of speculation. On any other subject no one's opinions deserve the name of knowledge, except so far as he has either had forced upon him by others, or gone through of himself, the same mental process which would have been required of him in carrying on an active controversy with opponents. That, therefore, which when absent, it is so indispensable, but so difficult, to create, how worse than absurd it is to forego, when spontaneously offering itself! If there are any persons who contest a received opinion, or who will do so if law or opinion will let them, let us thank them for it, open our minds to listen to them, and rejoice that there is some one to do for us what we otherwise ought, if we have any regard for either the certainty or the vitality of our convictions, to do with much greater labor for ourselves. . . .

We have now recognized the necessity to the mental well-being of mankind (on which all their other well-being depends) of freedom of opinion, and freedom of the expression of opinion, on four distinct grounds; which we will now briefly recapitulate.

First, if any opinion is compelled to silence, that opinion may, for aught we can certainly know, be true. To deny this is to assume our own infallibility.

Secondly, though the silenced opinion be an error, it may, and very commonly does, contain a portion of truth; and since the general or prevailing opinion on any subject is rarely or never the whole truth, it is only by the collision of adverse opinions that the remainder of the truth has any chance of being supplied.

Thirdly, even if the received opinion be not only true, but the whole truth; unless it is suffered to be, and actually is, vigorously and earnestly contested, it will, by most of those who receive it, be held in the manner of a prejudice, with little comprehension or feeling of its rational grounds. And not only this, but, fourthly, the meaning of the doctrine itself will be in danger of being lost, or enfeebled, and deprived of its vital effect on the character and conduct: the dogma becoming a mere formal profession, inefficacious for good, but cumbering the ground, and preventing the growth of any real and heart-felt conviction, from reason or personal experience.

The social order
and production

Friedrich Engels (1820-1895)

In 1844 Friedrich Engels became the friend and collaborator of Karl Marx (1818–1883). Their joint research and writing—among which was The Communist Manifesto—*lasted until Marx's death. Engels developed the theory of dialectical materialism and what has come to be known as the "Marxist" philosophy of history. Our selection is from Engel's book,* Herr Eugen Dühring's Revolution in Science (Anti-Dühring), *first published in 1878. Here Engels presents a classic account of his conception of the dialectic of history, involving the material conditions of man's existence, the necessary antagonism between the laboring class and the capitalist class, the proletarian revolution, and the eventual classless society. We are presented with a view both of a certain social order and of man's alleged historical destiny shaping itself through the emergence of a new order.*

The materialist conception of history starts from the principle that production, and with production the exchange of its products, is the basis of every social order; that in every society which has appeared in history the distribution of the products, and with it the division of society into classes or estates, is determined by what is produced and how it is produced, and how the product is exchanged. According to this conception, the ultimate causes of all social changes and political revolutions are to be sought, not in the minds of men, in their increasing insight into eternal truth and justice, but in changes in the mode of production and exchange; they are to be sought not in the

From Friedrich Engels, *Herr Eugen Dühring's Revolution in Science (Anti-Dühring)*, Pt. III, Ch. 2, tr. Emile Burns, ed. C. P. Dutt. Copyright, 1939 by International Publishers, New York. Used by permission.

philosophy but in the *economics* of the epoch concerned. The growing realisation that existing social institutions are irrational and unjust, that reason has become nonsense and good deeds a scourge is only a sign that changes have been taking place quietly in the methods of production and forms of exchange with which the social order, adapted to previous economic conditions, is no longer in accord. This also involves that the means through which the abuses that have been revealed can be got rid of must likewise be present, in more or less developed form, in the altered conditions of productions. These means are not to be *invented* by the mind, but *discovered* by means of the mind in the existing material facts of production.

Where then, on this basis, does modern socialism stand?

The existing social order, as is now fairly

generally admitted, is the creation of the present ruling class, the bourgeoisie. The mode of production peculiar to the bourgeoisie—called, since Marx, the capitalist mode of production—was incompatible with the local privileges and privileges of birth as well as with the reciprocal personal ties of the feudal system; the bourgeoisie shattered the feudal system, and on its ruins established the bourgeois social order, the realm of free competition, freedom of movement, equal rights for commodity owners, and all the other bourgeois glories. The capitalist mode of production could now develop freely. From the time when steam and the new tool-making machinery had begun to transform the former manufacture into large-scale industry, the productive forces evolved under bourgeois direction developed at a pace that was previously unknown and to an unprecedented degree. But just as manufacture, and the handicraft industry which had been further developed under its influence, had previously come into conflict with the feudal fetters of the guilds, so large-scale industry, as it develops more fully, comes into conflict with the barriers within which the capitalist mode of production holds it confined. The new forces of production have already outgrown the bourgeois form of using them; and this conflict between productive forces and mode of production is not a conflict which has risen in men's heads, as for example the conflict between original sin and divine justice; but it exists in the facts, objectively, outside of us, independently of the will or purpose even of the men who brought it about. Modern socialism is nothing but the reflex in thought of this actual conflict, its ideal reflection in the minds first of the class which is directly suffering under it—the working class.

In what, then, does this conflict consist?

Previous to capitalist production, that is to say, in the Middle Ages, small-scale production was general, on the basis of the private ownership by the workers of their means of production; the agricultural industry of the small peasant, freeman or serf, and the handicraft industry of the towns. The instruments of labour—land, agricultural implements, the workshop and tools—were the instruments of labour of individuals, intended only for individual use, and therefore necessarily puny, dwarfish, restricted. But just because of this they belonged, as a rule, to the producer himself. To concentrate and enlarge these scattered, limited means of production, to transform them into the mighty levers of production of the present day, was precisely the historic role of the capitalist mode of production and of its representative, the bourgeoisie. In Part IV of *Capital* Marx gives a detailed account of how, since the fifteenth century, this process has developed historically through the three stages of simple co-operation, manufacture and large-scale industry. But as Marx also points out, the bourgeoisie was unable to transform those limited means of production into mighty productive forces except by transforming them from individual means of production into *social* means of production, which could be used only *by a body of men as a whole*. The spinning wheel, the hand loom and the blacksmith's hammer were replaced by the spinning machine, the mechanical loom and the steam hammer; and the factory, making the co-operation of hundreds and thousands of workers necessary, took the place of the individual work-room. And, like the means of production, production itself changed from a series of individual operations into a series of social acts, and the products from the products of individuals into social products. The yarn, the cloth and the metal goods which now came from the factory were the common product of many workers through whose hands it had to pass successively before it was ready. No individual can say of such products: I made it, that is *my* product. . . .

In commodity production as it had developed in the Middle Ages, the question could never arise of who should be the owner of the product of labour. The individual producer had produced it, as a rule, from raw material which belonged to him and was often produced by himself, with his own instruments of labour, and by his own manual labour or that of his family. There was no need whatever for the product to be appropriated by him; it belonged to him as an absolute matter of course. His ownership of the product was therefore based *upon his own labour*. Even where outside help was used, it was as a rule subsidiary, and in many cases received other compensation in addition to wages; the guild apprentice and journeyman worked less for the sake of their board and wages than to train themselves to become master craftsmen. Then came the concentration of the means of production in large workshops and manufactories, their transformation into means of production that were in fact social. But the social means of production and the social products were treated as if they were still, as they had been before, the means of production and the products of individuals. Hitherto, the owner of the instruments of labour had appropriated the product because it was as a rule his own product, the auxiliary labour of other persons being the exception; now, the owner of the instruments of labour continued to appropriate the product, although it was no longer *his* product, but exclusively the product of *other's labour*. Thus, therefore, the products, now socially produced, were not appropriated by those who had really set the means of production in motion and really produced the products, but by the *capitalists*. Means of production and production itself had in essence become social. But they were subjected to a form of appropriation which has as its presupposition private production by individuals, with each individual owning his own product and bringing it on to the market. The mode of production is subjected to this form of appropriation, although it removes the presuppositions on which the latter was based.[1] In this contradiction, which gives the new mode of production its capitalist character, *the whole conflict of today is already present in germ*. The more the new mode of production gained the ascendancy on all decisive

fields of production and in all countries of decisive economic importance, supplanting individual production except for insignificant relics, the *more glaring necessarily became the incompatibility of social production with capitalist appropriation.*

The first capitalists found, as we have said, the form of wage labour already in existence; but wage labour as the exception, as an auxiliary occupation, as a supplementary, as a transitory phase. The agricultural labourer who occasionally went to work as a day labourer had a few acres of his own land, from which if necessary he could get his livelihood. The regulations of the guilds ensured that the journeyman of today became the master craftsman of tomorrow. But as soon as the means of production had become social and were concentrated in the hands of capitalists, this situation changed. Both the means of production and the products of the small, individual producer lost more and more of their value; there was nothing left for him to do but to go to the capitalist, and work for wages. Wage labour, hitherto an exception and subsidiary, became the rule and the basic form of all production; hitherto an auxiliary occupation, it now became the labourer's exclusive activity. The occasional wage worker became the wage worker for life. The number of lifelong wage workers was also increased to a colossal extent by the simultaneous disintegration of the feudal system, the dispersal of the retainers of the feudal lords, the eviction of peasants from their homesteads, etc. The separation between the means of production concentrated in the hands of the capitalists, on the one side, and the producers now possessing nothing but their labour power, on the other, was made complete. *The contradiction between social production and capitalist appropriation became manifest as the antagonism between proletariat and bourgeoisie....*

[1] There is no need here to explain that although the form of appropriation remains the same, the *character* of the appropriation is revolutionised by the process described above, to no less a degree than production. My appropriation of my own product and my appropriation of another person's product are certainly two very different forms of appropriation. It may be noted in passing that wage labour, in which the whole capitalist mode of production is already present in embryo form, is a very old institution; in isolated and scattered form it developed alongside slavery for centuries. But the germ could only develop into the capitalist mode of production when the necessary historical conditions had come into existence. [Note by F. Engels.]

With the extension of commodity production, however, and especially with the emergence of the capitalist mode of production, the laws of commodity production, previously latent, also began to operate more openly and more potently. The old bonds were loosened, the old dividing barriers broken through, the producers more and more transformed into independent, isolated commodity producers. The anarchy of social production became obvious, and was carried to further and further extremes. But the chief means through which the capitalist mode of production accentuated this anarchy in social production was the direct opposite of anarchy: the increasing organisation of production on a social basis in each individual productive establishment. This was the lever with which it put an end to the former peaceful stability. In whatever branch of industry it was introduced, it could suffer no older method of production to exist alongside it; where it laid hold of a handicraft, that handicraft was wiped out. The field of labour became a field of battle. The great geographical discoveries and the colonisation which followed on them multiplied markets and hastened on the transformation of handicraft into manufacture. The struggle broke out not only between the individual local producers; the local struggles developed into national struggles, the trade wars of the seventeenth and eighteenth centuries. Finally, large-scale industry and the creation of the world market have made the struggle universal and at the same time given it an unparalleled intensity. Between individual capitalists, as between whole industries and whole countries, advantages in natural or artificial conditions of production decide life or death. The vanquished are relentlessly cast aside. It is the Darwinian struggle for individual existence, transferred from Nature to society with intensified fury. The standpoint of the animal in Nature appears as the last word in human development. The contradiction between social production and capitalist appropriation reproduces itself as *the antithesis between the organisation of production in the individual factory and the anarchy of production in society as a whole.*

The capitalist mode of production moves in these two forms of manifestation of the contradiction immanent in it from its very nature, without hope of escaping from that "vicious circle" which Fourier long ago discovered in it. But what Fourier in his day was as yet unable to see is that this circle is gradually narrowing; that the motion is rather in the form of a spiral and must meet its end, like the motion of the planets, by collision with the centre. It is the driving force of the social anarchy of production which transforms the immense majority of men more and more into proletarians, and it is in turn the proletarian masses who will ultimately put an end to the anarchy of production. It is the driving force of the social anarchy of production which transforms the infinite perfectibility of the machine in large-scale industry into a compulsory commandment for each individual industrial capitalist to make his machinery more and more perfect, under penalty of ruin. But the perfecting of machinery means rendering human labour superfluous. If the introduction and increase of machinery meant the displacement of millions of hand workers by a few machine workers, the improvement of machinery means the displacement of larger and larger numbers of the machine workers themselves, and ultimately the creation of a mass of available wage workers exceeding the average requirements of capital for labour—a complete industrial reserve army, as I called it as long ago as 1845 [2]—a reserve that would be available at periods when industry was working at high pressure, but would be thrown out onto the streets by the crash inevitably following the boom; a reserve that would at all times be like a leaden weight on the feet of the working class in their fight for existence against capital, a regulator to keep wages down to the low level which suits the needs of capital. Thus it comes about that machinery, to use Marx's phrase, becomes the most powerful weapon in the war of capital against the working class, that the instruments of labour constantly tear the means of subsistence out of the hands of the labourer, that the very product of the labourer is turned

[2] *The Condition of the Working Class in England,* p. 109. German edition. [Note by F. Engels.]

into an instrument for his subjection. Thus it comes about that the economising of the instruments of labour becomes from the outset a simultaneous and absolutely reckless waste of labour power and robbery of the normal conditions necessary for the labour function; that machinery, "the most powerful instrument for shortening labour time, becomes the most unfailing means for placing every moment of the labourer's time and that of his family at the disposal of the capitalist for the purpose of expanding the value of his capital." [3]

Thus it comes about that the excessive labour of some becomes the necessary condition for the lack of employment of others, and that large-scale industry, which hunts all over the world for new consumers, restricts the consumption of the masses at home to a starvation minimum and thereby undermines its own internal market. "The law that always equilibrates the relative surplus population, or industrial reserve army, to the extent and energy of accumulation, this law rivets the labourer to capital more firmly than the wedges of Vulcan did Prometheus to the rock. It establishes an accumulation of misery, corresponding with accumulation of capital. Accumulation of wealth at one pole is, therefore, at the same time accumulation of misery, agony of toil, slavery, ignorance, brutality, mental degradation, at the opposite pole, *i.e.*, on the side of the class that *produces its own products in the form of capital.*" [4]

And to expect any other distribution of the products from the capitalist mode of production is like expecting the electrodes of a battery, while they are in contact with the battery, not to decompose water, not to develop oxygen at the positive pole and hydrogen at the negative....

And in fact, since 1825, when the first general crisis broke out, the whole industrial and commercial world, the production and exchange of all civilised peoples and of their more or less barbarian dependent people have been dislocated practically once in every ten

years. Trade comes to a standstill, the markets are glutted, the products lie in great masses, unsalable, ready money disappears, credit vanishes, the factories are idle, the working masses go short of the means of subsistence because they have produced too much of them, bankruptcy follows upon bankruptcy, forced sale upon forced sale. The stagnation lasts for years, both productive forces and products are squandered and destroyed on a large scale, until the accumulated masses of commodities are at last disposed of at a more or less considerable depreciation, until production and exchange gradually begin to move again. By degrees the pace quickens; it becomes a trot; the industrial trot passes into a gallop, and the gallop in turn passes into the headlong onrush of a complete industrial commercial, credit and speculative steeplechase, only to land again in the end, after the most breakneck jumps—in the ditch of a crash. And so on again and again. We have now experienced it five times since 1825, and at this moment (1877) we are experiencing it for the sixth time. And the character of these crises is so clearly marked that Fourier hit them all off when he described the first as *crise pléthorique*, a crisis of superabundance.

In these crises, the contradiction between social production and capitalist appropriation comes to a violent explosion. The circulation of commodities is for the moment reduced to nothing; the means of circulation, money, becomes an obstacle to circulation; all the laws of commodity production and commodity circulation are turned upside down. The economic collision has reached its culminating point: *the mode of production rebels against the mode of exchange; the productive forces rebel against the mode of production, which they have outgrown.*

The fact that the social organisation of production within the factory has developed to the point at which it has become incompatible with the anarchy of production in society which exists alongside it and above it—this fact is made palpable to the capitalists themselves by the violent concentration of capitals which takes place during crises through the ruin of many big and even more small capitalists. The whole

---

[3] *Capital*, vol. I, p. 445 (Kerr edition).
[4] *Capital*, vol. I, p. 709 (Kerr edition).

mechanism of the capitalist mode of production breaks down under the pressure of the productive forces which it itself created. It is no longer able to transform the whole of this mass of means of production into capital; they lie idle, and for this very reason the industrial reserve army must also lie idle. Means of production, means of subsistence, available labourers, all the elements of production and of general wealth are there in abundance. But "abundance becomes the source of distress and want" (Fourier), because it is precisely abundance that prevents the conversion of the means of production and subsistence into capital. For in capitalist society the means of production cannot begin to function unless they have first been converted into capital, into means for the exploitation of human labour power. The necessity for the means of production and subsistence to take on the form of capital stands like a ghost between them and the workers. It alone prevents the coming together of the material and personal levers of production; it alone forbids the means of production to function, the workers to work and to live. Thus on the one hand the capitalist mode of production stands convicted of its own incapacity any longer to control these productive forces. And on the other hand these productive forces themselves press forward with increasing force to put an end to the contradiction, to rid themselves of their character as capital, *to the actual recognition of their character as social productive forces.* . . .

If the crises revealed the incapacity of the bourgeoisie any longer to control the modern productive forces, the conversion of the great organisations for production and communication into joint-stock companies and state property shows that for this purpose the bourgeoisie can be dispensed with. All the social functions of the capitalists are now carried out by salaried employees. The capitalist has no longer any social activity save the pocketing of revenues, the clipping of coupons and gambling on the Stock Exchange, where the different capitalists fleece each other of their capital. Just as at first the capitalist mode of production displaced the workers, so now it displaces

the capitalists, relegating them, just as it did the workers, to the superfluous population, even if in the first instance not to the industrial reserve army.

But neither the conversion into joint-stock companies nor into state property deprives the productive forces of their character as capital. In the case of joint-stock companies this is obvious. And the modern state, too, is only the organisation with which bourgeois society provides itself in order to maintain the general external conditions of the capitalist mode of production against encroachments either by the workers or by individual capitalists. The modern state, whatever its form, is an essentially capitalist machine; it is the state of the capitalists, the ideal collective body of all capitalists. The more productive forces it takes over as its property, the more it becomes the real collective body of all the capitalists, the more citizens it exploits. The workers remain wage-earners, proletarians. The capitalist relationship is not abolished; it is rather pushed to an extreme. But at this extreme it is transformed into its opposite. State ownership of the productive forces is not the solution of the conflict, but it contains within itself the formal means, the key to the solution.

This solution can only consist in the recognition in practice of the social nature of the modern productive forces, in bringing, therefore, the mode of production, appropriation and exchange into accord with the social character of the means of production. And this can only be brought about by society, openly and without deviation, taking possession of the productive forces which have outgrown all control other than that of society itself. Thereby the social character of the means of production and of the products—which today operates against the producers themselves, periodically breaking through the mode of production and exchange and enforcing itself only as a blind law of Nature, violently and destructively—is quite consciously asserted by the producers, and is transformed from a cause of disorder and periodic collapse into the most powerful lever of production itself.

The forces operating in society work exactly

like the forces operating in Nature: blindly, violently, destructively, so long as we do not understand them and fail to take them into account. But when once we have recognised them and understood how they work, their direction and their effects, the gradual subjection of them to our will and the use of them for the attainment of our aims depends entirely upon ourselves. And this is quite especially true of the mighty productive forces of the present day. So long as we obstinately refuse to understand their nature and their character—and the capitalist mode of production and its defenders set themselves against any such attempt—so long do these forces operate in spite of us, against us, and so long do they control us, as we have shown in detail. But once their nature is grasped, in the hands of the producers working in association they can be transformed from demoniac masters into willing servants. It is the difference between the destructive force of electricity in the lightning of a thunderstorm and the tamed electricity of the telegraph and the arc light; the difference between a conflagration and fire in the service of man. This treatment of the productive forces of the present day, on the basis of their real nature at last recognised by society, opens the way to the replacement of the anarchy of social production by a socially planned regulation of production in accordance with the needs both of society as a whole and of each individual. The capitalist mode of appropriation, in which the product enslaves first the producer, and then also the appropriator, will thereby be replaced by the mode of appropriation of the products based on the nature of the modern means of production themselves: on the one hand direct social appropriation as a means to the maintenance and extension of production, and on the other hand direct individual appropriation as a means to life and pleasure.

By more and more transforming the great majority of the population into proletarians, the capitalist mode of production brings into being the force which, under penalty of its own destruction, is compelled to carry out this revolution. By more and more driving towards the conversion of the vast socialised means of production into state property, it itself points the way for the carrying through of this revolution. *The proletariat seizes the state power, and transforms the means of production in the first instance into state property.* But in doing this, it puts an end to itself as the proletariat, it puts an end to all class differences and class antagonisms, it puts an end also to the state as the state. Former society, moving in class antagonisms, had need of the state, that is, an organisation of the exploiting class at each period for the maintenance of its external conditions of production; that is, therefore, for the forcible holding down of the exploited class in the conditions of oppression (slavery, villeinage or selfdom, wage labour) determined by the existing mode of production. The state was the official representative of society as a whole, its embodiment in a visible corporation; but it was this only in so far as it was the state of that class which itself, in its epoch, represented society as a whole; in ancient times, the state of the slave-owning citizens; in the Middle Ages, of the feudal nobility; in our epoch, of the bourgeoisie. When ultimately it becomes really representative of society as a whole, it makes itself superfluous. As soon as there is no longer any class of society to be held in subjection; as soon as, along with class domination and the struggle for individual existence based on the former anarchy of production, the collisions and excesses arising from these have also been abolished, there is nothing more to be repressed which would make a special repressive force, a state, necessary. The first act in which the state really comes forward as the representative of society as a whole—the taking possession of the means of production in the name of society—is at the same time its last independent act as a state. The interference of the state power in social relations becomes superfluous in one sphere after another, and then ceases of itself. The government of persons is replaced by the administration of things and the direction of the processes of production. The state is not "abolished," *it withers away.* It is from this standpoint that we must appraise the phrase "free people's state"—both its justification at times for agitational purposes, and its ultimate scientific inadequacy—and also the demand of the so-called anarchists that the state should be abolished overnight. . . .

The seizure of the means of production by society puts an end to commodity production, and therewith to the domination of the product over the producer. Anarchy in social production is replaced by conscious organisation on a planned basis. The struggle for individual existence comes to an end. And at this point, in a certain sense, man finally cuts himself off from the animal world, leaves the conditions of animal existence behind him and enters conditions which are really human. The conditions of existence forming man's environment, which up to now have dominated man, at this point pass under the dominion and control of man, who now for the first time becomes the real conscious master of Nature, because and in so far as he has become master of his own social organisation. The laws of his own social activity, which have hitherto confronted him as external, dominating laws of Nature, will then be applied by man with complete understanding, and hence will be dominated by man. Men's own social organisation which has hitherto stood in opposition to them as if arbitrarily decreed by Nature and history, will then become the voluntary act of men themselves. The objective, external forces which have hitherto dominated history, will then pass under the control of men themselves. It is only from this point that men, with full consciousness, will fashion their own history; it is only from this point that the social causes set in motion by men will have, predominantly and in constantly increasing measure, the effects willed by men. It is humanity's leap from the realm of necessity into the realm of freedom.

To carry through his world-emancipating act is the historical mission of the modern proletariat. And it is the task of scientific socialism, the theoretical expression of the proletarian movement, to establish the historical conditions and, with these, the nature of this act, and thus to bring to the consciousness of the now oppressed class the conditions and nature of the act which it is its destiny to accomplish.

Reflections on the guillotine

Albert Camus (1913-1960)

Camus was born in Mondovi, Algeria. He took a degree in philosophy, had a variety of jobs, and established himself as a journalist, editing the French Resistance paper Combat *during World War II. His first novel,* The Stranger *(1942), received much attention and was widely praised. His collection of essays,* The Myth of Sisyphus, *published in the same year, developed his "absurdist" position, that of a man who accepts life on earth as the only grandeur, steadfastly denying any universal significance to man's existence. Camus' second novel,* The Plague *(1947), his major philosophical attempt,* The Rebel *(1951), and his novella,* The Fall *(1956), enhanced his international reputation, which was marked by the award of the Nobel Prize for literature in 1957, the year in which his volume of six short stories,* Exile and the Kingdom, *was published. Camus was killed in an auto accident in February, 1960. A collection of essays, editorials, and other pieces was published in English with the title* Resistance, Rebellion, and Death *in 1961. Camus wrote several plays which have been given production, and volumes of his notebooks have been published.*

The essay, "Reflections on the Guillotine," from which our selection is taken, is an attempt to analyze the death penalty in terms of the prevailing assumptions of a society that rejects a God who gives meaning to life and judges mankind.

. . . What does the death penalty mean for us, half-way through the twentieth century? For the sake of simplification, let us say that our civilization has lost the only values that, to a certain degree, could justify the death penalty, and that it suffers, on the contrary, from every evil that necessitates its suppression. In other words, the abolition of the death penalty should be demanded by the conscious members of our society on grounds of both logic and fidelity to the facts.

Of logic, first of all. To decide that a man must be definitively punished is to deny him any further opportunity whatsoever to make reparation for his acts. It is at this juncture, we repeat, that the arguments for and against capital punishment confront one another blindly, eventuating in a fruitless checkmate. Yet it is exactly here that none of us can afford to be positive, for we are all judges, all party to the dispute. Hence our uncertainty about our

From Albert Camus, "Reflections on the Guillotine," tr. Richard Howard. Originally published in *Evergreen Review,* Vol. 1, No. 3. Copyright, 1957, by Grove Press, Inc. Used by permission.

right to kill and our impotence to convince others on either side. Unless there is absolute innocence, there can be no supreme judge. Now we have all committed some transgression in our lives, even if this transgression has not put us within the power of the law and has remained an unknown crime: there are no just men, only hearts more or less poor in justice. The mere fact of living permits us to know this, and to add to the sum of our actions a little of the good that might partially compensate for the evil we have brought into the world. This right to live that coincides with the opportunity for reparation is the natural right of every man, even the worst. The most abandoned criminal and the worthiest judge here find themselves side by side, equally miserable and jointly responsible. Without this right, the moral life is strictly impossible. None among us, in particular, is entitled to despair of a single man, unless it be after his death, which transforms his life into destiny and admits of a final judgment. But to pronounce this final judgment before death, to decree the closing of accounts when the creditor is still alive, is the privilege of no man. On these grounds, at least, he who judges absolutely condemns himself absolutely.

Barnard Fallot of the Masuy gang, who worked for the Gestapo, confessed to the entire list of terrible crimes of which he was accused and later went to his death with great courage, declaring himself beyond hope of reprieve: "My hands are too red with blood," he said to one of his fellow prisoners.[1] Public opinion and that of his judges certainly classified him among the irrecoverables, and I would have been tempted to put him in that category myself, had I not read one astonishing piece of evidence: after having declared that he wanted to die bravely, Fallot told the same prisoner: "Do you know what I regret most of all? Not having known sooner about the Bible they gave me here. If I had, I wouldn't be where I am now." It is not a question of surrendering to the sentimentality of conventional imagery and

[1] Jean Bobognano, *Quartier des fauves, prison de Fresnes, Édition du Fuseau.*

conjuring up Victor Hugo's good convicts. The age of enlightenment, as it is called, wished to abolish the death penalty under the pretext that man was fundamentally good. We know, of course, that he is not (he is simply better or worse). After the last twenty years of our splendid history we know it very well. But it is because man is not fundamentally good that no one among us can set himself up as an absolute judge, for no one among us can pretend to absolute innocence. The verdict of capital punishment destroys the only indisputable human community there is, the community in the face of death, and such a judgment can only be legitimated by a truth or a principle that takes its place above all men, beyond the human condition.

Capital punishment, in fact, throughout history has always been a religious punishment. When imposed in the name of the king, representative of God on earth, or by priests, or in the name of a society considered as a sacred body, it is not the human community that is destroyed but the functioning of the guilty man as a member of the divine community which alone can give him his life. Such a man is certainly deprived of his earthly life, yet his opportunity for reparation is preserved. The real judgment is not pronounced in this world, but in the next. Religious values, especially the belief in an eternal life, are thus the only ones on which the death penalty can be based, since according to their own logic they prevent that penalty from being final and irreparable: it is justified only insofar as it is not supreme.

The Catholic Church, for example, has always admitted the necessity of the death penalty. It has imposed the penalty itself, without avarice, at other periods. Today, its doctrines still justify capital punishment, and concede the State the right to apply it. No matter how subtle this doctrine may be, there is at its core a profound feeling which was directly expressed by a Swiss councilor from Fribourg during a discussion of capital punishment by the national council in 1937; according to M. Grand, even the worst criminal examines his own conscience when faced with the actuality of execution. "He repents, and his preparation for death is made easier. The Church has saved one of its members, has accomplished its divine mission. This is why the Church has steadfastly countenanced capital punishment, not only as a means of legitimate protection, but *as a powerful means of salvation....* [My italics.] Without becoming precisely a matter of doctrine, the death penalty, like war itself, can be justified by its quasi-divine efficacy."

By virtue of the same reasoning, no doubt, one can read on the executioner's sword in Fribourg the motto "Lord Jesus, thou art the Judge." The executioner is thereby invested with a divine function. He is the man who destroys the body in order to deliver the soul to its divine judgment, which no man on earth can foresee. It will perhaps be considered that such mottos imply rather outrageous confusions, and certainly those who confine themselves to the actual teachings of Jesus will see this handsome sword as yet another outrage to the body of Christ. In this light can be understood the terrible words of a Russian prisoner whom the excutioners of the Tsar were about to hang in 1905, when he turned to the priest who was about to console him with the image of Christ and said: "Stand back, lest you commit a sacrilege." An unbeliever will not fail to remark that those who have placed in the very center of their faith the overwhelming victim of a judicial error should appear more reticent, to say the least, when confronted by cases of legal murder. One might also remind the believer that the emperor Julian, before his conversion, refused to give official posts to Christians because they systematically refused to pronounce the death sentence or to aid in administering it. For five centuries Christians believed that the strict moral teaching of their master forbade them to kill. But the Catholic faith is derived not only from the teachings of Christ, it is nourished by the Old Testament, by Saint Paul, and by the Fathers as well. In particular the immortality of the soul and the universal resurrection of the body are articles of dogma. Hence, capital punishment, for the believer, can be regarded as a provisional punishment which does not in the least affect the definite sentence, but remains a disposition necessary to the terrestrial order, an administrative measure which, far from making an end of the guilty man, can promote, on the contrary, his redemption in heaven. I do not say that all believers follow this reasoning, and I can imagine without much difficulty that most Catholics stand closer to Christ than to Moses or Saint Paul. I say only that the belief in the immortality of the soul has permitted Catholicism to formulate the problem of capital punishment in very different terms, and to justify it.

But what does such a justification mean to the society we live in, a society which in its institutions and manners alike has become almost entirely secular? When an atheist—or skeptic—or agnostic judge imposes the death penalty on an unbelieving criminal, he is pronouncing a definitive punishment that cannot be revised. He sits upon God's throne,[2] but without possessing God's powers and, moreover, without believing in them. He condemns to death, in fact, because his ancestors believed in eternal punishment. Yet the society which he claims to represent pronounces, in reality, a purely eliminative measure, destroys the human community united against death, and sets itself up as an absolute value because it pretends to absolute power. Of course society traditionally assigns a priest to the condemned man, and the priest may legitimately hope that fear of punishment will help effect the condemned man's conversion. Yet who will accept this casuistry as the justification of a punishment so often inflicted and so often received in an entirely different spirit? It is one thing to believe and "therefore know not fear," and another to find one's faith through fear. Conversion by fire or the knife will always be suspect, and one can well understand why the Church renounced a triumph by terror over infidel hearts. In any case, a secularized society has nothing to gain from a conversion concerning which it professes complete disinterest: it enacts a consecrated punishment, and at the same time deprives that punishment of its justification and its utility alike. Delirious in its own behalf,

[2] The decision of the jury is preceded by the formula "before God and my conscience. . . ."

society plucks the wicked from its bosom as if it were virtue personified. In the same way, an honorable man might kill his son who had strayed from the path of duty, saying, "Really, I didn't know what else I could do!" Society thus usurps the right of selection, as if it were nature, and adds a terrible suffering to the eliminative process, as if it were a redeeming god.

To assert, in any case, that a man must be absolutely cut off from society because he is absolutely wicked is the same as saying that society is absolutely good, which no sensible person will believe today. It will not be believed—in fact, it is easier to believe the contrary. Our society has become as diseased and criminal as it is only because it has set itself up as its own final justification, and has had no concern but its own preservation and success in history. Certainly it is a secularized society, yet during the nineteenth century it began to fashion a kind of ersatz religion by proposing itself as an object of adoration. The doctrines of evolution, and the theories of selection that accompanied such doctrines, have proposed the future of society as its final end. The political utopias grafted onto these doctrines have proposed, at the end of time, a Golden Age that justifies in advance all intermediary enterprises. Society has grown accustomed to legalizing whatever can minister to its future, and consequently to usurping the supreme punishment in an absolute fashion: it has regarded as a crime and a sacrilege everything that contradicts its own intentions and temporal dogmas. In other words, the executioner, formerly a priest, has become a civil servant. The results surround us. Half-way through the century, our society, which has forfeited the logical right to pronounce the death penalty, must now abolish it for reasons of realism.

Confronted with crime, how does our civilization in fact define itself? The answer is easy: for 30 years crimes of state have vastly exceeded crimes of individuals. I shall not even mention wars—general or local—although blood is a kind of alcohol that eventually intoxicates like the strongest wine. I am referring here to the number of individuals killed directly by the State, a number that has grown to astronomical proportions and infinitely exceeds that of "private" murders. There are fewer and fewer men condemned by common law, and more and more men executed for political reasons. The proof of this fact is that each of us, no matter how honorable he is, can now envisage the *possibility* of someday being put to death, whereas such an eventuality at the beginning of the century would have appeared farcical at best. Alphonse Karr's famous remark, "Let my lords the assassins begin," no longer has any meaning: those who spill the most blood are also those who believe they have right, logic, and history on their side.

It is not so much against the individual killer that our society must protect itself then, as against the State. Perhaps this equation will be reversed in another thirty years. But for the present, a legitimate defense must be made against the State, before all else. Justice and the most realistic sense of our time require that the law protect the individual against a State given over to the follies of sectarianism and pride. "Let the State begin by abolishing the death penalty" must be our rallying cry today.

Bloody laws, it has been said, make bloody deeds. But it is also possible for a society to suffer that state of ignominy in which public behavior, no matter how disorderly, comes nowhere near being so bloody as the laws. Half of Europe knows this state. We have known it in France and we risk knowing it again. The executed of the Occupation produced the executed of the Liberation whose friends still dream of revenge. Elsewhere, governments charged with too many crimes are preparing to drown their guilt in still greater massacres. We kill for a nation or for a deified social class. We kill for a future society, likewise deified. He who believes in omniscience can conceive of omnipotence. Temporal idols that demand absolute faith tirelessly mete out absolute punishments. And religions without transcendance murder those they condemn en masse and without hope.

How can European society in the twentieth century survive if it does not defend the individual by every means within its power against the oppression of the State? To forbid putting a man to death is one means of publicly proclaiming that society and the State are not absolute values, one means of demonstrating that nothing authorizes them to legislate definitively, to bring to pass the irreparable. Without the death penalty, Gabriel Péri and Brasillach would perhaps be among us still; we could then judge them, according to our lights, and proudly speak out our judgment, instead of which they now judge us, and it is we who must remain silent. Without the death penalty, the corpse of Rajk would not still be poisoning Hungary, a less guilty Germany would be received with better grace by the nations of Europe, the Russian Revolution would not still be writhing in its shame, and the blood of Algeria would weigh less heavily upon us here in France. Without the death penalty, Europe itself would not be infected by the corpses accumulated in its exhausted earth for the last twenty years. Upon our continent all values have been overturned by fear and hatred among individuals as among nations. The war of ideas is waged by rope and knife. It is no longer the natural human society that exercises its rights of repression, but a ruling ideology that demands its human sacrifices. "The lesson the scaffold always provides," Francart wrote, "is that human life ceases to be sacred when it is considered useful to suppress it." Apparently it has been considered increasingly useful, the lesson has found apt pupils, and the contagion is spreading everywhere. And with it, the disorders of nihilism. A spectacular counter-blow is required: it must be proclaimed, in institutions and as a matter of principle, that the human person is above and beyond the State. Every measure which will diminish the pressure of social forces on the individual will also aid in the decongestion of a Europe suffering from an afflux of blood, will permit us to think more clearly, and to make our way toward recovery. The disease of Europe is to believe in nothing and to claim to know everything. But Europe does not know everything, far from it, and to judge by the rebellion and the hope in which we find ourselves today, Europe does believe in something: Europe believes that the supreme misery of man, at its mysterious limit, borders on his supreme greatness. For the majority of Europeans faith is lost, and with it the justifications faith conferred upon the order of punishment. But the majority of Europeans are also sickened by that idolatry of the State which has claimed to replace their lost faith. From now on, with divided goals, certain and uncertain, determined never to submit and never to oppress, we must recognize both our hope and our ignorance, renounce all absolute law, all irreparable institutions. We know enough to be able to say that this or that great criminal deserves a sentence of perpetual forced labor. But we do not know enough to say that he can be deprived of his own future, which is to say, of our common opportunity for reparation. In tomorrow's united Europe, on whose behalf I write, the solemn abolition of the death penalty must be the first article of that European Code for which we all hope.

From the humanitarian idylls of the eighteenth century to its bloody scaffolds the road runs straight and is easily followed; we all know today's executioners are humanists. And therefore we cannot be too suspicious of humanitarian ideologies applied to a problem like that of capital punishment. I should like to repeat, by way of conclusion, that my opposition to the death penalty derives from no illusions as to the natural goodness of the human creature, and from no faith in a golden age to come. On the contrary, the abolition of capital punishment seems necessary to me for reasons of qualified pessimism, reasons I have attempted to explain in terms of logic and the most realistic considerations. Not that the heart has not made its contribution to what I have been saying: for anyone who has spent several weeks among these texts, these memories, and these men— all, intimately or remotely, connected with the scaffold—there can be no question of leaving their dreadful ranks unaffected by what one has seen and heard. Nevertheless, I do not believe there is no responsibility in this world for what I have found, or that one should submit to our modern propensity for absolving victim and killer in the same moral confusion. This purely sentimental confusion involves more cowardice than generosity, and ends up by justifying whatever is worst in this world: if everything is blessed, then slave camps are blessed, and organized murder, and the cynicism of the great political bosses—and ultimately, blessing everything alike, one betrays one's own brothers. We can see this happening all around us. But indeed, with the world in its present condition the man of the twentieth century asks for laws and institutions of *convalescence* that will check without crushing, lead without hampering. Hurled into the unregulated dynamism of history, man needs a new physics, new laws of equilibrium. He needs, most of all, a reasonable society, not the anarchy into which his own pride and the State's inordinate powers have plunged him.

It is my conviction that the abolition of the death penalty will help us advance toward that society. In taking this initiative, France could propose its extension on either side of the iron curtain; in any case she could set an example. Capital punishment would be replaced by a sentence of perpetual forced labor for criminals judged incorrigible, and by shorter terms for others. As for those who believe that such punishment is still more cruel than capital punishment itself, I wonder why, in that case, they do not reserve it for Landru and his like and relegate capital punishment to secondary offenders. One might also add that such forced labor leaves the condemned man the possibility of choosing his death, whereas the guillotine is a point of no return. On the other hand, I would answer those who believe that a sentence of perpetual forced labor is too mild a punishment by remarking first on their lack of imagination and then by pointing out that the privation of liberty could seem to them a mild punishment only to the degree that contemporary society has taught them to despise what liberty they have.[3]

That Cain was not killed, but bore in the sight of all men a mark of reprobation is, in any case, the lesson we should draw from the Old Testament, not to mention the Gospels, rather than taking our inspiration from the cruel examples of the Mosaic law. There is no reason why at least a limited version of such an experiment should not be attempted in France (say for a ten-year period), if our government is still capable of redeeming its vote for alcohol by the great measure in behalf of civilization which total abolition would represent. And if public opinion and its representatives cannot renounce our slothful law which confines itself to eliminating what it cannot amend, at least, while waiting for a day of regeneration and of truth, let us not preserve as it is this "solemn shambles" (in Tarde's expression) which continues to disgrace our society. The death penalty, as it is imposed, even as rarely as it is imposed, is a disgusting butchery, an outrage inflicted on the spirit and body of man. This truncation, this living severed head, these long gouts of blood, belong to a barbarous epoch that believed it could subdue the people by offering them degrading spectacles. Today, when this ignoble death is secretly administered, what meaning can such torture have? The truth is that in an atomic age we kill as we did in the age of steelyards: where is the man of normal sensibility whose stomach is not turned at the mere idea of such clumsy surgery? If the French state is incapable of overcoming its worst impulses to this degree, and of furnishing Europe with one of the remedies it needs most, let it at least reform its means of administering capital punishment. Science, which has taught us so much about killing, could at least teach us to kill decently. An anesthetic which would permit the accused to pass from a state of sleep to death, which

[3] See also the report on the death penalty made by Representative Dupont to the National Assembly on May 31, 1791: "He [*the assassin*] is consumed by a bitter, burning temper; what he fears above all is repose, a state that leaves him to himself, and to escape it he continually faces death and seeks to inflict it; solitude and his conscience are his real tortures. Does this not tell us what kind of punishment we should impose, to what agonies he is most sensitive? *Is it not in the very nature of the disease that we must seek the remedy which can cure it?*" I italicize this last sentence, which makes this little-known Representative a real precursor of our modern psychological theories.

would remain within his reach for at least a day so that he could make free use of it, and which in cases of refusal or failure of nerve could then be administered to him, would assure the elimination of the criminal, if that is what we require, but would also provide a little decency where today there is nothing but a sordid and obscene exhibition.

I indicate these compromises only to the degree that one must sometimes despair of seeing wisdom and the principles of civilization impose themselves upon those responsible for our future. For certain men, more numerous than is suppposed, knowing what the death penalty really is and being unable to prevent its application is physically insupportable. In their own way, they suffer this penalty too, and without any justification. If we at least lighten the weight of the hideous images that burden these men, society will lose nothing by our actions. But ultimately even such measures will be insufficient. Neither in the hearts of men nor in the manners of society will there be a lasting peace until we outlaw death.

Method and Value
in the Sciences

Many of the issues discussed in the previous parts appear under a new light in Part V. Here we deal with a method of obtaining knowledge which has won the approval of countless strong minds and which provides a contrast to the ways of developing ideas found in the various branches of philosophy. It has become banal to say that in our time there is a great need to understand what the sciences do, how they win acceptance of their theories, and, most importantly, what they may or may not say about problems of value. What bearing do the sciences have on the major objectives of human action?

PART V

Although scientific observation was certainly carried on in ancient times, widespread practice of science and understanding of its method seem to be late acquisitions of human culture. Once the practice of science has taken firm hold of a civilization, however, its method becomes the standard for valid investigation of the natural world. The results of scientific investigation, to be sure, transform civilizations in important ways. But perhaps more important than any scientific achievement is the attitude of mind which characterizes those who practice scientific method.

There is, of course, a great deal of variety in the procedures in the different disciplines which we call "science." Despite the differences between the work of the physicist and the zoologist, the astronomer and the geologist or botanist, certain common patterns are present which enable us to speak of a method belonging to science as a whole. It is this common method that our first selection, by Cohen and Nagel, seeks to describe. To understand what is meant by scientific method is to grasp one of the key factors to be taken into account in any contemporary formulation of a world view.

We often hear it said that mathematics, with its precision and exactitude, is the ideal of the sciences, and that every science ought to progress as far as possible in the direction of mathematics. These claims seem to be borne out by the development of such sciences as physics and chemistry, which have made great strides as they have become more and more mathematical; but not all thinkers would agree that mathematics represents the ideal for every science.

The twentieth century has seen a great deal of activity in what are called the social or behavioral sciences. Study of the many facets of human behavior has increasingly appropriated some of the concepts and procedures which have been found to work in the natural sciences, though with necessary modifications. Whether the social sciences, occupied as they are with the subject of man and culture, can ever achieve the rigor and exactitude of some of the natural sciences is a much disputed matter. Are their difficulties attributable to their relative immaturity, to the *complexity* of their subject matter, or, perhaps, to the *unique nature* of their subject matter? Whatever the state of these disciplines with respect to formulation and confirmation of theory, each of them has amassed a great fund of data which have helped in the understanding of many types of phenomena.

The proliferation of data in the behavioral sciences and the fecundity of investigators in producing ideas for experiment point up one of their chief problems: What principles are social scientists to be guided by in developing explanatory hypotheses? This problem is central in one of our readings.

The first two readings in this part have to do with the method of science and with the issues involved in the acceptance of scientific theories. Other readings of this part are occupied with some aspects of another set of issues: the implications of the sciences for human values. This broad area of problems is opened up in the discussion by Philipp Frank of the acceptance of scientific theories. The issue which Frank raises, as to whether scientific theories ought ever to be disconnected from their bearing on human conduct, to some extent underlies each of the subsequent readings.

Science, no matter how high its prestige, functions in a milieu of attitudes, beliefs, and purposes in which a great many competing interests are at stake. Are these human attitudes, beliefs, and purposes unrelated to the pursuits of the scientist, or must they be taken into account before scientific theory can achieve its significance? And a furthur issue: Do these attitudes, beliefs, and purposes, including religious and social values, help to determine what investigations the scientist will make? If so, is this a justifiable state of affairs? Should we accept the idea of a "republic of science," as Michael Polanyi calls it, in which only "purely scientific" reasons should be allowed to function, or is science in all its phases inseparable from the totality of human functions and fated to take its chances along with many much less rational approaches to the world, and at times to be subject to these approaches?

But, we might ask, shouldn't the practice of science somehow affect men's prevailing attitudes, beliefs, and purposes? We have already seen in Part III, on ethics, that John Dewey, among others, attempted to bring scientific attitudes to bear on ethical thought. The Darwinian theory of evolution has been one of the most influential of all scientific hypotheses, especially in the realm of ethical thought. What are the implications of the theory of evolution, properly understood, for the moral life? What are the differences, first of all, between biological and cultural evolutionary processes? What are the chief factors affecting furthur human development?

The American evolutionist G. G. Simpson, in our selection, carefully outlines proposals for a set of moral principles which he calls an "ethic" of knowledge and responsibility. These proposals are founded upon an evolutionist's understanding of the unique capacities possessed by man, and they are proposals made by a thinker with intimate knowledge of the data and theories of biological evolution. Are they also an attempt to make normative inferences from a theory of the nature of man? (See the introduction to Part III.) Is it legitimate to argue that because man possesses the capacity for knowledge, he has the obligation to use his knowledge in some particular way? In general, also, may we infer an obligation to be responsible from the fact that a certain power for responsibility exists in us? Here the reader should recall the position stated by Hume, in the part dealing with ethics, a position which challenges the legitimacy of any argument from fact to value, from a description of what is, to an assertion of what ought to be. Would Hume's position also prohibit an argument from capacity to duty?

Of special interest, also, is Simpson's discussion of the nonexpert's responsibility for evaluating the credentials of experts. This is certainly an important matter for our time. Is Simpson's position feasible, and is it really a solution of the problem? Are there alternative approaches that might be more desirable? If so, what might they be?

Perhaps no single issue is more pressing for students of the behavioral sciences than that of the nature of explanation. What does it mean to explain human behavior? Should we follow the same patterns in explaining why a killer has committed an act of murder and in explaining why bodies in the earth's gravitational field fall with a certain rate of acceleration? Should a behavioral scientist seek general laws, expressing regularities, from which to deduce particular cases, when he is trying to explain human action? Or, should he seek a pattern of explanation specifically tailored to entities—human beings—who are conceived to be not subject to general laws but self-determining, because of their ability to use language and to act for definite reasons? Should he rather emphasize the uniqueness of individuals; should he explain their behavior by pointing to intentions and reasons for particular acts instead of to the generalizations of causal law? Should he found his approach on the assumption that man is simply a "thing" or on the supposition that man is a free agent? Here the question of human self-knowledge enters a new context, where it becomes linked up with another question: What kinds of disciplines are the sciences of human behavior? Should they be modeled after the natural sciences, say, physics, where the aim is to discover general causal laws, or should they try to explain human action from the "inside," say, in the way that the novelist or the practicing psychotherapist does?

In a discussion touching on several facets of these problems, in our first part, Adolf Grünbaum offered a defense of determinism which was, at the same time, an argument for dealing "with man as with the rest of nature." As though in reply to Grünbaum, Theodore Mischel considers an alternative approach for psychology, one which regards the causal-law, deductive pattern of explanation as unsuited to a description of human action, and seeks, rather, to explain in terms of the reasons for action in individual cases. His approach is closer to the type of explanation found in novels and plays. From Mischel's point of view, does Grünbaum's defense of determinism confuse a *motive* with a *cause*? Mischel argues, too, that his view of explanation is able to justify the approaches found among existential analysts, who emphasize man's uniqueness, his distinctness from all other types of being. Would Mischel's approach to psychology in any way undermine the claim of that discipline to be called a science?

The question of the relation between descriptive and normative discourse appears now in a new form. Ruth Benedict, a distinguished anthropologist, well-acquainted with a variety of culture systems, offers the thesis that each culture system has a dominant style of its own which results from the emphasis on certain values. This pattern of value constitutes the standard or norm for conduct within a given culture. While there are marked differences among cultural patterns, Benedict holds that none can be said to be better or more valid than others, and that there are no universal norms. Her position, then, is one of ethical relativity founded on cultural relativity. The values of different cultures can be described, and within a given culture its value choices are prescriptive of action, but no inferences are to be made from anthropological facts to universal normative statements. Benedict agrees with Hume that morals are a matter of preference and convention, but for her the unit expressing its preference is a culture system. The sciences of human behavior, she believes, cannot be in a position to determine norms.

Gordon Allport rejects the position of Benedict in contending that social scientists can help to confirm or disconfirm the proposals of moral philosophers. Moral principles, he argues, are subject to confirmation by appeal to evidence gathered by the investigators of human behavior. Scientific knowledge of human nature, Allport holds, has a definite bearing on norms of action. What justifies a moral principle is not that it is approved of by a certain number of persons or that a philosopher can present arguments in its favor, but rather that it agrees with certain observed facts. This view also involves the rejection of both ethical and cultural relativity. Some values, Allport holds, are universally chosen and accord with certain prominent capacities and needs of all men. The sciences of human behavior are able to identify and investigate these capacities and needs and by so doing are able to confirm or disconfirm ethical theories.

Is Benedict's relativistic position justified? Is Allport right in thinking that the same or similar anthropological facts are capable of a nonrelativistic interpretation? Does Allport give any reason for our regarding moral principles as a type of hypothesis that is subject to being confirmed or disconfirmed? Does this interpretation of the nature of moral principles accord with the opinion of most moral philosophers? (Recall von Wright's classification of these principles in our third part.) If moral principles are viewed as prescriptions or directives, do the data of social science have any bearing on them?

Scientific method

Morris R. Cohen (1880-1947) and Ernest Nagel (b. 1901)

Born in Russia, Morris R. Cohen came to the United States as a boy. He took his doctorate in 1906 at Harvard. There he was a student of William James and Josiah Royce. He taught mathematics before joining the philosophy department at the City College of New York, where he remained until his retirement in 1938. His writings embrace many philosophic problems, but he is best known for his contributions to the philosophy of science and the philosophy of law. Among his works are Reason and Nature (1931) *and* An Introduction to Logic and Scientific Method (1934), *written with his former student, Ernest Nagel, who is professor of philosophy at Columbia University. Professor Nagel is the author of* Sovereign Reason, and Other Studies in the Philosophy of Science (1954) *and of* The Structure of Science (1961). *In the following selection from their book, Cohen and Nagel give a concise account of the most important features of scientific method.*

Facts and scientific method

The method of science does not seek to impose the desires and hopes of men upon the flux of things in a capricious manner. It may indeed be employed to satisfy the desires of men. But its successful use depends upon seeking, in a deliberate manner, and irrespective of what men's desires are, to recognize, as well as to take advantage of, the structure which the flux possesses.

1. Consequently, scientific method aims to discover what the facts truly are, and the use of the method must be guided by the discovered facts. But, as we have repeatedly

From *An Introduction to Logic and Scientific Method* by Morris R. Cohen and Ernest Nagel, copyright, 1934, by Harcourt, Brace & World, Inc.; renewed 1962 by Ernest Nagel and Leonora Cohen Rosenfield. Reprinted by permission of the publishers, Harcourt, Brace & World, Inc., and Routledge & Kegan Paul, Ltd.

pointed out, what the facts are cannot be discovered without reflection. Knowledge of the facts cannot be equated to the brute immediacy of our sensations. When our skin comes into contact with objects having high temperatures or with liquid air, the immediate experiences may be similar. We cannot, however, conclude without error that the temperatures of the substances touched are the same. Sensory experience sets the *problem* for knowledge, and just because such experience is immediate and final it must become informed by reflective analysis before knowledge can be said to take place.

2. Every inquiry arises from some felt problem, so that no inquiry can even get under way unless some selection or sifting of the subject matter has taken place. Such selection requires, we have been urging all along, some hypothesis, preconception, prejudice, which guides the research as well as delimits the subject matter of inquiry. Every inquiry is specific in the sense that it has a definite problem to solve, and such **259**

solution terminates the inquiry. It is idle to collect "facts" unless there is a problem upon which they are supposed to bear.

3. The ability to formulate problems whose solution may also help solve other problems is a rare gift, requiring extraordinary genius. The problems which meet us in daily life can be solved, if they can be solved at all, by the application of scientific method. But such problems do not, as a rule, raise far-reaching issues. The most striking applications of scientific method are to be found in the various natural and social sciences.

4. The "facts" for which every inquiry reaches out are propositions for whose truth there is considerable evidence. Consequently what the "facts" are must be determined by inquiry, and cannot be determined antecedently to inquiry. Moreover, what we believe to be the facts clearly depends upon the stage of our inquiry. There is therefore no sharp line dividing facts from guesses or hypotheses. During any inquiry the status of a proposition may change from that of hypothesis to that of fact, or from that of fact to that of hypothesis. Every so-called fact, therefore, *may* be challenged for the evidence upon which it is asserted to be a fact, even though no such challenge is actually made.

Hypotheses and scientific method

The method of science would be impossible if the hypotheses which are suggested as solutions could not be elaborated to reveal what they imply. The full meaning of a hypothesis is to be discovered in its implications.

1. Hypotheses are suggested to an inquirer by something in the subject matter under investigation, and by his previous knowledge of other subject matters. No rules can be offered for obtaining fruitful hypotheses, any more than rules can be given for discovering significant problems.

2. Hypotheses are required at every stage of an inquiry. It must not be forgotten that what are called general principles or laws (which may have been confirmed in a previous inquiry) can be applied to a present, still un-

terminated inquiry only with some risk. For they may not in fact be applicable. The general laws of any science function as hypotheses, which guide the inquiry in all its phases.

3. Hypotheses can be regarded as suggestions of possible connections between actual facts or imagined ones. The question of the truth of hypotheses need not, therefore, always be raised. The necessary feature of a hypothesis, from this point of view, is that it should be statable in a determinate form, so that its implications can be discovered by logical means.

4. The number of hypotheses which may occur to an inquirer is without limit, and is a function of the character of his imagination. There is a need, therefore, for a technique to choose between the alternative suggestions, and to make sure that the alternatives are in fact, and not only in appearance, *different* theories. Perhaps the most important and best explored part of such a technique is the technique of formal inference. For this reason, the structure of formal logic has been examined at some length. The object of that examination has been to give the reader an adequate sense of what formal validity means, as well as to provide him with a synoptic view of the power and range of formal logic.

5. It is convenient to have on hand—in storage, so to speak—different hypotheses whose consequences have been carefully explored. It is the task of mathematics to provide and explore alternative hypotheses. Mathematics receives hints concerning what hypotheses to study from the natural sciences; and the natural sciences are indebted to mathematics for suggestions concerning the type of order which their subject matter embodies.

6. The deductive elaboration of hypotheses is not the sole task of scientific method. Since there is a plurality of possible hypotheses, it is the task of inquiry to determine which of the possible explanations or solutions of the problem is in best agreement with the facts. Formal considerations are therefore never sufficient to establish the material truth of any theory.

7. No hypothesis which states a general proposition can be demonstrated as absolutely true. We have seen that all inquiry which deals

with matters of fact employs probable inference. The task of such investigations is to select that hypothesis which is the most probable on the factual evidence; and it is the task of further inquiry to find other factual evidence which will increase or decrease the probability of such a theory.

Evidence and scientific method

Scientific method pursues the road of systematic doubt. It does not doubt *all* things, for this is clearly impossible. But it does question whatever lacks adequate evidence in its support.

1. Science is not satisfied with psychological certitude, for the mere intensity with which a belief is held is no guarantee of its truth. Science demands and looks for logically adequate grounds for the propositions it advances.

2. No single proposition dealing with matters of fact is beyond every significant doubt. No proposition is so well supported by evidence that other evidence may not increase or decrease its probability. However, while no single proposition is indubitable, the body of knowledge which supports it, and of which it is itself a part, is better grounded than any alternative body of knowledge.

3. Science is thus always ready to abandon a theory when the facts so demand. But the facts must really demand it. It is not unusual for a theory to be modified so that it may be retained in substance even though "facts" contradicted an earlier formulation of it. Scientific procedure is therefore a mixture of a willingness to change, and an obstinacy in holding on to, theories apparently incompatible with facts.

4. The verification of theories is only approximate. Verification simply shows that, within the margin of experimental error, the experiment is *compatible* with the verified hypothesis.

System in the ideal of science

The ideal of science is to achieve a systematic interconnection of facts. Isolated propositions do not constitute a science. Such propositions serve merely as an opportunity to find the logical connection between them and other propositions.

1. "Common sense" is content with a miscellaneous collection of information. As a consequence, the propositions it asserts are frequently vague, the range of their application is unknown, and their mutual compatibility is generally very questionable. The advantages of discovering a system among facts is therefore obvious. A condition for achieving a system is the introduction of accuracy in the assertions made. The limit within which propositions are true is then clearly defined. Moreover, inconsistencies between propositions asserted become eliminated gradually because propositions which are part of a system must support and correct one another. The extent and accuracy of our information is thus increased. In fact, scientific method differs from other methods in the accuracy and number of facts it studies.

2. When, as frequently happens, a science abandons one theory for another, it is a mistake to suppose that science has become "bankrupt" and that it is incapable of discovering the structure of the subject matter it studies. Such changes indicate rather that the science is progressively realizing its ideal. For such changes arise from correcting previous observations or reasoning, and such correction means that we are in possession of more reliable facts.

3. The ideal of system requires that the propositions asserted to be true should be connected without the introduction of further propositions for which the evidence is small or nonexistent. In a system the number of unconnected propositions and the number of propositions for which there is no evidence are at a minimum. Consequently, in a system the requirements of simplicity, as expressed in the principle of Occam's razor, are satisfied in a high degree. For that principle declares that entities should not be multiplied beyond necessity. This may be interpreted as a demand that whatever is capable of proof should be proved. But the ideal of system requires just that.

4. The evidence for propositions which are

elements in a system accumulates more rapidly than that for isolated propositions. The evidence for a proposition may come from its own verifying instances, or from the verifying instances of *other* propositions which are connected with the first in a system. It is this systematic character of scientific theories which gives such high probabilities to the various individual propositions of a science.

The self-corrective nature of scientific method

Science does not desire to obtain conviction for its propositions in *any* manner and at *any* price. Propositions must be supported by logically acceptable evidence, which must be weighed carefully and tested by the well-known canons of necessary and probable inference. It follows that the *method* of science is more stable, and more important to men of science, than any particular result achieved by its means.

1. In virtue of its method, the enterprise of science is a self-corrective process. It appeals to no special revelation or authority whose deliverances are indubitable and final. It claims no infallibility, but relies upon the methods of developing and testing hypotheses for assured conclusions. The canons of inquiry are themselves discovered in the process of reflection, and may themselves become modified in the course of study. The method makes possible the noting and correction of errors by continued application of itself.

2. General propositions can be established only by the method of repeated sampling. Consequently, the propositions which a science puts forward for study are either confirmed in all possible experiments or modified in accordance with the evidence. It is this self-corrective nature of the method which allows us to challenge any proposition, but which also assures us that the theories which science accepts are more probable than any alternative theories. By not claiming more certainty than the evidence warrants, scientific method succeeds in obtaining more logical certainty than any other method yet devised.

3. In the process of gathering and weighing

evidence, there is a continuous appeal from facts to theories or principles, and from principles to facts. For there is nothing intrinsically indubitable, there are no absolutely first principles, in the sense of principles which are self-evident or which must be known prior to everything else.

4. The method of science is thus essentially circular. We obtain evidence for principles by appealing to empirical material, to what is alleged to be "fact"; and we select, analyze, and interpret empirical material on the basis of principles. In virtue of such give and take between facts and principles, everything that is dubitable falls under careful scrutiny at one time or another.

The abstract nature of scientific theories

No theory asserts *everything* that can possibly be asserted about a subject matter. Every theory selects certain aspects of it and excludes others. Unless it were possible to do this—either because such other aspects are irrelevant or because their influence on those selected is very minute—science as we know it would be impossible.

1. All theories involve abstraction from concrete subject matter. No rule can be given as to which aspects of a subject matter should be abstracted and so studied independently of other aspects. But in virtue of the goal of science—the achievement of a systematic interconnection of phenomena—in general those aspects will be abstracted which make a realization of this goal possible. Certain common elements in the phenomenon studied must be found, so that the endless variety of phenomena may be viewed as a system in which their structure is exhibited.

2. Because of the abstractness of theories, science often seems in patent contradiction with "common sense." In "common sense" the unique character and the pervasive character of things are not distinguished, so that the attempt by science to disclose the invariant features often gives the appearance of artificiality. Theories are then frequently regarded

as "convenient fictions" or as "unreal." However, such criticisms overlook the fact that it is just certain *selected invariant relations* of things in which science is interested, so that many familiar properties of things are necessarily neglected by the sciences. Moreover, they forget that "common sense" itself operates in terms of abstractions, which are familiar and often confused, and which are inadequate to express the complex structure of the flux of things.

Types of scientific theories

Scientific explanation consists in subsuming under some rule or law which expresses an invariant character of a group of events, the particular events it is said to explain. Laws themselves may be explained, and in the same manner, by showing that they are consequences of more comprehensive theories. The effect of such progressive explanation of events by laws, laws by wider laws or theories, is to reveal the interconnection of many apparently isolated propositions.

1. It is clear, however, that the process of explanation must come to a halt at some point. Theories which cannot be shown to be special consequences from a wider connection of facts must be left unexplained, and accepted as a part of the brute fact of existence. Material considerations, in the form of contingent matters of fact, must be recognized in at least two places. There is contingency at the level of sense: just *this* and not *that* is given in sense experience. And there is contingency at the level of explanation: a definite system, although not the only possible one from the point of view of formal logic, is found to be exemplified in the flux of things.

2. In a previous chapter we have enumerated several kinds of "laws" which frequently serve as explanations of phenomena. There is, however, another interesting distinction between theories. Some theories appeal to an easily imagined *hidden mechanism* which will explain the observable phenomena; other theories eschew all reference to such hidden mechanisms, and make use of *relations* abstracted from the phenomena actually observable. The former are called *physical* theories; the latter are called *mathematical* or *abstractive* theories.

It is important to be aware of the difference between these two kinds of theories, and to understand that some minds are especially attracted to one kind, while others are comfortable only with the other kind. But it is also essential not to suppose that either kind of theory is more fundamental or more valid than the other. In the history of science there is a constant oscillation between theories of these two types; sometimes both types of theories are used successfully on the same subject matter. Let us, however, make clear the differences between them.

The English physicist Rankine explained the distinction as follows: There are two methods of framing a theory. In a mathematical or abstractive theory, "a class of objects or phenomena is defined ... by describing ... that assemblage of properties which is common to all the objects or phenomena composing the class, as perceived by the senses, without introducing anything hypothetical." In a physical theory "a class of objects is defined ... as being constituted, in a manner not apparent to the senses, by a modification of some other class of objects or phenomena whose laws are already known." [1]

In the second kind of theory, some visualizable model is made the pattern for a mechanism hidden from the senses. Some physicists, like Kelvin, cannot be satisfied with anything less than a mechanical explanation of observable phenomena, no matter how complex such a mechanism may be. Examples of this kind of theory are the atomic theory of chemistry, the kinetic theory of matter as developed in thermodynamics and the behavior of gases, the theory of the gene in studies on heredity, the theory of lines of force in electrostatics, and the recent Bohr model of the atom in spectroscopy.

In the mathematical type of theory, the appeal to hidden mechanisms is eliminated, or at

[1] W. J. M. Rankine, *Miscellaneous Scientific Papers*, 1881, p. 210.

any rate is at a minimum. How this may be done is graphically described by Henri Poincaré: "Suppose we have before us any machine; the initial wheel work and the final wheel work alone are visible, but the transmission, the intermediary machinery by which the movement is communicated from one to the other, is hidden in the interior and escapes our view; we do not know whether the communication is made by gearing or by belts, by connecting-rods or by other contrivances. Do we say that it is impossible for us to understand anything about this machine so long as we are not permitted to take it to pieces? You know well we do not, and that the principle of the conservation of energy suffices to determine for us the most interesting point. We easily ascertain that the final wheel turns ten times less quickly than the initial wheel, since these two wheels are visible; we are able thence to conclude that a couple applied to the one will be balanced by a couple ten times greater applied to the other. For that there is no need to penetrate the mechanism of this equilibrium and to know how the forces compensate each other in the interior of the machine." Examples of such theories are the theory of gravitation, Galileo's laws of falling bodies, the theory of the flow of heat, the theory of organic evolution, and the theory of relativity.

As we suggested, it is useless to quarrel as to which type of theory is the more fundamental and which type should be universally adopted. Both kinds of theories have been successful in coördinating vast domains of phenomena, and fertile in making discoveries of the most important kind. At some periods in the history of a science, there is a tendency to mechanical models and atomicity; at others, to general principles connecting characteristics abstracted from directly observable phenomena; at still others, to a fusion or synthesis of these two points of view. Some scientists, like Kelvin, Faraday, Lodge, Maxwell, show an exclusive preference for "model" theories; other scientists, like Rankine, Ostwald, Duhem, can work best with the abstractive theories; and still others, like Einstein, have the unusual gift of being equally at home with both kinds.

The acceptance of scientific theories

Philipp G. Frank (b. 1884)

Philipp Frank was born in Vienna and received the Ph.D. from the University of Vienna in 1907. He was professor of theoretical physics in the University of Prague, Czechoslovakia, from 1912 to 1938. After coming to the United States, he taught at Harvard, retiring in 1958.

Frank's study of physics led him to an interest in the philosophy of science. His writings include The Law of Causality and Its Limitations *(1932),* Interpretations and Misinterpretations of Modern Physics *(1938),* Modern Science and Its Philosophy *(1949), and* Philosophy of Science *(1957). In the following paper Frank challenges the commonly held belief that scientific theories are accepted for "purely scientific" reasons. He considers the variety of reasons men have, including religious beliefs and social values, for accepting a scientific theory and contends that these reasons are not to be ignored.*

Among scientists it is taken for granted that a theory "should be" accepted if and only if it is "true"; to be true means in this context to be in agreement with the observable facts that can be logically derived from the theory. Every influence of moral, religious, or political considerations upon the acceptance of a theory is regarded as "illegitimate" by the so-called "community of scientists." This view certainly has had a highly salutary effect upon the evolution of science as a human activity. It tells the truth—but not the whole truth. It has never happened that all the conclusions drawn from a theory have agreed with the observable

From Philipp G. Frank, "The Variety of Reasons for the Acceptance of Scientific Theories," *Scientific Monthly,* September, 1954, pp. 139–145. Copyright, 1954, by American Association for the Advancement of Science. Reprinted from *Scientific Monthly* by permission.

facts. The scientific community has accepted theories only when a vast number of facts has been derived from few and simple principles. A familiar example is the derivation of the immensely complex motions of celestial bodies from the simple Newtonian formula of gravitation, or the large variety of electromagnetic phenomena from Maxwell's field equations.

If we restrict our attention to the two criterions that are called "agreement with observations" and "simplicity," we remain completely within the domain of activities that are cultivated and approved by the community of scientists. But, if we have to choose a certain theory for acceptance, we do not know what respective weight should be attributed to these two criterions. There is obviously no theory that agrees with *all* observations and no theory that has "perfect" simplicity. Therefore, in every individual case, one has to make a choice **265** of a theory by a compromise between both criterions. However, when we try to specify the degree of "simplicity" in different theories, we soon notice that attempts of this kind lead us far beyond the limits of physical science. Everybody would agree that a linear function is simpler than a function of the second or higher degree; everybody would also admit that a circle is simpler than an ellipse. For this reason, physics is filled with laws that express proportionality, such as Hooke's law in elasticity or Ohm's law in electrodynamics. In all these cases, there is no doubt that a nonlinear relationship would describe the facts in a more accurate way, but one tries to get along with a linear law as much as possible.

There was a time when, in physics, laws that could be expressed without using differential calculus were preferred, and in the long struggle between the corpuscular and the wave theories of light, the argument was rife that the corpuscular theory was mathematically simpler, while the wave theory required the solution of boundary problems of partial differential equations, a highly complex matter. We note that even a purely mathematical estimation of simplicity depends upon the state of culture of a certain period. People who have grown up in a mathematical atmosphere—that is, saturated with ideas about invariants—will find that Einstein's theory of gravitation is of incredible beauty and simplicity; but to people for whom ordinary calculus is the center of interest, Einstein's theory will be of immense complexity, and this low degree of simplicity will not be compensated by a great number of observed facts.

However, the situation becomes much more complex, if we mean by *simplicity* not only simplicity of the mathematical scheme but also simplicity of the whole discourse by which the theory is formulated. We may start from the most familiar instance, the decision between the Copernican (heliocentric) and the Ptolemaic (geocentric) theories. Both parties, the Roman Church and the followers of Copernicus, agreed that Copernicus' system, from the purely mathematical angle, was simpler than Ptolemy's. In the first one, the orbits of planets

were plotted as a system of concentric circles with the sun as center, whereas in the geocentric system, the planetary orbits were sequences of loops. The observed facts covered by these systems were approximately the same ones. The criterions of acceptance that are applied in the community of scientists today are, according to the usual way of speaking, in agreement with observed facts and mathematical simplicity. According to them, the Copernican system had to be accepted unhesitatingly. Since this acceptance did not happen before a long period of doubt, we see clearly that the criterions "agreement with observed facts" and "mathematical simplicity" were not the only criterions that were considered as reasons for the acceptance of a theory.

As a matter of fact, there were three types of reasons against the acceptance of the Copernican theory that remained unchallenged at the time when all "scientific" reasons were in favor of that theory. First, there was the incompatibility of the Copernican system with the traditional interpretation of the Bible. Second, there was the disagreement between the Copernican system and the prevailing philosophy of that period, the philosophy of Aristotle as it was interpreted by the Catholic schoolmen. Third, there was the objection that the mobility of the earth, as a real physical fact, is incompatible with the common-sense interpretation of nature. Let us consider these three types of reasons more closely. In the Book of Joshua this leader prays to God to stop the sun in its motion in order to prolong the day and to enable the people of Israel to win a decisive victory. God indeed "stopped the sun." If interpreted verbally, according to the usage of words in our daily language, this means that the sun is moving, in flagrant contradiction with the Copernican theory. One could, of course, give a more sophisticated interpretation and say that "God stopped the sun" means that he stopped it in its motion relative to the earth. This is no longer contradictory to the Copernican system. But now the question arises: Should we adopt a simple mathematical description and a complicated, rather "unnatural" interpretation of the Bible or a more complicated mathematical description (motion in loops) and a simple "natural" interpretation of the biblical text? The decision certainly cannot be achieved by any argument taken from physical science.

If one believes that all questions raised by science must be solved by the "methods" of this special science, one must say: Every astronomer who lived in the period between Copernicus and Galileo was "free" to accept either the Copernican or the Ptolemaic doctrine; he could make an "arbitrary" decision. However, the situation is quite different if one takes into consideration that physical science is only a part of science in general. Building up astronomical theories is a particular act of human behavior. If we consider human behavior in general, we look at physical science as a part of a much more general endeavor that embraces also psychology and sociology. It is called by some authors "behavioristics." From this more general angle, the effect of a simplification in the mathematical formula and the simplification in biblical interpretation are quite comparable with each other. There is meaning in asking by which act the happiness of human individuals and groups is more favorably influenced. This means that, from the viewpoint of a general science of human behavior, the decision between the Copernican and Ptolemaic systems was never a matter of arbitrary decision.

The compatibility of a physical theory with a certain interpretation of the Bible is a special case of a much more general criterion: the compatibility of a physical theory with theories that have been advanced to account for observable phenomena outside the domain of physical science. The most important reason for the acceptance of a theory beyond the "scientific criterions" in the narrower sense (agreement with observation and simplicity of the mathematical pattern) is the fitness of a theory to be generalized, to be the basis of a new theory that does not logically follow from the original one, and to allow prediction of more observable facts. This property is often called the "dynamical" character or the "fertility" of a theory. In this sense, the Copernican theory is much superior to the geocentric one.

Newtonian laws of motion have a simple form only if the sun is taken as a system of reference and not the earth. But the decision in favor of the Copernican theory on this basis could be made only when Newton's laws came into existence. This act requires, however, creative imagination or, to speak more flippantly, a happy guessing that leads far beyond the Copernican and Ptolemaic systems.

However, long before the "dynamical" character of the Copernican system was recognized, the objection was raised that the system was incompatible with "the general laws of motion" that could be derived from principles regarded as "immediately intelligible" or, in other words, "self-evident" without physical experiment or observations. From such "self-evident" principles there followed, for example, the physical law that only celestial bodies (like sun or moon) moved "naturally" in circular orbits, while terrestrial bodies (like our earth) moved naturally along straight lines as a falling stone does. Copernicus' theory of a "motion of the earth in a circular orbit" was, therefore, incompatible with "self-evident" laws of nature.

Medieval scientists were faced with the alternatives: Should they accept the Copernican theory with its simple mathematical formulas and drop the self-evident laws of motion, or should they accept the complicated mathematics of the Ptolemaic system along with the intelligible and self-evident general laws of motion. Acceptance of Copernicus' theory would imply dropping the laws of motion that had been regarded as self-evident and looking for radically new laws. This would also mean dropping the contention that a physical law can be derived from "intelligible" principles. Again, from the viewpoint of physical science, this decision cannot be made. Although an arbitrary decision may seem to be required, if one looks at the situation from the viewpoint of human behavior it is clear that the decision, by which the derivation of physical laws from self-evident principles is abandoned, would alter the situation of man in the world fundamentally. For example, an important argument for the existence of spiritual beings would lose its validity. Thus, social science had to decide whether the life of man would become happier or unhappier by the acceptance of the Copernican system.

The objections to this system, on the basis of self-evident principles, have also been formulated in a way that looks quite different but may eventually, when the chips are down, not be so very different. Francis Bacon, the most conspicuous adversary of Aristotelianism in the period of Galileo, fought the acceptance of the Copernican theory on the basis of common-sense experience. He took it for granted that the principles of science should be as analogous as possible to the experience of our daily life. Then, the principles could be presented in the language that has been shaped for the purpose of describing, in the most convenient way, the experience of our daily existence—the language that everyone has learned as a child and that is called "common-sense language." From this daily experience, we have learned that the behavior of the sun and the planets is very different from that of the earth. While the earth does not emit any light, the sun and the planets are brilliant; while every earthly object that becomes separated from the main body will tend to fall back toward the center and stop there, the celestial objects undergo circular motion eternally around the center.

To separate the sun from the company of the planets and put the earth among these brilliant and mobile creatures, as Copernicus suggested, would have been not only unnatural but a serious violation of the rule to keep the principles of science as close to common sense as possible. We see by this example that one of the reasons for the acceptance of a theory has frequently been the compatibility of this theory with daily life experience or, in other words, the possibility of expressing the theory in common-sense language. Here is, of course, the source of another conflict between the "scientific" reasons for the acceptance of a theory and other requirements that are not "scientific" in the narrower sense. Francis Bacon rejected the Copernican system because it was not compatible with common sense.

In the eighteenth and nineteenth centuries, Newton's mechanics not only had become compatible with common sense but had even been identified with common-sense judgment. As a result, in twentieth century physics, the theory of relativity and the quantum theory were regarded by many as incompatible with common sense. These theories were regarded as "absurd" or, at least, "unnatural." Lenard in Germany, Bouasse in France, O'Rahilly in Ireland, and Timiryaseff in Russia rejected the theory of relativity, as Francis Bacon had rejected the Copernican system. Looking at the historical record, we notice that the requirement of compatibility with common sense and the rejection of "unnatural theories" have been advocated with a highly emotional undertone, and it is reasonable to raise the question: What was the source of heat in those fights against new and absurd theories? Surveying these battles, we easily find one common feature, the apprehension that a disagreement with common sense may deprive scientific theories of their value as incentives for a desirable human behavior. In other words, by becoming incompatible with common sense, scientific theories lose their fitness to support desirable attitudes in the domain of ethics, politics, and religion.

Examples are abundant from all periods of theory-building. According to an old theory that was prevalent in ancient Greece and was accepted by such men as Plato and Aristotle, the sun, planets, and other celestial bodies were made of a material that was completely different from the material of which our earth consists. The great gap between the celestial and the terrestrial bodies was regarded as required by our common-sense experience. There were men—for example, the followers of Epicurus—who rejected this view and assumed that all bodies in the universe, earth and stars, consist of the same material. Nevertheless, many educators and political leaders were afraid that denial of the exceptional status of the celestial bodies in physical science would make it more difficult to teach the belief in the existence of spiritual beings as distinct from material bodies; and since it was their general conviction that the belief in spiritual beings is a powerful instrument to bring about a desirable conduct among citizens, a physical theory that supported this belief seemed to be highly desirable.

Plato, in his famous book *Laws*, suggested that people in his ideal state who taught the "materialistic" doctrine about the constitution of sun and stars should be jailed. He even suggested that people who knew about teachers of that theory and did not report them to the authorities should also be jailed. We learn from this ancient example how scientific theories have served as instruments of indoctrination. Obviously, fitness to support a desirable conduct of citizens or, briefly, to support moral behavior, has served through the ages as a reason for acceptance of a theory. When the "scientific criterions" did not uniquely determine a theory, its fitness to support moral or political indoctrination became an important factor for its acceptance. It is important to learn that the interpretation of a scientific theory as a support of moral rules is not a rare case but has played a role in all periods of history.

This role probably can be traced back to a fact that is well known to modern students of anthropology and sociology. The conduct of man has always been shaped according to the example of an ideal society; on the other hand, this ideal has been represented by the "behavior" of the universe, which is, in turn, determined by the laws of nature, in particular, by the physical laws. In this sense, the physical laws have always been interpreted as examples for the conduct of man or, briefly speaking, as moral laws. Ralph Waldo Emerson wrote in his essay *Nature* that "the laws of physics are also the laws of ethics." He used as an example the law of the lever, according to which "the smallest weight may be made to lift the greatest, the difference of weight being compensated by time."

We see the connection of the laws of desirable human conduct with the physical laws of the universe when we glance at the Book of Genesis. The first chapter presents a physical theory about the creation of the world. But the story of the creation serves also as an example for the moral behavior of men; for instance, because the creation took 7 days, we all

feel obliged to rest on each seventh day. Perhaps the history of the Great Flood is even more instructive. When the Flood abated, God established a Covenant with the human race: "Never again shall all flesh be cut off by the waters of a flood; neither shall there any more be a flood to destroy the earth." As a sign of the Covenant the rainbow appeared: "When I bring clouds over the earth and the bow is seen in the clouds, I will remember the Covenant which is between me and you, and the waters shall never again become a flood to destroy all flesh." If we read the biblical text carefully, we understand that what God actually pledged was to maintain, without exception, the validity of the physical laws or, in other words, of the causal law. God pledged: "While the earth remains, seedtime and harvest, cold and heat, summer and winter, day and night shall not cease."

All the physical laws, including the law of causality, were given to mankind as a reward for moral behavior and can be canceled if mankind does not behave well. So even the belief in the validity of causal laws in the physical world has supported the belief in God as the supreme moral authority who would punish every departure from moral behavior by abolishing causality. We have seen that Epicurean physics and Copernican astronomy were rejected on moral grounds. We know that Newton's physics was accepted as supporting the belief in a God who was an extremely able engineer and who created the world as a machine that performed its motions according to his plans. Even the generalization of Newtonian science that was advanced by 18th century materialism claimed to serve as a support for the moral behavior of man. In his famous book *Man a Machine*, which has often been called an "infamous book," La Mettrie stresses the point that by regarding men, animals, and planets as beings of the same kind, man is taught to regard them all as his brothers and to treat them kindly.

It would be a great mistake to believe that this situation has changed in the nineteenth and twentieth centuries. A great many authors have rejected the biological theory that organisms have arisen from inanimate matter (spontaneous generation), because such a theory would weaken the belief in the dignity of man and in the existence of a soul and would, therefore, be harmful to moral conduct. In twentieth century physics, we have observed that Einstein's theory of relativity has been interpreted as advocating an "idealistic" philosophy, which, in turn, would be useful as a support of moral conduct. Similarly, the quantum theory is interpreted as supporting a weakening of mechanical determinism and, along with it, the introduction of "indeterminism" into physics. In turn, a great many educators, theologians, and politicians have enthusiastically acclaimed this "new physics" as providing a strong argument for the acceptance of "indeterminism" as a basic principle of science.

The special mechanism by which social powers bring about a tendency to accept or reject a certain theory depends upon the structure of the society within which the scientist operates. It may vary from a mild influence on the scientist by friendly reviews in political or educational dailies to promotion of his book as a best seller, to ostracism as an author and as a person, to loss of his job, or, under some social circumstances, even to imprisonment, torture, and execution. The honest scientist who works hard in his laboratory or computation-room would obviously be inclined to say that all this is nonsense—that his energy should be directed toward finding out whether, say, a certain theory is "true" and that he "should not" pay any attention to the fitness of a theory to serve as an instrument in the fight for educational or political goals. This is certainly the way in which the situation presents itself to most active scientists. However, scientists are also human beings and are definitely inclined toward some moral, religious, or political creed. Those who deny emphatically that there is any connection between scientific theories and religious or political creeds believe in these creeds on the basis of indoctrination that has been provided by organizations such as churches or political parties. This attitude leads to the conception of a

"double truth" that is not only logically confusing but morally dangerous. It can lead to the practice of serving God on Sunday and the devil on weekdays.

The conviction that science is independent of all moral and political influences arises when we regard science either as a collection of facts or as a picture of objective reality. But today, everyone who has attentively studied the logic of science will know that science actually is an instrument that serves the purpose of connecting present events with future events and deliberately utilizes this knowledge to shape future physical events as they are desired. This instrument consists of a system of propositions —principles—and the operational definitions of their terms. These propositions certainly cannot be derived from the facts of our experience and are not uniquely determined by these facts. Rather they are hypotheses from which the facts can be logically derived. If the principles or hypotheses are not determined by the physical facts, by what are they determined? We have learned by now that, besides the agreement with observed facts, there are other reasons for the acceptance of a theory: simplicity, agreement with common sense, fitness for supporting a desirable human conduct, and so forth. All these factors participate in the making of a scientific theory. We remember, however, that according to the opinion of the majority of active scientists, these extrascientific factors "should not" have any influence on the acceptance of a scientific theory. But who has claimed and who can claim that they "should not"?

This firm conviction of the scientists comes from the philosophy that they have absorbed since their early childhood. The theories that are built up by "scientific" methods, in the narrower sense, are "pictures" of physical reality. Presumably they tell us the "truth" about the world. If a theory built up exclusively on the ground of its agreement with observable facts tells the "truth" about the world, it would be nonsense to assume seriously that a scientific theory can be influenced by moral or political reasons. However, we learned that "agreement with observed facts" does not single out one individual theory. We never have one theory that is in full agreement but several theories that are in partial agreement, and we have to determine the final theory by a compromise. The final theory has to be in fair agreement with observations and also has to be sufficiently simple to be usable. If we consider this point, it is obvious that such a theory cannot be "the truth." In modern science, a theory is regarded as an instrument that serves toward some definite purpose. It has to be helpful in predicting future observable facts on the basis of facts that have been observed in the past and the present. It should also be helpful in the construction of machines and devices that can save us time and labor. A scientific theory is, in a sense, a tool that produces other tools according to a practical scheme.

In the same way that we enjoy the beauty and elegance of an airplane, we also enjoy the "elegance" of the theory that makes the construction of the plane possible. In speaking about any actual machine, it is meaningless to ask whether the machine is "true" in the sense of its being "perfect." We can ask only whether it is "good" or sufficiently "perfect" for a certain purpose. If we require speed as our purpose, the "perfect" airplane will differ from one that is "perfect" for the purpose of endurance. The result will be different again if we choose safety, or fun, or convenience for reading and sleeping as our purpose. It is impossible to design an airplane that fulfills all these purposes in a maximal way. We have to make some compromises. But then, there is the question: Which is more important, speed or safety, or fun or endurance? These questions cannot be answered by any agreement taken from physical science. From the viewpoint of "science proper" the purpose is abitrary, and science can teach us only how to construct a plane that will achieve a specified speed with a specified degree of safety. There will be a debate, according to moral, political, and even religious lines, by which it will be determined how to produce the compromise. The policymaking authorities are, from the logical viewpoint, "free" to make their choice of which

type of plane should be put into production. However, if we look at the situation from the viewpoint of a unified science that includes both physical and social science, we shall understand how the compromise between speed and safety, between fun and endurance is determined by the social conditions that produce the conditioned reflexes of the policymakers. The conditioning may be achieved, for example, by letters written to congressmen. As a matter of fact, the building of a scientific theory is not essentially different from the building of an airplane.

If we look for an answer to the question of whether a certain theory, say the Copernican system or the theory of relativity, is perfect or true, we have to ask the preliminary questions: What purpose is the theory to serve? Is it only the purely technical purpose of predicting observable facts? Or is it to obtain a simple and elegant theory that allows us to derive a great many facts from simple principles? We choose the theory acccording to our purpose. For some groups, the main purpose of a theory may be to serve as a support in teaching a desirable way of life or to discourage an undesirable way of life. Then, we would prefer theories that give a rather clumsy picture of observed facts, provided that we can get from the theory a broad view of the universe in which man plays the role that we desire to give him. If we wish to speak in a more brief and general way, we may distinguish just two purposes of a theory: the usage for the construction of devices (technological purpose) and the usage for guiding human conduct (sociological purpose).

The actual acceptance of theories by man has always been a compromise between the technological and the sociological usage of science. Human conduct has been influenced directly by the latter, by supporting specific religious or political creeds, while the technological influence has been rather indirect. Technological changes have to produce social changes that manifest themselves in changing human conduct. Everybody knows of the Industrial Revolution of the nineteenth century and the accompanying changes in human life from a rural into an urban pattern. Probably the rise of atomic power will produce analogous changes in man's way of life.

The conflict between the technological and the sociological aims of science is the central factor in the history of science as a human enterprise. If thoroughly investigated, it will throw light upon a factor that some thinkers, Marxist as well as religious thinkers, regard as responsible for the social crisis of our time: the backwardness of social progress compared with technological progress. To cure this illness of our time, an English bishop recommended, some years ago, the establishment of a "truce" in the advancement in technology, in order to give social progress some time to keep up with technological advancement. We have seen examples of this conflict in Plato's indictment of astrophysical theories that could be used as a support of "materialism." We note the same purpose in the fight against the Copernican system and, in our own century, against the Darwinian theory of evolution, against Mendel's laws of heredity, and so forth.

A great many scientists and educators believe that such a conflict no longer exists in our time, because now it is completely resolved by "the scientific method," which theory is the only valid one. This opinion is certainly wrong if we consider theories of high generality. In twentieth century physics, we note clearly that a formulation of the general principles of subatomic physics (quantum theory) is accepted or rejected according to whether we believe that introduction of "indeterminism" into physics gives comfort to desirable ethical postulates or not. Some educators and politicians have been firmly convinced that the belief in "free will" is necessary for ethics and that "free will" is not compatible with Newtonian physics but is compatible with quantum physics. The situation in biology is similar. If we consider the attitude of biologists toward the question whether living organisms have developed from inanimate matter, we shall find that the conflict between the technological and the sociological purposes of theories is in full bloom. Some prominent biologists say that the existence of "spontaneous generation" is highly probable, while others of equal prominence claim that it is highly improbable. If we investigate the reasons for these conflicting attitudes, we shall easily discover that, for one group of scientists, a theory that claims the origin of man not merely from the "apes" but also from "dead matter" undermines their belief in the dignity of man, which is the indispensable basis of all human morality. We should note in turn that, for another group, desirable human behavior is based on the belief that there is a unity in nature that embraces all things.

In truth, many scientists would say that scientific theories "should" be based only on purely scientific grounds. But, exactly speaking, what does the word *should* mean in this context? With all the preceding arguments it can mean only: If we consider exclusively the technological purpose of scientific theories, we could exclude all criterions such as agreement with common sense or fitness for supporting desirable conduct. But even if we have firmly decided to do away with all "nonsense," there still remains the criterion of "simplicity," which is necessary for technological purposes and also contains, as we learned previously, a certain sociological judgment. Here, restriction to the purely technological purpose does not actually lead unambiguously to a scientific theory. The only way to include theory-building in the general science of human behavior is to refrain from ordering around scientists by telling them what they "should" do and to find how each special purpose can be achieved by a theory. Only in this way can science as a human activity be "scientifically" understood and the gap between the scientific and the humanistic aspect be bridged.

Evolution and human responsibility

George Gaylord Simpson (b. 1902)

G. G. Simpson is a distinguished vertebrate paleontologist and one of the world's foremost authorities on biological evolution. He was born in Chicago and educated at the University of Colorado and Yale University. From 1924 until 1958 he served in a number of capacities on the staff of the American Museum of Natural History in New York City. He has been chairman of the museum's department of geology and paleontology and professor of vertebrate paleontology at Columbia University. Since 1959 he has been Agassiz Professor of Vertebrate Paleontology at Harvard's Museum of Comparative Zoology.

Simpson has published numerous papers and books in his special field, including Horses *(1951). Our selection is taken from his book,* The Meaning of Evolution *(1949), widely regarded as one of the most authoritative works of its kind. Drawing on his knowledge of man's biological capacities, Simpson proposes ethical principles that he regards as suited to a being who has also the capacity for knowledge and responsibility.*

The meaning that we are seeking in evolution is its meaning to us, to man. The ethics of evolution must be human ethics. It is one of the many unique qualities of man, the new sort of animal, that he is the only ethical animal. The ethical need and its fulfillment are also products of evolution, but they have been produced in man alone.

Man's knowledge that he exists is, at the least, more conscious and particular than that of any other animal. Man alone knows that he has evolved and is still doing so. Man alone places himself in a conceptual framework of space and time. Man possesses purpose and ex-

ercises deliberate choice to a unique degree, even if, indeed, these capacities can be said to be the same in kind in any other animals. It is most improbable that any other animal has more than an inchoate or largely instinctual sense of values, while in man this is normally conscious, orderly, and controlled. (This does not contradict the fact that, even in man, the *origin* of his valuations is in considerable part unconscious and may be quite uncontrolled.)

Conscious knowledge, purpose, choice, and values carry as an inevitable corollary responsibility. Capacity for knowledge involves responsibility for finding out the truth and, in our social system, for communicating this. The possibility of choice brings an ethical responsibility for selection of what is right. The sense of values implies means and responsibility for

From George Gaylord Simpson, *The Meaning of Evolution*, Ch. 19. Copyright, 1949, by Yale University Press. Used by permission.

decision as to what is right. Purpose confers the power and, again, the responsibility for translating choice and value into right action. These capacities and responsibilities are not qualities of life in general or of its evolution, but specifically of man. Man is much the most knowing or thinking animal, as our predecessors rightly recognized in bestowing on him the distinctive qualification of *sapiens*. Man is also the responsible animal. This is more basic than his knowledge, although dependent on it, for some other animals surely know and think in a way not completely inhuman, but no other animal can truly be said to be responsible in anything like the same sense in which man is responsible.

The search for an absolute ethic, either intuitive or naturalistic, has been a failure. Survival, harmony, increase of life, integration of organic or social aggregations, or other such suggested ethical standards are characteristics which may be present in varying degrees, or absent, in organic evolution but they are not really ethical principles independent and absolute. They become ethical principles only if man chooses to make them such. Man cannot evade the responsibility of the choice. As his knowledge embraces facts about these characteristics in evolution, they become part of the basis on which his ethical principles should be developed, but they supply no automatic guide to good and bad.

Man has risen, not fallen. He can choose to develop his capacities as the highest animal and to try to rise still farther, or he can choose otherwise. The choice is his responsibility, and his alone. There is no automatism that will carry him upward without choice or effort and there is no trend solely in the right direction. Evolution has no purpose; man must supply this for himself. The means to gaining right ends involve both organic evolution and human evolution, but human choice as to what *are* the right ends must be based on human evolution. It is futile to search for an absolute ethical criterion retroactively in what occurred before ethics themselves evolved. The best human ethical standard must be relative and particular to man and is to be sought rather in the new evolution, peculiar to man, than in the old, universal to all organisms. The old evolution was and is essentially amoral. The new evolution involves knowledge, including the knowledge of good and evil.

The most essential material factor in the new evolution seems to be just this: knowledge, together, necessarily, with its spread and inheritance. As a first proposition of evolutionary ethics derived from specifically human evolution, it is submitted that promotion of knowledge is essentially good. This is a basic material ethic. "Promotion" involves both the acquisition of new truths or of closer approximations to truth (metaphorically the mutations of the new evolution) and also its spread by communication to others and by their acceptance and learning of it (metaphorically its heredity). This ethic of knowledge is not complete and independent. In itself knowledge is necessarily good, but it is effective only to the degree that it does spread in a population, and its results may then be turned by human choice and responsible action for either good or evil.

These considerations suggest some notice of the mechanisms for acquiring knowledge, of values in knowledge, and of its right and wrong utilization—subjects obviously too vast for adequate discussion here and yet too important to be passed over in total silence. Knowledge is of many sorts and is to be sought in no one way. Perception of tenderness and of security acquired at the mother's breast is as truly knowledge as is determination of the fabric of an alloy acquired at the electron microscope. Science is, however, our most successful and systematic means of acquiring knowledge and, at present, almost alone in the power to acquire knowledge wholly new to man. It used to be usual to claim that value judgments have no part in science, but we are coming more and more to perceive how false this was. Science is essentially interwoven with such judgments. The very existence of science demands the value judgment and essential ethic that knowledge is good. The additional and still more fundamental ethic of responsibility makes scientists individually responsible for evaluating the knowledge that they acquire, for transmitting it as may be right, and for its ultimate utilization for good.

A broad classification of the sciences into physical, biological, and social corresponds with three levels of organization of matter and energy, and not levels only, but also quite distinct kinds of organization. The three are of sharply increasing orders of complexity and each includes the lower grades. Vital organization is more intricate than physical organization and it is added to and does not replace physical organization, which is also fully involved in vital organization. Social organization retains and sums the complexities of both of these and adds its own still greater complexities.

Many of the dangers and ethical problems of science arise from these relationships. At one end, the universal basis of scientific knowledge is in the physical sciences, and they can produce most far-reaching results, for good or evil. The physical sciences are much the simplest of the three groups. Discoveries here are made more readily and more rapidly, so that advances of knowledge in this field are accelerated. But the physical sciences, which for these reasons need for their guidance the most rigid and continuous application of ethical standards, are farthest removed from the source of those standards and the means of their application. At the other end, this source and these means lie in the social sciences, but they are by far the most difficult and intricate. Their discoveries demand much more travail and are slower to be reached, far slower to be disseminated and utilized. Their ethical guidance is no less important than that of the physical sciences, but they have the added complication that they are themselves the lumber room of ethics, crowded with old, conflicting, and certainly partly false ethical systems and the battleground of these. To mention only one dilemma arising from this situation, the physical sciences have put man in possession of the awful secret of atomic energy before the social sciences have produced any means of controlling this or of securing its ethical application. The inequity of knowledge is in itself unethical and is one of man's great blunders. It could be his last.

The possibilities of wrong in the unequal development or in the results of the spread of knowledge reveal the need for another ethic, one that may be more profound or, at least, that shall have a moral rather than a mainly material basis. A second essential feature arising from the unique status of man in the history of life was seen to be his possession of personal responsibility. It is now submitted that the highest and most essential moral ethical standards are involved in the fact of man's personal responsibility.

This responsibility is not in itself an ethic. It is a fact, a fundamental and peculiar characteristic of the human species established by his evolution and evident in his relationship to the rest of the cosmos. Recognition of this responsibility and its proper exercise are the firm basis on which right and moral human action must be based. From it arises a pervasive ethic which, among other things, may ensure the right interpretation and action of the ethic of knowledge. Human responsibility requires, in each individual as well as in society as a whole, that the search for knowledge be a search for truth, as unbiased as is possible to human beings; that probable truths as discovered be tested by every means that can be devised, that these truths be communicated in such a way as is most likely to ensure their right utilization and incorporation into the general body of human knowledge, and that those who should receive this knowledge seek it, share in its communication, and in their turn examine and test with as little prejudice as possible whatever is submitted as truth. This is a large order, indeed, but a necessary one. It involves responsibilities for every living person, and responsibilities that cannot be ethically evaded; that is, their evasion is morally wrong. Among other consequences of this morality, it follows that blind faith (simple acceptance without review of evidence or rational choice between alternatives) is immoral. Such faith is immoral whether it is placed in a theological doctrine, a political platform, or a scientific theory.

Of course this does not mean that every individual must become a theologian before it is moral for him to join a church, a political economist before it is moral to vote, or a research biologist before it is moral to believe in evolution. The field of knowledge is obviously far too vast, and human mentality far too limited, for each of us to grasp all these intricacies. It is a social requirement that there be specialists in each field whose profession it is to examine and to test such truths as pertain to it. It is the moral duty of these specialists to submit their qualifications, the results of their judgment, and such general evidence for it as is essential for its substantiation. When such judgments conflict, as they often do on a given point, the moral duty of the nonspecialist is to choose the judgments of that authority whose qualifications are greatest in the pertinent field and whose submitted evidence is best. The individual remains personally responsible for making the choice, even if he must do so on the basis of the knowledge of others and not his personal knowledge.

Neither this nor any other process can rigidly guarantee making the right choice. It is not to be taken as an appeal to authority in the sense of belief in the absolute validity of any one opinion or of infallibility in science or in religion. The important point is responsibility for using the right *method* of choice. The right method is evaluation of evidence and avoidance of pure intuition and of authoritarian dogma. Recourse to authority, in this context, demands judgment that the accepted opinion is based on rational consideration of known evidence. It is the rejection of revelation or of emotional reaction when knowledge is available. It further rejects the absolute nature of any authority. Choice must be prepared to change if increase in knowledge or its better interpretation occurs.

Beyond its relationship to the ethic of knowledge, the fact of responsibility has still broader ethical bearings. The responsibility is basically personal and becomes social only as it is extended in society among the individuals composing the social unit. It is correlated with another human evolutionary characteristic, that of high individualization. From this relationship arises the ethical judgment that it is good, right, and moral to recognize the integrity and dignity of the individual and to promote the realization or fulfillment of individual capacities. It is bad, wrong, and immoral to fail in such recognition or to impede such fulfillment. This ethic applies first of all to the individual himself and to the integration and development of his own personality. It extends farther to his social group and to all mankind. Negatively, it is wrong to develop one individual at the expense of any other. Positively, it is right to develop all in the greatest degree possible to each within the group as a whole. Individuals vary greatly in other capacities, but integrity and dignity are capable of equal development in all.

Socialization and individualization may conflict, but they may also work together for the advancement of each. Here again choice is possible, and not only a possibility but also an unavoidable responsibility. Individual integration and welfare can be secured at the expense of others, but they may also be achieved, and reach their highest degree, by interaction which promotes others along with the self. Under this system of ethical standards a definition of the good society might indeed be simply that it is a society in which this interaction is usual.

An individual in society leads no existence wholly apart from that society, any more than the most solitary individual of any species of organisms can exist without reference to its environment. The social group is part of the human environment, a largely self-constructed part. It is the medium in which the individual exists and it is one of the molding, evolutionary influences on the individual. The abstraction of a human individual not so molded and influenced is completely unreal. Flexibility in reaction to the environment, especially including the social environment, is a major characteristic of the human species and is the essence of human individualization. A human organism that developed outside of such a framework, if this were possible, would certainly be far less individualized than one developed within it. Human personality and accompanying individualization, with all its amazing variety, depend on interaction with the environment to a far greater degree than does the lesser individualization of any other organisms. The sorts of human society that we call civilized all demand and are based on a rather high minimum of variability and of individualization in its members, a minimum far above that reached by any nonhuman species. In turn, such a society provides the possibility of degrees of individualization far greater than could ever be achieved outside it. In biological terms, it provides a variety of ecological niches much greater than those of primitive tribal society and tremendously greater than those available to any other species of organisms. The niches are filled by individual adjustability to larger extent than by genetic adjustment.

The apparent conflict of socialization and individualization thus does not really exist, and suggestion of choice between one or the other presents unreal alternatives. Individualization is a means of socialization and socialization provides enriched opportunities for individualization.

Another equally false set of alternatives is presented by any contrasting of collective action or security with personal responsibility. The collective aspects of the state are, or ethically should be, achieved by means of personal responsibility in all its members. Collective social measures, including provision for the underprivileged, are, or ethically should be, undertaken to prevent unethical development of some individuals at the expense of others and to promote the ethical equal development of all to the extent of their capacities. Such measures should not, and in the nature of things cannot, replace or eliminate personal responsibility but on the contrary require this and guarantee it, if they are both ethical and effective.

Collective action to promote individual development and to prevent exploitation is evidently required in an ethically good society, but its results can also be ethically bad. It can reinforce but can also contravene the ethical principles of personal responsibility and of individual integrity and dignity. This inevitably results if the members of society feel that their responsibility is delegated in the collective action and ceases to be individual. The in-

dividual who needs protection and help is not relieved of his responsibility for himself by the existence of a social mechanism for his assistance. Under our ethic, it is equally wrong for the individual to fail to seek such help as he needs and for him to demand or even to accept such help as a replacement for self-responsibility. On the other side, the social provision under this ethic must, if it is to be ethically right, be only the required means by which each individual carries out his personal responsibility toward any other individual who needs protection or aid. The responsibility is not diminished and it remains in the individual; it is not transferred to the mechanism that implements it.

It is fundamental in all this that responsibility is rooted in the true nature of man. It has arisen from and is inherent in his evolutionary history and status. Responsibility is something that he has just because he is human, and not something that he can choose to accept or to refuse. It cannot be rejected or unconditionally handed over to others. The attempt to do this is ethically wrong, and the responsibility remains where it was. The delegation of responsibility, to the extent that this is possible and proper, involves continuing responsibility for the actions of the delegate. In the last analysis, personal responsibility is nondelegable. Not only is every individual personally responsible for any actions by delegates or representatives of his, but he cannot ethically, even in semblance, delegate any responsibility for his own actions and for all their results.

The sweeping and impersonal nature of these generalizations may suggest difficulties and exceptions when particular and personal situations are considered. Is, for instance, the individual or society responsible if a jobless workman steals to feed his starving family? On reflection, this will be seen to be another false alternative. Everyone involved is necessarily responsible. The workman is certainly responsible for his action. On the stated facts alone the action itself may be ethically either good or bad. It is good if there was no alternative involving a lesser total of injury and indignity, determined by striking a balance between the good done for the family and the harm done morally to the workman himself and materially to his victim and to others who might otherwise have obtained the stolen food or who must indirectly pay for it. It is bad if avoidable harm is done, if, for instance, the workman has merely evaded responsibility for obtaining help in the social service available or for helping himself in a more proper way, such as accepting or seeking work. And in any case all other individuals in his society have a responsibility, which they may or may not have lived up to in the given case, first to see that sufficiently compensated work is available to the workman and second, in case of unavoidable failure in this, to see that the family is helped when help is needed beyond their own capacities.

As one more example, there is the old ethical problem of responsibility when an army officer orders a private to kill another human being. The situation is inherently bad: destruction of an individual is necessarily unethical on our premises. In a truly good society there would be no officer and no private. Pending the arrival of a good society, it is possible for such evil to be overbalanced by good resulting from the action. Whether the action was, in fact, more conducive to evil or to good in the particular circumstances, the officer and the private both have complete personal responsibility for it. The officer could not delegate the responsibility by giving an order and is as responsible as if the shot were fired by his own hand. The private who does fire the shot cannot turn responsibility for his personal action back on the person or the circumstances inducing him to take the action. He has acquiesced in a situation where he knows that he is bound to carry out the orders of others. It was right for him to do so if in his judgment the ultimate result would be better than the result of his refusal to acquiesce. He remains responsible not only for this decision but also for any immediate actions, good or bad, that result from his being under orders.

Ethical standards based on the fundamental evolutionary characteristics of man, particularly on human knowledge and human responsibility, have the widest applications to human conduct and respond fully to the human need for judgment of right and wrong. The broadest problem now facing mankind is choice between conflicting ideologies. These evolutionary ethics here lead to unequivocal decisions.

Authoritarianism is wrong. The assignment of authority on a fixed basis, without constant check and periodic review, inevitably involves an attempt to delegate nondelegable responsibility and to evade responsibility for subsequent actions of the delegate. This is an ethically wrong denial of the personal responsibility inherent in man's nature. The system inevitably leads to exploitation of all by the authoritarian leader and the development of a hierarchy in which each higher group exploits those below it. This is a morally wrong development of some individuals not along with but at the expense of others.

Totalitarianism is wrong. The concept of a state as a separate entity with its own rights and responsibilities contravenes the biological and social fact that all rights and responsibilities are vested by nature in the individuals that compose the state. The claim that the welfare of the state is superior to that of any or all its component individuals is thus absurd on the face of it, and the claim inevitably is used to excuse denial of maximum opportunities for individual development by all, a denial which is immoral. Concomitants sure to occur in such a state are regimentation of individuals, policing of all conduct (including conduct ethically good), judgment of knowledge and of ideas on a basis other than that of their truth and falsity, and consequent suppression of truth and unethical control of the dissemination of knowledge. Totalitarianism cannot conceivably be reconciled with any ethical system that admits the goodness of knowledge, the ineradicable existence of personal responsibility, and the value of individual integrity and dignity.

Democracy is wrong in many of its current aspects and under some current definitions, but democracy is the only political ideology which can be made to embrace an ethically good society by the standards of ethics here maintained. Laissez faire capitalism, or any other societal activity that promotes or permits selfish or unfair utilization of some individuals by others, is obviously wrong by these standards. Capitalism, not further restricted, is perfectly consistent with authoritarianism or totalitarianism and is of course wrong if involved in either of those morally wrong systems. In a socialized democracy, controlled capitalism without improper exploitation may be ethically good. Majority rule is wrong if it involves suppression or oppression of any minority, but decision of problems by the majority of all those affected by them, accompanied by free expression of all opinions and full preserval of minority rights is, so far as has yet been demonstrated, the only possible ethically good means of reaching collective action. Attempts to assign personal responsibility to the government are ethically wrong (and biologically futile, to boot), but government by representatives or delegates for whose actions each one of their constituents remains personally responsible seems to be the only practicable method of ethical government for large groups of people.

Governments called democracies are by no means all ethically right by our standards, and none is free of many ethically bad aspects. Yet an ethically good state, one based on the fact of personal responsibility by each of its members and organized to promote the acquisition, dissemination, and acceptance of truth in all fields, to maintain the integrity and dignity of every individual, and to enable maximum possible realization of personal capacities—such a government would necessarily be a democracy.

Below these broadest aspects of the ethical problems of our times, application of these evolutionary ethics to personal problems and actions may be complex but is usually pertinent and decisive. A basic problem for all of us is the integration and ethical development of our own personalities. A major factor in this is certainly the acceptance and exercise of our personal responsibility. There is often no essential clinical difference in neurotic trends and strains or underlying personality factors between those who are socially normal, workably adjusted and integrated and those who are pathologically maladjusted. The difference is essentially that the former have the ethically

good will toward integration and take the responsibility for achievement of this in themselves. It follows, of course, that the maladjusted are in such cases (which admit of certain exceptions, as in the case of some traumatic psychoses) responsible for their own condition. The responsibility extends to the necessity for seeking help, from psychiatrists or others, when personal resources are not wholly sufficient, and it is a responsibility of every other member of society to see that such help is available and sufficient for those who do seek it.

It is, indeed, another inescapable biological fact that no individual is fully self-sufficient, and the doctrine of personal responsibility carries no such illogical corollary. It is a responsibility not only with relationship to the self but also with relationship to others, ultimately embracing all of mankind, a responsibility for cooperation and for both giving and obtaining aid. This aspect of evolutionary ethics, above all others, begins in the cradle and follows us to the grave. Normal development of the human infant requires the presence of a mother and frequent contact with her. Her responsibility in this matter is another that cannot be delegated. Withholding of continual affectionate contact or unnecessary assignment of care to an impersonal agency is immoral because it impedes normal integration of the infant's individuality.

In such a situation, and in many others, the bearing of these ethics is perfectly clear. They provide, however, no guide by which every action of daily life need be judged and channeled into a single possible direction. In most respects wide latitude remains between "right" and "wrong." It is, in fact, a part of the sense of values arising from these considerations that diversity in personality and in action is a good and positively valuable characteristic of mankind, so long as it does not overstep broad ethical bounds or impinge unfavorably on other personalities. Regimentation of personality or suppression of individuality is ethically bad by these standards. Respect for others is ethically good. Appreciation rather than bigoted disapproval of differences from ourselves is one of the means of enriching our own experiences and personalities, and this too is one of the ethical goods.

It should, finally, again be emphasized that these ethical standards are relative, not absolute. They are relative to man as he now exists on the earth. They are based on man's place in nature, his evolution, and the evolution of life, but they do not arise automatically from these facts or stand as an inevitable and eternal guide for human—or any other—existence. Part of their basis is man's power of choice and they, too, are subject to choice, to selection or rejection in accordance with their own principles. They are also subject to future change as man evolves; after all, if mankind does pursue the ethic of knowledge it should be able progressively to improve and refine any ethical system based on knowledge.

There is no ethical absolute that does not arise from error and illusion. These relativistic ethics have, at least, the merit of being honestly derived from what seems to be demonstrably true and clear.

Psychology and explanations

of human behavior

Theodore Mischel (b. 1925)

Born in Vienna, Austria, Theodore Mischel received graduate training in both physics and philosophy in the United States. He holds an M.S. degree in physics from the University of Illinois and a Ph.D. in philosophy from Columbia University. From 1950 to 1951 he was a Fulbright Fellow in the University of Paris, and he has been a Visiting Faculty Fellow in the department of the history of science and medicine at Yale University. He is at present professor of philosophy at Colgate University in Hamilton, New York. He has published articles in such periodicals as The Journal of Philosophy, Mind, *and* The Psychological Review.

In the article reprinted here he challenges the belief of many philosophers of science that all scientific explanation requires the formulation of a theory involving a generalization, or causal law, from which all particular instances can be deduced. Mischel argues that in explaining human behavior we should look for motives and intentions which account for the acts of individuals rather than attempt to make generalizations. Man, he argues, is different in kind from other things in nature, a fact which makes it necessary to explain his behavior in a unique way.

Empirical psychologists are often deeply suspicious of the "understanding" of human behavior which novelists and playwrights can give us. As one recent book puts it

> Shakespeare and Dostoevsky may be "better psychologists than the psychologists" in their ability to touch closely and movingly on some widely held prototheory of behavior; they may even provide a prodigality of

plausible initial statements in their building of convincing portraits, but they and the nonempirical psychologists in general, apparently never feel the sharpest goad of the research psychologist—to find out by looking whether or not he is right.[1]

On this view, explanations like those given by Shakespeare and Dostoevsky are "nonempirical" in a very damaging sense—they are based on some "prototheory" of behavior, and one gives them without bothering "to find out by looking whether or not he is right."

What leads these writers to think that Shake-

Theodore Mischel, "Psychology and Explanations of Human Behavior," *Philosophy and Phenomenological Research*, Vol. XXIII, No. 4, June 1963. Used by permission of the author and editor. An earlier version of this paper was read to the W. A. White Institute for Psychoanalysis, New York City, May 11, 1961.

[1] Mandler and Kessen, *The Language of Psychology*, p. 250.

speare's explanations are based on a "proto-theory" is their belief that all "explanations share the characteristic of making the statement to be explained an instance of some wider generalization. They all involve in a more or less rigorous way the *deduction* of the statement to be explained." [2] If this is what it means to explain, then what Shakespeare tells us about human behavior can be an "explanation" only insofar as it tacitly assumes some generalizations or laws about human behavior. Since Shake-speare neither formulated nor tested any such laws, it is held that he must have taken them for granted—they constitute his "prototheory." This view is also supported by methodologists primarily concerned with the natural sciences, like C. G. Hempel and E. Nagel. These writers claim that we can explain an action in terms of the agent's motives only by virtue of an empirical generalization linking the motive to the ensuing action. In other words, the motive is taken to be an initial condition which can explain the action only when the latter can be deduced from the motive by means of an appropriate general law. In this way explanations in terms of motives are assimilated to the pattern of explanation characteristic of the physical sciences —i.e., to explanations which subsume what is to be explained under some law or law-like regularity.[3]

In contrast to this, I want to defend the view that novelists, playwrights, and other students of distinctively human behavior, can give us responsible, empirical explanations without using any generalizations, laws, or theories. For when they explain what men do in terms of their "motives" they are not explaining in terms of regularities or patterns of behavior; their explanations differ in type from those

based on laws, law-like statements, or theories. After defending the use of such explanations, I will try to show that at least some of the explanations actually given in psychology are similar to those given by novelists and play-wrights, rather than to those given by phys-ical scientists when they explain things other than human actions. Finally, I will suggest that recognition of this difference in explanation type allows us to see what is valid in the "existential" approach to psychology without committing us to excess metaphysical baggage.

I

How does Shakespeare explain behavior? Why, for example is Iago plotting against Othello? Well, he resents Othello for having appointed Cassio to the lieutenancy, he suspects the "lusty Moor" of an intrigue with his wife, and he sets out to serve his turn upon him. By leading Othello to think that Cassio is too familiar with Desdemona, Iago can gain his revenge, become the logical candidate for the lieutenancy, and yet remain "honest Iago" to all the world. But even when his profit in Cas-sio's ruin has been achieved, Iago continues to plot against Othello. What motivates him now is a desire to reduce the nobility that confronts him to baseness. To strip Othello of his self-respect, to harry him until he collapses at his feet, and thus to demonstrate his own superior-ity and power—this is Iago's aim when he plots against Othello.

No doubt, much more needs to be said in elucidating Shakespeare's explanation; but this may suffice to show that while his explanation involves reasons, aims, motives and intentions, it does not seem to involve any theory, or gen-eral laws, of behavior. Shakespeare is explaining why Iago acted in this way, but he is not saying anything about how all men, or all men of a certain kind, act under specified circumstances. To think that Shakespeare must have assumed that all men, or all vain, envious men, will act as Iago did under the circumstances would be silly—for such an assumption is patently false. We could, of course, improve our gen-eralization by replacing "all vain, envious men"

[2] *Ibid.*, p. 217 [their italics]. See also chaps. 11–13, *passim*.

[3] See Hempel & Oppenheim, "The Logic of Explanation" in Feigl & Brodbeck, *Rdgs. in Philo. of Science,* pp. 319–352; Hempel, "The Function of General Laws in History" in Feigl and Sellars, *Rdgs. in Philosophical Analysis,* pp. 459–471; E. Nagel, *The Structure of Science,* pp. 551–563. Hempel & Oppenheim say that "There is no for-mal difference on this account between motiva-tional and causal explanations." (*op. cit.* p. 328).

with a more and more detailed statement of Iago's character and background. But in order to get a generalization which we can assert with confidence we will have to fill in more and more detail until only someone "just like Iago" would fit. And in that case our "generalization" pertains to an individual rather than a class and thus is not a "general law" in the required sense. That is, when we explain Iago's action in terms of *his* particular character and background, we subsume that action under the pattern of an individual's past behavior, but not under a pattern that holds for all people of a certain kind. Consequently, the regularity in terms of which the explanation is given is not a "law" in the sense in which experimental psychologists claim that explanations of human behavior must be based on empirically tested "laws." [4]

When we explain what someone does in terms of a pattern in his past behavior, the regularity we appeal to is more like what Ryle calls a "dispositional statement of a law-like kind." According to Ryle motive explanations are of this dispositional type. For in his view, to say that someone is, e.g., envious, is to say that he is inclined to do and say certain sorts of things, to make certain sorts of plans, to feel certain sorts of feelings in certain situations. And "to say that he did something from that motive is to say that his action, done in its particular circumstances, was just the sort of thing that that was an inclination to do. It is to say 'he *would* do that.' " [5]

Now such dispositional explanations share one crucial characteristic of explanations based on general laws: both explain by showing that what happened is not surprising in view of what happened in the past. But while we often explain behavior in that way, there are times when such explanations completely fail to tell us what we wanted to know in asking "Why did he do it?" For we may ask this question because we do not understand the agent's *reason* for acting that way. Why, for example, did the driver fail to stop at the red light? If we were to ask him, *he* could not reply by citing a disposition to drive recklessly. To explain his action he would have to represent it as the right, the appropriate, thing to do under the circumstances—e.g., he had to get home in a hurry, it was late at night and he had looked ahead to see if anyone was coming, etc. Though we might not accept the explanation he gives us, we would at least begin by looking for his reasons when we are trying to understand why he did it. If we cannot find a satisfactory explanation in terms of reasons we may alleviate our surprise by pointing to a disposition: one could have expected this in view of his past, it is the sort of thing he would do. But we might still wonder what the point of his doing it was.

Since most human actions are intentional, they puzzle us when we fail to understand the agent's intentions. Usually the puzzle is solved, the action explained, when we succeed in discovering something about the agent, or the situation confronting him, which brings out the reason for his action. This may involve discovering the agent's goals and these may, of course, be odd ones; or his beliefs, including, possibly, mistaken ones, about the situation confronting him. And since the way in which people seek their goals is often regulated by rules, the reason for an action may become clear when we understand the rules—be they social and legal norms or individual rules (e.g., the strategy of a chessplayer or a general)—which the agent was following. Ordinarily, when we ask for the explanation of an intentional action we are asking for the "calculation" [6] which shows the considerations that lead the agent to decide on this as the right,

---

[4] "Scarcely anyone would be interested in a recitation of the doings of Rat A, then Rat B, then Rat C.... Scientific statements are made about "rats," not about "Rat A," about "people," not about "Miss A," usually with reference to the behavior of groups of organisms." Mandler and Kessen, *op. cit.*, p. 167.

[5] G. Ryle, *The Concept of Mind*, pp. 92–93. See also pp. 83–93 and 123–124.

[6] I take this concept from W. Dray, to whose excellent analysis of "rational explanations" in history my discussion is indebted. See W. Dray, *Laws and Explanation in History*, esp. chap. 5.

the appropriate, thing to do under the circumstances. Understanding this, we understand why he did it.

When we explain an action in this way we make a judgment to the effect that, given the agent's goals, etc., this was the thing for him to do. The explanation "justifies" the action in the sense that it represents it as the appropriate thing to do from the agent's point of view. But to show that an action was right *given* the agent's goals and beliefs, the rules he was following, etc., is not to justify his holding these beliefs and goals, or his adherence to these rules. Consequently, to explain in terms of reasons is not to certify the agent's "rationality," but only to show that this would seem the right (reasonable, appropriate) thing to do *if* one held the agent's beliefs, etc.

It should also be noted that in giving such explanations we are not implying that the agent actually went through such a calculation. For an explanation in terms of reasons can be given for any purposive, or intentional, action and a man may act intentionally without doing any mental planning—e.g., I drive my car without thinking what to do next, but my actions are purposive and if asked I could give reasons for what I did. Moreover, it is not only our words but also our actions that reveal our intentions. Because the pattern of my behavior may reveal a purpose different from the one I profess, it is possible for someone (including myself) to doubt that my professed intention is my real one. Nevertheless, though we may ascribe an intention to someone who in fact denies having it, it must be logically possible for the agent to acknowledge his own intention. So while intentional actions are not necessarily accompanied by bits of mental planning, they do involve a purposive pattern of behavior and the possibility of acknowledging the intention (at least in the "long run").

Explanations in terms of reasons thus differ in type from explanations based on laws or dispositions. While the latter explain by showing that what happened is not surprising in view of past regularities, the former explain by showing that what was done is intelligible because, from the agent's point of view, it was the thing to do. When we explain human behavior in terms of laws or dispositions we explain from "outside," in terms of regularity rather than rationale, in a way similar to that in which we explain the behavior of animals and things. But when we explain in terms of reasons we take the agent's point of view and look for the considerations which lead him to choose this deed as the right thing to do under these circumstances—in this sense we explain his behavior from "inside."

Before asking whether such explanations can be scientifically acceptable—a question I will consider in the next section—let us note that this, surely, is the kind of explanation Shakespeare and Dostoevsky give us. To assume that they must have written their characters on the basis of "some widely held prototheory of behavior" is *prima facie* absurd since it is a commonplace of criticism that a character whose development is a mere illustration of some theory about human behavior is a poor creation. What distinguishes "wooden," "mechanical" characters from those which seem to "live" is precisely that the former keep on doing what that sort of character *would* do, while the latter surprise us with each new turn in their development. But, though the development of a character like Othello is unexpected, it is also "inevitable." Killing Desdemona is clearly not the sort of thing Othello would do; but when he does it it seems the only thing for him to do. We are surprised because this is a genuine development and not the sort of thing we could have expected from the start. Yet we understand it because Shakespeare has made it possible for us to see the considerations which lead Othello to decide on this as the only thing to do. Seeing this we see that he could do no other—it was "inevitable." But saying that Othello could do no other is not like saying that the glass could only shatter when the stone hit it. It is more like saying "I cannot betray my friend" and explaining why we cannot. There are reasons, not causes or dispositions, why he could do no other. We understand the inevitability of the action from "inside" rather than "outside."

If Shakespeare and Dostoevsky can teach us

something about human psychology, this is not because they have discovered surprising *laws* or *regularities* in human behavior, but because they have discovered the surprising *reasons* why some people do the things they do.

II

While explanations in terms of reasons differ in type from explanations in terms of dispositions, laws or theories, they are not "unscientific" or "unempirical" in any damaging sense. For in explaining an action by representing it as the right thing to do from the agent's point of view, we are ascribing certain beliefs and intentions to the agent. We are saying something about him which is either true or false; we are making claims which have to be supported by evidence. And the evidence consists of some of the things the agent says and does, or some of the things he would do or say under certain circumstances. Sometimes it is very hard to find out what a man's motives and intentions really are—in word and deed, men sometimes deceive others and sometimes deceive themselves. But no matter how much deception or self-deception may be involved, a man's actions and words are always in some way significant for seeing what he really has "in mind." And in practice skilled observation —the sort of observation at which clinical psychologists and psychoanalysts are especially good—can often, though not always, bring us to the point where we can assert with confidence that this or that is what the agent really had "in mind." Moreover, when we fail to reach this point the difficulty is empirical, not logical—we fail because we lack relevant evidence, not because it is logically impossible for one person to "inspect the contents" of another person's mind.

So explaining an action in terms of the agent's reasons for acting is certainly not something one can do without bothering "to find out by looking whether or not he is right." But the place to look is not the psychologist's "laboratory" where empirical generalizations are tested, but the individual's behavior—what he says and does, what he would say and do

under certain circumstances. And when we are dealing with the explanations which Shakespeare and Dostoevsky give us, there is no place to look other than the play or novel—since they construct all the things their characters say or do, it is only an examination of their constructions that can tell us whether they have really explained the things they make their characters say and do.

In sciences like physics the claim that we cannot adequately explain without using laws is plausible. For suppose we try to explain one event (e.g., the bursting of the radiator) in terms of another (e.g., a fall in temperature). How could we know that one event really explains the other, or even that it has anything to do with the other, without knowing that these two events are "connected?" And what connection can there be between events other than a law which enables us to predict the occurrence of one of the events from the occurrence of the other? So the statements offered in explanation of the bursting of the radiator must meet two conditions: (1) they must be *true*, and (2) they must *really explain*—i.e., the fact being explained must be "connected" with the facts offered in explanation. Unless our explanation includes a law connecting the two sets of facts, we cannot know that one really explains the other. This is what leads Hempel to claim that:

> The use of universal empirical hypotheses as explanatory principles distinguishes genuine from pseudo-explanation . . . [pseudo-explanations] are based on metaphor rather than laws; they convey pictorial and emotional appeals instead of insight into factual connections.[7]

But the situation is radically different when we explain a human action in terms of the

[7] C. Hempel, "The Function of General Laws in History," *op. cit.*, p. 461. In the same vein, E. Nagel, in discussing one of Maitland's explanations, argues that only if "Maitland tacitly assumed some sort of generalization about human conduct" is there any ground for holding that his explanation "had anything to do" with the matter being explained (Nagel, *op. cit.*, p. 553).

agent's reason for doing it. To use a trivial example: suppose we explain why a man took a taxi by saying that it was raining, the taxi was most convenient, he could afford the fare, and he did not want to get wet. Clearly, one could challenge the truth of this explanation. But would it make any sense to grant the truth of the facts cited, and then to ask whether these facts can really explain why he took the taxi? Do we need some sort of empirical law asserting a "factual connection" in order that our explanation be "genuine" rather than "pseudo?" Surely not. For when we explain in this way we are not offering one set of facts (e.g., rain and a desire not to get wet) as conditions from which to predict, on the basis of some general law, the occurrence of another fact (e.g., taking the taxi). A man who says "I will take a taxi because it is raining" is not *predicting* what he will do; he is *justifying* what he intends to do as the right thing to do in view of an end. So when we explain an action by representing it as the right thing to do, from the agent's point of view, the "connection" between the action and the reasons which explain it is not a "factual connection." We do not need to be empirical scientists in order to know that taking a taxi is the thing to do when it is raining.

Of course, an empirical connection which the agent knows, or believes, to be true *may* be what makes something relevant as a reason —e.g., the chemist's decision to put litmus paper into a solution in order to test its acidity depends on his knowledge of an empirical regularity. If we did not understand that the chemist knew this regularity, we would not understand why he regarded what he did as the right thing to do. But in explaining his action we are showing the point of what he did, the reasons which led him to decide on this as the right means to his end. And a false empirical belief held by the agent—e.g., a criminal's belief that he would not be caught because . . . —may do this as well as a true one.

That the connection between an action and the reasons which explain it is not a "factual connection" certainly does not imply that anything and everything can be cited as a reason

for the action. For something is not a reason simply because a man says it is. If a New Yorker were to say that his reason for taking a taxi is that it is raining in China, we would ask "What has that to do with it, how is that relevant to your decision?" He might be able to show its relevance, but the possibility of this depends on the fact that in any given context certain things are accepted as evidently related to others as reasons for action. Only the relation is one of *relevance* rather than *regularity*.

So Nagel misses the point when he tries to support the claim that explanations in terms of reasons require generalizations about human conduct by arguing that even if we have shown that certain factors were in fact present, this

> clearly does not establish *which* of these factors (or for that matter, whether any of them) was the actual reason for the actor's conduct . . . Thus the fact that a person on trial for murder is known to have hated the victim does not suffice to show that he committed the murder . . . *because* of his hatred —for . . . he may have killed the deceased by accident, because he was paid to do so, or for a number of other reasons.[8]

Of course, showing that the murderer hated his victim does not suffice to show that this was his reason for killing him. But it is not true that we can support the claim that F was the "actual reason" for the murder only if we assume that "when the given factor is a circumstance under which men act, they *generally* conduct themselves in a manner similar to the particular action described in the imputation, so that the individual . . . presumably also acted the way he did because the given factor was present." [9] Instead of appealing to such "generalizations," what we ordinarily do when we want to know what the "actual reason" was is to find out all we can about the agent's relevant aims and beliefs, the "strategy" he was following, etc.—an empirical inquiry in the course of which we may appeal to dispositions or

[8] E. Nagel, *op. cit.*, p. 555 [his italics].
[9] *Ibid.*

draw inferences from laws.[10] On the basis of what we so discover, we try to construct a calculation which makes the crime intelligible by showing that *if* one had held these beliefs, etc., then committing the crime would have seemed the thing to do under these circumstances. And if we succeed in showing this, then we can properly claim to have found the "actual reason" for the crime. Surely something like this is what actually happens in a court of law when the prosecution tries to establish the accused's "motive." No generalizations are required because we don't need them in order to understand how the accused's hatred *could* "really explain" why he killed the victim—as could money, or "a number of other reasons." Generalizations are not needed because reasons for murder are not, as Nagel seems to think, causal "factors" in whose presence people will, generally, kill. They are considerations relevant to a decision to kill, and they do not need to be "factually connected" with murdering— as a fall in temperature does have to be synthetically "connected" with the bursting of the radiator—in order for us to understand how one *could* explain the other. To show that R was the "actual reason" for the murder is not to show that one can predict that people will, generally, kill in the presence of R; it is to show that R is the consideration which led this particular man to decide that killing the deceased was the thing for him to do under these circumstances.[11]

But the action is not entailed by the calculation; the explanans cannot be logically

[10] Laws and dispositions may thus be evidence supporting the premises used in our explanation. But this in no way shows that we are "really" explaining in terms of them rather than in terms of reasons. For if we explain something by deducing it from a law, the evidence which justifies our use of this law as an explanatory premise is no part of the explanation, nor is the explanation "really" given in terms of it. If it were, we could not explain anything without explaining everything.

[11] Of course, I am not denying that there may be cases where we cannot find an explanation in terms of reasons—e.g., "There was no reason in it; he was driven by a mad fit of passion."

deduced from the explanandum. How then do we know that we have "really" explained the action? In general terms one could say that a good explanation in terms of reasons is one in which the explanandum can be used to "justify" the explanans. That is, R is a good explanation of why A chose to do X if, given A's beliefs, aims, etc., it is a good reason for doing X. But how do we know that the considerations adduced in our explanation really constitute "good reasons," how do we know that they really suffice to "justify" the action as the right one from the agent's point of view? One cannot and need not specify in advance the criteria which any and every explanation in terms of reasons must meet in order to be a good one. This is not because there are no criteria, but because the criteria are contextual so that it is only within a specific explanatory context that we can decide when the considerations adduced "really" explain the action. For example, why does Iago "look dead with grieving" and make a show of not wanting to say anything against Cassio when Othello asks who began the brawl? (*Othello*, II, iii). Because it was essential to his plot that he maintain the role of "honest Iago," because he could count on Othello to "compel" him to tell the "truth" and thus get Cassio disgraced anyhow, and because this stratagem enabled him to make further use of Cassio in his plot —as a "good friend" he could easily suggest to Cassio that he ask Desdemona to intercede with Othello. And then "I'll pour this pestilence into his ear/That she repeals him for her body's lust." This is why Iago, who really hated Cassio, decided to put on this show of friendship. Of course, Iago's action cannot be logically deduced from this explanation. But if someone were to greet it with "Yes, but why did he do it?", we would not understand what he is asking for. What other, or better, reasons could Iago have had? The question may not be senseless, but it makes sense only if the questioner has something in mind which casts doubt on our explanation—either some evidence against the truth of one of the explanatory premises, or some consideration which we have overlooked and which may throw the "justification" out of joint, i.e., require us to revise the judgment that, from Iago's point of view, this was "good reason," this was the right thing to do under the circumstances. Barring this, one cannot, in this context, go on asking "Why did he do it?" We have found a good explanation of Iago's behavior—it is based on the evidence and, in its context, it leaves no further room for "Why did he do it?"—though it does not, of course, logically entail Iago's action. Why should it when we are explaining in terms of reasons rather than by deduction from a general law? One could not claim that the action has not "really" been explained because it cannot be deduced from the explanans without begging the question of what it means to explain.

The logical possibility of error does remain —an explanation in terms of reasons may have to be revised in light of new evidence. But surely this is no argument against such explanation. After all, explanations in terms of empirical laws and dispositions are not infallible either. Why should we expect logical certainty when dealing with questions of fact?

In sum, we can give responsible, empirical explanations of intentional actions in terms of the agent's reasons without using any generalizations or theories about human behavior in our explanation. For when we explain in this way there is never any problem about whether explanans and explanandum are connected in fact; the only problem is that of discovering what, as a matter of fact, the agent's reasons were. Discovering this is an empirical process which may involve inference based on laws and dispositions. But explaining the action by showing that the agent decided that this was the right, the appropriate, thing to do for such and such reasons is a rational process which requires no empirical laws or theories of behavior.

III

I now want to show that some of the explanations given in psychology are also of this type. While I think that many of the approaches developed by clinical psychologists who stress the importance of understanding the patient's point of view—Kelly's *Psychology of Personal Constructs* is one example [12]—are best construed as attempts at explanation in terms of reasons, I will here confine myself to the sort of explanation psychoanalysts often give in terms of the patient's unconscious motives (e.g., she acted this way because of an unconscious hatred of her mother). I choose this illustration because it is familiar and because it may help to show that it would be a mistake to think that explanations in terms of reasons can only apply to a limited range of "rational" behavior.

As a number of writers have pointed out, Freud's explanations often shift between talk about the neurotic's unconscious purpose and intentions and talk about the causes of his acts.[13] For example, in explaining a woman's obsessive behavior Freud tells us that "the deepest secret of her illness was that it enabled her to shield him [i.e., her husband] from malicious gossip, and to make a comfortable existence apart from her possible for him." [14] This certainly sounds as if the "secret of her illness" is that her obsessive behavior has a point to it, just as if it were something she decided to do for a reason. This is also suggested when Freud tells us that "the purpose she had in performing the action ... was to correct a painful event of the past." [15] But while this sounds like

[12] Kelly explains a person's actions in terms of the "constructs" he uses to "anticipate" what will happen if he acts one way or another; his psychology is thus an *"anticipatory* rather than a *reactive* system" of explanation. (*op. cit.,* p. 170, his italics). Unfortunately, Kelly fails to see that explaining in terms of "constructs" is explaining in terms of reasons rather than in terms of "predictive hypotheses." [See the author's "Personal Constructs, Rules and the Logic of Clinical Activity," *The Psychological Review,* 71 (3): 180–192, May, 1964. Ed.]

[13] See the articles by S. Toulmin and A. Flew in *Philosophy and Analysis* (M. Macdonald, ed.), A. C. MacIntyre's *The Unconscious,* and A. Flew, "Motives and the Unconscious," *Minnesota Studies in Philo. of Science,* vol. I, pp. 155–172.

[14] S. Freud, *General Introduction to Psychoanalysis,* Permabook ed., p. 274.

[15] *Ibid.,* p. 288.

an explanation in terms of reasons, it is odd because her behavior is obsessive—she could not help doing it, so how could it be something she "decided" to do?—and because she did not know that she had any such "reason"—since this was not a consideration for her when she acted that way, how could it be her "reason?" This oddness, as well as the fact that Freud often speaks of psychic "forces" and "mechanisms" causing various kinds of behavior—e.g., in connection with the same case he says "it took a long time and much effort for her to grasp and admit to me that such a motive as this could alone have been the driving force behind her obsessive act" [16] —has led many students to regard his explanations in terms of unconscious motives as explanations in terms of causes, laws and theories, rather than reasons.

Now the neurotic's behavior obviously differs in at least two important ways from that of a person who acts intentionally (i.e., for a reason). In the first place, it is "obsessive"—the woman cannot control her own behavior in the way someone who acts purposively can. Secondly, she does not know her "reason" for acting and the "not knowing" is dynamic—in contrast to someone whose motive is "preconscious" rather than "unconscious," she can be brought to admit her "reason" only after "a long time and much effort" in analysis. These differences between normal and neurotic behavior clearly call for explanation in terms of laws and theories. Why does this happen to some people under some conditions and not to others? Freud's answer is his theory about repression and the way in which neurotic symptoms can be produced by unconscious conflicts. By means of this theory Freud traces the obsession to its causes in the patient's past—i.e., the scene on the morning after the unhappy bridal night. Insofar as Freud gives us such theories about symptom formation, they are similar to those used in the physical sciences and their merits can be discussed in much the same way.

But what of Freud's explanation of, e.g.,

the obsessive ritual, in terms of the agent's unrecognized purpose? Is it logically dependent on his causal explanation of why people of a certain kind develop neurotic symptoms under conditions of a certain kind? It seems that Freud is here raising an entirely different kind of question, namely: What "reason" did she have for using this stratagem? What did she "achieve" by her obsession? Why did she "decide" to be ill? No doubt these are very odd-sounding questions. But Freud seems to be asking and answering just such questions when he tells us "the purpose she had in performing the action" or claims that "her symptoms enabled her to continue her relationship with him." [17] Could we not make better sense of these explanations in terms of unconscious motives if we regarded them as extensions of explanations in terms of reasons rather than as odd, speculative and, probably, unwarranted explanations in terms of laws and theories? Though neurotic actions differ significantly from normal, intentional ones, the differences may not be such as to preclude the possibility of explaining the former in a way analogous to that in which we typically explain the latter. After all, as we noted earlier, a man may act intentionally without doing any "calculating" beforehand. And it is also true that a man may sincerely think that he has acted for one reason but, after searching his own conscience or probing his motives with the help of another, he may see quite clearly that he really acted for a different reason. No doubt this is a case where the motive is "preconscious" and so it differs importantly from that of the neurotic who has repressed his motives and can admit them only after "a long time and much effort" in psychotherapy. Yet the neurotic's actions do show a purposive pattern—what he does loses its puzzling character and becomes intelligible when we see him as trying to achieve this and to avoid that. And when the analyst proceeds to ascribe an "unconscious motive" to the patient, though the latter's denial of this motive does not overthrow the analyst's interpretation, if the

[16] *Ibid.*, p. 288.

[17] *Ibid.*, p. 284.

interpretation is correct it is expected that the patient will, at least ideally, come to agree with it in the end. Surely what the psychoanalyst does when he gives such an interpretation of the patient's unconscious motives is more like what the trial lawyer, or the man of affairs, does when he tests his "interpretation" of another person's reasons for acting, than it is like what the physicist does when he tests his hypothesis about the cause of a certain phenomenon. When Freud's patient finally admits that this was the motive for her obsessive acts, is she giving assent to the theoretical considerations which show that this was the "driving force" causing her behavior? Clearly she is in no position to do that. But she, and only she, can finally admit that this really was the "reason" for her curious actions.[18]

The compulsive character of the neurotic's behavior does, of course, make it odd to say that she "decided" to do what she apparently does not want to do (i.e., suffer from her obsession and other neurotic symptoms). Yet psychoanalysts contend, e.g., that the neurotic "became so ill in order to be unable to marry and so to remain with her father," [19] or, more generally, that neurosis is "precisely the method the individual uses to preserve his own center, his own existence." [20] Surely this implies that in their view neurosis is not just something that happens to a person (like an infection caused by a germ), but is something he does; that there is some sense in which one can adduce "considerations" relevant to the neurotic's "decision" to be ill. Moreover, it is hard to see how the difference between compulsive and free behavior—i.e., the obsessive ritual vs the freedom achieved when the patient rids himself

of the obsession through analysis—can be made out without the introduction of unconscious "purposes," etc. For the difference between them is not that in one case behavior is caused while in the other it isn't; causal explanations can, presumably, be given in both cases. To say that the causes are different is true, but fails to bring out the point of the distinction between "compulsive" and "free" behavior. For the difference is that while the normal person does what he wants and knows (or can easily become aware of) the reasons why he does it, this is not true of the neurotic. And one of the contentions of psychoanalysis seems to be that there is a sense in which the neurotic does what he (unconsciously) "wants" to do, that there are (unconscious) "reasons" for his actions—but he has repressed these wishes and purposes and cannot become aware of them without psychotherapy. The difference between free and compulsive behavior might then be construed as the difference between acting in accordance with one's aims and intentions, and being "driven" by aims and intentions which one cannot (without therapy) acknowledge as one's own.

Thus the behavior of Freud's patient seems mad and unintelligible—what possible "reason" could she have for having to run several times a day into another room and having to stand there in a certain position, by the table with a spot on it, until the maid appears on the scene? But then Freud sees a purposive pattern in her actions: if she identifies herself with her husband and identifies the table bearing the spot with her wedding bed, then we can see that "the obsessive act thus says: 'No, it is not true, he was not disgraced before the servant, he was not impotent.' " [21] The obsessive act becomes intelligible—there is a "reason" for her action—when we see that "it serves the purpose of restoring her husband's credit after that unfortunate incident." [22] Though it will take "a long time and much effort" in analysis before the patient can admit to having this motive and be cured of her obsession, all of her symptoms become *meaningful* when we "per-

---

[18] Kelly asks clinical psychologists to follow this adage: "If you do not know what is wrong with a person, ask him; he may tell you. The clinician who asks such a question will have to be prepared to do some careful listening." Kelly, *op. cit.*, pp. 322–323.

[19] Freud, *op. cit.*, p. 285.

[20] R. May, "Existential Bases of Psychotherapy," in R. May (ed.), *Existential Psychology*, p. 76. Freud's claim that "symptoms are actually substitutes for the missing satisfaction" (Freud, *op. cit.*, p. 353) seems to involve a similar point.

[21] Freud, *op. cit.*, p. 274.

[22] *Ibid.*, p. 274.

ceive in them the voices which pleaded for him, excused him, exalted him, lamented his loss." [23] So we come to see that there really is a point to the obsessive ritual and the other symptoms; given her unconscious "aims" and distorted "beliefs" about the situation this would seem to her the thing to do.

Psychoanalysis thus makes it possible to see that while the neurotic's behavior is irrational, it is not a-rational: there is method in the madness. What seems a-rational becomes intelligible in terms of unconscious "purposes" and "intentions." For in terms of these the psychoanalyst can construct a "calculation" which shows us that from the neurotic's distorted "point of view" this strange behavior would seem "justified," would seem the "right," the "appropriate," the "rational" thing to do; and the patient can, at least ideally, be helped to see that he has really been operating in terms of this distorted "rationale" whose nature he has been hiding from himself. Irrational actions can thus be explained by extending the model used in explaining rational actions. This, I suggest, is why "Freudian psychology is exactly the stuff upon which the poet has always exercised his art. . . . Yet the relationship is reciprocal, and the effect of Freud upon literature has been no greater than the effect of literature upon Freud." [24]

IV

Recognition of the role of rational explanations sheds some light on the "existential" approach to psychology with its insistence that "the present dominant images of man in psychology and psychiatry are inadequate." [25] Writers who champion this view hold that we must develop a "psychology that will be relevant to man's distinguishing characteristics as man," a psychology which sees man as a unique individual who makes real decisions and acts responsibly with a view to the future.[26] This approach appeals to clinical psychologists who think that there is a conflict between what they believe as "scientists" and what they do as therapists. As Carl Rogers formulates the issue, to be "scientific" one has to understand the person as an "object" that is "manipulated" in therapy; but to be an effective therapist and understand one's patients one cannot do this.[27] As a result, there is said to be a conflict in psychology between the "objective" view that "the way to understand is from the outside" and the "existential" view that "the way to understand is from within." [28] And Rogers has suggested that this conflict might be reconciled by a "changed view of science" which recognizes that "science too, at its inception, is an 'I-Thou' relationship with the world of perceived objects, just as therapy at its deepest is an 'I-Thou' relationship wth a person." [29]

But surely one can do justice to the legitimate concern of psychologists like Rogers, May and Maslow, without adopting the desperate expedient of a Buberian interpretation of physics. What is distinctive of man as man is his developed capacity for using language. This capacity makes it possible for man to act intentionally (i.e., for a reason). For even though a man may do something intentionally without ever formulating his reasons for doing it, we would not describe men as acting intentionally if they could never put into words what they are doing and why they are doing it. To talk of a stone's reason for falling is to talk nonsense, and to speak of a rat as moving "in order to" avoid an electric shock is to speak in a weak, analogical sense. But the descriptions which we ordinarily apply to characteristically human activities—i.e., he telephoned, signed, plotted, paid, bought, married, etc.—are descriptions of intentional actions

[23] *Ibid.*, p. 284.

[24] L. Trilling, "Freud and Literature," *The Liberal Imagination*, p. 44.

[25] R. May (ed.), *Existential Psychology*, p. 7.

[26] R. May, *op. cit.*, pp. 39–51; see also, in the same volume, A. H. Maslow, pp. 55–58, and G. Allport, p. 95.

[27] C. Rogers, "Persons or Science? A Philosophical Question," *American Psychologist*, 10: 267–278, 1955.

[28] C. Rogers, "Two Divergent Trends," in R. May, *op. cit.*, esp. pp. 86–88.

[29] C. Rogers, "Persons or Science?" *op. cit.*, p. 278. In a similar vein Maslow calls for a "revolution in the theory of science . . . (which) will affect not only the science of psychology but all other sciences as well," in R. May (ed.), *op. cit.*, p. 58.

and the agent, typically, has a reason for doing them.

Now consider an intentional action like Iago's plotting against Othello. No doubt Iago makes various movements and sounds, and these are "hard data" of direct sense perception which can be described from "outside" without any reference to what is going on in Iago's mind. Psychologists who claim that "the behavior of the subject, verbal or not, is an event in the external world of the scientist, just as is the behavior of a rat" [30] are claiming that psychology, as a science, must confine itself to this external, spectatorial point of view. But if it does, then it is not dealing with "verbal behavior" if this means more than the emission of sounds. For if we describe men as "speaking" then our description presupposes that they are using words which have meanings, words which are combined in accordance with a system of rules. But meanings and rules are not "events in the external world." So if we describe what happens from a purely external point of view as the mere occurrence of events (i.e., the emission of certain sounds), we cannot at the same time describe it as "speaking."

Nor can we confine ourselves to the "outside" if we are to describe what Iago does *as* plotting. For "plotting" is not logically equivalent to a physical description of some complicated series of movements and sounds. If Iago is really plotting then he must *understand* what he is doing, he must be aware of the relation between what he does now and the consequences this will have for Othello. His action is purposive, he is using means to attain an end, and we can ask whether what he did was the right, the appropriate, the rational thing to do—questions which make no sense when asked of a purely physical description of his movements. If Iago's actions were not intended to have certain consequences in the future, then we could not describe what he does as "plotting." So if we describe Iago in this way, we take his words and deeds to have a significance which is not open to direct sense

inspection, a significance which is understood only when we understand his intentions. But intentions are not merely "events in the external world." [31]

To be sure, when we describe Iago as "plotting" (or performing some other intentional action), we are not asserting the occurrence of any events other than, or additional to, those referred to in a physical description of the movements and sounds he makes. The same activity can be described in a number of ways, and what a man does when he plots can also be described as a complicated series of movements and sounds. Insofar as we describe what happens in this way we are dealing with "events in the external world" which can be explained from the "outside," perhaps in terms of some neuro-physiological theory. But when we do this we are not dealing with what concerns students of distinctively human behavior—e.g., plotting, marrying, etc.—but are dealing instead with what concerns the physiologist—i.e., the movements and sounds made by human organisms under certain conditions. If, on the other hand, we are concerned with intentional actions, then we are concerned with behavior that is described as having a point to it, a point that can only be understood from "inside" in terms of the considerations which lead the agent to decide on this as the right thing to do. Neuro-physiological talk cannot tell us why Iago plotted against Othello, but "to get the lieutenancy" can. And when we explain in terms of reasons our "image of man" is the one championed by the existential approach—here we see the responsible agent who makes choices and acts with a view to the future.

Because men alone can act rationally, they alone can act irrationally. And their irrationality, like their rationality, can be explained in a way in which the behavior of things that never act for reasons cannot be explained. This, I suggest, is the valid insight of "existential psychology."

---

[30] Mandler and Kessen, *op. cit.*, p. 37.

[31] Of course, I am not denying that we discover his intentions from the things he says and does, or would say and do under certain conditions. But then the things he says and does are not *merely* "events in the external world."

What is "normal"?

Ruth Benedict (1887-1948)

One of America's foremost anthropologists, Ruth Benedict was educated at Vassar and at Columbia University. She was on the Columbia faculty from 1923 until her death. Her studies of primitive cultures have been widely read. Her books include Patterns of Culture (*1934*), *which is one of the best known of recent works in anthropology,* Zuñi Mythology (*1935*), Race, Science and Politics (*1940*), *and* The Chrysanthemum and the Sword (*1946*), *a study of Japanese culture.*

Miss Benedict came to believe that different culture systems expressed different choices of values which constituted their basic styles or emphases. She believed that cultures differ sharply from one another but that all are equally valid. Each culture makes a norm of its preferential pattern, but there are no universal standards. In the following selection from one of her articles she argues the case for cultural relativity.

Modern social anthropology has become more and more a study of the varieties and common elements of cultural environment and the consequences of these in human behavior. For such a study of diverse social orders primitive peoples fortunately provide a laboratory not yet entirely vitiated by the spread of a standardized world-wide civilization. Dyaks and Hopis, Fijians and Yakuts are significant for psychological and sociological study because only among these simpler peoples has there been sufficient isolation to give opportunity for the development of localized social forms. In the higher cultures the standardization of custom and belief over a couple of continents has given a false sense of the inevitability of the particular forms that have gained currency, and we need to turn to a wider survey in order to check the conclusions we hastily base upon this near-universality of familiar customs. Most of

From Ruth Benedict, "Anthropology and the Abnormal," in *The Journal of General Psychology*, vol. 10 (1934), pp. 59–82. Reprinted by permission of The Journal Press.

the simpler cultures did not gain the wide currency of the one which, out of our experience, we identify with human nature, but this was for various historical reasons, and certainly not for any that gives us as its carriers a monopoly of social good or of social sanity. Modern civilization, from this point of view, becomes not a necessary pinnacle of human achievement but one entry in a long series of possible adjustments.

These adjustments, whether they are in mannerisms like the ways of showing anger, or joy, or grief in any society, or in major human drives like those of sex, prove to be far more variable than experience in any one culture would suggest. In certain fields, such as that of religion or of formal marriage arrangements, these wide limits of variability are well known and can be fairly described. In others it is not yet possible to give a generalized account, but that does not absolve us of the task of indicating the significance of the work that has been done and of the problems that have arisen.

One of these problems relates to the cus- **293**

tomary modern normal-abnormal categories and our conclusions regarding them. In how far are such categories culturally determined, or in how far can we with assurance regard them as absolute? In how far can we regard inability to function socially as diagnostic of abnormality, or in how far is it necessary to regard this as a function of the culture?

As a matter of fact, one of the most striking facts that emerge from a study of widely varying cultures is the ease with which our abnormals function in other cultures. It does not matter what kind of "abnormality" we choose for illustration, those which indicate extreme instability, or those which are more in the nature of character traits like sadism or delusions of grandeur or of persecution, there are well-described cultures in which these abnormals function at ease and with honor, and apparently without danger or difficulty to the society.

The most notorious of these is trance and catalepsy. Even a very mild mystic is aberrant in our culture. But most peoples have regarded even extreme psychic manifestations not only as normal and desirable, but even as characteristic of highly valued and gifted individuals. . . . It is hard for us, born and brought up in a culture that makes no use of the experience, to realize how important a rôle it may play and how many individuals are capable of it, once it has been given an honorable place in any society. . . .

The most spectacular illustrations of the extent to which normality may be culturally defined are those cultures where an abnormality of our culture is the cornerstone of their social structure. It is not possible to do justice to these possibilities in a short discussion. A recent study of an island of northwest Melanesia by Fortune [*Sorcerers of Dobu*] describes a society built upon traits which we regard as beyond the border of paranoia. In this tribe the exogamic groups look upon each other as prime manipulators of black magic, so that one marries always into an enemy group which remains for life one's deadly and unappeasable foes. They look upon a good garden crop as a confession of theft, for everyone is engaged in making magic to induce into his garden the productive-

ness of his neighbors'; therefore no secrecy in the island is so rigidly insisted upon as the secrecy of a man's harvesting of his yams. Their polite phrase at the acceptance of a gift is, "And if you now poison me, how shall I repay you this gift?" Their preoccupation with poisoning is constant; no woman ever leaves her cooking pot for a moment unattended. Even the great affinal economic exchanges that are characteristic of this Melanesian culture area are quite altered in Dobu since they are incompatible with this fear and distrust that pervades the culture. They go farther and people the whole world outside their own quarters with such malignant spirits that all-night feasts and ceremonials simply do not occur here. They have even rigorous religiously enforced customs that forbid the sharing of seed even in one family group. Anyone else's food is deadly poison to you, so that communality of stores is out of the question. For some months before harvest the whole society is on the verge of starvation, but if one falls to the temptation and eats up one's seed yams, one is an outcast and a beachcomber for life. There is no coming back. It involves, as a matter of course, divorce and the breaking of all social ties.

Now in this society where no one may work with another and no one may share with another, Fortune describes the individual who was regarded by all his fellows as crazy. He was not one of those who periodically ran amok and, beside himself and frothing at the mouth, fell with a knife upon anyone he could reach. Such behavior they did not regard as putting anyone outside the pale. They did not even put the individuals who were known to be liable to these attacks under any kind of control. They merely fled when they saw the attack coming on and kept out of the way. "He would be all right tomorrow." But there was one man of sunny, kindly disposition who liked work and liked to be helpful. The compulsion was too strong for him to repress it in favor of the opposite tendencies of his culture. Men and women never spoke of him without laughing; he was silly and simple and definitely crazy. Nevertheless, to the ethnologist used to a culture that has, in Christianity, made his type the model of all virtue, he seemed a pleasant fellow.

An even more extreme example, because it is of a culture that has built itself upon a more complex abnormality, is that of the North Pacific Coast of North America. The civilization of the Kwakiutl, at the time when it was first recorded in the last decades of the nineteenth century, was one of the most vigorous in North America. It was built up on an ample economic supply of goods, the fish which furnished their food staple being practically inexhaustible and obtainable with comparatively small labor, and the wood which furnished the material for their houses, their furnishings, and their arts being, with however much labor, always procurable. They lived in coastal villages that compared favorably in size with those of any other American Indians and they kept up constant communication by means of sea-going dug-out canoes.

It was one of the most vigorous and zestful of the aboriginal cultures of North America, with complex crafts and ceremonials, and elaborate and striking arts. It certainly had none of the earmarks of a sick civilization. The tribes of the Northwest Coast had wealth, and exactly in our terms. That is, they had not only a surplus of economic goods, but they made a game of the manipulation of wealth. It was by no means a mere direct transcription of economic needs and the filling of those needs. It involved the idea of capital, of interest, and of conspicuous waste. It was a game with all the binding rules of a game, and a person entered it as a child. His father distributed wealth for him, according to his ability, at a small feast or potlatch, and each gift the receiver was obliged to accept and to return after a short interval with interest that ran to about 100 per cent a year. By the time the child was grown, therefore, he was well launched, a larger potlatch had been given for him on various occasions of exploit or initiation, and he had wealth either out at usury or in his own possession. Nothing in the civilization could be enjoyed without validating it by the distribution of this wealth. Everything that was valued, names and songs as well as material objects, were passed down in family lines, but they were always publicly assumed with accompanying sufficient distributions of property. It was the game of validating and exercising all the privileges one could accumulate from one's various forbears, or by gift, or by marriage, that made the chief interest of the culture. Everyone in his degree took part in it, but many, of course, mainly as spectators. In its highest form it was played out between rival chiefs representing not only themselves and their family lines but their communities, and the object of the contest was to glorify oneself and to humiliate one's opponent. On this level of greatness the property involved was no longer represented by blankets, so many thousand of them to a potlatch, but by higher units of value. These higher units were like our bank notes. They were incised copper tablets, each of them named, and having a value that depended upon their illustrious history. This was as high as ten thousand blankets, and to possess one of them, still more to enhance its value at a great potlatch, was one of the greatest glories within the compass of the chiefs of the Northwest Coast.

The details of this manipulation of wealth are in many ways a parody on our own economic arrangements, but it is with the motivations that were recognized in this contest that we are concerned in this discussion. The drives were those which in our own culture we should call megalomaniac. There was an uncensored self-glorification and ridicule of the opponent that it is hard to equal in other cultures outside of the monologues of the abnormal. . . . All of existence was seen in terms of insult. Not only derogatory acts performed by a neighbor or an enemy, but all untoward events, like a cut when one's axe slipped, or a ducking when one's canoe overturned, were insults. All alike threatened first and foremost one's ego security, and the first thought one was allowed was how to get even, how to wipe out the insult. . . .

In their behavior at great bereavements this set of the culture comes out most strongly. Among the Kwakiutl it did not matter whether a relative had died in bed of disease, or by the hand of an enemy, in either case death was an affront to be wiped out by the death of another person. The fact that one had been caused to mourn was proof that one had been put upon. A chief's sister and her daughter had gone up to Victoria, and either because they drank bad whiskey or because their boat capsized they never came back. The chief called together his warriors. "Now I ask you, tribes, who shall wail? Shall I do it or shall another?" The spokesman answered, of course, "Not you, Chief. Let some other of the tribes." Immediately they set up the war pole to announce their intention of wiping out the injury, and gathered a war party. They set out, and found seven men and two children asleep and killed them. "Then they felt good when they arrived at Sebaa in the evening."

The point which is of interest to us is that in our society those who on that occasion would feel good when they arrived at Sebaa that evening would be definitely abnormal. There would be some, even in our society, but it is not a recognized and approved mood under the circumstances. On the Northwest Coast those are favored and fortunate to whom that mood under those circumstances is congenial, and those to whom it is repugnant are unlucky. This latter minority can register in their own culture only by doing violence to their congenial responses and acquiring others that are difficult for them. The person, for instance, who, like a Plains Indian whose wife has been taken from him, is too proud to fight, can deal with the Northwest Coast civilization only by ignoring its strongest bents. If he cannot achieve it, he is the deviant in that culture, their instance of abnormality. . . .

Behavior honored upon the Northwest Coast is one which is recognized as abnormal in our civilization, and yet it is sufficiently close to the attitudes of our own culture to be intelligible to us and to have a definite vocabulary with which we may discuss it. The megalomaniac paranoid trend is a definite danger in our society. It is encouraged by some of our major preoccupations, and it confronts us with a choice of two possible attitudes. One is to brand it as abnormal and reprehensible, and is the attitude we have chosen in our civilization. The other is to make it an essential attribute of

ideal man, and this is the solution in the culture of the Northwest Coast.

These illustrations, which it has been possible to indicate only in the briefest manner, force upon us the fact that normality is culturally defined. An adult shaped to the drives and standards of either of these cultures, if he were transported into our civilization would fall into our categories of abnormality. He would be faced with the psychic dilemmas of the socially unavailable. In his own culture, however, he is the pillar of society, the end result of socially inculcated mores, and the problem of personal instability in his case simply does not arise.

No one civilization can possibly utilize in its mores the whole potential range of human behavior. Just as there are great numbers of possible phonetic articulations, and the possibility of language depends on a selection and standardization of a few of these in order that speech communication may be possible at all, so the possibility of organized behavior of every sort, from the fashions of local dress and houses to the dicta of a people's ethics and religion, depends upon a similar selection among the possible behavior traits. In the field of recognized economic obligations or sex tabus this selection is as non-rational and subconscious a process as it is in the field of phonetics. It is a process which goes on in the group for long periods of time and is historically conditioned by innumerable accidents of isolation or of contact of peoples. In any comprehensive study of psychology, the selection that different cultures have made in the course of history within the great circumference of potential behavior is of great significance.

Every society, beginning with some slight inclination in one direction or another, carries its preference farther and farther, integrating itself more and more completely upon its chosen basis, and discarding those types of behavior that are uncongenial. Most of those organizations of personality that seem to us most incontrovertibly abnormal have been used by different civilizations in the very foundations of their institutional life. Conversely the most valued traits of our normal individuals have been looked on in differently organized cultures as aberrant. Normality, in short, within a very wide range, is culturally defined. It is primarily a term for the socially elaborated segment of human behavior in any culture; and abnormality, a term for the segment that that particular civilization does not use. The very eyes with which we see the problem are conditioned by the long traditional habits of our own society.

It is a point that has been made more often in relation to ethics than in relation to psychiatry. We do not any longer make the mistake of deriving the morality of our own locality and decade directly from the inevitable constitution of human nature. We do not elevate it to the dignity of a first principle. We recognize that morality differs in every society, and is a convenient term for socially approved habits. Mankind has always preferred to say, "It is morally good," rather than "It is habitual," and the fact of this preference is matter enough for a critical science of ethics. But historically the two phrases are synonymous.

The concept of the normal is properly a variant of the concept of the good. It is that which society has approved. A normal action is one which falls well within the limits of expected behavior for a particular society. Its variability among different peoples is essentially a function of the variability of the behavior patterns that different societies have created for themselves, and can never be wholly divorced from a consideration of culturally institutionalized types of behavior.

Each culture is a more or less elaborate working-out of the potentialities of the segment it has chosen. In so far as a civilization is well integrated and consistent within itself, it will tend to carry farther and farther, according to its nature, its initial impulse toward a particular type of action, and from the point of view of any other culture those elaborations will include more and more extreme and aberrant traits.

Each of these traits, in proportion as it reinforces the chosen behavior patterns of that culture, is for that culture normal. Those individuals to whom it is congenial either con-

genitally, or as the result of childhood sets, are accorded prestige in that culture, and are not visited with the social contempt or disapproval which their traits would call down upon them in a society that was differently organized. On the other hand, those individuals whose characteristics are not congenial to the selected type of human behavior in that community are the deviants, no matter how valued their personality traits may be in a contrasted civilization.

The Dobuan who is not easily susceptible to fear of treachery, who enjoys work and likes to be helpful, is their neurotic and regarded as silly. On the Northwest Coast the person who finds it difficult to read life in terms of an insult contest will be the person upon whom fall all the difficulties of the culturally unprovided for. The person who does not find it easy to humiliate a neighbor, nor to see humiliation in his own experience, who is genial and loving, may, of course, find some unstandardized way of achieving satisfactions in his society, but not in the major patterned responses that his culture requires of him. If he is born to play an important rôle in a family with many hereditary privileges, he can succeed only by doing violence to his whole personality. If he does not succeed, he has betrayed his culture; that is, he is abnormal.

I have spoken of individuals as having sets toward certain types of behavior, and of these sets as running sometimes counter to the types of behavior which are institutionalized in the culture to which they belong. From all that we know of contrasting cultures it seems clear that differences of temperament occur in every society. The matter has never been made the subject of investigation, but from the available material it would appear that these temperament types are very likely of universal recurrence. That is, there is an ascertainable range of human behavior that is found wherever a sufficiently large series of individuals is observed. But the proportion in which behavior types stand to one another in different societies is not universal. The vast majority of the individuals in any group are shaped to the fashion of that culture. In other words, most individuals are plastic to the moulding force of the society into which they are born. In a society that values trance, as in India, they will have supernormal experience. In a society that institutionalizes homosexuality, they will be homosexual. In a society that sets the gathering of possessions as the chief human objective, they will amass property. The deviants, whatever the type of behavior the culture has institutionalized, will remain few in number, and there seems no more difficulty in moulding the vast malleable majority to the "normality" of what we consider an aberrant trait than to the normality of such accepted behavior patterns as acquisitiveness. The small proportion of the number of the deviants in any culture is not a function of the sure instinct with which that society has built itself upon the fundamental sanities, but of the universal fact that, happily, the majority of mankind quite readily take any shape that is presented to them.

Social science and norms

Gordon W. Allport (b. 1897)

Gordon W. Allport, one of America's leading psychologists, was born in Indiana and educated in the public schools of Cleveland, Ohio, and at Harvard, where he earned a doctor's degree. He has been a member of the Harvard faculty since 1930, and is now professor of psychology in the department of social relations. During World War II he served on the Emergency Committee in Psychology, specializing in problems of civilian morale and in the psychology of rumor. Among his published works are The Psychology of Radio, *with Hadley Cantril (1935),* Personality: A Psychological Interpretation *(1937),* The Psychology of Rumor, *with Leo Postman (1947),* The Individual and His Religion *(1950),* The Nature of Prejudice *(1954), and* Becoming: Basic Considerations for a Psychology of Personality *(1955).*

The following selection is an address given by Allport at the conference on New Knowledge in Human Values held in October, 1957, at Massachusetts Institute of Technology. In this paper he draws on his broad knowledge of the field of psychology to argue the thesis that social science can now help to confirm or disconfirm the ethical theories which philosophers have held. In the process of making this point, Allport challenges implicitly the position of cultural relativity adopted by Ruth Benedict.

Several of the contributors to this symposium have made the point that although moral values cannot be derived from natural data nor from science, they can in some sense be validated (confirmed or disconfirmed) by the activity of science. This point has been made by both natural scientists and social scientists on our program. I find myself in full agreement.

Likewise I agree with Professor Maslow when he says that the validating capacity of social science is still somewhat feeble. Its data and methods are coarse and imprecise. One critic complained that "social science is nothing but journalism without a dateline." However that may be, I offer my paper in support of the proposition that modern social science, for all its imperfections, can now aid us in selecting from among the moral imperatives prescribed by various philosophers as guides to social policy. It can do so by helping us test broad types of ethical theory in the light of our modern knowledge of human nature and human collectivities.

"Normative Compatibility in the Light of Social Science," by Gordon W. Allport in *New Knowledge in Human Values,* edited by Abraham H. Maslow. Reprinted with the permission of Harper & Row, Publishers, Incorporated.

Testing ethical theory by social science

By way of illustration, and without offering detailed evidence at this time, let me mention some of the broad types of ethical theory that seem to fare badly when they are exposed to social-scientific analysis.

299

Theories of *renunciation or asceticism*, to give one example, make the error of assuming that men seek a life that is one-sided rather than one that is full and abundant. According to this view morality is largely a matter of repression or negation—a denial of much or most of man's endowment for growth. We cannot, of course, deny that this path of life, with its implied beatific vision, may be well suited for a few; but it is doomed to failure if it is prescribed for the masses of mankind.

Authoritarian morality, of which we have seen much in our day, defines goodness merely in terms of obedience. The adult, with all his potentialities for growth, is kept at the childhood level. While it is easy for many people to adopt the authoritarian code in order to "escape from freedom," the result, we know, is stultification, tyranny, and war and therefore the destruction of virtually all values.

Legalistic theories prescribe morality in terms of "thou shalts" or "thou shalt nots." The psychological error here is that the letter of the law, being inflexible, does not guide men in the novel and changing encounters of daily life.

Utopian theories are inept, not because they counsel perfection—because all morality does that—but because they plot no pathway from today's quandaries to the ultimate beatitude they depict.

Utilitarian ethics—in fact every version of *hedonism*—fixes men's minds on a will o' the wisp. Happiness can never be a tangible goal; it can only be a by-product of otherwise motivated activity. We may add that in the mid-nineteenth century ethical hedonism (*laissez-faire*) was given an explicit trial in the social policies of Britain and America and succeeded in creating moral dilemmas not in solving them. In short, its failure was experimentally demonstrated much as the failure of authoritarian morality has been demonstrated in our own day.

With these negative examples before us, we now ask what type of ethical theory does social science find most congruent with recent researches on human nature and on human aggregates.

Before answering this question let us remind ourselves that all theories of moral conduct have one primary purpose: they set before us some appropriate formula for handling conflict —whether the conflict be between warring interests in one individual or among individuals. In testing rival ethical theories, therefore, it is necessary to know a good deal about the interests of men—about the motives that are likely to come into conflict within the person or between persons or groups of persons.

Desires versus demands

Although our present interest is in validatable moral theory, and not in motivation, let me refer to one relevant finding concerning motivation that comes from industrial research. Summarizing a number of studies of motivation and morale in industry, Likert concludes that workers have, in effect, two primary sets of interests. They want ego-recognition, a broad motivational category that includes credit for work done, economic security, praise, and many other forms of self-esteem. But they also want, no less urgently, affiliation with the group, a dimension that includes pleasant relations with the foreman, a sense of participation in team work, and above all the satisfaction of conducting themselves in terms of the values and normative expectations prevailing within the group of co-workers.[1]

The point is important. In industry, and probably in any form of human association, men wish to preserve their self-esteem—their self-love—and simultaneously wish to have warm, affiliative relations with their fellows. No one seems initially to want to hate. Hatred grows up as a consequence of blocked self-esteem and blocked affection.

Now it has been further discovered that high production, high morale, and successful relations can be achieved only when formulae

[1] Rensis Likert, *Motivational Dimensions in Administration*, University of Michigan, Ann Arbor, Mich., 1951.

are discovered that permit the adequate expression of these two sets of interests on the part of all participants. The movement called "human relations in industry" teaches this lesson over and over again, whether it be in terms of labor-management councils, group decision, the retraining of foremen, or basic changes in managerial philosophy.[2] In former days industry ran almost entirely on the basis of punishment, or, we may say, subtraction. Workers were asked to give up their identity, their pride, their social impulses during the hours they were earning a living. Today the saying is, "The whole man goes to work." Realizing this fact, certain industries now have counsellors on personal and family problems. Through improved communication the individual is given a means of participating in his own destiny. His private life and his work life are integrated; the interests of management and employees come together to a greater degree than formerly. I am not saying that Utopia is achieved in industry, but only that experimentation has already gone far enough to demonstrate the validity of ethical theory that advocates the resolution of conflict through the harmonious *integration of interests*.

This approach to morality does not aim at the reconciling of conflicting *demands*. Demands are usually nothing more than ways and means prematurely conceived to be the only channels for the realization of desires. All theories of the enlargement of interests stress the distinction between demands and desires, that is to say, between instrumental and intrinsic values, and insist that the moral individual himself must at every step distinguish between his demands and his desires. E. B. Holt calls the process *discrimination*, Ralph Barton Perry calls it *reflection*.[3]

I can illustrate the distinction by borrowing a classic incident from Mary Follett. It seems that, in a certain part of Vermont, dairy farmers who lived up the hill from the railway station and those who lived down the hill from the station both claimed the right to unload their milk supply first at the platform. Their demands were irreconcilable, and for a long time a feud prevailed. Finally they perceived their error. Their root desire was not, as they thought, to "unload first." This was a demand. The underlying desire of both factions was not to be kept waiting. Profiting from this discriminative insight they joined forces on a Saturday afternoon, lengthened the railway platform and thereafter were both able to unload "first."

Although the illustration may seem a bit pat, it does contain the paradigm for moral action: two or more conflicting sets of apparent purposes collide; they are analyzed reflectively and so purged of preconceived ways and means; the root desires themselves are then brought to fulfillment through the invention of a larger framework that renders them compatible rather than incompatible as they at first seemed to be. In Professor Weisskopf's terms, a "union upward" is achieved.

The principle of enlargement of interests

Wartime research is filled with examples of our principle. I shall cite one study, drawn from Stouffer's investigation of the American soldier.[4] Men in combat, we should expect, would show the maximum of destructive, self-preserving motivation. They were asked the question, "When the going was tough, how much did it help you to think that you couldn't let the other men down?" Approximately *two-thirds* said that it "helped a lot." Thus the affiliative motive even under extreme stress seems to hold twice as many men to their task

---

[2] The story is told in F. Roethlisberger and W. J. Dickson, *Management and the Worker*, Harvard University Press, Cambridge, Mass., 1939; and in S. D. Hoslett, *Human Factors in Management*, Harper & Row, Publishers, Incorporated, New York, 1946.

[3] E. B. Holt, *The Freudian Wish and Its Place in Ethics*, Henry Holt and Company, Inc., New York, 1915; R. B. Perry, *Realms of Value: a*

Critique of Human Civilization, Harvard University Press, Cambridge, Mass., 1954, chap. 6.

[4] S. A. Stouffer et al., *The American Soldier*, Princeton University Press, Princeton, N.J., 1949, vol. 2, p. 178.

as does the motive of hate. The point to note is that an enlargement of interest systems to include one's comrades is, even in the time of physical combat, a natural bent of man.

Successful psychotherapy offers a basic illustration of the principle. The most elementary formula for encouraging a patient is to assure him that "lots of people suffer from your difficulty." Most patients brighten when they know that they are not alone in their misery. Such assurance does not, of course, solve the patient's problem but he finds that even this imaginative integration of interests proves helpful. True neuroses, we know, are best defined as stubborn self-centeredness. No therapist can cure a phobia, obsession, prejudice, or hostility by the method of subtraction. He can only assist the patient to achieve a value-system and outlook that will blanket or absorb the troublesome factor.

The successful resolution of *social* conflict proceeds always along the same lines. Take the issue of desegregation, a problem of the first magnitude not only in this country but in the world at large. On the social level it is a matter of bringing resistant provincial interests in line with more inclusive national and world values. On the personal level, it is a problem of enlarging the outlook of individuals who live now according to an exclusionist formula that secures for them self-esteem at the expense of dark-skinned people. At present they are willing to form no inclusive unit with the federal majority in this country nor with the world majority; nor will they form inclusive units with the Negro minority in their midst. They are not able even to resolve the moral dilemma in their own breasts. In all directions the principle of inclusion fails.

At the moment this particular problem is most acute in the United States and in South Africa. Although I have not the space to diagnose the situation in detail, let me say briefly that so far as South Africa is concerned the chief blunder of the Nationalist Party government, morally and politically, lies in its failure to consult with the Bantu peoples concerning their own destiny. The master group *tells* the servant group, who outnumber the masters

three to one, that they have nothing to contribute to the life of the multiracial society excepting manual labor. Thus the cultural pride, love of homeland, and all other normal human aspirations and abilities of the Bantus are excluded from the existing matrix of values. The policy of apartheid extends to housing, transportation, schools, public assemblies, recreation, and politics, so that there is no legal opportunity to become acquainted. And needless to say the precondition of all normative compatibility *is* communication.

Both South Africa and the United States are exciting test cases for social science at the present time, the one following officially a policy of *excluding* interests, the other an official policy of *inclusion*. The world is watching the outcome.

We could pile up evidence from areas of conflict I have not yet touched upon—from family, classroom, neighborhood, municipality, and deliberative assemblies, but I shall limit myself to the question of how far it is possible for people, especially for children, to learn the moral principle of discrimination and inclusion.

The process of enlargement in childhood

A study by Piaget and his associates is enlightening.[5] These investigators find that the children around six and seven years of age, living in the city of Geneva, are unable to think of themselves as both Genevese and as Swiss. Given a crayon and asked to draw a circle for Geneva and for Switzerland, they ordinarily draw two circles side by side. And they insist that if they are Genevese they cannot simultaneously be Swiss. As for foreign lands, the children suffer from even greater cognitive impoverishment. Concerning Italy they know only that their father visited Italy, or an aunt comes from there. Even loyalty to the homeland does not yet exist. The child's

[5] J. Piaget and Anne-Marie Weil, "The Development in Children of the Idea of the Homeland of Relations with Other Countries," *International Soc. Sci. Bull.*, 3:561–578, 1951.

affective reactions are wholly egocentric. "I like Lausanne because I ate chocolate there." "I like Bern because my uncle lives there." In Piaget's language, these children have not yet commenced the process of "decentering," that is, from the unit of self to any larger social unit.

Ages eight and nine are transitional. Although the child draws a circle for Geneva properly inside the circle for Switzerland, he still has difficulty translating spatial enclosure into terms of social enclosure. He may say, for example, "I'm Swiss now so I can't be Genevese any longer." True, the concept of the homeland is gradually growing, but in a self-centered way. The child says, "I like Switzerland because I was born there." As for foreign lands, he knows of their existence but commonly views them with scorn. The French are dirty; the Americans want war; and people living in other lands all wish they were Swiss, of course. The child at this age has taken bits of conversation from his home and school and fitted them to his own affective self-centeredness.

Only at the age of ten and eleven do we find that decentering has made appreciable progress. Egocentricity begins to give way to the principles of reciprocity and inclusion. The child of ten or eleven understands his dual membership in a smaller and larger political unit. He also gives fewer personal reasons for his affective attachment to his homeland. Switzerland now becomes the land of the Red Cross; it is the country without war. Further, the child understands that members of other countries are as attached to their own lands as he is to his—this is the principle of "reciprocity." But cognitive reciprocity does not necessarily mean that the child is capable of seeing good in all the peoples he knows about. He may still despise them. Whether the child outgrows his affective provincialism along with his cognitive provincialism seems to depend largely on the attitudes he learns from his parents.

Now this study teaches us certain lessons. For one thing, it shows that maturation and time are needed to achieve a decentering from the unit of self to a progressively larger social unit. Further, this process may be arrested at any stage along the way, especially in its affective aspects. It is significant Piaget gives no evidence that his children (at least up to fourteen years of age) discern the possibility of membership in any supranational grouping. Decentering has not reached the point where the child feels himself as belonging to the European region, to be a supporter of the United Nations; certainly none mentions his membership in the inclusive collective of mankind. Even if in later years such a cognitive enlargement takes place, the chances are that the corresponding affective enlargement will be lacking. Using Piaget's terms, we may then say that adults in all nations are still incompletely decentered. Cognitively they may stumble at the threshold of supranational chambers, but affectively they fail to enter.

Resolving international conflicts

A study conducted in Belgium by de Bie shows how few adults are concerned with identification across national boundaries. Even those of a higher level of education have little sense of international relationships. Membership in any unit larger than the nation simply is not a psychological reality. Let international problems be handled by our leaders, they say.[6] And most, though not all, leaders, we know, lack affective, or even cognitive, decentering beyond the sphere of purely national interests.

In its *Tensions and Technology* Series, UNESCO has recenty published a volume entitled *The Nature of Conflict*, surveying much relevant research. In summing up the results, R. C. Angell concludes that interacting nations will enjoy peace only when they become parts of a social system that embraces them.[7] It is not necessary to destroy national loyalties, but only to include them. In Angell's words,

[6] P. de Bie, "Certain Psychological Aspects of Benelux," *International Soc. Sci. Bull.*, 3: 540–552, 1951.

[7] R. C. Angell, "Discovering Paths to Peace," chap. 4 in *The Nature of Conflict*, UNESCO, 1957.

"The social system which is painfully coming to birth will grow out of national states, but their structures will not be annihilated in the process." J. C. Flugel has made the same point: "We must probably agree that intra-group behavior is on the whole far more moral than inter-group behavior; and in so far as the latter is moral it is often because the groups in question are for certain purposes themselves members of a larger group, so that it can at bottom be reduced to behavior of the intra-group variety." [8]

Such conclusions are based on a considerable amount of historical and contemporary research. This research, broadly speaking, indicates the relative futility of the moral creeds and strategies that are hortatory, authoritarian, hedonistic, legalistic, or Utopian. To abolish war some of these theories have said: let us give up our prejudices, our malice and our fear; let us remove barriers to trade, to communications and travel; let nations surrender land, money, aspirations, armaments, pride, and sovereignty. Though it is necessary that some of these subtractions take place, they will not do so if the approach is negative. Each and every local interest, deplored by us as making for international discord, serves a legitimate purpose so long as no social system exists to transcend nationhood. To state the case psychologically, individuals who favor the conditions making for war do so because they have no embracing circle of loyalties or expectations that would render these present conditions maladaptive to their purposes. Conflicts of value are never solved by the process of direct collision or defeat, nor by the double-edged subtraction that comes through compromise, but only through a process of inclusion and recentering.

Although the subtractive, authoritarian, legalistic, and utopian moralities still prevail, we view with hope certain signs of progress. The United Nations, of course, is organized for the express purpose of resolving conflict through the enlargement of interest systems. True, its major activities seem for the present to be hopelessly blocked by a centering on national interests. There are even signs of regress in the present violent upsurge of national, religious, and linguistic provincialism. So we must count our gains humbly: evidences of regional grouping, increased student and personnel exchanges (though evaluative studies of this policy seem to show somewhat less gain than we might hope).[9] We note progress against illiteracy which eventually may establish a firmer ground for communication. International bodies of scientists and other scholars are all to the good. So too the Olympic games. But perhaps our firmest gain is the widening circle of enlightenment and discussion that our common problems have evoked, as exemplified in the present symposium.

Returning to Piaget's research for a moment, we can surely say of the average adult that cognitively and affectively he is potentially capable of considerable decentering. The average man has no difficulty at all thinking of himself at one and the same time as a member of his family, neighborhood, town, state, and nation. Along the way he manages to include his church, lodge, and friendship circles. The principle is thus established that larger loyalties do not clash so long as they allow for the maximum possible inclusion of smaller loyalties. Trouble, to be sure, arises when values conflict at the same level. A bigamist cannot comfortably apportion his loyalty between two wives, nor a traitor serve two countries. But still it is clearly within the capacity of men to continue the decentering process illustrated by Piaget's children, and to go well beyond them. Empirically we can point, as Professor Sorokin and Professor Maslow have done, to individuals who have already realized this capacity.[10] Unfor-

---

[8] J. C. Flugel, "Some Neglected Aspects of World Integration," chap. 6 in T. H. Pear (ed.), *Psychological Factors of Peace and War*, Hutchinson & Co. (Publishers), Ltd., London, 1950.

[9] *Journal of Social Issues,* vol. 12, no. 1, 1956; *Annals of the American Academy of Political and Social Science,* vol. 295, 1954.

[10] P. A. Sorokin, *Altruistic Love: A Study of American Good Neighbors and Christian Saints,* Beacon Press, Boston, 1950; A. H. Maslow, *Motivation and Personality,* Harper & Row, Publishers, Incorporated, New York, 1954.

tunately, they are still relatively few in numbers.

Nothing that I have said is intended to detract from the positive values of rivalry, or of pride in one's kin and kind. Rival scientists struggle vigorously to prove their respective theories against their opponents but they do so within the frame of loyalty to science as a whole. What is good in free enterprise comes from competition regulated by common loyalty to the rules of the game. One's pride in one's way of life is not incompatible with an attitude of "let both grow together until the harvest." To critics who reply that conflict is the essence of existence, that "to live is to struggle; to survive is to conquer," we reply that we do not aim to eliminate struggle but to establish it within a framework that will actually lead to survival in a fully human sense and not to extermination in a strictly literal sense.

Preparing the individual

The root of the matter, of course, lies in the posture of the individual's mentality. Psychologists today like to speak of "cognitive style." Now the style of mind that welcomes rivalry within the constraints of potential inclusion is marked by a kind of *tentativeness*. It does not insist upon the absolute validity of its equations; it prefers a way of life without prescribing it for all; it possesses humor; it maintains its loyalties within an expanding and yet discriminating frame. Its judgments are tentative, its religion heuristic, its ultimate sentiment compassion. There are, as we have said, people with this outlook. It is they who in this period of rapid social change give the world such stability as it possesses. Our problem is to increase their numbers.

On this particular problem I will say only one thing at this time. The cognitive style I have defined is the precise opposite of the prejudiced style of life. The past decade or so has produced hundreds of studies of the sources and correlates of prejudice.[11] If the prejudiced

[11] G. W. Allport, *The Nature of Prejudice*, Addison-Wesley Publishing Company, Inc., Reading, Mass., 1954.

style of life can be learned—and certainly it is not innate—then surely the tentative style, or, in Gandhi's terms, the "equi-minded" outlook can also be acquired. There is no simple formula for teaching it, but the books lie open for those who can adapt current research to educational policy for the home, school, and church. In the home there is much to be said for the method of the family conference wherein all the members from the oldest to the articulate youngest can seek a rational inclusive plan for the fulfillment of their interests. In schools, I suggest, we discard if necessary up to 10 per cent of the present content and replace it with suitably chosen instruction and experience in the principle of integration of interests. The lesson should include classroom and playground activities as well as studies in neighborhood, national, and international experiments in inclusion. In my opinion our knowledge to date warrants this deliberate change in educational policies.

Final word

But, of course, our knowledge, solid as some of it is, has many deficiencies. And since the emphasis of this Society is upon research, let me conclude by stating explicitly four implications of my remarks for a possible research program.

First, at the level of the individual person we need to know much more about the frame of mind that I have called tentative or equi-minded, for to me it seems to be the very essence of altruism. Research by Sorokin and by Maslow has given us valuable insights, but much more of the same order is needed.

Second, a problem of joint concern to psychology, anthropology, and philosophy confronts us. The moral guideline we have laid down requires discrimination between root desires and demands, between intrinsic values and instrumentals. Now it seems probable that the root desires (not the demands) of men in all countries are very similar and therefore not incompatible. Hence I advocate cross-cultural investigations that will compare men's motives in many lands but always with a view to distinguishing their root desires from their demands.

Third, how can we develop symbols of inclusion that will assist children, and citizens, and statesmen to look beyond the confines of egocentricity? Without images it is impossible to form attitudes. Our symbols today are overwhelmingly local and nationalistic. We continue to view our membership circles, as did Piaget's children, as lying side by side, not as concentric. We have few symbols of inclusion, but even if effective supranational symbols existed, they would, of course, have no magic property. Men's choices can be only among sequences they have known, and so our problem of training involves also the giving of experience, especially in childhood, that will enlarge the cognitive style and turn the mind automatically toward the integrative mode of handling conflict.

Finally, continued philosophical research is needed concerning the principle I have outlined. The harmonious realization of abilities, interests, and purposes is, of course, a familiar theme in philosophies as diverse as those of Plato, Spinoza, Kant, Dewey, and Perry—to name but a few. What philosophy needs now to do, with the aid of social science, is to specify which inclusive sets of interest can best be achieved by which available techniques—in industry, in education, and in statescraft. Philosophy has the further critical task of refining the principle and examining instances where it may not fully apply. I am aware that not all conflicts are easily brought under our formula. Yet the philosophical task, I am convinced, is one of refinement and not of refutation, for the principle of maximal inclusion has the overwhelming testimony of social science in its support.

Creativity,
Beauty, and the Arts

Human creativity expresses itself in many forms of action and reflection. We recognize creativity in scientific discoveries, in the actions of social and political reformers, in the work of religious leaders, and in the writings of philosophers. Most often, however, we apply the term "creative" to the work of artists. Their only concern seems to be to make something integral that has not been made before, something constructed out of sensuous material, which has no purpose beyond simply being. In the creation of the work of art we seem to recognize the purest expression of human creativity. We tend also to associate works of art with something present in our experience which we call "beauty." What beauty is, whether it is a quality belonging to objects or a feeling present in a subject, whether it is an essential property of works of art or of the response to them—these questions have often been asked by artists, critics, and philosophers. They constitute some of the central problems of the branch of philosophy known as aesthetics.

Philosophers have asked themselves the fundamental question, What is art? Although numerous definitions have been offered throughout the history of aesthetic thought, some major types of theory have emerged. One, the imitation theory, was associated with ancient Greek philosophy. Plato, without giving a clear answer to the question, What is art?, wanted to limit severely the role of the poets and painters in his ideal state, because many of them were imitators of appearing things, which themselves were imitations of the Forms. Plato held that instead of leading us toward intelligible objects, imitative art leads us away from truth toward mere shadows and images. Aristotle, on the other hand, though he regarded tragic drama as the imitation of an action, valued tragedy over history, because it gives us knowledge of what is universal and possible in human affairs.

The imitation theory dominated aesthetic thought until modern times. The expression theory seems to be the characteristically modern theory, although its antecedents certainly existed even in ancient times. There is no single expression theory, since the word "expression" can have several meanings. To "express" might mean to "convey" or "communicate," to "embody," or to "clarify." The emphasis might be placed on a transaction between the artist and the audience, on the qualities embodied in the work, or on some process occurring in the mind of the artist. Whether the artist is to be distinguished from the nonartist by the experiences which he has or by his capacity to transform experiences into a work is a question which has given rise to much dispute.

One of the recurring problems in aesthetic thought concerns what has been called the "cognitive significance" of art. Is art a way of knowing what exists in fact? If so, how does it differ from other kinds of knowledge? If it is not a kind of knowledge, then what does it give us? In what way is it valuable?

Often it is said that art has basically to do with our emotional life, that it orders for us or reveals to us the qualities of our feelings. Sometimes this has been regarded as a cognitive function; that is, it is said that art allows us to "understand" emotion. Other theorists have maintained that art enables us to enjoy a richer emotional life but does not give us anything that ought to be called knowledge. Sometimes art has been regarded as a basic mode of insight into the nature of what is, more basic even than science and philosophy.

Let us now look at some of the specific problems considered in our readings. In his treatise on poetry, a short work that has had an unusual influence, Aristotle not only describes what he has observed to be the elements of successful tragic drama but also provides rules for constructing tragedies. In addition, he connects this poetic form—tragedy—with the philosopher's wider concerns. As we have noted, Aristotle sees the drama as superior to history because of its universality. Can we say that tragic drama helps us in some way to understand the conflicts of our own individual lives? If so, exactly how does it do this?

It is interesting to consider whether the qualities of the action and of the character of the tragic hero, as Aristotle describes them, are necessary to what we, in our time, would want to call tragedy. Can we say that Aristotle gives us critical standards for evaluating modern tragic drama? A great deal of attention has been given to Aristotle's unities of time, place, and action. Are these to be regarded, as they were by neoclassical interpreters, as absolute requirements for drama or are they rather more like provisional generalizations based on observation of the works of Aristotle's time? What, also, is the interpretation to be given to the catharsis, or purging of the emotions of pity and fear, which Aristotle says is effected by tragedy? Does catharsis have a moral effect, a psychotherapeutic effect, both, or neither? Are pity and fear the only emotions aroused by tragedy, or are they simply representative of the range of emotions involved in this kind of drama?

In our selection R. G. Collingwood offers his view of art as expression. Collingwood says that we mean something very definite by "expression" when speaking of art. When one says that an artist "expresses" emotion, he means that the artist clarifies and individualizes emotion. An emotion which is at first vague, merely a state of excitement, is explored, developed, and made evident to the artist himself and to other men through the process of creating the work of art. The artist proper, according to Collingwood, is to be distinguished sharply from the craftsman. The artist is not seeking to achieve a certain end, and it is not his function to employ specific techniques to achieve specific ends. His objective is not to arouse a certain feeling in his audience. Rather, by following through his indefinite emotion to clarity, he enables his audience to perceive their own emotions, that is, to give them expression. The artist differs from the ordinary man only in having solved the problem of how to bring his emotions to expression. After the artist has shown him how, the ordinary man is able to express emotion as well as the artist. Collingwood lays stress on the view that the emotion clarified in art is highly individual; the artist is interested in making definite not a certain kind of emotion but a certain particular emotion.

The views of both Aristotle and Collingwood, with their emphasis on the particular qualities of works of art and especially on the emotional factor in art, lead us to ask this question: Does artistic experience, whether of the creator, the performer, or the spectator, produce a special kind of value distinct from values of other kinds? If so, how are we to rank this aesthetic value in relation to other values? If not, of what kind of value is it an instance?

Our selection from Jacques Maritain gives us a characterization of poetic intuition and knowledge. The essence of Maritain's position is that the knowledge given the poet is knowledge by "connaturality," that is, knowledge based on an inclination or likeness or "affective union" between the knower and the known. The world enters the inwardness of the poet and becomes inseparable from the movements of his own inner life. The poet's only objective is to create, not to satisfy a particular need but to express the free creativity that is in him. In this respect, the poet, Maritain suggests, is something like God. The knowledge achieved in the poet's creative act is inseparable from its expression in the work of art. Maritain holds that the intelligence is involved in poetic knowledge "in its preconscious activity." Does Maritain's view depend on a certain doctrine of the human self, and, if so, how might one describe this doctrine in so far as it is suggested in the reading?

George Santayana's analysis of beauty is an attempt to make sense of this prominent quality of our experience in terms of a "naturalistic" outlook, that is, one which seeks to explain human conscious experience as an aspect of physical nature. Beauty consists of the quality of pleasure given in our interested experience of the world, Santayana holds, but it is a quality which we read back into objects, instead of locating it in our selves. Feeling, for Santayana, belongs to the same order of things as physical nature, and beauty is a feeling. It is a feature of our mental life which we treat in a peculiar way: we expel it from ourselves and allow it to cling to objects. The experience of beauty, Santayana contends, has all of the individual character of other aspects of our emotional life, and it is intimately connected with our desires as particular beings.

A number of the preceding selections are brought into focus in Paul Weiss's discussion of the likenesses and the differences between science and art. The sciences and the arts, Weiss maintains, are more alike than is often admitted. Among their likenesses are these: both take human experience as their point of departure and construct new worlds related to the experienced world. They differ, however, in that scientists try to discover the connections among phenomena, while artists attempt to reveal a reality which underlies the phenomenal world. The scientist emphasizes meanings that are the same for everyone and features of reality that can be reproduced for anyone, while the artist illuminates the qualitatively unique not otherwise available to all men.

One of Weiss's important points is that we are not justified in taking either the portrait of the world sketched by science or an artistic vision of the world as the whole of the real world. Each major discipline grasps an aspect of the real, and the real is richer than the formulations or expressions of any inquiry.

Weiss's view seems to challenge Collingwood on a significant point: As Collingwood sees it, the artist differs from other men only in being able to solve the problem of expressing emotion; Weiss apparently believes that the artist is distinguished from his audience by being capable of feeling and seeing in ways in which other men do not feel and see. If we take Collingwood's view of the artist's function, we should be interested in works of art because they clarify for us our own emotional life. If we take Weiss's view of the artist's function, why exactly should we concern ourselves with the works that artists produce?

Art as imitation

Aristotle (384-323 B.C).*

Aristotle's Poetics *is the most influential work in aesthetics to come down from ancient times, in fact one of the most influential ever produced. Employing his characteristic capacity for observation and analysis, Aristotle scrutinizes tragic drama and distinguishes its major elements. His account of the dramatic unities, his singling out of the emotions of pity and fear aroused in the spectator, and his view of tragedy as revealing the universal have rendered this brief and incomplete work remarkably authoritative. The general view of art as imitation and the particular account of tragedy as the imitation of an action have been of special interest to philosophers of the arts.*

I propose to treat of Poetry in itself and of its various kinds, noting the essential quality of each; to inquire into the structure of the plot as requisite to a good poem; into the number and nature of the parts of which a poem is composed; and similarly into whatever else falls within the same inquiry. Following, then, the order of nature, let us begin with the principles which come first.

2. Epic poetry and Tragedy, Comedy also and Dithyrambic poetry, and the music of the flute and of the lyre in most of their forms, are all in their general conception modes of imitation. 3. They differ, however, from one another in three respects,—the medium, the objects, the manner or mode of imitation, being in each case distinct.

4. For as there are persons who, by conscious art or mere habit, imitate and represent various objects through the medium of colour and form, or again by the voice; so in the arts above mentioned, taken as a whole, the imita-

tion is produced by rhythm, language, or "harmony," either singly or combined.

Thus in the music of the flute and of the lyre, "harmony" and rhythm alone are employed; also in other arts, such as that of the shepherd's pipe, which are essentially similar to these. 5. In dancing, rhythm alone is used without "harmony"; for even dancing imitates character, emotion, and action, by rhythmical movement.

6. There is another art which imitates by means of language alone, and that either in prose or verse—which verse, again, may either combine different metres or consist of but one kind—but this has hitherto been without a name. 7. For there is no common term we could apply to the mimes of Sophron and Xenarchus and the Socratic dialogues on the one hand; and, on the other, to poetic imitations in iambic, elegiac, or any similar metre. People do, indeed, add the word "maker" or "poet" to the name of the metre, and speak of elegiac poets, or epic (that is, hexameter) poets, as if it were not the imitation that makes the poet, but the verse that entitles them all indiscriminately to the name. 8. Even when a treatise on medicine or natural science is

From Aristotle, *Poetics,* Ch. 1–15, tr. S. H. Butcher (London: The Macmillan Company, Ltd., 1911).

* See the introductory note on Aristotle on page 151.

311

brought out in verse, the name of poet is by custom given to the author; and yet Homer and Empedocles have nothing in common but the metre, so that it would be right to call the one poet, the other physicist rather than poet. 9. On the same principle, even if a writer in his poetic imitation were to combine all metres, as Chaeremon did in his *Centaur*, which is a medley composed of metres of all kinds, we should bring him too under the general term poet. So much then for these distinctions.

10. There are, again, some arts which employ all the means above mentioned,—namely, rhythm, tune and metre. Such are Dithyrambic and Nomic poetry, and also Tragedy and Comedy; but between them the difference is, that in the first two cases these means are all employed in combination, in the latter, now one means is employed, now another.

Such, then, are the differences of the arts with respect to the medium of imitation.

2

Since the objects of imitation are men in action, and these men must be either of a higher or a lower type (for moral character mainly answers to these divisions, goodness and badness being the distinguishing marks of moral differences), it follows that we must represent men either as better than in real life, or as worse, or as they are. It is the same in painting. Polygnotus depicted men as nobler than they are, Pauson as less noble, Dionysius drew them true to life.

2. Now it is evident that each of the modes of imitation above mentioned will exhibit these differences, and become a distinct kind in imitating objects that are thus distinct. 3. Such diversities may be found even in dancing, flute-playing, and lyre-playing. So again in language, whether prose or verse unaccompanied by music. Homer, for example, makes men better than they are; Cleophon as they are; Hegemon the Thasian, the inventor of parodies, and Nicochares, the author of the *Deliad*, worse than they are. 4. The same thing holds good of Dithyrambs and Nomes; here too one may portray different types, as Timo-

theus and Philoxenus differed in representing their Cyclopes. The same distinction marks off Tragedy from Comedy; for Comedy aims at representing men as worse, Tragedy as better than in actual life.

3

There is still a third difference—the manner in which each of these objects may be imitated. For the medium being the same, and the objects the same, the poet may imitate by narration—in which case he can either take another personality as Homer does, or speak in his own person, unchanged—or he may present all his characters as living and moving before us.

2. These, then, as we said at the beginning, are the three differences which distinguish artistic imitation—the medium, the objects and the manner. So that from one point of view, Sophocles is an imitator of the same kind as Homer—for both imitate higher types of character; from another point of view, of the same kind as Aristophanes—for both imitate persons acting and doing. 3. Hence, some say, the name of "drama" is given to such poems, as representing action. For the same reason the Dorians claim the invention both of Tragedy and Comedy. The claim to Comedy is put forward by the Megarians,—not only by those of Greece proper, who allege that it originated under their democracy, but also by the Megarians of Sicily, for the poet Epicharmus, who is much earlier than Chionides and Magnes, belonged to that country. Tragedy too is claimed by certain Dorians of the Peloponnese. In each case they appeal to the evidence of language. Villages, they say, are by them called κῶμαι, by the Athenians δῆμοι: and they assume that Comedians were so named not from κωμάζειν, "to revel," but because they wandered from village to village (κατὰ κώμας), being excluded contemptuously from the city. They add also that the Dorian word for "doing" is δρᾶν, and the Athenian, πράττειν.

4. This may suffice as to the number and nature of the various modes of imitation.

4

Poetry in general seems to have sprung from two causes, each of them lying deep in our nature. 2. First, the instinct of imitation is implanted in man from childhood, one difference between him and other animals being that he is the most imitative of living creatures; and through imitation he learns his earliest lessons; and no less universal is the pleasure felt in things imitated. 3. We have evidence of this in the facts of experience. Objects which in themselves we view with pain, we delight to contemplate when reproduced with minute fidelity: such as the forms of the most ignoble animals and of dead bodies. 4. The cause of this again is, that to learn gives the liveliest pleasure, not only to philosophers but to men in general; whose capacity, however, of learning is more limited. 5. Thus the reason why men enjoy seeing a likeness is, that in contemplating it they find themselves learning or inferring, and saying perhaps, "Ah, that is he." For if you happen not to have seen the original, the pleasure will be due not to the imitation as such, but to the execution, the colouring, or some such other cause.

6. Imitation, then, is one instinct of our nature. Next, there is the instinct for "harmony" and rhythm, metres being manifestly sections of rhythm. Persons, therefore, starting with this natural gift developed by degrees their special aptitudes, till their rude improvisations gave birth to Poetry.

7. Poetry now diverged in two directions, according to the individual character of the writers. The graver spirits imitated noble actions, and the actions of good men. The more trivial sort imitated the actions of meaner persons, at first composing satires, as the former did hymns to the gods and the praises of famous men. 8. A poem of the satirical kind cannot indeed be put down to any author earlier than Homer; though many such writers probably there were. But from Homer onward, instances can be cited,—his own *Margites*, for example, and other similar compositions. The appropriate metre was also here introduced; hence the measure is still called the iambic or lampooning measure, being that in which people lampooned one another. 9. Thus the older poets were distinguished as writers of heroic or of lampooning verse.

As, in the serious style, Homer is preeminent among poets, for he alone combined dramatic form with excellence of imitation, so he too first laid down the main lines of Comedy, by dramatizing the ludicrous instead of writing personal satire. His *Margites* bears the same relation to Comedy that the *Iliad* and *Odyssey* do to Tragedy. 10. But when Tragedy and Comedy came to light, the two classes of poets still followed their natural bent: the lampooners became writers of Comedy, and the Epic poets were succeeded by Tragedians, since the drama was a larger and higher form of art.

11. Whether Tragedy has as yet perfected its proper types or not; and whether it is to be judged in itself, or in relation also to the audience,—this raises another question. 12. Be that as it may, Tragedy—as also Comedy—was at first mere improvisation. The one originated with the leaders of the Dithyramb, the other with those of the phallic songs, which are still in use in many of our cities. Tragedy advanced by slow degrees; each new element that showed itself was in turn developed. Having passed through many changes, it found its natural form, and there it stopped.

13. Aeschylus first introduced a second actor; he diminished the importance of the Chorus, and assigned the leading part to the dialogue. Sophocles raised the number of actors to three, and added scene-painting. 14. Moreover, it was not till late that the short plot was discarded for one of greater compass, and the grotesque diction of the earlier satyric form for the stately manner of Tragedy. The iambic measure then replaced the trochaic tetrameter, which was originally employed when the poetry was of the satyric order, and had greater affinities with dancing. Once dialogue had come in, Nature herself discovered the appropriate measure. For the iambic is, of all measures, the most colloquial: we see it in the fact that conversational speech runs into iambic

form more frequently than into any other kind of verse; rarely into hexameters, and only when we drop the colloquial intonation. 15. The additions to the number of "episodes" or acts, and the other improvements of which tradition tells, must be taken as already described; for to discuss them in detail would, doubtless, be a large undertaking.

5

Comedy is, as we have said, an imitation of characters of a lower type—not, however, in the full sense of the word bad, the Ludicrous being merely a subdivision of the ugly. It consists in some defect or ugliness which is not painful or destructive. To take an obvious example, the comic mask is ugly and distorted, but does not imply pain.

2. The successive changes through which Tragedy passed, and the authors of these changes, are well known, whereas Comedy has had no history, because it was not at first treated seriously. It was late before the Archon granted a comic chorus to a poet; the performers were till then voluntary. Comedy had already taken definite shape when comic poets, distinctively so called, are heard of. 3. Who introduced masks, or prologues, or increased the number of actors—these and other similar details remain unknown. As for the plot, it came originally from Sicily; but of Athenian writers Crates was the first who, abandoning the "iambic" or lampooning form, generalized his themes and plots.

4. Epic poetry agrees with Tragedy in so far as it is an imitation in verse of characters of a higher type. They differ, in that Epic poetry admits but one kind of metre, and is narrative in form. They differ, again, in their length: for Tragedy endeavours, as far as possible, to confine itself to a single revolution of the sun, or but slightly to exceed this limit; whereas the Epic action has no limits of time. This, then, is a second point of difference; though at first the same freedom was admitted in Tragedy as in Epic poetry.

5. Of their constituent parts some are common to both, some peculiar to Tragedy. Whoever, therefore, knows what is good or bad Tragedy, knows also about Epic poetry: for all the elements of an Epic poem are found in Tragedy, but the elements of a Tragedy are not all found in the Epic poem.

6

Of the poetry which imitates in hexameter verse, and of Comedy, we will speak hereafter. Let us now discuss Tragedy, resuming its formal definition, as resulting from what has been already said.

2. Tragedy, then, is an imitation of an action that is serious, complete, and of a certain magnitude; in language embellished with each kind of artistic ornament, the several kinds being found in separate parts of the play; in the form of action, not of narrative; through pity and fear effecting the proper purgation of these emotions. 3. By "language embellished," I mean language into which rhythm, "harmony," and song enter. By "the several kinds in separate parts," I mean, that some parts are rendered through the medium of verse alone, others again with the aid of song.

4. Now as tragic imitation implies persons acting, it necessarily follows, in the first place, that Spectacular equipment will be a part of Tragedy. Next, Song and Diction, for these are the medium of imitation. By "Diction" I mean the mere metrical arrangement of the words: as for "Song," it is a term whose sense every one understands.

5. Again, Tragedy is the imitation of an action; and an action implies personal agents, who necessarily possess certain distinctive qualities both of character and thought; for it is by these that we qualify actions themselves, and these—thought and character—are the two natural causes from which actions spring, and on actions again all success or failure depends. 6. Hence, the Plot is the imitation of the action:—for by plot I here mean the arrangement of the incidents. By Character I mean that in virtue of which we ascribe certain qualities to the agents. Thought is required wherever a statement is proved, or, it may be, a general truth enunciated. 7. Every Tragedy, therefore, must have six parts, which parts determine its quality—namely, Plot, Character,

Diction, Thought, Spectacle, Song. Two of the parts constitute the medium of imitation, one the manner, and three the objects of imitation. And these complete the list. 8. These elements have been employed, we may say, by the poets to a man; in fact, every play contains Spectacular elements as well as Character, Plot, Diction, Song, and Thought.

9. But most important of all is the structure of the incidents. For Tragedy is an imitation, not of men, but of an action and of life, and life consists in action, and its end is a mode of action, not a quality. 10. Now character determines men's qualities, but it is by their actions that they are happy or the reverse. Dramatic action, therefore, is not with a view to the representation of character: character comes in as subsidiary to the actions. Hence the incidents and the plot are the end of a tragedy; and the end is the chief thing of all. 11. Again, without action there cannot be a tragedy; there may be without character. The tragedies of most of our modern poets fail in the rendering of character; and of poets in general this is often true. It is the same in painting; and here lies the difference between Zeuxis and Polygnotus. Polygnotus delineates character well: the style of Zeuxis is devoid of ethical quality. 12. Again, if you string together a set of speeches expressive of character, and well finished in point of diction and thought, you will not produce the essential tragic effect nearly so well as with a play which, however deficient in these respects, yet has a plot and artistically constructed incidents. 13. Besides which, the most powerful elements of emotional interest in Tragedy—Peripeteia or Reversal of the situation, and Recognition scenes—are parts of the plot. 14. A further proof is, that novices in the art attain to finish of diction and precision of portraiture before they can construct the plot. It is the same with almost all the early poets.

The Plot, then, is the first principle, and, as it were, the soul of a tragedy: Character holds the second place. 15. A similar fact is seen in painting. The most beautiful colors, laid on confusedly, will not give as much pleasure as the chalk outline of a portrait. Thus Tragedy is the imitation of an action, and of the agents mainly with a view to the action.

16. Third in order is Thought,—that is, the faculty of saying what is possible and pertinent in given circumstances. In the case of oratory, this is the function of the political art and of the art of rhetoric: and so indeed the older poets make their characters speak the language of civic life; the poets of our time, the language of the rhetoricians.

17. Character is that which reveals moral purpose, showing what kind of things a man chooses or avoids. Speeches, therefore, which do not make this manifest, or in which the speaker does not choose or avoid anything whatever, are not expressive of character. Thought, on the other hand, is found where something is proved to be or not to be, or a general maxim is enunciated.

18. Fourth among the elements enumerated comes Diction; by which I mean, as has been already said, the expression of the meaning in words; and its essence is the same both in verse and prose.

19. Of the remaining elements Song holds the chief place among the embellishments.

The Spectacle has, indeed, an emotional attraction of its own, but, of all the parts, it is the least artistic, and connected least with the art of poetry. For the power of Tragedy, we may be sure, is felt even apart from representation and actors. Besides, the production of spectacular effects depends more on the art of the stage machinist than on that of the poet.

7

These principles being established, let us now discuss the proper structure of the Plot, since this is the first and most important thing in Tragedy.

2. Now, according to our definition, Tragedy is an imitation of an action that is complete, and whole, and of a certain magnitude; for there may be a whole that is wanting in magnitude. 3. A whole is that which has a beginning, a middle, and an end. A beginning is that which does not itself follow anything by causal necessity, but after which something naturally is or comes to be. An end, on the contrary, is that which itself naturally follows

some other thing, either by necessity, or as a rule, but has nothing following it. A middle is that which follows something as some other thing follows it. A well constructed plot, therefore, must neither begin nor end at haphazard, but conform to these principles.

4. Again, a beautiful object, whether it be a picture of a living organism or any whole composed of parts, must not only have an orderly arrangement of parts, but must also be of a certain magnitude; for beauty depends on magnitude and order. Hence an exceedingly small picture cannot be beautiful; for the view of it is confused, the object being seen in an almost imperceptible moment of time. Nor, again, can one of vast size be beautiful; for as the eye cannot take it all in at once, the unity and sense of the whole is lost for the spectator; as for instance if there were one a thousand miles long. 5. As, therefore, in the case of animate bodies and organisms a certain magnitude is necessary, and a magnitude which may be easily embraced in one view; so in the plot, a certain length is necessary, and a length which can be easily embraced by the memory. 6. The limit of length in relation to dramatic competition and sensuous presentment, is no part of artistic theory. For had it been the rule for a hundred tragedies to compete together, the performance would have been regulated by the water-clock,—as indeed we are told was formerly done. 7. But the limit as fixed by the nature of the drama itself is this:—the greater the length, the more beautiful will the piece be by reason of its size, provided that the whole be perspicuous. And to define the matter roughly, we may say that the proper magnitude is comprised within such limits, that the sequence of events, according to the law of probability or necessity, will admit of a change from bad fortune to good, or from good fortune to bad.

8

Unity of plot does not, as some persons think, consist in the unity of the hero. For infinitely various are the incidents in one man's life, which cannot be reduced to unity; and so, too, there are many actions of one man out of which we cannot make one action. 2. Hence the error, as it appears, of all poets who have composed a *Heracleid*, a *Theseid*, or other poems of the kind. They imagine that as Heracles was one man, the story of Heracles must also be a unity. 3. But Homer, as in all else he is of surpassing merit, here too—whether from art or natural genius—seems to have happily discerned the truth. In composing the *Odyssey* he did not include all the adventures of Odysseus—such as his wound on Parnassus, or his feigned madness at the mustering of the host—incidents between which there was no necessary or probable connexion: but he made the *Odyssey*, and likewise the *Iliad*, to center round an action that in our sense of the word is one. 4. As therefore, in the other imitative arts, the imitation is one when the object imitated is one, so the plot, being an imitation of an action, must imitate one action and that a whole, the structural union of the parts being such that, if any one of them is displaced or removed, the whole will be disjointed and disturbed. For a thing whose presence or absence makes no visible difference, is not an organic part of the whole.

9

It is, moreover, evident from what has been said, that it is not the function of the poet to relate what has happened, but what may happen,—what is possible according to the law of probability or necessity. 2. The poet and the historian differ not by writing in verse or in prose. The work of Herodotus might be put into verse, and it would still be a species of history, with metre no less than without it. The true difference is that one relates what has happened, the other what may happen. 3. Poetry, therefore, is a more philosophical and a higher thing than history: for poetry tends to express the universal, history the particular. 4. By the universal I mean how a person of a certain type will on occasion speak or act, according to the law of probability or necessity; and it is this universality at which poetry aims in the names she attaches to the personages. The particular is—for example—what Alcibiades did or suffered. 5. In Comedy this is already apparent: for here the poet first constructs the plot on the lines of probability, and then inserts characteristic names;—unlike the lampooners who write about particular individuals. 6. But tragedians still keep to real names, the reason being that what is possible is credible: what has not happened we do not at once feel sure to be possible: but what has happened is manifestly possible: otherwise it would not have happened. 7. Still there are some tragedies in which there are only one or two well known names, the rest being fictitious. In others, none are well known,—as in Agathon's *Antheus*, where incidents and names alike are fictitious, and yet they give none the less pleasure. 8. We must not, therefore, at all costs keep to the received legends, which are the usual subjects of Tragedy. Indeed, it would be absurd to attempt it; for even subjects that are known are known only to a few, and yet give pleasure to all. 9. It clearly follows that the poet or "maker" should be the maker of plots rather than of verses; since he is a poet because he imitates, and what he imitates are actions. And even if he chances to take an historical subject, he is none the less a poet; for there is no reason why some events that have actually happened should not conform to the law of the probable and possible, and in virtue of that quality in them he is their poet or maker.

10. Of all plots and actions the epeisodic are the worst. I call a plot "epeisodic" in which the episodes or acts succeed one another without probable or necessary sequence. Bad poets compose such pieces by their own fault, good poets, to please the players; for, as they write show pieces for competition, they stretch the plot beyond its capacity, and are often forced to break the natural continuity.

11. But again, Tragedy is an imitation not only of a complete action, but of events inspiring fear or pity. Such an effect is best produced when the events come on us by surprise; and the effect is heightened when, at the same time, they follow as cause and effect. 12. The tragic wonder will then be greater than if they

happened of themselves or by accident; for even coincidences are most striking when they have an air of design. We may instance the statue of Mitys at Argos, which fell upon his murderer while he was a spectator at a festival, and killed him. Such events seem not to be due to mere chance. Plots, therefore, constructed on these principles are necessarily the best.

10

Plots are either Simple or Complex, for the actions in real life, of which the plots are an imitation, obviously show a similar distinction. 2. An action which is one and continuous in the sense above defined, I call Simple, when the change of fortune takes place without Reversal of the Situation and without Recognition.

A Complex action is one in which the change is accompanied by such Reversal, or by Recognition, or by both. 2. These last should arise from the internal structure of the plot, so that what follows should be the necessary or probable result of the preceding action. It makes all the difference whether any given event is a case of *propter hoc* or *post hoc*.

11

Reversal of the Situation is a change by which the action veers round to its opposite, subject always to our rule of probability or necessity. Thus in the *Oedipus*, the messenger comes to cheer Oedipus and free him from his alarms about his mother, but by revealing who he is, he produces the opposite effect. Again in the *Lynceus*, Lynceus is being led away to his death, and Danaus goes with him, meaning to slay him; but the outcome of the action is, that Danaus is killed and Lynceus saved.

2. Recognition, as the name indicates, is a change from ignorance to knowledge, producing love or hate between the persons destined by the poet for good or bad fortune. The best form of recognition is coincident with a Reversal of the Situation, as in the *Oedipus*. 3. There are indeed other forms. Even in-

animate things of the most trivial kind may sometimes be objects of recognition. Again, we may recognize or discover whether a person has done a thing or not. But the recognition which is most intimately connected with the plot and action is, as we have said, the recognition of persons. 4. This recognition, combined with Reversal, will produce either pity or fear; and actions producing these effects are those which, by our definition, Tragedy represents. Moreover, it is upon such situations that the issues of good or bad fortune will depend. 5. Recognition, then, being between persons, it may happen that one person only is recognized by the other—when the latter is already known—or it may be necessary that the recognition should be on both sides. Thus Iphigenia is revealed to Orestes by the sending of the letter; but another act of recognition is required to make Orestes known to Iphigenia.

6. Two parts, then, of the Plot—Reversal of the Situation and Recognition—turn upon surprises. A third part is the Scene of Suffering. The Scene of Suffering is a destructive or painful action, such as death on the stage, bodily agony, wounds, and the like.

12

[The parts of Tragedy which must be treated as elements of the whole, have been already mentioned. We now come to the quantitative parts—the separate parts into which Tragedy is divided—namely, Prologue, Episode, Exode, Choric song; this last being divided into Parode and Stasimon. These are common to all plays: peculiar to some are the songs of actors from the stage and the Commoi.

2. The Prologue is that entire part of a tragedy which precedes the Parode of the Chorus. The Episode is that entire part of a tragedy which is between complete choric songs. The Exode is that entire part of a tragedy which has no choric song after it. Of the Choric part the Parode is the first undivided utterance of the Chorus: the Stasimon is a Choric ode without anapaests or trochaic tetrameters: the Commos is a joint lamentation of Chorus and actors. 3. The parts of Tragedy which must be treated as elements of the whole have been already mentioned. The quantitative parts—the separate parts into which it is divided—are here enumerated.]

13

As the sequel to what has already been said, we must proceed to consider what the poet should aim at, and what he should avoid, in constructing his plots; and by what means the specific effect of Tragedy will be produced.

2. A perfect tragedy should, as we have seen, be arranged not on the simple but on the complex plan. It should, moreover, imitate actions which excite pity and fear, this being the distinctive mark of tragic imitation. It follows plainly, in the first place, that the change of fortune presented must not be the spectacle of a virtuous man brought from prosperity to adversity: for this moves neither pity nor fear; it merely shocks us. Nor, again, that of a bad man passing from adversity to prosperity: for nothing can be more alien to the spirit of Tragedy; it possesses no single tragic quality; it neither satisfies the moral sense, nor calls forth pity or fear. Nor, again, should the downfall of the utter villain be exhibited. A plot of this kind would, doubtless, satisfy the moral sense, but it would inspire neither pity nor fear; for pity is aroused by unmerited misfortune, fear by the misfortune of a man like ourselves. Such an event, therefore, will be neither pitiful nor terrible. 3. There remains, then, the character between these two extremes,—that of a man who is not eminently good and just, yet whose misfortune is brought about not by vice or depravity, but by some error or frailty. He must be one who is highly renowned and prosperous,—a personage like Oedipus, Thyestes, or other illustrious men of such families.

4. A well constructed plot should, therefore, be single in its issue, rather than double as some maintain. The change of fortune should be not from bad to good, but, reversely, from good to bad. It should come about as the result not of vice, but of some great error or frailty, in a character either such as we have described,

or better rather than worse. 5. The practice of the stage bears out our view. At first the poets recounted any legend that came in their way. Now, the best tragedies are founded on the story of a few houses,—on the fortunes of Alcmaeon, Oedipus, Orestes, Meleager, Thyestes, Telephus, and those others who have done or suffered something terrible. A tragedy, then, to be perfect according to the rules of art should be of this construction. 6. Hence they are in error who censure Euripides just because he follows this principle in his plays, many of which end unhappily. It is, as we have said, the right ending. The best proof is that on the stage and in dramatic competition, such plays, if well worked out, are the most tragic in effect; and Euripides, faulty though he may be in the general management of his subject, yet is felt to be the most tragic of the poets.

7. In the second rank comes the kind of tragedy which some place first. Like the *Odyssey*, it has a double thread of plot, and also an opposite catastrophe for the good and for the bad. It is accounted the best because of the weakness of the spectators; for the poet is guided in what he writes by the wishes of his audience. 8. The pleasure, however, thence derived is not the true tragic pleasure. It is proper rather to Comedy, where those who, in the piece, are the deadliest enemies—like Orestes and Aegisthus—quit the stage as friends at the close, and no one slays or is slain.

14

Fear and pity may be aroused by spectacular means; but they may also result from the inner structure of the piece, which is the better way, and indicates a superior poet. For the plot ought to be so constructed that, even without the aid of the eye, he who hears the tale told will thrill with horror and melt to pity at what takes place. This is the impression we should receive from hearing the story of the *Oedipus*. 2. But to produce this effect by the mere spectacle is a less artistic method, and dependent on extraneous aids. Those who employ spectacular means to create a sense not of the terrible but only of the monstrous, are strangers to the purpose of Tragedy; for we must not demand of Tragedy any and every kind of pleasure, but only that which is proper to it. 3. And since the pleasure which the poet should afford is that which comes from pity and fear through imitation, it is evident that this quality must be impressed upon the incidents.

Let us then determine what are the circumstances which strike us as terrible or pitiful.

4. Actions capable of this effect must happen between persons who are either friends or enemies or indifferent to one another. If an enemy kills an enemy, there is nothing to excite pity either in the act or the intention,—except so far as the suffering in itself is pitiful. So again with indifferent persons. But when the tragic incident occurs between those who are near or dear to one another—if, for example, a brother kills, or intends to kill, a brother, a son his father, a mother her son, a son his mother, or any other deed of the kind is done —these are the situations to be looked for by the poet. 5. He may not indeed destroy the framework of the received legends—the fact, for instance, that Clytemnestra was slain by Orestes and Eriphyle by Alcmaeon—but he ought to show invention of his own, and skilfully handle the traditional material. Let us explain more clearly what is meant by skilful handling.

6. The action may be done consciously and with knowledge of the persons, in the manner of the older poets. It is thus too that Euripides makes Medea slay her children. Or, again, the deed of horror may be done, but done in ignorance, and the tie of kinship or friendship be discovered afterwards. The *Oedipus* of Sophocles is an example. Here, indeed, the incident is outside the drama proper; but cases occur where it falls within the action of the play: one may cite the *Alcmaeon* of Astydamas, or Telegonus in the *Wounded Odysseus*. 7. Again, there is a third case,—<to be about to act with knowledge of the persons and then not to act. The fourth case is>when some one is about to do an irreparable deed through ignorance, and makes the discovery before it is done. These are the only possible ways. For the deed must either be done or not done,— and that wittingly or unwittingly. But of all

these ways, to be about to act knowing the persons, and then not to act, is the worst. It is shocking without being tragic, for no disaster follows. It is, therefore, never, or very rarely, found in poetry. One instance, however, is in the *Antigone*, where Haemon threatens to kill Creon. 8. The next and better way is that the deed should be perpetrated. Still better, that it should be perpetrated in ignorance, and the discovery made afterwards. There is then nothing to shock us, while the discovery produces a startling effect. 9. The last case is the best, as when in the *Cresphontes* Merope is about to slay her son, but recognizing who he is, spares his life. So in the *Iphigenia*, the sister recognizes the brother just in time. Again in the *Helle*, the son recognizes the mother when on the point of giving her up. This, then, is why a few families only, as has been already observed, furnish the subjects of tragedy. It was not art, but happy chance, that led poets to look for such situations and so impress the tragic quality upon their plots. They are compelled, therefore, to have recourse to those houses whose history contains moving incidents like these.

Enough has now been said concerning the structure of the incidents, and the proper constitution of the plot.

15

In respect of Character there are four things to be aimed at. First, and most important, it must be good. Now any speech or action that manifests moral purpose of any kind will be expressive of character: the character will be good if the purpose is good. This rule is relative to each class. Even a woman may be good, and also a slave; though the woman may be said to be an inferior being, and the slave quite worthless. 2. The second thing to aim at is propriety. There is a type of manly valour; but valour in a woman, or unscrupulous cleverness, is inappropriate. 3. Thirdly, character must be true to life: for this is a distinct thing from goodness and propriety, as here described. 4. The fourth point is consistency: for though the subject of the imitation, who suggested the

type, be inconsistent, still he must be consistently inconsistent. 5. As an example of motiveless degradation of character, we have Menelaus in the *Orestes*: of character indecorous and inappropriate, the lament of Odysseus in the *Scylla*, and the speech of Melanippe: of inconsistency, the *Iphigenia at Aulis*,—for Iphigenia the suppliant in no way resembles her later self.

6. As in the structure of the plot, so too in the portraiture of character, the poet should always aim either at the necessary or the probable. Thus a person of a given character should speak or act in a given way, by the rule either of necessity or of probability; just as this event should follow that by necessity or probable sequence. 7. It is therefore evident that the unravelling of the plot, no less than the complication, must arise out of the plot itself, it must not be brought about by the *Deus ex Machina*—as in the *Medea*, or in the Return of the Greeks in the *Iliad*. The *Deus ex Machina* should be employed only for events external to the drama,—for antecedent or subsequent events, which lie beyond the range of human knowledge, and which require to be reported or foretold; for to the gods we ascribe the power of seeing all things. Within the action there must be nothing irrational. If the irrational cannot be excluded, it should be outside the scope of the tragedy. Such is the irrational element in the *Oedipus* of Sophocles.

8. Again, since Tragedy is an imitation of persons who are above the common level, the example of good portrait-painters should be followed. They, while reproducing the distinctive form of the original, make a likeness which is true to life and yet more beautiful. So too the poet, in representing men who are irascible or indolent, or have other defects of character, should preserve the type and yet ennoble it. In this way Achilles is portrayed by Agathon and Homer.

9. These then are rules the poet should observe. Nor should he neglect those appeals to the senses, which, though not among the essentials, are the concomitants of poetry; for here too there is much room for error. But of this enough has been said in our published treatises.

Art as expression

R. G. Collingwood (1889-1943)

R. G. Collingwood, a distinguished English philosopher and historian, was born in Lancashire. His father was the friend and biographer of the famous art historian John Ruskin. Educated at Oxford, Collingwood became interested in Roman Britain and eventually was recognized as the leading authority on that period. His historical interests were surpassed, however, by his concern with philosophical problems. He served as Waynflete Professor of Metaphysical Philosophy in Magdalen College, Oxford, from 1935 until ill health forced his retirement in 1941.

Collingwood attempted to unite the approaches and insights of the historian with the interests of the philosopher. He believed that it was the task of philosophy to uncover the prevailing assumptions of a civilization and to probe the dominant ideas of history and science. He was also especially interested in art, having been a painter and a composer. In The Principles of Art (*1938*) *he attempted to distinguish what is properly art from other things which are given that name. For Collingwood, art is the expression of emotion. To express means to clarify and individualize.*

Among his other major works are Essay on Philosophical Method (*1933*), The Idea of History (*1946*), *and* The New Leviathan (*1942*).

Expressing emotion and arousing emotion

Our first question is this. Since the artist proper has something to do with emotion, and what he does with it is not to arouse it, what is it that he does? It will be remembered that the kind of answer we expect to this question is an answer derived from what we all know and all habitually say; nothing original or recondite, but something entirely commonplace.

Nothing could be more entirely commonplace than to say he expresses them. The idea is familiar to every artist, and to every one else who has any acquaintance with the arts. To state it is not to state a philosophical theory or

From R. G. Collingwood, *The Principles of Art*, Oxford, the Clarendon Press, 1938. Used by permission of the Clarendon Press, Oxford.

definition of art; it is to state a fact or supposed fact about which, when we have sufficiently identified it, we shall have later to theorize philosophically. For the present it does not matter whether the fact that is alleged, when it is said that the artist expresses emotion, is really a fact or only supposed to be one. Whichever it is, we have to identify it, that is, to decide what it is that people are saying when they use the phrase. Later on, we shall have to see whether it will fit into a coherent theory.

They are referring to a situation, real or supposed, of a definite kind. When a man is said to express emotion, what is being said about him comes to this. At first, he is conscious of having an emotion, but not conscious of what this emotion is. All he is conscious of is a perturbation or excitement, which he feels **321** going on within him, but of whose nature he is ignorant. While in this state, all he can say about his emotion is: "I feel . . . I don't know what I feel." From this helpless and oppressed condition he extricates himself by doing something which we call expressing himself. This is an activity which has something to do with the thing we call language: he expresses himself by speaking. It has also something to do with consciousness: the emotion expressed is an emotion of whose nature the person who feels it is no longer unconscious. It has also something to do with the way in which he feels the emotion. As unexpressed, he feels it in what we have called a helpless and oppressed way; as expressed, he feels it in a way from which this sense of oppression has vanished. His mind is somehow lightened and eased.

This lightening of emotions which is somehow connected with the expression of them has a certain resemblance to the "catharsis" by which emotions are earthed through being discharged into a make-believe situation; but the two things are not the same. Suppose the emotion is one of anger. If it is effectively earthed, for example by fancying oneself kicking some one down stairs, it is thereafter no longer present in the mind as anger at all: we have worked it off and are rid of it. If it is expressed, for example by putting it into hot and bitter words, it does not disappear from the mind; we remain angry; but instead of the sense of oppression which accompanies an emotion of anger not yet recognized as such, we have that sense of alleviation which comes when we are conscious of our own emotion as anger, instead of being conscious of it only as an unidentified perturbation. This is what we refer to when we say that it "does us good" to express our emotions.

The expression of an emotion by speech may be addressed to some one; but if so it is not done with the intention of arousing a like emotion in him. If there is any effect which we wish to produce in the hearer, it is only the effect which we call making him understand how we feel. But, as we have already seen, this is just the effect which expressing our emotions has on ourselves. It makes us, as well as the people to whom we talk, understand how we feel. A person arousing emotion sets out to affect his audience in a way in which he himself is not necessarily affected. He and his audience stand in quite different relations to the act, very much as physician and patient stand in quite different relations towards a drug administered by the one and taken by the other. A person expressing emotion, on the contrary, is treating himself and his audience in the same kind of way; he is making his emotions clear to his audience, and that is what he is doing to himself.

It follows from this that the expression of emotion, simply as expression, is not addressed to any particular audience. It is addressed primarily to the speaker himself, and secondarily to any one who can understand. Here again, the speaker's attitude towards his audience is quite unlike that of a person desiring to arouse in his audience a certain emotion. If that is what he wishes to do, he must know the audience he is addressing. He must know what type of stimulus will produce the desired kind of reaction in people of that particular sort; and he must adapt his language to his audience in the sense of making sure that it contains stimuli appropriate to their peculiarities. If what he wishes to do is to express his emotions intelligibly, he has to express them in such a way as to be intelligible to himself; his audience is then in the position of persons who overhear [1] him doing this. Thus the stimulus-and-reaction terminology has no applicability to the situation.

The means-and-end, or technique, terminology too is inapplicable. Until a man has expressed his emotion, he does not yet know what emotion it is. The act of expressing it is therefore an exploration of his own emotions. He is trying to find out what these emotions are. There is certainly here a directed process: an effort, that is, directed upon a certain end; but the end is not something foreseen and preconceived, to which appropriate means can be thought out in the light of our knowledge of

[1] Further development of the ideas expressed in this paragraph will make it necessary to qualify this word and assert a much more intimate relation between artist and audience.

its special character. Expression is an activity of which there can be no technique.

Expression and individualization

Expressing an emotion is not the same thing as describing it. To say "I am angry" is to describe one's emotion, not to express it. The words in which it is expressed need not contain any reference to anger as such at all. Indeed, so far as they simply and solely express it, they cannot contain any such reference. The curse of Ernulphus, as invoked by Dr. Slop on the unknown person who tied certain knots, is a classical and supreme expression of anger; but it does not contain a single word descriptive of the emotion it expresses.

This is why, as literary critics well know, the use of epithets in poetry, or even in prose where expressiveness is aimed at, is a danger. If you want to express the terror which something causes, you must not give it an epithet like "dreadful." For that describes the emotion instead of expressing it, and your language becomes frigid, that is inexpressive, at once. A genuine poet, in his moments of genuine poetry, never mentions by name the emotions he is expressing.

Some people have thought that a poet who wishes to express a great variety of subtly differentiated emotions might be hampered by the lack of a vocabulary rich in words referring to the distinctions between them; and that psychology, by working out such a vocabulary, might render a valuable service to poetry. This is the opposite of the truth. The poet needs no such words at all; the existence or nonexistence of a scientific terminology describing the emotions he wishes to express is to him a matter of perfect indifference. If such a terminology, where it exists, is allowed to affect his own use of language, it affects it for the worse.

The reason why description, so far from helping expression, actually damages it, is that description generalizes. To describe a thing is to call it a thing of such and such a kind: to bring it under a conception, to classify it. Expression, on the contrary, individualizes. The anger which I feel here and now, with a cer-

tain person, for a certain cause, is no doubt an instance of anger, and in describing it as anger one is telling truth about it; but it is much more than mere anger: it is a peculiar anger, not quite like any anger that I ever felt before, and probably not quite like any anger I shall ever feel again. To become fully conscious of it means becoming conscious of it not merely as an instance of anger, but as this quite peculiar anger. Expressing it, we saw, has something to do with becoming conscious of it; therefore, if being fully conscious of it means being conscious of all its peculiarities, fully expressing it means expressing all its peculiarities. The poet, therefore, in proportion as he understands his business, gets as far away as possible from merely labelling his emotions as instances of this or that general kind, and takes enormous pains to individualize them by expressing them in terms which reveal their difference from any other emotion of the same sort.

This is a point in which art proper, as the expression of emotion, differs sharply and obviously from any craft whose aim it is to arouse emotion. The end which a craft sets out to realize is always conceived in general terms, never individualized. However accurately defined it may be, it is always defined as the production of a thing having characteristics that could be shared by other things. A joiner, making a table out of these pieces of wood and no others, makes it to measurements and specifications which, even if actually shared by no other table, might in principle be shared by other tables. A physician treating a patient for a certain complaint is trying to produce in him a condition which might be, and probably has been, often produced in others, namely, the condition of recovering from that complaint. So an "artist" setting out to produce a certain emotion in his audience is setting out to produce not an individual emotion, but an emotion of a certain kind. It follows that the means appropriate to its production will be not individual means but means of a certain kind: that is to say, means which are always in principle replaceable by other similar means. As every good craftsman insists, there is always a "right way" of performing any operation. A "way" of acting is a general pattern to which various individual actions may conform. In order that the "work of art" should produce its intended psychological effect, therefore, whether this effect be magical or merely amusing, what is necessary is that it should satisfy certain conditions, possess certain characteristics: in other words be, not this work and no other, but a work of this kind and of no other. . . .

Art proper, as expression of emotion, has nothing to do with all this. The artist proper is a person who, grappling with the problem of expressing a certain emotion, says, "I want to get this clear." It is no use to him to get something else clear, however like it this other thing may be. Nothing will serve as a substitute. He does not want a thing of a certain kind, he wants a certain thing. This is why the kind of person who takes his literature as psychology, saying "How admirably this writer depicts the feelings of women, or busdrivers, or homosexuals . . . ," necessarily misunderstands every real work of art with which he comes into contact, and takes for good art, with infallible precision, what is not art at all. . . .

The artist and the ordinary man

I have been speaking of "the artist," in the present chapter, as if artists were persons of a special kind, differing somehow either in mental endowment or at least in the way they use their endowment from the ordinary persons who make up their audience. But this segregation of artists from ordinary human beings belongs to the conception of art as craft; it cannot be reconciled with the conception of art as expression. If art were a kind of craft, it would follow as a matter of course. Any craft is a specialized form of skill, and those who possess it are thereby marked out from the rest of mankind. If art is the skill to amuse people, or in general to arouse emotions in them, the amusers and the amused form two different classes, differing in their respectively active and passive relation to the craft of exciting determinate emotions; and this difference will be due, according to whether the artist is "born"

or "made," either to a specific mental endowment in the artist, which in theories of this type has gone by the name of "genius," or to a specific training.

If art is not a kind of craft, but the expression of emotion, this distinction of kind between artist and audience disappears. For the artist has an audience only in so far as people hear him expressing himself, and understand what they hear him saying. Now, if one person says something by way of expressing what is in his mind, and another hears and understands him, the hearer who understands him has that same thing in his mind. The question whether he would have had it if the first had not spoken need not here be raised; however it is answered, what has just been said is equally true. If some one says "Twice two is four" in the hearing of some one incapable of carrying out the simplest arithmetical operation, he will be understood by himself, but not by his hearer. The hearer can understand only if he can add two and two in his own mind. Whether he could do it before he heard the speaker say those words makes no difference. What is here said of expressing thoughts is equally true of expressing emotions. If a poet expresses, for example, a certain kind of fear, the only hearers who can understand him are those who are capable of experiencing that kind of fear themselves. Hence, when some one reads and understands a poem, he is not merely understanding the poet's expression of his, the poet's, emotions, he is expressing emotions of his own in the poet's words, which have thus become his own words. As Coleridge put it, we know a man for a poet by the fact that he makes us poets. We know that he is expressing his emotions by the fact that he is enabling us to express ours.

Thus, if art is the activity of expressing emotions, the reader is an artist as well as the writer. There is no distinction of kind between artist and audience. This does not mean that there is no distinction at all. When Pope wrote that the poet's business was to say "what all have felt but none so well express'd," we may interpret his words as meaning (whether or no Pope himself consciously meant this when he wrote them) that the poet's difference from his audience lies in the fact that, though both do exactly the same thing, namely express this particular emotion in these particular words, the poet is a man who can solve for himself the problem of expressing it, whereas the audience can express it only when the poet has shown them how. The poet is not singular either in his having that emotion or in his power of expressing it; he is singular in his ability to take the initiative in expressing what all feel, and all can express. . . .

Expressing emotion and betraying emotion

Finally, the expressing of emotion must not be confused with what may be called the betraying of it, that is, exhibiting symptoms of it. When it is said that the artist in the proper sense of that word is a person who expresses his emotions, this does not mean that if he is afraid he turns pale and stammers; if he is angry he turns red and bellows; and so forth. These things are no doubt called expressions; but just as we distinguish proper and improper senses of the word "art," so we must distinguish proper and improper senses of the word "expression," and in the context of a discussion about art this sense of expression is an improper sense. The characteristic mark of expression proper is lucidity or intelligibility; a person who expresses something thereby becomes conscious of what it is that he is expressing, and enables others to become conscious of it in himself and in them. Turning pale and stammering is a natural accompaniment of fear, but a person who in addition to being afraid also turns pale and stammers does not thereby become conscious of the precise quality of his emotion. About that he is as much in the dark as he would be if (were that possible) he could feel fear without also exhibiting these symptoms of it.

Confusion between these two senses of the word "expression" may easily lead to false critical estimates, and so to false aesthetic theory. It is sometimes thought a merit in an actress that when she is acting a pathetic scene she can work herself up to such an extent as to weep real tears. There may be some ground

for that opinion if acting is not an art but a craft, and if the actress's object in that scene is to produce grief in her audience; and even then the conclusion would follow only if it were true that grief cannot be produced in the audience unless symptoms of grief are exhibited by the performer. And no doubt this is how most people think of the actor's work. But if his business is not amusement but art, the object at which he is aiming is not to produce a preconceived emotional effect on his audience but by means of a system of expressions, or language, composed partly of speech and partly of gesture, to explore his own emotions: to discover emotions in himself of which he was unaware, and, by permitting the audience to witness the discovery, enable them to make a similar discovery about themselves. In that case it is not her ability to weep real tears that would mark out a good actress; it is her ability to make it clear to herself and her audience what the tears are about.

This applies to every kind of art. The artist never rants. A person who writes or paints or the like in order to blow off steam, using the traditional materials of art as means for exhibiting the symptoms of emotion, may deserve praise as an exhibitionist, but loses for the moment all claim to the title of artist. Exhibitionists have their uses; they may serve as an amusement, or they may be doing magic. The second category will contain, for example, those young men who, learning in the torment of their own bodies and minds what war is like, have stammered their indignation in verses, and published them in the hope of infecting others and causing them to abolish it. But these verses have nothing to do with poetry.

Thomas Hardy, at the end of a fine and tragic novel in which he has magnificently expressed his sorrow and indignation for the suffering inflicted by callous sentimentalism on trusting innocence, spoils everything by a last paragraph fastening his accusation upon "the president of the immortals." The note rings false, not because it is blasphemous (it offends no piety worthy of the name), but because it is rant. The case against God, so far as it exists, is complete already. The concluding paragraph adds nothing to it. All it does is to spoil the effect of the indictment by betraying a symptom of the emotion which the whole book has already expressed; as if a prosecuting counsel, at the end of his speech, spat in the prisoner's face.

The same fault is especially common in Beethoven. He was confirmed in it, no doubt, by his deafness; but the cause of it was not his deafness but a temperamental inclination to rant. It shows itself in the way his music screams and mutters instead of speaking, as in the soprano part of the Mass in D, or the layout of the opening page in the *Hammerklavier* Sonata. He must have known his failing and tried to overcome it, or he would never have spent so many of his ripest years among string quartets, where screaming and muttering are almost, one might say, physically impossible. Yet even there, the old Adam struts out in certain passages of the *Grosse Fuge*.

It does not, of course, follow that a dramatic writer may not rant in character. The tremendous rant at the end of *The Ascent of F6*, like the Shakespearian [2] ranting on which it is modelled, is done with tongue in cheek. It is not the author who is ranting, but the unbalanced character he depicts; the emotion the author is expressing is the emotion with which he contemplates that character; or rather, the emotion he has towards that secret and disowned part of himself for which the character stands.

[2] Shakespeare's characters rant (1) when they are characters in which he takes no interest at all, but which he uses simply as pegs on which to hang what the public wants, like Henry V; (2) when they are meant to be despicable, like Pistol; or (3) when they have lost their heads, like Hamlet in the graveyard.

Poetic knowledge

Jacques Maritain (b. 1882)

Jacques Maritain was born in Paris and educated in philosophy and natural sciences at the University of Paris and in Rome. He also studied biological science at the University of Heidelberg. He was converted to Catholicism in 1906 and in 1908 began the study of Scholastic thought, an occupation which he has continued all his life. He became professor of philosophy at the Institut Catholique in Paris in 1914. Since 1934 he has specialized in the study of Thomistic thought, becoming one of the foremost contemporary interpreters of the thought of St. Thomas Aquinas. He has lectured throughout Europe and the United States. He served as French Ambassador to the Holy See from 1945 to 1948, and from 1948 to 1953 he taught at Princeton University. Among his many books are Art and Scholasticism *(rev. ed. 1927),* The Degrees of Knowledge *(1938),* Existence and the Existent *(1948), and* The Range of Reason *(1952). Our selection is from his book* Creative Intuition in Art and Poetry *(1953), originally the Mellon Lectures at the National Gallery of Art in Washington, D.C. Maritain gives an account of the nature of "poetic intuition." Earlier in his book he defines "poetry" not as a particular art but as "that intercommunication between the inner being of things and the inner being of the human Self which is a kind of divination . . ." and "the secret life of each and all of the arts."*

Poetic intuition

. . . The problem, then, that I should like to discuss now deals with that kind of knowledge which is involved in poetic activity.

Clearly, what we are considering at this point is not the previous (theoretical) knowledge, in any field whatever of human experience and culture, that is *presupposed* by art and poetry, and which provides them with external materials to be integrated in, and transformed by, the fire of creative virtues.

From Jacques Maritain, *Creative Intuition in Art and Poetry,* Ch. 4. Copyright, 1953, by the Bollingen Foundation, Inc. Used by permission of the Bollingen Foundation and Curtis Brown, Ltd.

What we are considering is the kind of inherent knowledge that is immanent in and *consubstantial* with poetry, one with its very essence.

Here our first signpost is, I think—the notion, which I have previously pointed out, of the free creativity of the spirit. In the craftsman the creativity of the spirit is, as it were, bound or tied up to a particular aim, which is the satisfying of a particular need. In the poet it is free creativity, for it only tends to engender in beauty, which is a transcendental, and involves an infinity of possible realizations and possible choices. In this respect the poet is like a god. And in order to discover the first essentials of poetry there is nothing better for us to do than to look to the First Poet.

327

God's creative Idea, from the very fact that it is creative, does not receive anything from things, since they do not yet exist. It is in no way *formed* by its creatable object, it is only and purely *formative* and *forming*. And that which will be expressed or manifested in the things made is nothing else than their Creator Himself, whose transcendent Essence is enigmatically signified in a diffused, dispersed, or parceled-out manner, by works which are deficient likenesses of and created participations in it. And God's Intellect is determined or specified by nothing else than His own essence. It is by knowing Himself, in an act of intellection which is His very Essence and His very Existence, that He knows His works, which exist in time and have begun in time, but which He eternally is in the free act of creating.

Such is the supreme analogate of poetry. Poetry is engaged in the free creativity of the spirit. And thus it implies an intellective act which is not formed by things but is, by its own essence, formative and forming. Well, it is too clear that the poet is a poor god. He does not know himself. And his creative insight miserably depends on the external world, and on the infinite heap of forms and beauties already made by men, and on the mass of things that generations have learned, and on the code of signs which is used by his fellow men and which he receives from a language he has not made. Yet, for all that he is condemned both to subdue to his own purpose all these extraneous elements and to manifest his own substance in his creation.

At this point we see how essential to poetry is the subjectivity of the poet. I do not mean the inexhaustible flux of superficial feelings in which the sentimental reader recognizes his own cheap longings, and with which the songs to the Darling and Faithless One of generations of poets have desperately fed us. I mean subjectivity in its deepest ontologic sense, that is, the substantial totality of the human person, a universe unto itself, which the spirituality of the soul makes capable of containing itself through its own immanent acts, and which, at the center of all the subjects that it knows as objects, grasps only itself as subject. In a way similar to that in which divine creation presupposes the knowledge God has of His own essence, poetic creation presupposes, as a primary requirement, a grasping, by the poet, of his own subjectivity, in order to create. The poet's aim is not to know himself. He is not a guru. To attain, through the void, an intuitive experience of the existence of the Self, of the Atman, in its pure and full actuality, is the specific aim of natural mysticism. It is not the aim of poetry. The essential need of the poet is to create; but he cannot do so without passing through the door of the knowing, as obscure as it may be, of his own subjectivity. For poetry means first of all an intellective act which by its essence is creative, and forms something into being instead of being formed by things: and what can such an intellective act possibly express and manifest in producing the work if not the very being and substance of the one who creates? Thus it is that works of painting or sculpture or music or poetry the closer they come to the sources of poetry the more they reveal, one way or another, the subjectivity of their author.

But the substance of man is obscure to himself. He knows not his soul, except in the fluid multiplicity of passing phenomena which emerge from it and are more or less clearly attained by reflective consciousness, but only increase the enigma, and leave him more ignorant of the essence of his Self. He knows not his own subjectivity. Or, if he knows it, it is formlessly, by feeling it as a kind of propitious and enveloping night. Melville, I think, was aware of that when he observed that "no man can ever feel his own identity aright except his eyes be closed; as if darkness were indeed the proper element of our essences." Subjectivity *as subjectivity* is inconceptualizable; is an unknowable abyss. How, then, can it be revealed to the poet?

The poet does not know himself in the light of his own essence. Since man perceives himself only through a repercussion of his knowledge of the world of things, and remains empty to himself if he does not fill himself with the universe, the poet knows himself only on the condition that things resound in him, and that in him, at a single wakening, they and he come forth together out of sleep. In other words, the primary requirement of poetry, which is the obscure knowing, by the poet, of his own subjectivity, is inseparable from, is one with another requirement—the grasping, by the poet, of the objective reality of the outer and inner world: not by means of concepts and conceptual knowledge, but by means of an obscure knowledge which I shall describe in a moment as knowledge through affective union.

Hence the perplexities of the poet's condition. If he hears the passwords and the secrets that are stammering in things, if he perceives realities, correspondences, ciphered writings that are at the core of actual existence, if he captures those more things which are in heaven and earth than are dreamt of in our philosophy, he does not do so by knowing all this in the ordinary sense of the word to know, but by receiving all this into the obscure recesses of his passion. All that he discerns and divines in things, he discerns and divines not as something *other* than himself, according to the law of speculative knowledge, but, on the contrary, as inseparable from himself and from his emotion, and in truth as identified with himself.

His intuition, the creative intuition, is an obscure grasping of his own Self and of things in a knowledge through union or through connaturality which is born in the spiritual unconscious, and which fructifies only in the work. So the germ of which I spoke some pages back, and which is contained in the spiritual night of the free life of the intellect, tends from the very start to a kind of revelation—not to the revelation of the *Übermensch* or of the omnipotency of man, as the Surrealists believe, but to the humble revelation, virtually contained in a small lucid cloud of inescapable intuition, both of the Self of the poet and of some particular flash of reality in the God-made universe; a particular flash of reality bursting forth in its unforgettable individuality, but infinite in its meanings and echoing capacity—

To see a World in a Grain of Sand,
And a Heaven in a Wild Flower.

Such is the answer of philosophical analysis to the problem which had imposed itself on our consideration at the end of the merely descriptive or inductive inquiry conducted in the first chapter of this book. At that moment we observed that Oriental art, only intent on Things, nevertheless reveals obscurely, together with Things (and to the very extent to which it truly succeeds in revealing Things), the creative subjectivity of the artist; and that, on the other hand, Occidental art, more and more intent on the artist's Self, nevertheless reveals obscurely, together with this Self (and to the very extent to which it succeeds in revealing it), the transapparent reality and secret significance of Things. And we concluded that at the root of the creative act there must be a quite particular intellectual process, a kind of experience or knowledge without parallel in logical reason, through which Things and the Self are obscurely grasped together.

Now, availing ourselves of the self-awareness which the progress of reflexivity has developed in modern art and poetry, and which causes poets to say with Pierre Reverdy that "the value of a work is proportional to the poignant contact of the poet with his own destiny," we come to perceive in philosophical terms how and why the process in question takes place. A direct inquiry into the inner functioning of the intellect in its preconceptual life makes us realize that poetic intuition and poetic knowledge are both one of the basic manifestations of man's spiritual nature, and a primary requirement of the creativity of the spirit steeped in imagination and emotion.

Nature of poetic knowledge

I used a moment ago the expression "knowledge through connaturality." It refers to a basic distinction made by Thomas Aquinas, when he explains that there are two different ways to judge of things pertaining to a moral virtue, say fortitude. On the one hand we can possess in our mind moral science, the conceptual and rational knowledge of virtues, which produces in us a merely intellectual conformity with the truths involved. Then, if we are asked a question about fortitude, we will give the right answer by merely looking at and consulting the intelligible objects contained in our concepts. A moral philosopher may possibly not be a virtuous man and know everything about virtues.

On the other hand, we can possess the virtue in question in our own powers of will and desire, have it embodied in ourselves, and thus be in accordance with it or connatured with it in our very being. Then, if we are asked a question about fortitude, we will give the right answer, no longer through science, but through inclination, by looking at and consulting what we are and the inner bents or propensities of our own being. A virtuous man may possibly be utterly ignorant in moral philosophy, and know as well (probably better) everything about virtues—through connaturality.

In this knowledge through union or inclination, connaturality or congeniality, the intellect is at play not alone, but together with affective inclinations and the dispositions of the will, and as guided and shaped by them. It is not rational knowledge, knowledge through the conceptual, logical, and discursive exercise of reason. But it is really and genuinely knowledge, though obscure and perhaps incapable of giving account of itself.

St. Thomas explains in this way the difference between the knowledge of divine reality acquired by theology and the knowledge of divine reality provided by mystical experience. For the spiritual man, he says, knows divine things through inclination or connaturality: not only because he has learned them, but because he suffers them, as the Pseudo-Dionysius put it.

Knowledge through connaturality plays an immense part in human life. Modern philosophers have thrown it into oblivion, but the ancient Doctors paid careful attention to it and established upon it all their theory of God-given contemplation. I think that we have to restore it, and to recognize its basic role and importance in such domains as moral practical knowledge and natural or supernatural mystical experience—and in the domain of art and poetry. Poetic knowledge, as I see it, is a specific kind of knowledge through inclination or connaturality—let us say a knowledge through affective connaturality which essentially relates to the creativity of the spirit and tends to express itself in a work. So that in such a knowledge it is the object created, the poem, the painting, the symphony, in its own existence as a world of its own, which plays the part played in ordinary knowledge by the concepts and judgments produced within the mind.

Hence it follows that poetic knowledge is fully expressed only in the work. In the mind of the poet, poetic knowledge arises in an unconscious or preconscious manner, and emerges into consciousness in a sometimes almost imperceptible though imperative and irrefragable way, through an impact both emotional and intellectual or through an unpredictable experiential insight, which gives notice of its existence, but does not express it.

This particular kind of knowledge through connaturality comes about, I think, by means of emotion. That is why, at first glance, one believes, and often the poet himself believes, that he is like the Ahab of *Moby Dick:* "Here's food for thought, had Ahab time to think; but Ahab never thinks; he only feels, feels, feels; *that's* tingling enough for mortal man! to think's audacity. God only has that right and privilege." Well, in this people are mistaken. The poet also thinks. And poetic knowledge proceeds from the intellect in its most genuine and essential capacity as intellect, though through the indispensable instrumentality of feeling, feeling, feeling. At this point I would wish to insist that it is in no way a merely emotional or a sentimentalist theory of poetry that I am suggesting. First, I am speaking of a certain kind of knowledge, and emotion does not know: the intellect knows, in this kind of knowledge as in any other. Second, the emotion of which I am speaking is in no way that "brute or merely subjective emotion" to which I alluded in the first chapter, and which is extraneous to art. It is not an emotion expressed or *depicted* by the poet, an emotion as *thing* which serves as a kind of matter or material in the making of the work, nor is it a thrill in the poet which the poem will "send down the spine" of the reader. It is an emotion as *form*, which, being one with the creative intuition, gives form to the poem, and which is *intentional*, as an idea is, or carries within itself infinitely more than itself. (I use the word "intentional" in the Thomistic sense, reintroduced by Brentano and Husserl into modern philosophy, which refers to the purely tendential existence through which a thing—for instance, the object known—is present, in an immaterial or suprasubjective manner, in an "instrument"—an idea for instance, which, in so far as it determines the act of knowing, is a mere immaterial tendency or *intentio* toward the object.)

How can emotion be thus raised to the level of the intellect and, as it were, take the place of the concept in becoming for the intellect a determining means or instrumental vehicle through which reality is grasped?

That's a difficult question, as are all similar questions dealing with the applicaton of the general concept of knowledge through connaturality to the various particular fields in which this kind of knowledge is at play. I think that in all these cases, where the soul "suffers things more than it learns them," and experiences them through resonance in subjectivity, we have to find out a certain specific way in which the great notion developed by John of St. Thomas apropos of mystical knowledge—*amor transit in conditionem objecti*, love passes on to the sphere of the intentional means of objective grasping—has to be used analogically. Here I would say that in poetic knowledge emotion carries the reality which the soul suffers—a world in a grain of sand— into the depth of subjectivity, and of the spiritual unconscious of the intellect, because in the poet, contrary to other men (especially those involved in the business of civilized life), the soul remains, as it were, more available to itself, and keeps a reserve of spirituality which is not absorbed by its activity toward the outside and by the toil of its powers. And this deep unemployed reserve of the spirit, being unemployed, is like a sleep of the soul; but, being spiritual, is in a state of virtual vigilance and vital tension, owing to the virtual reversion of the spirit on itself and on everything in itself. The soul sleeps, but her heart is awake; allow her to sleep . . .

Well, let us suppose that in the density of such a secretly alert sleep and such a spiritual tension, emotion intervenes (whatever this emotion may be; what matters is where it is received). On the one hand it spreads into the entire soul, it imbues its very being, and thus certain particular aspects in things become connatural to the soul affected in this way. On the other hand, emotion, falling into the living springs, is received in the vitality of intelligence, I mean intelligence permeated by the diffuse light of the Illuminating Intellect and virtually turned toward all the harvests of experience and memory preserved in the soul, all the universe of fluid images, recollections, associations, feelings, and desires latent, under pressure, in the subjectivity, and now stirred. And it suffices for emotion disposing or inclining, as I have said, the entire soul in a certain determinate manner to be thus received in the undetermined vitality and productivity of the spirit, where it is permeated by the light of the Illuminating Intellect: then, while remaining emotion, it is made—with respect to the aspects in things which are connatural to, or *like*, the soul it imbues—into an instrument of intelligence judging through connaturality, and plays, in the process of this knowledge through *likeness* between reality and subjectivity, the part of a nonconceptual intrinsic determination of intelligence in its preconscious activity. By this very fact it is transferred into the state of objective intentionality; it is spiritualized, it becomes intentional, that is to say, conveying, in a state of immateriality, things other than itself. It becomes for the intellect a determining means or instrumental vehicle through which the things which have impressed this emotion on the soul, and the deeper, invisible things that are contained in them or connected with them, and which have ineffable correspondence or coaptation with the soul thus affected, and which resound in it, are grasped and known obscurely.

It is by means of such a spiritualized emotion that poetic intuition, which in itself is an intellective flash, is born in the unconscious of the spirit. In one sense it is, as I said a moment ago, a privilege of those souls in which the margin of dreaming activity and introverted natural spirituality, unemployed for the business of human life, is particularly large. In another sense, because it emanates from a most natural capacity of the human mind, we must say that every human being is potentially capable of it: among those who do not know it, many, in point of fact, have repressed it or murdered it within themselves. Hence their instinctive resentment against the poet.

Of itself poetic intuition proceeds from the natural and supremely spontaneous movement of the soul which seeks itself by communicating with things in its capacity as a spirit endowed with senses and passions. And sometimes it is in mature age, when the spirit has been fed with experience and suffering, and turns back toward itself, that it best experiences the sapid sleep in which poetic intuition awakes—and which also exists, in another fashion, and with the acrid taste of greenness, in the child and the primitive. Poetic knowledge is as natural to the spirit of man as the return of the bird to his nest; and it is the universe which, together with the spirit, makes its way back to the mysterious nest of the soul. For the content of poetic intuition is both the reality of the things of the world and the subjectivity of the poet, both obscurely conveyed through an intentional or spiritualized emotion. The soul is known in the experience of the world and the world is known in the experience of the soul, through a knowledge which does not know itself. For such knowledge knows, not in order to know, but in order to produce. It is toward creation that it tends.

"*Je est un autre,*" Rimbaud said: "I is another." In poetic intuition objective reality and subjectivity, the world and the whole of the soul, coexist inseparably. At that moment sense and sensation are brought back to the heart, blood to the spirit, passion to intuition. And through the vital though nonconceptual actuation of the intellect all the powers of the soul are also actuated in their roots.

Pleasure and beauty

George Santayana (1863-1952)

Born in Spain of an American mother, Santayana grew up in the United States. He was educated at Harvard and taught there from 1889 to 1912, while William James and Josiah Royce were on the faculty. After coming into a modest inheritance, Santayana left Harvard to live abroad and to devote all his time to study and writing. He produced a great many books, written in a finely cultivated style, as well as poems, essays, and one novel. His two major cycles, The Life of Reason *and* The Realms of Being, *are systematic explorations of the concepts of Nature, Mind, and Value. Throughout these works Santayana unwaveringly maintains his materialism and naturalism but seeks also for the ideal goals of human existence.*

Our selection is from Santayana's book, The Sense of Beauty, *published in 1896. In this work he presents a naturalistic theory of beauty, regarding it as "pleasure objectified." In other portions of the book he explores the notions of form, content, and expression in art. Part of his purpose in this book was to challenge some of the prevailing conceptions in the philosophy of art, for example, that art requires a "disinterested" attitude.*

The differentia of æsthetic pleasure not its disinterestedness.

The distinction between pleasure and the sense of beauty has sometimes been said to consist in the unselfishness of æsthetic satisfaction. In other pleasures, it is said, we gratify our senses and passions; in the contemplation of beauty we are raised above ourselves, the passions are silenced and we are happy in the recognition of a good that we do not seek to possess. The painter does not look at a spring of water with the eyes of a thirsty man, nor at a beautiful woman with those of a satyr. The difference lies, it is urged, in the impersonality of the enjoyment. But this distinction is one of intensity and

Reprinted with the permission of Charles Scribner's Sons, from *The Sense of Beauty*, pp. 37-52, by George Santayana. (1896). Used by permission also of Constable & Company, Ltd.

delicacy, not of nature, and it seems satisfactory only to the least æsthetic minds.[1]

In the second place, the supposed disinterestedness of æsthetic delights is not very fundamental. Appreciation of a picture is not identical with the desire to buy it, but it is, or ought to be, closely related and preliminary to that desire. The beauties of nature and of the plastic arts are not consumed by being enjoyed; they retain all the efficacy to impress a second beholder. But this circumstance is

[1] Schopenhauer, indeed, who makes much of it, was a good critic, but his psychology suffered much from the pessimistic generalities of his system. It concerned him to show that the will was bad, and, as he felt beauty to be a good if not a holy thing, he hastened to convince himself that it came from the suppression of the will. But even in his system this suppression is only relative. The desire of individual objects, indeed, is absent in the perception of beauty, but there is still present that initial love of the gen-

accidental, and those æsthetic objects which depend upon change and are exhausted in time, as are all performances, are things the enjoyment of which is an object of rivalry and is coveted as much as any other pleasure. And even plastic beauties can often not be enjoyed except by a few, on account of the necessity of travel or other difficulties of access, and then this æsthetic enjoyment is as selfishly pursued as the rest.

The truth which the theory is trying to state seems rather to be that when we seek æsthetic pleasures we have no further pleasure in mind; that we do not mix up the satisfactions of vanity and proprietorship with the delight of contemplation. This is true, but it is true at bottom of all pursuits and enjoyments. Every real pleasure is in one sense disinterested. It is not sought with ulterior motives, and what fills the mind is no calculation, but the image of an object or event, suffused with emotion. A sophisticated consciousness may often take the idea of self as the touchstone of its inclinations; but this self, for the gratification and aggrandizement of which a man may live, is itself only a complex of aims and memories, which once had their direct objects, in which he had taken a spontaneous and unselfish interest. The gratifications which, merged together, make the selfishness are each of them ingenuous, and no more selfish than the most altruistic, impersonal emotion. The content of selfishness is a mass of unselfishness. There is no reference to the nominal essence called oneself either in one's appetites or in one's natural affections; yet a man absorbed in his meat and drink, in his houses and lands, in his children and dogs, is called selfish because these inter-

eral type and principles of things which is the first illusion of the absolute, and drives it on to the fatal experiment of creation. So that, apart from Schopenhauer's mythology, we have even in him the recognition that beauty gives satisfaction to some dim and underlying demand of our nature, just as particular objects give more special and momentary pleasures to our individualized wills. His psychology was, however, far too vague and general to undertake an analysis of those mysterious feelings.

ests, although natural and instinctive in him, are not shared by others. The unselfish man is he whose nature has a more universal direction, whose interests are more widely diffused.

But as impersonal thoughts are such only in their object, not in their subject or agent, since all thoughts are the thoughts of somebody: so also unselfish interests have to be somebody's interests. If we were not interested in beauty, if it were of no concern to our happiness whether things were beautiful or ugly, we should manifest not the maximum, but the total absense of æsthetic faculty. The disinterestedness of this pleasure is, therefore, that of all primitive and intuitive satisfactions, which are in no way conditioned by a reference to an artificial general concept, like that of the self, all the potency of which must itself be derived from the independent energy of its component elements. I care about myself because "myself" is a name for the things I have at heart. To set up the verbal figment of personality and make it an object of concern apart from the interests which were its content and substance, turns the moralist into a pedant, and ethics into a superstition. The self which is the object of *amour propre* is an idol of the tribe, and needs to be disintegrated into the primitive objective interests that underlie it before the cultus of it can be justified by reason.

The differentia of æsthetic pleasure not its universality.

The supposed disinterestedness of our love of beauty passes into another characteristic of it often regarded as essential,—its universality. The pleasures of the senses have, it is said, no dogmatism in them; that anything gives me pleasure involves no assertion about its capacity to give pleasure to another. But when I judge a thing to be beautiful, my judgment means that the thing is beautiful in itself, or (what is the same thing more critically expressed) that it should seem so to everybody. The claim to universality is, according to this doctrine, the essence of the æsthetic; what makes the perception of beauty a judgment rather than a sensation. All æsthetic precepts would be impossible, and all criticism arbitrary and subjective, unless we admit a paradoxical universality in our judgment, the philosophical implications of which we may then go on to develope. But we are fortunately not required to enter the labyrinth into which this method leads; there is a much simpler and clearer way of studying such questions, which is to challenge and analyze the assertion before us and seek its basis in human nature. Before this is done, we should run the risk of expanding a natural misconception or inaccuracy of thought into an inveterate and pernicious prejudice by making it the centre of an elaborate construction.

That the claim of universality is such a natural inaccuracy will not be hard to show. There is notoriously no great agreement upon æsthetic matters; and such agreement as there is, is based upon similarity of origin, nature, and circumstance among men, a similarity which, where it exists, tends to bring about identity in all judgments and feelings. It is unmeaning to say that what is beautiful to one man *ought* to be beautiful to another. If their senses are the same, their associations and dispositions similar, then the same thing will certainly be beautiful to both. If their natures are different, the form which to one will be entrancing will be to another even invisible, because his classifications and discriminations in perception will be different, and he may see a hideous detached fragment or a shapeless aggregate of things, in what to another is a perfect whole—so entirely are the unities of objects unities of function and use. It is absurd to say that what is invisible to a given being *ought* to seem beautiful to him. Evidently this obligation of recognizing the same qualities is conditioned by the possession of the same faculties. But no two men have exactly the same faculties, nor can things have for any two exactly the same values.

What is loosely expressed by saying that any one ought to see this or that beauty is that he would see it if his disposition, training, or attention were what our ideal demands for him; and our ideal of what any one should be has complex but discoverable sources. We take, for instance, a certain pleasure in having our own judgments supported by those of others; we are intolerant, if not of the existence of a nature different from our own, at least of its expression in words and judgments. We are confirmed or made happy in our doubtful opinions by seeing them accepted universally. We are unable to find the basis of our taste in our own experience and therefore refuse to look for it there. If we were sure of our ground, we should be willing to acquiesce in the naturally different feelings and ways of others, as a man who is conscious of speaking his language with the accent of the capital confesses its arbitrariness with gayety, and is pleased and interested in the variations of it he observes in provincials; but the provincial is always zealous to show that he has reason and ancient authority to justify his oddities. So people who have no sensations, and do not know why they judge, are always trying to show that they judge by universal reason.

Thus the frailty and superficiality of our own judgments cannot brook contradiction. We abhor another man's doubt when we cannot tell him why we ourselves believe. Our ideal of other men tends therefore to include the agreement of their judgments with our own; and although we might acknowledge the fatuity of this demand in regard to natures very different from the human, we may be unreasonable enough to require that all races should admire the same style of architecture, and all ages the same poets.

The great actual unity of human taste within the range of conventional history helps the pretension. But in principle it is untenable. Nothing has less to do with the real merit of a work of imagination than the capacity of all men to appreciate it; the true test is the degree and kind of satisfaction it can give to him who appreciates it most. The symphony would lose nothing if half mankind had always been deaf, as nine-tenths of them actually are to the intricacies of its harmonies; but it would have lost much if no Beethoven had existed. And more: incapacity to appreciate certain types of beauty may be the condition *sine qua non* for the appreciation of another kind; the greatest capacity both for enjoyment and creation is highly specialized and exclusive, and hence the greatest ages of art have often been strangely intolerant.

The invectives of one school against another, perverse as they are philosophically, are artistically often signs of health, because they indicate a vital appreciation of certain kinds of beauty, a love of them that has grown into a jealous passion. The architects that have pieced out the imperfections of ancient buildings with their own thoughts, like Charles V. when he raised his massive palace beside the Alhambra, may be condemned from a certain point of view. They marred much by their interference; but they showed a splendid confidence in their own intuitions, a proud assertion of their own taste, which is the greatest evidence of æsthetic sincerity. On the contrary, our own gropings, eclecticism, and archæology are the symptoms of impotence. If we were less learned and less just, we might be more efficient. If our appreciation were less general, it might be more real, and if we trained our imagination into exclusiveness, it might attain to character.

The differentia of æsthetic pleasure: its objectification.

There is, however, something more in the claim to universality in æsthetic judgments than the desire to generalize our own opinions. There is the expression of a curious but well-known psychological phenomenon, viz., the transformation of an element of sensation into the quality of a thing. If we say that other men should see the beauties we see, it is because we think those beauties *are in the object*, like its colour, proportion, or size. Our judgment appears to us merely the perception and discovery of an external existence, of the real excellence that is without. But this notion is radically absurd and contradictory. Beauty, as we have seen, is a value; it cannot be conceived as an independent existence which affects our senses and which we consequently perceive. It exists in perception, and cannot exist otherwise. A beauty not perceived is a pleasure not felt, and a contradiction. But modern philosophy has taught us to say the same thing of every element of the perceived world; all are sensations; and their grouping into objects imagined to be permanent and external is the work of certain habits of our intelligence. We should be incapable of surveying or retaining the diffused experiences of life, unless we organized and classified them, and out of the chaos of impressions framed the world of conventional and recognizable objects.

How this is done is explained by the current theories of perception. External objects usually affect various senses at once, the impressions of which are thereby associated. Repeated experiences of one object are also associated on account of their similarity; hence a double tendency to merge and unify into a single percept, to which a name is attached, the group of those memories and reactions which in fact had one external thing for their cause. But this percept, once formed, is clearly different from those particular experiences out of which it grew. It is permanent, they are variable. They are but partial views and glimpses of it. The constituted notion therefore comes to be the reality, and the materials of it merely the appearance. The distinction between substance and quality, reality and appearance, matter and mind, has no other origin.

The objects thus conceived and distinguished from our ideas of them, are at first compacted of all the impressions, feelings, and memories, which offer themselves for association and fall within the vortex of the amalgamating imagination. Every sensation we get from a thing is originally treated as one of its qualities. Experiment, however, and the practical need of a simpler conception of the structure of objects lead us gradually to reduce the qualities of the object to a minimum, and to regard most perceptions as an effect of those few qualities upon us. These few primary qualities, like extension which we persist in treating as independently real and as the quality of a substance, are those which suffice to explain the order of our experiences. All the rest, like colour, are relegated to the subjective sphere, as merely effects upon our minds, and apparent or secondary qualities of the object.

But this distinction has only a practical justification. Convenience and economy of thought alone determine what combination of our sensations we shall continue to objectify and treat as the cause of the rest. The right and tendency to be objective is equal in all, since they are all prior to the artifice of thought by which we separate the concept from its materials, the thing from our experiences.

The qualities which we now conceive to belong to real objects are for the most part images of sight and touch. One of the first classes of effects to be treated as secondary were naturally pleasures and pains, since it could commonly conduce very little to intelligent and successful action to conceive our pleasures and pains as resident in objects. But emotions are essentially capable of objectification, as well as impressions of sense; and one may well believe that a primitive and inexperienced consciousness would rather people the world with ghosts of its own terrors and passions than with projections of those luminous and mathematical concepts which as yet it could hardly have formed.

This animistic and mythological habit of thought still holds its own at the confines of knowledge, where mechanical explanations are not found. In ourselves, where nearness makes observation difficult, in the intricate chaos of animal and human life, we still appeal to the efficacy of will and ideas, as also in the remote night of cosmic and religious problems. But in all the intermediate realm of vulgar day, where mechanical science has made progress, the inclusion of emotional or passionate elements in the concept of the reality would be now an extravagance. Here our idea of things is composed exclusively of perceptual elements, of the ideas of form and of motion.

The beauty of objects, however, forms an exception to this rule. Beauty is an emotional element, a pleasure of ours, which nevertheless we regard as a quality of things. But we are now prepared to understand the nature of this exception. It is the survival of a tendency originally universal to make every effect of a thing upon us a constituent of its conceived nature. The scientific idea of a thing is a great abstraction from the mass of perceptions and re-

actions which that thing produces; the æsthetic idea is less abstract, since it retains the emotional reaction, the pleasure of the perception, as an integral part of the conceived thing.

Nor is it hard to find the ground of this survival in the sense of beauty of an objectification of feeling elsewhere extinct. Most of the pleasures which objects cause are easily distinguished and separated from the perception of the object: the object has to be applied to a particular organ, like the palate, or swallowed like wine, or used and operated upon in some way before the pleasure arises. The cohesion is therefore slight between the pleasure and the other associated elements of sense; the pleasure is separated in time from the perception, or it is localized in a different organ, and consequently is at once recognized as an effect and not as a quality of the object. But when the process of perception itself is pleasant, as it may easily be, when the intellectual operation, by which the elements of sense are associated and projected, and the concept of the form and substance of the thing produced, is naturally delightful, then we have a pleasure intimately bound up in the thing, inseparable from its character and constitution, the seat of which in us is the same as the seat of the perception. We naturally fail, under these circumstances, to separate the pleasure from the other objectified feelings. It becomes, like them, a quality of the object, which we distinguish from pleasures not so incorporated in the perception of things, by giving it the name of beauty.

The definition of beauty.

We have now reached our definition of beauty, which, in the terms of our successive analysis and narrowing of the conception, is value positive, intrinsic, and objectified. Or, in less technical language, Beauty is pleasure regarded as the quality of a thing.

This definition is intended to sum up a variety of distinctions and identifications which should perhaps be here more explicitly set down. Beauty is a value, that is, it is not a perception of a matter of fact or of a relation: it is an emotion, an affection of our volitional and appreciative nature. An object cannot be beautiful if it can give pleasure to nobody: a beauty to which all men were forever indifferent is a contradiction in terms.

In the second place, this value is positive, it is the sense of the presence of something good, or (in the case of ugliness) of its absence. It is never the perception of a positive evil, it is never a negative value. That we are endowed with the sense of beauty is a pure gain which brings no evil with it. When the ugly ceases to be amusing or merely uninteresting and becomes disgusting, it becomes indeed a positive evil: but a moral and practical, not an æsthetic one. In æsthetics that saying is true—often so disingenuous in ethics—that evil is nothing but the absence of good: for even the tedium and vulgarity of an existence without beauty is not itself ugly so much as lamentable and degrading. The absence of æsthetic goods is a moral evil: the æsthetic evil is merely relative, and means less of æsthetic good than was expected at the place and time. No form in itself gives pain, although some forms give pain by causing a shock of surprise even when they are really beautiful: as if a mother found a fine bull pup in her child's cradle, when her pain would not be æsthetic in its nature.

Further, this pleasure must not be in the consequence of the utility of the object or event, but in its immediate perception; in other words, beauty is an ultimate good, something that gives satisfaction to a natural function, to some fundamental need or capacity of our minds. Beauty is therefore a positive value that is intrinsic; it is a pleasure. These two circumstances sufficiently separate the sphere of æsthetics from that of ethics. Moral values are generally negative, and always remote. Morality has to do with the avoidance of evil and the pursuit of good: æsthetics only with enjoyment.

Finally, the pleasures of sense are distinguished from the perception of beauty, as sensation in general is distinguished from perception; by the objectification of the elements and their appearance as qualities rather of things than of consciousness. The passage from sensation to perception is gradual, and the path may be sometimes retraced: so it is with beauty and the pleasures of sensation. There is no sharp line between them, but it depends upon the degree of objectivity my feeling has attained at the moment whether I say "It pleases me," or "It is beautiful." If I am self-conscious and critical, I shall probably use one phrase; if I am impulsive and susceptible, the other. The more remote, interwoven, and inextricable the pleasure is, the more objective it will appear; and the union of two pleasures often makes one beauty. In Shakespeare's LIVth sonnet are these words:

O how much more doth beauty beauteous
　　seem
By that sweet ornament which truth doth
　　give!
The rose looks fair, but fairer we it deem
For that sweet odour which doth in it live.
The canker-blooms have full as deep a dye
As perfumèd tincture of the roses,
Hang on such thorns, and play as wantonly
When summer's breath their maskèd buds
　　discloses.
But, for their beauty only is their show,
They live unwooed and unrespected fade;
Die to themselves. Sweet roses do not so:
Of their sweet deaths are sweetest odours
　　made.

One added ornament, we see, turns the deep dye, which was but show and mere sensation before, into an element of beauty and reality; and as truth is here the co-operation of perceptions, so beauty is the co-operation of pleasures. If colour, form, and motion are hardly beautiful without the sweetness of the odour, how much more necessary would they be for the sweetness itself to become a beauty! If we had the perfume in a flask, no one would think of calling it beautiful: it would give us too detached and controllable a sensation. There would be no object in which it could be easily incorporated. But let it float from the garden, and it will add another sensuous charm to objects simultaneously recognized, and help to make them beautiful. Thus beauty is constituted by the objectification of pleasure. It is pleasure objectified.

Science and art

Paul Weiss (b. 1901)

One of the foremost of contemporary American philosophers and a leading metaphysical thinker, Paul Weiss was born in New York City and educated at the College of the City of New York and at Harvard, where he received the Ph.D. degree. He has taught at Harvard and Bryn Mawr. Since 1946 he has been at Yale University, where he now holds the Sterling chair of philosophy.

His books include Reality *(1938),* Nature and Man *(1947),* Man's Freedom *(1950),* Modes of Being *(1958),* The World of Art *(1961) and its companion volume* Nine Basic Arts, *and* The God We Seek *(1964); he has, as well, written works on social and political philosophy and on the philosophy of history and of religion. In addition, he has published numerous articles, edited, with Charles Hartshorne, the* Collected Papers of Charles Sanders Peirce, *and founded and edited the* Review of Metaphysics.

In The World of Art *Weiss examines a variety of problems encountered by the philosophic investigator of the arts and relates the activity of the artist to the complexus of human activities. In the following selection, he seeks to answer a question that frequently arises in discussions of the arts: How does the contribution of the artist compare with that of the scientist?*

. . . If we are to have stable and reliable knowledge, we must refine the crude knowledge of common sense. Science offers one way of doing this. But we should also make use of other means, particularly if we are to understand spheres of existence beyond the interest or reach of science. It is the task of both scientific and nonscientific inquirers to free us from error, the one doing it in one way, the other in another. Neither suffices by itself. Each needs the protection of the other in order to make sure that some of the things maintained by common sense ought to be eliminated, and some of the things unknown to common sense accepted, because they belong to the whole of

From "Science and Art," from *The World of Art* by Paul Weiss. Copyright © 1961 by Southern Illinois University Press. Reprinted by permission of Southern Illinois University Press.

what is true and ought to be known. To bring all knowledge into one harmonious whole, we must have recourse to a speculatively achieved view. This relates to what lies behind all special inquiries, and helps prevent any one of these from obscuring the light of the others. The speculatively achieved view looks at all beliefs, common or specialized, from a vantage point which requires all of them to be justified, but not necessarily only by the means which the established sciences provide.

Both science and the humanities, then, are opposed to error. Both do much to free us from it. Both accept some common-sense data. Both would deny themselves if they reject the data which warrants the other. A defense of the possibility and worth of science is in part a defense of philosophy and other inquiries as well. And the converse is also true.

But it might be said, "The language of science is precise and is available to all. Other subjects speak in metaphors and then with an emphasis and stress which varies the meaning from man to man." This contention, though, like the previous one, is not altogether justifiable. So far as what it claims is true, it in fact shows that there is something more to be known than could be known by the methods of science. It points, in other words, to a conclusion opposite to that which it was intended to support.

Physics, certainly on its elementary levels, is precise, predictive, and universally knowable. But physics is not the only science. Nor are those disciplines which put their expressions in quantitative terms the only ones which are entitled to the designation "scientific." Chemistry is a science; so are biology, astronomy, geology. Yet none of these is wholly or merely quantitative. The chemist remarks on the colors of his compounds, the botanist and the astronomer classify, the biological unit is the observable cell, the geologist has no hesitancy of speaking of faults in rocks. Each uses notions which have not been quantified completely. No one of them is so precisely expressed that no diversity of understanding is possible.

The language of the sciences is not as precise as it is popularly supposed to be. On the other hand, the terms and grammar of other subjects are not as loose as their critics say they are. It is possible for fellow workers in nonscientific fields to understand one another, to agree and disagree on a given issue, and it is possible for them to teach and communicate what they have discovered. Terms like "the historic past," "beauty," "truth," "prayer" are not in the vocabulary of the accepted sciences. Yet in their appropriate contexts they have an appropriate precision.

Where a topic is complex and has multiple facets presenting a host of problems, what is needed is not an expression which dissects it and arbitrarily limits the field, but a characterization which roughly marks it off from others and allows for the possibility of conquering it from many angles. If we use only those terms which the sciences have made precise in meaning, reference, and use, we will not be able to locate the common-sense world from which those sciences issued and to which they may refer. If we want to deal with the world as experienced and with every kind of question it might raise, it would be wrong to prohibit the use of the very terms which, though metaphorical and in some respects vague and undefined, point to that world and no other.

The languages of the sciences are more precise than those of other subjects, and particularly of art and philosophy. Scientists can now state more precisely than ever before what they mean by genes, electrons, elements, gravitation, but artists and philosophers seem to be just where they have always been. On questions relating to beauty, creativity, the soul, substance or divinity, men today seem to be at least as incoherent and obscure as they were in the past.

Part of the advance in precision on the part of scientists is due to the fact that places where they could not obtain a desired precision were abandoned by them. Also, the sciences abstract from the concrete, the individual, the private, and substantial—and sometimes even from the sensuous and observable—to end with terms which are tissues of universals capable of complete and exhaustive analysis and definition. "Electron" means the same thing for a host of scientists in part because what is intended by the term is not a concrete entity but the universal "electronicity"—the character which all electrons share and perhaps exemplify in diverse ways. Like every abstract universal, "electronicity" is capable of sharp definition; but like every other universal it does not reveal anything about the individual natures and specific differences which distinguish one electron from another.

He who is willing to ignore the individual, indeterminate or substantial nature of beings can make his discourse in other fields as precise as that of the sciences. The classical economist is a case in point. He has few friends, not because he is too vague but because he formulates his principles and conclusions with too great a precision. What was wanted of him was not a knowledge of the way in which an abstract or ideal "economic man" might behave, but a knowledge of the character of a concrete economic process which could not be obtained by manipulating the economist's abstractions. Descriptions of the exact course of individual events in the world, like sensuous portrayals of the real, require the use of elements which are more flexible, more comprehensive, and more emotionally palatable than those which the sciences employ. Those who are interested in such descriptions acquire knowledge despite an inability to express themselves except in metaphor or by reference to qualities or impressions.

Science, it is also sometimes claimed, alone is coherent and intelligible. It alone is supposed to be disinterested, disowning the flavor of words and concentrating on the pure, nuclear, distilled meaning of terms. Its counters are said to be duplicable and fixed, well-defined elements which keep their meanings in context after context. Primarily concerned with concepts and not with feelings, enjoyments, qualities or impressions, it is said to ignore the emotional aspects, the music, the psychological associations, the ineffable tonality characteristic of other modes of communication. Putting aside the fact that psychological associations, emotions, and tonality intrude into the most austere and abstract discourse, and the fact that artists communicate quite well with others in quite distant places and with large groups of spectators, there is some truth in this contrast. But it shows merely that science follows a different method from the others; it does not show that it either gets more or less of the truth than they. An artist reads into his product the alterations which must be made in order to have his work relate to the world beyond. The alterations which a scientific discourse requires are not mentioned in it; they are provided by the instruments that are used when scientific formulae and hypotheses are made pertinent to something experienced.

A related point is made in the contention that science by making use of true universals, the only items that can be properly dealt with by the intellect, alone can hope to be universally understood. Only it, it is said, can provide knowledge free from the limitations and em-

phasis that the senses and emotions inevitably impose on observed material. Only such knowledge can be communicated; only this can be grasped by a multitude. The supposition is doubly questionable. First, though the same universals can be known in the same way by many intellects, each intellect is rooted in an individual body and grasps things in a different way. The same content has a different meaning for each. Second, the senses and the emotions offer us content which is one with the content others confront. Both points require some elaboration.

All men may be able to understand the definitions and usages which the sciences give to their basic terms. But that knowledge alone will not suffice to make them scientists. The knowledge must be supported by common habits of response and work. The reason why scientific truths are universally intelligible is not simply because they make use of universals but because individual scientists, despite the different weights which these truths have for them, are habituated to respond to them in common ways. In the same sense, the language of carpenters is also universal; even though they have no commonly accepted names or definitions, they view wood and their tools in similar ways at similar times.

A truly universal language presupposes either a set of habits in the respondents which enable all of them to isolate a common meaning in diverse contents, or the use of terms in such a way that they prompt individuals to so respond to different meanings that the outcome is the same for each. Science follows the former procedure. Other subjects follow the latter; they use a universal language in that they say different things to different men with a corresponding difference of appeal, thereby enabling the different men to know a common truth.

There is of course a difference between the languages of the sciences and other subjects. The sciences use a comparatively cold language, a language about the nature of things as they might be when all human interests, preferences and insights are suppressed; the language of the others is warmer, more subjective, humanized. It is not enough, however, to be concerned only with those truths which can be universally acknowledged. Since the language of science expresses the least common denominator of knowledge, the aspect of things which anyone could affirm at any time, it can provide only a minimum of content. But then, since some men are capable of noting things which others cannot, what the sciences report cannot be all that there is to know. If we try to deal only with that aspect of things which every man can affirm, we run the risk of denying the truths that men of genius and sudden insight can reach. Artists present truths in a guise which most men fail to see. That does not mean the artists are mistaken; on the contrary, those who take account of what the artists portray learn truths they never knew or otherwise could have known.

There is a sense in which all men could be said to have a knowledge of things not expressed or expressable in the sciences. The senses and emotions provide them with content which, though differing from individual to individual in specific nature, is as common and constant as it is vague and general. Though Tom may see red where John sees blue, both see a color and not a set of vibrations. If we ignore such content, we leave out the most reliable data we have about the nature of the real so far as this can be gleaned through perception.

The sciences are not as precise as they are supposed to be; nor strictly speaking are their languages necessarily or exclusively suited for universal communication. The sciences are precise to some degree; inside the frame of special habits and customs they speak a universal language. But a comparable precision and universality is evident in other disciplines as well. So far as a science neglects or rejects what cannot be made to conform to its ideal of a precise and communicable expression, other subjects must be brought to play on the facts so that full justice can be done to them. Supplementing what is open to dispassionate thought, the quantifiable and duplicable, is the concrete, the unique, the qualitative, what is open to men of insight. The truth is all together, only fragmentarily grasped in any inquiry

whose reach is less than the whole of things.

Science and other disciplines are then closer in nature, topic, objective, method, value and truth than is currently supposed. All take their start with what is experienced. Science, unlike the others, tries to find intelligible links between the various parts; the others try to get to first principles or to create what none can adequately cognize. No less than the others, science turns away from obtrusive reality to construct a world that never was encountered, but unlike them it does this in order to forge fruitful ways for interrelating phenomena, thereby making it possible to explain and control them.

A sharp contrast can be made between science and art if one attends to the way they reach their truths. Scientists tend to make distinctions, refine divisions, use sharp and steady definitions, whereas the artists are inclined to encompass, unify, merge, bridge, combine. But if truth means, as it does, the conveying of the intent of an entire situation, of its general import or meaning as well as of the structure and interrelation of its parts, then art must be said to convey truth as surely as science does. A work of art is a unified, substantial whole representing a world beyond. Its various parts interpenetrate to function in it in ways quite different from the ways they function in ordinary life. An interpenetration of terms, though, is not altogether alien to science as a whole. The assertions, experiments, and contributions of individual scientists are so many words in a single, organic, creative discourse engaged in by all the scientists together. Their total work constitutes a single whole, having a value somewhat analogous to that which is provided by a single artistic work.

Science, taken as one enterprise, is a cooperative discipline involving the employment of many independent workers. These provide the focussed terms, phrases, and occasional lines which make up the final single "poetic" discourse of science. The artist, on the other hand, though he does attend to the tonality of his items, does not build up his unity in terms of these alone. While taking some account of the meaning of his words, the natural affiliations of shapes, positions, textures, colors and sounds, he uses them in new ways to create a new syntax, thereby making it possible to tell a story which cannot be heard if one keeps too close to the relations that its terms have with that odd miscellany which makes up this world of ours. He alone is able to convey the sensuous nature of the basic reality which common-sense obscures and from which science abstracts.

Scientific workers are constantly helping one another. This is a signal fact about them, setting them over against the students of the humanities and particularly artists. Artists are strikingly individualistic, not very cooperative—though without genuine cooperation there would of course be no theatre, no opera, and little architecture, music, or dance. Artists may pool hints and suggestions, but they rarely add to one another's knowledge or production. Even inside a school artists function more like a colony of concurrent workers than as an integrated body of men, mutually supportive. Their works do not form a systematic whole. Scientists, in contrast, add vital units to one another to build bigger than they know.

Close cooperation and a common outlook are desirable in science but not necessarily in art. Since art is not trying to do what science is doing, it would be foolish for art to accept the conditions for work which are essential to science. The converse is also true. Nor does it follow that if art does not conform to the conditions to which science submits, it cannot lay hold of reality or that it cannot convey a truth. This would be the case if reality is only what science can convey and if truth can be had only in a scientific way—the very questions at issue.

In both science and art there are innovations in techniques. These relate primarily to the craft aspects of these enterprises. The current doctrine tends to exaggerate the place such innovations have in art and minimize their importance for science. The making of microscopes for the first time, the use of new surgical instruments, the grafting of plants, differ only in locus and purpose from the innovations of artists in the use of new materials and media, in the way to make and preserve paint, and so on. Artists tend to make their innovations integral to the production of their works; the scientists take them to be essentially preliminary, more like the finger exercises of the musician or the practicing at the barre of the dancer than they are like the usages of the full-fledged performing artist. Nevertheless science is interested in great innovators, perhaps because their achievements so signally affect the instruments, habits, experiments, outlooks, and lives of great numbers in a rather short time. Since the artist allows less of a break to occur between preparation and achievement, between what he takes to be instrumental to his art and the art work itself,[1] than the scientist does, he is more ready than the scientist to make the great innovations an incidental part of the entire work.

It is perhaps primarily experimentation that is at the focus of the attention of those who insist on making a radical distinction between art and science. Science alone, it is thought, experiments; it alone therefore can learn what is and is not the case. But art makes no experiments; it merely weaves idle fancies together, making no claim to be true of anything at all. This contrast is forced and largely mistaken. Not all scientists experiment. Theoretical physicists do not; astronomers and many botanists do not—unless by experiment one means a constant process of exploration, modification, reorganization, a trial and error use of means and procedures in the attempt to get to some desired result. But such experimentation is also to be found in the arts. The tentative tacking back and forth in an effort to resolve a difficulty or problem is characteristic of all probing men, scientists and politicians, artists and philosophers. For every color applied to canvas, for every form cut in metal, for every incident marked out in a story, another must be altered or replaced. That modification might require

---

[1] The innovations of doctors are closer to the innovations of artists than they are to those of scientists. The improvisations of a dancer are like the practice of the doctor; they are part of the work itself. The practicing dancer does not of course perform in public; the doctor unfortunately doctors while he practices.

a return to the beginning, which must be changed in the light of what had just been done. Art is as much remaking as making, retreat as advance, more trial and error than clear purpose made evident.

The scientist tends to allow the world to set the conditions for the type of result which is to be achieved. His experiment is primarily a way of enabling nature to answer his questions. The material with which the artist deals has its own nature and rationale; no less than the material which occupies the scientist, it is brute, objective, to be molded but never entirely mastered. But the artist insists on being in control; he experiments with the very material which is to provide him with his product. Indeed, it would not be amiss to say that the artist is even more of an experimenter, even more empirical, than the scientist. For it is the artist, not the scientist, who loses himself in the activity of manipulating material then and there available. Experimentation for the artist is a way of finding out the promise of the material, his own capacities, and the kind of transformation his intentions must undergo in being realized. What he elicits from his material is incorporated in the object he produces. The scientist instead tends to experiment just for the sake of getting clues to what lies hidden.

Each work of art is an experiment in that the desired result is in good measure achieved by trial and error. It is not, however, an experiment in the scientific sense of a designed set of traps and sluices through which nature may be led and thereby made to yield results not otherwise knowable. Scientific experimentation is concerned with means for the effective evidencing of nature's ways; artistic experimentation is concerned with means for the effective production of an artistic whole. This is an important difference between the two disciplines. Another is that the scientific experimenter usually has a definitive question to put

to nature. The artist in contrast has a not clearly-defined outcome which he desires.

The scientist, though concerned with what he experiences, looks beyond this for the laws and forces which serve to bind the phenomenal world into a cohesive, intelligible realm. The artist, though primarily concerned with grasping the subterranean aspects of reality, confines himself to his material. He adumbrates what lies below by reorganizing what lies above. The attempt of the scientist is to cut through incidental particularity to the laws and principles which the particulars illustrate, and to the presumed elements in terms of which phenomena can at least in theory be transformed into one another. As we saw, it is not necessary that he express his principles or elements in quantitative or mathematical terms. These are but agencies making possible easier deductions and more precise expressions of what is to be expected if such and such modifications are imposed on such and such phenomena. But in the end the scientist would like to express himself in precise terms, and if possible in formulae having a mathematical form. He is more speculative than the artist, more ready to leave the phenomenal world behind in order to express laws and isolate the elements which provide phenomena with their explanation and ground.

He who attended to science alone would know what is real, but he would not make contact with it in its concreteness; he who attended to art alone would grasp the real, but he would not know how to make this evident to an inquiring mind. From the standpoint of science, art exhibits an over-sensuous world, outside science's interest and beyond the reach of its methods. Art from its side sees science as presenting reality in an over-formalized guise. When it is said that art is just a tissue of fictions or that science is empty and futile, it is usually because one has mistakenly taken science or art alone to possess the truth.

Language,
Thought, and Meaning

Whatever else they may be engaged in, philosophers have very frequently to occupy themselves with the clarification of the expressions which they employ. From Plato onward, the literature of philosophy contains many instances of the attempt to clarify concepts through analysis of the meanings of words. In the twentieth century especially a great deal of attention has been given to problems of linguistic meaning and generally to the analysis of language. A number of twentieth-century philosophers have judged philosophy to be like a sick patient in need of therapy. They have diagnosed the disease to be primarily the malfunctioning of language and have proceeded to try to cure it by treating such things as "systematically misleading expressions," to use the phrase of Gilbert Ryle. This approach to philosophy has been centered in England and developed under the influence of the philosophers G. E. Moore and Ludwig Wittgenstein, especially the latter.

Prior to the development of the school of analytic philosophy in England, logical positivism (often called logical empiricism), an outgrowth of the "Vienna Circle" of the twenties, had also made proposals concerning the analysis of meaning. The so-called "verification principle" or "verifiability criterion" of meaningfulness offered by positivists such as A. J. Ayer was a sweeping proposal for reform in the approach to language and meaning.

The recent critical movement concerned with analyzing meaning had begun even in the nineteenth century, as the first of the readings in this part shows. Here the American philosopher Charles Sanders Peirce, regarded as the founder of "Pragmatism," proposes a criterion of meaning close to that of Hume in the eighteenth century and of the logical empiricists in the twentieth. Peirce makes the meaning of a belief equivalent to its practical effects and holds that beliefs without practical consequences are meaningless. Moreover, two seemingly different ideas whose practical effects are nevertheless identical cannot really be said to be different. Thus, Peirce regards his pragmatic test of meaning to be a powerful tool to eliminate needless disputes.

It is important to recognize that Peirce limits the practical consequences of an idea to the sensible effects which it produces, effects which are available to any number of observers. Here he shows the influence of his training in physics and his work as an experimental scientist. His emphasis in analyzing the meaning of a concept is on the observational results available to the impartial investigator. Is Peirce's pragmatic criterion of meaning applicable only to scientific concepts, or is it also to be applied to the whole range of ideas in everyday life? Do all investigators deal with concepts whose range of meanings is as definite as that of the concepts employed by physicists and chemists?

We come next to consider the criterion of meaning offered by recent logical empiricists. The criterion presented by A. J. Ayer makes the test of the cognitive meaningfulness of what is thought to be a factual statement the logical possibility of either showing it to be probably true or showing it to be probably false by observation. Statements that in no way can be thought of as subject to a procedure of empirical verification or falsification are not to be regarded as cognitively meaningful. (Cognitive meaning is meaning which involves representation of the factual world or reference to some actual state of affairs. Other kinds of meaning are also recognized, for example, emotive. See Ayer's discussion of emotive meaning and also Carnap's reply to Henle.)

Thinkers such as Ayer and Rudolf Carnap are especially concerned with establishing a standard for philosophical discussion. They argue that one should not regard as cognitively meaningful certain statements of metaphysics which allegedly tell us something about the whole of reality, because there is in principle no way of showing these statements to be true or false by observation of the world. Such statements have only a semblance of cognitive meaning; the empiricist criterion, often called the "verification principle," is offered as a means which, if accepted, would enable us to discover whether, behind the semblance, there is any genuine meaning. The logical empiricist, of course, takes as his standard of verification the empirical methods of the sciences. One cannot correctly apply this criterion if he employs some subjective interpretation of verification. Also it was recognized, especially by Carnap, that even in the sciences the requirement of complete verification is too strong. The notion of "confirmability" to a high degree has tended to replace that of verifiability.

If the positivists' criterion of meaning had been accepted by all philosophers some of the statements of philosophers would no longer be interpreted or discussed since they would be regarded as meaningless.

Paul Henle, in our selection, subjects the criterion to a searching examination, asking what the grounds are for its acceptance. Is it to be accepted because of empirical considerations? If so, what is the evidence in support of it? Do the responses which people make when asked to judge meaningfulness, indicating the presence or the absence of "phenomena of understanding," that is, evidence that they do perceive meaning, support the adoption of such a criterion? Henle asks especially whether this is the case with the language of scientists and finds that scientific language does not imply a verifiability criterion of meaningfulness. He also holds that metaphysical statements often have empirical content; that is, their truth or falsity depends on matters of fact, and those that do not have empirical content are nevertheless understood.

Alternatively, Henle asks, is the criterion to be accepted on normative grounds, as a proposal about how we should limit the range of meaningful statements? If so, Henle asks, what are the advantages of agreeing to this? After considering both assessments of the sort of thing the principle is, he concludes that on neither interpretation should it be adopted, though a much milder interpretation of the principle, one which urges us always to think rigorously, might well be accepted.

In replying to Henle, Rudolf Carnap, one of the most influential of all logical empiricists, employs the notion of confirmability rather than of verifiability. Carnap presents his view of "pseudo-statements," of which, he maintains, many metaphysical statements are examples. These are devoid of cognitive meaning but may evoke many of the same "phenomena of understanding" that genuine statements do. For this reason, he holds, Henle's test, employing the presence or absence of phenomena of understanding, is inconclusive. Carnap also discusses the empirical content of metaphysical statements and asserts that if a metaphysician were to tell us the "possible observational results which he would regard as confirming or disconfirming evidence for his thesis if they were to occur," then his thesis would become a cognitive one.

A. J. Ayer is known not only for his forceful statement of some of the basic principles of the logical empiricists, but also for his version of what is called the "emotive" theory of ethics. Ayer takes the position that sentences using value expressions have no cognitive import, only emotive import: they are only expressions of our feelings. Not only do they tell us nothing about the world; they are not even statements about our feelings. Such sentences simply evince our feelings. Ayer's emotive theory must be understood as implicit criticism of most of the tradition of ethical thought, which has treated sentences using such terms as "good" and "bad" as cognitively significant and has regarded the debate over moral principles as a meaningful one. On Ayer's view, when we call something "good" we are simply applauding it. There is no question of justifying our expression, since we have said nothing. In other words, the whole realm of value is noncognitive, and it is senseless to speak of any such thing as knowledge of value.

It is instructive to take Henle's approach to this aspect of Ayer's thought. If we were to regard the emotivist ethical theory as justifiable on empirical grounds and were to subject it to empirical testing, would we find evidence that people do regard ethical sentences as mere interjections? Or, if we interpret it as a normative theory, what are the benefits of not regarding these sentences as having cognitive significance?

In the paper by Gilbert Ryle we see another way of performing the task of sharpening the philosopher's linguistic tools. One of the most fertile thinkers among the Oxford philosophers, Ryle shows very clearly the distinction which he makes between the "ordinary" use of language and its philosophic use. In performing our everyday tasks, he argues, we operate *with* language, we use it well enough and are not misled by it. In philosophic thought we must operate *upon* language, seeking to examine one concept in relation to neighboring concepts, and digging at the roots of expressions which may systematically mislead us. The view of concepts which Ryle and others influenced by Ludwig Wittgenstein hold is that concepts are constantly becoming entangled one with another, that their boundaries are often vague, and that all of the things denoted by a general word, such as "games" or "art" or "norms," are not necessarily held together by a common thread, but rather have likenesses which are more in the nature of "family resemblances." The place to look in order to disentangle concepts is to "ordinary" language, that is, to the *uses* we make of language in fulfilling our everyday tasks. Thus the meanings of locutions employed in more specialized spheres, such as philosophy or the sciences, are grounded in ordinary meanings, that is, in the everyday uses of locutions.

Should ordinary language be held up for esteem in the manner of many British philosophers? In our selection, Friedrich Waismann says no. A mathematician and early positivist, Waismann challenges the position taken by Ryle and others of the Oxford school who trust in ordinary language. In a searching examination of the many capacities of language, Waismann emphasizes the desirability of attempting creatively to expand and reform language. The stress, he argues, should not be put on the paths already taken by language, but on those not yet entered. As he sees it, human language is a means of expanding our grasp of the world. To employ language in new ways, he suggests, can be more creative and ultimately of more value than to return continually to the frame of ordinary language.

We see in these two discussions, and in the previous ones of this part, the overriding importance which recent philosophers have given to an examination of their chief instrument—language. Philosophers have become extraordinarily self-conscious about the means they have at their disposal to do what they are trying to do. And, we must recognize that what they try to do is influenced by their view of the means they have available.

To clarify the complex interrelationships between language and thought, between conceptual thought and feeling, between mythical expression and rational language—these were some of the major tasks undertaken by Ernst Cassirer, one of the most productive of recent thinkers. In our selection he develops the thesis that mythical thought, beginning with the enthralling moment of immediate sensory impressions, moves toward a more permanent, but figurative and emotional, presentation of an objective power. The overwhelming awareness of the "momentary gods" becomes recognition of a persisting superior being. Language, too, Cassirer holds, shows a similar movement from immediate sensory detail, viewed in terms of human action and purpose, to a fixed, definite, and objective conceptual ordering of the world. Cassirer also maintains that language develops its view of the world primarily by a functional approach, that the poetic, dynamic, emotional perspective is the primary focus of human speech. Language and mythico-religious thought, Cassirer holds, develop together; the structures of language and of myth affect one another.

This discussion is important in connection with the earlier readings in this part and also with the readings in the next part. Cassirer tries to show that the symbolic phase of language, in which word-sounds are understood to stand for the concepts of things and their relations, is the last phase of its development, a phase which builds on earlier phases in which the primary use of language was to concentrate the experience of the moment. The other writers of this part have been overwhelmingly concerned with words as symbols of concepts, as indeed have most philosophers since Plato. The writers of the next part, usually called "existentialist," raise the question, at least implicitly, whether philosophy should not also consider those aspects of man's existence with which mythical thought is preoccupied—the individual, subjective, affective, and momentary. Is there perhaps suggested in Cassirer's writing the possibility of developing a philosophic approach in which conceptual frames of thought are brought to bear upon the emotional and subjective?

How to make our ideas clear

Charles Sanders Peirce (1839-1914)

A highly original thinker, Peirce was born in Cambridge, Massachusetts, the son of Benjamin Peirce, a famous mathematician and professor at Harvard. As a youth he was taught mathematics by his father, who also encouraged him to do experimental work in physics and astronomy, sciences to which he later made contributions. His most important work, however, was in philosophy, especially in logic and epistemology. Though he never published a single complete and systematic work, his numerous papers and articles collected and edited after his death are often brilliant, and it is Peirce who is credited with originating the philosophic movement known as "Pragmatism."

A man of somewhat irregular habits, Peirce never succeeded in obtaining a university professorship, though he lectured for a time at Johns Hopkins and occasionally at Harvard. For thirty years he held jobs with the U.S. Coast and Geodetic Survey, and in 1891 retired on a small legacy to Milford, Pennsylvania. Toward the end of his life he was extremely poor and had to depend on the charity of friends, among them William James. After his death his papers were sold by his widow to Harvard for a modest sum.

In our selection from his famous essay, Peirce proposes that the meaning of a belief be identified with the sum of its practical effects, and that beliefs without consequences observable through the senses be considered meaningless.

...The very first lesson that we have a right to demand that logic shall teach us is how to make our ideas clear; and a most important one it is, depreciated only by minds who stand in need of it. To know what we think, to be masters of our own meaning, will make a solid foundation for great and weighty thought. It

Reprinted by permission of the publishers from *Collected Papers of Charles Sanders Peirce,* ed. Charles Hartshorne and Paul Weiss. Cambridge, Mass.: The Belknap Press of Harvard University Press, Vol. V. Copyright, 1934, 1935, 1962, by the President and Fellows of Harvard College. (Originally published in 1878.)

is most easily learned by those whose ideas are meagre and restricted; and far happier they than such as wallow helplessly in a rich mud of conceptions. A nation, it is true, may, in the course of generations, overcome the disadvantage of an excessive wealth of language and its natural concomitant, a vast, unfathomable deep of ideas. We may see it in history, slowly perfecting its literary forms, sloughing at length its metaphysics, and, by virtue of the untirable patience which is often a compensation, attaining great excellence in every branch of mental acquirement. The page of history is not yet unrolled which is to tell us whether such a people will or will not in the long run prevail **351** over one whose ideas (like the words of their language) are few, but which possesses a wonderful mastery over those which it has. For an individual, however, there can be no question that a few clear ideas are worth more than many confused ones. A young man would hardly be persuaded to sacrifice the greater part of his thoughts to save the rest; and the muddled head is the least apt to see the necessity of such a sacrifice. Him we can usually only commiserate, as a person with a congenital defect. Time will help him, but intellectual maturity with regard to clearness comes rather late, an unfortunate arrangement of nature, inasmuch as clearness is of less use to a man settled in life, whose errors have in great measure had their effect, than it would be to one whose path lies before him. It is terrible to see how a single unclear idea, a single formula without meaning, lurking in a young man's head, will sometimes act like an obstruction of inert matter in an artery, hindering the nutrition of the brain, and condemning its victim to pine away in the fullness of his intellectual vigor and in the midst of intellectual plenty. Many a man has cherished for years as his hobby some vague shadow of an idea, too meaningless to be positively false; he has, nevertheless, passionately loved it, has made it his companion by day and by night, and has given to it his strength and his life, leaving all other occupations for its sake, and in short has lived with it and for it, until it has become, as it were, flesh of his flesh and bone of his bone; and then he has waked up some bright morning to find it gone, clean vanished away like the beautiful Melusina of the fable, and the essence of his life gone with it. I have myself know such a man; and who can tell how many histories of circle-squarers, metaphysicians, astrologers, and what not, may not be told in the old German story?

II

The principles set forth in the first of these papers [1] lead, at once, to a method of reaching

[1] ["The Fixation of Belief." Ed.]

a clearness of thought of a far higher grade than the "distinctness" of the logicans. We have there found that the action of thought is excited by the irritation of doubt, and ceases when belief is attained; so that the production of belief is the sole function of thought. All these words, however, are too strong for my purpose. It is as if I had described the phenomena as they appear under a mental microscope. Doubt and Belief, as the words are commonly employed, relate to religious or other grave discussions. But here I use them to designate the starting of any question, no matter how small or how great, and the resolution of it. If, for instance, in a horsecar, I pull out my purse and find a five-cent nickel and five coppers, I decide, while my hand is going to the purse, in which way I will pay my fare. To call such a question Doubt, and my decision Belief, is certainly to use words very disproportionate to the occasion. To speak of such a doubt as causing an irritation which needs to be appeased, suggests a temper which is uncomfortable to the verge of insanity. Yet, looking at the matter minutely, it must be admitted that, if there is the least hesitation as to whether I shall pay the five coppers or the nickel (as there will be sure to be, unless I act from some previously contracted habit in the matter), though irritation is too strong a word, yet I am excited to such small mental activity as may be necessary to deciding how I shall act. Most frequently doubts arise from some indecision, however momentary, in our action. Sometimes it is not so. I have, for example, to wait in a railway-station, and to pass the time I read the advertisements on the walls, I compare the advantages of different trains and different routes which I never expect to take, merely fancying myself to be in a state of hesitancy, because I am bored with having nothing to trouble me. Feigned hesitancy, whether feigned for mere amusement or with a lofty purpose, plays a great part in the production of scientific inquiry. However the doubt may originate, it stimulates the mind to an activity which may be slight or energetic, calm or turbulent. Images pass rapidly through consciousness, one incessantly melting into another, until at last, when all is over—it may be in a fraction of a second, in an hour, or after long years—we find ourselves decided as to how we should act under such circumstances as those which occasioned our hesitation. In other words, we have attained belief.

In this process we observe two sorts of elements of consciousness, the distinction between which may best be made clear by means of an illustration. In a piece of music there are the separate notes, and there is the air. A single tone may be prolonged for an hour or a day, and it exists as perfectly in each second of that time as in the whole taken together; so that, as long as it is sounding, it might be present to a sense from which everything in the past was as completely absent as the future itself. But it is different with the air, the performance of which occupies a certain time, during the portions of which only portions of it are played. It consists in an orderliness in the succession of sounds which strike the ear at different times; and to perceive it there must be some continuity of consciousness which makes the events of a lapse of time present to us. We certainly only perceive the air by hearing the separate notes; yet we cannot be said to directly hear it, for we hear only what is present at the instant, and an orderliness of succession cannot exist in an instant. These two sorts of objects, what we are *immediately* conscious of and what we are *mediately* conscious of, are found in all consciousness. Some elements (the sensations) are completely present at every instant so long as they last, while others (like thought) are actions having beginning, middle, and end, and consist in a congruence in the succession of sensations which flow through the mind. They cannot be immediately present to us, but must cover some portion of the past or future. Thought is a thread of melody running through the succession of our sensations.

We may add that just as a piece of music may be written in parts, each part having its own air, so various systems of relationship of succession subsist together between the same sensations. These different systems are distinguished by having different motives, ideas, or

functions. Thought is only one such system; for its sole motive, idea, and function is to produce belief, and whatever does not concern that purpose belongs to some other system of relations. The action of thinking may incidentally have other results. It may serve to amuse us, for example, and among *dilettanti* it is not rare to find those who have so perverted thought to the purposes of pleasure that it seems to vex them to think that the questions upon which they delight to exercise it may ever get finally settled; and a positive discovery which takes a favorite subject out of the arena of literary debate is met with ill-concealed dislike. This disposition is the very debauchery of thought. But the soul and meaning of thought, abstracted from the other elements which accompany it, though it may be voluntarily thwarted, can never be made to direct itself toward anything but the production of belief. Thought in action has for its only possible motive the attainment of thought at rest; and whatever does not refer to belief is no part of the thought itself.

And what, then, is belief? It is the demi-cadence which closes a musical phrase in the symphony of our intellectual life. We have seen that it has just three properties: first, it is something that we are aware of; second, it appeases the irritation of doubt; and, third, it involves the establishment in our nature of a rule of action, or, say for short, a *habit*. As it appeases the irritation of doubt, which is the motive for thinking, thought relaxes, and comes to rest for a moment when belief is reached. But, since belief is a rule for action, the application of which involves further doubt and further thought, at the same time that it is a stopping-place, it is also a new starting-place for thought. That is why I have permitted myself to call it thought at rest, although thought is essentially an action. The *final* upshot of thinking is the exercise of volition, and of this thought no longer forms a part; but belief is only a stadium of mental action, an effect upon our nature due to thought, which will influence future thinking.

The essence of belief is the establishment of a habit, and different beliefs are distinguished by the different modes of action to which they give rise. If beliefs do not differ in this respect, if they appease the same doubt by producing the same rule of action, then no mere differences in the manner of consciousness of them can make them different beliefs, any more than playing a tune in different keys is playing different tunes. Imaginary distinctions are often drawn between beliefs which differ only in their mode of expression—the wrangling which ensues is real enough, however. To believe that any objects are arranged among themselves as in Fig. 1, and to believe that

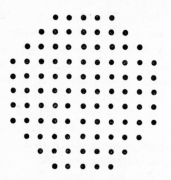

Fig. 1

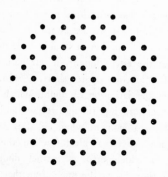

Fig. 2

they are arranged as in Fig. 2, are one and the same belief; yet it is conceivable that a man should assert one proposition and deny the other. Such false distinctions do as much harm as the confusion of beliefs really different, and are among the pitfalls of which we ought constantly to beware, especially when we are upon metaphysical ground. One singular deception of this sort, which often occurs, is to mistake the sensation produced by our own

unclearness of thought for a character of the object we are thinking. Instead of perceiving that the obscurity is purely subjective, we fancy that we contemplate a quality of the object which is essentially mysterious; and if our conception be afterward presented to us in a clear form we do not recognize it as the same, owing to the absence of the feeling of unintelligibility. So long as this deception lasts, it obviously puts an impassable barrier in the way of perspicuous thinking; so that it equally interests the opponents of rational thought to perpetuate it, and its adherents to guard against it.

Another such deception is to mistake a mere difference in the grammatical construction of two words for a distinction between the ideas they express. In this pedantic age, when the general mob of writers attend so much more to words than to things, this error is common enough. When I just said that thought is an *action*, and that it consists in a *relation*, although a person performs an action but not a relation, which can only be the result of an action, yet there was no inconsistency in what I said, but only a grammatical vagueness.

From all these sophisms we shall be perfectly safe so long as we reflect that the whole function of thought is to produce habits of action; and that whatever there is connected with a thought, but irrelevant to its purpose, is an accretion to it, but no part of it. If there be a unity among our sensations which has no reference to how we shall act on a given occasion, as when we listen to a piece of music, why, we do not call that thinking. To develop its meaning, we have, therefore, simply to determine what habits it produces, for what a thing means is simply what habits it involves. Now, the identity of a habit depends on how it might lead us to act, not merely under such circumstances as are likely to arise, but under such as might possibly occur, no matter how improbable they may be. What the habit is depends on *when* and *how* it causes us to act. As for the *when*, every stimulus to action is derived from perception; as for the *how*, every purpose of action is to produce some sensible result. Thus, we come down to what is tangible and practical as the root of every real distinction of thought, no matter how subtile it may be; and there is no distinction of meaning so fine as to consist in anything but a possible difference of practice.

To see what this principle leads to, consider in the light of it such a doctrine as that of transubstantiation. The Protestant churches generally hold that the elements of the sacrament are flesh and blood only in a tropical sense; they nourish our souls as meat and the juice of it would our bodies. But the Catholics maintain that they are literally just that, meat and blood; although they possess all the sensible qualities of wafer-cakes and diluted wine. But we can have no conception of wine except what may enter into a belief, either—

1. That this, that, or the other, is wine; or,

2. That wine possesses certain properties. Such beliefs are nothing but self-notifications that we should, upon occasion, act in regard to such things as we believe to be wine according to the qualities which we believe wine to possess. The occasion of such action would be some sensible perception, the motive of it to produce some sensible result. Thus our action has exclusive reference to what affects the senses, our habit has the same bearing as our action, our belief the same as our habit, our conception the same as our belief; and we can consequently mean nothing by wine but what has certain effects, direct or indirect, upon our senses; and to talk of something as having all the sensible characters of wine, yet being in reality blood, is senseless jargon. Now, it is not my object to pursue the theological question; and having used it as a logical example I drop it, without caring to anticipate the theologian's reply. I only desire to point out how impossible it is that we should have an idea in our minds which relates to anything but conceived sensible effects of things. Our idea of anything *is* our idea of its sensible effects; and if we fancy that we have any other we deceive ourselves, and mistake a mere sensation accompanying the thought for a part of the thought itself. It is absurd to say that thought has any meaning unrelated to its only function. It is foolish for Catholics and Protestants to fancy themselves in disagreement about the elements of the sacrament, if they agree in regard to all their sensible effects, here or hereafter.

It appears, then, that the rule for attaining the third grade of clearness of apprehension is as follows: consider what effects, which might conceivably have practical bearings, we conceive the object of our conception to have. Then, our conception of these effects is the whole of our conception of the object.

III

Let us illustrate this rule by some examples; and, to begin with the simplest one possible, let us ask what we mean by calling a thing *hard*. Evidently that it will not be scratched by many other substances. The whole conception of this quality, as of every other, lies in its conceived effects. There is absolutely no difference between a hard thing and a soft thing so long as they are not brought to the test. Suppose, then, that a diamond could be crystallized in the midst of a cushion of soft cotton, and should remain there until it was finally burned up. Would it be false to say that that diamond was soft? This seems a foolish question, and would be so, in fact, except in the realm of logic. There such questions are often of the greatest utility as serving to bring logical principles into sharper relief than real discussions ever could. In studying logic we must not put them aside with hasty answers, but must consider them with attentive care, in order to make out the principles involved. We may, in the present case, modify our question, and ask what prevents us from saying that all hard bodies remain perfectly soft until they are touched, when their hardness increases with the pressure until they are scratched. Reflection will show that the reply is this: there would be no *falsity* in such modes of speech. They would involve a modification of our present usage of speech with regard to the words "hard" and "soft," but not of their meanings. For they represent no fact to be different from what it is; only they involve arrangements of facts which would be exceedingly maladroit.

This leads us to remark that the question of what would occur under circumstances which do not actually arise is not a question of fact, but only of the most perspicuous arrangement of them. For example, the question of free-will and fate in its simplest form, stripped of verbiage, is something like this: I have done something of which I am ashamed; could I, by an effort of the will, have resisted the temptation, and done otherwise? The philosophical reply is that this is not a question of fact, but only of the [possible] arrangement of facts. Arranging them so as to exhibit what is particularly pertinent to my question—namely, that I ought to blame myself for having done wrong —it is perfectly true to say that, if I had willed to do otherwise than I did, I should have done otherwise. On the other hand, arranging the facts so as to exhibit another important consideration, it is equally true that when a temptation has once been allowed to work, it will, if it has a certain force, produce its effect, let me struggle how I may. There is no objection to a contradiction in what would result from a false supposition. The *reductio ad absurdum* consists in showing that contradictory results would follow from a hypothesis which is consequently judged to be false. Many questions are involved in the free-will discussion, and I am far from desiring to say that both sides are equally right. On the contrary, I am of opinion that one side [determinism] denies important facts, and that the other does not. But what I do say is that the above single question was the origin of the whole doubt; that, had it not been for this question, the controversy would never have arisen; and that this question is perfectly solved in the manner which I have indicated. . . .

IV

Let us now approach the subject of logic, and consider a conception which particularly concerns it, that of *reality*. Taking clearness in the sense of familiarity, no idea could be clearer than this. Every child uses it with perfect confidence, never dreaming that he does not

understand it. As for clearness in its second grade, however, it would probably puzzle most men, even among those of a reflective turn of mind, to give an abstract definition of the real. Yet such a definition may perhaps be reached by considering the points of difference between reality and its opposite, fiction. A figment is a product of somebody's imagination; it has such characters as his thought impresses upon it. That those characters are independent of how you or I think is an external reality. There are, however, phenomena within our own minds, dependent upon our thought, which are at the same time real in the sense that we really think them. But though their characters depend on how we think, they do not depend on what we think those characters to be. Thus, a dream has a real existence as a mental phenomenon, if somebody has really dreamt it; that he dreamt so and so, does not depend on what anybody thinks was dreamt, but is completely independent of all opinion on the subject. On the other hand, considering, not the fact of dreaming, but the thing dreamt, it retains its peculiarities by virtue of no other fact than that it was dreamt to possess them. Thus we may define the real as that whose characters are independent of what anybody may think them to be.

But, however satisfactory such a definition may be found, it would be a great mistake to suppose that it makes the idea of reality perfectly clear. Here, then, let us apply our rules. According to them, reality, like every other quality, consists in the peculiar, sensible effects which things partaking of it produce. The only effect which real things have is to cause belief, for all the sensations which they excite emerge into consciousness in the form of beliefs. The question, therefore, is, how is true belief (or belief in the real) distinguished from false belief (or belief in fiction). Now, as we have seen in the former paper, the ideas of truth and falsehood, in their full development, appertain exclusively to the scientific method of settling opinion. A person who arbitrarily chooses the propositions which he will adopt can use the word truth only to emphasize the expression of his determination to hold on to his choice. Of course, the method of tenacity never prevailed exclusively; reason is too natural to men for that. But in the literature of the Dark Ages we find some fine examples of it. When Scotus Erigena is commenting upon a poetical passage in which hellebore is spoken of as having caused the death of Socrates, he does not hesitate to inform the inquiring reader that Helleborus and Socrates were two eminent Greek philosophers, and that the latter having been overcome in argument by the former took the matter to heart and died of it! What sort of an idea of truth could a man have who could adopt and teach, without the qualification of a "perhaps," an opinion taken so entirely at random? The real spirit of Socrates, who I hope would have been delighted to have been "overcome in argument," because he would have learned something by it, is in curious contrast with the naïve idea of the glossist, for whom (as for the "born missionary" of today) discussion would seem to have been simply a struggle. When philosophy began to awake from its long slumber, and before theology completely dominated it, the practice seems to have been for each professor to seize upon any philosophical position he found unoccupied and which seemed a strong one, to intrench himself in it, and to sally forth from time to time to give battle to the others. Thus, even the scanty records we possess of those disputes enable us to make out a dozen or more opinions held by different teachers at one time concerning the question of nominalism and realism. Read the opening part of the *Historia Calamitatum* of Abélard, who was certainly as philosophical as any of his contemporaries, and see the spirit of combat which it breathes. For him, the truth is simply his particular stronghold. When the method of authority prevailed, the truth meant little more than the Catholic faith. All the efforts of the scholastic doctors are directed toward harmonizing their faith in Aristotle and their faith in the Church, and one may search their ponderous folios through without finding an argument which goes any further. It is noticeable that where different faiths flourish side by side, renegades are looked upon with contempt even by the party whose

belief they adopt; so completely has the idea of loyalty replaced that of truth-seeking. Since the time of Descartes, the defect in the conception of truth has been less apparent. Still, it will sometimes strike a scientific man that the philosophers have been less intent on finding out what the facts are than on inquiring what belief is most in harmony with their system. It is hard to convince a follower of the *a priori* method by adducing facts; but show him that an opinion he is defending is inconsistent with what he has laid down elsewhere, and he will be very apt to retract it. These minds do not seem to believe that disputation is ever to cease; they seem to think that the opinion which is natural for one man is not so for another, and that belief will, consequently, never be settled. In contenting themselves with fixing their own opinions by a method which would lead another man to a different result, they betray their feeble hold of the conception of what truth is.

On the other hand, all the followers of science are fully persuaded that the processes of investigation, if only pushed far enough, will give one certain solution to each question to which they can be applied. One man may investigate the velocity of light by studying the transits of Venus and the aberration of the stars; another by the oppositions of Mars and the eclipses of Jupiter's satellites; a third by the method of Fizeau; a fourth by that of Foucault; a fifth by the motions of the curves of Lissajous; a sixth, a seventh, an eighth, and a ninth, may follow the different methods of comparing the measures of statical and dynamical electricity. They may at first obtain different results, but, as each perfects his method and his processes, the results will move steadily together toward a destined center. So with all scientific research. Different minds may set out with the most antagonistic views, but the progress of investigation carries them by a force outside of themselves to one and the same conclusion. This activity of thought by which we are carried, not where we wish, but to a foreordained goal, is like the operation of destiny. No modification of the point of view taken, no selection of other facts for study, no natural bent of mind even, can enable a man to escape the predestinate opinion. This great law is embodied in the conception of truth and reality. The opinion which is fated [2] to be ultimately agreed to by all who investigate is what we mean by the truth, and the object represented in this opinion is the real. That is the way I would explain reality.

But it may be said that this view is directly opposed to the abstract definition which we have given of reality, inasmuch as it makes the characters of the real depend on what is ultimately thought about them. But the answer to this is that, on the one hand, reality is independent, not necessarily of thought in general, but only of what you or I or any finite number of men may think about it; and that, on the other hand, though the object of the final opinion depends on what that opinion is, yet what that opinion is does not depend on what you or I or any man thinks. Our perversity and that of others may indefinitely postpone the settlement of opinion; it might even conceivably cause an arbitrary proposition to be universally accepted as long as the human race should last. Yet even that would not change the nature of the belief, which alone could be the result of investigation carried sufficiently far; and if, after the extinction of our race, another should arise with faculties and disposition for investigation, that true opinion must be the one which they would ultimately come to. "Truth crushed to earth shall rise again," and the opinion which would finally result from investigation does not depend on how anybody may actually think. But the reality of that which is real does depend on the real fact that investigation is destined to lead, at last, if continued long enough, to a belief in it.

But I may be asked what I have to say to all the minute facts of history, forgotten never to

[2] Fate means merely that which is sure to come true, and can nohow be avoided. It is a superstition to suppose that a certain sort of events are ever fated, and it is another to suppose that the word "fate" can never be freed from its superstitious taint. We are all fated to die.

be recovered, to the lost books of the ancients, to the buried secrets.

Full many a gem of purest ray serene
  The dark, unfathomed caves of ocean bear;
Full many a flower is born to blush unseen,
  And waste its sweetness on the desert air.

Do these things not really exist because they are hopelessly beyond the reach of our knowledge? And then, after the universe is dead (according to the prediction of some scientists), and all life has ceased forever, will not the shock of atoms continue though there will be no mind to know it? To this I reply that, though in no possible state of knowledge can any number be great enough to express the relation between the amount of what rests unknown to the amount of the known, yet it is unphilosophical to suppose that, with regard to any given question (which has any clear meaning), investigation would not bring forth a solution of it, if it were carried far enough. Who would have said, a few years ago, that we could ever know of what substances stars are made whose light may have been longer in reaching us than the human race has existed? Who can be sure of what we shall not know in a few hundred years? Who can guess what would be the result of continuing the pursuit of science for ten thousand years, with the activity of the last hundred? And if it were to go on for a million, or a billion, or any number of years you please, how is it possible to say that there is any question which might not ultimately be solved?

But it may be objected, "Why make so much of these remote considerations, especially when it is your principle that only practical distinctions have a meaning?" Well, I must confess that it makes very little difference whether we say that a stone on the bottom of the ocean, in complete darkness, is brilliant or not—that is to say, that it *probably* makes no difference, remembering always that that stone *may* be fished up tomorrow. But that there are gems at the bottom of the sea, flowers in the untraveled desert, etc., are propositions which, like that about a diamond being hard when it is not pressed, concern much more the arrangement of our language than they do the meaning of our ideas.

It seems to me, however, that we have, by the application of our rule, reached so clear an apprehension of what we mean by reality, and of the fact which the idea rests on, that we should not, perhaps, be making a pretension so presumptuous as it would be singular, if we were to offer a metaphysical theory of existence for universal acceptance among those who employ the scientific method of fixing belief. However, as metaphysics is a subject much more curious than useful, the knowledge of which, like that of a sunken reef, serves chiefly to enable us to keep clear of it, I will not trouble the reader with any more Ontology at this moment. I have already been led much further into that path than I should have desired; and I have given the reader such a dose of mathematics, psychology, and all that is most abstruse, that I fear he may already have left me, and that what I am now writing is for the compositor and proofreader exclusively. I trusted to the importance of the subject. There is no royal road to logic, and really valuable ideas can only be had at the price of close attention. But I know that in the matter of ideas the public prefer the cheap and nasty; and in my next paper I am going to return to the easily intelligible, and not wander from it again. The reader who has been at the pains of wading through this paper shall be rewarded in the next one by seeing how beautifully what has been developed in this tedious way can be applied to the ascertainment of the rules of scientific reasoning.

We have, hitherto, not crossed the threshold of scientific logic. It is certainly important to know how to make our ideas clear, but they may be ever so clear without being true. How to make them so, we have next to study. How to give birth to those vital and procreative ideas which multiply into a thousand forms and diffuse themselves everywhere, advancing civilization and making the dignity of man, is an art not yet reduced to rules, but of the secret of which the history of science affords some hints.

The verifiability criterion;

On emotivism

A. J. Ayer (b. 1910)

Educated at Christchurch College, Oxford, Alfred Jules Ayer was appointed fellow and lecturer in philosophy there immediately after receiving the B.A. in 1932. In 1946 he was named professor of philosophy at the University of London. He resigned this post in 1959 to accept an Oxford professorship. He is one of the best-known logical positivists. His books include Language, Truth & Logic *(1936; 2d ed., 1946),* Foundations of Empirical Knowledge *(1940),* Philosophical Essays *(1954), and* The Problem of Knowledge *(1956). In his first book he presents with great vigor and lucidity a defense of logical empiricism as well as proposals concerning the status of ethical, religious, and aesthetic statements. In the first part of our selection from that book he explains the verifiability criterion of meaningfulness, which, in one form or another, has played an important role in the logical empiricist movement, though it has been subjected to severe criticism by positivists themselves. In the second part of the selection Ayer offers his view that ethical statements are neither true nor false but serve only to express the speaker's feelings or to arouse those of his hearers. The reader should keep in mind that in the introduction to the second edition of* Language, Truth & Logic *Ayer reconsidered and emended some of the formulations given in the original edition.*

The verifiability criterion

... The criterion which we use to test the genuineness of apparent statements of fact is the criterion of verifiability. We say that a sentence is factually significant to any given person, if, and only if, he knows how to verify the proposition which it purports to express—that is, if he knows what observations would lead him, under certain conditions, to accept the proposition as being true, or reject it as being false. If, on the other hand, the putative proposition is of such a character that the assumption of its truth, or falsehood, is consistent with any assumption whatsoever concerning the nature of his future experience, then, as far as he is concerned, it is, if not a tautology, a mere pseudo-proposition. The sentence expressing it may be emotionally significant to him; but it is not literally significant. And with regard to questions the procedure is the same. We enquire in every case what observations would lead us to answer the question, one way or the other; and, if none can be discovered, we must conclude that the

From *Language, Truth & Logic* by Alfred J. Ayer. Published by Dover Publications, Inc., New York 14, N.Y. at $1.25, and reprinted through permission of the publishers, Dover Publications, Inc. and Victor Gollancz, Ltd.

sentence under consideration does not, as far as we are concerned, express a genuine question, however strongly its grammatical appearance may suggest that it does.

As the adoption of this procedure is an essential factor in the argument of this book, it needs to be examined in detail.

In the first place, it is necessary to draw a distinction between practical verifiability, and verifiability in principle. Plainly we all understand, in many cases believe, propositions which we have not in fact taken steps to verify. Many of these are propositions which we could verify it we took enough trouble. But there remain a number of significant propositions, concerning matters of fact, which we could not verify even if we chose; simply because we lack the practical means of placing ourselves in the situation where the relevant observations could be made. A simple and familiar example of such a proposition is the proposition that there are mountains on the farther side of the moon.[1] No rocket has yet been invented which would enable me to go and look at the farther side of the moon, so that I am unable to decide the matter by actual observation. But I do know what observations would decide it for me, if, as is theoretically conceivable, I were once in a position to make them. And therefore I say that the proposition is verifiable in principle, if not in practice, and is accordingly significant. On the other hand, such a metaphysical pseudo-proposition as "the Absolute enters into, but is itself incapable of, evolution and progress,"[2] is not even in principle verifiable. For one cannot conceive of an observation which would enable one to determine whether the Absolute did, or did not, enter into evolution and progress. Of course it is possible that the author of such a remark is using English words in a way in which they are not commonly used by English-speaking people, and that he does, in fact, intend to assert something which could be empirically verified. But until he makes us understand how the

proposition that he wishes to express would be verified, he fails to communicate anything to us. And if he admits, as I think the author of the remark in question would have admitted, that his words were not intended to express either a tautology or a proposition which was capable, at least in principle, of being verified, then it follows that he has made an utterance which has no literal significance even for himself.

A further distinction which we must make is the distinction between the "strong" and the "weak" sense of the term "verifiable." A proposition is said to be verifiable, in the strong sense of the term, if, and only if, its truth could be conclusively established in experience. But it is verifiable, in the weak sense, if it is possible for experience to render it probable. In which sense are we using the term when we say that a putative proposition is genuine only if it is verifiable?

It seems to me that if we adopt conclusive verifiability as our criterion of significance, as some positivists have proposed,[3] our argument will prove too much. Consider, for example, the case of general propositions of law—such propositions, namely, as "arsenic is poisonous"; "all men are mortal"; "a body tends to expand when it is heated." It is of the very nature of these propositions that their truth cannot be established with certainty by any finite series of observations. But if it is recognised that such general propositions of law are designed to cover an infinite number of cases, then it must be admitted that they cannot, even in principle, be verified conclusively. And then, if we adopt conclusive verifiability as our criterion of significance, we are logically obliged to treat these general propositions of law in the same fashion as we treat the statements of the metaphysician.

In face of this difficulty, some positivists[4]

[1] This example has been used by Professor Schlick to illustrate the same point.

[2] A remark taken at random from *Appearance and Reality*, by F. H. Bradley.

[3] e.g., M. Schlick, "Positivismus und Realismus," *Erkenntnis*, vol. I, 1930. F. Waismann, "Logische Analyse des Warscheinlichkeitsbegriffs," *Erkenntnis*, vol. I, 1930.

[4] e.g., M. Schlick, "Die Kausalität in der gegenwärtigen Physik," *Naturwissenschaft*, vol. 19, 1931.

have adopted the heroic course of saying that these general propositions are indeed pieces of nonsense, albeit an essentially important type of nonsense. But here the introduction of the term "important" is simply an attempt to hedge. It serves only to mark the authors' recognition that their view is somewhat too paradoxical, without in any way removing the paradox. Besides, the difficulty is not confined to the case of general propositions of law, though it is there revealed most plainly. It is hardly less obvious in the case of propositions about the remote past. For it must surely be admitted that, however strong the evidence in favour of historical statements may be, their truth can never become more than highly probable. And to maintain that they also constituted an important, or unimportant, type of nonsense would be unplausible, to say the very least. Indeed, it will be our contention that no proposition, other than a tautology, can possibly be anything more than a probable hypothesis. And if this is correct, the principle that a sentence can be factually significant only if it expresses what is conclusively verifiable is self-stultifying as a criterion of significance. For it leads to the conclusion that it is impossible to make a significant statement of fact at all.

Nor can we accept the suggestion that a sentence should be allowed to be factually significant if, and only if, it expresses something which is definitely confutable by experience.[5] Those who adopt this course assume that, although no finite series of observations is ever sufficient to establish the truth of a hypothesis beyond all possibility of doubt, there are crucial cases in which a single observation, or series of observations, can definitely confute it. But, as we shall show later on, this assumption is false. A hypothesis cannot be conclusively confuted any more than it can be conclusively verified. For when we take the occurrence of certain observations as proof that a given hypothesis is false, we presuppose the existence of certain conditions. And though, in any given case, it may be extremely improbable that this as-

sumption is false, it is not logically impossible. We shall see that there need be no self-contradiction in holding that some of the relevant circumstances are other than we have taken them to be, and consequently that the hypothesis has not really broken down. And if it is not the case that any hypothesis can be definitely confuted, we cannot hold that the genuineness of a proposition depends on the possibility of its definite confutation.

Accordingly, we fall back on the weaker sense of verification. We say that the question that must be asked about any putative statement of fact is not, Would any observations make its truth or falsehood logically certain? but simply, Would any observations be relevant to the determination of its truth or falsehood? And it is only if a negative answer is given to this second question that we conclude that the statement under consideration is nonsensical.

To make our position clearer, we may formulate it in another way. Let us call a proposition which records an actual or possible observation an experiential proposition. Then we may say that it is the mark of a genuine factual proposition, not that it should be equivalent to an experiential proposition, or any finite number of experiential propositions, but simply that some experiential propositions can be deduced from it in conjunction with certain other premises without being deducible from those other premises alone.[6]

This criterion seems liberal enough. In contrast to the principle of conclusive verifiability,

[5] This has been proposed by Karl Popper in his *Logik der Forschung.*

[6] This is an oversimplified statement, which is not literally correct. I give what I believe to be the correct formulation in the Introduction... ["There remains the more serious objection that my criterion, as it stands, allows meaning to any indicative statement whatsoever. To meet this, I shall emend it as follows. I propose to say that a statement is directly verifiable if it is either itself an observation-statement, or is such that in conjunction with one or more observation-statements it entails at least one observation-statement which is not deducible from these other premises alone; and I propose to say that a statement is indirectly verifiable if it satisfies the following conditions: first, that in conjunction with certain other premises it entails one or more directly verifiable statements which are not de-

it clearly does not deny significance to general propositions or to propositions about the past. Let us see what kinds of assertion it rules out.

A good example of the kind of utterance that is condemned by our criterion as being not even false but nonsensical would be the assertion that the world of sense-experience was altogether unreal. It must, of course, be admitted that our senses do sometimes deceive us. We may, as the result of having certain sensations, expect certain other sensations to be obtainable which are, in fact, not obtainable. But, in all such cases, it is further sense-experience that informs us of the mistakes that arise out of sense-experience. We say that the senses sometimes deceive us, just because the expectations to which our sense-experiences give rise do not always accord with what we subsequently experience. That is, we rely on our senses to substantiate or confute the judgements which are based on our sensations. And therefore the fact that our perceptual judgements are sometimes found to be erroneous has not the slightest tendency to show that the world of sense-experience is unreal. And, indeed, it is plain that no conceivable observation, or series of observations, could have any tendency to show that the world revealed to us by sense-experience was unreal. Consequently, anyone who condemns the sensible world as a world of mere appearance, as opposed to reality, is saying something which, according to our criterion of significance, is literally nonsensical. . . .

Emotivism in ethics

We begin by admitting that the fundamental ethical concepts are unanalysable, inasmuch as there is no criterion by which one can test the

[ducible from these other premises alone; and secondly, that these other premises do not include any statement that is not either analytic, or directly verifiable, or capable of being independently established as indirectly verifiable. And I can now reformulate the principle of verification as requiring of a literally meaningful statement, which is not analytic, that it should be either directly or indirectly verifiable, in the foregoing sense."]

validity of the judgements in which they occur. So far we are in agreement with the absolutists. But, unlike the absolutists, we are able to give an explanation of this fact about ethical concepts. We say that the reason why they are unanalysable is that they are mere pseudo-concepts. The presence of an ethical symbol in a proposition adds nothing to its factual content. Thus if I say to someone, "You acted wrongly in stealing that money," I am not stating anything more than if I had simply said, "You stole that money." In adding that this action is wrong I am not making any further statement about it. I am simply evincing my moral disapproval of it. It is as if I had said, "You stole that money," in a peculiar tone of horror, or written it with the addition of some special exclamation marks. The tone, or the exclamation marks, adds nothing to the literal meaning of the sentence. It merely serves to show that the expression of it is attended by certain feelings in the speaker.

If now I generalise my previous statement and say, "Stealing money is wrong," I produce a sentence which has no factual meaning—that is, expresses no proposition which can be either true or false. It is as if I had written "Stealing money!!"—where the shape and thickness of the exclamation marks show, by a suitable convention, that a special sort of moral disapproval is the feeling which is being expressed. It is clear that there is nothing said here which can be true or false. Another man may disagree with me about the wrongness of stealing, in the sense that he may not have the same feelings about stealing as I have, and he may quarrel with me on account of my moral sentiments. But he cannot, strictly speaking, contradict me. For in saying that a certain type of action is right or wrong, I am not making any factual statement, not even a statement about my own state of mind. I am merely expressing certain moral sentiments. And the man who is ostensibly contradicting me is merely expressing his moral sentiments. So that there is plainly no sense in asking which of us is in the right. For neither of us is asserting a genuine proposition.

What we have just been saying about the

symbol "wrong" applies to all normative ethical symbols. Sometimes they occur in sentences which record ordinary empirical facts besides expressing ethical feeling about those facts: sometimes they occur in sentences which simply express ethical feeling about a certain type of action, or situation, without making any statement of fact. But in every case in which one would commonly be said to be making an ethical judgement, the function of the relevant ethical word is purely "emotive." It is used to express feeling about certain objects, but not to make any assertion about them.

It is worth mentioning that ethical terms do not serve only to express feeling. They are calculated also to arouse feeling, and so to stimulate action. Indeed some of them are used in such a way as to give the sentences in which they occur the effect of commands. Thus the sentence "It is your duty to tell the truth" may be regarded both as the expression of a certain sort of ethical feeling about truthfulness and as the expression of the command "Tell the truth." The sentence "You ought to tell the truth" also involves the command "Tell the truth," but here the tone of the command is less emphatic. In the sentence "It is good to tell the truth" the command has become little more than a suggestion. And thus the "meaning" of the word "good," in its ethical usage, is differentiated from that of the word "duty" or the word "ought." In fact we may define the meaning of the various ethical words in terms both of the different feelings they are ordinarily taken to express, and also the different responses which they are calculated to provoke.

We can now see why it is impossible to find a criterion for determining the validity of ethical judgments. It is not because they have an "absolute" validity which is mysteriously independent of ordinary sense-experience, but because they have no objective validity whatsoever. If a sentence makes no statement at all, there is obviously no sense in asking whether what it says is true or false. And we have seen that sentences which simply express moral judgements do not say anything. They are pure expressions of feeling and as such do not come

under the category of truth and falsehood. They are unverifiable for the same reason as a cry of pain or a word of command is unverifiable—because they do not express genuine propositions.

Thus, although our theory of ethics might fairly be said to be radically subjectivist, it differs in a very important respect from the orthodox subjectivist theory. For the orthodox subjectivist does not deny, as we do, that the sentences of a moralizer express genuine propositions. All he denies is that they express propositions of a unique non-empirical character. His own view is that they express propositions about the speaker's feelings. If this were so, ethical judgements clearly would be capable of being true or false. They would be true if the speaker had the relevant feelings, and false if he had not. And this is a matter which is, in principle, empirically verifiable. Furthermore they could be significantly contradicted. For if I say, "Tolerance is a virtue," and someone answers, "You don't approve of it," he would, on the ordinary subjectivist theory, be contradicting me. On our theory, he would not be contradicting me, because, in saying that tolerance was a virtue, I should not be making any statement about my own feelings or about anything else. I should simply be evincing my feelings, which is not at all the same thing as saying that I have them.

The distinction between the expression of feeling and the assertion of feeling is complicated by the fact that the assertion that one has a certain feeling often accompanies the expression of that feeling, and is then, indeed, a factor in the expression of that feeling. Thus I may simultaneously express boredom and say that I am bored, and in that case my utterance of the words, "I am bored," is one of the circumstances which make it true to say that I am expressing or evincing boredom. But I can express boredom without actually saying that I am bored. I can express it by my tone and gestures, while making a statement about something wholly unconnected with it, or by an ejaculation, or without uttering any words at all. So that even if the assertion that one has a certain feeling always involves the expression of that feeling, the expression of a feeling assuredly does not always involve the assertion that one has it. And this is the important point to grasp in considering the distinction between our theory and the ordinary subjectivist theory. For whereas the subjectivist holds that ethical statements actually assert the existence of certain feelings, we hold that ethical statements are expressions and excitants of feeling which do not necessarily involve any assertions.

We have already remarked that the main objection to the ordinary subjectivist theory is that the validity of ethical judgements is not determined by the nature of their author's feelings. And this is an objection which our theory escapes. For it does not imply that the existence of any feelings is a necessary and sufficient condition of the validity of an ethical judgement. It implies, on the contrary, that ethical judgements have no validity.

There is, however, a celebrated argument against subjectivist theories which our theory does not escape. It has been pointed out by Moore that if ethical statements were simply statements about the speaker's feelings, it would be impossible to argue about questions of value.[7] To take a typical example: if a man said that thrift was a virtue, and another replied that it was a vice, they would not, on this theory, be disputing with one another. One would be saying that he approved of thrift, and the other that *he* didn't; and there is no reason why both these statements should not be true. Now Moore held it to be obvious that we do dispute about questions of value, and accordingly concluded that the particular form of subjectivism which he was discussing was false.

It is plain that the conclusion that it is impossible to dispute about questions of value follows from our theory also. For as we hold that such sentences as "Thrift is a virtue" and "Thrift is a vice" do not express propositions at all, we clearly cannot hold that they express incompatible propositions. We must therefore admit that if Moore's argument really refutes

[7] cf. "The Nature of Moral Philosophy," *Philosophical Studies.*

the ordinary subjectivist theory, it also refutes ours. But, in fact, we deny that it does refute even the ordinary subjectivist theory. For we hold that one really never does dispute about questions of value.

This may seem, at first sight, to be a very paradoxical assertion. For we certainly do engage in disputes which are ordinarily regarded as disputes about questions of value. But, in all such cases, we find, if we consider the matter closely, that the dispute is not really about a question of value, but about a question of fact. When someone disagrees with us about the moral value of a certain action or type of action, we do admittedly resort to argument in order to win him over to our way of thinking. But we do not attempt to show by our arguments that he has the "wrong" ethical feeling towards a situation whose nature he has correctly apprehended. What we attempt to show is that he is mistaken about the facts of the case. We argue that he has misconceived the agent's motive: or that he has misjudged the effects of the action, or its probable effects in view of the agent's knowledge; or that he has failed to take into account the special circumstances in which the agent was placed. Or else we employ more general arguments about the effects which actions of a certain type tend to produce, or the qualities which are usually manifested in their performance. We do this in the hope that we have only to get our opponent to agree with us about the nature of the empirical facts for him to adopt the same moral attitude towards them as we do. And as the people with whom we argue have generally received the same moral education as ourselves, and live in the same social order, our expectation is usually justified. But if our opponent happens to have undergone a different process of moral "conditioning" from ourselves, so that, even when he acknowledges all the facts, he still disagrees with us about the moral value of the actions under discussion, then we abandon the attempt to convince him by argument. We say that it is impossible to argue with him because he has a distorted or undeveloped moral sense; which signifies merely that he employs a different set of values from our own. We feel that our own system of values is superior, and therefore speak in such derogatory terms of his. But we cannot bring forward any arguments to show that our system is superior. For our judgement that it is so is itself a judgement of value, and accordingly outside the scope of argument. It is because argument fails us when we come to deal with pure questions of value, as distinct from questions of fact, that we finally resort to mere abuse.

In short, we find that argument is possible on moral questions only if some system of values is presupposed. If our opponent concurs with us in expressing moral disapproval of all actions of a given type *t*, then we may get him to condemn a particular action A, by bringing forward arguments to show that A is of type *t*. For the question whether A does or does not belong to that type is a plain question of fact. Given that a man has certain moral principles, we argue that he must, in order to be consistent, react morally to certain things in a certain way. What we do not and cannot argue about is the validity of these moral principles. We merely praise or condemn them in the light of our own feelings.

If anyone doubts the accuracy of this account of moral disputes, let him try to construct even an imaginary argument on a question of value which does not reduce itself to an argument about a question of logic or about an empirical matter of fact. I am confident that he will not succeed in producing a single example. And if that is the case, he must allow that its involving the impossibility of purely ethical arguments is not, as Moore thought, a ground of objection to our theory, but rather a point in favour of it.

Having upheld our theory against the only criticism which appeared to threaten it, we may now use it to define the nature of all ethical enquiries. We find that ethical philosophy consists simply in saying that ethical concepts are pseudo-concepts and therefore unanalysable. The further task of describing the different feelings that the different ethical terms are used to express, and the different reactions that they customarily provoke, is a task for the psychologist. There cannot be such a thing as ethical science, if by ethical science one means the elaboration of a "true" system of morals. For we have seen that, as ethical judgements are mere expressions of feeling, there can be no way of determining the validity of any ethical system, and, indeed, no sense in asking whether any such system is true. All that one may legitimately enquire in this connection is, What are the moral habits of a given person or group of people, and what causes them to have precisely those habits and feelings? And this enquiry falls wholly within the scope of the existing social sciences.

It appears, then, that ethics, as a branch of knowledge, is nothing more than a department of psychology and sociology. And in case anyone thinks that we are overlooking the existence of casuistry, we may remark that casuistry is not a science, but is a purely analytical investigation of the structure of a given moral system. In other words, it is an exercise in formal logic.

Meaning and verifiability

Paul Henle (1908-1962) and Rudolf Carnap (b. 1891)

Born in New York City, Paul Henle studied at Harvard University, where he received a Ph.D. in 1933 with a dissertation in symbolic logic. That same year he published, with F. M. Chapman, Fundamentals of Logic, *one of the first modern elementary textbooks in logic. He taught at Smith College and the University of Michigan, saw service in World War II, and then taught at Northwestern University, where he was chairman of the philosophy department. In 1950 he returned to the University of Michigan, remaining there until his death. Henle became especially interested in problems in the theory of language. He contributed a number of articles to professional journals and edited* Language, Thought and Culture *(1958), a volume based on a cooperative study of language and symbolism undertaken at the University of Michigan.*

A native of Ronsdorf, Germany, Rudolf Carnap became one of the most important figures in the logical empiricist movement. From 1910 to 1914, Carnap studied philosophy, mathematics, and physics at the Universities of Jena and Freiburg. At Jena he attended the lectures of Gottlob Frege (1848–1925) on symbolic logic and the foundations of mathematics. His studies were interrupted by World War I, during which he served as an army officer. After the war he continued his study and research in philosophy, doing work on the foundations of physics. From 1926 to 1931 he taught at the University of Vienna and was a member of the "Vienna Circle." In 1931 he went to teach in Prague, Czechoslovakia, where he remained until 1935. Carnap moved to the United States in 1936 and joined the faculty of the University of Chicago. From 1952 to 1954 he was at the Institute for Advanced Studies at Princeton, New Jersey, and in 1954 accepted a chair at the University of California at Los Angeles, where he remained until his retirement. Among his many writings, some of the most important are Der Logische Aufbau der Welt (The Logical Construction of the World) *(1928),* Testability and Meaning *(1936),* The Logical Syntax of Language *(1937),* Introduction to Semantics *(1942),* Meaning and Necessity *(1947), and* Logical Foundations of Probability *(1950).*

In the following selections Henle and Carnap debate one of the most prominent issues in logical empiricist thought: whether or not to accept a verifiability criterion for cognitive meaningfulness.

From Paul Henle, "Meaning and Verifiability," and Rudolf Carnap, "Paul Henle on Meaning and Verifiability," in *The Philosophy of Rudolf Carnap,* ed. Paul A. Schilpp. Copyright 1963 by *The Library of Living Philosophers, Inc.* Used by permission of The Open Court Publishing Co., La Salle, Ill.

Meaning and Verifiability, by Paul Henle

... The problems regarding a theory of meaning may ... be reduced to two: First, what are the empirical facts regarding actual use of expressions on which it rests; and, second, what are the ideals such as simplicity, clarity, and the like, which it embodies. Whether these considerations be taken as themselves constitutive of a theory or whether they are the motives of a stipulation need not be a matter of primary concern. ...

II

To consider the empirical evidence relevant to a theory of meaning is to consider what people understand. If language is used and comprehended, then it must be meaningful, and any theory of meaning which claims empirical sanction may begin with a reference to what is understood. There would be no advantage to bringing in the notion of understanding if there were not empirical evidence of a definitely describable sort for a statement's being understood. There is, for example, a peculiar sort of feeling of comprehension and of being in control of the situation which most often accompanies understanding. This is in marked contrast to the feeling of blankness and being at a loss which is the usual concomitant of not understanding. The contrast is perhaps most marked when one comes upon an unintelligible sentence in a paragraph which otherwise is clear. For a while everything has been going along smoothly, one has been in complete control, suddenly he is faced with an obstacle. One re-reads the sentence to be sure he has not mis-read it, but, finding no error here, he stops to conjecture what possibly might be meant, then, perhaps, gives up this sentence as a bad job and goes on to others. There is quite the opposite feeling when the meaning of a passage which hitherto has been obscure suddenly dawns on one. The irresolution and confusion are replaced by mastery and one goes ahead serenely untroubled. It would be foolish, of course, to claim that this sense of understanding is infallible, for, certainly, there have been cases where a person thought he understood something which subsequent experience showed he had failed to. There have even been cases where persons have understood what they thought they had failed to, as when they expected something profound and heard something trivial. Granted all these exceptions, however, it would still be the case that this feeling of understanding is evidence and strong evidence that actually something has been understood.

Subjective feelings are not, of course, the only sort of evidence available. Any experienced lecturer can tell by watching his audience whether it is understanding him. The members of an audience which is perplexed twist and shuffle, they look at one another, they frown. In part, this conduct is similar to that of a bored audience, but the frowning and turning to neighbors are sufficiently distinctive to leave no doubt in the mind of the lecturer. Examinations, to take another case from the class-room, are often tests of comprehension. Once again, no one would claim them to be infallible, but on the whole they would generally be conceded to be a pretty fair index of understanding. Along the same lines also, even casual conversation may reveal understanding or lack of it. Ability to obey commands constitutes a similar criterion.

We may speak of all these occurrences, interpersonal as well as subjective, as the *phenomena of understanding*. The paragraphs above are by no means intended to be exhaustive of these phenomena but merely to suggest their range. The reason for calling attention to them, however, is to formulate more precisely the requirements for empirical justification of any meaning theory. We may say that a theory of meaning is empirically justified to the extent that the class of statements which it designates as meaningful coincides with the class of statements in conjunction with which all or most of the phenomena of meaning occur.

So far this discussion has been completely general, intended to indicate the considerations by which any theory of meaning is to be judged. Without narrowing the discussion more than is necessary, I should now like to restrict it to verifiability theories of meaning and for this purpose it is sufficient to characterize verifiability theories as those which make the meaningfulness of synthetic statements dependent on their being capable of some sort of empirical verification. This characterization is not precise but to make it more precise would be to restrict it to one type of verifiability theory rather than another. For the present, it is accurate enough; restrictions as to types of verifiability theories will be introduced later. Given verifiability theories characterized in this broad way, this section will consider the empirical evidence for and against them. The normative considerations which may favor or oppose such theories are reserved for another section.

One of the aspects of unformalized language to which the positivists have called violent attention is the occurrence of utterances called metaphysical. These utterances, allegedly characteristic of treatises on metaphysics, are claimed to be totally without possibility of verification. These claims must be investigated because, if they can be substantiated, they lead to the further question of whether the phenomena of meaning occur in connection with such statements. If so, any empirical basis would be destroyed for a verifiability theory of languages as a whole. There would still be the possibility, of course, that there were normative reasons for holding a verifiability theory or that a verifiability theory applied to some more restricted linguistic domain, such as a language for some science. Still the matter is of sufficient importance to be considered.

In what follows I shall argue that, on the whole, the positivist accusation against traditional metaphysics has been mistaken and that metaphysical hypotheses do have empirical content. This is not universally the case, however, and there are some metaphysical statements which seem to lack such content. Where this is the case, however, the statements none the less exhibit many phenomena of understanding and therefore on an empirical basis should be accounted meaningful.

On the first point, the empirical content of many metaphysical hypotheses, one of the more striking phenomena in the history of philosophy, is the way in which metaphysical theories are refuted by later scientific discovery. Critics of philosophy have, in fact, made much of the point. Thus, with whatever assurance we believe in contemporary physics, with that assurance, we must disbelieve in Lucretius's cosmology. According to modern physics, the atoms out of which Lucretius builds his universe simply do not exist. Again, with whatever assurance we believe in the conservation of momentum, we must disbelieve in the Cartesian theory of interaction of mind and body. Again, on one interpretation of Aristotle at least, everything would increase in perfection until it became identical with God, if it were not for absolute limitations imposed by the fixity of species. On this interpretation, one must either construe the term "species" in some non-biological sense or else admit that Aristotle is flatly wrong. Again, there are certainly metaphysical implications to Kant's work, even though he did not consider himself a metaphysician, and notice how much harder it is to accept Kant's position since the physical employment of non-Euclidean geometries. All these are cases in which philosophers have maintained doctrines as important aspects of their metaphysical views which subsequent empirical investigations have shown to be false. And if empirical investigations can disprove them, they must have some empirical content.

We may trace the same sort of connections even where a philosophy accords with empirical investigations. Notice the reliance on the theory of evolution in such metaphysicians as Bergson and Alexander. If evolution were conclusively disproved, these philosophies would be as good as refuted. Again, there is no doubt as to what would be the fate of Whitehead's doctrine of the self-determination of each actual occasion if empirical investigations would give overwhelming support to a doctrine of universal determinism, extending even to the minutest particle. There is no doubt either as to what would be the fate of Santayana's materialism if strong arguments could be adduced for the existence of mental telepathy without any physical basis.

Here again are cases in which characteristic metaphysical doctrines have their probabilities affected by empirical investigations. These are not peripheral opinions, accidental accretions to the philosopher's central thought, but the characteristic and distinctive doctrines of the systems in question. I shall not here claim that all metaphysical statements are empirical in this sense, but it is clear that at least some are and important ones.

Granted that much of metaphysics has at least some verifiable content, it would still, I believe, have to be admitted that there are exceptions and some cases of unverifiable statements could be found. Consider, for example, such a statement as "God exists" in a system in which a deity is thought of as a supremely perfect being and in which the ontological argument is rejected, so that the statement is synthetic. Suppose furthermore the statement is asserted without reference to response to prayer or to mystical communion and even without reference to any design in nature. It would seem in this case that we had here a metaphysician's assertion, held to be meaningful, for which, even ideally, no empirical verification could be given. I have not, I realize, thus far in this discussion taken up the question of how far the notion of verifiability can be stretched, how far "verifiability in principle" may extend, but if the requirement is intended to exclude anything, the statement in question must be excluded.

There is a further question, however, as to whether the phenomena of understanding occur in connection with the statement. Here I think the answer must be in the affirmative. With many people at least, there will be no feeling of bafflement on encountering the statement, an audience will not look blank when it hears it, and a group of students may even write a clear examination involving it. It may be that the people who evince these phenomena of understanding are not keeping in mind all the restrictions mentioned above which are necessary to make the statement synthetic and without empirically verifiable content. In many cases this might be admitted, but there is no evidence to show that it need be admitted in all cases and, particularly in the case of trained theologians, there is every reason to believe that the conditions would be kept in mind.

In this case then, and in others of a similar sort, the phenomena of understanding are the opposite of what one should expect if there is to be empirical confirmation of verifiability theories. The evidence all goes to show that metaphysical statements are understood, and if, according to the verifiability theories, they are said to be incapable of being understood, this is a defect of the theories. Depending on which formulation of the theories one uses, one must say either that they fail the empirical test as theories or else that they lack the motive of conformity to actual practice which might lead to adopting them as stipulations.

The point may be made in another way. Roughly, the positivistic argument against metaphysics might be expressed in the syllogism:

Unverifiable utterances are meaningless
Metaphysical utterances are unverifiable
∴ Metaphysical utterances are meaningless.

The minor premise is objectionable as not being universally true, but as being true only for a subclass of metaphysical utterances. Instead of drawing the stated conclusion for these cases, however, I have argued that it is false on empirical grounds. The denial of the conclusion taken together with the modified minor allows an inference of the falsity of the major, that is, of verifiability theories. Or the argument of this section is capable of still another alternative formulation. According to verifiability theories, theological discussions cannot be understood. Without pretending to understand all such discussions, I am more sure that I have understood some of them than I am that the verifiability theories are correct.

III

Even though, according to the argument of the last section, verifiability theories of meaning receive no empirical confirmation from the phenomena of understanding when taken as theories of language as a whole, it may be that they receive such confirmation from some part of language. In particular, it may be that verifiability theories account for meaning as it occurs in the sciences. Indeed, the theory is most often put forth as an account of scientific meaning and everyone would admit that there is a verifiability requirement for scientific theories. As has often been remarked, science is an interpersonal enterprise, not concerned with truths supported by insight alone, but requiring publicly available support for each assertion made. Given this requirement, there must be evidence for any scientific hypotheses and this evidence is the verifiable aspect of the theory.

The matter may be put in another way—a theory equally compatible with every conceivable state of affairs in the world would not be counted as a scientific theory at all. It might be a mathematical theorem or perhaps a metaphysical hypothesis, but it would not be science. Every scientific theory, then, is at least materially equivalent to the denial of some possible state of affairs. In principle at least, one must be able to investigate whether this state of affairs obtains, and a verifiability requirement is therefore implicit in any scientific theory.

Thus it may be admitted that scientific theories have a requirement of verifiability and it is doubtful if anyone would seriously deny the point. This is not the same, however, as saying that scientific laws are subject to a verifiability requirement of meaning. It must be admitted that a statement which is not verifiable is not worth discussing for scientific purposes, but this is not equivalent to saying that it is unintelligible. The scientific verifiability requirement is in fact a good deal more stringent than any positivist theory of meaning has imposed, for statements which are verifiable in principle only, while admitted to be intelligible, are relegated to a limbo of conjecture, not perhaps totally condemned, but certainly considered unworthy of the serious attention of a scientist in the practice of his profession. This is, however, a judgment as to what is a part of science and even perhaps as to what is worth discussing, not a judgment as to what is intelligible. Thus, while granting that there is a verifiability requirement of scientific laws and indeed a stringent one, this gives no reason to claim that this is a requirement for meaning.

An apparent exception to what I have been claiming is found in the doctrine of operationalism, the view that scientific concepts are to be defined in terms of physical operations, that mass is to be defined in terms of the operation of weighing, length in terms of the manipulation of measuring sticks, and the like. Once again no one would deny that these operational characteristics are desirable in a scientific concept, but the desirability, as before, may be explained in different ways. It may be that, apart from operational standards, concepts are not intelligible, or it may be that concepts, though intelligible if not meeting these standards, are lacking in a desirable sort of precision. From this latter point of view, though operational concepts possess certain advantages, other forms of concepts may also be intelligible. So construed, operationalism is not a theory of meaning but a demand for a certain sort of scientific practice. Even the author of the term "operationalism" claims no more for it at present. He says:

> It is often supposed that the operational criterion of meaning demands that the operations which give meaning to a physical concept *must* be instrumental operations. This is, I believe, palpably a mistaken point of view for simple observation shows that physicists do profitably employ concepts the meaning of which is not to be found in the instrumental operations of the laboratory, and which cannot be reduced to such operations without residue. Nearly all the concepts of theoretical or mathematical physics are of this character.[1]

The correctness of this point of view is further substantiated by some developments in the social sciences. Psychoanalytic theory though rich and clinically productive, lacks the sort of precision and verifiability which is characteristic of the more advanced sciences. Recently there have been attempts to determine some sort of operational meanings for the Freudian concepts, to translate them, or at least to turn part of their meaning into more rigorously formulated and experimentally applicable concepts. This may be regarded as an attempt to operationalize Freudian psychology. Similarly,

[1] P. W. Bridgman, *The Nature of Some of Our Physical Concepts,* New York, 1952, p. 8.

I have heard discussions as to how Veblen's notion of conspicuous consumption could be reduced to operational concepts or how tests might be devised which would similarly transform some of Benjamin Lee Whorf's notions of the influence of language upon thought. This is not the place to comment on the utility of such attempts or their probable success, but one aspect of them is pertinent to the present discussion: If they represent the attempt to displace non-operational concepts by operational ones, the non-operational concepts must be meaningful. Without this assumption there could be no comprehension of what one was doing or of whether one had done it correctly. Thus the attempt to extend operationalism serves only to confirm the position that operationalism, like verifiability requirements in science generally, serves as an ideal of scientific discourse which is independent of meaningfulness.

Much of what has been claimed in the preceding discussion might be summarized by claiming that the verifiability theory has confused a requirement that scientific questions be decidable with a claim that unverifiable statements are meaningless. This confusion has been aided by an ambiguity characteristic of such terms as "meaningful," "meaningless," "nonsense" and the like. In one sense, an event is meaningful if it signifies something important —if it portends something. There is a matching sense of "significant" to go with it where "significant" implies having an important meaning. A significant book in this sense is not merely one which is composed of comprehensible standard sentences, but it is one which is especially worth reading. In these senses "meaningful" and "significant" can be equated, roughly at least, and can be opposed to what is meaningless or insignificant. These latter terms comprehend not merely what is not a sign at all and so literally has no meaning or significance, but also what signifies something unimportant and which therefore may be neglected safely. Because of the emphasis on what is important the senses which have been discussed may be referred to as *evaluative* senses of "meaningful," "significant" and kindred

terms. It must, of course, be remembered that this evaluative use is relative and that what is meaningful from one point of view or assuming a given set of goals may be meaningless if the context is shifted.

In opposition to the evaluative sense of these terms is their *semantic* sense, their functioning to indicate what is intelligible and what not. There is no assertion of importance here, merely the claim that something can be understood. In this sense a statement is meaningful or significant—once more the terms are roughly synonymous—if it is comprehended, if it conveys intelligence to someone. There is no requirement that what is conveyed be vital or that any evaluation be made, but merely that something be understood. Similarly, in this sense, the meaningless is the unintelligible, what can't be grasped. In this sense, it is perhaps better to use "non-significant" rather than "insignificant" as an antonym of "significant." In the semantic use as well as the evaluative there is a relativism, but a relativism to a person rather than to a goal. Something is intelligible not in itself but to some one under some determinate conditions.

The term "nonsense" likewise has its evaluative and semantic senses. In the former sense one accuses people of talking nonsense if they hold views with which one is in violent disagreement. Yet they cannot be talking nonsense in the semantic sense, otherwise there would be no view expressed with which to disagree.

In terms of this distinction, it is possible to summarize the objection to finding in science a basis for a verifiability theory of meaning. At most scientific practice shows that unverifiable statements are meaningless in the evaluative sense of "meaningless." If theory of meaning is to be something distinct from theory of value, it is necessary to establish meaninglessness in the semantic sense; and this has not been done. The existence of the two senses of the same words has made this confusion easier. . . .

IV

So far, the verifiability theory has been treated as a descriptive hypothesis without consideration of the norms which it might embody. This remains to be done. Fortunately, the normative and descriptive elements are related and this discussion can be brief.

One might hold a verifiability theory, not on grounds that meanings as actually used all conformed to it, but for the reason that the meanings which did conform were in some manner preferable to others. Such a feeling might lead to a suggestion for the reform of language in the direction of a verifiability theory or even to a stipulative definition of meaning. This sort of motive has, I think, been strong among the holders of the theory and it may be well to survey these advantages.

If one adheres to a verifiability criterion of meaning, all questions which he raises will be answerable in principle and discussions will be avoided which are incapable of solution. This certainly is an advantage and it is desirable to start a discussion with the assurance that it is not impossible to reach a conclusion. Again, concepts seem clearer to the extent to which they can be expressed in terms of observable characteristics. If this is coupled with some such device as a linguistic system admitting of a clear-cut set of stated descriptions, such as Carnap employs, the resulting feeling of clarity is even greater.

If I have stated these advantages briefly it is not because I under-estimate them or fail to feel their force. While admitting every advantage of concepts which conform to the verifiability requirement, the upshot of our previous discussion is that they are simply not sufficient to deal with the range of meanings actually employed. If one is to have any respect for the phenomena of meaning, other forms of meaning must be admitted. To call these other forms meaningless is to belie the facts of understanding.

Any sort of investigation must have as its goals both rigor and breadth, but one of these goals may momentarily be placed ahead of the other. Different groups may differ in their stress, as is illustrated in the field of psychology where academic psychology stresses rigor and psychoanalysis emphasizes scope, though in the end each hopes for a comprehensive theory both

exact and broad. If the verifiability theories similarly were conceived as one approach to philosophy stressing rigor at the expense of broadness, but hoping ultimately to achieve greater scope, there could be no objection to them. They would be compatible with other attempts which place primary emphasis on breadth. In Kantian language this would be a regulative use of the theories and they would amount merely to an injunction to be as rigorous as possible. Instead, however, they have most often been used constitutively as definitive of meaning rather than a plea to use rigorous concepts wherever possible. This use does not seem justified.

Paul Henle on Meaning and Verifiability, a reply by Rudolf Carnap

As a basis for my discussion, I shall formulate *two theses of empiricism,* and then make comments to elucidate them and to reply to Henle's arguments.

T1. Principle of confirmability. If it is in principle impossible for any conceivable observational result to be either confirming or disconfirming evidence for a linguistic expression A, then expression A is devoid of cognitive meaning.

Note that what is denied here is only cognitive (theoretical, referential, descriptive) meaning. The thesis implies that the expression A is neither true nor false, in other words, that A does not express a proposition. A may still have meaning components of other kinds, e.g., pictorial, emotive, or motivative meaning.

Definition. We say that an expression A is a *pseudo-statement* if A is devoid of cognitive meaning, but has the grammatical form of a declarative sentence and may therefore lead to psychological effects which are similar to those of a genuine statement.

Among the psychological effects of a pseudo-statement may be associations that resemble the genuine understanding of a propositional statement. This possibility explains why not only the listener but even the speaker sometimes

374 LANGUAGE, THOUGHT, AND MEANING

mistakes a pseudo-statement for a genuine one. It follows from these explanations that the occurrence of the psychological phenomenon of subjective "understanding" of an expression A cannot be taken as a proof that A is a cognitive statement.

Henle regards a theory of significance (meaningfulness) as empirically justified to the extent that the class of statements which it takes as significant coincides with the class of those statements which lead to the psychological phenomenon of understanding. This criterion may often be useful in simple cases; but it can only be accepted as a crude approximation. The subjective impression of the existence of a material object may be taken as evidence for the actual existence of that object; but it is clear that this evidence is not conclusive, as is shown by sensory illusions. Analogously, the subjective phenomenon of understanding may be taken as evidence for significance, as Henle says; but this evidence cannot be regarded as necessarily conclusive.

T2. Some of the main theses in certain systems of traditional metaphysics are incapable of confirmation or disconfirmation by any conceivable observational data, and are therefore pseudo-statements.

Note that the characterization as pseudo-statements does not refer to all systems or theses in the field of metaphysics. At the time of the Vienna Circle, the characterization was applied mainly to those metaphysical systems which had exerted the greatest influence upon continental philosophy during the last century, viz., the post-Kantian systems of German idealism and, among contemporary ones, those of Bergson and Heidegger. On the basis of later, more cautious analyses, the judgment was not applied to the main theses of those philosophers whose thinking had been in close contact with the science of their times, as in the cases of Aristotle and of Kant; the latter's epistemological theses about the synthetic a priori character of certain judgments were regarded by us as false, not as meaningless. Nor was it applied to those philosophers who tried to explain the

world by audacious generalizations on the basis of experience, though perhaps on insufficient observational evidence. They might be regarded as the precursors of science taking the first tentative steps towards a scientific explanation of the world. Furthermore, the judgment is not meant to apply to those systems which are sometimes called "metaphysical," but which start explicitly from empirical knowledge and inductively infer from it a system of cosmology. Henle gives examples of metaphysical statements which were refuted, or in some cases confirmed, by the later development of science. Theses of this kind, at least in the interpretation given to them by Henle, which may be historically correct, are confirmable and therefore are not regarded by us as pseudo-statements.

Henle discusses certain statements of theology which, in his view, are not confirmable but are nevertheless understood. As an example, he gives the statement "God exists." (Incidentally, I think it would be clearer to use a formulation like "there is at least one god" or "there is exactly one god," containing the predicate "god" instead of the alleged proper name "God.") In this context, it is important to distinguish between the mythical (or magical) and the metaphysical uses of the word "God" or "god." Neurath [2] emphasized the difference between the magic of primeval periods and later metaphysics. Magic was this-worldly and empirical; metaphysics, on the other hand, was transcendent and non-empirical. Neurath regarded theology as a transition phenomenon; in its primitive form it was magical, but later it became more and more metaphysical, although it preserved some of its original formulations. I made the same distinction in [*The Elimination of Metaphysics through Logical Analysis of Language*, sec. 3 (1932)].[3] I pointed out that the word "God," in its mythical use, has a clear, empirical mean-

[2] Otto Neurath, "From Magic to Unified Science," *Empirische Soziologie*, Wien, 1931, chap. 1.

[3] [English translation by Arthur Pap in *Logical Positivism*, ed. A. J. Ayer, The Free Press of Glencoe, New York, 1959. Ed.]

ing. In its metaphysical use, on the other hand, its old empirical meaning vanishes; since no new meaning is supplied, the term "God" becomes meaningless. I added that in theology the use of the word "God" is sometimes mythical and thus empirical, sometimes metaphysical, and sometimes ambiguous. In order to classify a theological statement, we have to take its interpretation or its context into consideration. The psychological phenomenon of the subjective understanding of theological statements, even in the later metaphysical phase, can easily be explained by those associations connected with the word "God" which are remnants of the earlier mythical phase.

The hypotheses of telepathy and other forms of extra-sensory perception, of psychokinesis, and the like, are certainly empirical hypotheses, not fundamentally different from other hypotheses in science. If the evidence for a hypothesis of this kind should finally be so strong that the hypothesis would be regarded as scientifically acceptable, this result might possibly, though not necessarily, lead to a fundamental change in the system of science. It seems to me, however, that some analytic philosophers ascribe to hypotheses of this kind a greater importance for analytic-philosophical problems than is warranted; they would expect them, for example, to decide the issue between physicalism and dualistic emergentism. Henle seems to think that the acceptance of "mental telepathy with-

out any physical basis" would constitute a refutation of Santayana's materialism. (Incidentally, it is not quite clear to me what is meant by "without any physical basis." In all telepathic experiments made so far, two human organisms have been involved in the situation.) In a similar sense, Rhine has asserted that the hypothesis of extra-sensory perception, which he accepts, constitutes a proof for idealism. In contrast to these views, I do not think that the thesis of materialism or idealism could be confirmed or disconfirmed by any observational evidence. . . . I think that, in general, a representative of a metaphysical thesis of this kind is not willing to specify possible observational results which he would regard as confirming or disconfirming evidence for his thesis if they were to occur. But if he should be willing to do so, his specifications would make his thesis cognitive. Henle seems to think that if our criterion of significance is taken in the liberalized form as "confirmability in principle," then there are hardly any metaphysical theses left which would be excluded. I think, however, that our principle excludes not only a great number of assertions in systems like those of Hegel and Heidegger, especially since the latter says explicitly that logic is not applicable to statements in metaphysics, but also in contemporary discussions, e.g., those concerning the reality of space or of time.

Ordinary language and

philosophy

Gilbert Ryle (b. 1900)

Gilbert Ryle is Waynflete Professor of Metaphysical Philosophy in Magdalen College, Oxford, and editor of the influential British journal, Mind. *One of the leading members of the British school of analytic philosophy, Ryle published an article in 1932 entitled "Systematically Misleading Expressions," which helped to generate a great deal of activity in the philosophic study of linguistic problems. Influenced by the work of Ludwig Wittgenstein, Ryle has pursued his own directions in three books,* Philosophical Arguments *(1945),* The Concept of Mind *(1949), where he shows how philosophic misconceptions arise out of a misuse of language, and* Dilemmas *(1954).*

Our selection is a more recent article published in the Canadian journal, Dialogue. *Here, with characteristic grace and wit, Ryle distinguishes between what he calls the "morning" and "afternoon" concern with language. In the former we use language to get through our everyday tasks, and in the latter we are interested in understanding certain abstract concepts symbolized by words which we use effectively enough in the "morning."*

St. Augustine said "When you do not ask me what Time is, I know perfectly well; but when you do ask me, I cannot think what to say." What, then, was it that he knew perfectly well, and what was it that he did not know? Obviously he knew perfectly well such things as these, that what happened yesterday is more recent than what happened a month ago; that a traveller who walks four miles in an hour, goes twice as fast as a traveller who takes two hours over the same journey. He knew how to say things and how to understand things said to him which specified dates, durations

From Gilbert Ryle, "Abstractions," in *Dialogue,* Vol. 1, No. 1 (June, 1962), pp. 5–16. Copyright 1962 by *Dialogue.* Used by permission of the author and editor.

and times of day; epochs, seasons and moments. He knew when it was midday and he could use the calendar. He could cope efficiently and easily with concrete chronological and chronometrical tasks. He could use and understand tensed verbs. What he could not do is to give any reply at all to such abstract questions as these: what is it that there is twice as much of in a fortnight as in a week? Why could Time, unlike a battle, never have started, and why can Time, unlike a concert, never come to a stop? Does Time flow on at an uniform or an irregular speed, and in either case, is its speed measured in a second sort of Time? In short, what is Time—is it a Thing or a Process or a Relation? Is it a sort of cosmic river, only one without any tangible water between its nonexisting banks? One which flows out of no spring and pours out into no ocean?

We might say that Augustine, like anyone else, could answer concrete factual questions about times; but that, like everyone else, he could not answer abstract questions about the concept of Time. But what is this difference between concrete or factual questions and abstract or conceptual questions?

Take another example. Hume, like any other sensible person, knew perfectly well how to distinguish between one occasion when he met a friend by appointment and another occasion when he met a friend by chance; or between one game of cards when the dealer dealt himself all the aces by trickery, and another when the dealer dealt himself all the aces by sheer luck. None the less, when Hume, as a philosopher, asks himself What is Chance? he actually gives an answer which we can swiftly prove to be wrong. He says that since whatever comes about is due to some cause, and since chance is not a cause, therefore, to say that something, like a meeting between friends, has come about by chance can only mean that it has come about from some cause of which we are ignorant. But this answer must be wrong, for though we are ignorant of the cause of cancer, we should never say that cancer comes about by chance. The phrase "by chance" cannot therefore be equivalent to the phrase "from an unknown cause." Hume tried but failed to answer his abstract question about the concept of chance, though in everyday life he knew perfectly well how to distinguish fortuitous coincidence from nonfortuitous conjunctions of affairs. We are tempted to say that he did not know the meaning of the abstract noun "Chance," despite the fact that he knew perfectly well the meaning of the adverbial phrase "by chance." Yet how could he possibly know the one without knowing the other?

To change the example once more, you yourselves would find it difficult to tell me what Knowledge is and how it differs from True Belief, yet your difficulty, whatever it is, does not continue to embarrass you when asked such concrete questions as these:—Do you still know the date of the Battle of Waterloo? At what age did you learn or come to know Pythagoras' Theorem? Why are memorised gibberish syllables easier to forget, i.e. cease to know, than significant sentences, and sentences in prose easier to forget than sentences in verse?

Notice that in this case, while my abstract epistemological question employed the abstract noun "knowledge," in my concrete questions this abstract noun did not occur, but only the active verbs "know," "learn" and "forget." So we are tempted to say that we do not know the meaning of the abstract noun, though we are perfectly at home with the meanings of the active verbs. Yet this cannot be right, for if a person understands perfectly well the active verbs "know," "learn" and "forget" he knows all that he needs in order to understand the abstract noun "knowledge." If a child has learned what it is for someone to conquer or protect someone else, he needs no further lessons in order to understand the abstract nouns "conquest" and "protection."

Similarly with adjectives. A person who is quite familiar with the idea of things being probable or improbable is fully equipped to understand the abstract noun "probability"— yet is not thereby equipped to answer the abstract, conceptual question "What is probability?" or "Is probability a property of happenings, though only some future ones, or is it a property of some of our thoughts about happenings?" Questions like those that perplexed Augustine and defeated Hume, namely the abstract questions about Time and Chance, can be classified as conceptual questions. They are questions *about* Concepts. But a question such as "How long did the battle last?" or "Did the friends meet by chance or by design?" is a question *about* a battle or a meeting. Here the ideas of temporal duration and of fortuitousness are being operated *with*; but they are not here being operated *upon*. Somewhat similarly, the sculptor operates with a chisel, but it is the stone that he is operating upon. It would be the business of the mechanic, not the sculptor, to operate upon the chisel itself.

With some exaggeration we might try saying that a conceptual question or conceptual statement typically has for its grammatical subject an abstract noun, like "Time" or "Chance" or "Probability," where a factual question about a battle, or a meeting, or the weather would incorporate the corresponding concrete ideas only by means of its verbs or adjectives or adverbs. The weather-forecast that tells us that in a certain region there will probably be snowstorms tomorrow, has for its subject the weather in a certain place, and not the concept of probability. This idea comes in only adverbially, as a qualification of the expectations about the weather. But to say this would be too violent. For the weather-forecast might just as well be worded in this way: "There is the probability" or "There is a high probability of snowstorms in such and such a region." This forecast employs the abstract noun "probability," though its author would certainly tell us, if asked, that he was not talking about the concept of probability, but only talking about the weather. The presence of the abstract noun "probability" or "time" does not prove that the sentence incorporating it expressed a proposition about the concept of Probability or the concept of Time. It can do so, but it need not. Correspondingly, a philosopher or logician might be discussing the concept of Knowledge, Time, Chance or Probability, although he abstained from employing those abstract nouns or any others.

How is an abstract assertion, however it is worded, about the concept of Time, or Probability or Knowledge related to the concrete assertions in which, perhaps, a battle is said to have lasted for three days, snowstorms are asserted to be probable, or the schoolboy is said no longer to know Pythagoras' Theorem? (1) Clearly the abstract assertion about the concept is, in an important way, more sophisticated than the concrete assertions. A child who had not yet progressed far enough to understand that snow would probably be falling tomorrow, would *a fortiori* not yet be equipped to understand assertions about the concepts of Probability and Time. (2) But more than this. Abstract assertions about the concepts of Probability and Knowledge are parasitic upon concrete assertions expressed, perhaps, with the adverb "probably" and the verb "know," "learn" or "forget"—parasitic in this way, that the maker of an assertion about Probability or Time or Knowledge is saying in perfectly general terms something *about* what is said when, for example, it is said that snow will probably be falling tomorrow, or that the schoolboy has forgotten what he had once learned, namely, Pythagoras' Theorem. What functioned as predicate or a part of the predicate of the concrete assertion is itself the subject matter that is being talked about in the abstract assertion. Statements about Probability are, in an important way, statements *about* what it is that is stated when we state that something will probably happen or what it is that is asked when someone asks whether it is more likely to snow than to rain. To put it over-grammatically, the abstract noun "probability" is parasitic upon, *inter alia*, the adverb "probably," and the abstract noun "Time" is parasitic upon, *inter alia*, the tenses of ordinary tensed verbs. The chisel with which, this morning, the sculptor was carving the stone, is, this afternoon, the object upon which the mechanic is working. But he is always working upon the chisel *as* the tool with which stone-carving has been done and is to be done again, though stone-carving is not being done with it this afternoon.

Maybe we can now begin to see part of what it was that perplexed Augustine. It puzzled him that, so to speak, in the morning he could, without error or confusion, produce and follow ordinary remarks containing tensed verbs and specifications of dates, hours and epochs, and yet, so to speak, in the afternoon he could not answer questions about the concept of Time. The morning task and the afternoon task belong to different levels; and the afternoon task requires re-considering, in a special way, features of what had been done, perfectly efficiently perhaps, but still naïvely, in the morning. In the morning he had talked good sense about everyday topics in, *inter alia*, temporal dictions; but in the afternoon he had to try to talk good sense about the good sense that, in the morning, he had talked in those temporal dictions.

But now for a further point. The persons responsible for publishing weather-forecasts are constantly having to tell their hearers that, for example, snowstorms are likely in certain regions, while in other regions, though snowstorms are possible, rainy weather is much more probable; and so on. From what intellectual motive can they or anyone else raise what I am calling the "afternoon"-conceptual questions, namely the questions about what had been contributed to their morning forecasts by their expressions "probably," "possible, but less likely" and so on? If, in the morning, they knew quite well what they were saying, why do they or other people need, in the afternoon, to try to say things about the well-understood things that they had said in the morning? How are any conceptual problems left requiring a solution, if the meteorologist had, in the morning, said with truth, consistency and clarity all that he meant to say about tomorrow's weather? What light is there for a conceptual discussion in the afternoon to throw on themes in which the meteorologist had in the morning been in no darkness at all? He and his hearers knew what he meant, so how can he need to be given an autopsy on what he meant? What questions about Time are left to perplex Augustine, after he has said and understood all the chronological and chronometrical things about the everyday world that he had needed to say and understand before lunch?

Let us take a new example. We are all, in everyday life, constantly having to consider concrete questions of existence and non-existence. How long ago did mammoths exist and how long have they been extinct or non-extinct? Does there exist a prime number between 23 and 29? Is this island uninhabited or do there exist some human beings on it? Even when we speak of people constructing or demolishing bridges or houses we are speaking of them as bringing bridges or houses into existence, and as rendering them no longer

existent. When theists and atheists dispute about the existence of God, they may not come to an agreement on their problem; but they do not differ in their employment of the notions of existence or non-existence.

None the less, there do arise, so to speak, in the afternoon, well-known problems about the concepts of existence and non-existence. How can non-existence be ascribed to anything, say a prime number between 23 and 29, or to a 20th century mammoth, if there *is*, i.e. if there *exists* nothing of which this or any other predicate can be predicated? Just how do 100 imaginary dollars differ from 100 real or existent dollars, if I can imagine my 100 imaginary dollars as having all the properties of the real dollars, including that of being real? Once again we have to ask how it is that we are, in the morning, perfectly at home with the idea of things existing or being extinct or non-existent, and yet, in the afternoon, find ourselves challenged to describe what it was that we had earlier been at home with. Yet we do, somehow, need to be able to describe it. What sort of a need is this? To ask this is to ask what sorts of problems are specifically philosophical problems. Why do we need to philosophise?

Let us try out this suggested answer. A man at the dinner table may know very well the difference between an onion and a beetroot. He knows their names, he knows how they taste, he can tell them apart from their looks and smells; maybe he even knows how to cultivate and cook them. But he cannot classify them; he cannot say to what different botanical *sorts* onions and beetroots belong. So perhaps we are in a similar position. We can, in concrete cases, tell existence from non-existence, knowledge from ignorance, a month from a minute; but we cannot say what sort of a thing it is for something to exist, what sort of a thing knowing is, or what sort of a thing a minute is a short stretch of. Perhaps problems about concepts are classificatory problems. I daresay that this is how Socrates thought of his philosophical problems, namely as problems the solution to which, if he could ever find them, would be of the pattern "Virtue is a species of Knowledge, differing from other species of Knowledge in such and such respects."

I do not think that this suggested answer is right, and for this reason. The philosophically interesting and crucial problems are problems about concepts which are, typically, too pervasive or too catholic to be treated as mere species of higher genera. The concepts of Time, Knowledge, Probability, Cause, Chance, Existence, Negation, and so on, are not departmental notions, and *a fortiori* not sub-departmental notions; they are inter-departmental. They belong, to put it metaphorically, not to this or that special vocabulary but to the topic-neutral syntax of our thoughts about the world.

So now let us consider another suggestion. Instead of thinking of a man who knows onions from beetroots but cannot tell us to what botanical sorts they belong, let us now think instead of the inhabitant of a village who knows well every house, field, stream, road and pathway in the neighbourhood and is, for the first time, asked to draw or consult a map of his village—a map which shall join on properly to the maps of adjacent districts and in the end to the map of his country and even of his continent. He is being asked to think about his own familiar terrain in a way that is at the start entirely strange, despite the fact that every item that he is to inscribe or identify in his map is to be something that he is entirely familiar with. In the morning he can walk from the church to the railway station without ever losing his way. But now, in the afternoon, he has to put down with compass bearings and distances in kilometres and metres the church, the railway station and the paths and roads between. In the morning he can show us the route from anywhere to anywhere; but it still puzzles him in the afternoon to describe those routes—describe them not just in words but in such cartographical terms that his local map will fit in with the maps of his entire region and country. He has, so to speak, to *translate* and therefore to re-think his local topographical knowledge into

universal cartographical terms. Now he has to survey even his own dear home as if through the transparent pages of an international atlas.

I think you will agree that Augustine's puzzlement about the concept of Time has a good deal in common with the puzzlement of our villager who is asked to think about his home-village in cartographical terms.

We should notice that part of what perplexes the villager when for the first time asked to draw or to read a map of a place in which he is entirely at home is that he has to describe it in perfectly general, cartographical terms—terms, that is, which are shared by all other places. Where he normally thinks of *his* home, *his* church and *his* railway station in personal terms, now he has to think of them in impersonal, neutral terms. For him his village is unlike every other village in being the centre of his own life; but the map is neutral as between his village and any other. It represents them all by different arrangements of the same dots, lines and colours. All their distances, compass bearings and heights above sea level are given in the same unemphatic, impartial, impersonal code. The map is not a local snapshot; or an album of local snapshots; it is a slice out of an universal diagram. When he is out of the country, a snapshot of his home may make him feel homesick; but the map-reference of his home will not do this.

None the less the map is a store of knowledge about his district, for which his own personal familiarity with it can never deputise. Besides being personally intimate with his neighbourhood, he does also need to know its geography. He has learned something valuable when he has made the, at first, perplexing transition from thinking of his neighbourhood in only personal and practical terms, to thinking of it also in neutral, public, cartographical terms. Unlike Augustine, he can now say "When, in the morning, you do not ask me questions, I can guide you on foot from anywhere in the district to anywhere else; but, when in the afternoon, you do ask me questions, I can now *also* tell you the distances in kilometres and the compass-bearings between anywhere in the district and anywhere else in the district, or anywhere else in the country or even anywhere else in the whole wide world." Not only can he cope with the familiar morning tasks, but he can now also cope with the sophisticated afternoon tasks. Both are territorial tasks about one and the same region; but they are tasks of different levels. The "afternoon" or cartographical task is more sophisticated than the "morning" task of merely guiding someone from the church to the station. But this "afternoon" task is also in an important way parasitic upon tasks of the "morning" type, since the "cash-value," so to speak, of what the code-symbols in the map represent consists wholly in such things as the fields, bridges, paths, rivers and railway-stations with which the local inhabitants and visitors and even the Ordnance Surveyors themselves became familiar, not by studying maps but *ambulando*.

How should we apply this analogy of the two levels of topographical knowledge to the difference on which we have been concentrating, namely the difference between concrete and abstract, morning and afternoon, factual and conceptual considerations? In this way. In making my everyday unphilosophical statements, in asking my ordinary factual questions or in giving my concrete, practical advice, I say what I have to say with a variety of familiar words and phrases. These may be quite untechnical expressions or they may be technical or semi-technical expressions. Some of them may be unfamiliar to some people, but if I myself am not familiar with them, either I avoid trying to use them, or I am in doubt whether I have said what I wished to say.

Now every word or phrase that I so employ —with a few exceptions, such as expletives— so contributes to my statement, question or advice that it would have been a different statement, etc., had I used a different non-synonymous word or phrase instead. It would have been a different statement, different in having different implications, in requiring different tests for truth or falsehood, in being compatible and incompatible with different affiliated statements, in being evidence for or against different corollaries, and so on. Let us

label these for brevity its "implication-threads." If I am familiar with a word or phrase, then I know, *ambulando*, the particular differences, of these sorts, that it contributes to the particular statements etc. in which I employ it. Having said something sensible with it, I know how to go on saying particular things that continue to make co-sense with what I said. So far I am like the villager who, on leaving the church, turns right in order to walk home and never has to nullify his first steps by turning back in his tracks. He is continuously on the correct route all the way—unless he is absent-minded or distracted; and this reservation applies to my talking and thinking too.

But now we have to notice a new point. The things that we say often, indeed usually, contain a mixture or plurality of words or phrases. We have to marry the contribution made by one to the contributions made by all the others; and sometimes the implication-threads generated by one of them pull or seem to pull across or away from the implication-threads generated by another. For example, I might truly and intelligibly describe a weary sailor in a storm as having toiled voluntarily, although reluctantly; and then I find myself in a perplexity. For I seem to be saying that he toiled not under compulsion but because he volunteered to do it, despite the fact that he did not want to do it. The natural implication-threads of "voluntarily" seem to pull away from the natural implication-threads of "reluctantly." So now it is not enough to be familiar with the separate contributions of the two adverbs. I need to be able to *say* how their apparent conflict is an unreal one, as it must be if my original statement was intelligible and true. I am now confronted by a conceptual problem, though doubtless a fairly elementary and local one. But still it is a problem the solution of which requires consideration in perfectly general terms of the notions of *action, motive, preference, strength of desires, choice* and so on, with no particular reference to this sailor or this storm. I have, so to speak, now to place on the same regional map the ideas of "voluntarily" and "reluctantly" with each of which by itself I am quite at home. I have to orientate them together with one another, and also orientate them together with the other familiar ideas with which they must or may come into conjunction. I have to fix what I may call their "logical bearings" *vis-à-vis* one another and *vis-à-vis* all other normal or possible neighbours. Of course the big philosophical issues are not those which, like my specimen about the sailor, just happen more or less accidentally to crop up now and then, but those which inevitably present themselves over and over again. When we speak, as we constantly have to speak, in the very same breath, of a responsible human agent acting in a world which is, as he himself also is, a field of chemical, mechanical and biological causes and effects, we are not merely liable, but bound, to find ourselves perplexed by the seeming interferences between the implication-threads belonging to our causal ideas and the implication-threads belonging to our moral ideas. Men *must*, we feel, be free; yet they *must*, we also feel, be amenable to prediction and explanation. Their actions cannot be mechanical. Yet also they cannot be unmechanical.

But how? And now we can see, I hope, that the answer to this question "But how?" is not one the answer to which can be provided either out of our morning familiarity with the ideas of culpability and merit; or out of our morning familiarity with the ideas of impact, attraction, pressure and tension, stimulus and response. We have now, instead, suspiciously to trace and test in their own right the implication-threads which ordinarily we naïvely rely upon. We have now to operate *upon* what we ordinarily operate readily and unquestioningly *with*. We now need the theory of our daily practice, the geography of our daily walks. When two or twenty familiar implication-threads seem to pull across and against one another, it is no longer enough to be able unperplexedly to follow along each one by itself. We need to be able to state their directions, their limits and their interlockings; to think systematically *about* what normally we merely think competently and even dexterously

with. Our familiarities are now at seeming loggerheads with themselves; so an afternoon discipline and method have to be superimposed upon our morning habits. However forcibly a man may, in the morning, argue on this or that concrete topic, he may still need to learn a quite new kind of lesson, namely how, in the afternoon, to assess the forces of those arguments and how to compare and correlate them with the forces of seemingly interfering or cooperating arguments.

It follows *first* that the philosophical examination of a concept, like that, say, of Time or Probability or Voluntariness, can never be the examination of that concept by itself, but only the examination of it *vis-à-vis* its numerous neighbour-concepts, and then *vis-à-vis* their innumerable neighbours too. Even the cartographer cannot produce a map that is the map just of one boulder by itself, or one stretch of water by itself. It follows *second* that the procedure of the philosophical examination of a concept is necessarily an argumentative or, if you prefer, a dialectical procedure. The philosopher has done nothing at all until he has shown the directions and the limits of the implication-threads that a concept contributes to the statements in which it occurs; and to show this he has, so to speak, to tug these threads through their neighbouring threads, which, in their turn, he must simultaneously be tugging.

What cross-bearings are to the cartographer, crossing implication-threads are for the philosopher. Augustine's after-breakfast ability to say things in temporal terms and to understand things said in temporal terms was not enough by itself to enable him, after lunch, to coordinate the contributions to statements of these temporal terms with the contributions made to them by associated terms of different sorts. He was like the sailor, who, though perfectly at home in his own ship, is asked about the disposition and organisation of the fleet to which the ship belongs. This is not just a new question of an old sort. It is a question of a new sort.

The creative capacities
of language

Friedrich Waismann (1896-1959)

Friedrich Waismann was trained as a mathematician and philosopher. A native of Vienna, he became closely associated with the group of scientists and philosophers called the "Vienna Circle." These men, among them Moritz Schlick, Rudolf Carnap, and Hans Reichenbach, developed the principles of logical positivism. Waismann took refuge in England in 1937 and taught first at Cambridge University. Two years afterward he accepted the post of reader in the philosophy of mathematics at the University of Oxford, a position which he retained until his death. He wrote Introduction to Mathematical Thinking *(1951) as well as many articles and papers.*

Our selection, originally entitled "Analytic-Synthetic V," is the fifth installment of a long article which remained unfinished, though six installments were published. In it Waismann conducts a sensitive exploration of some features of language. He dissents from the view that "the ordinary use of language" is adequate and reliable. Taking issue with some contemporary philosophers, he calls for a "departure from the beaten track" in the approach to language, arguing that a creative use of language requires such independence.

Language is always changing. That is a commonplace, yet, oddly enough, one not enough heeded by those who are clamoring for "the ordinary use of language," quite prepared, it seems, to damn everything out of hand—in philosophy—if it fails to conform to its standards. While appreciating the service done to clear thinking by the insistence on the normal use, I feel that the time has come to say a word of warning against the cult of it, for such it has almost become. Like any cult,

From Friedrich Waismann, "Analytic-Synthetic V," in *Analysis,* XIII, October, 1952. Copyright 1952 by *Analysis.* Used by permission of the publisher, Basil Blackwell.

while it is likely to protect its votaries from certain dangers—getting trapped in the vagaries of speech—it is apt to make them blind to the obvious narrowness of such a view, particularly when it is just on the point of becoming one of the major influences of our time. It tends to instil, in the faithful and in the not-so-faithful alike, a belief, a complacent one, in the adequacy of language which is far from the truth. In actual fact, language is a deficient instrument, and treacherous in many ways. As this opens a subject of vast dimensions I shall confine myself to a few scattered observations.

First, I shall try to argue that a departure 383

from the beaten track need not only not be anathematized, but may be the *very thing* to be strived for—in poetry, science and in philosophy. My second point is that language, far from serving merely to report facts, is a collective instrument of thought that enters experience itself, shaping and molding the whole apprehension of phenomena (such as color and luster, e.g.) in a certain definite way, and, who knows, giving to them just that subtle bias which makes all the difference. How curiously different, for instance, must the world of color have appeared to the Romans who had in their language no word for gray, brown, nor any *generic* word for blue (though they had a number of words to denote particular shades of this color). How curiously different, it would seem, must human action appear when seen through the filter of Eskimo language where, owing to the lack of transitive verbs, it is likely to be perceived as a sort of happening without an active element in it. (In Greenlandic one cannot say "I kill him," "I shoot the arrow," but only "He dies to me," "The arrow is flying away from me," just as "I hear" is expressed by "me-sound-is.") Eskimo philosophers, if there were any, would be likely to say that what we call action is "really" a pattern, or gestalt, of succeeding impressions. Just as Greenlandic assimilates action to impression—which strikes us as strange—so our language tends to bias us in just the opposite way: it makes us assimilate perception to action. We say not only "I cut the tree," but also "I see the tree": the use of the same construction makes it appear as if the "I" was the *subject* from which issued the seeing, and as if the seeing was a sort of action directed at the tree; nor are we any better off if we use the passive voice "The tree is seen by me"—for now it almost looks as if something *happened* to the tree, as if it had to undergo or suffer my seeing it. Following the clues of speech, we are led to interpret the world of experience one-sidedly, just as "owing to the common philosophy of grammar," as Nietzsche put it, i.e. "owing to the unconscious domination and guidance of similar grammatical functions the way seems barred against certain other possi-bilities of world-interpretation." In other words, every language contains, deep-sunken in it, certain molds, designs, forms to apprehend phenomena, human action, etc. It is hardly going too far to say that a whole world picture is wedded to the use of the transitive verb and the actor-action scheme that goes with it—that if we spoke a different language we would perceive a different world. By growing up in a certain language, by thinking in its semantic and syntactical grooves, we acquire a certain more or less uniform outlook on the world—an outlook we are scarcely aware of until (say) by coming across a language of a totally different structure we are shocked into seeing the oddity of the obvious, or what seemed to be obvious. Finally, I want to say that philosophy *begins* with distrusting language—that medium that pervades, and warps, our very thought. But this is perhaps too strong an expression. I do not mean to say that language *falsifies* experience, twists it into something else; the point is that it supplies us with certain categorical forms without which the formation of a coherent system of experience, a world picture, would be impossible. In this sense, language shapes and fashions the frame in which experience is set, and different languages achieve this in different ways. A philosopher, more than others, should be sensitive to this sort of influence, alive to the dangers that lie dormant in the forms of expression—the very thing, that is, which, so misguidedly, has been raised to the standard in philosophical controversy.

When I spoke of the change of language I was not thinking of those cases which delight the heart of a philologist—umlaut, ablaut, and the like. Nor was I referring to changes in meaning and vocabulary—what was originally stupid, wanton, Latin *nescius*, becomes "nice"; a horse that is well fed and grows a smooth, shiny coat is "glad"—*glatt* in German; what is now silly was formerly "sely" corresponding to German *selig*—happy, blessed; for while such changes are instructive in many ways, they are hardly such as to deserve the philosopher's attention. Neither was I thinking of those more subtle changes in the *valeurs* for a word which

—as in the case of "romantic"—are significant of a change in the tone of thought of a whole period—of a half-conscious awakening of new ways of feeling and responses to nature, so elusive and yet, to the historian, so important. What I had in mind were cases which are best illustrated by a few examples.

Nothing is so opposed as day and night; yet there is a sense, as when we speak of a "three days' journey," in which "day" includes night. "Man" is used in contrast to woman, but occasionally as a term including woman; and a similar shift of sense is perceptible in "he" and "she"—as an arguer, also woman is "he." We say of a child that he is two years "old," not two years "young," just as we inquire "How *long* (not how *short*) will you stay?" or "How *far* (not how *near*) is it from here to the station?" The word "quality," while for the most part used indifferently, is sometimes uttered in a peculiar tone—as when we say "He has quality." White and black are commonly contrasted with colors in the strict and proper sense ("illustrations in color" *versus* "illustrations in black and white"), yet in certain contexts we are inclined to reckon them amongst the colors; as when we say "Look round you—everything you see has some color or other," thinking, perhaps, that even air and vapor, or glass and water are possessed by some very pale, some very pearly tone. Thus "color" tends to absorb into its meaning all shades, even black and white, the otherwise "colorless" hues. But these are instances betraying a deeper drift. In the ordinary sense, motion is opposed to rest, speed to slowness, size to littleness, numerous to a few, depth to shallowness, strength to weakness, value to worthlessness, just as far is opposed to near, hot to cold, dry to wet, dark to bright, heavy to light, and true to false. And this was, roughly, the way in which Greek philosophers regarded such contrasts. "Up" for them was simply "not-down," "soft" "not-hard," "dry" "not wet," and so on.[1] The fact that two polar terms were in use

[1] See, e.g., A. P. Rossiter, *The Growth of Science,* Pitman Publishing Corporation, New York, 1939.

may have played a role in underpinning the belief that things which are hot and cold, or hard and soft, etc., are different, not in degree, but in kind—a fateful belief, for on it hinged their understanding—no, their lack of understanding of change. They signally failed to penetrate it. The Greeks never mastered the problem of motion—which is but the simplest case—they never evolved a science of dynamics, which is surprising enough in view of their genius for mathematics. They give the impression that they somehow got started on the wrong track—for them heavenly and terrestrial motion were entirely different, the one governed by law, eternal and unchanging, the other lawless, corrupt, confused; if faced with a change, such as a thing getting heated, they thought that one quality must be destroyed to let the opposite quality take its place. Thus they were, perhaps as a consequence of their quaint ideas, mightily impeded in coming to grips with the problem of change.

In science a language has come into use in which those contrasted terms are looked upon as degrees of one and the same quality—darkness as light intensity of illumination, slowness as the lower range of speed, rest as the limiting case of motion; there is a scale only of hardness, not of softness, only a physical theory of heat, not a theory of coldness; what we measure is the strength of a rope, a current, etc., not its weakness, what we count is number, not fewness; the air has a degree of moisture, not of dryness; and everything has weight and mass, even an electron. Again, we speak of health irrespective of whether it is good or bad health, and of the value of things which are of no value. Under the influence of such examples, it would seem, a term like "truth-value" has been coined to cover both truth and falsity of a statement, just as "verification" is, prevalently, used to include falsification. "Distance," "width," "wealth," "intelligence" are further nouns which had the same career; though the same is not so true of the adjectives—"distant," "wealthy," "intelligent" are not yet relativized, any more than "hard," "hot," "speedy," "weighty" are, or "healthy," "valuable" and "worthy"; on the contrary, they retain the original sense. Adjectives, it would appear, have a much tougher life than nouns, and not only in English. But that only in passing.

Here we see a whole array of terms shifting in a parallel way, and in a way which is of far-reaching consequence: for the construction of modern science is bound up with it and would not have been possible without it. The changeover from the static view—where the adjective is seen as the expression of a permanent quality—to a dynamic which apprehends quality as a variable degree within a certain scale made possible "functional thinking" (I use the word as mathematicians do), the kind of thinking that can cope with change and the conceptual difficulties it presents. What happened was obviously this: one term of a pair of contraries had a tendency to swallow up the other and stand for the whole range of variation. Whether this tendency can be traced to the rationalizing influence of science, or whether it is prior to science and has itself given an impetus to that revolution of thought is a question still undecided.[2] It is in this context, perhaps, not without significance that Latin and Greek were lacking in all the finer means to express continuous change and functional dependence: in Latin, for instance, there are no *general* terms to express the relation "the more—the less"; the phrases used for "the more—the more" are confined to simple *proportionality*, the analogue to *statics*.[3] Nor has any classical language an equivalent for "to become" (*devenir* in French, *devenire* in medieval Latin) so essential to our way of describing a change in quality, for neither *fieri* nor γίγνεσθαι can be used in the same way to express the idea of *continuous* change. There are no uses of intransitive verbs such as "to soften," (*rubesco* is inceptive), etc.

The new idiom, which sprang up first in the vernacular about the 14th century, has not entirely displaced the older one (as can still be seen from the adjectives cited above). Both exist side by side. Though the use of "moisture" for dry as well as wet (as in meteorology), or of "truth-value" in logic still has the ring of jargon, in other instances the new idiom has become completely naturalised—as with "distance" for near and far, "age" for young and old, "size" for big and small, "density" for thick and thin. Yet even so, we can use any such term in two distinct ways—we may ask "*Is* he old?" or "*How* old is he?"; and so in the other cases.

At the time of Nicole Oresme, Bishop of Lisieux, when a new way of looking at change was growing up, and with it a new way of speaking of qualities, this must have been felt as a shocking departure from the ordinary use, supported and sanctioned as it was by old tradition. How the cloisters of the schoolmen must have resounded with "intensio et remissio formarum"—the disputes as to whether a quality might have degrees and, in changing, could yet remain the same, or whether this was patent nonsense. One may imagine the indignant outcries of the purists of the time, their loathing of what must have appeared to them as "new-fangled ways of speaking" and as a "complete perversion" of grammar. The latter, more even than the vocabulary, embodies a good deal of the conservatism of mankind, and progress had often to be made in the teeth of the enormous resistance offered by its structure to ways of thinking which do not, or not smoothly, fit its grooves. (See what has been said in the foregoing on Greek language and absence of dynamics.) Grammar draws a *cordon sanitaire* against any rebellious ideas that dare to crop up.

The importance of functional correlation can, moreover, be seen in a different domain: in perspective, and the enthusiasm with which it was universally greeted when it was discovered—another coincidence?—at the very time when new aspects of thought and feeling were just about to take shape: Duccio's Maesta and Giotto's wall paintings in the Capella degli Scrovegni in Padua both belong to the early 14th century. The "strange fascination which perspective had for the Renaissance mind can-

[2] My attention has been drawn to this aspect of the matter by my former pupil, J. L. Hevesi.

[3] Cf. Karl Ettmayer, Ritter von, *Analytische Syntax der französischen Sprache,* N. Niemeyer, Halle, 1936, vol. II, pp. 935ff.

not be accounted for exclusively by a craving for verisimilitude," as Panofsky [4] observes. A sensibility to functional relation is apparent in this, and the interest in perspective—so alien to the Greeks—is almost symbolic of the time. A reflex of it can still be caught from the writings of Leonardo da Vinci and Dürer. As perspective rests essentially on a clear understanding of the way in which two variables, the apparent size of an object and its distance from the beholder, are connected, Leonardo saw in painting a "science." He certainly must have been struck by the affinity between this "science" and the philosophical speculations on dynamics of the schoolmen of which he was fully aware (he even employed their ideas in his theory of painting).

If those pedantic schoolmen and -masters had had their way, there would today be no science and no dynamics; but, for consolation, "correct" grammar. To look at any departure from the norm as a crime is nothing but a blind prejudice; and a fateful one at that as it tends to drain the life-blood of any independent inquiry. Language is an instrument that must as occasion requires, be bent to one's purpose. To stick to language as it is can only lead to a sort of Philistinism which insists on the observance of the cliché and will end up with a harakiri of living thought. Indeed, the guardian of language who jealously watches over its "correctness" is in the long run bound to turn into a reactionary who looks askance at any innovation. Correctness is a useful, but a negative virtue. Follow those prophets, and you will soon find yourself imprisoned in a language cage, clean, disinfected, and unpleasant like a sanatorium room.

Understandably enough, there is an instinctive prejudice against neologisms, in part springing from a wholesome fear that novelty of speech may screen poverty of thought. We all dislike new words. And yet there is another and perfectly proper urge to give expression to meanings so far unexpressed, or, in the present language, indeed inexpressible. When

Freud, for instance, says *der Patient erinnert den Vorfall* he is using the verb *erinnern* in a novel manner; in the ordinary way, the verb is used reflexively, *sich an etwas erinnern*. Why has Freud (who wrote a very good style) diverged at this point? There is a queer way in which a neurotic person who is under treatment may suddenly remember long-forgotten scenes of his early life which, as Freud puts it, have been "repressed" and are now being relived. What has been inaccessible to the patient, however hard he may have tried, breaks, in a violent storm of emotion, through to consciousness. In order to set apart this kind of remembrance from the ordinary one where we remember at will, Freud uses the verb transitively, in a way no one has done before; and with this syntactical innovation goes a semantic change. By this use Freud has enriched the German language. Such stray deviations, hit upon in a lucky hour and accepted by custom, these little, yet expressive departures from the beaten track, have not only a vividness, a sparkle of their own, but they sharpen the tools of thought and keep language from going blunt. So why cavil at them?

What those sticklers for correctness prefer not to see is that we are living in a *changing world*, and that language is always lagging behind these changes. To cite only one sort of examples out of a great many parallel ones— in psychological experiments one constantly comes across situations which call for new ways of describing. If Maxwell disks, for instance, are rotated one sees, so long as the movement is slow, several color sectors, and when the disk is spinning rapidly, a uniform color, the result of fusion, but in between there is a certain point where a flicker is seen. There are cases in which the color itself is seen flickering, and others, as when the disk is watched through a small screen-hole, which are more aptly described by saying that there is a flickering *across* the disk or *before* it in space, or again that the disk's surface is seen *behind* the flicker. These modes of expression, though perfectly natural and instantly understood by every one, yet digress from the norm. For "before" and "behind," while clearly denoting spatial

[4] E. Panofsky, *Albrecht Dürer*, Princeton University Press, Princeton, N.J., 1945, vol. I, p. 260.

relations, are used in such a way that it makes no longer sense to ask, "Exactly how many millimeters before the disk is the flickering?" Here we have a sense of "before" which admits of no distance. To cite a few similar cases —if we look at a metal its color seems to lie *behind* its surface, just as its glitter appears *in front of*, or *superimposed* on it; the glow of a piece of red-hot iron is seen not simply as color that lies on its surface but as *extending* back into the object. Again, it has been said that, when a person is speaking with someone in complete darkness, the voice of the other sounds distinctly *behind* the darkness, not *in* the darkness. In some cases an object is seen as "desurfaced," with a filmy, fluffy sort of outline, a bit unreal perhaps. Queer idioms which say what cannot quite be said by anything else: but condemn them on account of that? Notice with what unerring instinct language contrives to say, at the cost of a slight departure, what would be unsayable if we moved along the rigid grooves of speech. Indeed, how should one describe such phenomena if not by breaking away from the clichés? Is there anything objectionable in that? If so, language could never keep pace with life. Yet new situations, unforeseen, arise, and with them the need of describing them; it can only be met by adjusting language—either by coining new words, or, as the word-creating faculty is scanty, by pressing old ones into new services, in this way cutting through the dead mass of convention. It is precisely because speech runs so much in ready-made molds that an occasional anomaly, a happy flouting of the laws of grammar, an uncommon phrasing, arouses our attention and lends luster to the point we want to bring out. It is in this way, by *transgressing*, that language manages to achieve what it is meant to achieve, and that it grows. Why, then, the squeamishness?

Not only should the scientist be free to deviate from common language, where the need arises, but he is bound to do so if he is to convey a new insight not in conformity with the ideas dominant of the time, with ideas, moreover, precipitated in language. The classical example of this is Einstein. When he was groping his way, there was, in his own words, "a feeling of direction," of going towards something he didn't quite know—which centered more and more on a suspicion that all was not well with the idea of simultaneity. He could at first not say what was wrong with it, and yet felt that here, if anywhere, was the key to all the dark puzzles that troubled the physicists at that time. Had he been brought up as a pupil of G. E. Moore, imbued with a belief in the infallibility of the ordinary modes of expression, he could never have made his discovery, clogged as he would have been by the dead weight of usage. As it was, he paid no respect to common sense, let alone the common speech. He insisted on asking himself, Do I *really* understand what I mean when I say that two events are simultaneous? Once the question was brought into sharp focus, he came to see, gradually perhaps and to his surprise, that there was a gap in his understanding. For the sense in which we speak of two events happening at the same time, when they are in the same place, or nearby, cannot be applied to events in distant places. It would be *blind*, he felt, to apply the familiar meaning of "simultaneous" to these other cases—it would only land us in perplexities beyond resolve. Einstein saw that the term "simultaneous" had first to be *defined* for the case of distant events, and defined in such a way that the definition supplies us with a method to decide experimentally whether or not two events are simultaneous. This "seeing" of a crucial point in the meaning of "simultaneous" has *absolutely* nothing to do with the way the word is actually used in language. It is as well to remind you that in 1905, when Einstein's first essay appeared, there was only *one* use, not two uses of "simultaneous," and that it would be absurd to pretend that, when Einstein found a difference in meaning, he was making a *linguistic* discovery. (A sidelight on how wrong the philosophical equation meaning $=$ is.) On the contrary, anyone who had taken ordinary language, or common sense, for his guide, and had been asked whether he understood what "simultaneous" meant, would have replied with a decided Yes—no matter whether he could, or could not, specify a method for finding out. He would have said that the meaning of the word is clear in itself and needs no further explanation. In fact, no one before Einstein, whether a plain man, a scientist, or a philosopher, doubted for a minute that the concept was clear to him, so clear that he need not trouble. That's precisely what made people slur over the decisive point. Einstein *saw:* that is how he freed himself from the thought-habits imposed on us by speech, radically so. By following the lead of language, or of the common sense philosophers one would have barred oneself from the spark of insight which was to be the dawn of a new era in physics.

These facts speak for themselves. That science cannot live under the tutelage of any ideas on "correctness," will perhaps be conceded. But this is true not only of science. Poetry is forever groping along the borders of the unspeakable, wresting new land from the vast void of the unexpressed. It is its mission to break through the wall of conventional views that encloses us, to startle us into seeing the world through fresh eyes. This is what all the great poets from Dante to Baudelaire have performed, and that is their glory. However, it is a large subject, too large to be treated here. I shall pick out only one tiny point, and one, moreover, that concerns prose—Flaubert's style which, in Proust's phrase, has "renewed our vision of things." In a work of fiction, nature is usually treated as background to men; against this background stand out the main characters of the story, the way they act, think, speak, feel and behave. The contrast between the uniformity of nature and the uniqueness of the human world is, in French, expressed by the use of two tenses—the imperfect for things and processes, and the perfect for men and actions. But with Flaubert, what men do is, in essence, always the same—it is like the succession of rain and sunshine, spring and summer, the ripening of the corn, and the phases of the moon. There is something dull and repetitive about them which pervades them with a sort of dispassionate sadness. There is a passage in *Madame Bovary* where Flaubert speaks of "the eternal monotony of passion which has ever the

same forms and the same language." A revealing passage; for what he has tried to do and has done is to bring about something like a shift in our way of seeing people and things; and this he achieves, simply, by his relentless use of the imperfect, assimilating, in language, his apprehension of men to that of things (remember Greenlandic!). Everything, including human action, is resolved into a perpetual and monotonous flux, revealing the melancholy essence of human existence. Describing people in the forms appropriate to things produces a peculiar effect indeed—"what, up to the time of Flaubert, had been merely action, has become impression," as Proust puts it. As we read over the pages of his novels, we are made to feel in what people say that they would always say precisely the same thing, that their whole life can be poured into a phrase as into a little vial. And when the perfect is used—on rare occasions only as when the narrative changes direction—it is again with a queer effect: it gives to a thing (when it occupies the place of a subject) a character of activity, it is as if a furtive ray of sunlight was falling on it, imparting to it, for a fleeting instant, a life of its own: change suddenly turns into action. And from this arises that unique Flaubertian vision of things which, like any artist's vision, can only be communicated through his style. Besides the tenses, the conjunction "and" is used in an entirely new way. It hardly ever binds phrase to phrase, but has a more musical function—to mark a pause in the beat of the rhythm, to indicate that the moving wave we have been following has spent itself, and that another is about to build itself up. To this must be added a novel use of the present participles, of adverbs, and of certain pronouns and prepositions—grammatical peculiarities which all contribute to give shape to a world picture in which life is seen as a smooth change of one state passing into another without the persons taking any active part in the action—a picture that reminds one of some huge escalator which goes on and on, never stopping, never breaking its monotony. But where an "action" does intervene in the flow of events, its protagonists are, in general, *things*, acting on a plane of nonhuman drama.

What a vision! And yet a vision attained by distorting syntax. This, I think, should be enough to instil a drop of scepticism into the belief that all is well with ordinary language; it makes one wonder whether there is not, after all, a hard atom of truth in the view that ordinary speech is only good for saying things that are no longer worth saying.

By giving so copious examples my aim was to drive home the point defended here—that the ideal of correctness is a deadening one, that it is in vain to set up a language police to stem living developments. (I have always suspected that correctness is the last refuge of those who have nothing to say.)

Poets and literary critics feel, today perhaps more keenly than ever before, that there is something disquieting about language. If I correctly read the signs, there is a susceptibility to the perils of words, a growing one, and a suspicion that language comes between us and the things we want to say. "In speaking one always says more than one intends to" observes Sartre; and T. S. Eliot, having noticed the vanity of words to express what is unique in experience, says "The particular has no language." Philosophers, on the other hand, are on the whole more likely to be found in the opposite camp—"debunking" all this talk as "pseudo-complaints which masquerade as genuine." [5] I think that this is a mistaken attitude for a number of reasons, and this is perhaps the place to set out some of them.

First, to talk of *the* ordinary use of language is, as I have already hinted in a previous article, unrealistic. Though I would not go so far as Ezra Pound in saying that our whole speech is "churning and chugging" today, the fact remains that language is in a state of flux. But, it will be said, that is the concern of the historian of language, not of the philosopher. All the philosopher needs to know is the *stock* use of a word or phrase, as it is employed at

present, in contrast with its nonstock uses.[6] This answer is unsatisfactory. Though it would be silly to pretend that one did not know the stock use of "cat" or "shut the door," there are other cases where one would feel less sure. Is a "taste of onions" the stock use and a "taste for history" derived, secondary, figurative? (But it is not *felt* as a metaphor!) Is only a "brilliant sunshine" standard use and a "brilliant style" nonstandard? Is "day" as opposed to night, or as including night the norm? What about speaking of a "wild laughter," a "brooding silence," or saying that a "recollection of this experience moved in his eyes"? It is easy to see that the "stock use" shifts with the context, and shifts in time. What was stock use may become obsolescent and fall into the limbo of silence, just as new uses may spring up and may, in their turn, become standard language; but where is one to draw the line? It is well to remember that almost all expressions which refer to the mental are derived from others whose primary sense was sensuous and that this is a process which goes on to the present day; just as a good many words, under the influence of science, philosophy, or something still more elusive, have only in fairly recent times undergone a change in meaning—e.g. "organic," "nervous," "unconscious," "original," "creative," "objective," "curiosity," "to entail," etc. There is continuous change and continuous creation in language. Finally, there is such a thing as ambiguity which—except in exceptional cases—mars any attempt to single out one use as the stock one. Exactly how many standard uses has "nature"? What about "in," "on," "about" etc.? "The Engish prepositions," says Empson, "from being used in so many ways and in combination with so many verbs, have acquired not so much a number of meanings as a body of meaning continuous in several dimensions." [7] If so, or if the uses

[5] Alice Ambrose, "The Problems of Linguistic Inadequacy," in Max Black (ed.), *Philosophical Analysis,* Cornell University Press, Ithaca, N.Y., 1950.

[6] I am indebted here to Prof. G. Ryle for letting me read an article of his in which such distinctions are discussed.

[7] William Empson, *Seven Types of Ambiguity,* Harcourt, Brace & World, Inc., New York, 1931, p. 5.

shade off into one another imperceptibly, how can one peel off and throw away all the non-stock uses and retain the stock ones? Yes, this view *is* unrealistic.

Next, and this raises a bigger issue, even if there was such a thing as a stock use, it need not matter much to the philosopher. I mean, he need not be *bound* to this use; I should even go further and say that, sooner or later, he is bound to commit the crime and depart from it—that is, if he has something new to say. In this respect, his position is not altogether different from that of the poet or the scientist, and for similar reasons. He, too, may have come to see something which, in the ordinary way, cannot quite be said. I shall argue later that this is a characteristic feature of some philosophising. To mention here just one small point, the English language has been enriched by many words coined by philosophers who were sensitive to gaps in our vocabulary. "Optimism," for instance, is due to Leibniz, and was borrowed from him by Voltaire. "Impression" in its modern sense was introduced by Hume, "intuition" by De Quincey, "intuitionism" by Sidgwick, "intuitionist" by H. Spencer. "Scientist" is an invention of Whewell, "aesthetic" one of Baumgarten, and so on. That even the laws of grammar can be flouted with salubrious effect can be seen from Lichtenberg's remark that one should say "It thinks in me."

My third point is that certain features of ones' own language are noticed and appreciated in their full significance only when it is compared with other languages—with German (verbal way of expressing color), Greenlandic (dominance of the impression verb), Latin (absence of words for blue, grey, and brown), etc. Is, then, the philosopher to go to the Eskimos to learn his trade? Not exactly; yet the mere *awareness* of other possibilities is, philosophically, of the utmost importance: it makes us see in a flash other ways of world interpretation of which we are unaware, and thus drives home what is conventional in our outlook. The technique of the ordinary-use philosophers has suffered from the fact that they restricted themselves to the study of one language to the exclusion of any other—with the result that they became blind to those ubiquitous features of their own language on which their whole mode of thinking, indeed their world picture, depends.

Connected with this is another large point —the misleadingness of our speech forms. That language, "the embodied and articulated Spirit of the Race," as Coleridge put it, is in many ways inadequate can, I take it, by no one be doubted. In particular, it is the syntax and the field of analogies embedded in language which, unperceived, hold our thought in thrall, or push it along perilous lines. We shall soon have occasion to substantiate this point.

But there are still more reasons for guarding against this official doctrine. The one is that its champions pay heed only to the actual use of language not to its gaps revealing as they are. Suppose, for instance, that I say "I ought to do so-and-so"; when I say that it is obvious that the I is here only a pseudo-subject from which the ought seems to proceed, whereas in fact it is more a *point d'appui* to which it is directed. We regard a rule of ethics, politeness, etc., as something outside ourselves which applies to us as objects. We are rather in a passive (obedient) frame of mind, and what is active is, at most, the consent we give to that duty. "I am under an obligation," "it is my duty" are therefore phrases which are more appropriate. That "ought" does not refer to an occult activity betrays itself in a number of features; thus we do not say "I will ought," "I choose (decide) to ought," any more than we say "I ought to ought," or "I am resolved upon oughting." There is no such thing as a "will to ought." The complete absence of these idioms *is* revealing. That philosophers have concentrated on the use, and neglected the nonuse of expressions is a further weakness of their technique.

Language and myth

Ernst Cassirer (1874-1945)

Ernst Cassirer was a thinker who made contributions to nearly every field of philosophy. He was born and educated in Germany and lectured for many years at the University of Berlin. In 1919 he was appointed to the professorship of philosophy at Hamburg. Finding himself in the exposed position of a Jew in the Germany of 1932, Cassirer resigned his post. He spent the succeeding years at Oxford and at Sweden's University of Göteborg before coming to the United States in 1941. Here he was invited to teach at Yale University. He died while on leave as a visiting professor at Columbia.

A prolific writer, Cassirer made notable contributions to the philosophy of language and culture and did distinguished work in the history of philosophy and in the philosophy of science. Among his best-known works are Substance and Function (1910), *the influential three-volume* Philosophy of Symbolic Forms (1923–1929), An Essay on Man (1944), *and* The Myth of the State (1946). *All his later works reflect his belief that man is best defined as the symbolizing animal and that each aspect of culture, such as art, science, or history, is a symbolic form by which man constructs the world of reality. In our selection, a chapter from his* Language and Myth, *Cassirer examines the complex interrelationships between linguistic concepts and mythico-religious feeling and thought. He discusses a dimension of language not explored in the previous selections.*

To know and understand the peculiar nature of mythico-religious conception not only through its results, but through the very principle of its formation, and to see, furthermore, how the growth of linguistic concepts is related to that of religious ideas and in what essential traits they coincide—this requires us, indeed, to reach far back into the past. We must not hesitate to take a roundabout way through general logic and epistemology, for it is only upon this basis that we may hope to determine precisely the *function* of this sort of ideation and to distinguish it clearly from the conceptual forms which serve theoretical thinking. According to the traditional teachings of logic, the mind forms concepts by taking a certain number of objects which have common properties, i.e., coincide in certain respects, together in thought and abstracting from their differences, so that only the similarities are retained and reflected upon, and in this way a general idea of such-and-such a class of objects is formed in consciousness. Thus the concept (*notio, conceptus*) is that idea which represents the totality of *essential* properties, i.e., the *essence* of the objects in question. In this apparently simple and obvious explanation, every-

"Language and Conception" from *Language and Myth* by Ernst Cassirer as translated by Susanne K. Langer. Copyright 1946 by Susanne Langer. Reprinted with the permission of Harper & Row, Publishers.

thing depends on what one means by a "property," and how such properties are supposed to be originally determined. The formulation of a general concept presupposes *definite* properties; only if there are fixed characteristics by virtue of which things may be recognized as similar or dissimilar, coinciding or not coinciding, is it possible to collect objects which resemble each other into a class. But—we cannot help asking at this point—how can such differentiae exist prior to language? Do we not, rather, *realize* them only by means of language, through the very act of naming them? And if the latter be the case, then by what rules and what criteria is this act carried out? What is it that leads or constrains language to collect just *these* ideas into a single whole and denote them by a word? What causes it to select, from the ever-flowing, ever-uniform stream of impressions which strike our senses or arise from the autonomous processes of the mind, certain pre-eminent forms, to dwell on them and endow them with a particular "significance"? As soon as we cast the problem in this mold, traditional logic offers no support to the student and philosopher of language; for its explanation of the origin of generic concepts presupposes the very thing we are seeking to understand and derive—the formulation of linguistic notions.[1] The problem becomes even more difficult, as well as more urgent, if one considers that the form of that ideational synthesis which leads to the primary verbal concepts and denotations is not simply and unequivocally determined by the object itself, but allows scope for the free operation of language and for its specific mental stamp. Of course, even this freedom must have its rules, and this original, creative power has a law of its own. Can this law be set forth, and can it be brought into relation with the principles that govern other spheres of spiritual expression, especially the rules of mythical, religious, and purely theoretical, i.e., scientific, conception?

[1] For more detailed discussion of this point see my *Philosophie der symbolischen Formen*, vol. I, pp. 244ff.

Beginning with the last of these branches, we can show that all the intellectual labor whereby the mind forms general concepts out of specific impressions is directed toward breaking the isolation of the datum, wresting it from the "here and now" of its actual occurrence, relating it to other things and gathering it and them into some inclusive order, into the unity of a "system." The logical form of conception, from the standpoint of theoretical knowledge, is nothing but a preparation for the logical form of judgment; all judgment, however, aims at overcoming the illusion of singularity which adheres to every particular content of consciousness. The apparently singular fact becomes known, understood and conceptually grasped only in so far as it is "subsumed" under a general idea, recognized as a "case" of a law or as a member of a manifold or a series. In this sense every genuine judgment is synthetic; for what it intends and strives for is just this synthesis of parts into a whole, this weaving of particulars into a system. This synthesis cannot be achieved immediately and at a single stroke; it has to be worked out step by step, by a progressive activity of relating separate notions or sense impressions with each other, and then gathering up the resultant wholes into greater complexes, until finally the union of all these separate complexes yields the coherent picture of the totality of things. The will to this totality is the vivifying principle of our theoretical and empirical conception. This principle, therefore, is necessarily "discursive"; that is to say, it starts with a particular case, but instead of dwelling upon it, and resting content in sheer contemplation of the particular, it lets the mind merely start from this instance to run the whole gamut of Being in the special directions determined by the empirical concept. By this process of running through a realm of experience, i.e., of discursive thinking, the particular receives its fixed intellectual "meaning" and definite character. It has different appearances according to the ever-broadening contexts in which it is taken; the place it holds in the totality of Being, or rather the place which the progressive march of thought assigns to it, determines its content and its theoretical significance.

How this ideal of knowledge controls the rise of science, especially the construction of mathematical physics, requires no further elucidation. All the concepts of physics have no other aim than to transform the "rhapsody of perceptions," by which the world of sense is actually presented to us, into a system, a coherent epitome of laws. Each individual datum becomes a phenomenon and object of "nature" only as it meets this requirement—for "nature" in the theoretical sense, according to the Kantian definition, is nothing but the existence of things as determined by general laws.

A distinction has often been drawn between the "individualizing" mode of historical thought and the "generalizing" mode of science. While in the latter any concrete case is merely regarded as an instance of a general law, and while the "here" and "now" has no significance save in so far as it reveals a universal rule, it is said that history deliberately seeks out this here and now, in order to grasp it ever more precisely in just this character. But even in historical thinking the particular fact is significant only by virtue of the relationships into which it enters. Although it cannot be regarded as an instance of a general law, yet in order to be historically conceived, to appear *sub specie* the mode of history, it must take its place as a *member* of a course of events or belong to some teleological nexus. Its determination in time is the exact opposite of its temporal separateness; for historically it has meaning only if and as it refers back to a past and forward to a future. Thus all genuine historical reflection, instead of losing itself in contemplation of the *merely* singular and nonrecurrent, must strive, like the morphological thought of Goethe, to find those "pregnant" moments in the course of events where, as in focal points, whole series of occurrences are epitomized. In such points, phases of reality that are temporally widely separated become connected and linked for historical conception and understanding. As certain high moments are culled from the uniform stream of time, and are related to each other, and concatenated

in series, the origin and end of all happenings, their whence and whither, is gradually illumined. So historical conception, too, is characterized by the fact that through it a thousand connections are forged by one stroke; and it is not so much the contemplation of particulars as an awareness of such relationships that constitutes the peculiar historicity, or what we call the historical significance of facts.

But let us not dwell longer on such general observations, because our concern is not primarily with the structure of scientific concepts; we are considering this structure only in order to clarify another, namely, the form and character of the primordial linguistic concepts. While this remains to be done, the purely logical theory of conception cannot be completely developed. For all the concepts of theoretical knowledge constitute merely an upper stratum of logic which is founded upon a lower stratum, that of the logic of language. Before the intellectual work of conceiving and understanding of phenomena can set in, the work of *naming* must have preceded it, and have reached a certain point of elaboration. For it is this process which transforms the world of sense impression, which animals also possess, into a mental world, a world of ideas and meanings. All theoretical cognition takes its departure from a world already preformed by language; the scientist, the historian, even the philosopher, lives with his objects only as language presents them to him. This immediate dependence is harder to realize than anything that the mind creates mediately, by conscious thought processes. It is easy to see that logical theory, which traces concepts back to an act of generalizing "abstraction," is of little use here; for this "abstraction" consists of selecting from the wealth of *given* properties certain ones which are common to several sensory or intuitive experiences; but our problem is not the choice of properties already given, but the *positing* of the properties themselves. It is to comprehend and illuminate the nature and direction of *noticing*, which must precede mentally the function of "denoting." Even those thinkers who have concerned themselves most actively with the problem of the "origin of language" have thought it necessary to stop at this point, and have simply assumed a "faculty" of the soul for the process of "noticing."

"When man attained that condition of reflection which is peculiar to him," says Herder in his essay on the origins of language, "and when this reflection first achieved free play, he invented speech." Suppose a certain animal, say a lamb, to pass before the eyes of a human being: what image, what view of it will present itself to him? Not the same that would arise for wolves or lions; they would smell and taste it mentally, be overcome by sensuality, and instinct would throw them upon it. Nor would man's image be like that of another animal to whom the lamb was of no direct interest; for such an animal would let it glide vaguely past, because its own instinct was turned in another direction. "But with man, not so! As soon as he is in a position to become acquainted with the lamb, there is no instinct to interfere with him; there is no sensuality to draw him into too close contact with it, or to repel him from it; it stands before him just as it meets his senses. White, gentle, woolly—his mind in its conscious exercise seeks a characteristic for it— the lamb bleats! He has found the differentia. His inner sense is activated. This bleating, which has made the liveliest impression on his mind, that freed itself from all other properties of sight and touch, stood forth, and entered most deeply into his experience—'Ah! You are the bleating one!'—remains with him; he feels that he has recognized it *humanly*, has interpreted it, in that he knows it by a property. . . . By a property, then? And is that anything but by an inward *denoting word*? The sound of bleating, thus apprehended by a human being as the character of the sheep, became, through the medium of reflection, the *name* of the sheep, even though his tongue had never attempted to utter it." [2]

In these statements of Herder's one can still hear quite clearly the echoes of those theories which he was combating—the traces of the language theories of the Enlightenment, which

[2] "Ueber den Ursprung der Sprache," *Werke* (ed. Supham), vol. V, pp. 35f.

derived language from conscious reflection and considered it as something "invented." Man looks for a differentia because he needs it; because his reason, his specific faculty of "reflection" demands it. This demand itself remains something underived—a "basic power of the soul." Thus the explanation has really progressed in a circle: for the end and goal of language formation, the act of denotation by specific properties, must be regarded as also the principle of its beginning.

Humboldt's notion of the "inward form of language" seems to lead in another direction. For he no longer considers the "whence" of linguistic concepts, but is concerned purely with their "what"; not their origin, but the demonstration of their character constitutes his problem. The form of observation, which underlies all speech and language development, always expresses a peculiar spiritual character, a special way of conceiving and apprehending. The difference between the several languages, therefore, is not a matter of different sounds and marks, but of different world conceptions. If the moon is denoted in Greek as the Measuring One ($\mu\acute{\eta}\nu$), in Latin as the Shining One (luna), or if even in one and the same language, as in Sanskrit, the elephant is called now the Twice Drinker, now the Two-Tusked One, now the Handed One—that goes to show that language never denotes simply objects, things as such, but always conceptions arising from the autonomous activity of the mind. The nature of concepts, therefore, depends on the way this active viewing is directed.

But even this notion of the inward form of language really has to presuppose that which it professes to prove and reveal. For, on the one hand, speech is here the vehicle of any world perspective, the medium through which thought must pass before it can find itself and assume a definite theoretical form; but, on the other hand, just this sort of form, this definite perspective has to be presupposed, in order to explain the particular character of any given language, its special way of seeing and denoting. So the question of the origin of language tends always to become—even for the thinkers who have taken it most profoundly and struggled hardest with it—a veritable monkey puzzle. All the energy devoted to it seems only to lead us about in a circle and finally leave us at the point from which we started.

And yet the very nature of such fundamental problems entails that the mind, though it despairs of ever finally solving them, can never quite let them alone. And we receive something like a new hope of a solution if, instead of comparing the primary linguistic forms with the forms of logical conception, we try to compare them with those of mythical ideation. What holds these two kinds of conception, the linguistic and the mythical, together in one category, and opposes both of them to the form of logical thought, is the fact that they both seem to reveal the same sort of intellectual apprehension, which runs counter to that of our theoretical thought processes. The aim of theoretical thinking, as we have seen, is primarily to deliver the contents of sensory or intuitive experience from the isolation in which they originally occur. It causes these contents to transcend their narrow limits, combines them with others, compares them, and concatenates them in a definite order, in an all-inclusive context. It proceeds "discursively," in that it treats the immediate content only as a point of departure, from which it can run the whole gamut of impressions in various directions, until these impressions are fitted together into one unified conception, one closed system. In this system there are no more isolated points; all its members are reciprocally related, refer to one another, illumine and explain each other. Thus every separate event is ensnared, as it were, by invisible threads of thought, that bind it to the whole. The theoretical significance which it receives lies in the fact that it is stamped with the character of this totality.

Mythical thinking, when viewed in its most elementary forms, bears no such stamp; in fact, the character of intellectual unity is directly hostile to its spirit. For in this mode, thought does not dispose freely over the data of intuition, in order to relate and compare them to each other, but is captivated and enthralled by the intuition which suddenly confronts it. It comes to rest in the immediate experience; the sensible present is so great that everything else dwindles before it. For a person whose apprehension is under the spell of this mythico-religious attitude, it is as though the whole world were simply annihilated; the immediate content, whatever it be, that commands his religious interest so completely fills his consciousness that nothing else can exist beside and apart from it. The ego is spending all its energy on this single object, lives in it, loses itself in it. Instead of a widening of intuitive experience, we find here its extreme limitation; instead of expansion that would lead through greater and greater spheres of being, we have here an impulse toward concentration; instead of extensive distribution, intensive compression. This focusing of all forces on a single point is the prerequisite for all mythical thinking and mythical formulation. When, on the one hand, the entire self is given up to a single impression, is "possessed" by it and, on the other hand, there is the utmost tension between the subject and its object, the outer world; when external reality is not merely viewed and contemplated, but overcomes a man in sheer immediacy, with emotions of fear or hope, terror or wish fulfillment: then the spark jumps somehow across, the tension finds release, as the subjective excitement becomes objectified, and confronts the mind as a god or a daemon.

Here we have the mythico-religious protophenomenon which Usener has sought to fix with the term "momentary god." "In absolute immediacy," he says, "the individual phenomenon is deified, without the intervention of even the most rudimentary class concept; that *one* thing which you see before you, that and nothing else is the god." To this day, the life of primitive races shows us certain features in which this process is almost tangibly clear. We may recall the examples of it which Spieth adduces: water found by a thirsty person, a termite mound that hides and saves someone, any new object that inspires a man with sudden terror—all these are transformed directly into gods. Spieth summarizes his observations with the words: "To the mind of the Evé, the moment in which an object or any striking attributes of it enter into any noticeable relation, pleasant or unpleasant, with the life and spirit of man, that moment a Tro is born in his consciousness." It is as though the isolated occurrence of an impression, its separation from the totality of ordinary, commonplace experience produced not only a tremendous intensification, but also the highest degree of *condensation*, and as though by virtue of this condensation the objective form of the god were created so that it veritably burst forth from the experience.

Now it is here, in this intuitive creative form of myth, and not in the formation of our discursive theoretical concepts, that we must look for the key which may unlock for us the secrets of the original conceptions of language. The formulation of language, too, should not be traced back to any sort of reflective contemplation, to the calm and clearheaded comparison of given sense impressions and the abstraction of definite attributes; but here again we must abandon this static point of view for the comprehension of the dynamic process which produces the verbal sound out of its own inner drive. To be sure, this retrospect in itself is not enough; for through it we are merely brought to the further, more difficult question, how it is possible for anything permanent to result from such a dynamism, and why the vague billowing and surging of sensory impressions and feelings should give rise to an objective, verbal "structure." The modern science of language, in its efforts to elucidate the "origin" of language, has indeed gone back frequently to Hamann's dictum, that poetry is "the mother-tongue of humanity"; its scholars have emphasized the fact that speech is rooted not in the prosaic, but in the poetic aspect of life, so that its ultimate basis must be sought not in preoccupation with the objective view of things and their classification according to certain attributes, but in the primitive power of subjective feeling.[3] But although this doctrine may seem, at first sight, to evade the vicious circle into which the theory of logical expression is ever lapsing, in the end it also

cannot bridge the gulf between the purely denotative and the expressive function of speech. In this theory, too, there always remains a sort of hiatus between the lyrical aspect of verbal expression and its logical character; what remains obscure is exactly that *emancipation* whereby a sound is transformed from an emotional utterance into a denotative one.

Here we may be guided once more by consideration of how the "momentary gods" were generated. If such a god is, in his origin, the creation of a moment, if he owes his existence to some entirely concrete and individual, never-recurring situation, he yet achieves a certain substantiality which lifts him far above this accidental condition of his origin. Once he has been divorced from the immediate exigency, the fear or hope of the moment, he becomes an independent being, which henceforth lives on by a law of its own, and has gained form and continuity. He appears to men not as a creature of the hour, but as an objective and superior power, which they adore and which their cult endows with more and more definite form. The image of the momentary god, instead of merely preserving the memory of what he originally meant and was—a deliverance from fear, the fulfillment of a wish and a hope—persists and remains long after that memory has faded and finally disappeared altogether.

The same function which the image of the god performs, the same tendency to permanent existence, may be ascribed to the uttered sounds of language. The word, like a god or a daemon, confronts man not as a creation of his own, but as something existent and significant in its own right, as an objective reality. As soon as the spark has jumped across, as soon as the tension and emotion of the moment has found its discharge in the word or the mythical image, a sort of turning point has occurred in human mentality: the inner excitement which was a mere subjective state has vanished, and has been resolved into the objective form of myth or of speech. And now an ever-progressive objectification can begin. In the same measure in which the autonomous activity of man extends over a widening sphere, and becomes adjusted and organized within that sphere, his

[3] See Otto Jespersen, *Progress in Language,* London, 1894, esp. pp. 332ff.

mythical and verbal *world* undergoes a progressive organization and ever more definite articulation. The "momentary gods" are succeeded by gods of activity, as Usener has shown us through the examples of the Roman "functional gods" and the corresponding Lithuanian deities. Wissowa summarizes the basic character of Roman religion with the words: "All their deities are entirely practically conceived, so to speak—conceived as being effective in those things with which the Roman dealt in his ordinary life: the local environment in which he moved, the various occupations in which he engaged, the occasions that determine and shape the life of the individual as well as the community—all these things are in the keeping of clearly conceived gods with definitely recognized powers. For the Roman, even Jupiter and Tellus were gods of the Roman community, gods of the hearth and the heath, of wood and wold, seedtime and harvest, of growth and flower and fruit." [4] Here one can trace directly how humanity really attains its insight into objective reality only through the medium of its own activity and the progressive differentiation of that activity; before man thinks in terms of logical concepts, he holds his experiences by means of clear, separate, mythical images. And here, too, the development of language appears to be the counterpart of the development which mythical intuition and thought undergo; for one cannot grasp the true nature and function of linguistic concepts if one regards them as copies, as representations of a definite world of facts, whose components are given to the human mind *ab initio* in stark and separate outlines. Again, the limits of things must first be posited, the outlines drawn, by the agency of language; and this is accomplished as man's activity becomes internally organized, and his conception of Being acquires a correspondingly clear and definite pattern.

We have already demonstrated that the primary function of linguistic concepts does not consist in the comparison of experiences and the selection of certain common attributes, but

in the concentration of such experiences, so to speak, in distilling them down to one point. But the manner of this concentration always depends upon the direction of the subject's interest, and is determined not so much by the content of the experience as by the teleological perspective from which it is viewed. Whatever appears important for our wishing and willing, our hope and anxiety, for acting and doing: that and only that receives the stamp of verbal "meaning." Distinctions in meaning are the prerequisite for that solidification of impressions which, as we said above, is a necessary condition for their denotation by words. For only what is related somehow to the focus point of willing and doing, only what proves to be essential to the whole scheme of life and activity, is selected from the uniform flux of sense impressions, and is "noticed" in the midst of them—that is to say, receives a special linguistic accent, a name. The beginnings of this process of "noticing" must undoubtedly be attributed even to animal mentality; for in their world of experience, too, those elements upon which their impulses and instincts center are singled out by their conscious apprehension. Only something that arouses a single impulse, such as the nutritional or the sexual impulse, or anything that relates to it, "is there" for an animal as an objective content of its feeling and apperception. But such a presence always fills just the actual moment in which the impulse is evoked, is directly stimulated. As soon as the excitation abates, and the desire is fulfilled, the world of Being, the order of perceptions collapses again. When a new stimulus reaches the animal's consciousness, this world may be resurrected; but it is always held in the narrow confines of actual drives and excitations. Its successive beginnings always fill just the present moment, without ranging themselves in any progression; the past is but dimly retained, the future does not become an image, a *prospect*. Only symbolic expression can yield the possibility of prospect and retrospect, because it is only by symbols that distinctions are not merely *made*, but *fixed* in consciousness. What the mind has once created, what has been culled from the total sphere of conscious-

[4] G. Wissowa, *Religion und Kultus der Römer,* Munich, 1912, vol. 2, pp. 24f.

ness, does not fade away again when the spoken word has set its seal upon it and given it definite form.

Here, too, the recognition of function precedes that of Being. The aspects of Being are distinguished and coordinated according to a measure supplied by action—hence they are guided, not by any "objective" similarity among things, but by their appearance through the medium of practice, which relates them within a purposive nexus. This teleological character of verbal concepts may be readily supported and clarified by means of examples from the history of language.[5] A great many of the phenomena which philologists commonly treat under the general heading of "changes of meaning" can really be understood in principle only from this angle. If altered conditions of life, the changes that attend the advance of culture, have brought men into a new practical relation with their environment, the concepts inherent in language do not retain their original "sense." They begin to shift, to move about, in the same measure as the bounds of human activity tend to vary and efface each other. Wherever, for any reason, the distinction between two activities loses its importance and meaning, there is wont to be a corresponding shift of verbal meanings, namely, of the words which marked that distinction. A very characteristic instance of this sort of thing may be found in an article which Meinhof has published under the title, "On the Influence of Occupation on the Language of the Bantu Tribes in Africa." According to Meinhof, "The Herero have a word, *rima*, to denote sowing, which is phonetically identical with *lima*, the word for hoeing, cultivating, in other Bantu languages. The reason for this peculiar change of meaning is that the Herero neither sow nor cultivate the ground. They are cowherds, and their whole vocabulary smells of cows. Sowing and cultivating they deem unworthy occupations for a man; so they do not find it worth

while to draw nice distinctions among such inferior tasks." [6]

Primitive languages especially furnish many further examples in support of the principle that the order of nomenclature does not rest on the external similarities among things or events, but that different items bear the same name, and are subsumed under the same concept, whenever their *functional* significance is the same, i.e., whenever they hold the same place or at least analogous places in the order of human activities and purposes. Certain Indian tribes, for instance, are said to use the same word for "dancing" and for "working" [7] —obviously because the distinction between these two activities is not immediately apparent to them, since in their scheme of things dance and agriculture serve essentially the same purpose of providing the means of livelihood. The growth and prosperity of their crops seems to them to depend as much or more on the correct performance of their dances, their magical and religious ceremonies, than on prompt and proper attention to the soil.[8] Such a fusion of activities gives rise to the identification of their respective names, the "concepts" of language. When the natives along the Swan River in Africa were first introduced to the sacrament of Communion, they called it a dance; [9] which goes further to show how a unity may be posited by language in spite of all distinctions and even complete disparity of appearances, as long as the contents of experience agree in their functional import—in this case, their religious significance.[10]

[6] "Ueber die Einwirkung der Beschäftigung auf die Sprache bei den Bantustämmen Afrikas," *Globus*, 75:361, 1899.

[7] "Die Tarahumara tanzen überhaupt nur zu Zauberzwecken bzw. als 'Gebet.' Tanzen ist ihnen daher...gleich arbeiten, was aus der Bedeutung des Wortes tanzen nolávoa hervorgeht." Preuss, "Der Ursprung der Religion and Kunst," *Globus*, 87:336, 1905.

[8] E. Reclus, *Le primitif d'Australie*, p. 28.

[9] Cf. Preuss, *Religion und Mythologie der Uitoto*, Göttingen and Leipzig, 1923, vol. I, pp. 123ff., and vol. II, pp. 637f.

[10] Here we may adduce a further striking example of this "teleological" construction of language, which I owe to a verbal communication

[5] In regard to the "teleological" structure of language, cf. the more detailed study in my *Philosophie d. symbolischen Formen*, vol. I, pp. 254ff.

Here is one of the basic motives by virtue of which mythical thinking transcends the original vagueness of "complex" intuitions and proceeds to concretely defined, distinctly sundered, and individualized mental constructions. This process, too, is determined primarily by the lines which activity takes; so much so that the forms of mythical invention reflect, not the objective character of *things*, but the forms of human practices. The primitive god, like primitive action, is limited to a very restricted sphere. Not only does every occupation have its particular god, but each phase of the total action becomes the domain of an independent god or daemon who governs this precise sphere of action. The Roman *Fratres Arvales*, when making atonement for the removal of trees from the sacred grove of the goddess Dia, divided the deed into a number of separate acts, for each of which a special deity was invoked: *Deferenda* for fetching down the wood, *Commolenda* for chopping it up, *Coinquenda* for splitting it, and *Adolenda* for burning up the brushwood.[11] The same phenomenon may be seen in primitive languages, which often divide an action into several subactions, and instead of comprehending it all under one term, denote each part by a separate verb, as though they had to break up the idea into little pieces in order to handle it. Perhaps it

is not mere chance that in the language of the Evé, who have such a wealth of "momentary gods" and "special gods," this peculiarity should be very pronounced.[12] And even where both language and myth have risen considerably above such momentary, sense-bound intuition, where they have broken through their original fetters, they long remain quite inseparably involved with each other. Their connection is, in fact, so close that it is impossible to determine on a basis of empirical data which of them takes the lead in their progress toward universal formulation and conception, and which one merely follows suit. Usener, in a section of his work that is philosophically one of the most significant parts, has sought to prove that all general terms in language have had to go through a certain mythical phase. The fact that in the Indo-Germanic languages abstract concepts are usually denoted by feminine nouns, with the feminine ending -a (-η), proves, according to Usener, that the idea this feminine form expresses was originally not conceived as an abstractum, but apprehended and felt as a female *deity*.

"Can there be any doubt," he asks further, "whether Φόβος came first, or φόβος, the divine image or the condition? Why should the condition be denoted as something of masculine gender, not as neuter, like τὸ δέος? The first creation of the word must have been inspired by some idea of a living, personal Being, the 'Startler,' the 'Flight Producer'; in countless applications of the supposed abstract word, this Being still appears: εἰσῆλθεν or ἐνέπεσε Φόβος, the Startler stalks, or attacks, me! The same process must be assumed for the making of all feminized abstractions. The feminine adjective only became an abstraction after it had denoted a female personage, and in primitive times this could not have been conceived as anything but a goddess" (p. 375).

But does not the science of language as well as that of religion show signs of a converse process as well? Should we not suppose, for instance, that the way which inflected lan-

---

from my colleague Professor Otto Dempwolff. In the Kâte language, which is current in New Guinea, there is a word *bilin,* which denotes a certain kind of grass with tough stems and roots that are wedged firmly in the soil; the latter are said to hold the earth together during earthquakes, so that it does not break apart. When nails were first introduced by Europeans, and when their use became popularly known, the natives applied this word to them—as also to wire and to iron rods, in short, to everything that served the purpose of holding things together.

Similarly, one may often observe in nursery language the creation of such teleological identities, which do not meet our class concepts at all, and seem even to defy them. Cf. Clara and William Stern, *Die Kindersprache,* Leipzig, 1906, pp. 26, 172, et al.

[11] Wissowa, *Religion und Kultus der Römer,* vol. 2, p. 25.

[12] Westermann, *Grammatik der Ewe-Sprache,* Berlin, 1907, p. 95.

guages have of endowing every noun with a particular gender may have influenced the conceptions of mythico-religious imagination and bent them after its own fashion? Or may we deem it mere chance that among peoples whose language does not differentiate genders, but employs other and more complex principles of classification, the realm of myth and religion also exhibits an entirely different structure—that it represents all phases of existence not under the auspices of personal, divine powers, but orders it according to totemic groups and classes? We shall content ourselves with merely proposing this question, which would have to be answered by detailed scientific research. But whatever the verdict might be, it is evident that myth and language play similar roles in the evolution of thought from momentary experience to enduring conceptions, from sense impression to formulation, and that their respective functions are mutually conditioned. Together and in combination they prepare the soil for the great syntheses from which our mental creation, our unified vision of the cosmos springs.

Philosophy and
Personal Commitment

Having worked through the selections up to now, the reader may have received the impression that philosophy is a sort of discipline in which certain types of problems are raised and an effort is made to analyze and solve these problems as well as can be done during business hours, so to speak. On this view, the work of the philosopher is like the work of anyone else with a profession, distinguished only by the kinds of problem which are considered. The purpose of this part is twofold: first, to present another contemporary view of philosophy, one which sees philosophy more nearly as the "philosophic way of life" than as a special field of study or analysis; and second, to present some of the issues about which existentialist thinkers have been especially concerned.

These issues arise when one turns his attention to the mode of existence of the thinker rather than to the content or method of his thought. The thinker is not viewed as a "thinking substance" self-contained in his act of thought, but as a "flesh-and-blood" individual, one whose thinking is inseparable from his concrete existence. One of the central problems for the existentialist thinker concerns the discrepancy between objective knowledge and personal action and commitment, or between truth conceived as objective, universal, and impersonal, and truth viewed as subjective, individual, and personal.

Though treated with special urgency by modern existentialists, this issue, or one very much like it, has also appeared in traditional philosophy. In the past, philosophy has at times been concerned with the development of wisdom in the conduct of life. What philosophic wisdom is has been difficult to specify. It has usually been conceived as something other than practical wisdom in the handling of everyday affairs. It seems to involve self-knowledge as well as the knowledge of other beings and things and also certain attitudes which are difficult to define. The reader may wish to return to Plato's *Apology* for some suggestions as to the nature of these attitudes.

Many thinkers, especially in England and the United States, would argue that philosophic reflection is one thing and the achievement of wisdom another, that the philosopher and the sage are two distinct persons, and that no effort should be made to unite them. Yet the attempt to do so has supplied one of the most vital strains of philosophic thought, one to which Plato and the early pre-Socratic philosophers contributed.

In his dialogue, the *Symposium*, Plato has Socrates relate the speech of the mythical priestess, Diotima. Drawing on all the considerable poetic capacity at his command, Plato presents a vision of the interconnection of love, knowledge, beauty, and philosophic wisdom. In an idiom quite different from that of modern existentialist thought and rich in imaginative power, Plato expresses an ideal of human wholeness, in which all aspects of the person are bound together in active harmony. In Plato's vision, man, in his finite and changing situation, is seen in relation to, and in intercommunication with, an eternal unchanging order.

In the selections of this part, Kierkegaard, Nietzsche, Buber, and Jaspers, four unique modern thinkers, confront, each from his own standpoint, the human condition as this enters a personal world of thought and action. Kierkegaard, in his passionate concern with the task of becoming a Christian, takes the full measure of human subjectivity, developing a sense of truth which has to do with the subject's *relationship* to the object of his belief, rather than with the nature of that object. Viewing Christian belief as faith in "the paradox," Kierkegaard finds genuine faith only in the believer who holds with "infinite passion" to an "objective uncertainty."

Kierkegaard, the immensely gifted and tormented nineteenth-century Danish thinker, was a philosopher, a theologian, and a polemicist against the complacency of the Danish church. Perhaps more acutely than any other modern thinker, he was aware of an absolute gulf between man and God and also of an irreconcilable divergence between the world which appears to objective thought and the inner demand of the thinker for his thought to accord with his feeling and will. The true thinker, Kierkegaard believes, must choose through his thought, and Kierkegaard chooses by developing the subjective notion of truth, one which is concerned with the believer's being "in" the truth. Truth is not conceived here as the agreement of an idea with its object, as in one traditional doctrine, but as a mode of personal existence. It is truth to oneself, or "authenticity." Kierkegaard was deeply opposed to the dominant philosophy of his day—the "System" of Hegel—on the grounds that it attempted to harmonize all aspects of reality under the category of the Intellectual and so had falsified what is most important in an individual: his existence as a being who is called upon to decide. Personal decision is a matter of "either/or" and cannot be treated in the manner of the Hegelian synthesis, which effects an intellectual reconciliation of opposing alternatives.

In his trenchant and ironic style, Kierkegaard makes us consider an extremely critical problem for modern thought: Must the major part of man's personal life, his religious and moral commitments, his mythical and artistic vision, be cut off from his objective view of the world, the product of science and rational reflection? This issue has already appeared in earlier readings, but it now achieves added urgency. A good many thinkers have charged that Kierkegaard's position is one which champions the irrational and helps only to widen the rift between the human subject and the objective world. Is this a fair assessment of Kierkegaard? Does he in fact abandon reason? Or does he rather attempt to recognize the limits of reason? Are there conditions which justify holding to his view of truth? The reader may wish to return at this point to Merleau-Ponty's discussion of freedom, in the first part, for another view of the relation between the subjective and objective realms.

Nietzsche's thought is inclined in a different direction from Kierkegaard's, toward the future of the Superman or Overman who expresses through himself the fundamental will to power that, in Nietzsche's view, underlies all being. Opposing Christian morality, Nietzsche dreams of those who are strong enough to overcome all morality, to "'transvaluate all values," to assume the burden of commanding themselves, and who act without resentment or pity. In the poetic vision of his *Thus Spoke Zarathustra*, Nietzsche addresses himself to the task of establishing a relationship not to the Absolute or God, but to one's own will to power.

Nietzsche's complex vision of the man who surpasses man singles out for praise the bold, self-assertive, aggressive, and intellectually powerful individual who can transform his ideals into reality, who has, in effect, mastered himself. Between this individual and ordinary men, Nietzsche sees a more significant difference than between mankind and the other animals. Man, in Nietzsche's view, is always a task for himself; he should be a creation of his own making, the meaning of whose existence is to surpass himself. Not one norm for all men, but mankind made up of individuals, each expressing his uniqueness, is Nietzsche's ideal. The Nietzschean Overman has learned to live fully in the moment, desiring an "eternal recurrence" even of moments of pain. In such an attitude he experiences, according to Nietzsche, the true upsurge of power.

What sort of ideal for mankind has Nietzsche provided? Is his emphasis on power as the standard of human value justified? Can the existence of the Nietzschean Overman be reconciled with life in the social order? Is Nietzsche correct in believing that the individual is to be considered the source of values?

In the thought of Martin Buber the emphasis on subjectivity and individual responsibility which Kierkegaard and Nietzsche shared is tempered by an equally strong insistence on the inseparability of individual existence from the presence of other persons. Influenced by Biblical and Hasidic Judaism and by philosophers such as Kant and Feuerbach, Buber stresses the coexistence of man *with* man. Human existence is "dialogue," in which a man is addressed by others or by God and responds through his actions. The individual, in Buber's view, achieves full existence only as he develops mutuality with others. No one can be fully a person by and through himself. One is a person when he responds to the Other as Thou, as a concrete, fully present being, rather than as an It, or mere object. Buber sees the ethical life and the religious life as inseparable. The man who takes upon himself responsibility for each of his actions meets God in his life. Thus, for Buber, value ultimately resides in certain relations between persons and in the relation between man and God.

Does Buber offer a plausible approach to individual existence? Or is there a dimension of existence in which the individual must stand isolated from all other men? Should religion be defined in such a way that the demands of religious faith are always compatible with moral demands?

In our final selection, Karl Jaspers describes an ideal of philosophizing which refuses to separate the life of the thinker from his thought. Jaspers portrays the philosophic life as an ongoing task which never achieves any final unities and in which man strives to grasp himself as part of the "Comprehensive." The Comprehensive is Jaspers' name for the totality which includes man along with the being that is not man. Man, having to think of himself as a subject set over against an objective world, strives through reason to comprehend the relationships among all aspects of being. In Jaspers' view, being, in its full richness and variety, must always finally elude the categories of man's thinking. Thus the philosopher is always fated to suffer "shipwreck" but never to give up his quest, since his dedication is to reason and to the fullest use of reason. Reason is a striving to establish unity out of the most complex and diverse materials.

Truth is subjectivity

Søren Kierkegaard (1813-1855)

Denmark's foremost thinker and the inspiring genius of contemporary existentialism, Kierkegaard felt that his one task was to "become a Christian." He was the son of a prosperous and gloomy merchant with a strong sense of sin. Kierkegaard studied theology, literature, and philosophy at the University of Copenhagen, and though for a time he led the life of a young Bohemian, he settled down to pass his theological examinations in 1840. The following year he broke his engagement to the youthful Regina Olsen, an event which had a marked effect upon his spiritual life. Beginning with Either/Or (*1843*), *he produced a number of remarkably original works, in which he developed his view of the aesthetic, ethical, and religious categories or stages of life. In such works as* Fear and Trembling (*1843*), Repetition (*1843*), The Concept of Dread (*1844*), and* Stages on Life's Road (*1845*), *he probed the meaning of faith and sin and carried forward his attack on the Danish church and the Hegelian system of philosophy. Obliged to publish his works at his own expense and embattled against church leaders, Kierkegaard nevertheless continued to write with intense concentration for much of the time until his death. In the book entitled* Concluding Unscientific Postscript (*1846*), *following the* Philosophical Fragments (*1844*), *he developed his view of "subjectivity." His account of the "authentic" relation of faith has had a great influence on later existentialists.*

...In an attempt to make clear the difference of way that exists between an objective and a subjective reflection, I shall now proceed to show how a subjective reflection makes its way inwardly in inwardness. Inwardness in an existing subject culminates in passion; corresponding to passion in the subject the truth becomes a paradox; and the fact that the truth becomes a paradox is rooted precisely in its having a relationship to an existing subject. Thus the one corresponds to the other. By

Reprinted from *Concluding Unscientific Postscript* by Søren Kierkegaard, tr. D. F. Swenson and W. Lowrie, by permission of Princeton University Press. Copyright, 1941, by Princeton University Press.

forgetting that one is an existing subject, passion goes by the board and the truth is no longer a paradox; the knowing subject becomes a fantastic entity rather than a human being, and the truth becomes a fantastic object for the knowledge of this fantastic entity.

When the question of truth is raised in an objective manner, reflection is directed objectively to the truth, as an object to which the knower is related. Reflection is not focussed upon the relationship, however, but upon the question of whether it is the truth to which the knower is related. If only the object to which he is related is the truth, the subject is accounted to be in the truth. When the question of the truth is raised subjectively, reflec- **407** *tion is directed subjectively to the nature of the individual's relationship; if only the mode of this relationship is in the truth, the individual is in the truth even if he should happen to be thus related to what is not true.*[1] Let us take as an example the knowledge of God. Objectively, reflection is directed to the problem of whether this object is the true God; subjectively, reflection is directed to the question whether the individual is related to a something *in such a manner* that his relationship is in truth a God-relationship. On which side is the truth now to be found? Ah, may we not here resort to a mediation, and say: It is on neither side, but in the mediation of both? Excellently well said, provided we might have it explained how an existing individual manages to be in a state of mediation. For to be in a state of mediation is to be finished, while to exist is to become. Nor can an existing individual be in two places at the same time— he cannot be an identity of subject and object. When he is nearest to being in two places at the same time he is in passion; but passion is momentary, and passion is also the highest expression of subjectivity.

The existing individual who chooses to pursue the objective way enters upon the entire approximation-process by which it is proposed to bring God to light objectively. But this is in all eternity impossible, because God is a subject, and therefore exists only for subjectivity in inwardness. The existing individual who chooses the subjective way apprehends instantly the entire dialectical difficulty involved in having to use some time, perhaps a long time, in finding God objectively; and he feels this dialectical difficulty in all its painfulness, because every moment is wasted in which he does not have God.[2] That very instant he has God, not by virtue of any objective deliberation, but by virtue of the infinite passion of inwardness. The objective inquirer, on the other hand, is not embarrassed by such dialectical difficulties as are involved in devoting an entire period of investigation to finding God—since it is possible that the inquirer may die tomorrow; and if he lives he can scarcely regard God as something to be taken along if convenient, since God is precisely that which one takes *a tout prix*, which in the understanding of passion constitutes the true inward relationship to God.

It is at this point, so difficult dialectically, that the way swings off for everyone who knows what it means to think, and to think existentially; which is something very different from sitting at a desk and writing about what one has never done, something very different from writing *de omnibus dubitandum* and at the same time being as credulous existentially as the most sensuous of men. Here is where the way swings off, and the change is marked by the fact that while objective knowledge rambles comfortably on by way of the long road of approximation without being impelled by the urge of passion, subjective knowledge counts every delay a deadly peril, and the decision so infinitely important and so instantly pressing that it is as if the opportunity had already passed.

Now when the problem is to reckon up on which side there is most truth, whether on the side of one who seeks the true God objectively, and pursues the approximate truth of the God-idea; or on the side of one who, driven by the infinite passion of his need of God, feels an infinite concern for his own relationship to God in truth (and to be at one and the same time on both sides equally, is as we have noted not possible for an existing individual, but is

---

[1] The reader will observe that the question here is about essential truth, or about the truth which is essentially related to existence, and that it is precisely for the sake of clarifying it as inwardness or as subjectivity that this contrast is drawn.

[2] In this manner God certainly becomes a postulate, but not in the otiose manner in which **this word** is commonly understood. It becomes **clear** rather that the only way in which an exist-

ing individual comes into relation with God, is when the dialectical contradiction brings his passion to the point of despair, and helps him to embrace God with the "category of despair" (faith). Then the postulate is so far from being arbitrary that it is precisely a life-necessity. It is then not so much that God is a postulate, as that the existing individual's postulation of God is a necessity.

merely the happy delusion of an imaginary I-am-I): the answer cannot be in doubt for anyone who has not been demoralized with the aid of science. If one who lives in the midst of Christendom goes up to the house of God, the house of the true God, with the true conception of God in his knowledge, and prays, but prays in a false spirit; and one who lives in an idolatrous community prays with the entire passion of the infinite, although his eyes rest upon the image of an idol: where is there most truth? The one prays in truth to God though he worships an idol; the other prays falsely to the true God, and hence worships in fact an idol.

When one man investigates objectively the problem of immortality, and another embraces an uncertainty with the passion of the infinite: where is there most truth, and who has the greater certainty? The one has entered upon a never-ending approximation, for the certainty of immortality lies precisely in the subjectivity of the individual; the other is immortal, and fights for his immortality by struggling with the uncertainty. Let us consider Socrates. Nowadays everyone dabbles in a few proofs; some have several such proofs, others fewer. But Socrates! He puts the question objectively in a problematic manner: *if* there is an immortality. He must therefore be accounted a doubter in comparison with one of our modern thinkers with the three proofs? By no means. On this "if" he risks his entire life, he has the courage to meet death, and he has with the passion of the infinite so determined the pattern of his life that it must be found acceptable—*if* there is an immortality. Is any better proof capable of being given for the immortality of the soul? But those who have the three proofs do not at all determine their lives in conformity therewith; if there is an immortality it must feel disgust over their manner of life: can any better refutation be given of the three proofs? The bit of uncertainty that Socrates had, helped him because he himself contributed the passion of the infinite; the three proofs that the others have do not profit them at all, because they are dead to spirit and enthusiasm, and their three proofs, in lieu of proving anything else,

prove just this. A young girl may enjoy all the sweetness of love on the basis of what is merely a weak hope that she is beloved, because she rests everything on this weak hope; but many a wedded matron more than once subjected to the strongest expressions of love, has in so far indeed had proofs, but strangely enough has not enjoyed *quod erat demonstrandum*. The Socratic ignorance, which Socrates held fast with the entire passion of his inwardness, was thus an expression for the principle that the eternal truth is related to an existing individual, and that this truth must therefore be a paradox for him as long as he exists; and yet it is possible that there was more truth in the Socratic ignorance as it was in him, than in the entire objective truth of the System, which flirts with what the times demand and accommodates itself to *Privatdocents*.

The objective accent falls on WHAT is said, the subjective accent on HOW it is said. This distinction holds even in the aesthetic realm, and receives definite expression in the principle that what is in itself true may in the mouth of such and such a person become untrue. In these times this distinction is particularly worthy of notice, for if we wish to express in a single sentence the difference between ancient times and our own, we should doubtless have to say: "In ancient times only an individual here and there knew the truth; now all know it, except that the inwardness of its appropriation stands in an inverse relationship to the extent of its dissemination.[3] Aesthetically the contradiction that truth becomes untruth in this or that person's mouth, is best construed comically: In the ethico-religious sphere, ac-

[3] *Stages on Life's Way,* Note: Though ordinarily not wishing an expression of opinion on the part of reviewers, I might at this point almost desire it, provided such opinions, so far from flattering me, amounted to an assertion of the daring truth that what I say is something that everybody knows, even every child, and that the cultured know infinitely much better. If it only stands fast that everyone knows it, my standpoint is in order, and I shall doubtless make shift to manage with the unity of the comic and the tragic. If there were anyone who did not know it I might perhaps be in danger of being dislodged from my position of equilib-

cent is again on the "how." But this is not to be understood as referring to demeanor, expression, or the like; rather it refers to the relationship sustained by the existing individual, in his own existence, to the content of his utterance. Objectively the interest is focussed merely on the thought-content, subjectively on the inwardness. At its maximum this inward "how" is the passion of the infinite, and the passion of the infinite is the truth. But the passion of the infinite is precisely subjectivity, and thus subjectivity becomes the truth. Objectively there is no infinite decisiveness, and hence it is objectively in order to annul the difference between good and evil, together with the principle of contradiction, and therewith also the infinite difference between the true and the false. Only in subjectivity is there decisiveness, to seek objectivity is to be in error. It is the passion of the infinite that is the decisive factor and not its content, for its content is precisely itself. In this manner subjectivity and the subjective "how" constitute the truth.

But the "how" which is thus subjectively accentuated precisely because the subject is an existing individual, is also subject to a dialectic with respect to time. In the passionate moment of decision, where the road swings away from objective knowledge, it seems as if the infinite decision were thereby realized. But in the same moment the existing individual finds himself in the temporal order, and the subjective "how" is transformed into a striving, a striving which receives indeed its impulse and a repeated renewal from the decisive passion of the infinite, but is nevertheless a striving.

When subjectivity is the truth, the conceptual determination of the truth must include an expression for the antithesis to objectivity, a momento of the fork in the road where the way swings off; this expression will at the same time serve as an indication of the tension of the subjective inwardness. Here is such a definition of truth: *An objective uncertainty held fast in an appropriation-process of the most passionate inwardness is the truth*, the highest truth attainable for an *existing* individual. At the point where the way swings off (and where this is cannot be specified objectively, since it is a matter of subjectivity), there objective knowledge is placed in abeyance. Thus the subject merely has, objectively, the uncertainty; but it is this which precisely increases the tension of that infinite passion which constitutes his inwardness. The truth is precisely the venture which chooses an objective uncertainty with the passion of the infinite. I contemplate the order of nature in the hope of finding God, and I see omnipotence and wisdom; but I also see much else that disturbs my mind and excites anxiety. The sum of all this is an objective uncertainty. But it is for this very reason that the inwardness becomes as intense as it is, for it embraces this objective uncertainty with the entire passion of the infinite. In the case of a mathematical proposition the objectivity is given, but for this reason the truth of such a proposition is also an indifferent truth.

But the above definition of truth is an equivalent expression for faith. Without risk there is no faith. Faith is precisely the contradiction between the infinite passion of the individual's inwardness and the objective uncertainty. If I am capable of grasping God objectively, I do not believe, but precisely because I cannot do this I must believe. If I wish to preserve myself in faith I must constantly be intent upon holding fast the objective uncertainty, so as to remain out upon the deep, over seventy thousand fathoms of water, still preserving my faith.

In the principle that subjectivity, inwardness, is the truth, there is comprehended the Socratic wisdom, whose everlasting merit it was to have become aware of the essential significance of existence, of the fact that the knower

---

rium by the thought that I might be in a position to communicate to someone the needful preliminary knowledge. It is just this which engages my interest so much, this that the cultured are accustomed to say: that everyone knows what the highest is. This was not the case in paganism, nor in Judaism, nor in the seventeen centuries of Christianity. Hail to the nineteenth century! Everyone knows it. What progress has been made since the time when only a few knew it. To make up for this, perhaps, we must assume that no one nowadays does it.

is an existing individual. For this reason Socrates was in the truth by virtue of his ignorance, in the highest sense in which this was possible within paganism. To attain to an understanding of this, to comprehend that the misfortune of speculative philosophy is again and again to have forgotten that the knower is an existing individual, is in our objective age difficult enough. But to have made an advance upon Socrates without even having understood what he understood, is at any rate not "Socratic." Compare the "Moral" of the *Fragments*.

Let us now start from this point, and as was attempted in the *Fragments*, seek a determination of thought which will really carry us further. I have nothing here to do with the question of whether this proposed thought-determination is true or not, since I am merely experimenting; but it must at any rate be clearly manifest that the Socratic thought is understood within the new proposal, so that at least I do not come out behind Socrates.

When subjectivity, inwardness, is the truth, the truth becomes objectively a paradox; and the fact that the truth is objectively a paradox shows in its turn that subjectivity is the truth. For the objective situation is repellent; and the expression for the objective repulsion constitutes the tension and the measure of the corresponding inwardness. The paradoxical character of the truth is its objective uncertainty; this uncertainty is an expression for the passionate inwardness, and this passion is precisely the truth. So far the Socratic principle. The eternal and essential truth, the truth which has an essential relationship to an existing individual because it pertains essentially to existence (all other knowledge being from the Socratic point of view accidental, its scope and degree a matter of indifference), is a paradox. But the eternal essential truth is by no means in itself a paradox; but it becomes paradoxical by virtue of its relationship to an existing individual. The Socratic ignorance gives expression to the objective uncertainty attaching to the truth, while his inwardness in existing is the truth. To anticipate here what will be developed later, let me make the following remark. The Socratic ignorance is an analogue to the category of the absurd, only that there is still less

of objective certainty in the absurd, and in the repellent effect that the absurd exercises. It is certain only that it is absurd, and precisely on that account it incites to an infinitely greater tension in the corresponding inwardness. The Socratic inwardness in existing is an analogue to faith; only that the inwardness of faith, corresponding as it does, not to the repulsion of the Socratic ignorance, but to the repulsion exerted by the absurd, is infinitely more profound.

Socratically the eternal essential truth is by no means in its own nature paradoxical, but only in its relationship to an existing individual. This finds expression in another Socratic proposition, namely, that all knowledge is recollection. This proposition is not for Socrates a cue to the speculative enterprise, and hence he does not follow it up; essentially it becomes a Platonic principle. Here the way swings off; Socrates concentrates essentially upon accentuating existence, while Plato forgets this and loses himself in speculation. Socrates' infinite merit is to have been an *existing* thinker, not a speculative philosopher who forgets what it means to exist. For Socrates therefore the principle that all knowledge is recollection has at the moment of his leave-taking and as the constantly rejected possibility of engaging in speculation, the following two-fold significance: (1) that the knower is essentially *integer*, and that with respect to the knowledge of the eternal truth he is confronted with no other difficulty than the circumstance that he exists; which difficulty, however, is so essential and decisive for him that it means that existing, the process of transformation to inwardness in and by existing, is the truth; (2) that existence in time does not have any decisive significance, because the possibility of taking oneself back into eternity through recollection is always there, though this possibility is constantly nullified by utilizing the time, not for speculation, but for the transformation to inwardness in existing.[4]

The infinite merit of the Socratic position

[4] This will perhaps be the proper place to offer an explanation with respect to a difficulty in the plan of the *Fragments*, which had its ground in the fact that I did not wish at once to make the case as difficult dialectically as it

was precisely to accentuate the fact that the knower is an existing individual, and that the task of existing is his essential task. Making an advance upon Socrates by failing to understand this, is quite a mediocre achievement. This Socratic principle we must therefore bear in mind, and then inquire whether the formula may not be so altered as really to make an advance beyond the Socratic position.

Subjectivity, inwardness, has been posited as the truth; can any expression for the truth be found which has a still higher degree of inwardness? Aye, there is such an expression, provided the principle that subjectivity or inwardness is the truth begins by positing the opposite principle: that subjectivity is untruth. Let us not at this point succumb to such haste as to fail in making the necessary distinctions. Speculative philosophy also says that subjectivity is untruth, but says it in order to stimulate

a movement in precisely the opposite direction, namely, in the direction of the principle that objectivity is the truth. Speculative philosophy determines subjectivity negatively as tending toward objectivity. This second determination of ours, however, places a hindrance in its own way while proposing to begin, which has the effect of making the inwardness far more intensive. Socratically speaking, subjectivity is untruth if it refuses to understand that subjectivity is truth, but, for example, desires to become objective. Here, on the other hand, subjectivity in beginning upon the task of becoming the truth through a subjectifying process, is in the difficulty that it is already untruth. Thus, the labor of the task is thrust backward, backward, that is, in inwardness. So far is it from being the case that the way tends in the direction of objectivity, that the beginning merely lies still deeper in subjectivity.

---

is, because in our age terminologies and the like are turned so topsy-turvy that it is almost impossible to secure oneself against confusion. In order if possible clearly to exhibit the difference between the Socratic position (which was supposed to be the philosophical, the pagan-philosophical position) and the experimentally evoked thought-determination which really makes an advance beyond the Socratic, I carried the Socratic back to the principle that all knowledge is recollection. This is, in a way, commonly assumed, and only one who with a specialized interest concerns himself with the Socratic, returning again and again to the sources, only for him would it be of importance on this point to distinguish between Socrates and Plato. The proposition does indeed belong to both, only that Socrates is always departing from it, in order to exist. By holding Socrates down to the proposition that all knowledge is recollection, he becomes a speculative philosopher instead of an existential thinker, for whom existence is the essential thing. The recollection-principle belongs to speculative philosophy, and recollection is immanence, and speculatively and eternally there is no paradox. But the difficulty is that no human being is speculative philosophy; the speculative philosopher himself is an existing individual, subject to the claims that existence makes upon him. There is no merit in forgetting this, but a great merit in holding it fast, and this is precisely what Socrates did. To accentuate existence, which also involves the qualification of inwardness, is the Socratic position; the Platonic tendency, on the other hand,

is to pursue the lure of recollection and immanence. This puts Socrates fundamentally in advance of speculative philosophy; he does not have a fantastic beginning, in which the speculative philosopher first disguises himself, and then goes on and on to speculate, forgetting the most important thing of all, which is to exist. But precisely because Socrates is thus in advance of speculation, he presents, when properly delineated, a certain analogous resemblance to that which the experiment described as in truth going beyond the Socratic. The truth as paradox in the Socratic sense becomes analogous to the paradox *sensu eminentiori,* the passion of inwardness in existing becomes an analogue to faith *sensu eminentiori.* That the difference is none the less infinite, that the characterization which the *Fragments* made of that which in truth goes beyond the Socratic remains unchanged, it will be easy to show; but by using at once apparently the same determinations, or at any rate the same words, about these two different things, I feared to cause a misunderstanding. Now I think there can be no objection to speaking of the paradoxical and of faith in reference to Socrates, since it is quite correct to do so when properly understood. Besides, the old Greeks also used the word πίστις, though not by any means in the sense of the experiment; and they used it in such a manner that, especially with reference to a work of Aristotle where the term is employed, it would be possible to set forth some very enlightening considerations bearing upon its difference from faith *sensu eminentiori.*

But the subject cannot be untruth eternally, or eternally be presupposed as having been untruth; it must have been brought to this condition in time, or here become untruth in time. The Socratic paradox consisted in the fact that the eternal was related to an existing individual, but now existence has stamped itself upon the existing individual a second time. There has taken place so essential an alteration in him that he cannot now possibly take himself back into the eternal by way of recollection. To do this is to speculate; to be able to do this, but to reject the possibility by apprehending the task of life as a realization of inwardness in existing, is the Socratic position. But now the difficulty is that what followed Socrates on his way as a rejected possibility, has become an impossibility. If engaging in speculation was a dubious merit even from the point of view of the Socratic, it is now neither more nor less than confusion.

The paradox emerges when the eternal truth and existence are placed in juxtaposition with one another; each time the stamp of existence is brought to bear, the paradox becomes more clearly evident. Viewed Socratically the knower was simply an existing individual, but now the existing individual bears the stamp of having been essentially altered by existence.

Let us now call the untruth of the individual *Sin*. Viewed eternally he cannot be sin, nor can he be eternally presupposed as having been in sin. By coming into existence therefore (for the beginning was that subjectivity is untruth), he becomes a sinner. He is not born as a sinner in the sense that he is presupposed as being a sinner before he is born, but he is born in sin and as a sinner. This we might call *Original Sin*. But if existence has in this manner acquired a power over him, he is prevented from taking himself back into the eternal by way of recollection. If it was paradoxical to posit the eternal truth in relationship to an existing individual, it is now absolutely paradoxical to posit it in relationship to such an individual as we have here defined. But the more difficult it is made for him to take himself out of existence by way of recollection, the more profound is the inwardness that his existence may have in existence; and when it is made impossible for him, when he is held so fast in existence that

the back door of recollection is forever closed to him, then his inwardness will be the most profound possible. But let us never forget that the Socratic merit was to stress the fact that the knower is an existing individual; for the more difficult the matter becomes, the greater the temptation to hasten along the easy road of speculation, away from fearful dangers and crucial decisions, to the winning of renown and honors and property, and so forth. If even Socrates understood the dubiety of taking himself speculatively out of existence back into the eternal, although no other difficulty confronted the existing individual except that he existed, and that existing was his essential task, now it is impossible. Forward he must, backward he cannot go.

Subjectivity is the truth. By virtue of the relationship subsisting between the eternal truth and the existing individual, the paradox came into being. Let us now go further, let us suppose that the eternal essential truth is itself a paradox. How does the paradox come into being? By putting the eternal essential truth into juxtaposition with existence. Hence when we posit such a conjunction within the truth itself, the truth becomes a paradox. The eternal truth has come into being in time: this is the paradox. If in accordance with the determinations just posited, the subject is prevented by sin from taking himself back into the eternal, now he need not trouble himself about this; for now the eternal essential truth is not behind him but in front of him, through its being in existence or having existed, so that if the individual does not existentially and in existence lay hold of the truth, he will never lay hold of it.

Existence can never be more sharply accentuated than by means of these determinations. The evasion by which speculative philosophy attempts to recollect itself out of existence has been made impossible. With reference to this, there is nothing for speculation to do except to arrive at an understanding of this impossibility; every speculative attempt which insists on being speculative shows *eo ipso* that it has not understood it. The individual may thrust all this away from him, and take refuge in speculation; but it is impossible first to accept it, and then to revoke it by means of speculation, since it is definitely calculated to prevent speculation.

When the eternal truth is related to an existing individual it becomes a paradox. The paradox repels in the inwardness of the existing individual, through the objective uncertainty and the corresponding Socratic ignorance. But since the paradox is not in the first instance itself paradoxical (but only in its relationship to the existing individual), it does not repel with a sufficient intensive inwardness. For without risk there is no faith, and the greater the risk the greater the faith; the more objective security the less inwardness (for inwardness is precisely subjectivity), and the less objective security the more profound the possible inwardness. When the paradox is paradoxical in itself, it repels the individual by virtue of its absurdity, and the corresponding passion of inwardness is faith. But subjectivity, inwardness, is the truth; for otherwise we have forgotten what the merit of the Socratic position is. But there can be no stronger expression for inwardness than when the retreat out of existence into the eternal by way of recollection is impossible; and when, with truth confronting the individual as a paradox, gripped in the anguish and pain of sin, facing the tremendous risk of the objective insecurity, the individual believes. But without risk no faith, not even the Socratic form of faith, much less the form of which we here speak.

When Socrates believed that there was a God, he held fast to the objective uncertainty with the whole passion of his inwardness, and it is precisely in this contradiction and in this risk, that faith is rooted. Now it is otherwise. Instead of the objective uncertainty, there is here a certainty, namely, that objectively it is absurd; and this absurdity, held fast in the passion of inwardness, is faith. The Socratic ignorance is as a witty jest in comparison with the earnestness of facing the absurd; and the Socratic existential inwardness is as Greek light-mindedness in comparison with the grave strenuosity of faith.

What now is the absurd? The absurd is—that the eternal truth has come into being in time, that God has come into being, has been born, has grown up, and so forth, precisely like any other individual human being, quite indistinguishable from other individuals. For every assumption of immediate recognizability is pre-Socratic paganism, and from the Jewish point of view, idolatry; and every determination of what really makes an advance beyond the Socratic must essentially bear the stamp of having a relationship to God's having come into being; for faith *sensu strictissimo*, as was developed in the *Fragments*, refers to becoming. When Socrates believed that there was a God, he saw very well that where the way swings off there is also an objective way of approximation, for example by the contemplation of nature and human history, and so forth. His merit was precisely to shun this way, where the quantitative siren song enchants the mind and deceives the existing individual.

In relation to the absurd, the objective approximation-process is like the comedy, *Misunderstanding upon Misunderstanding*, which is generally played by *Privatdocents* and speculative philosophers. The absurd is precisely by its objective repulsion the measure of the intensity of faith in inwardness. Suppose a man who wishes to acquire faith; let the comedy begin. He wishes to have faith, but he wishes also to safeguard himself by means of an objective inquiry and its approximation-process. What happens? With the help of the approximation-process the absurd becomes something different; it becomes probable, it becomes increasingly probable, it becomes extremely and emphatically probable. Now he is ready to believe it, and he ventures to claim for himself that he does not believe as shoemakers and tailors and simple folk believe, but only after long deliberation. Now he is ready to believe it; and lo, now it has become precisely impossible to believe it. Anything that is almost probable, or probable, or extremely and emphatically probable, is something he can almost know, or as good as know, or extremely and emphatically almost *know*—but it is impossible to *believe*. For the absurd is the object of faith, and the only object that can be believed.

On self-overcoming

Friedrich Nietzsche (1844-1900)

One of the most controversial and many-sided of all philosophers, Nietzsche was born in a small Prussian village, the son of a Lutheran minister. He completed his education at the University of Leipzig, where he came under the influence of Schopenhauer's pessimism, an influence which did not prevent him from excelling in his studies. In 1868 he was appointed to the chair of classical philology at the University of Basel in Switzerland. Though he disliked teaching, he remained in this post until 1879. For several years afterward he traveled and wrote extensively. His books were largely collections of brief essays and aphorisms. The last eleven years of his life were spent in broken health, probably caused by intense literary effort, loneliness, and physical disease.

Nietzsche's books, from his first, The Birth of Tragedy (1872), to his last, a collection of his papers published by his sister after his death with the title The Will to Power, reflect his restless and intense reassessment of modern man. The driving concern of much of his work was the rejection of Christian and "herd" morality and the espousal of a "transvaluation of values." In his poetic work Thus Spoke Zarathustra (1883-1885), he developed one of his central ideas, that of "self-overcoming." Our selection, drawn from several parts of this work, expresses the main outlines of this theme and provides as well a portrait of the Nietzschean hero.

On the adder's bite

One day Zarathustra had fallen asleep under a fig tree, for it was hot, and had put his arms over his face. And an adder came and bit him in the neck, so that Zarathustra cried out in pain. When he had taken his arm from his face, he looked at the snake, and it recognized the eyes of Zarathustra, writhed awkwardly, and wanted to get away. "Oh no," said Zarathustra, "as yet you have not accepted my thanks. You waked me in time, my way is still long." "Your way is short," the adder said sadly; "my poison kills." Zarathustra smiled. "When has a dragon ever died of the poison of a snake?" he said. "But take back your poison. You are not rich enough to give it to me." Then the adder fell around his neck a second time and licked his wound.

When Zarathustra once related this to his disciples they asked: "And what, O Zarathustra, is the moral of your story?" Then Zarathustra answered thus:

The annihilator of morals, the good and just call me: my story is immoral.

But if you have an enemy, do not requite him evil with good, for that would put him to shame. Rather prove that he did you some good.

And rather be angry than put to shame.

From *Thus Spoke Zarathustra,* Pts. 1-4 in *The Portable Nietzsche* by Walter Kaufmann. Copyright, 1954, by The Viking Press, Inc. and reprinted by their permission.

And if you are cursed, I do not like it that you want to bless. Rather join a little in the cursing.

And if you have been done a great wrong, then quickly add five little ones: a gruesome sight is a person single-mindedly obsessed by a wrong.

Did you already know this? A wrong shared is half right. And he who is able to bear it should take the wrong upon himself.

A little revenge is more human than no revenge. And if punishment is not also a right and an honor for the transgressor, then I do not like your punishments either.

It is nobler to declare oneself wrong than to insist on being right—especially when one is right. Only one must be rich enough for that.

I do not like your cold justice; and out of the eyes of your judges there always looks the executioner and his cold steel. Tell me, where is that justice which is love with open eyes? Would that you might invent for me the love that bears not only all punishment but also all guilt! Would that you might invent for me the justice that acquits everyone, except him that judges!

Do you still want to hear this too? In him who would be just through and through even lies become kindness to others. But how could I think of being just through and through? How can I give each his own? Let this be sufficient for me: I give each my own.

Finally, my brothers, beware of doing wrong to any hermit. How could a hermit forget? How could he repay? Like a deep well is a hermit. It is easy to throw in a stone; but if the stone sank to the bottom, tell me, who would get it out again? Beware of insulting the hermit. But if you have done so—well, then kill him too.

Thus spoke Zarathustra. . . .

On self-overcoming

"Will to truth," you who are wisest call that which impels you and fills you with lust?

A will to the thinkability of all beings: this *I* call your will. You want to *make* all being thinkable, for you doubt with well-founded suspicion that it is already thinkable. But it shall yield and bend for you. Thus your will wants it. It shall become smooth and serve the spirit as its mirror and reflection. That is your whole will, you who are wisest: a will to power—when you speak of good and evil too, and of valuations. You still want to create the world before which you can kneel: that is your ultimate hope and intoxication.

The unwise, of course, the people—they are like a river on which a bark drifts; and in the bark sit the valuations, solemn and muffled up. Your will and your valuations you have placed on the river of becoming; and what the people believe to be good and evil, that betrays to me an ancient will to power.

It was you who are wisest who placed such guests in this bark and gave them pomp and proud names—you and your dominant will. Now the river carries your bark farther; it *has* to carry it. It avails nothing that the broken wave foams and angrily opposes the keel. Not the river is your danger and the end of your good and evil, you who are wisest, but that will itself, the will to power—the unexhausted procreative will of life.

But to make you understand my word concerning good and evil, I shall now say to you my word concerning life and the nature of all the living.

I pursued the living; I walked the widest and the narrowest paths that I might know its nature. With a hundredfold mirror I still caught its glance when its mouth was closed, so that its eyes might speak to me. And its eyes spoke to me.

But wherever I found the living, there I heard also the speech on obedience. Whatever lives, obeys.

And this is the second point: he who cannot obey himself is commanded. That is the nature of the living.

This, however, is the third point that I heard: that commanding is harder than obeying; and not only because he who commands must carry the burden of all who obey, and because this burden may easily crush him. An experiment and hazard appeared to me to be in all commanding; and whenever the living commands, it hazards itself. Indeed, even when it commands *itself*, it must still pay for its commanding. It must become the judge, the avenger, and the victim of its own law. How does this happen? I asked myself. What persuades the living to obey and command, and to practice obedience even when it commands?

Hear, then, my word, you who are wisest. Test in all seriousness whether I have crawled into the very heart of life and into the very roots of its heart.

Where I found the living, there I found will to power; and even in the will of those who serve I found the will to be master.

That the weaker should serve the stronger, to that it is persuaded by its own will, which would be master over what is weaker still: this is the one pleasure it does not want to renounce. And as the smaller yields to the greater that it may have pleasure and power over the smallest, thus even the greatest still yields, and for the sake of power risks life. That is the yielding of the greatest: it is hazard and danger and casting dice for death.

And where men make sacrifices and serve and cast amorous glances, there too is the will to be master. Along stealthy paths the weaker steals into the castle and into the very heart of the more powerful—and there steals power.

And life itself confided this secret to me: "Behold," it said, "I am *that which must always overcome itself.* Indeed, you call it a will to procreate or a drive to an end, to something higher, farther, more manifold: but all this is one, and one secret.

"Rather would I perish than forswear this; and verily, where there is perishing and a falling of leaves, behold, there life sacrifices itself—for power. That I must be struggle and a becoming and an end and an opposition to ends—alas, whoever guesses what is my will should also guess on what *crooked* paths it must proceed.

"Whatever I create and however much I love it—soon I must oppose it and my love; thus my will wills it. And you too, lover of knowledge, are only a path and footprint of my will; verily, my will to power walks also on the heels of your will to truth.

"Indeed, the truth was not hit by him who shot at it with the word of the 'will to existence': that will does not exist. For, what does not exist cannot will; but what is in existence, how could that still want existence? Only where there is life is there also will: not will to life but—thus I teach you—will to power.

"There is much that life esteems more highly than life itself; but out of the esteeming itself speaks the will to power."

Thus life once taught me; and with this I shall yet solve the riddle of your heart, you who are wisest.

Verily, I say unto you: good and evil that are not transitory, do not exist. Driven on by themselves, they must overcome themselves again and again. With your values and words of good and evil you do violence when you value; and this is your hidden love and the splendor and trembling and overflowing of your soul. But a more violent force and a new overcoming grow out of your values and break egg and eggshell.

And whoever must be a creator in good and evil, verily, he must first be an annihilator and break values. Thus the highest evil belongs to the highest goodness: but this is creative.

Let us speak of this, you who are wisest, even if it be bad. Silence is worse; all truths that are kept silent become poisonous.

And may everything be broken that cannot brook our truths! There are yet many houses to be built!

Thus spoke Zarathustra.

On those who are sublime

Still is the bottom of my sea: who would guess that it harbors sportive monsters? Imperturbable is my depth, but it sparkles with swimming riddles and laughters.

One who was sublime I saw today, one who was solemn, an ascetic of the spirit; oh, how my soul laughed at his ugliness! With a swelled chest and like one who holds in his breath, he stood there, the sublime one, silent, decked out with ugly truths, the spoil of his hunting, and rich in torn garments; many thorns too adorned him—yet I saw no rose.

As yet he has not learned laughter or

beauty. Gloomy this hunter returned from the woods of knowledge. He came home from a fight with savage beasts; but out of his seriousness there also peers a savage beast—one not overcome. He still stands there like a tiger who wants to leap; but I do not like these tense souls, and my taste does not favor all these who withdraw.

And you tell me, friends, that there is no disputing of taste and tasting? But all of life is a dispute over taste and tasting. Taste—that is at the same time weight and scales and weigher; and woe unto all the living that would live without disputes over weight and scales and weighers!

If he grew tired of his sublimity, this sublime one, only then would his beauty commence; and only then will I taste him and find him tasteful. And only when he turns away from himself, will he jump over his shadow—and verily, into *his* sun. All-too-long has he been sitting in the shadow, and the cheeks of this ascetic of the spirit have grown pale; he almost starved to death on his expectations. Contempt is still in his eyes, and nausea hides around his mouth. Though he is resting now, his rest has not yet lain in the sun. He should act like a bull, and his happiness should smell of the earth, and not of contempt for the earth. I would like to see him as a white bull, walking before the plowshare, snorting and bellowing; and his bellowing should be in praise of everything earthly.

His face is still dark; the shadow of the hand plays upon him. His sense of sight is still in shadows. His deed itself still lies on him as a shadow: the hand still darkens the doer. As yet he has not overcome his deed.

Though I love the bull's neck on him, I also want to see the eyes of the angel. He must still discard his heroic will; he shall be elevated, not merely sublime: the ether itself should elevate him, the will-less one.

He subdued monsters, he solved riddles: but he must still redeem his own monsters and riddles, changing them into heavenly children. As yet his knowledge has not learned to smile and to be without jealousy; as yet his torrential passion has not become still in beauty.

Verily, it is not in satiety that his desire shall grow silent and be submerged, but in beauty. Gracefulness is part of the graciousness of the great-souled.

His arm placed over his head: thus should the hero rest; thus should he overcome even his rest. But just for the hero the *beautiful* is the most difficult thing. No violent will can attain the beautiful by exertion. A little more, a little less: precisely this counts for much here, this matters most here.

To stand with relaxed muscles and unharnessed will: that is most difficult for all of you who are sublime.

When power becomes gracious and descends into the visible—such descent I call beauty.

And there is nobody from whom I want beauty as much as from you who are powerful: let your kindness be your final self-conquest.

Of all evil I deem you capable: therefore I want the good from you.

Verily, I have often laughed at the weaklings who thought themselves good because they had no claws.

You shall strive after the virtue of the column: it grows more and more beautiful and gentle, but internally harder and more enduring, as it ascends.

Indeed, you that are sublime shall yet become beautiful one day and hold up a mirror to your own beauty. Then your soul will shudder with godlike desires, and there will be adoration even in your vanity.

For this is the soul's secret: only when the hero has abandoned her, she is approached in a dream by the overhero.

Thus spoke Zarathustra. . . .

On the vision and the riddle

When it got abroad among the sailors that Zarathustra was on board—for another man from the blessed isles had embarked with him —there was much curiosity and anticipation. But Zarathustra remained silent for two days and was cold and deaf from sadness and answered neither glances nor questions. But on the evening of the second day he opened his ears again, although he still remained silent, for there was much that was strange and dangerous to be heard on this ship, which came from far away and wanted to sail even farther. But Zarathustra was a friend of all who travel far and do not like to live without danger. And behold, eventually his own tongue was loosened as he listened, and the ice of his heart broke. Then he began to speak thus:

To you, the bold searchers, researchers, and whoever embarks with cunning sails on terrible seas—to you, drunk with riddles, glad of the twilight, whose soul flutes lure astray to every whirlpool, because you do not want to grope along a thread with cowardly hand; and where you can *guess*, you hate to *deduce*—to you alone I tell the riddle that I *saw*, the vision of the loneliest.

Not long ago I walked gloomily through the deadly pallor of dusk—gloomy and hard, with lips pressed together. Not only one sun had set for me. A path that ascended defiantly through stones, malicious, lonely, not cheered by herb or shrub—a mountain path crunched under the defiance of my foot. Striding silently over the mocking clatter of pebbles, crushing the rock that made it slip, my foot forced its way upward. Upward—defying the spirit that drew it downward toward the abyss, the spirit of gravity, my devil and archenemy. Upward—although he sat on me, half dwarf, half mole, lame, making lame, dripping lead into my ear, leaden thoughts into my brain.

"O Zarathustra," he whispered mockingly, syllable by syllable; "you philosopher's stone! You threw yourself up high, but every stone that is thrown must fall. O Zarathustra, you philosopher's stone, you slingstone, you starcrusher! You threw yourself up so high; but every stone that is thrown must fall. Sentenced to yourself and to your own stoning—O Zarathustra, far indeed have you thrown the stone, but it will fall back on yourself."

Then the dwarf fell silent, and that lasted a long time. His silence, however, oppressed me; and such twosomeness is surely more lonesome than being alone. I climbed, I climbed, I dreamed, I thought; but everything oppressed me. I was like one sick whom his wicked torture makes weary, and who as he falls asleep is awakened by a still more wicked dream. But there is something in me that I call courage; that has so far slain my every discouragement. This courage finally bade me stand still and speak: "Dwarf! It is you or I!"

For courage is the best slayer, courage which *attacks*; for in every attack there is playing and brass.

Man, however, is the most courageous animal: hence he overcame every animal. With playing and brass he has so far overcome every pain; but human pain is the deepest pain.

Courage also slays dizziness at the edge of abysses: and where does man not stand at the edge of abysses? Is not seeing always—seeing abysses?

Courage is the best slayer: courage slays even pity. But pity is the deepest abyss: as deeply as man sees into life, he also sees into suffering.

Courage, however, is the best slayer—courage which attacks: which slays even death itself, for it says, "Was *that* life? Well then! Once more!"

In such words, however, there is much playing and brass. He that has ears to hear, let him hear! . . .

Before sunrise

O heaven above me, pure and deep! You abyss of light! Seeing you, I tremble with godlike desires. To throw myself into your height, that is *my* depth. To hide in your purity, that is *my* innocence.

Gods are shrouded by their beauty; thus you conceal your stars. You do not speak; thus you proclaim your wisdom to me. Today you rose for me silently over the roaring sea; your love and your shyness are a revelation to my roaring soul. That you came to me, beautiful, shrouded in your beauty, that you speak to me silently, revealing your wisdom—oh, how should I not guess all that is shy in your soul! *Before* the sun you came to me, the loneliest of all.

We are friends from the beginning: we share grief and ground and gray dread; we even share the sun. We do not speak to each other, because we know too much; we are silent to each other, we smile our knowledge at each other. Are you not the light for my fire? Have you not the sister soul to my insight? Together we have learned everything; together we have learned to ascend over ourselves to ourselves and to smile cloudlessly—to smile down cloudlessly from bright eyes and from a vast distance when constraint and contrivance and guilt steam beneath us like rain.

And when I wandered alone, for *whom* did my soul hunger at night, on false paths? And when I climbed mountains, *whom* did I always seek on the mountains, if not you? And all my wandering and mountain climbing were sheer necessity and a help in my helplessness: what I want with all my will is to *fly*, to fly up into *you*.

And whom did I hate more than drifting clouds and all that stains you? And I hated even my own hatred because it stained you. I loathe the drifting clouds, those stealthy great cats which prey on what you and I have in common —the uncanny, unbounded Yes and Amen. We loathe these mediators and mixers, the drifting clouds that are half-and-half and have learned neither to bless nor to curse from the heart.

Rather would I sit in a barrel under closed heavens, rather sit in the abyss without a heaven, than see you, bright heaven, stained by drifting clouds.

And often I had the desire to tie them fast with the jagged golden wires of the lightning, that, like thunder, I might beat the big drums on their kettle-belly—an angry kettle-drummer —because they rob me of your Yes and Amen, O heaven over me, pure and light! You abyss of light! Because they rob you of *my* Yes and Amen. For I prefer even noise and thunder and storm-curses to this deliberate, doubting cats' calm; and among men too I hate most of all the soft-treaders and those who are half-and-half and doubting, tottering drift clouds.

And "whoever cannot bless should *learn* to curse"—this bright doctrine fell to me from a bright heaven; this star stands in my heaven even in black nights.

But I am one who can bless and say Yes, if only you are about me, pure and light, you abyss of light; then I carry the blessings of my

Yes into all abysses. I have become one who blesses and says Yes; and I fought long for that and was a fighter that I might one day get my hands free to bless. But this is my blessing: to stand over every single thing as its own heaven, as its round roof, its azure bell, and eternal security; and blessed is he who blesses thus.

For all things have been baptized in the well of eternity and are beyond good and evil; and good and evil themselves are but intervening shadows and damp depressions and drifting clouds.

Verily, it is a blessing and not a blasphemy when I teach: "Over all things stand the heaven Accident, the heaven Innocence, the heaven Chance, the heaven Prankishness."

"By Chance"—that is the most ancient nobility of the world, and this I restored to all things: I delivered them from their bondage under Purpose. This freedom and heavenly cheer I have placed over all things like an azure bell when I taught that over them and through them no "eternal will" wills. This prankish folly I have put in the place of that will when I taught: "In everything one thing is impossible: rationality."

A *little* reason, to be sure, a seed of wisdom scattered from star to star—this leaven is mixed in with all things: for folly's sake, wisdom is mixed in with all things. A little wisdom is possible indeed; but this blessed certainty I found in all things: that they would rather *dance* on the feet of Chance.

O heaven over me, pure and high! That is what your purity is to me now, that there is no eternal spider or spider web of reason; that you are to me a dance floor for divine accidents, that you are to me a divine table for divine dice and dice players. But you blush? Did I speak the unspeakable? Did I blaspheme, wishing to bless you? Or is it the shame of twosomeness that makes you blush? Do you bid me go and be silent because the *day* is coming now?

The world is deep—and deeper than day had ever been aware. Not everything may be put into words in the presence of the day. But the day is coming, so let us part.

O heaven over me, bashful and glowing! O

you, my happiness before sunrise! The day is coming, so let us part!

Thus spoke Zarathustra....

On the higher man

... This crown of him who laughs, this rose-wreath crown: I myself have put on this crown, I myself have pronounced my laughter holy. Nobody else have I found strong enough for this today.

Zarathustra the dancer, Zarathustra the light, waves with his wings, ready for flight, waving at all birds, ready and heady, happily light-headed; Zarathustra the soothsayer, Zarathustra the sooth-laugher, not impatient, not unconditional, one who loves leaps and side-leaps: I myself have put on this crown!

Lift up your hearts, my brothers, high, higher! And do not forget your legs either. Lift up your legs too, you good dancers; and better yet, stand on your heads!

In happiness too there are heavy animals; there are ponderous-pedes through and through. Curiously they labor, like an elephant laboring to stand on its head. But it is still better to be foolish from happiness than foolish from unhappiness; better to dance ponderously than to walk lamely. That you would learn my wisdom from me: even the worst thing has two good reverse sides—even the worst thing has good dancing legs; that you would learn, you higher men, to put yourselves on your right legs! That you would unlearn nursing melancholy and all mob-sadness! Oh, how sad even the mob's clowns seem to me today! But this today is the mob's.

Be like the wind rushing out of his mountain caves: he wishes to dance to his own pipe; the seas tremble and leap under his feet.

What gives asses wings, what milks lionesses—praised be this good intractable spirit that comes like a cyclone to all today and to all the mob. What is averse to thistle-heads and casuists' heads and to all wilted leaves and weeds—praised be this wild, good, free storm spirit that dances on swamps and on melancholy as on meadows. What hates the mob's blethercocks and all the bungled gloomy brood—praised be this spirit of all free spirits, the laughing gale that blows dust into the eyes of all the black-sighted, sore-blighted.

You higher men, the worst about you is that all of you have not learned to dance as one must dance—dancing away over yourselves! What does it matter that you are failures? How much is still possible! So *learn* to laugh away over yourselves! Lift up your hearts, you good dancers, high, higher! And do not forget good laughter. This crown of him who laughs, this rose-wreath crown: to you, my brothers, I throw this crown. Laughter I have pronounced holy; you higher men, *learn* to laugh!

The life of dialogue

Martin Buber (1878-1965)

The foremost contemporary Jewish philosopher and theologian, Martin Buber was born in Vienna and grew up in the home of his grandfather, Solomon Buber, one of the last great scholars of an era of Judaism known as the Enlightenment. He studied philosophy and art history and received the Ph.D. in 1904 from the University of Berlin. A Zionist and leader of Jewish thought, Buber taught philosophy of religion at the University of Frankfurt from 1923 to 1933 and became the chief exponent of the movement in Judaism known as Hasidism. In 1938 he left Germany for Palestine to become professor at the Hebrew University. He retired in 1951 but continued to live in Jerusalem, Israel, until his death. Buber's published writings cover an unusual range. They include studies of the biblical prophets and of the religions of the Orient, discussions of pedagogical theory and of contemporary existentialist thinkers, as well as contributions to political thought. In his fictional writings he has retold the tales of the Hasidic rabbis. In his most influential work, I and Thou, *which first appeared in 1923, he presented in a poetic manner his view of the dialogical relation. In subsequent essays, collected in* Between Man and Man *and* Pointing the Way, *he has developed some of the consequences of his view of the I–Thou relation. In the following selection he expresses his central conception, that of the life of dialogue.*

Responsibility

The idea of responsibility is to be brought back from the province of specialized ethics, of an "ought" that swings free in the air, into that of lived life. Genuine responsibility exists only where there is real responding.

Responding to what?

To what happens to one, to what is to be seen and heard and felt. Each concrete hour allotted to the person, with its content drawn from the world and from destiny, is speech for the man who is attentive. Attentive, for no more than that is needed in order to make a beginning with the reading of the signs that are given to you. For that very reason, as I have already indicated, the whole apparatus of our civilization is necessary to preserve men from this attentiveness and its consequences. For the attentive man would no longer, as his custom is, "master" the situation the very moment after it stepped up to him: it would be laid upon him to go up to and into it. Moreover, nothing that he believed he possessed as always available would help him, no knowledge and no technique, no system and no programme; for now he would have to do with what cannot be classified, with concretion itself. This speech has no alphabet, each of its sounds is a new creation and only to be grasped as such.

It will, then, be expected of the attentive

Reprinted from *Between Man and Man* by Martin Buber, tr. Ronald Gregor Smith, with permission of the Macmillan Company, N.Y. and Routledge & Kegan Paul, Ltd. First published in 1947 by Routledge & Kegan Paul, Ltd.

man that he faces creation as it happens. It happens as speech, and not as speech rushing out over his head but as speech directed precisely at him. And if one were to ask another if he too heard and he said he did, they would have agreed only about an experiencing and not about something experienced.

But the sounds of which the speech consists —I repeat it in order to remove the misunderstanding, which is perhaps still possible, that I referred to something extraordinary and larger than life—are the events of the personal everyday life. In them, as they now are, "great" or "small," we are addressed, and those which count as great, yield no greater signs than the others.

Our attitude, however, is not yet decided through our becoming aware of the signs. We can still wrap silence about us—a reply characteristic of a significant type of the age—or we can step aside into the accustomed way; although both times we carry away a wound that is not to be forgotten in any productivity or any narcotism. Yet it can happen that we venture to respond, stammering perhaps—the soul is but rarely able to attain to surer articulation—but it is an honest stammering, as when sense and throat are united about what is to be said, but the throat is too horrified at it to utter purely the already composed sense. The words of our response are spoken in the speech, untranslatable like the address, of doing and letting—whereby the doing may behave like a letting and the letting like a doing. What we say in this way with the being is our entering upon the situation, into the situation, which has at this moment stepped up to us, whose appearance we did not and could not know, for its like has not yet been.

Nor are we now finished with it, we have to give up that expectation: a situation of which we have become aware is never finished with, but we subdue it into the substance of lived life. Only then, true to the moment, do we experience a life that is something other than a sum of moments. We respond to the moment, but at the same time we respond on its behalf, we answer for it. A newly-created concrete reality has been laid in our arms; we answer

for it. A dog has looked at you, you answer for its glance, a child has clutched your hand, you answer for its touch, a host of men moves about you, you answer for their need.

Morality and religion

Responsibility which does not respond to a word is a metaphor of morality. Factually, responsibility only exists when the court is there to which I am responsible, and "self-responsibility" has reality only when the "self" to which I am responsible becomes transparent into the absolute. But he who practises real responsibility in the life of dialogue does not need to name the speaker of the word to which he is responding—he knows him in the word's substance which presses on and in, assuming the cadence of an inwardness, and stirs him in his heart of hearts. A man can ward off with all his strength the belief that "God" is there, and he tastes him in the strict sacrament of dialogue.

Yet let it not be supposed that I make morality questionable in order to glorify religion. Religion, certainly, has this advantage over morality, that it is a phenomenon and not a postulate, and further that it is able to include composure as well as determination. The reality of morality, the demand of the demander, has a place in religion, but the reality of religion, the unconditioned being of the demander, has no place in morality. Nevertheless, when religion does itself justice and asserts itself, it is much more dubious than morality, just because it is more actual and inclusive. Religion as risk, which is ready to give itself up, is the nourishing stream of the arteries; as system, possessing, assured and assuring, religion which believes in religion is the veins' blood, which ceases to circulate. And if there is nothing that can so hide the face of our fellow-man as morality can, religion can hide from us as nothing else can the face of God. Principle there, dogma here, I appreciate the "objective" compactness of dogma, but behind both there lies in wait the— profane or holy—war against the situation's power of dialogue, there lies in wait the "once-for-all" which resists the unforeseeable moment. Dogma, even when its claim of origin remains uncontested, has become the most exalted form of invulnerability against revelation. Revelation will tolerate no perfect tense, but man with the arts of his craze for security props it up to perfectedness.

The realms

The realms of the life of dialogue and the life of monologue do not coincide with the realms of dialogue and monologue even when forms without sound and even without gesture are included. There are not merely great spheres of the life of dialogue which in appearance are not dialogue, there is also dialogue which is not the dialogue of life, that is, it has the appearance but not the essence of dialogue. At times, indeed, it seems as though there were only this kind of dialogue.

I know three kinds. There is genuine dialogue—no matter whether spoken or silent—where each of the participants really has in mind the other or others in their present and particular being and turns to them with the intention of establishing a living mutual relation between himself and them. There is technical dialogue, which is prompted solely by the need of objective understanding. And there is monologue disguised as dialogue, in which two or more men, meeting in space, speak each with himself in strangely tortuous and circuitous ways and yet imagine they have escaped the torment of being thrown back on their own resources. The first kind, as I have said, has become rare; where it arises, in no matter how "unspiritual" a form, witness is borne on behalf of the continuance of the organic substance of the human spirit. The second belongs to the inalienable sterling quality of "modern existence." But real dialogue is here continually hidden in all kinds of odd corners and, occasionally in an unseemly way, breaks surface surprisingly and inopportunely—certainly still oftener it is arrogantly tolerated than downright scandalizing—as in the tone of a railway guard's voice, in the glance of an old newspaper vendor, in the smile of the chimney-sweeper. And the third. . . .

A *debate* in which the thoughts are not expressed in the way in which they existed in the mind but in the speaking are so pointed that they may strike home in the sharpest way, and moreover without the men that are spoken to being regarded in any way present as persons; a *conversation* characterized by the need neither to communicate something, nor to learn something, nor to influence someone, nor to come into connexion with someone, but solely by the desire to have one's own self-reliance confirmed by marking the impression that is made, or if it has become unsteady to have it strengthened; a *friendly chat* in which each regards himself as absolute and legitimate and the other as relativized and questionable; a *lovers' talk* in which both partners alike enjoy their own glorious soul and their precious experience—what an underworld of faceless spectres of dialogue!

The life of dialogue is not one in which you have much to do with men, but one in which you really have to do with those with whom you have to do. It is not the solitary man who lives the life of monologue, but he who is incapable of making real in the context of being the community in which, in the context of his destiny, he moves. It is, in fact, solitude which is able to show the innermost nature of the contrast. He who is living the life of dialogue receives in the ordinary course of the hours something that is said and feels himself approached for an answer. But also in the vast blankness of, say, a companionless mountain wandering that which confronts him, rich in change, does not leave him. He who is living the life of monologue is never aware of the other as something that is absolutely not himself and at the same time something with which he nevertheless communicates. Solitude for him can mean mounting richness of visions and thoughts but never the deep intercourse, captured in a new depth, with the incomprehensibly real. Nature for him is either an *état d'âme*, hence a "living through" in himself, or it is a passive object of knowledge, either idealistically brought within the soul or realistically alienated. It does not become for him a word apprehended with senses of beholding and feeling.

Being, lived in dialogue, receives even in extreme dereliction a harsh and strengthening sense of reciprocity; being, lived in monologue, will not, even in the tenderest intimacy, grope out over the outlines of the self.

This must not be confused with the contrast between "egoism" and "altruism" conceived by some moralists. I know people who are absorbed in "social activity" and have never spoken from being to being with a fellow-man. I know others who have no personal relation except to their enemies, but stand in such a relation to them that it is the enemies' fault if the relation does not flourish into one of dialogue.

Nor is dialogic to be identified with love. I know no one in any time who has succeeded in loving every man he met. Even Jesus obviously loved of "sinners" only the loose, lovable sinners, sinners against the Law; not those who were settled and loyal to their inheritance and sinned against him and his message. Yet to the latter as to the former he stood in a direct relation. Dialogic is not to be identified with love. But love without dialogic, without real outgoing to the other, reaching to the other, and companying with the other, the love remaining with itself—this is called Lucifer.

Certainly in order to be able to go out to the other you must have the starting place, you must have been, you must be, with yourself. Dialogue between mere individuals is only a sketch, only in dialogue between persons is the sketch filled in. But by what could a man from being an individual so really become a person as by the strict and sweet experiences of dialogue which teach him the boundless contents of the boundary?

What is said here is the real contrary of the cry, heard at times in twilight ages, for universal unreserve. He who can be unreserved with each passer-by has no substance to lose; but he who cannot stand in a direct relation to each one who meets him has a fulness which is futile. Luther is wrong to change the Hebrew "companion" (out of which the Seventy had already made one who is near, a neighbour) into "nearest." If everything concrete is equally near, equally nearest, life with the world

ceases to have articulation and structure, it ceases to have human meaning. But nothing needs to mediate between me and one of my companions in the companionship of creation, whenever we come near one another, because we are bound up in relation to the same centre.

The basic movements

I term basic movement an essential action of man (it may be understood as an "inner" action, but it is not there unless it is there to the very tension of the eyes' muscles and the very action of the foot as it walks), round which an essential attitude is built up. I do not think of this happening in time, as though the single action preceded the lasting attitude; the latter rather has its truth in the accomplishing, over and over again, of the basic movement, without forethought but also without habit. Otherwise the attitude would have only æsthetic or perhaps also political significance, as a beautiful and as an effective lie. The familiar maxim, "An attitude must first be adopted, the rest follows of itself" ceases to be true in the circle of essential action and essential attitude—that is, where we are concerned with the wholeness of the person.

The basic movement of the life of dialogue is the turning towards the other. That, indeed, seems to happen every hour and quite trivially. If you look at someone and address him you turn to him, of course with the body, but also in the requisite measure with the soul, in that you direct your attention to him. But what of all this is an essential action, done with the essential being? In this way, that out of the incomprehensibility of what lies to hand this one person steps forth and becomes a presence. Now to our perception the world ceases to be an insignificant multiplicity of points to one of which we pay momentary attention. Rather it is a limitless tumult round a narrow breakwater, brightly outlined and able to bear heavy loads —limitless, but limited by the breakwater, so that, though not engirdled, it has become finite in itself, been given form, released from its own indifference. And yet none of the contacts of each hour is unworthy to take up from our essential being as much as it may. For no man is without strength for expression, and our turning towards him brings about a reply, however imperceptible, however quickly smothered, in a looking and sounding forth of the soul that are perhaps dissipating in mere inwardness and yet do exist. The notion of modern man that this turning to the other is sentimental and does not correspond to the compression of life today is a grotesque error, just as his affirmation that turning to the other is impractical in the bustle of this life today is only the masked confession of his weakness of initiative when confronted with the state of the time. He lets it dictate to him what is possible or permissible, instead of stipulating, as an unruffled partner, what is to be stipulated to the state of *every* time, namely, what space and what form it is bound to concede to creaturely existence.

The basic movement of the life of monologue is not turning away as opposed to turning towards; it is "reflexion."

When I was eleven years of age, spending the summer on my grandparents' estate, I used, as often as I could do it unobserved, to steal into the stable and gently stroke the neck of my darling, a broad dapple-grey horse. It was not a casual delight but a great, certainly friendly, but also deeply stirring happening. If I am to explain it now, beginning from the still very fresh memory of my hand, I must say that what I experienced in touch with the animal was the Other, the immense otherness of the Other, which, however, did not remain strange like the otherness of the ox and the ram, but rather let me draw near and touch it. When I stroked the mighty mane, sometimes marvellously smooth-combed, at other times just as astonishingly wild, and felt the life beneath my hand, it was as though the element of vitality itself bordered on my skin, something that was not I, was certainly not akin to me, palpably the other, not just another, really the Other itself; and yet it let me approach, confided itself to me, placed itself elementally in the relation of *Thou* and *Thou* with me. The horse, even when I had not begun by pouring oats for him into the manger, very gently raised his massive head, ears flicking, then

snorted quietly, as a conspirator gives a signal meant to be recognizable only by his fellow-conspirator; and I was approved. But once—I do not know what came over the child, at any rate it was childlike enough—it struck me about the stroking, what fun it gave me, and suddenly I became conscious of my hand. The game went on as before, but something had changed, it was no longer the same thing. And the next day, after giving him a rich feed, when I stroked my friend's head he did not raise his head. A few years later, when I thought back to the incident, I no longer supposed that the animal had noticed my defection. But at the time I considered myself judged.

Reflexion is something different from egoism and even from "egotism." It is not that a man is concerned with himself, considers himself, fingers himself, enjoys, idolizes and bemoans himself; all that can be added, but it is not integral to reflexion. (Similarly, to the turning towards the other, completing it, there can be added the realizing of the other in his particular existence, even the encompassing of him, so that the situations common to him and oneself are experienced also from his, the other's, end.) I term it reflexion when a man withdraws from accepting with his essential being another person in his particularity—a particularity which is by no means to be circumscribed by the circle of his own self, and though it substantially touches and moves his soul is in no way immanent in it—and lets the other exist only as his own experience, only as a "part of myself." For then dialogue becomes a fiction, the mysterious intercourse between two human worlds only a game, and in the rejection of the real life confronting him the essence of all reality begins to disintegrate.

The wordless depths

Sometimes I hear it said that every *I and Thou* is only superficial, deep down word and response cease to exist, there is only the one primal being unconfronted by another. We should plunge into the silent unity, but for the rest leave its relativity to the life to be lived, instead of imposing on it this absolutized

I and absolutized *Thou* with their dialogue.

Now from my own unforgettable experience I know well that there is a state in which the bonds of the personal nature of life seem to have fallen away from us and we experience an undivided unity. But I do not know—what the soul willingly imagines and indeed is bound to imagine (mine too once did it)—that in this I had attained to a union with the primal being or the godhead. That is an exaggeration no longer permitted to the responsible understanding. Responsibly—that is, as a man holding his ground before reality—I can elicit from those experiences only that in them I reached an undifferentiable unity of myself without form or content. I may call this an original prebiographical unity and suppose that it is hidden unchanged beneath all biographical change, all development and complication of the soul. Nevertheless, in the honest and sober account of the responsible understanding this unity is nothing but the unity of this soul of mine, whose "ground" I have reached, so much so, beneath all formations and contents, that my spirit has no choice but to understand it as the groundless. But the basic unity of my own soul is certainly beyond the reach of all the multiplicity it has hitherto received from life, though not in the least beyond individuation, or the multiplicity of all the souls in the world of which it is one—existing but once, single, unique, irreducible, this creaturely one: one of the human souls and not the "soul of the All"; a defined and particular being and not "Being"; the creaturely basic unity of a creature, bound to God as in the instant before release the creature is to the *creator spiritus*, not bound to God as the creature to the *creator spiritus* in the moment of release.

The unity of his own self is not distinguishable in the man's feeling from unity in general. For he who in the act or event of absorption is sunk beneath the realm of all multiplicity that holds sway in the soul cannot experience the cessation of multiplicity except as unity itself. That is, he experiences the cessation of his own multiplicity as the cessation of mutuality, as revealed or fulfilled absence of otherness. The being which has become one can no longer understand itself on this side of individuation nor indeed on this side of *I and Thou*. For to the border experience of the soul "one" must apparently mean the same as "the One."

But in the actuality of lived life the man in such a moment is not above but beneath the creaturely situation, which is mightier and truer than all ecstasies. He is not above but beneath dialogue. He is not nearer the God who is hidden above *I and Thou*, and he is farther from the God who is turned to men and who gives himself as the *I* to a *Thou* and the *Thou* to an *I*, than that other who in prayer and service and life does not step out of the position of confrontation and awaits no wordless unity, except that which perhaps bodily death discloses.

Nevertheless, even he who lives the life of dialogue knows a lived unity: the unity of *life*, as that which once truly won is no more torn by any changes, not ripped asunder into the everyday creaturely life and the "deified" exalted hours; the unity of unbroken, raptureless perseverance in concreteness, in which the word is heard and a stammering answer dared.

On the philosophical life

Karl Jaspers (b. 1883)

A psychiatrist who later became one of the towering figures of contemporary philosophy, Jaspers was born in Oldenburg, Germany, the son of a bank director. He studied law as a young man, and then medicine. He was a scientific assistant in the psychiatric clinic in Heidelberg before World War I and was appointed to the chair of philosophy there in 1921, after five years of teaching psychology. He was dismissed from this post by the Hitler government in 1937 for political reasons and was reinstated in 1945. Since 1948 he has been professor of philosophy at Basel, Switzerland.

Jaspers' major works include General Psychopathology *(1913),* Psychology of Weltanschauungen *(1919), the three-volume* Philosophy *(1932),* Reason and Existenz *(1935), and* Of Truth *(1947). He has also published several shorter and less systematic works, as well as studies of Nietzsche and Descartes and of a number of the great philosophers.*

Our selection consists of two portions of his book published in English with the title The Way to Wisdom *(1951). Jaspers rejects a philosophy of fixed content in favor of the process of philosophizing. In the following discussion he speaks of the philosophic life, or, as he prefers to call it, "the philosophic practice of life."*

The history of philosophy as methodical thinking began twenty-five hundred years ago, but as mythical thought much earlier.

The beginning however is something quite different from the source. The beginning is historical and provides those who follow with a mounting accumulation of insights. But it is always from the source that the impulsion to philosophize springs. The source alone lends meaning to present philosophy and through it alone is past philosophy understood.

This source is of many kinds. Wonderment gives rise to question and insight; man's doubt in the knowledge he has attained gives rise to critical examination and clear certainty; his

From Karl Jaspers, *The Way to Wisdom,* tr. Ralph Manheim, Chs. 2 and 11. Copyright, 1951, by Yale University Press. Used by permission.

awe and sense of forsakenness lead him to inquire into himself. And now let us examine these three drives.

First: Plato said that the source of philosophy was wonder. Our eyes gave us "the sight of the stars, the sun and the firmament." This "impelled us to examine the universe, whence grew philosophy, the greatest good conferred upon mortals by the gods." And Aristotle: "For it is owing to their wonder that men both now begin and at first began to philosophize: they wondered originally at the obvious difficulties, then advanced little by little and stated difficulties about the greater matters, e.g., about the phenomena of the moon, and those of the sun, and of the stars, and about the genesis of the universe."

Wonder impels man to seek knowledge. In my wonderment I become aware of my lack of knowledge. I seek knowledge, but for its own sake or not "to satisfy any common need."

In philosophical thought man awakens from his bondage to practical needs. Without ulterior purpose he contemplates things, the heavens, the world, and asks, what is all this? Where does it come from? From the answers to his questions he expects no profit but an intrinsic satisfaction.

Second: Once I have satisfied my wonderment and admiration by knowledge of what is, *doubt* arises. I have heaped up insights, but upon critical examination nothing is certain. Sensory perceptions are conditioned by our sense organs and hence deceptive; in any event they do not coincide with what exists in itself outside me, independently of my perception. Our categories are those of our human understanding. They become entangled in hopeless contradictions. Everywhere proposition stands against proposition. In my philosophical progress I seize upon doubt and attempt to apply it radically to everything, either taking pleasure in the sceptical negation which recognizes nothing but by itself cannot take a single step forward, or inquiring: Where then is there a certainty that rises above all doubt and withstands all critique?

Descartes' famous proposition, "I think, therefore I am," was for him a solid certainty, though he doubted everything else. For even a total fallacy in my thinking, a fallacy which may be beyond my understanding, cannot blind me to the realization that in order to be deluded in my thinking I must *be*.

Methodical doubt gives rise to a critical examination of all knowledge, and without radical doubt there can be no true philosophical thought. But the crucial question is: How and where has a foundation for certainty been gained through doubt itself?

And third: While I concentrate my energies upon the knowledge of things in the world, while I am engaged in doubt as a road to certainty, I am immersed in things; I do not think of myself, of my aims, my happiness, my salvation. In forgetfulness of my self I am content with the attainment of this knowledge.

This changes when I become aware of myself in my situation.

The Stoic Epictetus said, "Philosophy arises when we become *aware of our own weakness and helplessness.*" How shall I help myself in my weakness? His answer was: By looking upon everything that is not within my power as necessary and indifferent to me, but by raising what does depend on me, namely the mode and content of my ideas, to clarity and freedom by thought.

And now let us take a look at our human state. We are always in situations. Situations change, opportunities arise. If they are missed they never return. I myself can work to change the situation. But there are situations which remain essentially the same even if their momentary aspect changes and their shattering force is obscured: I must die, I must suffer, I must struggle, I am subject to chance, I involve myself inexorably in guilt. We call these fundamental situations of our existence ultimate situations.[1] That is to say, they are situations which we cannot evade or change. Along with wonder and doubt, awareness of these ultimate situations is the most profound source of philosophy. In our day-to-day lives we often evade them, by closing our eyes and living as if they did not exist. We forget that we must die, forget our guilt, and forget that we are at the mercy of chance. We face only concrete situations and master them to our profit, we react to them by planning and acting in the world, under the impulsion of our practical interests. But to ultimate situations we react either by obfuscation or, if we really apprehend them, by despair and rebirth: we become ourselves by a change in our consciousness of being.

[1] The term here translated as "ultimate situation" is *Grenzsituation*. This is a concept of central importance for the understanding of Jaspers' thought, as for the understanding of Existentialism. As the context above shows, the ultimate situations are the inescapable realities in relation to which alone human life can be made genuinely meaningful. Ultimate situations cannot be changed or surmounted; they can only be acknowledged. [Translator's note.]

Or we may define our human situation by saying that *no reliance can be placed in worldly existence.*

Ingenuously we mistake the world for being as such. In happy situations we rejoice at our strength, we are thoughtlessly confident, we know nothing but our actuality. In pain and weakness we despair. But if we come out of this situation alive we let ourselves slip back into forgetfulness of self and a life of happiness.

Such experience however has sharpened man's wits. The menace beneath which he lives drives him to seek security. He expects his mastery of nature and his community with other men to guarantee his existence.

Man gains power over nature in order to make it serve him; through science and technology he seeks to make it reliable.

But in man's domination of nature there remains an element of the incalculable which represents a constant threat, and the end is always failure: hard labour, old age, sickness and death cannot be done away with. Our dominated nature is reliable only in isolated cases; in the whole we can place no reliance.

Men band together in a community in order to limit and ultimately abolish the endless struggle of all against all; they seek to achieve security through mutual aid.

But here again there is a limit. Only if there were states in which every citizen stood to every other in a relation of absolute solidarity could justice and freedom be secure. For only then, if a citizen suffered injustice, would all others oppose it as one man. Such a state has never been seen. Those who have stood by one another in extremity and weakness have never been more than limited groups, and sometimes no more than a few individuals. No state, no church, no society offers absolute security. Such security has been a pleasing delusion of quiet times, in which the ultimate situations were veiled.

But there is a counterweight to the general unreliability of the world: there are in the world things worthy of faith, things that arouse confidence; there is a foundation which sustains us: home and country, parents and ancestors, brothers and sisters and friends, husbands and wives. There is a foundation of historical tradition, in native language, in faith, in the work of thinkers, poets, and artists. However, this tradition also gives no security, it is not absolutely reliable. For we encounter it always as the work of man; God is nowhere in the world. Tradition always implies a question. Keeping sight of the tradition, man must always derive what for him is certainty, being, the reliable, from his own primal source. But the precariousness of all worldly existence is a warning to us, it forbids us to content ourselves with the world; it points to something else.

The ultimate situations—death, chance, guilt, and the uncertainty of the world—confront me with the reality of failure. What do I do in the face of this absolute failure, which if I am honest I cannot fail to recognize?

The advice of the Stoic, to withdraw to our own freedom in the independence of the mind, is not adequate. The Stoic's perception of man's weakness was not radical enough. He failed to see that the mind in itself is empty, dependent on what is put into it, and he failed to consider the possibility of madness. The Stoic leaves us without consolation; the independent mind is barren, lacking all content. He leaves us without hope, because his doctrine affords us no opportunity of inner transformation, no fulfilment through self-conquest in love, no hopeful expectation of the possible.

And yet the Stoics' striving is toward true philosophy. Their thought, because its source is in ultimate situations, expresses the basic drive to find a revelation of true being in human failure.

Crucial for man is his attitude toward failure: whether it remains hidden from him and overwhelms him only objectively at the end or whether he perceives it unobscured as the constant limit of his existence; whether he snatches at fantastic solutions and consolations or faces it honestly, in silence before the unfathomable. The way in which man approaches his failure determines what he will become.

In ultimate situations man either perceives nothingness or senses true being in spite of and above all ephemeral worldly existence. Even despair, by the very fact that it is possible in the world, points beyond the world.

Or, differently formulated, man seeks redemption. Redemption is offered by the great, universal religions of redemption. They are characterized by an objective guarantee of the truth and reality of redemption. Their road leads to an act of individual conversion. This philosophy cannot provide. And yet all philosophy is a transcending of the world, analogous to redemption.

To sum up: The source of philosophy is to be sought in wonder, in doubt, in a sense of forsakenness. In any case it begins with an inner upheaval, which determines its goal.

Plato and Aristotle were moved by wonder to seek the nature of being.

Amid infinite uncertainty Descartes sought compelling certainty.

Amid the sufferings of life the Stoics sought the repose of the mind.

Each of these experiences has its own truth, clothed always in historical conceptions and language. In making these philosophies our own we penetrate the historical husk to the primal sources that are alive within us.

The inner drive is toward firm foundations, depth of being, eternity.

But for us perhaps none of these is the most fundamental, absolute source. The discovery that being can be revealed to wonder is a source of inspiration, but beguiles us into withdrawing from the world and succumbing to a pure, magical metaphysic. Compelling certainty is limited to the scientific knowledge by which we orient ourselves in the world. Stoic imperturbability serves us only as a makeshift in distress, as a refuge from total ruin, but in itself remains without content and life.

These three motives—wonder leading to knowledge, doubt leading to certainty, forsakenness leading to the self—cannot by themselves account for our present philosophical thought.

In this crucial turning point in history, in this age of unprecedented ruin and of potentialities that can only be darkly surmised, the three motives we have thus far considered remain in force, but they are not adequate. They can operate only if there is *communication* among men.

In all past history there was a self-evident bond between man and man, in stable communities, in institutions, and in universal ideas. Even the isolated individual was in a sense sustained in his isolation. The most visible sign of today's disintegration is that more and more men do not understand one another, that they meet and scatter, that they are indifferent to one another, that there is no longer any reliable community or loyalty.

Today a universal situation that has always existed in fact assumes crucial importance: That I can, and cannot, become one with the Other in truth; that my faith, precisely when I am certain, clashes with other men's faith; that there is always somewhere a limit beyond which there appears to be nothing but battle without hope of unity, ending inevitably in subjugation or annihilation; that softness and complaisance cause men without faith either to band blindly together or stubbornly to attack one another.

All this is not incidental or unimportant. It might be, if there were a truth that might satisfy me in my isolation. I should not suffer so deeply from lack of communication or find such unique pleasure in authentic communication if I for myself, in absolute solitude, could be certain of the truth. But I am only in conjunction with the Other, alone I am nothing.

Communication from understanding to understanding, from mind to mind, and also from existence to existence, is only a medium for impersonal meanings and values. Defence and attack then become means not by which men gain power but by which they approach one another. The contest is a loving contest in which each man surrenders his weapons to the other. The certainty of authentic being resides only in unreserved communication between men who live together and vie with one another in a free community, who regard their association with one another as but a preliminary stage, who take nothing for granted and question everything. Only in communication is all other truth fulfilled, only in communication am I myself not merely living but fulfilling life. God manifests Himself only indirectly, and only through man's love of man; compelling certainty is particular and relative, subordinated to the Whole. The Stoical attitude is in fact empty and rigid.

The basic philosophical atitude of which I am speaking is rooted in distress at the absence of communication, in the drive to authentic communication, and in the possibility of the loving contest which profoundly unites self and self.

And this philosophical endeavour is at the same time rooted in the three philosophical experiences we have mentioned, which must all be considered in the light of their meaning, whether favourable or hostile, for communication from man to man.

And so we may say that wonder, doubt, the experience of ultimate situations, are indeed sources of philosophy, but the ultimate source is the will to authentic communication, which embraces all the rest. This becomes apparent at the very outset, for does not all philosophy strive for communication, express itself, demand a hearing? And is not its very essence communicability, which is in turn inseparable from truth?

Communication then is the aim of philosophy, and in communication all its other aims are ultimately rooted: awareness of being, illumination through love, attainment of peace. . . .

Meditation teaches us the *power of thought*.

Thought is the beginning of human existence. In accurate knowledge of objects I experience the power of the rational, as in the operations of mathematics, in the natural sciences, in technical planning. As my method grows purer, the logic of my syllogisms becomes more compelling, I gain greater insight into chains of causality, my experience becomes more reliable.

But philosophical thought begins at the limits of this rational knowledge. Rationality cannot help us in the essentials: it cannot help us to posit aims and ultimate ends, to know the highest good, to know God and human freedom; this inadequacy of the rational gives rise

to a kind of thinking which, while working with the tools of the understanding, is more than understanding. Philosophy presses to the limits of rational knowledge and there takes fire.

He who believes that he understands everything is no longer engaged in philosophical thought. He who takes scientific insight for knowledge of being itself and as a whole has succumbed to scientific superstition. He who has ceased to be astonished has ceased to question. He who acknowledges no mystery is no longer a seeker. Because he humbly acknowledges the limits of possible knowledge the philosopher remains open to the unknowable that is revealed at those limits.

Here cognition ceases, but not thought. By technically applying my knowledge I can act outwardly, but nonknowledge makes possible an inner action by which I transform myself. This is another and deeper kind of thought; it is not detached from being and oriented toward an object but is a process of my innermost self, in which thought and being become identical. Measured by outward, technical power, this thought of inner action is as nothing, it is no applied knowledge that can be possessed, it cannot be fashioned according to plan and purpose; it is an authentic illumination and growth into being.

The understanding (*ratio*) broadens our horizons; it fixates objects, reveals the tensions of the existent, and also permits what it cannot apprehend to stand forth in full force and clarity. The clarity of the understanding makes possible clarity at its limits, and arouses the authentic impulses which are thought and action, inward and outward act in one.

The philosopher is expected to live according to his doctrine. This maxim expresses poorly the thought that lies behind it. For the philosopher has no doctrine if by doctrine is meant a set of rules under which the particular cases of empirical existence might be subsumed, as things are subsumed under empirical species or men's acts under juridical norms. Philosophical ideas cannot be applied; they are a reality in themselves, so that we may say: in the fulfillment of these thoughts the man himself lives; or life is permeated with thought. That is why the philosopher and the man are inseparable (while man can be considered apart from his scientific knowledge); and that is why we cannot explore philosophical ideas in themselves but must at the same time gain awareness of the philosophical humanity which conceived them.

Philosophical life is in constant peril of straying into perversions in justification of which philosophical propositions are invoked. The formulae which elucidate existence are distorted by the vital will:

Peace of mind is confused with passivity, confidence with an illusory faith in the harmony of all things, knowing how to die is mistaken for flight from the world, reason for total indifference. The best is perverted to the worst.

The will to communication is perverted into self-contradictory attitudes: we wish to be undisturbed, yet demand absolute self-certainty in self-illumination. We wish to be excused because of our nerves and yet ask to be recognized as free. We are cautious and taciturn, and secretly on our guard even while professing unreserved readiness for communication. We think of ourselves while we are supposedly speaking of the idea.

The philosopher who strives to understand and overcome these perversions in himself knows his uncertainty; he is always on the lookout for criticism, he seeks opposition and wishes to be called to question; he desires to listen, not in order to submit but in order to be spurred onward in self-illumination. Where there is open and unreserved communication this philosopher finds truth and unsought-for confirmation in harmony with the other.

Philosophy must even leave the possibility of full communication in uncertainty, though it lives by faith in communication and stakes everything on communication. We can believe in it but not know it. To believe that we possess it is to have lost it.

For there are terrible limits which philosophical thought has never recognized as definitive: limits at which we forget or at which we accept and recognize notions which we have

not thoroughly elucidated. Alas, we talk so much when what really matters can be stated so simply, not in a universal proposition to be sure, but in a concrete symbol.

In the face of perversions, involvements, and confusions, modern man calls the doctor. And indeed there are diseases and neuroses which strongly effect our mental condition. The attempt to diagnose them, to understand them, to treat them is perfectly realistic. There is no reason to shun the human agency of the physician, when through critical experience he has gained real knowledge and ability. But certain modern developments in the field of psychotherapy are no longer grounded in medical science but in philosophy, so that like any other philosophical effort they demand to be examined from the point of view of ethics and metaphysics.

The goal of a philosophical life cannot be formulated as a state of being, which is attainable and once attained, perfect. Our states of being are only manifestations of existential striving or failure. It lies in our very nature to be on-the-way. We strive to cut across time. That is possible only in polarities:

Only when we exist entirely in this time of our historicity can we experience something of the eternal present.

Only as determinate men, each in his specificity, can we experience humanity as such.

Only when we experience our own age as our Comprehensive reality can we apprehend this age as part of the unity of history, and this unity of history as part of eternity.

In our ascending journey the primal source grows clearer for us behind our empirical states, but there is constant danger that it will return to obscurity.

The ascent of philosophical life is the ascent of the individual man. He must accomplish it as an individual in communication and cannot shift responsibility to others.

We achieve this ascent in the historically concrete, elective acts of our life, not by electing any so-called weltanschauung laid down in propositions.

And now, in conclusion, let us venture a

metaphor that may characterize the situation of philosophy in the temporal world:

Having oriented himself on secure dry land —through realistic observation, through the special sciences, through logic and methodology —the philosopher, at the limits of this land, explores the world of ideas over tranquil paths. And now like a butterfly he flutters over the ocean shore, darting out over the water; he spies a ship in which he would like to go on a voyage of discovery, to seek out the one thing which as transcendence is present in his existence. He peers after the ship—the method of philosophical thought and philosophical life— the ship which he sees and yet can never fully reach; and he struggles to reach it, sometimes strangely staggering and reeling.

We are creatures of this sort, and we are lost if we relinquish our orientation to the dry land. But we are not content to remain there. That is why our flutterings are so uncertain and perhaps so absurd to those who sit secure and content on dry land, and are intelligible only to those who have been seized by the same unrest. For them the world is a point of departure for that flight upon which everything depends, which each man must venture on his own though in common with other men, and which can never become the object of any doctrine.